SOCIAL STATISTICS FOR A DIVERSE SOCIETY

Eighth Edition

SAGE was founded in 1965 by Sara Miller McCune to support the dissemination of usable knowledge by publishing innovative and high-quality research and teaching content. Today, we publish over 900 journals, including those of more than 400 learned societies, more than 800 new books per year, and a growing range of library products including archives, data, case studies, reports, and video. SAGE remains majority-owned by our founder, and after Sara's lifetime will become owned by a charitable trust that secures our continued independence.

Los Angeles | London | New Delhi | Singapore | Washington DC | Melbourne

SOCIAL STATISTICS FOR A DIVERSE SOCIETY

Eighth Edition

Chava Frankfort-Nachmias
University of Wisconsin

Anna Leon-Guerrero
Pacific Lutheran University

Los Angeles | London | New Delhi
Singapore | Washington DC | Melbourne

FOR INFORMATION:

SAGE Publications, Inc.
2455 Teller Road
Thousand Oaks, California 91320
E-mail: order@sagepub.com

SAGE Publications Ltd.
1 Oliver's Yard
55 City Road
London, EC1Y 1SP
United Kingdom

SAGE Publications India Pvt. Ltd.
B 1/I 1 Mohan Cooperative Industrial Area
Mathura Road, New Delhi 110 044
India

SAGE Publications Asia-Pacific Pte. Ltd.
3 Church Street
#10-04 Samsung Hub
Singapore 049483

Acquisitions Editor: Jeff Lasser
Development Editor: Jessica Miller
Editorial Assistant: Adeline Wilson
eLearning Editor: Gabrielle Piccininni
Production Editor: Kelly DeRosa
Copy Editor: QuADS Prepress (P) Ltd.
Typesetter: C&M Digitals (P) Ltd.
Proofreader: Jennifer Grubba
Indexer: Sheila Bodell
Cover Designer: Candice Harman
Marketing Manager: Kara Kindstrom

Printed in the United States of America

Library of Congress Cataloging-in-Publication Data

Names: Frankfort-Nachmias, Chava, author. | Leon-Guerrero, Anna, author.

Title: Social statistics for a diverse society / Chava Frankfort-Nachmias, University of Wisconsin, Anna Leon-Guerrero, Pacific Lutheran University.

Description: Eighth edition. | Los Angeles : SAGE, [2016] | Includes bibliographical references and index.

Identifiers: LCCN 2016039109 | ISBN 978-1-5063-4720-2 (pbk. : alk. paper)

Subjects: LCSH: Social sciences—Statistical methods. | Statistics.

Classification: LCC HA29 .N25 2016 | DDC 519.5—dc23 LC record available at https://lccn.loc.gov/2016039109

This book is printed on acid-free paper.

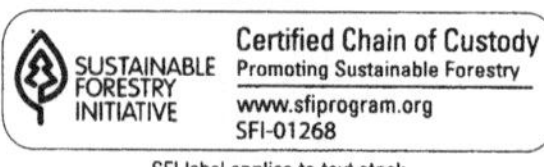

SFI label applies to text stock

17 18 19 20 21 10 9 8 7 6 5 4 3 2 1

BRIEF CONTENTS

DETAILED CONTENTS

CHAPTER 6 • Sampling and Sampling Distributions 151

CHAPTER 7 • Estimation 179

CHAPTER 9 • Bivariate Tables 235

CHAPTER 10 • The Chi-Square Test and Measures of Association 269

PREFACE

You may be reading this introduction on your first day of class. We know you have some questions and concerns about what your course will be like. Math, formulas, and calculations? Yes, those will be part of your learning experience. But there is more.

Throughout our text we highlight the relevance of statistics in our daily and professional lives. Data are used to predict public opinion, consumer spending, and even a presidential election. How Americans feel about a variety of political and social topics—race relations, gun control, immigration, the economy, health care reform, or terrorism—are measured by surveys and polls and reported daily by the news media. Your recent Amazon purchase didn't go unnoticed. The study of consumer trends, specifically focusing on young adults, helps determine commercial programming, product advertising and placement, and, ultimately, consumer spending. And as we prepare this text, just months before the 2016 Presidential election, weekly polls have begun predicting the historic election between Hillary Clinton and Donald Trump.

Statistics are not just a part of our lives in the form of news bits or information. And it isn't just numbers either. As social scientists we rely on statistics to help us understand our social world. We use statistical methods and techniques to track demographic trends, to assess social differences, and to better inform social policy. We encourage you to move beyond just being a consumer of statistics and determine how you can use statistics to gain insight into important social issues that affect you and others.

TEACHING AND LEARNING GOALS

Three teaching and learning goals continue to be the guiding principles of our book, as they were in previous editions.

Our first goal is to introduce you to social statistics and demonstrate its value. Although most of you will not use statistics in your own student research, you will be expected to read and interpret statistical information presented by others in professional and scholarly publications, in the workplace, and in the popular media. This book will help you understand the concepts behind the statistics so that you will be able to assess the circumstances in which certain statistics should and should not be used.

A special characteristic of this book is its integration of statistical techniques with substantive issues of particular relevance in the social sciences. Our second goal is to demonstrate that substance and statistical techniques are truly related in social science research. Your learning will not be limited to statistical calculations and formulas. Rather, you will become proficient in statistical techniques while learning about social differences and inequality through numerous substantive examples and real-world data applications. Because the world we live in is characterized by a growing diversity—where personal and social realities are increasingly shaped by race, class, gender, and other categories of experience—this book teaches you basic statistics while incorporating social science research related to the dynamic interplay of our social worlds.

Our third goal is to enhance your learning by using straightforward prose to explain statistical concepts and by emphasizing intuition, logic, and common sense over rote memorization and derivation of formulas.

DISTINCTIVE AND UPDATED FEATURES OF OUR BOOK

Our learning goals are accomplished through a variety of specific and distinctive features throughout this book.

A Close Link Between the Practice of Statistics, Important Social Issues, and Real-World Examples. This book is distinct for its integration of statistical techniques with pressing social issues of particular concern to society and social science. We emphasize how the conduct of social science is the constant interplay between social concerns and methods of inquiry. In addition, the examples throughout the book—mostly taken from news stories, government reports, public opinion polls, scholarly research, and the National Opinion Research Center's General Social Survey—are formulated to emphasize to students like you that we live in a world in which statistical arguments are common. Statistical concepts and procedures are illustrated with real data and research, providing a clear sense of how questions about important social issues can be studied with various statistical techniques.

A Focus on Diversity: The United States and International. A strong emphasis on race, class, and gender as central substantive concepts is mindful of a trend in the social sciences toward integrating issues of diversity in the curriculum. This focus on the richness of social differences within our society and our global neighbors is manifested in the application of statistical tools to examine how race, class, gender, and other categories of experience shape our social world and explain social behavior.

Chapter Reorganization and Content. Each revision presents many opportunities to polish and expand the content of our text. In this edition, we have made a number of changes in response to feedback from reviewers and fellow instructors. We merged frequency distributions and graphic presentation into one chapter. We expanded the discussion of probability in Chapters 6 and 7. We refined the discussion on the interpretation and application of descriptive statistics (variance and standard deviation) and inferential tests (t, Z, F ratio, and regression and correlation). End-of-chapter exercises have been organized into calculation and interpretation problems.

Reading the Research Literature, Statistics in Practice, A Closer Look, and Data at Work. In your student career and in the workplace, you may be expected to read and interpret statistical information presented by others in professional and scholarly publications. These statistical analyses are a good deal more complex than most class and textbook presentations. To guide you in reading and interpreting research reports written by social scientists, most of our chapters include a Reading the Research Literature and a Statistics in Practice feature, presenting excerpts of published research reports or specific SPSS calculations using the statistical concepts under discussion. Being statistically literate involves more than just completing a calculation; it also includes learning how to apply and interpret statistical information and being able to say what it means. We include A Closer Look discussion in each chapter, advising students about the common errors and limitations in quantitative data collection and analysis. A new chapter feature for this eighth edition is Data at Work, profiling men and women who use data in their work settings and professions.

SPSS and GSS 2014. IBM® SPSS® Statistics* is used throughout this book, although the use of computers is not required to learn from the text. Real data are used to motivate and make concrete the coverage of statistical topics. As a companion to the eighth edition's SPSS demonstrations and exercises, we provide two GSS 2014 data sets on the study site at **http://edge.sagepub.com/frankfort8e**. SPSS exercises at the end of each chapter rely on variables from both data modules. There is ample opportunity for instructors to develop their own exercises using these data.

Tools to Promote Effective Study. Each chapter concludes with a list of Main Points and Key Terms discussed in that chapter. Boxed definitions of the Key Terms also appear in the body of the chapter, as do Learning Checks keyed to the most important points. Key Terms are also clearly defined and explained in the Glossary, another special feature in our book. Answers to all the Odd-Numbered Exercises and Learning Checks in the text are included at the end of the book, as well as on the study site at **http://edge.sagepub.com/frankfort8e**. Complete step-by-step solutions are provided in the instructor's manual, available on the study site.

A NOTE ABOUT ROUNDING

Throughout this text and in ancillary materials, we followed these rounding rules: If the number you are rounding is followed by 5, 6, 7, 8, or 9, round the number up. If the number you are rounding is followed by 0, 1, 2, 3, or 4, do not change the number. For rounding long decimals, look only at the number in the place you are rounding to and the number that follows it.

edge.sagepub.com/frankfort8e

SAGE edge offers a robust online environment featuring an impressive array of tools and resources for review, study, and further exploration, keeping both instructors and students on the cutting edge of teaching and learning. **SAGE edge** content is open access and available on demand. Learning and teaching has never been easier!

SAGE edge for students provides a personalized approach to help students accomplish their coursework goals in an easy-to-use learning environment.

- Mobile-friendly **eFlashcards** strengthen understanding of key terms and concepts.
- Mobile-friendly practice **quizzes** allow for independent assessment by students of their mastery of course material.
- A customized online **action plan** includes tips and feedback on progress through the course and materials, which allows students to individualize their learning experience.
- **Web exercises** and meaningful web links facilitate student use of Internet resources, further exploration of topics, and responses to critical thinking questions.

*SPSS is a registered trademark of International Business Machines Corporation.

- EXCLUSIVE! Access to full-text **SAGE journal articles** that have been carefully selected to support and expand on the concepts presented in each chapter.
- Access to **GSS 2014 data sets.**

SAGE edge for instructors supports teaching by making it easy to integrate quality content and create a rich learning environment for students.

- **Test banks** provide a diverse range of pre-written options as well as the opportunity to edit any question and/or insert personalized questions to effectively assess students' progress and understanding.
- **Sample syllabus** provides a suggested model for instructors to use when creating the syllabi for their courses.
- Editable, chapter-specific **PowerPoint® slides** offer complete flexibility for creating a multimedia presentation for the course.
- EXCLUSIVE! Access to full-text **SAGE journal articles** have been carefully selected to support and expand on the concepts presented in each chapter to encourage students to think critically.
- **Multimedia content** includes web resources and web exercises that appeal to students with different learning styles.
- **Lecture notes** summarize key concepts by chapter to ease preparation for lectures and class discussions.
- Lively and stimulating ideas for **class activities** that can be used in class to reinforce active learning.
- Chapter-specific **discussion questions** help launch classroom interaction by prompting students to engage with the material and by reinforcing important content.
- A **course cartridge** provides easy LMS (Learning Management System) integration.

ACKNOWLEDGMENTS

We are both grateful to Jerry Westby, Series Editor for SAGE Publications, for his commitment to our book and for his invaluable assistance through the production process.

Many manuscript reviewers recruited by SAGE provided invaluable feedback. For their thoughtful comments to the eighth edition, we thank

Andrew S. Fullerton, Oklahoma State University

David A. Gay, University of Central Florida

Dr. Lindsey Peterson, Mississippi State University

Heather Macpherson Parrott, Long Island University-Post

Christopher Donoghue, Montclair State University

S. Michael Gaddis, The Pennsylvania State University

Jann W. MacInnes, University of Florida

Laura Sullivan, Brandeis University

Warren Waren, Texas A&M University

Joe Weinberg, University of Southern Mississippi

For their comments to the seventh edition, we thank

Walter F. Carroll, Bridgewater State University

Andrew S. Fullerton, Oklahoma State University

David A. Gay, University of Central Florida

Judith G. Gonyea, Boston University

Megan Henly, University of New Hampshire

Patricia A. Jaramillo, The University of Texas at San Antonio

Brett Lehman, Louisiana State University

James W. Love, California State University, Fullerton

Kay Kei-Ho Pih, California State University, Northridge

For their comments to the sixth edition, we thank

Diane Balduzy, Massachusetts College of Liberal Arts

Ellen Berg, California State University–Sacramento

Robert Carini, University of Louisville

Melissa Evans-Andris, University of Louisville

Meredith Greif, Georgia State University

Kristen Kenneavy, Ramapo College

Dave Rausch, West Texas A&M University

Billy Wagner, California State University–Channel Islands

Kevin Yoder, University of North Texas

For their comments to the fifth edition, we thank

Anna A. Amirkhanyan, The American University

Robert Carini, University of Louisville

Patricia Case, University of Toledo

Stanley DeViney, University of Maryland Eastern Shore

David Gay, University of Central Florida

Dusten R. Hollist, University of Montana

Ross Koppel, University of Pennsylvania

Benny Marcus, Temple University

Matt G. Mutchler, California State University Dominguez Hills

Mahasin C. Owens-Sabir, Jackson State University

Dave Rausch, West Texas A&M University

Kevin Yoder, University of North Texas

We are grateful to Jessica Miller and Kelly DeRosa for guiding the book through the production process. We would also like to acknowledge Laura Kirkhuff, Krishna Pradeep Joghee, and the rest of the SAGE staff for their assistance on this edition.

We extend our deepest appreciation to Michael Clark for his fine editing and data work. Among his many contributions, Michael would relate our revision goals to his student experience, reminding us of how students can learn and successfully master this material.

Chava Frankfort-Nachmias would like to thank and acknowledge her friends and colleagues for their unending support; she also would like to thank her students:

I am grateful to my students at the University of Wisconsin–Milwaukee, who taught me that even the most complex statistical ideas can be simplified. The ideas presented in this book are the products of many years of classroom testing. I thank my students for their patience and contributions.

Finally, I thank my partner, Marlene Stern, for her love and support.

Anna Leon-Guerrero would like to thank her Pacific Lutheran University students for inspiring her to be a better teacher. My love and thanks to my husband, Brian Sullivan.

Chava Frankfort-Nachmias

University of Wisconsin–Milwaukee

Anna Leon-Guerrero

Pacific Lutheran University

ABOUT THE AUTHORS

Chava Frankfort-Nachmias is an Emeritus Professor of Sociology at the University of Wisconsin–Milwaukee. She is the coauthor of *Research Methods in the Social Sciences* (with David Nachmias), coeditor of *Sappho in the Holy Land* (with Erella Shadmi), and numerous publications on ethnicity and development, urban revitalization, science and gender, and women in Israel. She was the recipient of the University of Wisconsin System teaching improvement grant on integrating race, ethnicity, and gender into the social statistics and research methods curriculum. She is also the coauthor (with Anna Leon-Guerrero) of *Essentials of Social Statistics.*

Anna Leon-Guerrero is Professor of Sociology at Pacific Lutheran University in Washington. She received her Ph.D. in sociology from the University of California–Los Angeles. A recipient of the university's Faculty Excellence Award and the K.T. Tang Award for Excellence in Research, she teaches courses in statistics, social theory, and social problems. She is also the author of *Social Problems: Community, Policy, and Social Action*.

1

THE WHAT AND THE WHY OF STATISTICS

Chapter Learning Objectives

1. Describe the five stages of the research process
2. Define independent and dependent variables
3. Distinguish between the three levels of measurement
4. Apply descriptive and inferential statistical procedures

Are you taking statistics because it is required in your major—not because you find it interesting? If so, you may be feeling intimidated because you associate statistics with numbers, formulas, and abstract notations that seem inaccessible and complicated. Perhaps you feel intimidated not only because you're uncomfortable with math but also because you suspect that numbers and math don't leave room for human judgment or have any relevance to your own personal experience. In fact, you may even question the relevance of statistics to understanding people, social behavior, or society.

In this book, we will show you that statistics can be a lot more interesting and easy to understand than you may have been led to believe. In fact, as we draw on your previous knowledge and experience and relate statistics to interesting and important social issues, you'll begin to see that statistics is not just a course you have to take but a useful tool as well.

There are two reasons why learning statistics may be of value to you. First, you are constantly exposed to statistics every day of your life. Marketing surveys, voting polls, and social research findings appear daily in the news media. By learning statistics, you will become a sharper consumer of statistical material. Second, as a major in the social sciences, you may be expected to read and interpret statistical information related to your occupation or work. Even if conducting research is not a part of your work, you may still be expected to understand and learn from other people's research or to be able to write reports based on statistical analyses.

Just what is statistics anyway? You may associate the word with numbers that indicate birthrates, conviction rates, per capita income, marriage and divorce rates, and so on. But the word **statistics** also refers to a set of procedures used by social scientists to organize, summarize, and communicate numerical information. Only information represented by numbers can be the subject of statistical analysis. Such information is called **data**; researchers use statistical procedures to analyze data to answer research questions and test theories. It is the latter usage—answering research questions and testing theories—that this textbook explores.

Statistics A set of procedures used by social scientists to organize, summarize, and communicate numerical information.

Data Information represented by numbers, which can be the subject of statistical analysis.

THE RESEARCH PROCESS

Research process A set of activities in which social scientists engage to answer questions, examine ideas, or test theories.

To give you a better idea of the role of statistics in social research, let's start by looking at the **research process**. We can think of the research process as a set of activities in which social scientists engage so that they can answer questions, examine ideas, or test theories.

As illustrated in Figure 1.1, the research process consists of five stages:

1. Asking the research question
2. Formulating the hypotheses
3. Collecting data
4. Analyzing data
5. Evaluating the hypotheses

Each stage affects the theory and is affected by it as well. Statistics is most closely tied to the data analysis stage of the research process. As we will see in later chapters, statistical analysis of the data helps researchers test the validity and accuracy of their hypotheses.

ASKING RESEARCH QUESTIONS

The starting point for most research is asking a research question. Consider the following research questions taken from a number of social science journals:

> How will the Affordable Care Act influence the quality of health care?
>
> Has support for same-sex marriage increased during the past decade?

Figure 1.1 The Research Process

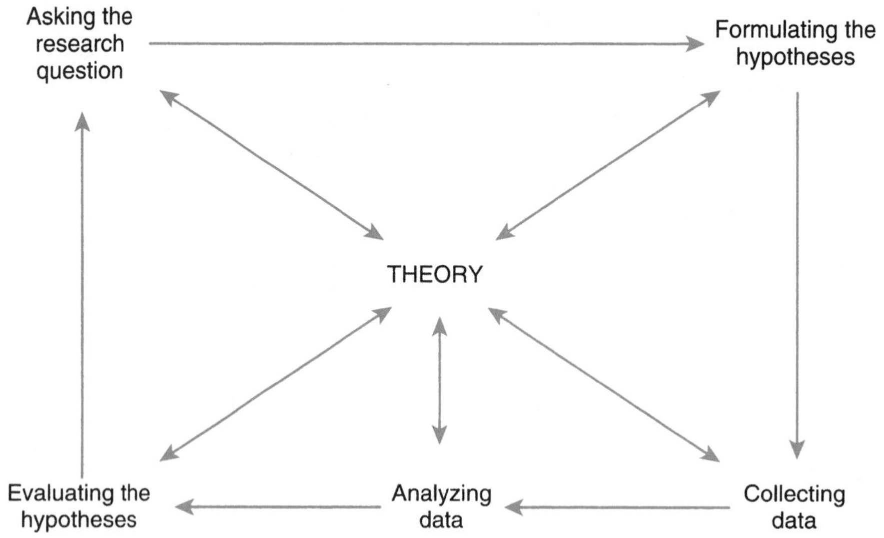

Does race or ethnicity predict voting behavior?

What factors affect the economic mobility of female workers?

These are all questions that can be answered by conducting **empirical research**—research based on information that can be verified by using our direct experience. To answer research questions, we cannot rely on reasoning, speculation, moral judgment, or subjective preference. For example, the questions "Is racial equality good for society?" and "Is an urban lifestyle better than a rural lifestyle?" cannot be answered empirically because the terms good and better are concerned with values, beliefs, or subjective preference and, therefore, cannot be independently verified. One way to study these questions is by defining good and better in terms that can be verified empirically. For example, we can define good in terms of economic growth and better in terms of psychological well-being. These questions could then be answered by conducting empirical research.

Empirical research Research based on evidence that can be verified by using our direct experience.

You may wonder how to come up with a research question. The first step is to pick a question that interests you. If you are not sure, look around! Ideas for research problems are all around you, from media sources to personal experience or your own intuition. Talk to other people, write down your own observations and ideas, or learn what other social scientists have written about.

Take, for instance, the relationship between gender and work. As a college student about to enter the labor force, you may wonder about the similarities and differences between women's and men's work experiences and about job opportunities when you graduate. Here are some facts and observations based on research reports: In 2015, women who were employed full time earned about $726 (in current dollars) per week on average; men who were employed full time earned $895 (in current dollars) per week on average.[1] Women's and men's work are also very different. Women continue to be the minority in many of the higher ranking and higher salaried positions in professional and managerial occupations. For example, in 2014, women made up 25.3% of architects, 16.5% of civil engineers, 12.4% of police and sheriff's patrol officers, and 2.4% of electricians. In comparison, among all those employed as preschool and kindergarten teachers, 98% were women. Among all receptionists and information clerks in 2014, 91% were women.[2] Another noteworthy development in the history of labor in the United States took place in January 2010: Women outnumbered men for the first time in the labor force by holding 50.3% of all nonfarm payroll jobs.[3] These observations may prompt us to ask research questions such as the following: How much change has there been in women's work over time? Are women paid, on average, less than men for the same type of work?

LEARNING CHECK 1.1

Identify one or two social science questions amenable to empirical research. You can almost bet that you will be required to do a research project sometime in your college career.

THE ROLE OF THEORY

You may have noticed that each preceding research question was expressed in terms of a relationship. This relationship may be between two or more attributes of individuals or groups, such as gender and income or gender segregation in the workplace and income disparity. The relationship between attributes or characteristics of individuals and groups lies at the heart of social scientific inquiry.

Most of us use the term theory quite casually to explain events and experiences in our daily life. You may have a theory about why your roommate has been so nice to you lately or why you didn't do so well on your last exam. In a somewhat similar manner, social scientists attempt to explain the nature of social reality. Whereas our theories about events in our lives are commonsense explanations based on educated guesses and personal experience, to the social scientist, a theory is a more precise explanation that is frequently tested by conducting research.

Theory A set of assumptions and propositions used to explain, predict, and understand social phenomena.

A **theory** is a set of assumptions and propositions used by social scientists to explain, predict, and understand the phenomena they study.[4] The theory attempts to establish a link between what we observe (the data) and our conceptual understanding of why certain phenomena are related to each other in a particular way.

For instance, suppose we wanted to understand the reasons for the income disparity between men and women; we may wonder whether the types of jobs men and women have and the organizations in which they work have something to do with their wages. One explanation for gender wage inequality is gender segregation in the workplace—the fact that American men and women are concentrated in different kinds of jobs and occupations. What is the significance of gender segregation in the workplace? In our society, people's occupations and jobs are closely associated with their level of prestige, authority, and income. The jobs in which women and men are segregated are not only different but also unequal. Although the proportion of women in the labor force has markedly increased, women are still concentrated in occupations with low pay, low prestige, and few opportunities for promotion. Thus, gender segregation in the workplace is associated with unequal earnings, authority, and status. In particular, women's segregation into different jobs and occupations from those of men is the most immediate cause of the pay gap. Women receive lower pay than men do even when they have the same level of education, skill, and experience as men in comparable occupations.

FORMULATING THE HYPOTHESES

So far, we have come up with a number of research questions about the income disparity between men and women in the workplace. We have also discussed a possible explanation—a theory—that helps us make sense of gender inequality in wages. Is that enough? Where do we go from here?

Our next step is to test some of the ideas suggested by the gender segregation theory. But this theory, even if it sounds reasonable and logical to us, is too general and does not contain enough specific information to be tested. Instead, theories suggest specific concrete predictions or **hypotheses** about the way that observable attributes of people or groups are interrelated in real life. Hypotheses are tentative because they can be verified only after they have been tested empirically.[5] For example, one hypothesis we can derive from the gender segregation theory is that wages in occupations in which the majority of workers are female are lower than the wages in occupations in which the majority of workers are male.

Hypothesis A statement predicting the relationship between two or more observable attributes.

Not all hypotheses are derived directly from theories. We can generate hypotheses in many ways—from theories, directly from observations, or from intuition. Probably, the greatest source of hypotheses is the professional or scholarly literature. A critical review of the scholarly literature will familiarize you with the current state of knowledge and with hypotheses that others have studied.

Table 1.1 Variables and Value Categories

Variable	Categories
Social class	Lower Working Middle Upper
Gender	Male Female
Education	Less than high school High school Some college College graduate

Let's restate our hypothesis:

> Wages in occupations in which the majority of workers are female are lower than the wages in occupations in which the majority of workers are male.

Note that this hypothesis is a statement of a relationship between two characteristics that vary: wages and gender composition of occupations. Such characteristics are called variables. A **variable** is a property of people or objects that takes on two or more values. For example, people can be classified into a number of social class categories, such as upper class, middle class, or working class. Family income is a variable; it can take on values from zero to hundreds of thousands of dollars or more. Similarly, gender composition is a variable. The percentage of females (or males) in an occupation can vary from 0 to 100. Wages is a variable, with values from zero to thousands of dollars or more. See Table 1.1 for examples of some variables and their possible values.

Variable A property of people or objects that takes on two or more values.

Social scientists must also select a **unit of analysis**; that is, they must select the object of their research. We often focus on individual characteristics or behavior, but we could also examine groups of people such as families, formal organizations like elementary schools or corporations, or social artifacts such as children's books or advertisements. For example, we may be interested in the relationship between an individual's educational degree and annual income. In this case, the unit of analysis is the individual. On the other hand, in a study of how corporation profits are associated with employee benefits, corporations are the unit of analysis. If we examine how often women are featured in prescription drug advertisements, the advertisements are the unit of analysis. Figure 1.2 illustrates different units of analysis frequently employed by social scientists.

Unit of analysis The object of research, such as individuals, groups, organizations, or social artifacts.

LEARNING CHECK 1.2

Remember that research question you came up with? Formulate a testable hypothesis based on your research question. Remember that your variables must take on two or more values and you must determine the unit of analysis. What is your unit of analysis?

Figure 1.2 Examples of Units of Analysis

Individual as unit of analysis:

How old are you?
What are your political views?
What is your occupation?

Family as unit of analysis:

How many children are in the family?
Who does the housework?
How many wage earners are there?

Organization as unit of analysis:

How many employees are there?
What is the gender composition?
Do you have a diversity office?

City as unit of analysis:

What was the crime rate last year?
What is the population density?
What type of government runs things?

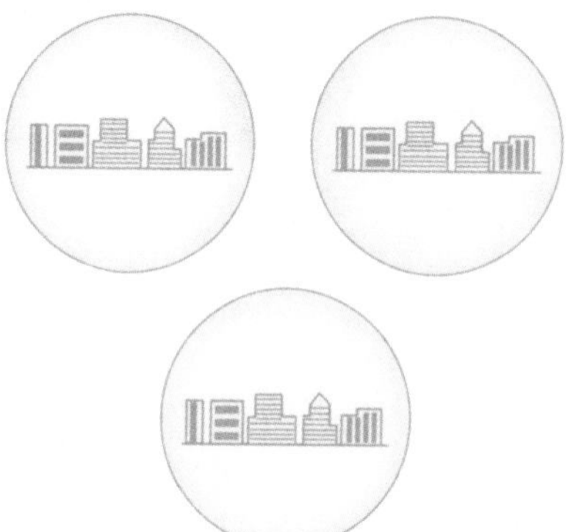

Independent and Dependent Variables: Causality

Hypotheses are usually stated in terms of a relationship between an independent and a dependent variable. The distinction between an independent and a dependent variable is important in the language of research. Social theories often intend to provide an explanation for social patterns or causal relations between variables. For example, according to the gender segregation theory, gender segregation in the workplace is the primary explanation (although certainly not the only one) of the male-female earning gap. Why should jobs where the majority of workers are women pay less than jobs that employ mostly men? One explanation is that

> societies undervalue the work women do, regardless of what those tasks are, because women do them. . . . For example, our culture tends to devalue caring or nurturant work at least partly because it is done by women. This tendency accounts for child care workers' low rank in the pay hierarchy.[6]

In the language of research, the variable the researcher wants to explain (the "effect") is called the **dependent variable**. The variable that is expected to "cause" or account for the dependent variable is called the **independent variable**. Therefore, in our example, *gender composition of occupations* is the independent variable, and *wages* is the dependent variable.

Dependent variable The variable to be explained (the effect).

Independent variable The variable expected to account for (the cause of) the dependent variable.

Cause-and-effect relationships between variables are not easy to infer in the social sciences. To establish that two variables are causally related, your analysis must meet three conditions: (1) The cause has to precede the effect in time, (2) there has to be an empirical relationship between the cause and the effect, and (3) this relationship cannot be explained by other factors.

Let's consider the decades-old debate about controlling crime through the use of prevention versus punishment. Some people argue that special counseling for youths at the first sign of trouble and strict controls on access to firearms would help reduce crime. Others argue that overhauling federal and state sentencing laws to stop early prison releases is the solution. In the early 1990s, Washington and California adopted "three strikes and you're out" legislation, imposing life prison terms on three-time felony offenders. Such laws are also referred to as habitual or persistent offender laws. Twenty-six other states and the federal government adopted similar measures, all advocating a "get tough" policy on crime; the most recent legislation was in 2012 in the state of Massachusetts. In 2012, California voters supported a revision to the original law, imposing a life sentence only when the new felony conviction is serious or violent. Let's suppose that years after the measure was introduced, the crime rate declined in some of these states (in fact, advocates of the measure have identified declining crime rates as evidence of its success). Does the observation that the incidence of crime declined mean that the new measure caused this reduction? Not necessarily! Perhaps the rate of crime had been going down for other reasons, such as improvement in the economy, and the new measure had nothing to do with it. To demonstrate a cause-and-effect relationship, we would need to show three things: (1) The reduction of crime actually occurred after the enactment of this measure, (2) the enactment of the "three strikes and you're out" measure was empirically associated with a decrease in crime, and (3) the relationship between the reduction in crime and the "three strikes and you're out" policy is not due to the influence of another variable (e.g., the improvement of overall economic conditions).

Independent and Dependent Variables: Guidelines

Because it is difficult to infer cause-and-effect relationships in the social sciences, be cautious about using the terms cause and effect when examining relationships between variables. However, using the terms independent variable and dependent variable is still appropriate even when this relationship is not articulated in terms of direct cause and effect. Here are a few guidelines that may help you identify the independent and dependent variables:

1. The dependent variable is always the property that you are trying to explain; it is always the object of the research.
2. The independent variable usually occurs earlier in time than the dependent variable.
3. The independent variable is often seen as influencing, directly or indirectly, the dependent variable.

The purpose of the research should help determine which is the independent variable and which is the dependent variable. In the real world, variables are neither dependent nor independent; they can be switched around depending on the research problem. A variable defined as independent in one research investigation may be a dependent variable in another.[7] For instance, *educational attainment* may be an independent variable in a study attempting to explain how education influences political attitudes. However, in an investigation of whether a person's level of education is influenced by the social status of his or her family of origin, *educational attainment* is the dependent variable. Some variables, such as race, age, and ethnicity, because they are primordial characteristics that cannot be explained by social scientists, are never considered dependent variables in a social science analysis.

LEARNING CHECK 1.3

Identify the independent and dependent variables in the following hypotheses:

- *Older Americans are more likely to support stricter immigration laws than younger Americans.*
- *People who attend church regularly are more likely to oppose abortion than people who do not attend church regularly.*
- *Elderly women are more likely to live alone than elderly men.*
- *Individuals with postgraduate education are likely to have fewer children than those with less education.*

What are the independent and dependent variables in your hypothesis?

COLLECTING DATA

Once we have decided on the research question, the hypothesis, and the variables to be included in the study, we proceed to the next stage in the research cycle. This step includes measuring our variables and collecting the data. As researchers, we must decide how to measure the variables of interest to us, how to select the cases for our research, and what kind of data collection techniques we will be using. A wide variety of data collection techniques are available to us, from direct observations to survey research, experiments, or secondary sources. Similarly, we can construct numerous measuring instruments. These instruments can be as simple as a single question included in a questionnaire or as complex as a composite measure constructed through the combination of two or more questionnaire items. The choice of a particular data collection method or instrument to measure our variables depends on the study objective. For instance, suppose we decide to study how one's social class is related to attitudes about women in the labor force. Since attitudes about working women are not directly observable, we need to collect data by asking a group of people questions about their attitudes and opinions. A suitable method of data collection for this project would be a survey that uses some kind of questionnaire or interview guide to elicit verbal reports from respondents. The questionnaire could include numerous questions designed to measure attitudes toward working women, social class, and other variables relevant to the study.

How would we go about collecting data to test the hypothesis relating the gender composition of occupations to wages? We want to gather information on the proportion of men and women in different occupations and the average earnings for these occupations. This kind of information is routinely collected and disseminated by the U.S. Department of Labor, the Bureau of Labor Statistics, and the U.S. Census Bureau. We could use these data to test our hypothesis.

Levels of Measurement

The statistical analysis of data involves many mathematical operations, from simple counting to addition and multiplication. However, not every operation can be used with every variable. The type of statistical operation we employ depends on how our variables are measured. For example, for the variable *gender*, we can use the number 1 to represent females and the number 2 to represent males. Similarly, 1 can also be used as a numerical code for the category "one child" in the variable *number of children*. Clearly, in the first example, the number is an arbitrary symbol that does not correspond to the property "female," whereas in the second example the number 1 has a distinct numerical meaning that does correspond to the property "one child." The correspondence between the properties we measure and the numbers representing these properties determines the type of statistical operations we can use. The degree of correspondence also leads to different ways of measuring—that is, to distinct levels of measurement. In this section, we will discuss three levels of measurement: (1) nominal, (2) ordinal, and (3) interval-ratio.

NOMINAL LEVEL OF MEASUREMENT At the **nominal** level of measurement, numbers or other symbols are assigned a set of categories for the purpose of naming, labeling, or classifying the observations. *Gender* is an example of a nominal-level variable (Table 1.2). Using the numbers 1 and 2, for instance, we can classify our observations into the categories "females" and "males," with 1 representing females and 2 representing males. We could use any of a variety of symbols to represent the different categories of a nominal variable; however, when numbers are used to represent the different categories, we do not imply anything about the magnitude or quantitative difference between the categories. Nominal categories cannot be rank-ordered. Because the different categories (e.g., males vs. females) vary in the quality inherent in each but not in quantity, nominal variables are often called qualitative. Other examples of nominal-level variables are political party, religion, and race.

Nominal measurement Numbers or other symbols are assigned to a set of categories for the purpose of naming, labeling, or classifying the observations. Nominal categories cannot be rank-ordered.

Nominal variables should include categories that are both exhaustive and mutually exclusive. Exhaustiveness means that there should be enough categories composing the variables to classify every observation. For example, the common classification of the variable marital status into the categories "married," "single," and "widowed" violates the requirement of exhaustiveness. As defined, it does not allow us to classify same-sex couples or heterosexual couples who are not legally married. We can make every variable exhaustive by adding the category "other"

Table 1.2 Nominal Variables and Value Categories

Variable	Categories
Gender	Male Female
Religion	Protestant Christian Jewish Muslim
Marital status	Married Single Widowed Other

to the list of categories. However, this practice is not recommended if it leads to the exclusion of categories that have theoretical significance or a substantial number of observations.

Mutual exclusiveness means that there is only one category suitable for each observation. For example, we need to define religion in such a way that no one would be classified into more than one category. For instance, the categories Protestant and Methodist are not mutually exclusive because Methodists are also considered Protestant and, therefore, could be classified into both categories.

LEARNING CHECK 1.4

Review the definitions of exhaustive and mutually exclusive. Now look at Table 1.2. What other categories could be added to each variable to be exhaustive and mutually exclusive?

Ordinal measurement Numbers are assigned to rank-ordered categories ranging from low to high.

ORDINAL LEVEL OF MEASUREMENT Whenever we assign numbers to rank-ordered categories ranging from low to high, we have an **ordinal** level of measurement. *Social class* is an example of an ordinal variable. We might classify individuals with respect to their social class status as "upper class," "middle class," or "working class." We can say that a person in the category "upper class" has a higher class position than a person in a "middle-class" category (or that a "middle-class" position is higher than a "working-class" position), but we do not know the magnitude of the differences between the categories—that is, we don't know how much higher "upper class" is compared with the "middle class."

Many attitudes that we measure in the social sciences are ordinal-level variables. Take, for instance, the following statement used to measure attitudes toward working women: "Women should return to their traditional role in society." Respondents are asked to identify the number representing their degree of agreement or disagreement with this statement. One form in which a number might be made to correspond with the answers can be seen in Table 1.3. Although the differences between these numbers represent higher or lower degrees of agreement with the statement, the distance between any two of those numbers does not have a precise numerical meaning.

Like nominal variables, ordinal variables should include categories that are mutually exhaustive and exclusive.

Table 1.3 Ordinal Ranking Scale

Rank	Value
1	Strongly agree
2	Agree
3	Neither agree nor disagree
4	Disagree
5	Strongly disagree

INTERVAL-RATIO LEVEL OF MEASUREMENT If the categories (or values) of a variable can be rank-ordered and if the measurements for all the cases are expressed in the same units, and equally spaced, then an interval-ratio level of measurement has been achieved. Examples of variables measured at the interval-ratio level are *age*, *income*, and *SAT scores*. With all these variables, we can compare values not only in terms of which is larger or smaller but also in terms of how much larger or smaller one is compared with another. In some discussions of levels of measurement, you will see a distinction made between interval-ratio variables that have a natural zero point (where zero means the absence of the property) and those variables that have zero as an arbitrary point. For example, weight and length have a natural zero point, whereas temperature has an arbitrary zero point. Variables with a natural zero point are also called *ratio variables*. In statistical practice, however, ratio variables are subjected to operations that treat them as interval and ignore their ratio properties. Therefore, we make no distinction between these two types in this text.

Interval-ratio measurement Measurements for all cases are expressed in the same units and equally spaced. Interval-ratio values can be rank-ordered.

CUMULATIVE PROPERTY OF LEVELS OF MEASUREMENT Variables that can be measured at the interval-ratio level of measurement can also be measured at the ordinal and nominal levels. As a rule, properties that can be measured at a higher level (interval-ratio is the highest) can also be measured at lower levels, but not vice versa. Let's take, for example, *gender composition of occupations*, the independent variable in our research example. Table 1.4 shows the percentage of women in five major occupational groups.

The variable *gender composition* (measured as the percentage of women in the occupational group) is an interval-ratio variable and, therefore, has the properties of nominal, ordinal, and interval-ratio measures. For example, we can say that the management group differs from the natural resources group (a nominal comparison), that service occupations have more women than the other occupational categories (an ordinal comparison), and that service occupations have 35 percentage points more women (56.7 - 21.7) than production occupations (an interval-ratio comparison).

The types of comparisons possible at each level of measurement are summarized in Table 1.5 and Figure 1.3. Note that differences can be established at each of the three levels, but only at the interval-ratio level can we establish the magnitude of the difference.

LEVELS OF MEASUREMENT OF DICHOTOMOUS VARIABLES A variable that has only two values is called a dichotomous variable. Several key social factors, such as gender, employment status, and marital status, are dichotomies—that is, you are male or female, employed or unemployed, married or not married. Such variables may seem to be measured at the nominal level: You fit in either one category or the other. No category is naturally higher or lower than the other, so they can't be ordered.

Dichotomous variable A variable that has only two values.

Table 1.4 Gender Composition of Five Major Occupational Groups, 2014

Occupational Group	Women in Occupation (%)
Management, professional, and related occupations	51.6
Service occupations	56.7
Production, transportation, and materials occupations	21.7
Sales and office occupations	61.8
Natural resources, construction, and maintenance occupations	4.4

Source: U.S. Department of Labor, 2015, *Labor Force Statistics from the Current Population Survey 2014*, Table 11

Table 1.5 Levels of Measurement and Possible Comparisons

Level	Different or Equivalent	Higher or Lower	How Much Higher
Nominal	Yes	No	No
Ordinal	Yes	Yes	No
Interval-ratio	Yes	Yes	Yes

Figure 1.3 Levels of Measurement and Possible Comparisons: Education Measured on Nominal, Ordinal, and Interval-Ratio Levels

LEARNING CHECK 1.5

Make sure you understand these levels of measurement. As the course progresses, your instructor is likely to ask you what statistical procedure you would use to describe or analyze a set of data. To make the proper choice, you must know the level of measurement of the data.

However, because there are only two possible values for a dichotomy, we can measure it at the ordinal or the interval-ratio level. For example, we can think of "femaleness" as the ordering principle for gender, so that "female" is higher and "male" is lower. Using "maleness" as the ordering principle, "female" is lower and "male" is higher. In either case, with only two classes, there is no way to get them out of order; therefore, gender could be considered at the ordinal level.

Dichotomous variables can also be considered to be interval-ratio level. Why is this? In measuring interval-ratio data, the size of the interval between the categories is meaningful: The distance between 4 and 7, for example, is the same as the distance between 11 and 14. But with a dichotomy, there is only one interval. Therefore, there is really no other distance to which we can compare it. Mathematically, this gives the dichotomy more power than other nominal-level variables (as you will notice later in the text).

For this reason, researchers often dichotomize some of their variables, turning a multicategory nominal variable into a dichotomy. For example, you may see race dichotomized into "white" and "nonwhite." Though we would lose the ability to examine each unique racial category and we may collapse categories that are not similar, it may be the most logical statistical step to take. When you dichotomize a variable, be sure that the two categories capture a distinction that is important to your research question (e.g., a comparison of the number of white vs. nonwhite U.S. senators).

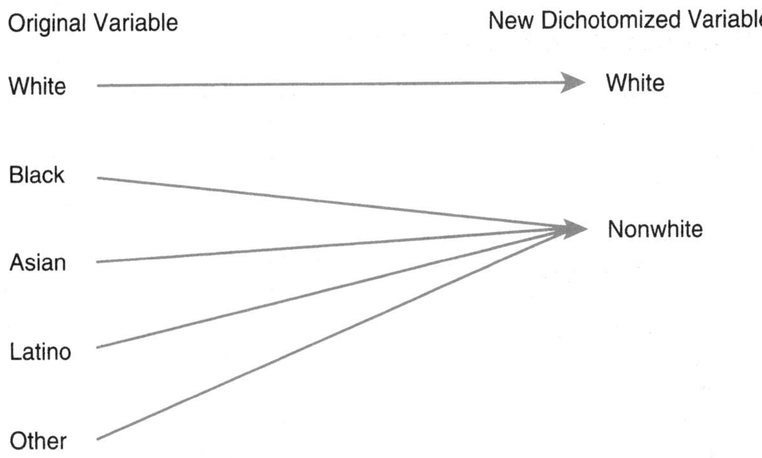

Discrete and Continuous Variables

The statistical operations we can perform are also determined by whether the variables are continuous or discrete. Discrete variables have a minimum-sized unit of measurement, which cannot be subdivided. The number of children per family is an example of a discrete variable because the minimum unit is one child. A family may have two or three children, but not 2.5 children. The variable *wages* in our research example is a discrete variable because currency has a minimum unit (1 cent), which cannot be subdivided. One can have $101.21 or $101.22 but not $101.21843. Wages cannot differ by less than 1 cent—the minimum-sized unit.

Unlike discrete variables, continuous variables do not have a minimum-sized unit of measurement; their range of values can be subdivided into increasingly smaller fractional values. *Length* is an example of a continuous variable because there is no minimum unit of length. A particular object may be 12 in. long, it may be 12.5 in. long, or it may be 12.532011 in. long. Although we cannot always measure all possible length values with absolute accuracy, it is possible for objects to exist at an infinite number of lengths.[8] In principle, we can speak of a tenth of an inch, a ten thousandth of an inch, or a ten trillionth of an inch. The variable *gender composition of occupations* is a continuous variable because it is measured in proportions or percentages (e.g., the percentage of women civil engineers), which can be subdivided into smaller and smaller fractions.

This attribute of variables—whether they are continuous or discrete—affects subsequent research operations, particularly measurement procedures, data analysis, and methods of inference and generalization. However, keep in mind that, in practice, some discrete variables can be treated as if they were continuous, and vice versa.

LEARNING CHECK 1.6

Name three continuous and three discrete variables. Determine whether each of the variables in your hypothesis is continuous or discrete.

A CLOSER LOOK 1.1

A CAUTIONARY NOTE: MEASUREMENT ERROR

Social scientists attempt to ensure that the research process is as error free as possible, beginning with how we construct our measurements. We pay attention to two characteristics of measurement: (1) reliability and (2) validity.

Reliability means that the measurement yields consistent results each time it is used. For example, asking a sample of individuals "Do you approve or disapprove of President Barack Obama's job performance?" is more reliable than asking "What do you think of President Donald Trump's job performance?" While responses to the second question are meaningful, the answers might be vague and could be subject to different interpretation. Researchers look for the consistency of measurement over time, in relationship with other related measures, or in measurements or observations made by two or more researchers. Reliability is a prerequisite for validity: We cannot measure a phenomenon if the measure we are using gives us inconsistent results.

Validity refers to the extent to which measures indicate what they are intended to measure. While standardized IQ tests are reliable, it is still debated whether such tests measure intelligence or one's test-taking ability. A measure may not be valid due to individual error (individuals may want to provide socially desirable responses) or method error (questions may be unclear or poorly written).

Specific techniques and practices for determining and improving measurement reliability and validity are the subject of research methods courses.

ANALYZING DATA AND EVALUATING THE HYPOTHESES

Following the data collection stage, researchers analyze their data and evaluate the hypotheses of the study. The data consist of codes and numbers used to represent their observations. In our example, each occupational group would be represented by two scores: (1) the percentage of women and (2) the average wage. If we had collected information on 100 occupations, we would end up with 200 scores, 2 per occupational group. However, the typical research project includes more variables; therefore, the amount of data the researcher confronts is considerably larger. We now must find a systematic way to organize these data, analyze them, and use some set of procedures to decide what they mean. These last steps make up the statistical analysis stage, which is the main topic of this textbook. It is also at this point in the research cycle that statistical procedures will help us evaluate our research hypothesis and assess the theory from which the hypothesis was derived.

Descriptive and Inferential Statistics

Statistical procedures can be divided into two major categories: (1) descriptive statistics and (2) inferential statistics. Before we can discuss the difference between these two types of statistics, we need to understand the terms population and sample. A **population** is the total set of individuals, objects, groups, or events in which the researcher is interested. For example, if we were interested in looking at voting behavior in the last presidential election, we would probably define our population as all citizens who voted in the election. If we wanted to understand the employment patterns of Latinas in our state, we would include in our population all Latinas in our state who are in the labor force.

Population The total set of individuals, objects, groups, or events in which the researcher is interested.

Although we are usually interested in a population, quite often, because of limited time and resources, it is impossible to study the entire population. Imagine interviewing all the citizens of the United States who voted in the last election or even all the Latinas who are in the labor force in our state. Not only would that be very expensive and time-consuming, but we would also probably have a very hard time locating everyone! Fortunately, we can learn a lot about a population if we carefully select a subset from that population. A subset of cases selected from a population is called a **sample**. The process of identifying and selecting this subset is referred to as **sampling**. Researchers usually collect their data from a sample and then generalize their observations to the population. The ultimate goal of sampling is to have a subset that closely resembles the characteristics of the population. Because the sample is intended to represent the population that we are interested in, social scientists take sampling seriously. We'll explore different sampling methods in Chapter 6.

Sample A subset of cases selected from a population.

Sampling The process of identifying and selecting the subset of the population for study.

Descriptive statistics includes procedures that help us organize and describe data collected from either a sample or a population. Occasionally data are collected on an entire population, as in a census. **Inferential statistics**, on the other hand, make predictions or inferences about a population based on observations and analyses of a sample. For instance, the General Social Survey (GSS), from which numerous examples presented in this book are drawn, is conducted every other year by the National Opinion Research Center (NORC) on a representative sample of several thousands of respondents (e.g., a total of 3,842 cases were included in the GSS 2014). The survey, which includes several hundred questions (the data collection interview takes approximately 90 minutes), is designed to provide social science researchers with a readily accessible database of socially relevant attitudes, behaviors, and attributes of a cross section of the U.S. adult population. NORC has verified that the composition of the GSS samples closely resembles census data. But because the data are based on a sample rather than on the entire population, the average of the sample does not equal the average of the population as a whole.

Descriptive statistics Procedures that help us organize and describe data collected from either a sample or a population.

Inferential statistics The logic and procedures concerned with making predictions or inferences about a population from observations and analyses of a sample.

Evaluating the Hypotheses

At the completion of these descriptive and inferential procedures, we can move to the next stage of the research process: the assessment and evaluation of our hypotheses and theories in light of the analyzed data. At this next stage, new questions might be raised about unexpected trends in the data and about other variables that may have to be considered in addition to our original variables. For example, we may have found that the relationship between gender composition of occupations and earnings can be observed with respect to some groups of occupations but not others. Similarly, the relationship between these variables may apply for some racial/ethnic groups but not for others.

These findings provide evidence to help us decide how our data relate to the theoretical framework that guided our research. We may decide to revise our theory and hypothesis to take account of these later findings. Recent studies are modifying what we know about gender segregation in the workplace. These studies suggest that race as well as gender shapes the occupational structure in the United States and helps explain disparities in income. This reformulation of the theory calls for a modified hypothesis and new research, which starts the circular process of research all over again.

Statistics provide an important link between theory and research. As our example on gender segregation demonstrates, the application of statistical techniques is an indispensable part of the research process. The results of statistical analyses help us evaluate our hypotheses and theories, discover unanticipated patterns and trends, and provide the impetus for shaping and reformulating our theories. Nevertheless, the importance of statistics should not diminish the significance of the preceding phases of the research process. Nor does the use of statistics lessen the importance of our own judgment in the entire process. Statistical analysis is a relatively small part of the research process, and even the most rigorous statistical procedures cannot speak for themselves. If our research questions are poorly conceived or our data are flawed due to errors in our design and measurement procedures, our results will be useless.

EXAMINING A DIVERSE SOCIETY

The increasing diversity of American society is relevant to social science. By the middle of this century, if current trends continue unchanged, the United States will no longer be comprised predominantly of European immigrants and their descendants. Due mostly to renewed immigration and higher birthrates, in time, nearly half the U.S. population will be of African, Asian, Latino, or Native American ancestry.

Less partial and distorted explanations of social relations tend to result when researchers, research participants, and the research process itself reflect that diversity. A consciousness of social differences shapes the research questions we ask, how we observe and interpret our findings, and the conclusions we draw. Though diversity has been traditionally defined by race, class, and gender, other social characteristics such as sexual identity, physical ability, religion, and age have been identified as important dimensions of diversity. Statistical procedures and quantitative methodologies can be used to describe our diverse society, and we will begin to look at some applications in the next chapter. For now, we will preview some of these statistical procedures.

In Chapter 2, we will learn how to organize information using descriptive statistics and graphic techniques. These statistical tools can also be employed to learn about the characteristics and experiences of groups in our society that have not been as visible as other groups. For example, in a series of special reports published by the U.S. Census Bureau over the past few years, these descriptive statistical techniques have been used to describe the characteristics and experiences of ethnic minorities and those who are foreign born. Using data published by the U.S. Census Bureau, we discuss various graphic devices that can be used to explore the differences and similarities among the many social groups coexisting within the American society. These devices are also used to emphasize the changing age composition of the U.S. population.

Whereas the similarities and commonalities in social experiences can be depicted using measures of central tendency (Chapter 3), the differences and diversity within social groups can be described using statistical measures of variation (Chapter 4). In Chapters 3 and 4, we examine a variety of social demographic variables including the ethnic composition of the 50 U.S. states.

We will learn about inferential statistics and bivariate analyses in Chapters 5 through 12. First, we review the bases of inferential statistics—the normal distribution, sampling and probability, and estimation—in Chapters 5 to 7. In Chapters 8 to 12, we examine the ways in which class, sex, or ethnicity influence various social behaviors and attitudes. Inferential statistics, such as the *t* test,

A TALE OF SIMPLE ARITHMETIC: HOW CULTURE MAY INFLUENCE HOW WE COUNT

A CLOSER LOOK 1.2

A second-grade schoolteacher posed this problem to the class: "There are four blackbirds sitting in a tree. You take a slingshot and shoot one of them. How many are left?"

"Three," answered the seven-year-old European with certainty. "One subtracted from four leaves three."

"Zero," answered the seven-year-old African with equal certainty. "If you shoot one bird, the others will fly away."[9]

chi-square, and the *F* statistic, help us determine the error involved in using our samples to answer questions about the population from which they are drawn. In addition, we review several methods of bivariate analysis, which are especially suited for examining the association between different social behaviors and attitudes and variables such as race, class, ethnicity, gender, and religion. We use these methods of analysis to show not only how each of these variables operates independently in shaping behavior but also how they interlock to shape our experience as individuals in society.[10]

Whichever model of social research you use—whether you follow a traditional one or integrate your analysis with qualitative data, whether you focus on social differences or any other aspect of social behavior—remember that any application of statistical procedures requires a basic understanding of the statistical concepts and techniques. This introductory text is intended to familiarize you with the range of descriptive and inferential statistics widely applied in the social sciences. Our emphasis on statistical techniques should not diminish the importance of human judgment and your awareness of the person-made quality of statistics. Only with this awareness can statistics become a useful tool for understanding diversity and social life.

LEARNING STATISTICS[11]

After years of teaching statistics, we have learned that what underlies many of the difficulties students have in learning statistics is the belief that it involves mainly memorization of meaningless formulas. There is no denying that statistics involves many strange symbols and unfamiliar terms. It is also true that you need to know some math to do statistics. But although the subject involves some mathematical computations, we will not ask you to know more than four basic operations: (1) addition, (2) subtraction, (3) multiplication, and (4) division.

The language of statistics may appear difficult because these operations (and how they are combined) are written in a code that is unfamiliar to you. These abstract notations are simply part of the language of statistics; much like learning any foreign language, you need to learn the alphabet before you can speak the language. Once you understand the vocabulary and are able to translate the symbols and codes into terms that are familiar to you, you will begin to see how statistical techniques simply provide another source of information with which you can analyze the diverse world around you.

Another strategy for increasing your statistical knowledge is to frame your new learning in a context that is relevant and interesting. Therefore, you will find that we rely on examples from recent sociological literature, pressing social issues, and current events to make real connections to your coursework and your life. A hallmark of our text is the use of real-world examples and data; there are some, but not many, cases of fictional data in this book. We emphasize intuition, logic, and common sense over rote memorization and the derivation of formulas. In each chapter,

DATA AT WORK

At the end of each chapter, the Data at Work feature will introduce you to women and men who use quantitative data and research methods in their professional lives. They represent a wide range of career fields—education, clinical psychology, international studies, public policy, publishing, politics, and research. Some may have been led to their current positions because of the explicit integration of quantitative data and research, while others are accidental data analysts—quantitative data became part of their work portfolio. Though "data" or "statistics" are not included in their job titles, these individuals are collecting, disseminating, and/or analyzing data.

We encourage you to review each profile and imagine how you could use quantitative data and methods at work.

you'll see "Learning Check" boxes where you can apply or test your new knowledge. The chapters also include "A Closer Look" boxes where we provide more detailed or background information about a particular statistical technique or interpretation. Beginning with Chapter 2, we include "Statistics in Practice" and "Reading the Research Literature" features, highlighting the interpretation of data, specific statistical calculations, or published research. We believe being statistically literate involves more than just completing a calculation; it also means learning how to apply and interpret statistical information and being able to say what it means.

What might also help develop confidence in your statistical ability is working with other students. We encourage you to collaborate with your peers as you learn this course material. We have learned that students who are intimidated by statistics do not like to admit it or talk about it. This avoidance mechanism may be an obstacle to overcoming statistics anxiety. Talking about your feelings with other students will help you realize that you are not the only one intimidated by the course. This sharing process is at the heart of the treatment of statistics anxiety—talking to others in a safe group setting will help you take risks and trust your own intuition and judgment. Ultimately, your judgment and intuition lie at the heart of your ability to translate statistical symbols and concepts into a language that makes sense and to interpret data using your newly acquired statistical tools.

MAIN POINTS

- Statistics are procedures used by social scientists to organize, summarize, and communicate information. Only information represented by numbers can be the subject of statistical analysis.
- The research process is a set of activities in which social scientists engage to answer questions, examine ideas, or test theories. It consists of the following stages: asking the research question, formulating the hypotheses, collecting data, analyzing data, and evaluating the hypotheses.
- A theory is a set of assumptions and propositions used for explanation, prediction, and understanding of social phenomena. Theories offer specific concrete predictions about the way observable attributes of people or groups would be interrelated in real life. These predictions, called hypotheses, are tentative answers to research problems.
- A variable is a property of people or objects that takes on two or more values. The variable that the researcher wants to explain (the "effect") is called the dependent variable. The variable that is expected to "cause" or account for the dependent variable is called the independent variable.

- Three conditions are required to establish causal relations: (1) The cause has to precede the effect in time; (2) there has to be an empirical relationship between the cause and the effect; and (3) this relationship cannot be explained by other factors.
- At the nominal level of measurement, numbers or other symbols are assigned to a set of categories to name, label, or classify the observations. At the ordinal level of measurement, categories can be rank-ordered from low to high (or vice versa). At the interval-ratio level of measurement, measurements for all cases are expressed in the same unit.
- A population is the total set of individuals, objects, groups, or events in which the researcher is interested. A sample is a relatively small subset selected from a population. Sampling is the process of identifying and selecting the subset.
- Descriptive statistics includes procedures that help us organize and describe data collected from either a sample or a population. Inferential statistics is concerned with making predictions or inferences about a population from observations and analyses of a sample.

KEY TERMS

data 1
dependent variable 7
descriptive statistics 15
dichotomous variable 11
empirical research 3
hypothesis 4
independent variable 7
inferential statistics 15
interval-ratio measurement 11
nominal measurement 9
ordinal measurement 10
population 15
research process 2
sample 15
sampling 15
statistics 1
theory 4
unit of analysis 5
variable 5

DIGITAL RESOURCES

Get the edge on your studies. **edge.sagepub.com/frankfort8e**

Take a quiz to find out what you've learned.
Review key terms with eFlashcards.
Dive into real research with SAGE Journal Articles.

SPSS DEMONSTRATION [GSS14SSDS-A]

Introduction to Data Sets and Variables

We'll be using a set of computer data and exercises at the end of each chapter. All computer exercises are based on the program IBM SPSS Version 24 or IBM SPSS Statistics Base Student Edition 23.

Throughout this textbook, you'll be working with two data sets. (1) The GSS14SSDS-A and (2) GSS14SSDS-B each contain a selection of 49 variables[12] and 1,500 cases from the 2014 General Social Survey (GSS). The GSS has been conducted biennially since 1972. Conducted by the NORC at the University of Chicago, with principal funding from the National Science Foundation, the GSS is designed to provide social science researchers with a readily accessible database of socially relevant attitudes, behaviors, and attributes of a cross section of the U.S. population. Next to the U.S. Census data, the GSS is the most frequently analyzed source of social science information by educators, legislators, and media outlets.

The SPSS appendix found on this text's study site explains the basic operation and procedures for SPSS for Windows Student Version. We strongly recommend that you refer to this appendix before beginning the SPSS exercises.

When you begin using a data set, you should take the time to review your variables. What are the variables called? What do they measure? What do they mean? There are several ways to do this.

To review your data, you must first open the data file. Files are opened in SPSS by clicking on *File*, then *Open*, and then *Data*. After switching directories and drives to the appropriate location of the files (which may be on a hard disk or on a ZIP drive), you select one data file and click on *Open*. This routine is the same each time you open a data file. SPSS automatically opens each data file in the SPSS Data Editor window labeled Data View. We'll use GSS14SSDS-A.SAV for this demonstration.

One way to review the complete list of variables in a file is to click on the *Utilities* choice from the main menu, then on *Variables* in the list of submenu choices. The SPSS variable names, which are limited to eight characters or less, are listed in the scroll box (refer to Figure 1.4). When a variable name is highlighted, the descriptive label for that variable is listed, along with any missing values and, if available, the value labels for each variable category. (As you use this feature, please note that sometimes SPSS mislabels the variable's measurement level. Always confirm that the reported SPSS measurement level is correct.) SPSS allows you to display data in alphabetical order (based on the variable name) or in the order presented in the file (which may not be alphabetical).

A second way to review all variables is through the Variable View window. Notice on the bottom of your screen that there are two tabs, one for *Data View* and the other for *Variable View*. Click on *Variable View*, and you'll see all the variables listed in the order in which they appear in the Data View window (as depicted in Figure 1.5). Each column provides specific information about the variables. The columns labeled "Label" and "Values" provide the variable label (a brief label of what it's measuring) and value labels (for each variable category).

Figure 1.4 Utilities-Variables Dialog Box

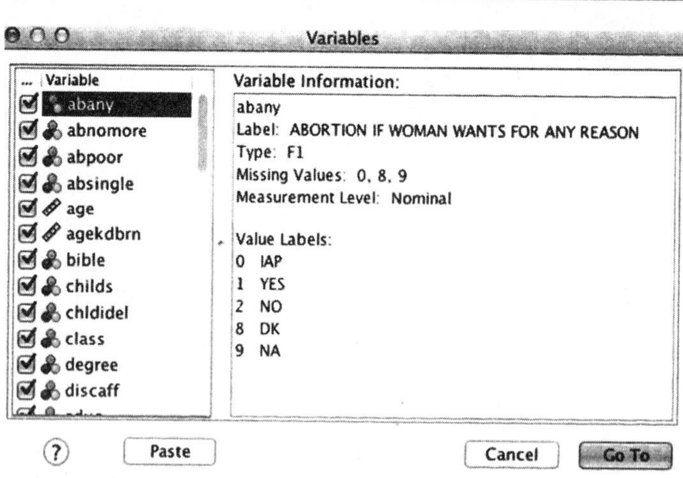

Figure 1.5 Variable View Window for GSS14SDSS-A

	Name	Type	Width	Decimals	Label	Values	Missing	Columns	Align	Measure	Role
1	abany	Numeric	1	0	ABORTION IF W...	{0, IAP}...	0, 8, 9	8	Right	Nominal	Input
2	abnomore	Numeric	1	0	MARRIED--WA...	{0, IAP}...	0, 8, 9	8	Right	Nominal	Input
3	abpoor	Numeric	1	0	LOW INCOME-...	{0, IAP}...	0, 8, 9	8	Right	Nominal	Input
4	absingle	Numeric	1	0	NOT MARRIED	{0, IAP}...	0, 8, 9	8	Right	Nominal	Input
5	age	Numeric	2	0	AGE OF RESPO...	{89, 89 OR ...	0, 98, 99	8	Right	Scale	Input

SPSS PROBLEM [GSS14SSDS-A]

Based on the *Utilities-Variables* option, review the variables from the GSS14SSDS-A. Can you identify three nominal variables, three ordinal variables, and at least one interval-ratio variable? Based on the information in the dialog box or Variable View window, you should be able to identify the variable name, variable label, and category values.

CHAPTER EXERCISES

1. In your own words, explain the relationship of data (collecting and analyzing) to the research process. (Refer to Figure 1.1.)

2. Construct potential hypotheses or research questions to relate the variables in each of the following examples. Also, write a brief statement explaining why you believe there is a relationship between the variables as specified in your hypotheses.

   a. Political party and support of the Affordable Care Act

   b. Income and race/ethnicity

   c. The crime rate and the number of police in a city

   d. Life satisfaction and marital status

   e. Age and support for marijuana legalization

   f. Care of elderly parents and ethnicity

3. Determine the level of measurement for each of the following variables:

   a. The number of people in your statistics class

   b. The percentage of students who are first-generation college students at your school

   c. The name of each academic major offered in your college

   d. The rating of the overall quality of a textbook, on a scale from "Excellent" to "Poor"

   e. The type of transportation a person takes to school (e.g., bus, walk, car)

   f. The number of hours you study for a statistics exam

   g. The rating of the overall quality of your campus coffee shop, on a scale from "Excellent" to "Poor"

4. For each of the variables in Exercise 3 that you classified as interval-ratio, identify whether it is discrete or continuous.

5. Why do you think men and women, on average, do not earn the same amount of money? Develop your own theory to explain the difference. Use three independent variables in your theory, with annual income as your dependent variable. Construct hypotheses to link each independent variable with your dependent variable.

6. For each of the following examples, indicate whether it involves the use of descriptive or inferential statistics. Justify your answer.

   a. The number of unemployed people in the United States

   b. Determining students' opinion about the quality of food at the cafeteria based on a sample of 100 students

   c. The national incidence of breast cancer among Asian women

   d. Conducting a study to determine the rating of the quality of a new smartphone, gathered from 1,000 new buyers

   e. The average GPA of various majors (e.g., sociology, psychology, English) at your university

   f. The change in the number of immigrants coming to the United States from Southeast Asian countries between 2010 and 2015

7. Adela García-Aracil (2007)[13] identified how several factors affected the earnings of young European higher education graduates. Based on data from several EU (European Union) countries, her statistical models included the following variables: annual income (actual dollars), gender (male or female), the number of hours worked per week (actual hours), and years of education (actual years) for each graduate. She also identified each graduate by current job title (senior officials and managers, professionals, technicians, clerks, or service workers).

   a. What is García-Aracil's dependent variable?

   b. Identify two independent variables in her research. Identify the level of measurement for each.

   c. Based on her research, García-Aracil can predict the annual income for other young graduates with similar work experiences and characteristics like the graduates in her sample. Is this an application of descriptive or inferential statistics? Explain.

8. Construct measures of political participation at the nominal, ordinal, and interval-ratio levels. (*Hint:* You can use behaviors such as voting frequency or political party membership.) Discuss the advantages and disadvantages of each.

9. Variables can be measured according to more than one level of measurement. For the following variables, identify at least two levels of measurement. Is one level of measurement better than another? Explain.

   a. Individual age

   b. Annual income

   c. Religiosity

   d. Student performance

   e. Social class

   f. Number of children

2

THE ORGANIZATION AND GRAPHIC PRESENTATION OF DATA

Demographers examine the size, composition, and distribution of human populations. Changes in the birth, death, and migration rates of a population affect its composition and social characteristics.[1] In order to examine a large population, researchers often have to deal with very large amounts of data. For example, imagine the amount of data it takes to describe the immigrant or elderly population in the United States. To make sense out of these data, a researcher has to organize and summarize the data in some systematic fashion. In this chapter, we review two such methods used by social scientists: (1) the creation of frequency distributions and (2) the use of graphic presentation.

Chapter Learning Objectives

1. Construct and analyze frequency, percentage, and cumulative distributions
2. Calculate proportions and percentages
3. Compare and contrast frequency and percentage distributions for nominal, ordinal, and interval-ratio variables
4. Construct and interpret a pie chart, bar graph, histogram, the statistical map, line graph, and time-series chart

FREQUENCY DISTRIBUTIONS

The most basic way to organize data is to classify the observations into a frequency distribution. A **frequency distribution** is a table that reports the number of observations that fall into each category of the variable we are analyzing. Constructing a frequency distribution is usually the first step in the statistical analysis of data.

Frequency distribution A table reporting the number of observations that fall into each category of the variable.

Immigration has been described as "remaking America with political, economic, and cultural ramifications."[2] Globalization has fueled migration, particularly since the beginning of the 21st century. Workers migrate because of the promise of employment and higher standards of living than what is attainable in their home countries. Data reveal that many migrants seek specifically to move to the United States.[3] The U.S. Census Bureau uses the term foreign born to refer to those who are not U.S. citizens at birth. The U.S. Census estimates that nearly 13% of the U.S. population or approximately 41 million people are foreign born.[4] Immigrants are not one homogeneous group but are many diverse groups. Table 2.1 shows the frequency distribution of the world region of birth for the foreign-born population.

The frequency distribution is organized in a table, which has a number (2.1) and a descriptive title. The title indicates the kind of data

Table 2.1 Frequency Distribution for Categories of Region of Birth for Foreign-Born Population, 2012

Region of Birth	Frequency (f)
Mexico	11,489,387
South and East Asia	10,443,902
Caribbean	3,882,592
Central America	3,172,307
South America	2,731,619
Middle East	1,578,801
All other	7,439,616
Total	40,738,224

Source: Anna Brown and Eileen Patton, *Statistical Portrait of the Foreign-Born Population of the United States, 2012,* 2014.

presented: "Categories of Region of Birth for Foreign-Born Population." The table consists of two columns. The first column identifies the variable (world region of birth) and its categories. The second column, with the heading "Frequency (f)," tells the number of cases in each category as well as the total number of cases (N = 40,738,224). Note also that the source of the table is clearly identified. It tells us that the data are from a 2014 report by Anna Brown and Eileen Patton (though the information is based on 2012 U.S. Census data). The source of the data can be reported as a source note or in the title of the table.

What can you learn from the information presented in Table 2.1? The table shows that as of 2012, approximately 41 million people were classified as foreign born. Out of this group, the majority, about 11.5 million people, were from Mexico, 10.4 million were from Asia, followed by 7.4 million from the category of all other countries.

PROPORTIONS AND PERCENTAGES

Frequency distributions are helpful in presenting information in a compact form. However, when the number of cases is large, the frequencies may be difficult to grasp. To standardize these raw frequencies, we can translate them into relative frequencies—that is, proportions or percentages.

Proportion A relative frequency obtained by dividing the frequency in each category by the total number of cases.

A **proportion** is a relative frequency obtained by dividing the frequency in each category by the total number of cases. To find a proportion (p), divide the frequency (f) in each category by the total number of cases (N):

$$p = \frac{f}{N} \tag{2.1}$$

where

f = frequency

N = total number of cases

We've calculated the proportion for the three largest groups of foreign born. First, the proportion of foreign born originally from Mexico is

$$\frac{11,489,387}{40,738,224} = .282$$

The proportion of foreign born who were originally from South and East Asia is

$$\frac{10,443,902}{40,738,224} = .256$$

The proportion of foreign born who were originally from all other countries is

$$\frac{7,439,616}{40,738,224} = .183$$

The proportion of foreign born who were originally from other reported areas (combining the Caribbean, Central and South America, and Middle East) is

$$\frac{11,365,319}{40,738,224} = .279$$

Proportions should always sum to 1.00 (allowing for some rounding errors). Thus, in our example, the sum of the six proportions is

$$0.28 + 0.26 + 0.18 + 0.28 = 1.0$$

To determine a frequency from a proportion, we simply multiply the proportion by the total N:

$$f = p(N) \tag{2.2}$$

Thus, the frequency of foreign born from South and East Asia can be calculated as

$$0.26(40,738,224) = 10,591,938$$

The obtained frequency differs somewhat from the actual frequency of 10,443,902. This difference is due to rounding off of the proportion. If we use the actual proportion instead of the rounded proportion, we obtain the correct frequency:

$$0.256366158\,(40,738,224) = 10,443,902$$

We can also express frequencies as percentages. A **percentage** is a relative frequency obtained by dividing the frequency in each category by the total number of cases and multiplying by 100. In most statistical reports, frequencies are presented as percentages rather than proportions. Percentages express the size of the frequencies as if there were a total of 100 cases.

Percentage A relative frequency obtained by dividing the frequency in each category by the total number of cases and multiplying by 100.

To calculate a percentage, multiply the proportion by 100:

$$\text{Percentage (\%)} = \frac{f}{N}(100) \tag{2.3}$$

or

$$\text{Percentage (\%)} = p(100) \tag{2.4}$$

Thus, the percentage of respondents who were originally from Mexico is

$$0.28(100) = 28\%$$

LEARNING CHECK 2.1

Calculate the proportion and percentage of males and females in your statistics class. What proportion is female?

PERCENTAGE DISTRIBUTIONS

Percentage distribution A table showing the percentage of observations falling into each category of the variable.

Percentages are usually displayed as percentage distributions. A **percentage distribution** is a table showing the percentage of observations falling into each category of the variable. For example, Table 2.2 presents the frequency distribution of categories of places of origin (Table 2.1) along with the corresponding percentage distribution. Percentage distributions (or proportions) should always show the base (N) on which they were computed. Thus, in Table 2.2, the base on which the percentages were computed is $N = 40{,}738{,}224$.

THE CONSTRUCTION OF FREQUENCY DISTRIBUTIONS

In this section, you will learn how to construct frequency distributions. Most often, we can use statistical software to accomplish this, but it is important to go through the process to understand how frequency distributions are actually constructed.

Table 2.2 Frequency and Percentage Distributions for Categories of Region of Birth for Foreign Born, 2012

Region of Birth	Frequency (f)	Percentage (%)
Mexico	11,489,387	28
South and East Asia	10,443,902	26
Caribbean	3,882,592	9
Central America	3,172,307	8
South America	2,731,619	7
Middle East	1,578,801	4
All other	7,439,616	18
Total	40,738,224	100

Source: Anna Brown and Eileen Patton, *Statistical Portrait of the Foreign-Born Population of the United States, 2012*, 2014. Retrieved from http://www.pewhispanic.org/2014/04/29/statistical-portrait-of-the-foreign-born-population-in-the-united-states-2012/

For nominal and ordinal variables, constructing a frequency distribution is quite simple. To do so, count and report the number of cases that fall into each category of the variable along with the total number of cases (*N*). For the purpose of illustration, let's take a small random sample of 40 cases from a General Social Survey (GSS) sample and record their scores on the following variables: gender, a nominal-level variable; degree, an ordinal measurement of education; and age and number of children, both interval-ratio variables. The use of "male" and "female" in parts of this book is in keeping with the GSS categories for the variable "sex" (respondent's sex).

The interviewer recorded the gender of each respondent at the beginning of the interview. To measure degree, researchers asked each individual to indicate the highest degree completed: less than high school, high school, some college, bachelor's degree, and graduate degree. The first category represented the lowest level of education. Researchers calculated respondents' age based on the respondent's birth year. The number of children was determined by the question, "How many children have you ever had?" The answers given by our subsample of 40 respondents are displayed in Table 2.3. Note that each row in the table represents a respondent, whereas each column represents a variable. This format is conventional in the social sciences.

You can see that it is going to be difficult to make sense of these data just by eyeballing Table 2.3. How many of these 40 respondents are males? How many said that they had a graduate degree? How many were older than 50 years of age? To answer these questions, we construct a frequency distribution for each variable.

Frequency Distributions for Nominal Variables

Let's begin with the nominal variable, gender. First, we tally the number of males, then the number of females (the column of tallies has been included in Table 2.4 for the purpose of illustration). The tally results are then used to construct the frequency distribution presented in Table 2.4. The table has a title describing its content ("Frequency Distribution of the Variable Gender: GSS Subsample"). Its categories (male and female) and their associated frequencies are clearly listed; in addition, the total number of cases (*N*) is also reported. The Percentage column is the percentage distribution for this variable. To convert the Frequency column to percentages, simply divide each frequency by the total number of cases and multiply by 100. Percentage distributions are routinely added to almost any frequency table and are especially important if comparisons with other groups are to be considered. Immediately, we can see that it is easier to read the information. There are 25 females and 15 males in this sample. Based on this frequency distribution, we can also conclude that the majority of sample respondents are female.

LEARNING CHECK 2.2

Construct a frequency and percentage distribution for males and females in your statistics class.

Frequency Distributions for Ordinal Variables

To construct a frequency distribution for ordinal-level variables, follow the same procedures outlined for nominal-level variables. Table 2.5 presents the frequency distribution for the variable degree. The table shows that 60.0%, a majority, indicated that their highest degree was a high school degree.

Table 2.3 A GSS Subsample of 40 Respondents

Gender of Respondent	Degree	Number of Children	Age
M	Bachelor	1	43
F	High school	2	71
F	High school	0	71
M	High school	0	37
M	High school	0	28
F	High school	6	34
F	High school	4	69
F	Graduate	0	51
F	Bachelor	0	76
M	Graduate	2	48
M	Graduate	0	49
M	Less than high school	3	62
F	Less than high school	8	71
F	High school	1	32
F	High school	1	59
F	High school	1	71
M	High school	0	34
M	Bachelor	0	39
F	Bachelor	2	50
M	High school	3	82
F	High school	1	45
M	High school	0	22
M	High school	2	40
F	High school	2	46
M	High school	0	29
F	High school	1	75
F	High school	0	23
M	Bachelor	2	35
M	Bachelor	3	44
F	High school	3	47
M	High school	1	84
F	Graduate	1	45
F	Less than high school	3	24
F	Graduate	0	47
F	Less than high school	5	67
F	High school	1	21
F	High school	0	24
F	High school	3	49
F	High school	3	45
F	Graduate	3	37

Note: M, male; F, female.

Table 2.4 Frequency Distribution of the Variable Gender, GSS Subsample

Gender	Tallies	Frequency (f)	Percentage (%)
Male	卌 卌 卌	15	37.5
Female	卌 卌 卌 卌 卌	25	62.5
Total (*N*)		40	100.0

Table 2.5 Frequency Distribution of the Variable Degree, GSS Subsample

Degree	Tallies	Frequency (f)	Percentage (%)
Less than high school	||||	4	10.0
High school	卌 卌 卌 卌 ||||	24	60.0
Bachelor	卌 |	6	15.0
Graduate	卌 |	6	15.0
Total (*N*)		40	100.0

The major difference between frequency distributions for nominal and ordinal variables is the order in which the categories are listed. The categories for nominal-level variables do not have to be listed in any particular order. For example, we could list females first and males second without changing the nature of the distribution. Because the categories or values of ordinal variables are rank-ordered, however, they must be listed in a way that reflects their rank—from the lowest to the highest or from the highest to the lowest. Thus, the data on degree in Table 2.5 are presented in declining order from "less than high school" (the lowest educational category) to "graduate" (the highest educational category).

Frequency Distributions for Interval-Ratio Variables

We hope that you agree by now that constructing frequency distributions for nominal- and ordinal-level variables is rather straightforward. Simply list the categories and count the number of observations that fall into each category. Building a frequency distribution for interval-ratio variables with relatively few values is also easy. For example, when constructing a frequency distribution for number of children, simply list the number of children and report the corresponding frequency, as shown in Table 2.6.

Very often interval-ratio variables have a wide range of values, which makes simple frequency distributions very difficult to read. For example, take a look at the frequency distribution for the variable *age* in Table 2.7. The distribution contains age values ranging from 21 to 84 years. For a more concise picture, the large number of different scores could be reduced into a smaller number of groups, each containing a range of scores. Table 2.8 displays such a grouped

Table 2.6 Frequency Distribution of Variable Number of Children, GSS Subsample

Number of Children	Frequency (f)	Percentage (%)
0	13	32.5
1	9	22.5
2	6	15.0
3	8	20.0
4	1	2.5
5	1	2.5
6	1	2.5
7+	1	2.5
Total (*N*)	40	100.0

Table 2.7 Frequency Distribution of the Variable Age, GSS Subsample

Age of Respondent	Frequency (f)	Age of Respondent	Frequency (f)
21	1	59	1
22	1	62	1
23	1	67	1
24	2	69	1
28	1	71	4
29	1	75	1
32	1	76	1
34	2	82	1
35	1	84	1
37	2		
39	1		
40	1		
43	1		
44	1		
45	3		
46	1		
47	2		
48	1		
49	2		
50	1		
51	1		

frequency distribution of the data in Table 2.7. Each group, known as a class interval, now contains 10 possible scores instead of 1. Thus, the ages of 21, 22, 23, 24, 28, and 29 all fall into a single class interval of 20–29. The second column of Table 2.8, Frequency, tells us the number of respondents who fall into each of the intervals—for example, that seven respondents fall into the class interval of 20–29. Having grouped the scores, we can clearly see that the biggest single age group is between 40 and 49 years (12 out of 40, or 30% of sample). The percentage distribution that we have added to Table 2.8 displays the relative frequency of each interval and emphasizes this pattern as well.

LEARNING CHECK 2.3

Can you verify that Table 2.8 was constructed correctly? Use Table 2.7 to determine the frequency of cases that fall into the categories of Table 2.8.

The decision as to how many groups to use and, therefore, how wide the intervals should be is usually up to the researcher and depends on what makes sense in terms of the purpose of the research. The rule of thumb is that an interval width should be large enough to avoid too many categories but not so large that significant differences between observations are concealed. Obviously, the number of intervals depends on the width of each. For instance, if you are working with scores ranging from 10 to 60 and you establish an interval width of 10, you will have five intervals.

Table 2.8 Grouped Frequency Distribution of the Variable Age, GSS Subsample

Age Category	Frequency (f)	Percentage (%)
20–29	7	17.5
30–39	7	17.5
40–49	12	30.0
50–59	3	7.5
60–69	3	7.5
70–79	6	15.0
80–89	2	5.0
Total (*N*)	40	100.0

LEARNING CHECK 2.4

If you are having trouble distinguishing between nominal, ordinal, and interval-ratio variables, review the section on levels of measurement in Chapter 1. The distinction between these levels of measurement will be important throughout the book.

CUMULATIVE DISTRIBUTIONS

Cumulative frequency distribution A distribution showing the frequency at or below each category (class interval or score) of the variable.

Sometimes, we may be interested in locating the relative position of a given score in a distribution. For example, we may be interested in finding out how many or what percentage of our sample was younger than 40 or older than 60. Frequency distributions can be presented in a cumulative fashion to answer such questions. A cumulative frequency distribution shows the frequencies at or below each category of the variable.

Cumulative frequencies are appropriate only for variables that are measured at an ordinal level or higher. They are obtained by adding to the frequency in each category the frequencies of all the categories below it.

Let's look at Table 2.9. It shows the cumulative frequencies based on the frequency distribution from Table 2.8. The cumulative frequency column, denoted by *Cf*, shows the number of persons at or below each interval. For example, you can see that 14 of the 40 respondents were 39 years old or younger, and 29 respondents were 59 years old or younger.

To construct a cumulative frequency distribution, start with the frequency in the lowest class interval (or with the lowest score, if the data are ungrouped), and add to it the

Table 2.9 Grouped Frequency Distribution and Cumulative Frequency for the Variable Age, GSS Subsample

Age Category	Frequency (f)	Cumulative Frequency (Cf)
20–29	7	7
30–39	7	14
40–49	12	26
50–59	3	29
60–69	3	32
70–79	6	38
80–89	2	40
Total (*N*)	40	

A CLOSER LOOK 2.1

REAL LIMITS, STATED LIMITS, AND MIDPOINTS OF CLASS INTERVALS

The intervals presented in Table 2.8 constitute the categories of the variable age that we used to classify the survey's respondents. In Chapter 1 ("The What and the Why of Statistics"), we noted that our variables need to be both exhaustive and mutually exclusive. These principles apply to the intervals here as well. This means that each of the 40 respondents can be classified into one and only one category. In addition, we should be able to classify all the possible scores.

In our example, these requirements are met: Each observation score fits into only one interval, and there is an appropriate category to classify each individual score as recorded in Table 2.8. However, if you looked closely at Table 2.8, you may have noticed that there is actually a gap of 1 year between adjacent intervals. A gap could create a problem with scores that have fractional values. Though age is conventionally rounded down, let's suppose for a moment that respondent's age had been reported with more precision. Where would you classify a woman who was 49.25 years old? Notice that her age would actually fall between the intervals 40–49 and 50–59! To avoid this potential problem, use the real limits shown in the following table rather than the stated limits listed in Table 2.8.

Real limits extend the upper and lower limits of the intervals by .5. For instance, the real limits for the interval 40–49 are 39.5–49.5; the real limits for the interval 50–59 are 49.5–59.5; and so on. (Scores that fall exactly at the upper real limit or the lower real limit of the interval [e.g., 59.5 or 49.5] are usually rounded to the closest even number. The number 59.5 would be rounded to 60 and would thus be included in the interval 59.5–69.5.) In the following table, we include both the stated limits and real limits for the grouped frequency distribution of respondent's age. So where would you classify a respondent who was 49.25 years old? (*Answer:* In the interval 39.5–49.5.) How about 19.9? (In the interval 19.5–29.5.)

The midpoint is a single number that represents the entire interval. A midpoint is calculated by adding the lower and upper real limits of the interval and dividing by 2. The midpoint of the interval 19.5–29.5, for instance, is (19.5 + 29.5) ÷ 2 = 24.5. The midpoint for all the intervals of the table are displayed in the third column.

Even though grouped frequency distributions are very helpful in summarizing information, remember that they are only a summary and therefore involve a considerable loss of detail. Since most researchers and students have access to computers, grouped frequencies are used only when the raw data are not available. Most of the statistical procedures described in later chapters are based on the raw scores.

Respondent's Age			
Stated Limits	Real Limits	Midpoint	Frequency (f)
20–29	19.5–29.5	24.5	7
30–39	29.5–39.5	34.5	7
40–49	39.5–49.5	44.5	12
50–59	49.5–59.5	54.5	3
60–69	59.5–69.5	64.5	3
70–79	69.5–79.5	74.5	6
80–89	79.5–89.5	84.5	2
Total (*N*)			40

frequencies in the next highest class interval. Continue adding the frequencies until you reach the last class interval. The cumulative frequency in the last class interval will be equal to the total number of cases (*N*). In Table 2.9, the frequency associated with the first class interval (20–29) is 7. The cumulative frequency associated with this interval is also 7, since there are no cases below this class interval. The frequency for the second class interval is 7. The cumulative frequency for this interval is 7 + 7 = 14. To obtain the cumulative frequency of 26 for the third interval, we add its frequency (12) to the cumulative frequency associated with the second class interval (14). Continue this process until you reach the last class interval. Therefore, the cumulative frequency for the last interval is equal to 40, the total number of cases (*N*).

Cumulative percentage distribution A distribution showing the percentage at or below each category (class interval or score) of the variable.

We can also construct a cumulative percentage distribution (*C*%), which has wider applications than the cumulative frequency distribution (*Cf*). A **cumulative percentage distribution** shows the percentage at or below each category (class interval or score) of the variable. A cumulative percentage distribution is constructed using the same procedure as for a cumulative frequency distribution except that the percentages—rather than the raw frequencies—for each category are added to the total percentages for all the previous categories.

In Table 2.10, we have added the cumulative percentage distribution to the frequency and percentage distributions shown in Table 2.8. The cumulative percentage distribution shows, for example, that 35% of the sample was 39 years or younger. Like the percentage distributions described earlier, cumulative percentage distributions are especially useful when you want to compare differences between groups. For an example of how cumulative percentages are used in a comparison, we used GSS data to contrast the opinions of whites and blacks about whether they believe immigrants take jobs away from native-born Americans. Respondents were asked, "How much do you agree or disagree with the following statement? Immigrants take jobs away." The percentage distribution and the cumulative percentage distribution for whites and blacks are shown in Table 2.11. (This table is referred to as a bivariate table, reporting the overlap between two variables—[1] respondent race and [2] level of agreement to the immigration statement. We'll discuss bivariate tables in depth in Chapter 9 ["Bivariate Tables"].)

The cumulative percentage distributions suggest that a higher percentage of blacks agree to the statement that immigrants take away jobs. The two groups are separated by 5 percentage

Table 2.10 Grouped Frequency Distribution and Cumulative Percentages for the Variable Age, GSS Subsample

Age Category	Frequency (f)	Percentage (%)	Cumulative Percentage (C%)
20–29	7	17.5	17.5
30–39	7	17.5	35.0
40–49	12	30.0	65.0
50–59	3	7.5	72.5
60–69	3	7.5	80.0
70–79	6	15.0	95.0
80–89	2	5.0	100.0
Total (*N*)	40	100.0	

Table 2.11 Cumulative Percentage Distribution for "Immigrants Take Away Jobs" by Race, GSS 2014

	Whites		Blacks	
	Percentage (%)	Cumulative Percentage (C%)	Percentage (%)	Cumulative Percentage (C%)
Strongly agree	7.3	7.3	10.7	10.7
Agree	31.7	39	33.3	44
Neither	19.8	58.8	28	72
Disagree	35	93.8	24	96
Strongly disagree	6.2	100.0	4	100.0
Total	100.0		100.0	

points—44% of black respondents indicated that they either strongly agreed or agreed to the statement, while 39% of white respondents said the same. (Note that a higher percentage of whites disagree with the statement than blacks.) These data prompt many other questions about the role that race or other variables may play in attitudes about legal and unauthorized immigration. What explains the difference between white and black respondents? What would the differences be if we compared men with women? Whites with Latinos? Employed with unemployed individuals?

RATES

Terms such as birthrate, unemployment rate, and marriage rate are often used by social scientists and demographers and then quoted in the popular media to describe population trends. But what exactly are rates, and how are they constructed? A rate is obtained by dividing the number of actual occurrences in a given time period by the number of possible occurrences.

Rate A number obtained by dividing the number of actual occurrences in a given time period by the number of possible occurrences.

$$\text{Rate} = \frac{f}{\text{Population}} \quad (2.5)$$

For example, to determine the poverty rate for 2014, the U.S. Census Bureau took the number of men and women in poverty in 2014 (actual occurrences) and divided it by the total population in 2014 (possible occurrences). The 2014 rate can be expressed as

$$\text{Poverty rate, 2014} = \frac{\text{Number of people in poverty in 2014}}{\text{Total population in 2014}}$$

Since 46,657,000 people were poor in 2014 and the number for the total population was 315,804,000, the poverty rate for 2014 is

$$\text{Poverty rate, 2014} = \frac{46{,}657{,}000}{315{,}804{,}000} = 0.15$$

The poverty rate in 2014 as reported by the U.S. Census Bureau was 15% (.15 × 100). This means that for every 1,000 people, 150 were poor according to the U.S. Census Bureau definition. Rates are often expressed as rates per thousand or hundred thousand to eliminate decimal points and make the number easier to interpret.

The preceding poverty rate can be referred to as a crude rate because it is based on the total population. Rates can be calculated on the general population or on a more narrowly defined select group. For instance, poverty rates are often given for the number of people who are 18 years or younger—highlighting how our young are vulnerable to poverty. The poverty rate for those 18 years or younger is as follows:

$$\text{Poverty rate for those 18 years or younger, 2014} = \frac{15{,}540{,}000}{73{,}556{,}000} = 0.21$$

We could even take a look at the poverty rate for older Americans:

$$\text{Poverty rate for those 65 years of age or older, 2014} = \frac{4{,}590{,}000}{45{,}994{,}000} = 0.10$$

LEARNING CHECK 2.5

Law enforcement agencies routinely record crime rates (the number of crimes committed relative to the size of a population), arrest rates (the number of arrests made relative to the number of crimes reported), and conviction rates (the number of convictions relative to the number of cases tried). What other variables can be expressed as rates?

READING THE RESEARCH LITERATURE: ACCESS TO PUBLIC BENEFITS

Statistical tables that display frequency distributions or other kinds of statistical information are found in virtually every book, article, or newspaper report that makes any use of statistics. However, the inclusion of statistical tables in a report or an article doesn't necessarily mean that the research is more scientific or convincing. You will always have to ask what the tables are saying and judge whether the information is relevant or accurately presented and analyzed. Most statistical tables presented in the social science literature are a good deal more complex than those we describe in this chapter.

The first step in reading any statistical table is to understand what the researcher is trying to tell you. Begin your inspection of the table by reading its title, as the title usually describes the central contents of the table. Check for any source notes to the table; such notes reveal the source of the data or the table and any additional information that the author considers important. Next, examine the column and row headings and subheadings. These identify the variables, their categories, and the kind of statistics presented, such as raw frequencies or percentages. The main body of the table includes the appropriate statistics (frequencies, percentages, rates, etc.) for each variable or group as defined by each heading and subheading.

Table 2.12 was included in an article written by Yolanda Padilla and her colleagues (2006) about the disadvantages faced by the young children of Mexican immigrants in unmarried families. For their analysis, the researchers relied on data from the Fragile Families and Child Wellbeing Study, a nationally representative, longitudinal survey that follows a cohort of new parents and their children for 5 years. They compared parental demographic and socio-economic characteristics, formal and informal support, and child well-being indicators for Mexican immigrant and U.S.-born unmarried mothers. Note that several categories of U.S.-born women (Mexican American, black non-Hispanic, white non-Hispanic) are presented. Social scientists are seldom interested in a single population. The most interesting questions pertain to differences between two or more groups.[5] Table 2.12 summarizes the utilization of public benefits and programs by immigrant and U.S.-born groups. The columns or rows do not add up to 100%.

Note that the frequency (*f*) for each category is not reported in Table 2.12. Although the table is quite simple, it is important to examine it carefully, including its title and headings, to make sure that you understand what the information means.

Table 2.12 Percentage Distribution of Access to Public Benefits Among Mexican Immigrant and U.S.-Born Unmarried Mothers

	Mexican Born	U.S. Born			
Variables	Mexican Immigrant	Mexican American	Black Non-Hispanic	White Non-Hispanic	Total U.S.-Born Population
Prenatal care in first 3 months of pregnancy	79	72.9	78.4	81.8	78.1
Health insurance					
Medicaid	77	79	70.2	70	69.1
Private	16.3	16.2	22.9	23.8	24.8
Other	6.7	4.8	6.9	5.2	6.1
TANF receipt[a]	12.2	20.4	38.9	14.8	29.6
Food stamp receipt	21.3	40.3	53.5	30.4	45.8
Rent assistance	7.2	22.3	24.4	99	21.0
Head Start	5.2	5.4	3.5	3.8	4.0
WIC receipt[b]	84.6	88.1	86.7	76	84.6

Source: Adapted from Yolanda Padilla, Melissa Dalton Radey, Robert Hummer, and Eunjeong Kim, "The Living Conditions of U.S.-Born Children of Mexican Immigrants in Unmarried Families," *Hispanic Journal of Behavioral Sciences* 28, no. 3 (2006), p. 343.

Notes:
a. TANF = Temporary Assistance for Needy Families.
b. WIC = Women, Infants, and Children Program.

LEARNING CHECK 2.6

Inspect Table 2.12 and answer the following questions:

What is the source of this table?

How many variables are presented? What are their names?

What is represented by the numbers presented in the second column? In the last row of the table?

What do the authors tell us about the table?

> Among unmarried mothers, there is no significant difference in access to prenatal care or infant health care (well-child visits) based on immigrant status. Differences in access to health insurance are evident only between Mexican immigrant mothers and non-Hispanic white mothers, who tend to have lower rates of Medicaid and higher rates of private insurance.
>
> Immigrant mothers are significantly less likely to receive welfare assistance in the form of Temporary Assistance for Needy Families (TANF) than are U.S.-born mothers. Only about 12.2% of Mexican immigrant mothers receive TANF compared with 20.4% of U.S.-born Mexican mothers and 38.9% of non-Hispanic black mothers. Unmarried Mexican immigrant mothers do not differ significantly from non-Hispanic white mothers in this measure. The same pattern is observed for food stamps and rent assistance. Only 21.3% of unmarried Mexican immigrant mothers receive food stamps, and only 7.2% receive rent assistance. In terms of assistance from Head Start/Early Head Start, we found no significant difference between Mexican immigrants and natives. Finally, rates of receipt of Women, Infants, and Children (WIC) Program benefits are similar across all groups, although Mexican immigrant mothers are slightly more likely to receive WIC benefits than are non-Hispanic white mothers.[6]

The authors conclude that in spite of having fewer resources, immigrant mothers are less likely than U.S.-born mothers to receive formal support (which includes access to public assistance and private health insurance).

Further analyses could examine why these differences exist. Other variables that explain the differences between these groups could be identified (such as educational attainment, social support networks, or employment status). For a more detailed analysis of the relationships between these variables, you need to consider some of the more complex techniques of bivariate (two variable) analysis and statistical inference. We consider these advanced techniques beginning with Chapter 8 ("Testing Hypotheses").

GRAPHIC PRESENTATION OF DATA

You have probably heard that "a picture is worth a thousand words." The same can be said about statistical graphs because they summarize hundreds or thousands of numbers. Graphs communicate information visually, rather than in words or numbers and are often utilized in news stories, research reports, and government documents. Information that is presented graphically may seem more accessible than the same information when presented in frequency distributions or in other tabular forms.

In this section, you will learn about some of the most commonly used graphical techniques. We concentrate less on the technical details of how to create graphs and more on how to choose the appropriate graphs to make statistical information coherent. We also focus on how to interpret graphically presented information.

As we introduce various graphical techniques, we also show you how to use graphs to tell a story. The particular story we tell here is that of the elderly in the United States and throughout the world. Demographers predict that over the next several decades, the U.S. overall population growth will be among middle-aged and older Americans, what demographers have referred to as the graying of America. "Population aging is a long-range trend that will characterize our society as we continue into the 21st century. It is a force we all will cope with for the rest of our lives," warns gerontologist Harry Moody.[7]

The different types of graphs demonstrate the many facets and challenges of our aging society. People have tended to talk about seniors as if they were a homogeneous group, but the different graphical techniques illustrate the wide variation in economic characteristics, living arrangements, and family status among people aged 65 years and older.

Here we focus on those graphical techniques most widely used in the social sciences. The first two, (1) the pie chart and (2) bar graph, are appropriate for nominal and ordinal variables. The next two, (3) histograms and (4) line graphs, are used with interval-ratio variables. We also discuss statistical maps and time-series charts. The statistical map is most often used with interval-ratio data. Finally, time-series charts are used to show how some variables change over time.

THE PIE CHART

The elderly population of the United States is racially heterogeneous. As the data in Table 2.13 show, of the total 43,177,961 elderly (defined as persons 65 years and older) in 2010–2014, the two largest racial groups were whites (84.5%) and blacks (8.7%).

A **pie chart** shows the differences in frequencies or percentages among the categories of a nominal or an ordinal variable. The categories are displayed as segments of a circle whose pieces add up to 100% of the total frequencies. The pie chart shown in Figure 2.1 displays the same information that Table 2.13 presents (notice that due to rounding the

Pie chart A graph showing the differences in frequencies or percentages among the categories of a nominal or an ordinal variable. The categories are displayed as segments of a circle whose pieces add up to 100% of the total frequencies.

Table 2.13 Five-Year Estimates of the U.S. Population 65 Years and Over by Race, 2010–2014

Race	Percentage (%)
White alone	84.5
Black alone	8.7
American Indian alone	0.5
Asian alone	3.8
Native Hawaiian or Pacific Islander alone	0.1
Some other race alone	1.5
Two or more races combined	1.0
Total	100.1

Source: U.S. Census Bureau, *American Fact Finder*, Table S0101, 2015.

Figure 2.1 Five-Year Estimates of the U.S. Population 65 Years and Over by Race, 2010–2014

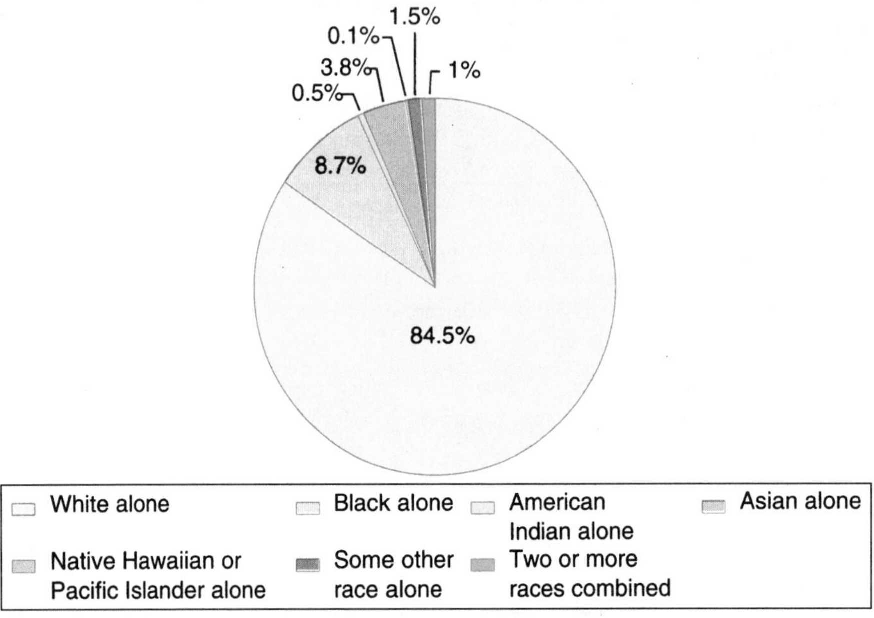

Source: U.S. Census Bureau, *American Fact Finder*, Table S0103, 2015.

Figure 2.2 Five-Year Estimates of U.S. Population 65 Years and Over by Race, 2010–2014

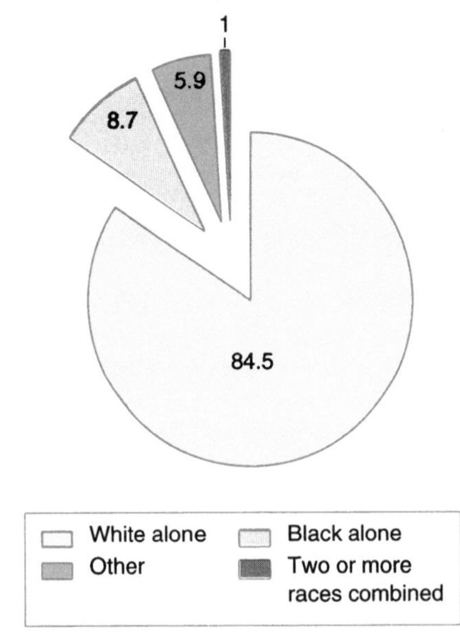

Source: U.S. Census Bureau, *American Fact Finder*, Table S01013, 2015.

percentages in Table 2.13 do not add up to 100%). Although you can inspect these data in Table 2.13, you can interpret the information more easily by seeing it presented in the pie chart in Figure 2.1.

Did you notice that the percentages for several of the racial groups are 3.8% or less? It might be better to combine categories—American Indian, Asian, native Hawaiian, some other race—into an "other races" category. This will leave us with three distinct categories: (1) white, (2) black, and (3) other and two or more races. The revised pie chart is presented in Figure 2.2. We can highlight the diversity of the elderly population by "exploding" the pie chart, moving the nonwhite segments representing these groups slightly outward to draw them to the viewer's attention. This also highlights the largest slice of the pie chart—white elderly comprised 84.5% of the U.S. elderly population in 2014–2015.

THE BAR GRAPH

The bar graph provides an alternative way to graphically present nominal or ordinal data. It shows the differences in frequencies or percentages among categories of a nominal or an ordinal variable. The categories are displayed as rectangles of equal width with their height proportional to the frequency or percentage of the category.

Bar graph A graph showing the differences in frequencies or percentages among the categories of a nominal or an ordinal variable. The categories are displayed as rectangles of equal width with their height proportional to the frequency or percentage of the category.

Let's illustrate the bar graph with an overview of the marital status of the elderly. Figure 2.3 is a bar graph displaying the percentage distribution of persons 65 years old and over by marital status in 2010. This chart is interpreted similar to a pie chart except that the categories of the variable are arrayed along the horizontal axis (sometimes referred to as the *X*-axis) and the percentages along the vertical axis (sometimes referred to as the *Y*-axis). This bar graph is easily interpreted: It shows that in 2010, the majority of the elderly population were married. Specifically, 54.2% were married, 28.6% were widowed, 11.2% divorced, 1.2% separated, and 4.2% never married. Due to rounding, the percentages add up to 99.4%.

Construct a bar graph by first labeling the categories of the variables along the horizontal axis. For these categories, construct rectangles of equal width, with the height of each

Figure 2.3 Marital Status of U.S. Elderly (65 Years and Older), Percentages, 2010

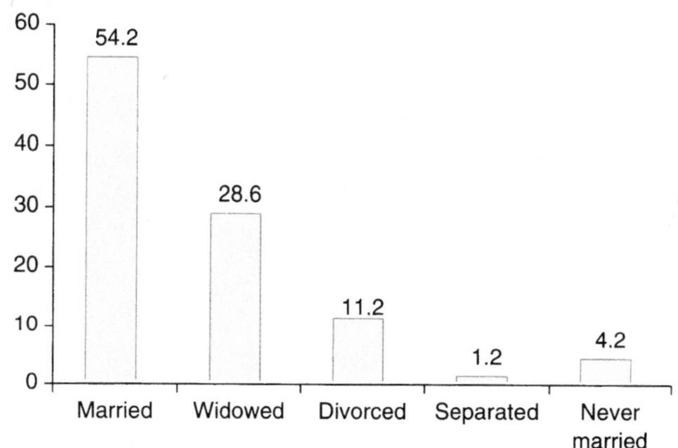

Source: Loraine West, Samantha Cole, Daniel Goodkind, and Wan He, 65+ *in the United States: 2010*, Current Population Report, P23-212, 2014.

Figure 2.4 Marital Status of U.S. Elderly (65 Years and Older) by Gender (Percentages), 2010

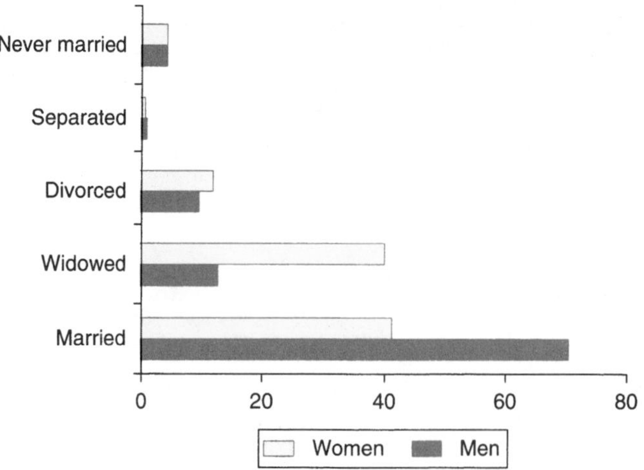

Source: Loraine West, Samantha Cole, Daniel Goodkind, and Wan He, 65+ *in the United States: 2010,* Current Population Report, P23-212, 2014.

proportional to the frequency or percentage of the category. Note that a space separates each of the categories to make clear that they are nominal categories.

Bar graphs are often used to compare one or more categories of a variable among different groups. Suppose we want to show how the patterns in marital status differ between men and women. The longevity of women is a major factor in the gender differences in marital and living arrangements.[8] Additionally, elderly widowed men are more likely to remarry than elderly widowed women.

Figure 2.4 compares the marital status for women and men 65 years and older in 2010. We can also construct bar graphs horizontally, with the categories of the variable arrayed along the vertical axis and the percentages or frequencies displayed on the horizontal axis, as displayed in Figure 2.4. This presentation allows for a side-by-side visual comparison. It shows that elderly women are more likely than elderly men to be widowed (40% vs. 13%), and elderly men are more likely to be married than elderly women (70% vs. 42%).

THE HISTOGRAM

Histogram A graph showing the differences in frequencies or percentages among the categories of an interval-ratio variable. The categories are displayed as contiguous bars, with width proportional to the width of the category and height proportional to the frequency or percentage of that category.

The **histogram** is used to show the differences in frequencies or percentages among categories of an interval-ratio or ordinal variable. The categories are displayed as contiguous bars, with width proportional to the width of the category and height proportional to the frequency or percentage of that category. A histogram looks very similar to a bar chart except that the bars are contiguous to each other (touching) and may not be of equal width. In a bar chart, the spaces between the bars visually indicate that the categories are separate. Examples of variables with separate categories are *marital status* (married, single), *gender* (male, female), and *employment status* (employed, unemployed). In a histogram, the touching bars indicate that the categories or intervals are ordered from low to high in a meaningful way. For example, the categories of the variables *hours spent studying*, *age*, and *years of school completed* are contiguous, ordered intervals.

Figure 2.5 is a histogram displaying the frequency distribution of the population 65 years and over by age. To construct the histogram, arrange the age intervals along the horizontal axis and

Figure 2.5 Age Distribution of U.S. Population 65 Years and Over, 2012 (Numbers in Thousands)

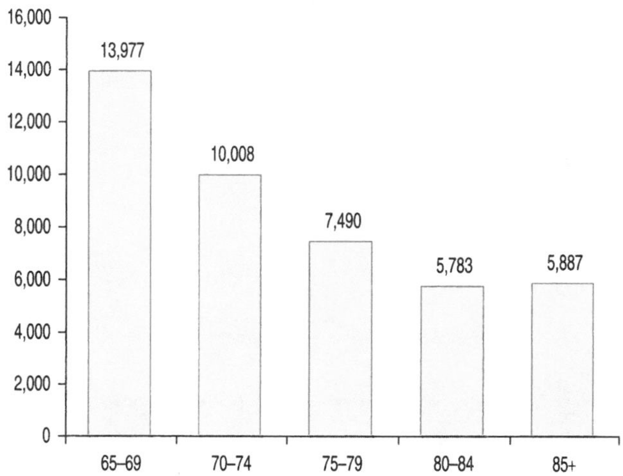

Source: Jennifer Ortman, Victoria Velkoff, and Howard Hogan, *An Aging Nation: The Older Population of the United States*, Current Population Reports, P25-1140, 2014.

the frequencies (or percentages) along the vertical axis. For each age category, construct a bar with the height corresponding to the frequency of the elderly in the population in that age category. The width of each bar corresponds to the number of years that the age interval represents. The area that each bar occupies tells us the number of individuals that falls into a given age interval. Note that the figure title includes the notation "numbers in thousands." You should multiply each reported frequency by 1,000. For example, the largest age category is 65–69 years with 13,977,000 (13,977 × 1,000). The smallest age group is 80–84 years with 5,783,000. The total number of elderly 65 years and over can be found by summing all the reported frequencies.

THE STATISTICAL MAP

Since the 1960s, the elderly have been relocating to the South and the West of the United States. It is projected that by 2020 the concentration of elderly in these areas will increase by as much as 80% (though recent census data reveal that the Great Recession halted this dominant immigration trend). We can display these dramatic geographical changes in American society by using a statistical map. A statistical map presents geographic data patterns or variations, such as population distribution, voting patterns, crime rates, or labor force composition.

Statistical map A visual presentation of geographic data patterns or variations, such as the population distribution.

Let's look at Figure 2.6. It presents a statistical map, by state, of the percentage of the population 65 years and over for 2010. The variable percentage of the population has four categories: (1) less than 11%, (2) 11% to 12.9%, (3) 13% to 14.9%, and (4) 15% or more. Each category is represented by a different shading (or color code), and the states are shaded depending on their classification into the different categories. To make it easier to read a map that you construct and to identify its patterns, keep the number of categories relatively small—say, not more than five.

Maps may also display geographical patterns on the level of cities, counties, city blocks, census tracts, and other units. Your choice of whether to display variations on the state level or for smaller units will depend on the research question you wish to explore.

Figure 2.6 Percentage of the Population 65 Years and Over by State, 2010

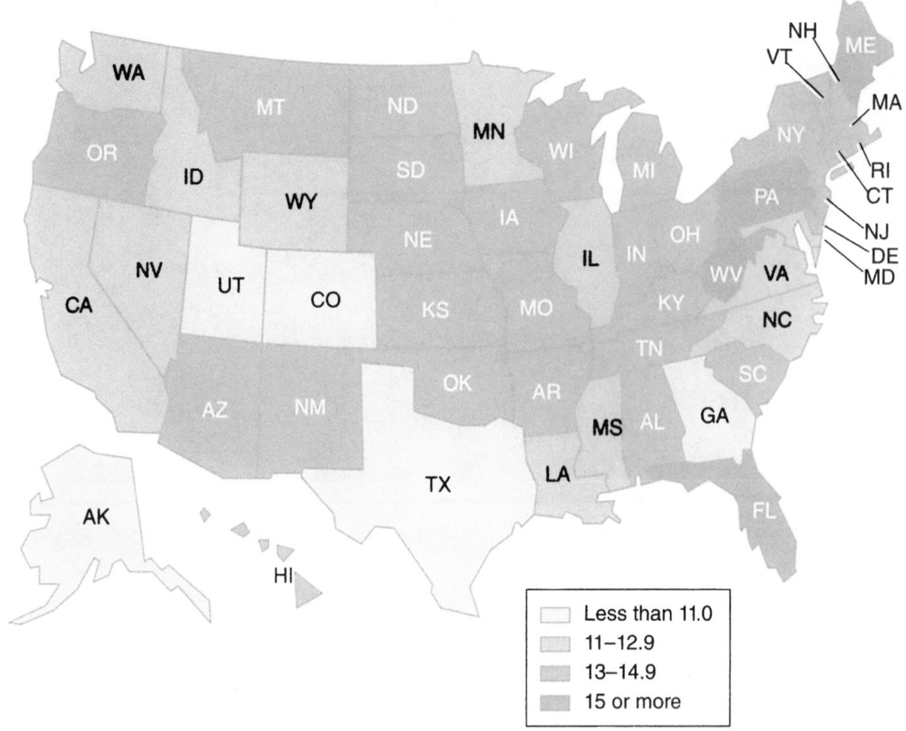

Source: Loraine West, Samantha Cole, Daniel Goodkind, and Wan He, *65+ in the United States: 2010*, Current Population Report, P23-212, 2014.

LEARNING CHECK 2.7

Can you think of a few other examples of data that could be described using a statistical map? What type of data are organized or reported at the state level?

THE LINE GRAPH

Line graph A graph showing the differences in frequencies or percentages among categories of an interval-ratio variable. Points representing the frequencies of each category are placed above the midpoint of the category and are joined by a straight line.

The elderly population is growing worldwide in both developed and developing countries. In 1994, 30 nations had elderly populations of at least 2 million; demographic projections indicate that there will be 55 such nations by 2020. Japan is one of the nations that is experiencing dramatic growth of its elderly population. Figure 2.7 is a line graph displaying the elderly population of Japan for 2010 and 2014.

The line graph is another way to display interval-ratio distributions; it shows the differences in frequencies or percentages among categories of an interval-ratio variable. Compared with histograms, line graphs are better suited for comparing how a variable is distributed across two or more groups or across two or more time periods as we've done in Figure 2.7. Points

Figure 2.7 Population of Japan, Age 65 and Above, 2010 and 2014

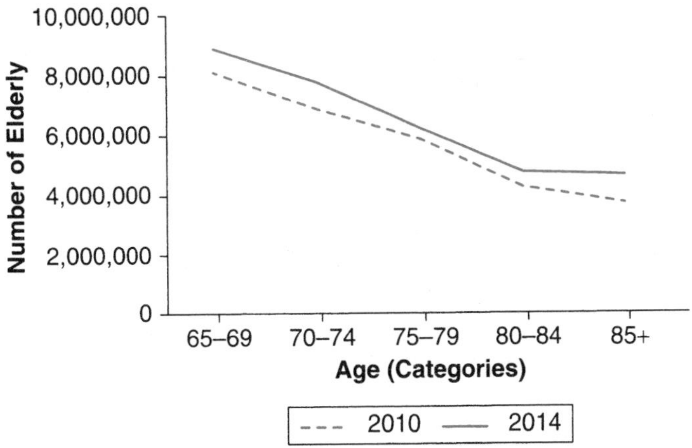

Source: United Nations Statistics Division, *Population by Age, Sex, and Urban/Rural Residence*, 2015. Retrieved from http://data.un.org/Data.aspx?d=POP&f=tableCode%3A22

representing the frequencies of each category are placed above the midpoint of the category and are joined by a straight line. Notice that in Figure 2.7, the age intervals are arranged on the horizontal axis and the frequencies along the vertical axis. Instead of using bars to represent the frequencies, however, points representing the frequencies of each interval are placed above the midpoint of the intervals. Adjacent points are then joined by straight lines.

Figure 2.7 shows how Japan's population of age 65 and over increased from 2010 to 2014. According to projections, Japan's oldest-old population, those 80 years or older, is projected to grow rapidly, from about 4.8 million (less than 4% of the total population) in 2014 to 10.8 million (8.9%) by 2020 (not depicted in the figure). This projected rise has already led to a reduction in retirement benefits and other adjustments to prepare for the economic and social impact of a rapidly aging society.[9]

THE TIME-SERIES CHART

We are often interested in examining how some variables change over time. For example, we may be interested in showing changes in the labor force participation of Latinas over the past decade, changes in the public's attitude toward same-sex marriage, or changes in divorce and marriage rates. A **time-series chart** displays changes in a variable at different points in time. It involves two variables: (1) *time*, which is labeled across the horizontal axis, and (2) another variable of interest whose values (frequencies, percentages, or rates) are labeled along the vertical axis. To construct a time-series chart, use a series of dots to mark the value of the variable at each time interval and then join the dots by a series of straight lines.

Time-series chart A graph displaying changes in a variable at different points in time. It shows time (measured in units such as years or months) on the horizontal axis and the frequencies (percentages or rates) of another variable on the vertical axis.

Figure 2.8 shows a time series from 2010 to 2050 of the percentage of the total population that is 65 years or older (the percentages for 2030 and 2050 are projections, as reported by the U.S. Census Bureau) for selected world regions. This time series enables us to see clearly the increase in the elderly population worldwide. As we have already mentioned, these demographic changes will have significant social, political, and economic implications, capturing the attention of policy makers and social scientists.

Figure 2.8 Percentage of Total Population 65 Years and Above for Selected World Regions, 2010, 2030, and 2050

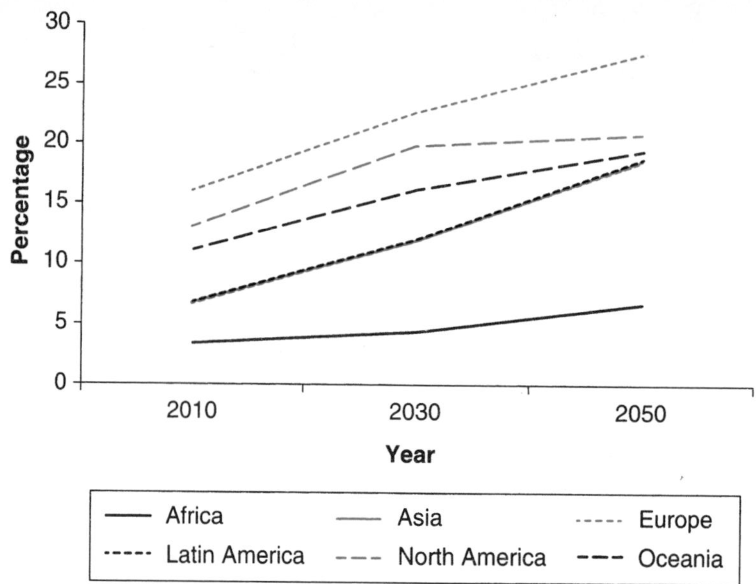

Source: Loraine West, Samantha Cole, Daniel Goodkind, and Wan He, *65+ in the United States: 2010*, Current Population Report, P23-212, 2014.

LEARNING CHECK 2.8

How does the time-series chart differ from a line graph? The difference is that line graphs display frequency distributions of a single variable, whereas time-series charts display two variables. In addition, time is always one of the variables displayed in a time-series chart.

STATISTICS IN PRACTICE: FOREIGN-BORN POPULATION 65 YEARS AND OVER

In their 2014 report *65+ in America*, U.S. Census Bureau researchers Loraine West, Samantha Cole, Daniel Goodkind, and Wan He describe the foreign-born population aged 65 and over in a series of tables and graphs. We present several for your review.

Frequencies and percentages presented in Table 2.14 summarize three characteristics of the 5,000,000 foreign-born elderly. The majority of these older men and women entered the U.S. prior to 1990. Almost 73% were naturalized citizens in 2010. In the same year, the largest percentage lived in the West (36%), followed by the South (29%).

Figure 2.10 is a pie chart, presenting one variable—world region of birth. We learn that the majority of the foreign-born elderly originally came from Latin America (37%), Asia (29%), and Europe (28%). The bar graph (Figure 2.11) presents the percentage of foreign-born elderly from each world region by their period of entry. Prior to 1990 and during 2000–2010, the largest percentage of foreign-born elderly came from Latin America and the Caribbean. However, from 1990 to 1999, the largest percentage of foreign-born elderly emigrated from Asia.

A CLOSER LOOK 2.2

A CAUTIONARY NOTE: DISTORTIONS IN GRAPHS

In this chapter, we have seen that statistical graphs can give us a quick sense of the main patterns in the data. However, graphs cannot only quickly inform us, they can also quickly deceive us. Because we are often more interested in general impressions than in detailed analyses of the numbers, we are more vulnerable to being swayed by distorted graphs. Edward Tufte in his 1983 book *The Visual Display of Quantitative Information* not only demonstrates the advantages of working with graphs but also offers a detailed discussion of some of the pitfalls in the application and interpretation of graphics.[10]

Probably the most common distortions in graphical representations occur when the distance along the vertical or horizontal axis is altered either by not using 0 as the baseline (as demonstrated in Figure 2.9a and b) or in relation to the other axis. Axes may be stretched or shrunk to create any desired result to exaggerate or disguise a pattern in the data. In Figure 2.9a and b, 2015 international data on female representation in national parliaments are presented. Without altering the data in any way, notice how the difference between the countries is exaggerated by using 30 as a baseline (as in Figure 2.9b).

Remember to interpret the graph in the context of the numerical information the graph represents.

Figure 2.9 Female Representation in National Parliaments, 2015: (a) Using 0 as the Baseline and (b) Using 30 as the Baseline

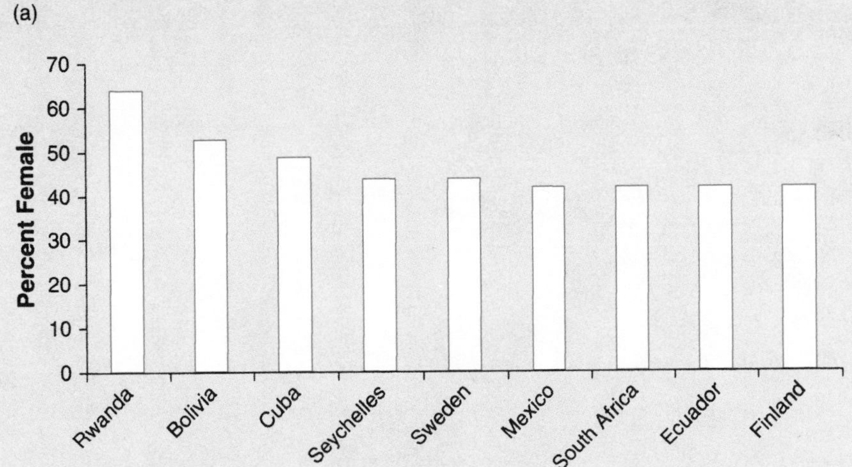

(Continued)

(Continued)

Figure 2.9 (Continued)

(b)

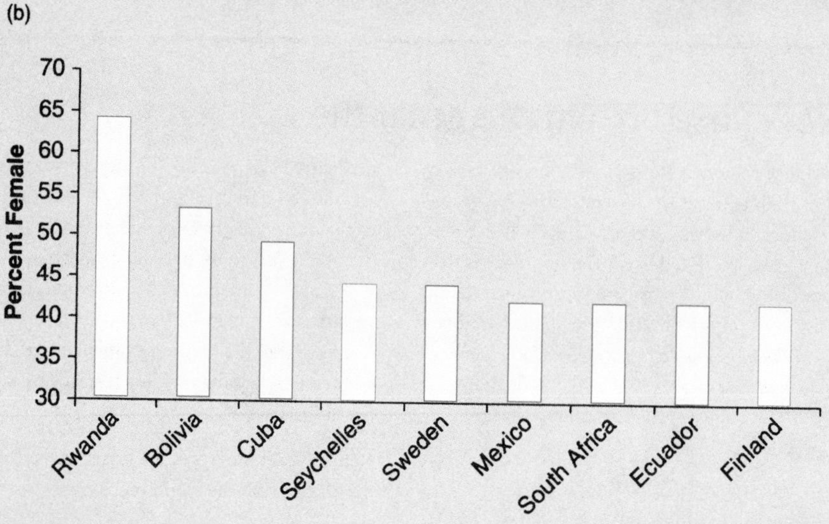

Source: Inter-Parliamentary Union, *Women in National Parliaments*, 2016. Retrieved from www.ipu.org/wmn-e/classif.htm

Table 2.14 Foreign-Born Population Aged 65 and Over by Period of Entry, Citizenship Status, and Region, 2010

Characteristic	Population (in Thousands)	Percentage (%)
Total	4,963	100
Period of entry		
Prior to 1990	3,769	76
1990 to 1999	644	13.0
2000 to 2010	550	11.1
Citizenship status		
Naturalized citizen	3,582	72.2
Not a U.S. citizen	1,381	27.8
Region		
Northwest	1,232	24.8
Midwest	504	10.1
South	1,442	29.1
West	1,784	36.0

Source: Loraine West, Samantha Cole, Daniel Goodkind, and Wan He, *65+ in the United States: 2010*, Current Population Report, P23-212, 2014.

Figure 2.10 Foreign-Born Population Aged 65 Years and Over by World Region of Birth, 2010

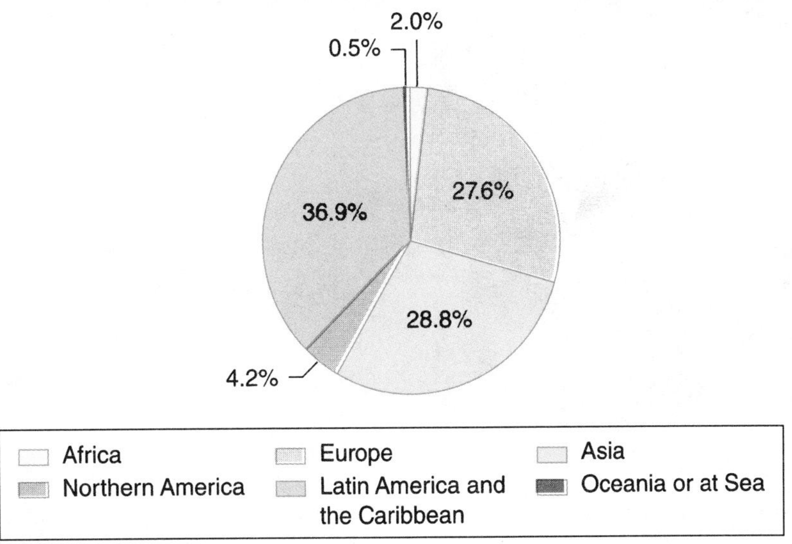

Source: Loraine West, Samantha Cole, Daniel Goodkind, and Wan He, 65+ *in the United States:* 2010, Current Population Report, P23-212, 2014.

Figure 2.11 Foreign-Born Population Aged 65 and Over by World Region of Birth and Period of Entry, 2010

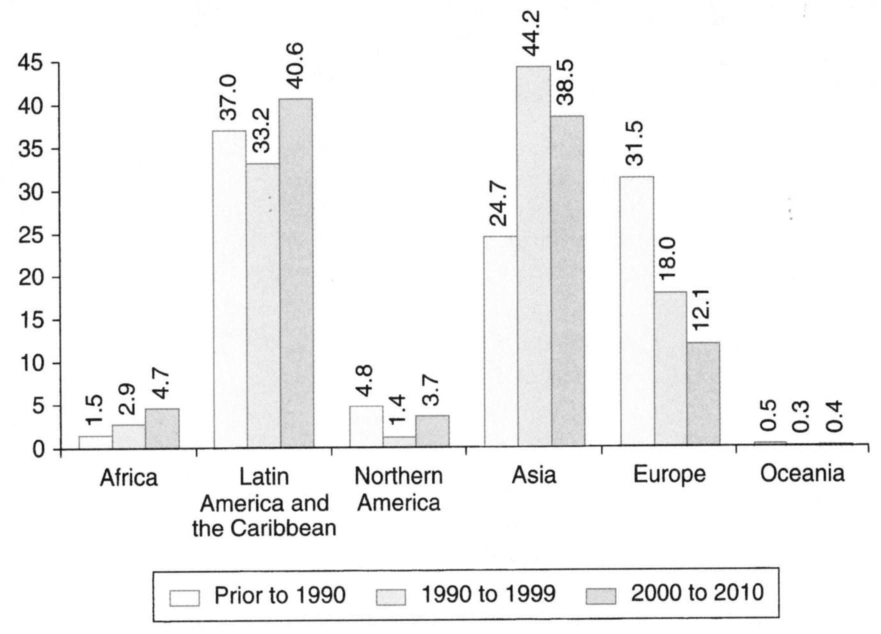

Source: Loraine West, Samantha Cole, Daniel Goodkind, and Wan He, 65+ *in the United States:* 2010, Current Population Report, P23-212, 2014.

DATA AT WORK

Kurt Taylor Gaubatz: Graduate Program in International Studies

Photo courtesy of Kurt Taylor Gaubatz

Though Kurt began his college career as a music major, after taking an economics class he was fascinated by the challenge of understanding and modeling human behavior. He came to see the importance of public policy. "All of the biggest problems we face as a society, indeed, as human beings, comes down to questions in the social sciences. . . . This is a very good area to work on the hardest and most important issues."

According to Kurt, "A research career is a life of posing and answering questions, of trying to think about things in new and more interesting ways. In that sense, then, in addition to getting to work on important social problems, research is a natural outlet for human curiosity."

He advises students to develop two essential research skills. "Information, a huge amount of information, is now increasingly available to everyone who carries a phone. The critical skill[s] [are] knowing how to build new ideas from the organization and analysis of that information, and being able to communicate those ideas effectively. Students need to focus on filling their toolbox with those analytic and communication skills."

MAIN POINTS

- The most basic way to organizing data is to classify the observations into a frequency distribution—a table that reports the number of observations that fall into each category of the variable being analyzed.
- Constructing a frequency distribution is usually the first step in the statistical analysis of data. To obtain a frequency distribution for nominal and ordinal variables, count and report the number of cases that fall into each category of the variable along with the total number of cases (N). To construct a frequency distribution for interval-ratio variables that have a wide range of values, first combine the scores into a smaller number of groups—known as class intervals—each containing a number of scores.
- Proportions and percentages are relative frequencies. To construct a proportion, divide the frequency (f) in each category by the total number of cases (N). To obtain a percentage, divide the frequency (f) in each category by the total number of cases (N) and multiply by 100.
- Percentage distributions are tables that show the percentage of observations that fall into each category of the variable. Percentage distributions are routinely added to almost any frequency table and are especially important if comparisons between groups are to be considered.
- Cumulative frequency distributions allow us to locate the relative position of a given score in a distribution. They are obtained

by adding to the frequency in each category the frequencies of all the categories below it.

- Cumulative percentage distributions have wider applications than cumulative frequency distributions. A cumulative percentage distribution is constructed by adding to the percentages in each category the percentages of all the categories below it.
- A rate is a number that expresses raw frequencies in relative terms. A rate can be calculated as the number of actual occurrences in a given time period divided by the number of possible occurrences for that period. Rates are often multiplied by some power of 10 to eliminate decimal points and make the number easier to interpret.
- A pie chart shows the differences in frequencies or percentages among categories of nominal or ordinal variable. The categories of the variable are segments of a circle whose pieces add up to 100% of the total frequencies.
- A bar graph shows the differences in frequencies or percentages among categories of a nominal or an ordinal variable. The categories are displayed as rectangles of equal width with their height proportional to the frequency or percentage of the category.
- Histograms display the differences in frequencies or percentages among categories of interval-ratio variables. The categories are displayed as contiguous bars with their width proportional to the width of the category and height proportional to the frequency or percentage of that category.
- A line graph shows the differences in frequencies or percentages among categories of an interval-ratio variable. Points representing the frequencies of each category are placed above the midpoint of the category (interval). Adjacent points are then joined by a straight line.
- A time-series chart displays changes in a variable at different points in time. It displays two variables: (1) time, which is labeled across the horizontal axis, and (2) another variable of interest whose values (e.g., frequencies, percentages, or rates) are labeled along the vertical axis.

KEY TERMS

DIGITAL RESOURCES

SAGE edge™

Get the edge on your studies. **edge.sagepub.com/frankfort8e**

Take a quiz to find out what you've learned.
Review key terms with eFlashcards.
Dive into real research with SAGE Journal Articles.

SPSS DEMONSTRATIONS [GSS14SSDS-A]

Demonstration 1: Producing Frequency Distributions

In SPSS, you can review the frequency distribution for a single variable or for several variables at once. The frequency procedure is found in the *Descriptive Statistics* menu under *Analyze*. For this chapter, we will use the GSS14SSDS-A data set.

In the Frequencies dialog box, click on the variable name(s) in the left column and transfer the name(s) to the Variable(s) box. More than one variable can be selected at one time.

For our demonstration, let's select the variable POLVIEWS (respondent's political views). Click on *OK* to process the frequency. Respondents were asked to answer the question by indicating 1= extremely liberal, 2 = liberal, 3 = slightly liberal, 4 = moderate, 5 = slightly conservative, 6 = conservative, and 7 = extremely conservative.

SPSS will produce two tables in a separate Output window, a small statistics table (not presented here), and a frequency table. Use the Window scroll keys to move up and down the window to find the statistics and frequency tables for POLVIEWS. What level of measurement is this variable? (Refer to Chapter 1 to review definitions.)

In the first table, Statistics, SPSS identifies all the valid and missing responses to this question. Responses are coded missing if no answer was given.

In the frequency table (see Figure 2.12), the variable label is reported. The first column lists the value and value label for each category of POLVIEWS. The next four columns contain important frequency information about the variable. The Frequency column shows the number of respondents who gave a particular response. Thus, we can see that 1,500 respondents are included in the data set, but only 1,442 provided a valid response, with 58 responses missing.

The Percent column calculates what percentage of the whole sample (1,500 cases) each of the responses represents. Thus, 10.9% of the total sample indicated slightly liberal political views. In most instances, percentages reported in the third column, Valid Percent, is more useful. This column removes all the cases defined as missing and recalculates percentages based only on the valid responses. Recalculated based only on valid cases (1,442), the percentage of those who answered slightly liberal is 11.3. The last column, Cumulative Percent, calculates cumulative percentages

Figure 2.12 Frequency Table for POLVIEWS

polviews THINK OF SELF AS LIBERAL OR CONSERVATIVE

		Frequency	Percent	Valid Percent	Cumulative Percent
Valid	1 EXTREMELY LIBERAL	50	3.3	3.5	3.5
	2 LIBERAL	187	12.5	13.0	16.4
	3 SLIGHTLY LIBERAL	163	10.9	11.3	27.7
	4 MODERATE	565	37.7	39.2	66.9
	5 SLGHTLY CONSERVATIVE	206	13.7	14.3	81.2
	6 CONSERVATIVE	218	14.5	15.1	96.3
	7 EXTRMLY CONSERVATIVE	53	3.5	3.7	100.0
	Total	1442	96.1	100.0	
Missing	8 DK	47	3.1		
	9 NA	11	.7		
	Total	58	3.9		
Total		1500	100.0		

beginning with the first response. We know that 27.7% of the valid sample reported that they were liberal (extremely liberal, liberal, or slightly liberal).

Demonstration 2: Recoding Variables

Some variables may need to be recoded or reduced into a smaller number of categories or intervals in order to better present and understand the data. We could, for example, collapse POLVIEWS into a variable with three categories: (1) liberal, (2) moderate, and (3) conservative. To accomplish this, we could use the SPSS commands *Transform–Recode Into Different Variables*.

For more detailed instruction on recoding variables, please refer to the section on Recoding Variables in the SPSS Appendix on the text's study site, which explains how to recode the variable EDUC (respondent's years of education).

After reviewing the SPSS Appendix, recode POLVIEWS into a new variable called RPOLVIEWS. Frequencies for RPOLVIEWS should look like Figure 2.13.

Demonstration 3: Producing a Bar Chart

SPSS greatly simplifies and improves the production of graphics. The program offers a separate choice from the main menu bar, *Graphs*, which lists more than a dozen types of graphs that SPSS can create.

Under the *Graphs* menu select *Legacy Dialogs*, and then *Bar*, which will produce various types of bar charts. We will use bar charts to display the distribution of the nominal variable MARITAL (marital status of respondent). After clicking on *Bar*, you will be presented with the initial dialog box, with the Simple bar charts option already selected.

Almost all graphics procedures in SPSS begin with a dialog box that allows you to choose exactly the type of chart you want to construct. Many graph types can display more than one variable (the Clustered or Stacked choices). We will keep things simple here, so click on *Simple*, then on *Define*. When you do so, the main dialog box for simple bar charts opens.

The variable MARITAL should be placed in the box labeled *Category Axis*. In the *Bars Represent* box, click on the *% of cases* radio button. This choice changes the default statistic from the number of cases to percentages, which are normally more useful for comparison purposes. Click on *OK* to submit your request. (SPSS automatically excludes missing values. You can change this by clicking on *Options*. Click in the box labeled *Display groups defined by missing values* to turn on this choice. Then, click on *Continue*, then on *OK* to submit your request to SPSS.)

The bar chart for MARITAL is presented in an output window labeled SPSS Viewer. You can see in Figure 2.14 that the bar chart for MARITAL has five bars because the only valid responses to this question are (1) "married," (2) "widowed," (3) "divorced," (4) "separated," and (5) "single, never been married."

SPSS graphs can be edited by selecting *Edit*, then *Edit Content, In Separate Window*, which moves the graph to its own window (*Chart Editor*) and displays various editing tools and choices.

Figure 2.13 Frequency Table for RPOLVIEWS

Rpolviews Recoded POLVIEWS

		Frequency	Percent	Valid Percent	Cumulative Percent
Valid	1.00 Liberal	400	26.7	27.7	27.7
	2.00 Moderate	565	37.7	39.2	66.9
	3.00 Conservative	477	31.8	33.1	100.0
	Total	1442	96.1	100.0	
Missing	System	58	3.9		
Total		1500	100.0		

Figure 2.14 Bar Graph for MARITAL

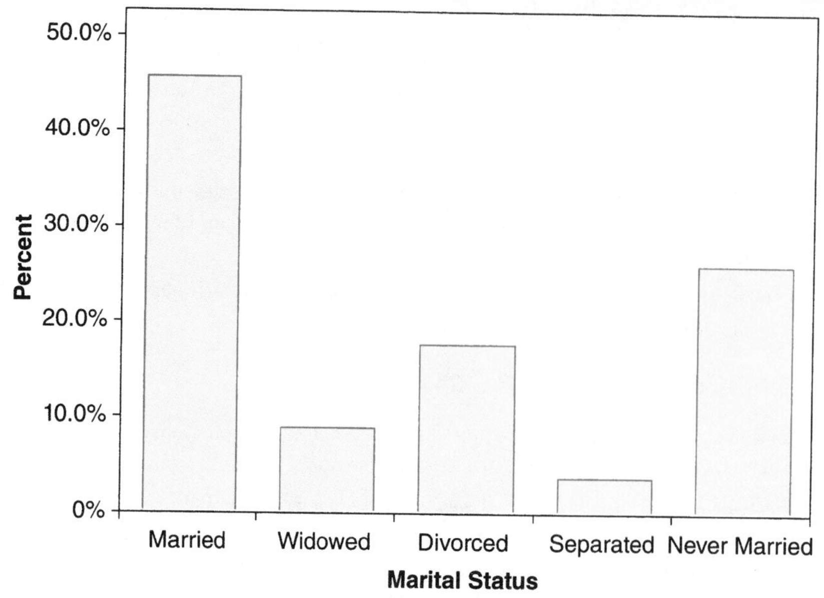

Demonstration 4: Producing a Histogram

Histograms are used to display interval or ratio variables. We'll use the variable AGEKDBRN—respondent's age when first child was born. Under the *Graphs–Legacy Dialogs* menu in SPSS, select the *Histogram*.

Figure 2.15 Histogram for AGEKDBRN

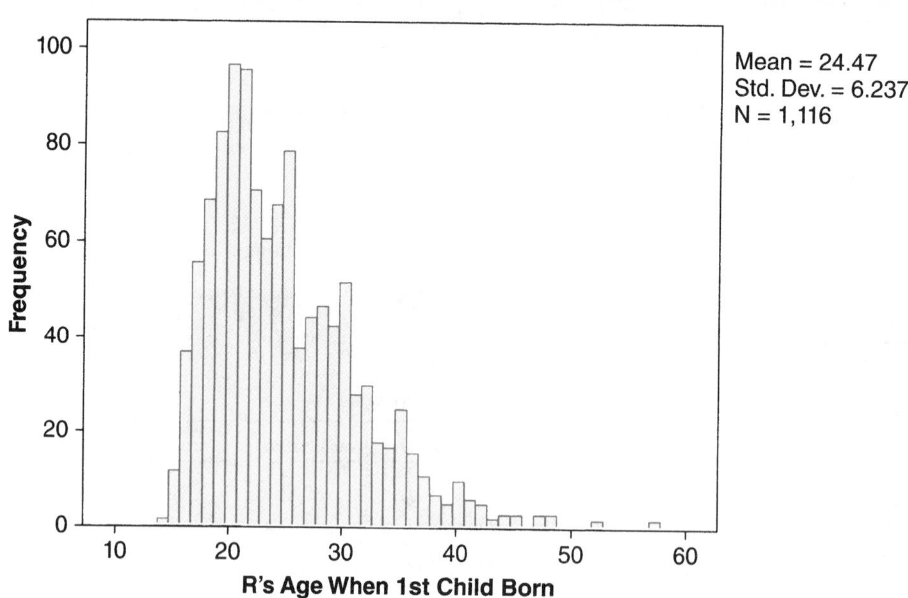

Histograms are created for one variable at a time (that's why there was no opening dialog box as for bar charts). You simply insert (drag) the variable you want to display in the first empty box. You don't need to worry about missing values in histograms; unlike the bar chart default, SPSS automatically deletes them from the display. Notice that SPSS includes icons to indicate the level of measurement for each variable. Interval-ratio variables (or scale variables as SPSS refers to them) is matched with a ruler icon. Click on the *OK* button (on the bottom left-hand corner) to process this request. The resulting histogram is shown in Figure 2.15.

SPSS automatically decided the appropriate width for each interval based on the range of the variable and the optimal number of bars to be displayed on a screen. The histogram also includes the calculation for mean and standard deviation, which will be discussed in Chapters 3 and 4.

SPSS PROBLEMS [GSS14SSDS-A]

1. Use the SPSS Frequencies command to produce a frequency table for the variable HEALTH.
   a. What is the number of valid respondents?
   b. Based on the valid number of respondents, what percentage of the sample reported being in excellent health? What proportion of the sample is in poor health?
   c. What is the best way to graphically display these data? Explain.
2. The GSS included a series of questions on respondent's attitudes about immigrants. In the chapter, we examined the relationship between race and attitudes about immigrants and jobs (IMMJOBS). There are two additional variables to consider—IMMCULT (Immigrants undermine American culture) and IMMEDUC (Legal immigrants should have the same education as Americans).
   a. Run frequencies for all the three variables (including IMMJOBS).
   b. Prepare a general statement summarizing your results from the three frequency tables. Identify the level of measurement for each variable. How would you describe respondents' attitudes about immigrants?
3. Produce the frequency table for GOODLIFE (the standard of living of the respondent will improve).
   a. What is the level of measurement for this variable?
   b. Identify two independent variables that may affect how someone responded to GOODLIFE. Explain the relationship between these variables and GOODLIFE.
   c. What is the best way to graphically display these data? Explain.
4. The GSS2014 respondents were asked to report their highest year of school (EDUC). Run the frequency table for this variable. Collapse this interval ratio variable into an ordinal measure (omitting those who did not respond to the question). How many categories do you have?
   a. Prepare a frequency and cumulative percentage table of your recoded EDUC variable.
   b. Prepare a graphic presentation of your recoded EDUC variable.
5. Determine how best to represent the following variables graphically:

a. PARTYID (respondent's political party identification)

b. NRINCOME06 (respondent's annual income)

c. LETIN1 (number of immigrants to America nowadays should be)

d. EMAILHR (e-mail hours per week)

Note: Before selecting/constructing your graph, you may want to review the variable by first using the *Frequencies* or *Utilities–Variables* command. The levels of measurement for several variables are mislabeled in SPSS. If you are using the *Utilities–Variables* option to review each variable and its level of measurement, you should confirm the level of measurement by reviewing the variable's frequency table (*Analyze–Descriptive–Frequencies*).

CHAPTER EXERCISES

1. Suppose you surveyed 30 people and asked them whether they are white (W) or nonwhite (N), and how many traumas (serious accidents, rapes, or crimes) they have experienced in the past year. You also asked them to tell you whether they perceive themselves as being in the upper, middle, working, or lower class. Your survey resulted in the raw data presented in the table below:

   a. Identify the level of measurement for each variable.

   b. Construct raw frequency tables for race.

   c. What proportion of the 30 individuals is nonwhite? What percentage is white?

Race	Class	Trauma	Race	Class	Trauma
W	L	1	W	W	0
W	M	0	W	M	2
W	M	1	W	W	1
N	M	1	W	W	1
N	L	2	N	W	0
W	W	0	N	M	2
N	W	0	W	M	1
W	M	0	W	M	0
W	M	1	N	W	1
N	W	1	W	W	0
N	W	2	W	W	0
N	M	0	N	M	0
N	L	0	N	W	0
W	U	0	N	W	1
W	W	1	W	W	0

Note: Race: W, white; N, nonwhite; Class: L, lower class; M, middle class; U, upper class; W, working class.

2. Using the data from Exercise 1, construct a frequency and percentage distribution for class.
   a. Which is the smallest perceived class group?
   b. Which two classes include the largest percentages of people?
3. Using the data from Exercise 1, construct a frequency distribution for trauma.
   a. What level of measurement is used for the trauma variable?
   b. Are people more likely to have experienced no traumas or only one trauma in the past year?
   c. What proportion has experienced one or more traumas in the past year?
4. Using the data from Exercise 1, construct appropriate graphs showing percentage distributions for race, class, and trauma.
5. GSS 2014 respondents were asked to rate their agreement to the statement, "Immigrants were good for America". Results are provided in the table below for the percentage in each category by political party. Do these data support the statement that people's views on immigration are related to their political party affiliation? Why or why not?

	Strong Democrat (%)	Independent (%)	Strong Republican (%)
Agree strongly	6.2	11.3	6.1
Agree	51.9	54.7	42.9
Neither agree nor disagree	29.6	22.6	14.3
Disagree	8.6	9.4	34.7
Strongly disagree	3.7	1.9	2.0
Total	100.0	99.9	100.0

6. How many hours per week do you spend on e-mail? Data are presented here for a GSS sample of 99 men and women, who each reported the number of hours they spent per week on e-mail.
   a. Compute the cumulative frequency and cumulative percentage distribution for the data.
   b. What proportion of the sample spent 3 hours or less per week on e-mail?
   c. What proportion of the sample spent 6 or more hours per week on e-mail?
   d. Construct a graph that best displays these data. Explain why the graph you selected is appropriate for these data.

E-mail Hours per Week	Frequency
0	19
1	20

(Continued)

(Continued)

E-mail Hours per Week	Frequency
2	13
3	5
4	2
5	6
6	5
7	2
8	3
9	1
10 or more	23

7. The time-series chart shown below displays trends for presidential election voting rates by race and Hispanic origin for 1966–2012. Analysts noted how for the first time in the 2012 Presidential election black voting rates exceeded the rates for non-Hispanic whites. Overall, votes cast were higher in 2012 than 2008 (131,948,000 vs. 131,144,000—data not reported in the figure), an increase attributed to minority voters. Describe the variation in voting rates for the four racial and Hispanic origin groups.

Voting Rates by Presidential Election, 1996-2012

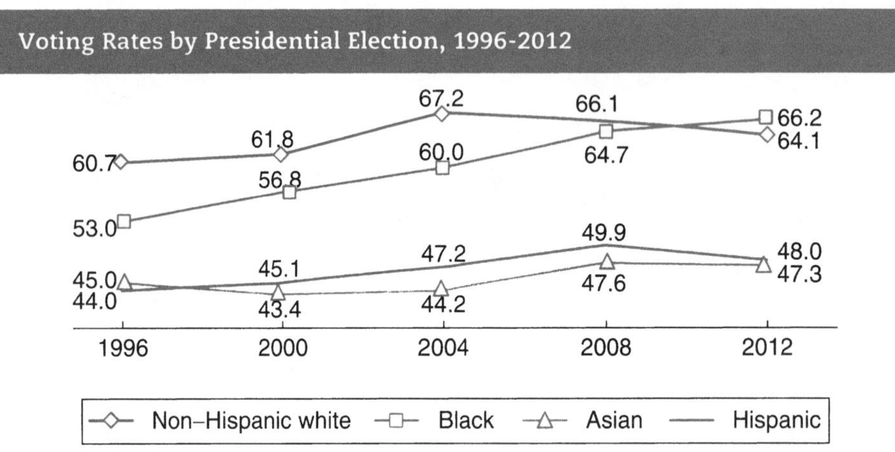

Source: Thom File, *The Diversifying Electorate—Voting Rates by Race and Hispanic Origin in 2012 (and other recent elections)*, Current Population Survey P20-568, 2013, Figure 1.

8. According to the Pew Research Center (2015) recent immigrants are better educated than earlier immigrants to the United States. The change was attributed to the availability of better education in each region or country of origin. The percentage of immigrants 25 years of age and older who completed at least high school are reported in this table for 1970 to 2013. Write a statement describing the change over time in the percentage who completed at least a high school degree.

	1970	1980	1990	2000	2013
Mexico	14	17	26	30	48
Other Central/South America	52	57	53	60	66
Asia	75	72	75	82	84
Europe	48	68	81	87	95
Caribbean	36	48	52	58	72
Africa	81	91	88	85	85

Source: Pew Research Center, *Modern Immigration Wave Brings 59 Million to U.S., Driving Population Grown and Change through 2065*, 2015.

9. Older Americans are often described as more politically engaged than younger Americans. One measure of political engagement is election voting. Loraine West and her U.S. Census Bureau colleagues (2014) presented the following bar graph reporting the 2012 Presidential election voting by age group. Note that the voting in the Presidential election is presented with frequencies (in millions) and by percentage. Based on the percentage data, are older Americans more likely to vote in the Presidential election than younger Americans? (Before you answer, define which age groups are younger vs. older.)

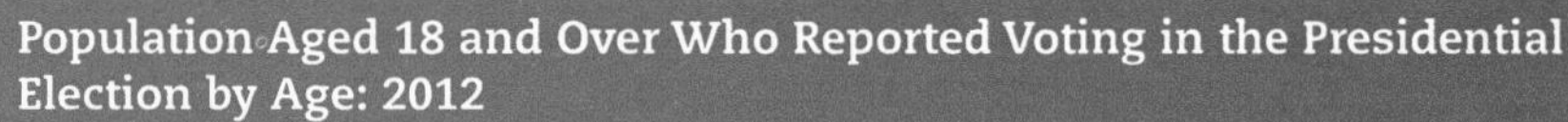

Population Aged 18 and Over Who Reported Voting in the Presidential Election by Age: 2012

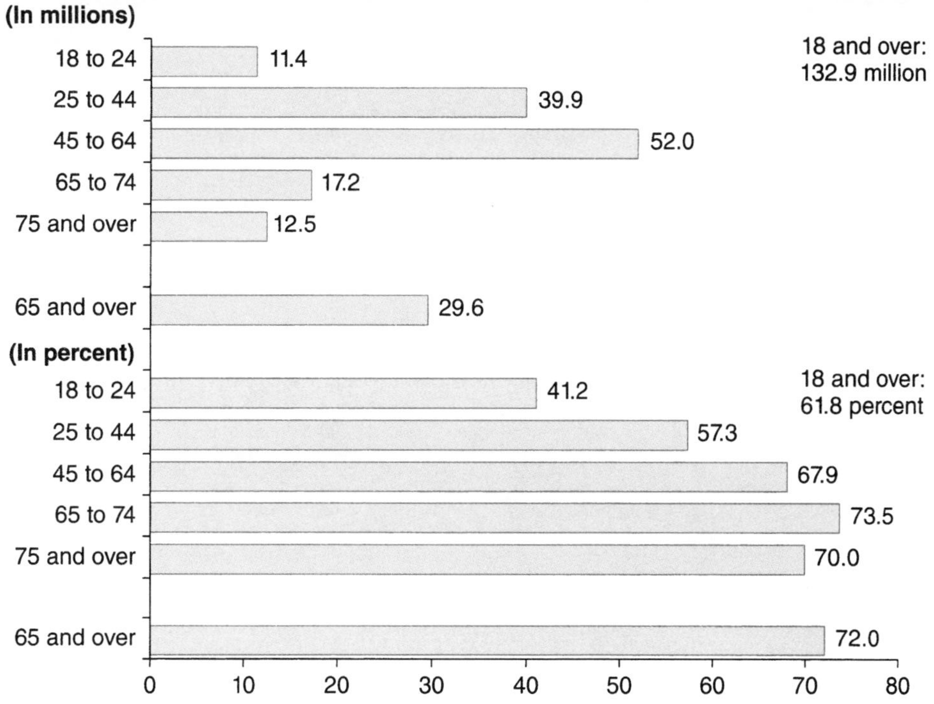

Source: Loraine West, Samantha Cole, Daniel Goodkind and Wan He, *65+ in the United States: 2010*. Current Population Report, P23-212, 2014.

10. The U.S. Bureau of Justice reports the estimated percentage of sentenced prisoners under state and federal jurisdiction by sex and age, as of December 31, 2014. Percentages are presented in the table below. Due to rounding, the totals may not equal 100%.

	All Males (%) Total Number (1,402,404)	All Females (%) Total Number (106,232)
18–19	1.0	.6
20–24	11.4	10.0
25–29	15.4	17.5
30–34	16.5	18.6
35–39	14.2	14.7
40–44	12.2	12.8
45–49	10.4	10.9
50–54	8.5	7.7
55–59	5.2	3.9
60–64	2.7	1.8
65+	2.3	1.2

Source: E. Ann Carson, "*Prisoners in 2014*," Bureau of Justice Statistics NCJ 248955, 2015.

a. Calculate a cumulative percentage distribution for males.

b. Calculate a cumulative percentage distribution for females.

11. In this exercise, we examine the percentage of 8th-, 10th-, and 12th-grade students who reported smoking cigarettes daily in the past 30 days as reported by the Monitoring the Future survey. Data are reported in this time-series graph from 1980 to 2014. Describe the smoking trends for each group of students.

Percentage of 8th-, 10th-, and 12th- Grade Students Who Reported Smoking Cigarettes Daily in the Past 30 Days by Grade, 1980-2014

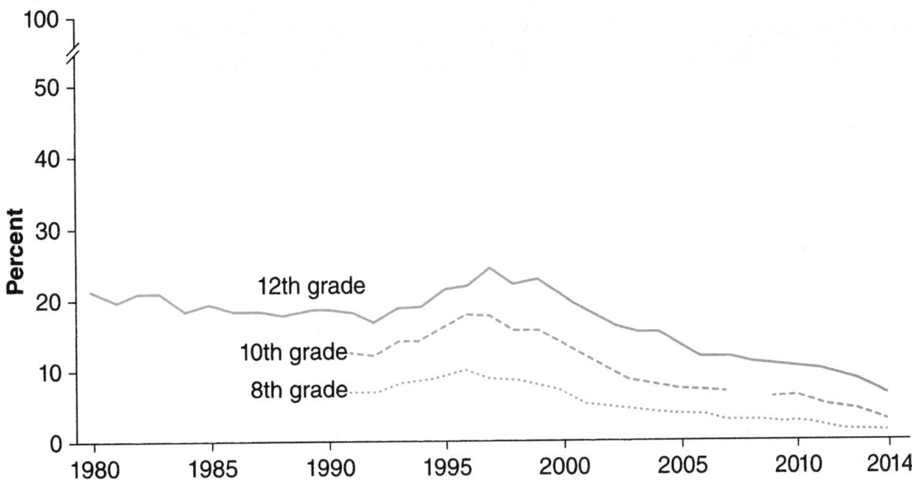

Source: Federal Interagency Forum on Child and Family Statistics. *America's Children: Key National Indicators of Well-Being, 2015*, 2015.

12. The Affordable Care Act was fully implemented in 2014, requiring citizens and all legal residents to purchase health insurance. The percentage of adults aged 18 to 64 years who were uninsured are reported in the bar chart. Describe the difference, if any, in the percentage of uninsured adults from 2013 to 2014.

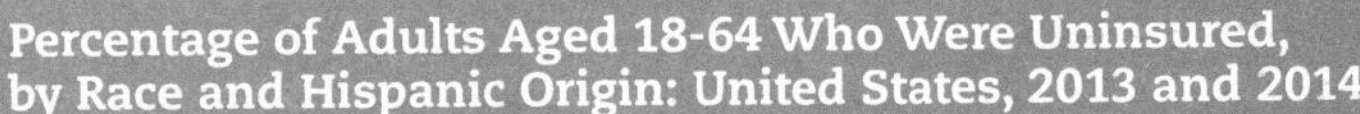

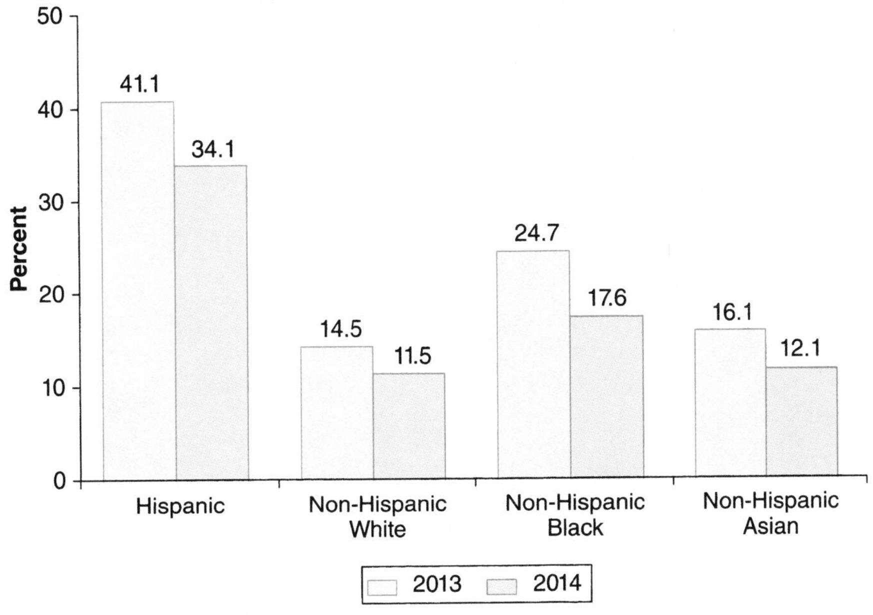

Source: Michael Martinez, Brian Ward, and Patricia Adams, *Health Care Access and Utilization Among Adults Aged 18-65 by Race and Hispanic Origin: United States, 2013 and 2014*, NCHS Data Brief No. 208, 2015.

13. Elizabeth Greico and her colleagues (2012) analyzed U.S. Census data on foreign-born individuals by country of origin and age for 2010. The data are presented in the table with row percentages totaling 100% (approximately).

	Less Than 18	18–44	45–64	65+
Africa	10.6	54.9	28.2	6.3
Asia	7	47.6	32.8	12.7
Europe	5.6	32.9	33	28.4
North America	7.3	30.7	36.1	25.9
Oceania	7.8	51.7	30.3	10.3
Latin America	7.2	56.1	28.1	8.6

Source: Elizabeth Greico, Yesenia Acosta, G. Patricia de la Cruz, Thomas Gryn, Luke Larsen, Edward Trevelyan, and Nathan Walters, *The Foreign Born Population in the United States: 2010* (American Community Survey Reports ACS-19; Washington, DC: U.S. Census Bureau), 2012.

a. Describe the relationship between immigrant age and country of origin.

b. Construct a graph that best displays these data.

3

MEASURES OF CENTRAL TENDENCY

Frequency distributions and graphical techniques are useful tools for describing data. The main advantage of using frequency distributions or graphs is to summarize quantitative information in ways that can be easily understood even by a lay audience. Often, however, we need to describe a large set of multivariate data for which graphs and tables may not be the most efficient tools. For instance, let's say that we want to present information on the income, education, and political party affiliation of both men and women. Presenting this information might require up to six frequency distributions or graphs. The more variables we add, the more difficult it becomes to present the information clearly.

We might also describe a distribution by selecting a single number that describes or summarizes the distribution more concisely. Such numbers describe what is typical about the distribution, for example, a single number could summarize income earnings among Latino college graduates or the most common political party identification for Millennials. Numbers that describe what is average or typical of the distribution are called measures of central tendency.

In this chapter, we will learn about three measures of central tendency: (1) the mode, (2) the median, and (3) the mean. You are probably somewhat familiar with these measures. Each describes what is most typical, central, or representative of the distribution. For example, the terms median income and average income are used frequently in the popular media. In this chapter, we will also learn about how these measures differ from one another. We will see that the choice of an appropriate measure of central tendency for representing a distribution depends on three factors: (1) the way the variables are measured (their level of measurement), (2) the shape of the distribution, and (3) the purpose of the research.

Chapter Learning Objectives

1. Explain the importance of measures of central tendency
2. Calculate and interpret the mode, the median, and the mean
3. Identify the relative strengths and weaknesses of the three measures
4. Determine and explain the shape of the distribution

Measures of central tendency Categories or scores that describe what is average or typical of the distribution.

THE MODE

The mode is the category or score with the largest frequency or percentage in the distribution. Of all the measures of central tendency

Mode The category or score with the highest frequency (or percentage) in the distribution.

discussed in this chapter, the mode is the easiest one to identify. Simply locate the category represented by the highest frequency in the distribution.

We can use the mode to determine, for example, the most common foreign language spoken in the United States today. English is clearly the language of choice in public communication in the United States, but you may be surprised by the U.S. Census Bureau's finding that at least 350 languages are spoken in U.S. homes. In the New York metro area alone, at least 192 languages are spoken; 38% of the metro population age 5 years and over speak a language other than English.[1]

What is the most common foreign language spoken in the United States today? To answer this question, look at Table 3.1, which lists the 10 most commonly spoken foreign languages in the United States during 2009–2013 and the number of people who speak each language. The table shows that Spanish is the most common; more than 37 million people speak Spanish. In this example, we refer to "Spanish" as the mode—the category with the largest frequency in the distribution.

The mode is always a category or score, *not* a frequency. Do not confuse the two. That is, the mode in the previous example is "Spanish," not its frequency of 37,458,624. The mode is not necessarily the category with the majority (i.e., more than 50%) of cases, as it is in Table 3.1; it is simply the category in which the largest number (or proportion) of cases fall.

The mode is the only measure of central tendency that can be used with nominal-level variables. Recall that with nominal variables—such as foreign languages spoken in the United States, race/ethnicity, or religious affiliation—we are only able to classify respondents based on a qualitative and not on a quantitative property. However, the mode can also be used to describe the most commonly occurring category in any distribution. For example, the variable GOODLIFE presented in Figure 3.1 is an ordinal variable, measuring responses to the question, "The way things are in America, people like me and my family have a good chance of improving our standard of living—do you agree or disagree?" Which is the modal category?

Table 3.1 Ten Most Common Foreign Languages Spoken in the United States, 2009–2013

Language	Number of Speakers
Spanish	37,458,624
Chinese	2,896,766
Tagalog	1,613,346
Vietnamese	1,399,936
French	1,307,742
Korean	1,117,343
German	1,063,773
Arabic	924,374
Russian	879,434
French Creole	739,725

Source: U.S. Census Bureau, *Census Bureau Reports at Least 350 Languages Spoken in U.S. Homes*, 2015.

Figure 3.1 Respondent's Prospects of Improving Standard of Living (GOODLIFE), GSS 2014

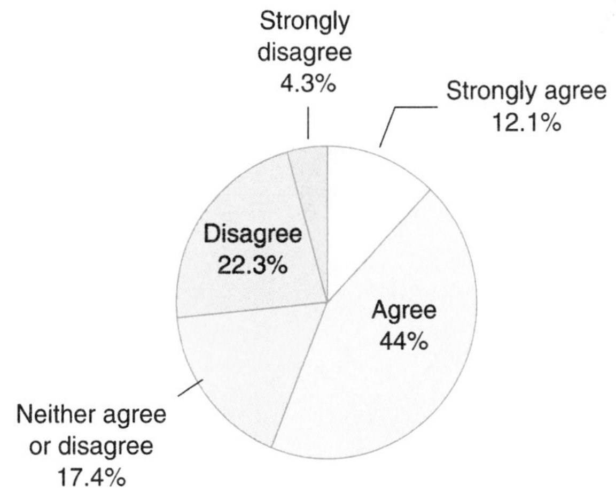

LEARNING CHECK 3.1

Listed below are the political party affiliations of 15 individuals. Find the mode.

Democrat	Republican	Democrat	Republican	Republican
Independent	Democrat	Democrat	Democrat	Republican
Independent	Democrat	Independent	Republican	Democrat

In some distributions, there are two scores or categories with the highest frequency. For instance, Figure 3.2 is a bar graph showing the response of GSS 2014 respondents to the following question: "If you were asked to use one of the four names for your social class, which would you say you belong to: the lower class, the working class, the middle class, or the upper class?" The same percentage of respondents (43%) identified themselves as "working" or "middle" class. Both response categories have the highest frequency, and therefore, both are the modes. We can describe this distribution as bimodal. When two scores or categories with the highest frequencies are quite close (but not identical) in frequency, the distribution is still "essentially" bimodal. In these situations, you should not rely on merely reporting the (true) mode, but instead report the two highest frequency categories.

THE MEDIAN

The median is a measure of central tendency that can be calculated for variables that are at least at an ordinal level of measurement. The median represents the exact middle of a distribution; it is the score that divides the distribution into two equal parts so that half the cases are above it and half below it. For example, according to the U.S. Bureau of Labor Statistics, the median weekly earnings of full-time wage and salary workers during the fourth quarter

Median The score that divides the distribution into two equal parts so that half the cases are above it and half below it.

Figure 3.2 Respondents' Social Class, GSS 2014

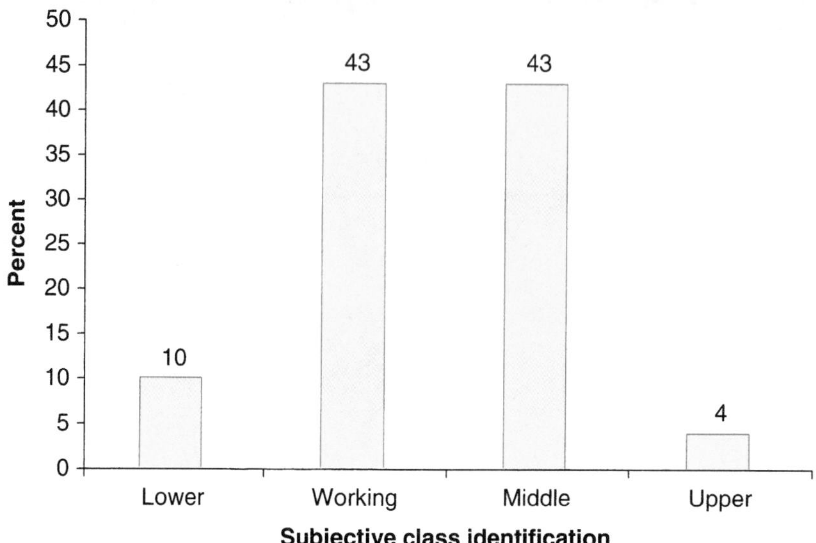

of 2015 was $825.[2] This means that half the workers in the United States earned more than $825 a week and half earned less than $825.

Because many variables used in social research are ordinal, the median is an important measure of central tendency. The median is a suitable measure for those variables whose categories or scores can be arranged in order of magnitude from the lowest to the highest. Therefore, the median can be used with ordinal or interval-ratio variables, for which scores can be at least rank-ordered, but cannot be calculated for variables measured at the nominal level.

Finding the Median in Sorted Data

It is very easy to find the median. In most cases, it can be done by a simple inspection of the sorted data. The location of the median score differs somewhat, depending on whether the number of observations is odd or even. Let's first consider two examples with an odd number of cases.

AN ODD NUMBER OF CASES Suppose we are looking at five individual responses to the question, "Thinking about the economy, how would you rate economic conditions in this country today?" Following are the responses of these five hypothetical persons:

Poor

Good

Only fair

Poor

Excellent
Total (N) = 5

To locate the median, first arrange the responses in order from the lowest to the highest (or the highest to the lowest):

Poor
Poor
Only fair
Good
Excellent
Total (N) = 5

The median is the response associated with the middle case. Find the middle case when N is odd by adding 1 to N and dividing by 2: $(N + 1)/2$. Because N is 5, you calculate $(5 + 1)/2 = 3$. The middle case is thus the third case, and the median is "only fair," the response associated with the third case. Notice that the median divides the distribution exactly into half so that there are two respondents who are more satisfied and two respondents who are less satisfied.

Now let's look at another example. The following is a list of the number of hate crimes reported in the nine most populous U.S. states in 2014.[3]

Number of Hate Crimes	States
145	Texas
759	California
65	Florida
545	New York
50	Pennsylvania
109	Illinois
311	Michigan
336	New Jersey
140	North Carolina
Total (N) = 9	

To locate the median, first arrange the number of hate crimes in order from the lowest to the highest (as illustrated in Figure 3.3). The middle case is $(9 + 1)/2 = 5$, the fifth state, Texas. The median is 145, the number of hate crimes associated with Texas. It divides the distribution exactly into half, so that there are four states with fewer hate crimes and four with more (this is illustrated in Figure 3.3a).

Figure 3.3 Finding the Median Number of Hate Crimes for (a) Nine States and (b) Eight States

(a) Odd Number of Cases

1. Order the cases from the lowest to the highest:

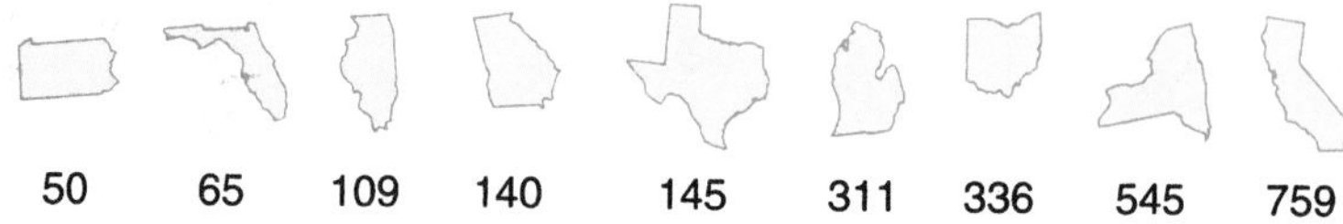

50 65 109 140 145 311 336 545 759

2. In this situation, we need the 5th case: $(9 + 1) \div 2 = 5$.

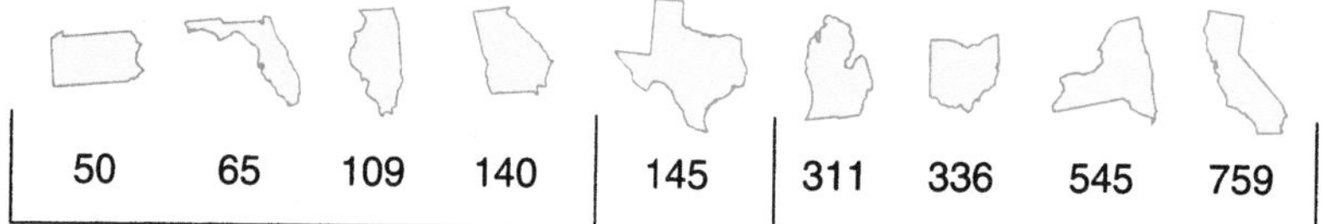

50 65 109 140 | 145 | 311 336 545 759

4 cases on this side of the median | 4 cases on this side of the median

(b) Even Number of Cases

1. Order the cases from the lowest to the highest:

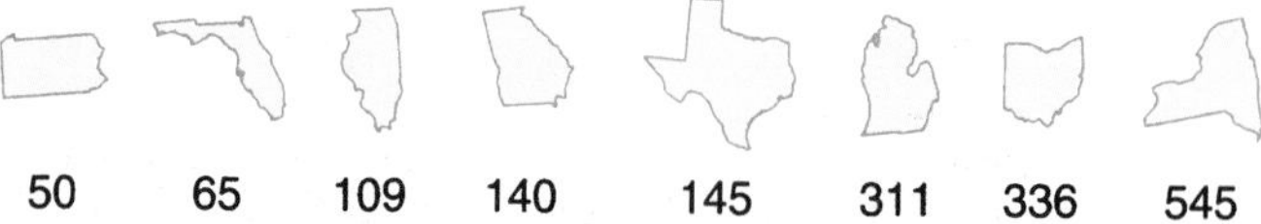

50 65 109 140 145 311 336 545

2. In this situation, we take the average of the two cases nearest the 4.5th case: $(8 + 1) \div 2 = 4.5$

Median: $(140 + 145)/2 = 142.5$

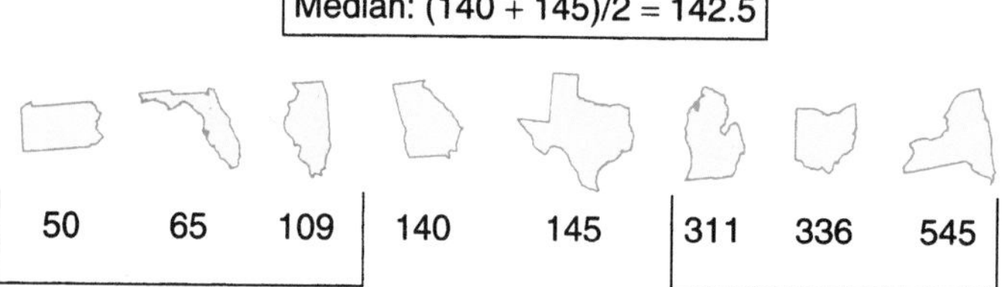

50 65 109 | 140 145 | 311 336 545

3 cases on this side of the median | 3 cases on this side of the median

AN EVEN NUMBER OF CASES Now let's delete the last score to make the number of states even (Figure 3.3b). The scores have already been arranged in ascending order.

Again, to locate the median, first arrange the number of hate crimes in order from the lowest to the highest:

Number of Hate Crimes	States
50	Pennsylvania
65	Florida

Number of Hate Crimes	States
109	Illinois
140	North Carolina
145	Texas
311	Michigan
759	California
545	New York
Total (N) = 8	

When N is even (eight states), we no longer have a single middle case. The median is therefore located halfway between the two middle cases. Find the two middle cases by using the previous formula: $(N + 1)/2$, or $(8 + 1)/2 = 4.5$. In our example, this means that you average the scores for the fourth and fifth states, North Carolina and Texas. The numbers of hate crimes associated with these states are 140 and 145. To find the median for this interval-ratio variable, simply average the two middle numbers:

$$\frac{140+145}{2}=142.5$$

The median is therefore 142.5.

As a note of caution, when data are ordinal, averaging the middle two scores is no longer appropriate. The median simply falls between two middle values.

LEARNING CHECK 3.2

Find the median of the following distribution of an interval-ratio variable: **22, 15, 18, 33, 17, 5, 11, 28, 40, 19, 8, 20.**

Finding the Median in Frequency Distributions

Often our data are arranged in frequency distributions. Take, for instance, the frequency distribution displayed in Table 3.2. It shows the political views of GSS 2014 respondents.

To find the median, we need to identify the category associated with the observation located at the middle of the distribution. We begin by specifying N, the total number of respondents. In this particular example, $N = 1{,}442$. We then use the formula $(N + 1)/2$, or $(1{,}442 + 1)/2 = 721.5$. The median is the value of the category associated with the 721.5th case. The cumulative frequency (*Cf*) of the 721.5th case falls in the category "moderate"; thus, the median is "moderate." This may seem odd; however, the median is always the value of the response category, not the frequency.

We can also locate the median in a frequency distribution by using the cumulative percentages column, as shown in the last column of Table 3.2. In this example, the percentages are cumulated from "extremely liberal" to "extremely conservative." We could also cumulate the other way, from "extremely conservative" to "extremely liberal." To find the median, we identify the

Table 3.2 Respondent's Political Views, GSS 2014

Political View	Frequency (f)	Cumulative Frequency (Cf)	Percentage (%)	Cumulative Percentage (C%)
Extremely liberal	50	50	3	3
Liberal	187	237	13	16
Slightly liberal	163	400	11	27
Moderate	565	965	39	66
Slightly conservative	206	1,171	14	80
Conservative	218	1,389	15	95
Extremely conservative	53	1,442	4	99
Total (*N*)	1,442		99[a]	

Note: a. Due to rounding, the percentage total does not add up to 100.

response category that contains a cumulative percentage value equal to 50%. The median is the value of the category associated with this observation.[4] Looking at Table 3.2, the percentage value equal to 50% falls within the category "moderate." The median for this distribution is therefore "moderate." If you are not sure why the middle of the distribution—the 50% point—is associated with the category "moderate," look again at the cumulative percentage column (*C*%). Notice that 33% of the observations are accumulated below the category "moderate" and that 66% are accumulated up to and including the category "moderate." We know, then, that the percentage value equal to 50% is located somewhere within the "moderate" category.

LEARNING CHECK 3.3

For a review of cumulative distributions, refer to Chapter 2.

Locating Percentiles in a Frequency Distribution

Percentile A score below which a specific percentage of the distribution falls.

The median is a special case of a more general set of measures of location called percentiles. A **percentile** is a score at or below which a specific percentage of the distribution falls. The *n*th percentile is a score below which *n*% of the distribution falls. For example, the 75th percentile is a score that divides the distribution so that 75% of the cases are below it. The median is the 50th percentile. It is a score that divides the distribution so that 50% of the cases fall below it. Like the median, percentiles require that data be ordinal or higher in level of measurement. Percentiles are easy to identify when the data are arranged in frequency distributions.

To help illustrate how to locate percentiles in a frequency distribution, we display in Table 3.3 the frequency distribution, the percentage distribution, and the cumulative percentage distribution of how often teens have dinner with their parents during an average week. The data were collected in the 2014 Monitoring the Future survey, a national survey measuring the behaviors and attitudes of 12th-grade students. As you can see from the cumulative percentage column, the 50th percentile (the median) falls somewhere in the fifth category, "4–5 days

Table 3.3 Days per Week Having Dinner With Parent(s), Monitoring the Future 2014

Days per Week Having Dinner With Parent	Frequency (f)	Percentage (%)	Cumulative Percentage (C%)
Less than 1 day	1,445	16	16
1 day per week	492	6	22
2 days per week	711	8	30
3 days per week	1,024	11	41
4–5 days per week	1,909	21	62
6–7 days per week	3,326	37	99
Total (*N*)	8,907	99[a]	

Note: a. Due to rounding, the percentage total does not add up to 100.

a week." Fifty percent of all teens have dinner with their parents 4–5 days a week or less, and 50% of all teens have dinner with their parents 4–5 days a week or more.

Percentiles are widely used to evaluate relative performance on standardized achievement tests, such as the SAT or ACT. Let's suppose that your ACT score was 29. To evaluate your performance for the college admissions officer, the testing service translated your score into a percentile rank. Your percentile rank was determined by comparing your score with the scores of all other students who took the test at the same time. Suppose for a moment that 90% of all students received a lower ACT score than you (and 10% scored above you). Your percentile rank would have been 90. If, however, there were more students who scored better than you—let's say that 15% scored above you and 85% scored lower than you—your percentile rank would have been 85.

Another widely used measure of location is the quartile. The lower quartile is equal to the 25th percentile and the upper quartile is equal to the 75th percentile. (Can you locate the upper quartile in Table 3.3?) A college admissions office interested in accepting the top 25% of its applicants based on their SAT scores could calculate the upper quartile (the 75th percentile) and accept everyone whose score is equivalent to the 75th percentile or higher. (Note that they would be calculating percentiles based on the scores of their applicants, not of all students in the nation who took the SAT.)

THE MEAN

The arithmetic mean is by far the best known and most widely used measure of central tendency. The mean is what most people call the "average." The mean is typically used to describe central tendency in interval-ratio variables such as income, age, and education. You are probably already familiar with how to calculate the mean. Simply add up all the scores and divide by the total number of scores.

Mean A measure of central tendency that is obtained by adding up all the scores and dividing by the total number of scores. It is the arithmetic average.

This calculation can be reflected in a mathematical formula. Beginning with this section, we introduce a number of formulas that will help you calculate some of the statistical concepts we review in each chapter. A formula is a shorthand way to explain what operations we need to follow to obtain a certain result. So instead of saying "add all the scores together and then divide by the number of scores," we can define the mean by the following formula:

$$\bar{Y} = \frac{\Sigma Y}{N} \tag{3.1}$$

Let's take a moment to consider these new symbols because we continue to use them in later chapters. We use Y to represent the raw scores in the distribution of the variable of interest; $\bar{Y}$ is pronounced "Y-bar" and is the mean of the variable of interest. The symbol represented by the Greek letter Σ is pronounced "sigma," and it is used often from now on. It is a summation sign (just like the Σ sign) and directs us to sum whatever comes after it. Therefore, ΣY means "add up all the raw Y scores." Finally, the letter N, as you know by now, represents the number of cases (or observations) in the distribution.

Let's summarize the symbols as follows:

Y = the raw scores of the variable Y

$\bar{Y}$ = the mean of Y

ΣY = the sum of all the Y scores

N = the number of observations or cases

Now that we know what the symbols mean, let's work through an example. The following are the ages of the 10 students in a graduate statistics class:

$$21, 32, 23, 41, 20, 30, 36, 22, 25, 27$$

What is the mean age of the students?

For these data, the ages included in this group are represented by Y; N = 10, the number of students in the class; and SY is the sum of all the ages:

$$\Sigma Y = 21 + 32 + 23 + 41 + 20 + 30 + 36 + 22 + 25 + 27 = 277$$

Thus, the mean age is

$$\bar{Y} = \frac{\Sigma Y}{N} = \frac{277}{10} = 27.7$$

Let's take a look at one more example. Table 3.4 shows the 2014 incarceration rates (per 100,000 population) for 10 of the most populous U.S. states. We want to summarize the information presented in this table by calculating some measure of central tendency. Because the variable "incarceration rate" is an interval-ratio variable, we will select the arithmetic mean as our measure of central tendency.

To find the mean incarceration rate (number of people in federal or state prison per 100,000 population) for the data presented in Table 3.4, add up the incarceration rates for all states and divide the sum by the number of states:

$$\frac{(349 + 584 + 513 + 265 + 375 + 394 + 444 + 517 + 358 + 437)}{10} = 423.6$$

The mean incarceration rate for 10 of the most populous states is 423.6.[5] For these 10 states, the average number of prisoners is 423.6.

The mean can also be calculated when the data are arranged in a frequency distribution. We have presented an example involving a frequency distribution in A Closer Look 3.1.

A CLOSER LOOK 3.1

FINDING THE MEAN IN A FREQUENCY DISTRIBUTION

When data are arranged in a frequency distribution, we must give each score its proper weight by multiplying it by its frequency. We can use the following modified formula to calculate the mean:

$$\bar{Y} = \frac{\Sigma(fY)}{N}$$

where

Y = the raw scores of the variable Y

$\bar{Y}$ = the mean of Y

$\Sigma(fY)$ = the sum of all the fYs

N = the number of observations or cases

We now illustrate how to calculate the mean from a frequency distribution using the preceding formula. In the 2014 GSS, respondents were asked about what they think is the ideal number of children for a family. Their responses are presented in the following table.

Ideal Number of Children, GSS 2014

Number of Children (Y)	Frequency (f)	Frequency Σ(fY)
0	13	0
1	16	16
2	506	1,012
3	240	720
4	76	304
5	15	75
6	2	12
Total	$N = 868$	$\Sigma fY = 2{,}139$

Notice that to calculate the value of ΣfY) (Column 3), each score (Column 1) is multiplied by its frequency (Column 2), and the products are then added together. When we apply the formula,

$$\bar{Y} = \frac{\Sigma fY}{N} = \frac{2{,}139}{868} = 2.46$$

we find that the mean for the ideal number of children is 2.46.

Table 3.4 2014 Incarceration Rates per 100,000 People for 10 of the Most Populous States

State	Incarceration per 100,000
California	349
Texas	584
Florida	513
New York	265
Illinois	375
Pennsylvania	394
Ohio	444
Georgia	517
North Carolina	358
Michigan	437

Source: E. Ann Carson. *Prisoners in 2014*. Bureau of Justice Statistics, NCJ 248955, 2015.

LEARNING CHECK 3.4

If you are having difficulty understanding how to find the mean in a frequency distribution, examine this illustrated table. It presents the process without using any notation.

Finding the Mean in a Frequency Distribution

Number of people per house	Number of houses like this	Number of people such houses contribute
1	3	3
2	5	10
3	1	3
4	1	4

Total number of people: 20
Total number of houses: 10
Mean number of people per house: 20/10 = 2

LEARNING CHECK 3.5

The following distribution is the same as the one you used to calculate the median in an earlier Learning Check: 22, 15, 18, 33, 17, 5, 11, 28, 40, 19, 8, 20. Calculate the mean. Is it the same as the median, or is it different?

Understanding Some Important Properties of the Arithmetic Mean

The following three mathematical properties make the mean the most important measure of central tendency. It is, in fact, a concept that is basic to numerous and more complex statistical operations.

INTERVAL-RATIO LEVEL OF MEASUREMENT Because it requires the mathematical operations of addition and division, the mean can be calculated only for variables measured at the interval-ratio level. This is the only level of measurement that provides numbers that can be added and divided.

CENTER OF GRAVITY Because the mean (unlike the mode and the median) incorporates all the scores in the distribution, we can think of it as the center of gravity of the distribution. That is, the mean is the point that perfectly balances all the scores in the distribution. If we subtract the mean from each score and add up all the differences, the sum will always be zero!

LEARNING CHECK 3.6

Why is the mean considered the center of gravity of the distribution? Think of the last time you were in a park on a seesaw (it may have been a long time ago) with a friend who was much heavier than you. You were left hanging in the air until your friend moved closer to the center. In short, to balance the seesaw a light person far away from the center (the mean) can balance a heavier person who is closer to the center. Can you illustrate this principle with a simple income distribution?

SENSITIVITY TO EXTREMES The examples we have used to show how to compute the mean demonstrate that, unlike with the mode or the median, every score enters into the calculation of the mean. This property makes the mean sensitive to extreme scores in the distribution. The mean is pulled in the direction of either very high or very low values. A glance at Figure 3.4 should convince you of that. Figure 3.4a and b show the incomes of 10 individuals. In Figure 3.4b, the income of one individual has shifted from $5,000 to $35,000. Notice the effect it has on the mean; it shifts from $3,000 to $6,000! The mean is disproportionately affected by the relatively high income of $35,000 and is misleading as a measure of central tendency for this distribution. Notice that the median's value is not affected by this extreme score; it remains at $3,000. Thus, the median gives us better information on the typical income for this group. In the next section, we will see that because of the sensitivity of the mean, it is not suitable as a measure of central tendency in distributions that have a few very extreme values on one side of the distribution. (A few extreme values are no problem if they are not mostly on one side of the distribution.)

Illustrating the Seesaw Principle

a. Three people, weights 60, 120, and 180, all stand on a seesaw. The fulcrum is placed at 120. The mean is (60 + 120 + 180)/3. The seesaw balances.

b. The 180-pound person is replaced by a 240-pound person, but we do not move the fulcrum. The seesaw slowly falls to the right.

c. We move the fulcrum to 140. The new mean is (60 + 120 + 240)/3. The seesaw balances again.

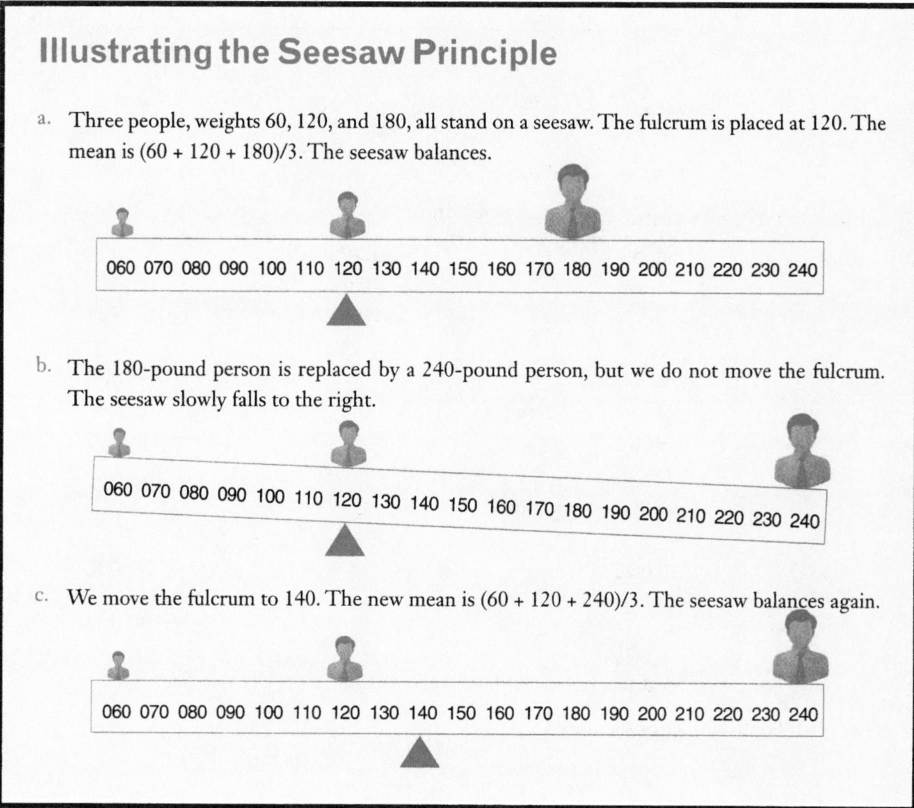

LEARNING CHECK 3.7

When asked to choose the appropriate measure of central tendency for a distribution, remember that the level of measurement is not the only consideration. When variables are measured at the interval-ratio level, the mean is usually the measure of choice, but remember that extreme scores in one direction make the mean unrepresentative and the median or mode may be the better choice.

Figure 3.4 The Value of the Mean Is Affected by Extreme Scores: (a) No Extreme Scores and (b) One Extreme Score

(a) No extreme scores: The mean is \$3,000

Income (Y)	Frequency (f)	fY
1,000	1	1,000
2,000	2	4,000
3,000	4	12,000
4,000	2	8,000
5,000	1	5,000
	$N = 10$	$\Sigma fY = 30,000$

$$\text{Mean} = \frac{\Sigma fY}{N} = \frac{30,000}{10} = \$3,000$$

Median = \$3,000

(b) One extreme score: The mean is \$6,000

Income (Y)	Frequency (f)	fY
1,000	1	1,000
2,000	2	4,000
3,000	4	12,000
4,000	2	8,000
35,000	1	35,000
	$N = 10$	$\Sigma fY = 60,000$

$$\text{Mean} = \frac{\Sigma fY}{N} = \frac{60,000}{10} = \$6,000$$

Median = \$3,000

READING THE RESEARCH LITERATURE: THE CASE OF REPORTING INCOME

Though income levels have changed for American men and women in the past few decades, as we already noted in Chapter 1 ("The What and the Why of Statistics"), gender income equality has yet to be achieved. We continue our investigation of gender income inequality by reviewing published income data.

As noted in the previous discussion (and in Figure 3.4), due to its sensitivity to extreme values, the mean may not be the best measure of central tendency for income. In fact, median earnings are routinely reported in scholarly research and by government publications such as those reported by U.S. Department of Labor and the U.S. Census Bureau.

Figure 3.5 compares the median weekly earnings of women and men who are full-time wage and salary workers by age for 2014. We can use these medians to note the differences between subgroups of the population or changes over time.

For 2014, women's median earnings were 83% of men's—on average, women's median usual weekly earnings was $719 and men's median usual weekly earnings was $871. The data presented in Figure 3.5 reveal that for each age-group, men earn more than women. The gender earnings gap is largest, $241 (1021 - 780), for the 55 to 64 years age-group. The smallest earnings gap is $42 (493 - 451) for Americans aged 16 to 24 years.

When mean income scores are reported, interpret with caution as extremely low or high income values may skew the distribution. When a researcher reports an "average" score, assess whether the calculation was based on a median or a mean.

Figure 3.5 Median Usual Weekly Earnings of Women and Men, Full-Time Wage and Salary Workers, by Age, 2014 Annual Averages

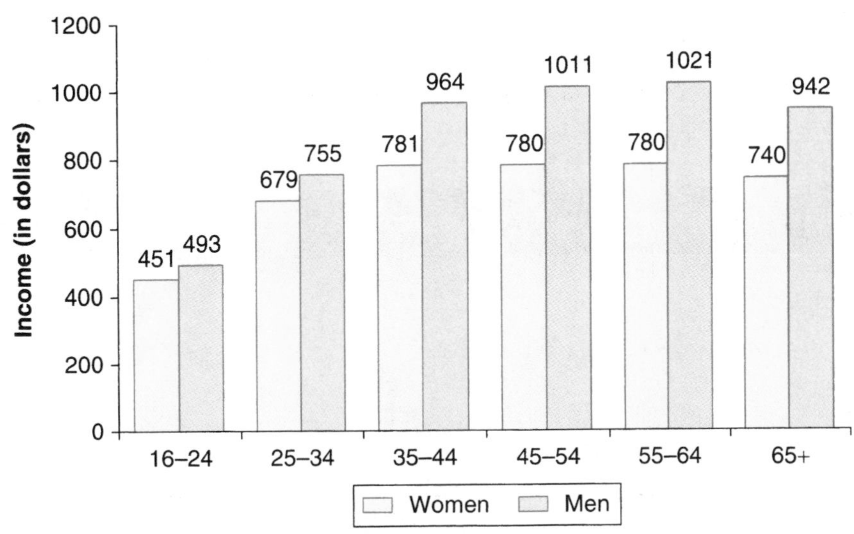

Source: U.S. Bureau of Labor Statistics. *TED: The Economics Daily*. "Women's earnings compared with men's earnings in 2014," 2015.

LEARNING CHECK 3.8

Examine Figure 3.5 and contrast the median weekly earnings of women and men. How else would you describe the relationship between age and median weekly earnings?

STATISTICS IN PRACTICE: THE SHAPE OF THE DISTRIBUTION

The distribution of interval-ratio variables can also be described by their general shape. As we learned in Chapter 2 ("The Organization and Graphic Presentation of Data"), histograms show the differences in frequencies or percentages on an interval-ratio variable. Using histograms, produced by SPSS, we will demonstrate how a distribution can be either symmetrical or skewed, depending on whether there are a few extreme values at one end of the distribution.

The Symmetrical Distribution

Symmetrical distribution The frequencies at the right and left tails of the distribution are identical; each half of the distribution is the mirror image of the other.

A distribution is symmetrical (Figure 3.6a) if the frequencies at the right and left tails of the distribution are identical, so that if it is divided into two halves, each will be the mirror image of the other. In a unimodal, symmetrical distribution, the mean, median, and mode are identical.

For example, refer to Figure 3.7, displaying the distribution of the number of children. Only categories 1–3 are shown. The distribution is symmetrical with the mean, the median, and the mode at 2.0 (the mean of 1.9 would be rounded to 2.0).

The Positively Skewed Distribution

Skewed distribution A distribution with a few extreme values on one side of the distribution.

As a general rule, for skewed distributions the mean, the median, and the mode do not coincide. The mean, which is always pulled in the direction of extreme scores, falls closest to the tail of the distribution where a small number of extreme scores are located.

Positively skewed distribution A distribution with a few extremely high values.

In Figure 3.8, we present a positively skewed distribution. The histogram reports hours per week on the Internet, with the mean (11.91) greater than the median (6.00) and the mode (1). Confirm how the shape of this distribution matches Figure 3.6c.

Figure 3.6 Types of Frequency Distributions

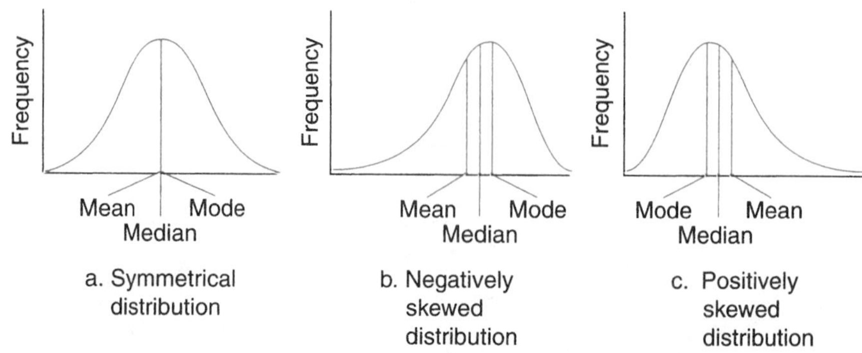

Figure 3.7 Number of Children, GSS 2014

Statistics

NChilds

N	Valid	690
	Missing	489
Mean		1.9855
Median		2.0000
Mode		2.00

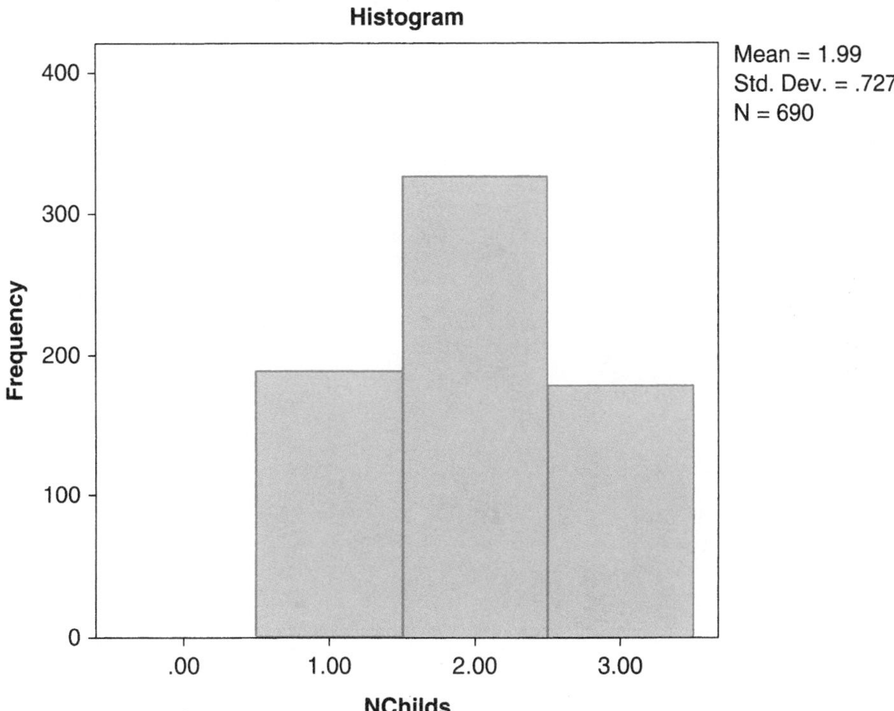

The Negatively Skewed Distribution

Now examine Figure 3.9 for the number of years spent in school among those respondents who did not finish high school. Here you can see the opposite pattern. The distribution of the number of years spent in school for those without a high school diploma is a **negatively skewed distribution** (similar to what is presented in Figure 3.6b). First, note that the largest number of years spent in school are concentrated at the high end of the scale (11 years) and that there are fewer respondents at the low end. The mean, the median, and the mode also differ in values as they did in the previous example. However, here the mode has the highest value (mode = 11.0), the median has the second highest value (median = 10.0), and the mean has the lowest value (mean = 8.89).

Negatively skewed distribution A distribution with a few extremely low values.

Figure 3.8 Number of WWW Hours per Week, GSS 2014 Subsample

Statistics

wwwhr WWW HOURS PER WEEK

N	Valid	423
	Missing	756
Mean		11.91
Median		6.00
Mode		1

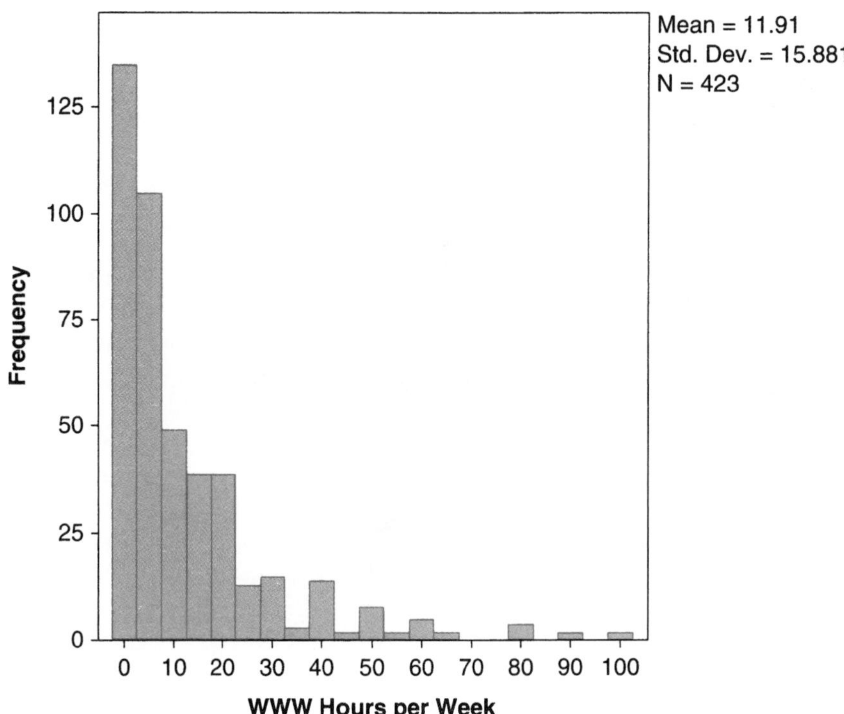

Guidelines for Identifying the Shape of a Distribution

Following are some useful guidelines for identifying the shape of a distribution.

1. In unimodal distributions, when the mode, the median, and the mean coincide or are almost identical, the distribution is symmetrical.

Figure 3.9 Years of School Among Respondents Without a High School Degree, GSS 2014

Statistics

educ HIGHEST YEAR OF SCHOOL COMPLETED

N	Valid	169
	Missing	0
Mean		8.89
Median		10.00
Mode		11

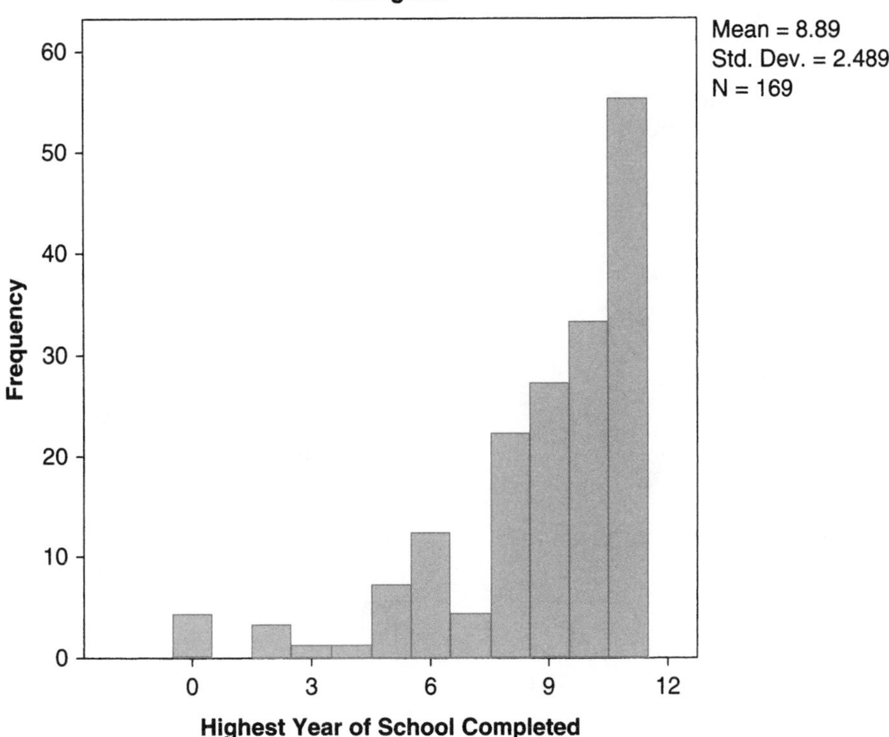

2. When the mean is higher than the median (or is positioned to the right of the median), the distribution is positively skewed.

3. When the mean is lower than the median (or is positioned to the left of the median), the distribution is negatively skewed.

A CLOSER LOOK 3.2

A CAUTIONARY NOTE: REPRESENTING INCOME

Personal income is frequently positively skewed because there are a few people with very high incomes; therefore, the mean may not be the most appropriate measure to represent average income. For example, the 2014 American Community Survey—an ongoing survey of economic and income statistics—reported the 2014 mean and median annual earnings of white, black, and Hispanic households in the United States. In Figure 3.10, we compare the mean and median income for each group.

As shown, for all groups in Figure 3.10, the reported mean is higher than the median. This discrepancy indicates that household income in the United States is highly skewed, with the mean overrepresenting those households in the upper-income bracket and misrepresenting the income of the average household. A preferable alternative is to use the median annual earnings of these groups.

Because the earnings of whites are the highest in comparison with all other groups, it is useful to look at each group's median earnings relative to the earnings of whites. For example, blacks were paid just 62 cents ($35,398/$56,866) and Hispanics were paid 75 cents ($42,491/$56,866) for every $1 paid to whites.

Figure 3.10 Household Mean and Median Income by Race, 2014

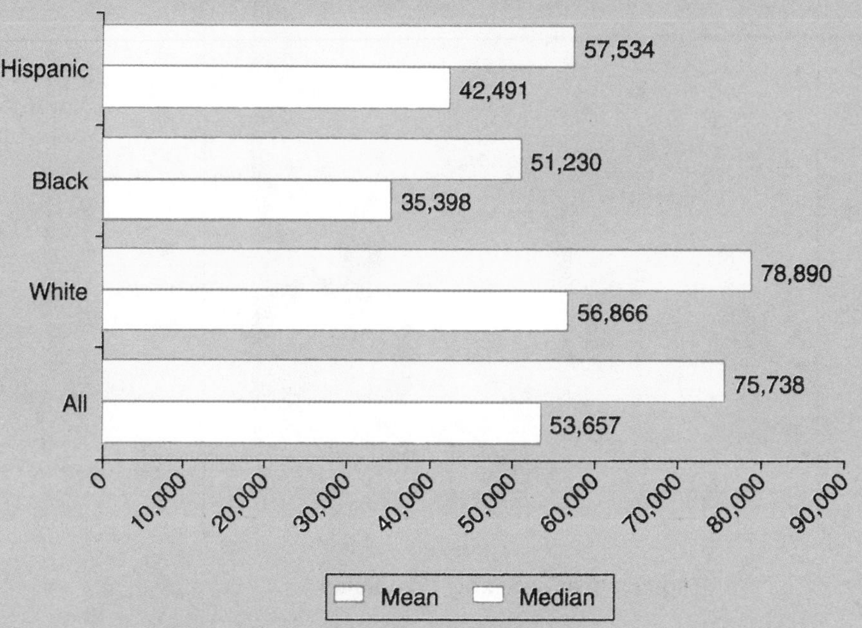

Source: U.S. Census Bureau, *Historical Income Tables: Households*, Table H-5, 2015.

CONSIDERATIONS FOR CHOOSING A MEASURE OF CENTRAL TENDENCY

So far, we have considered three basic kinds of measures: (1) the mode, (2) the median, and (3) the mean. Each can represent the central tendency of a distribution. But which one should we use? The mode? The median? The mean? Or, perhaps, all of them? There is no simple answer to this question. However, in general, we tend to use only one of the three measures of central tendency, and the choice of the appropriate one involves a number of considerations. These considerations and how they affect our choice of the appropriate measure are presented in the form of a decision tree in Figure 3.11.

Level of Measurement

The variable's level of measurement is the primary consideration in choosing a measure of central tendency. The measure of central tendency should be appropriate to the level of measurement. Thus, as shown in Figure 3.11, with nominal variables our choice is restricted to the mode as a measure of central tendency.

However, with ordinal data, we have two choices: (1) the mode or (2) the median (or sometimes both). Our choice depends on what we want to know about the distribution. If we are interested in showing what is the most common or typical value in the distribution, then our choice is the mode. If, however, we want to show which value is located exactly in the middle of the distribution, then the median is our measure of choice.

When the data are measured on an interval-ratio level, the choice between the appropriate measures is a bit more complex and is restricted by the shape of the distribution.

Skewed Distribution

When the distribution is skewed, the mean may give misleading information on the central tendency because its value is affected by extreme scores in the distribution. The median (see, e.g., A Closer Look 3.2) or the mode can be chosen as the preferred measure of central tendency because neither is influenced by extreme scores.

Figure 3.11 How to Choose a Measure of Central Tendency

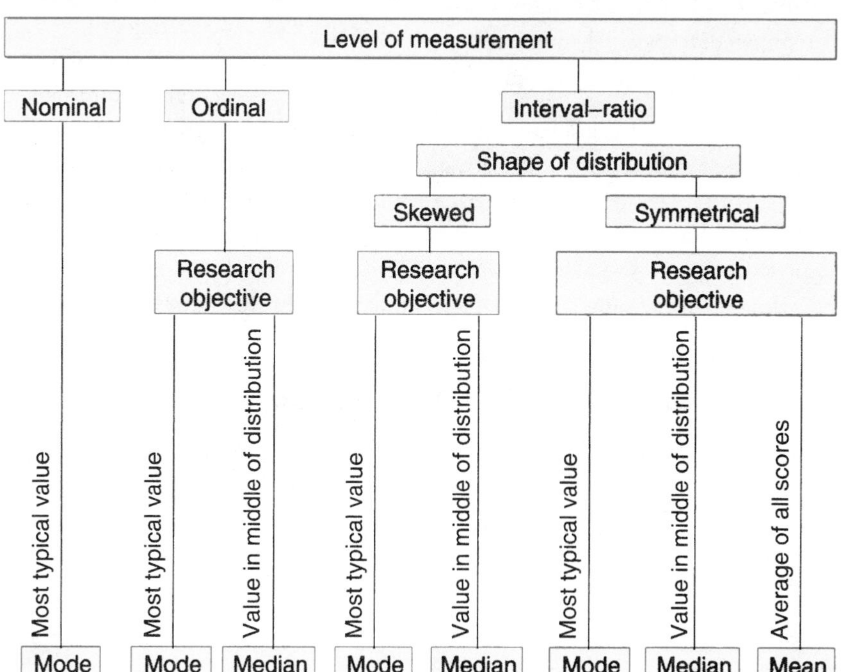

DATA AT WORK

Ben Anderstone: Political Consultant

Photo courtesy of Ben Anderstone

Ben's interest in politics is based on what he describes as a "decidedly nerdy perspective." As an undergraduate student, he began managing local campaigns in Washington State, applying his knowledge of political demographics, psychology, and microtargeting (which he defines as methods to enhance political communications by compiling and modeling information about individual voters).

Currently Ben is a political consultant in a small firm that focuses on local races. "Because our firm specializes in data-driving research, we often focus on solving some of the more cloying questions of politics—such as 'can I even win this thing?'—using a mix of quantitative data and experience."

It is not surprising that statistics is an integral part of Ben's work. He explains, "We do a lot of projects analyzing the viability of school levies and bonds and when school districts would be smartest to go to ballot. This involves wrangling a lot of variables together and—even in the absence of certainty—giving a probabilistic recommendation. In addition to complicated statistical techniques like regression analysis, we very frequently use descriptive statistics to, say, show the association between demographics of voting precincts and a bond/levy's past performance there. That helps our clients keep an eye on their political strengths and find ways that they might repair their political weaknesses."

Ben's advice for students interested in a career involving quantitative research begins simply, "Don't get daunted by the mathematical nature of statistics." Ben highlights the value of statistical data and the advantages of knowing how to use such data. "One of the most attractive aspects of the field is that statistics, however complicated it gets, fundamentally relates to very concrete, important things that come up in everyday life. It certainly can take a while to acquaint yourself with a statistics concept to the point where you feel fully comfortable explaining and applying it. But being able to explain these concepts is a hugely marketable and useful skill. It's often said that 'the data speaks for itself'—but, in fact, I find that few people are actually equipped to speak for the data, and those who do are in a great position in the professional world."

Symmetrical Distribution

When the distribution we want to analyze is symmetrical, we can use any of the three averages. Again, our choice depends on the research objective and what we want to know about the distribution. In general, however, the mean is our best choice because it contains the greatest amount of information and is easier to use in more advanced statistical analyses.

MAIN POINTS

- The mode, the median, and the mean are measures of central tendency—numbers that describe what is average or typical about the distribution.
- The mode is the category or score with the largest frequency (or percentage) in the distribution. It is often used to describe the most commonly occurring category of a nominal-level variable.
- The median is a measure of central tendency that represents the exact middle of the distribution. It is calculated for variables measured on at least an ordinal level of measurement.
- The mean is typically used to describe central tendency in interval-ratio variables, such as income, age, or education. We obtain the mean by summing all the scores and dividing by the total (N) number of scores.
- In a symmetrical distribution, the frequencies at the right and left tails of the distribution are identical. In skewed distributions, there are either a few extremely high (positive skew) or a few extremely low (negative skew) values.

KEY TERMS

mean 71
measures of central tendency 63
median 65
mode 63
negatively skewed distribution 79
percentile 70
positively skewed distribution 78
skewed distribution 78
symmetrical distribution 78

DIGITAL RESOURCES

SAGE edge™

Get the edge on your studies. **edge.sagepub.com/frankfort8e**

Take a quiz to find out what you've learned.
Review key terms with eFlashcards.
Dive into real research with SAGE Journal Articles.

SPSS DEMONSTRATIONS [GSS14SSDS-A]

Demonstration 1: Producing Measures of Central Tendency With Frequencies

The Frequencies command, which we demonstrated in Chapter 2, also has the ability to produce the three measures of central tendency discussed in this chapter. We will use Frequencies to calculate measures of central tendency for EMAILHR (number of e-mail hours per week) and TVHOURS (hours per day watching television).

Figure 3.12 Statistics Output for EMAILHR and TVHOURS

Statistics

		emailhr EMAIL HOURS PER WEEK	tvhours HOURS PER DAY WATCHING TV
N	Valid	568	1001
	Missing	932	499
Mean		6.43	2.94
Median		2.00	2.00
Mode		0	2

Click on *Analyze*, *Descriptive Statistics*, then *Frequencies*. Place EMAILHR and TVHOURS in the Variable(s) box. Then click on the *Statistics* button. You will see that the Central Tendency box lists four choices, but we will click on only the first three—(1) Mean, (2) Median, and (3) Mode. Then click on *Continue*, then on *OK* to process this request.

The statistics box for EMAILHR and TVHOURS is displayed here (Figure 3.12). Both variables are interval-ratio measurements. Though we have instructed you to select the Mean, Median, and Mode for your output, the mean is the most appropriate measure of central tendency. SPSS produces exactly the output we asked for, without regard for whether the output is correct for this type of variable. It is up to you to select the proper measure of central tendency.

Demonstration 2: Producing Measures of Central Tendency With Descriptives and Split File

Suppose we want our results split by sex, allowing us to separate results for males and females. Select *Data*, *Split File*, *Organize Output by Groups*. Insert the variable *sex* into the box labeled "Groups Based on." Click *OK*. Now SPSS will filter our results by SEX.

When you want to calculate the mean of interval-ratio variables but you don't need to view the actual frequency table listing the responses in each category, the Descriptives procedure is often the best choice. Descriptives can be found by clicking on *Analyze*, *Descriptive Statistics*, and then *Descriptives*.

The Descriptives dialog box is uncomplicated and requires only that you place the variables of interest (AGE, EMAILWK, and TVHOURS) in the Variable(s) box. By default, Descriptives will calculate the mean, standard deviation (to be discussed in the next chapter), minimum, maximum, and the number of cases with a valid response.

You will need to scroll through your SPSS output to locate the descriptive statistics for female respondents. Figure 3.13 displays these descriptive statistics for AGE, EMAILWK, and TVHOURS for female GSS respondents in 2014.

The output from Descriptives automatically lists the variables in the order that we specified in the dialog box. Based on the output, we can determine that on an average, female respondents were 50.52 years old, used their e-mail 6.27 hours per week, and watched 2.79 hours of television per day.

Figure 3.13 Descriptive Statistics for Females Only

sex RESPONDENTS SEX = 2 FEMALE

Descriptive Statistics[a]

	N	Minimum	Maximum	Mean	Std. Deviation
age AGE OF RESPONDENT	823	18	89	50.52	17.525
emailhr EMAIL HOURS PER WEEK	309	0	60	6.27	10.094
tvhours HOURS PER DAY WATCHING TV	564	0	24	2.79	2.392
Valid N (listwise)	309				

a. sex RESPONDENTS SEX = 2 FEMALE

SPSS EXERCISES [GSS14SSDS-A]

1. Based on the last SPSS Demonstration on Descriptives, compare the means for each variable (AGE, EMAILHR, and TVHOURS) for men and women.
   a. On average, which group is older, uses their e-mail more frequently, and watches more television per day?
   b. Program SPSS to split the file by DEGREE (respondent's educational attainment) and run Descriptives for EMAILHR. Rank the DEGREE groups by the highest to lowest e-mail use per day.
2. Picking an appropriate statistic to describe the central tendency of a distribution is a critical skill. Determine the appropriate measure(s) of central tendency for the following variables: (remember to reset the Split File option—*Analyze All Cases, Do Not Create Groups*)
   a. Respondent's marital status [MARITAL]
   b. Respondent's general level of happiness [HAPPY]
   c. Number of hours a respondent worked last week [HRS1]
   d. Which presidential candidate respondent voted for in 2012 [PRES12]
   e. Number of brothers and sisters of respondents [SIBS]
   f. Beliefs about the Bible [BIBLE]
3. Create a frequency distribution, including any appropriate measures of central tendency, for PREMARSX (Does the respondent approve of sex before marriage?).
   a. Which measure of central tendency is most appropriate to summarize the distribution of PREMARSX? Explain why.
   b. Suppose we are interested in whether attitudes about premarital sex vary by beliefs about the Bible. Create a frequency distribution, including any appropriate measures of central tendency, for PREMARSX, this time separating results for the categories in BIBLE. Are there any differences in their measures of central tendency? Explain.

4. Create a frequency distribution, including any appropriate measures of central tendency, for EDUC (years of education).

   a. Which measure of central tendency is most appropriate to summarize the distribution of EDUC? Explain why.

   b. Create a frequency distribution, this time separating results for SEX categories. Include in your analysis, the appropriate measure of central tendency. Are there any differences in their measures? Explain.

5. Some believe that social class influences an individual's decision on the number of children to have. Use SPSS to investigate this question with the GSS data file. The variable CHILDS measures the respondent's number of children. To produce the necessary information, have SPSS split the file by CLASS and then run Frequencies (and Statistics) for CHILDS.

   a. What is the best measure of central tendency to represent the number of children in a household? Why?

   b. Which social class has more children per respondent?

   c. Rerun your analysis, this time with the variable CHLDIDEL (ideal number of children). Is there a difference among the social class categories? Explain.

CHAPTER EXERCISES

1. The following GSS 2014 frequency distribution presents information about people's self-evaluations of their lives, based on three categories: (1) exciting, (2) routine, and (3) dull.

Respondent's Assessment of Life	Frequency	Percentage	Cumulative Percentage
Exciting	355	45.5	45.5
Routine	379	48.6	94.1
Dull	46	5.9	100.0
Total	780	100.0	

   a. Find the mode.

   b. Find the median.

   c. Interpret the mode and the median.

   d. Why would you not want to report the mean for this variable?

2. GSS 2014 respondents were asked their opinion on whether homosexuals should have the right to marry. (The data were collected before the 2015 U.S. Supreme Court decision granting same-sex couples the right to marry.) Responses were measured on a five-point scale from *strongly agree* to *strongly disagree*.

Homosexuals Should Have Right to Marry	Frequency	Percentage	Cumulative Percentage
Strongly agree	251	32.5	32.5
Agree	195	25.2	57.5
Neither agree nor disagree	74	9.6	67.3
Disagree	92	11.9	79.2
Strongly disagree	161	20.8	100.0
Total	773	100.0	

a. What is the level of measurement for this variable?

b. What is the mode?

c. Calculate the median for this variable. In general, how would you characterize the public's attitude about same-sex marriage?

3. This frequency distribution contains information on the number of hours worked last week for a sample of 32 Latino adults from the GSS 2010.

Hours Worked Last Week	Frequency	Percentage	Cumulative Percentage
20	3	9.4	9.4
25	2	6.3	15.6
28	1	3.1	18.8
29	1	3.1	21.9
30	3	9.4	31.3
32	1	3.1	34.4
40	14	43.8	78.1
50	2	6.3	84.4
52	1	3.1	87.5
55	1	3.1	90.6
60	1	3.1	93.8
64	1	3.1	96.9
70	1	3.1	100.0
Total	32	100.0	

a. What is the level of measurement, mode, and median for "hours worked last week"?

b. Construct quartiles for weeks worked last year. What is the 25th percentile? The 50th percentile? The 75th percentile? Why don't you need to calculate the 50th percentile to answer this question?

4. GSS 2014 respondents were asked, "Some people say the following things are important for being truly American. Others say they are not important. How important do you think each of the following is—to be a Christian?" Responses were measured on a 4-point scale: *very important*, *fairly important*, *not very important*, and *not important at all*.

Important to Be a Christian	Frequency
Very important	136
Fairly important	49
Not very important	89
Not important at all	118
Total	392

a. What is the modal category?

b. Calculate the median category for this variable.

c. Identify which categories contain the 20th and 80th percentiles.

5. Monitoring the Future is a longitudinal study of the behaviors and attitudes of American secondary school students. Data from the 2014 survey are presented, measuring the frequency of eating breakfast (an indicator of a healthy lifestyle) by student race. The table features a different format, presenting frequencies and percentages in a single column.

	Black	White	Hispanic
	f	f	f
	%	%	%
Never	4	14	5
	9.3%	6.4%	7.0%
Seldom	11	22	9
	25.6%	10.1%	12.7%
Sometimes	10	43	21
	23.3%	19.7%	29.6%
Most days	2	25	9
	4.7%	11.5%	12.7%
Nearly every day	7	30	2
	16.3%	13.8%	2.8%
Everyday	9	84	25
	20.9%	38.5%	35.2%
Total	43	218	71
	100%	100%	100%

a. Calculate the median and mode for each racial group.

b. Use this information to describe how teens' breakfast habits vary by race. In your opinion, which statistic provides a better description of the data—the median or mode?

6. Use this GSS 2014 data to determine whether labor force participation varies by sex. Not all labor categories are shown; some categories are collapsed. Calculate the appropriate measures of central tendency for males and females. Describe their labor force participation rate. Are they similar or different? Use your calculations to support your answer.

	Male	Female
Working full time	303	263
Working part time	55	86
School	12	21
Keeping house	8	107
Not working (laid off, temporary)	35	26
Total	413	503

7. U.S. households have become smaller over the years. The following table from the 2010 GSS contains information on the number of people currently aged 18 years or older living in a respondent's household. Calculate the mean number of people living in a U.S. household in 2010.

Household Size	Frequency
1	381
2	526
3	227
4	200
5	96
6	42
7	19
8	5
9	2
10	2
Total	1,500

8. SPSS output from the GSS 2014 is presented here, reporting respondents' ideal number of children.

chldidel IDEAL NUMBER OF CHILDREN

		Frequency	Percent	Valid Percent	Cumulative Percent
Valid	0	11	.9	1.6	1.6
	1	14	1.2	2.1	3.7
	2	395	33.5	58.2	61.9
	3	188	15.9	27.7	89.5
	4	56	4.7	8.2	97.8
	5	11	.9	1.6	99.4
	6	2	.2	.3	99.7
	7 SEVEN+	2	.2	.3	100.0
	Total	679	57.6	100.0	
Missing	-1 IAP	386	32.7		
	8 AS MANY AS WANT	114	9.7		
	Total	500	42.4		
Total		1179	100.0		

a. Which category contains the 90th percentile?

b. What is the median?

c. What is the mean? Calculate based only on the valid responses.

d. Given your findings, is the distribution symmetrical, positively skewed, or negatively skewed?

9. In Exercise 7, you examined U.S. household size in 2010. Using these data, construct a histogram to represent the distribution of household size.

a. From the appearance of the histogram, would you say the distribution is positively or negatively skewed? Why?

b. Now calculate the median for the distribution and compare this value with the value of the mean from Exercise 7. Do these numbers provide further evidence to support your decision about how the distribution is skewed? Why do you think the distribution of household size is asymmetrical?

10. Exercise 3 used GSS data on the number of hours worked per week for a sample of 32 Latino adults.

a. Calculate the mean number of hours worked per week.

b. Compare the value of the mean with those you have already calculated for the median. Without constructing a histogram, describe whether and how the distribution of weeks worked per year is skewed.

11. During the 2016 Democratic Presidential primaries, Secretary Hillary Clinton and Senator Bernie Sanders were criticized for defining the American middle class as any household that makes $250,000 or less a year. At the time, the U.S. Census Bureau reported that the median income was $53,657 and the mean income was $75,738 for 2014.[6] Would you agree or disagree with the Democratic candidates? How would you explain the median and mean income measures to the candidates?

12. Do homicide rates vary with country population? Investigate this question using United Nation's data for countries grouped by population size. Calculate the mean and median for each group. Describe the distribution for each group. Which group has the higher homicide rate?

2013 Homicide Rate per 100,000			
#1–10 Most Populated	Murder Rate	#11–20 Most Populated	Murder Rate
China	0.8	Mexico	18.9
India	3.3	Philippines	9.3
United States	3.8	Ethiopia	8.1
Indonesia	0.6	Vietnam	1.5
Brazil	26.5	Germany	.7
Pakistan	7.8	Egypt	3.4
Nigeria	10.3	Iran	4.8
Russia	9.0	Turkey	4.3
Japan	0.3	Democratic Republic of the Congo	13.5
Bangladesh	2.6	Thailand	4.9

Source: United Nations Office on Drugs and Crime, Statistics: *Intentional Homicide, Counts and Rates per 100,000 Population*, 2015. Retrieved from http://data.un.org/Data.aspx?d=UNODC&f=tableCode%3A1

13. The following table reports infant mortality rates for selected countries based on estimates reported in the Central Intelligence Agency's 2016 *World Factbook*. Infant morality rates have been associated with the quality of prenatal care and the overall quality of health care provided within a country.

Country	Infant Mortality Rates
Afghanistan	115.08
Canada	4.65
Colombia	14.58
Finland	2.52
Germany	3.43
Panama	10.41
Rwanda	58.19
Syria	15.61
Turkey	18.87
United States	5.87
Zimbabwe	26.11

Source: Central Intelligence Agency, *World Factbook*, 2016.

a. Calculate the mean and median infant mortalities reported for the 11 countries presented above.

b. Describe the shape of the distribution.

4

MEASURES OF VARIABILITY

Chapter Learning Objectives

1. Explain the importance of measuring variability
2. Calculate and interpret the index of qualitative variation, range, interquartile range, the variance, and the standard deviation
3. Identify the relative strengths and weaknesses of the measures

In the previous chapter, we looked at measures of central tendency: the mean, the median, and the mode. With these measures, we can use a single number to describe what is average for or typical of a given distribution. Although measures of central tendency can be very helpful, they tell only part of the story. In fact, when used alone, they may mislead rather than inform. Another way of summarizing a distribution of data is by selecting a single number that describes how much variation and diversity there is in the distribution. Numbers that describe diversity or variation are called **measures of variability**. Researchers often use measures of central tendency along with measures of variability to describe their data.

In this chapter, we discuss five measures of variability: (1) the index of qualitative variation, (2) the range, (3) the interquartile range, (4) the standard deviation, and (5) the variance. Before we discuss these measures, let's explore why they are important.

THE IMPORTANCE OF MEASURING VARIABILITY

Measures of variability Numbers that describe diversity or variability in the distribution of a variable.

The importance of looking at variation and diversity can be illustrated by thinking about the differences in the experiences of U.S. women. Are women united by their similarities or are they divided by their differences? The answer is *both*. To address the similarities without dealing with differences is "to misunderstand and distort that which separates as well as that which binds women together" (pp. 128–129).[1] Even when we focus on one particular group of women, it is important to look at the differences as well as the commonalities. Take, for example, Asian American women. As a group, they share a number of characteristics.

> Their participation in the workforce is higher than that of women in any other ethnic group. Many . . . live life supporting others, often allowing their lives to be subsumed by the needs of the extended family. . . . However, there are

> many circumstances when these shared experiences are not sufficient to accurately describe the condition of a particular Asian-American woman. Among Asian-American women there are those who were born in the United States . . . and . . . those who recently arrived in the United States. Asian-American women are diverse in their heritage or country of origin: China, Japan, the Philippines, Korea . . . and . . . India. . . . Although the majority of Asian-American women are working class—contrary to the stereotype of the "ever successful" Asians—there are poor, "middle-class," and even affluent Asian-American women. (pp. 129–130)[2]

One form of stereotyping is treating a group as if it were totally characterized by its central value, ignoring the diversity within the group. The complete story of a particular group, like Asian American women, can best be told by examining their commonalities and their differences. We learned in the previous chapter how measures of central tendency can be used to document what is common or average for a group of individuals, and in this chapter, we'll learn different measures of variation to understand the diversity of experiences. The concept of variability has implications not only for describing the diversity of social groups such as Asian American women but also for issues that are important in your everyday life.

One of the most important issues facing the academic community is how to reconstruct the curriculum to make it more responsive to the needs of students. Let's suppose that a university committee is examining how to better respond to the needs of students. In its attempt to evaluate statistics courses offered in different departments, the committee compares the grading policy in two courses. The first, offered in the sociology department, is taught by Professor Brown; the second, offered through the school of social work, is taught by Professor Yamato. The committee finds that over the years, the average grade for Professor Brown's class has been C+. The average grade in Professor Yamato's class is also C+. We could easily be misled by these statistics into thinking that the grading policy of both instructors is about the same. However, we need to look more closely into how the grades are distributed in each of the classes. The differences in the distribution of grades are illustrated in Figure 4.1, which displays the frequency polygon for the two classes.

Compare the shapes of these two distributions. Notice that while both distributions have the same mean, they are shaped very differently. The grades in Professor Yamato's class are more spread out ranging from A to F, whereas the grades for Professor Brown's class are clustered around the mean and range only from B to C. Although the means for both distributions are identical, the grades in Professor Yamato's class vary considerably more than the grades given by Professor Brown. The comparison between the two classes is more complex than we first thought it would be.

As this example demonstrates, information on how scores are spread from the center of a distribution is as important as information about the central tendency in a distribution. This type of information is obtained by measures of variability.

LEARNING CHECK 4.1

Look closely at Figure 4.1. Whose class would you choose to take? If you were worried that you might fail statistics, your best bet would be Professor Brown's class where no one fails. However, if you want to keep up your GPA and are willing to work, Professor Yamato's class is the better choice. If you had to choose one of these classes based solely on the average grades, your choice would not be well informed.

Figure 4.1 Distribution of Grades for Professors Brown's and Yamato's Statistics Classes

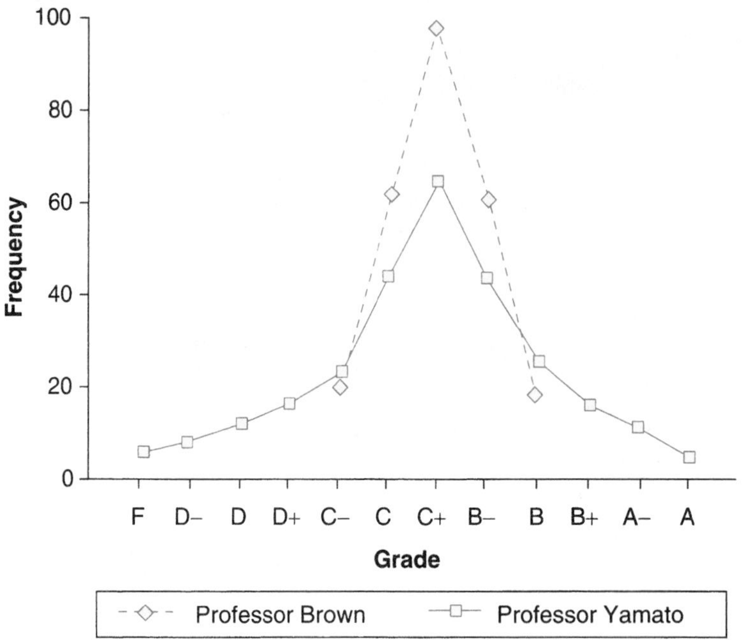

THE INDEX OF QUALITATIVE VARIATION

The United States is undergoing a demographic shift. Formerly a predominantly European population, the country is now characterized by racial, ethnic, and cultural diversity. These changes challenge us to rethink every conceptualization of society based solely on the experiences of European populations and force us to ask questions that focus on the experiences of different racial/ethnic groups. For instance, we may want to compare the racial/ethnic diversity in different cities, regions, or states or may want to find out if a group has become more racially and ethnically diverse over time.

Index of qualitative variation (IQV) A measure of variability for nominal variables. It is based on the ratio of the total number of differences in the distribution to the maximum number of possible differences within the same distribution.

The **index of qualitative variation (IQV)** is a measure of variability for nominal variables such as race and ethnicity. The index can vary from 0.00 to 1.00. When all the cases in the distribution are in one category, there is no variation (or diversity) and the IQV is 0.00. In contrast, when the cases in the distribution are distributed evenly across the categories, there is maximum variation (or diversity) and the IQV is 1.00.

Suppose you live in Maine, where the majority of residents are white and a small minority are Latino or Asian. Also suppose that your best friend lives in Hawaii, where almost half of the population is either Asian or Native Hawaiian. The distributions for these two states are presented in Table 4.1. Which is more diverse? Clearly, Hawaii, where half the population is either Asian or Native Hawaiian, is more diverse than Maine, where Asians and Latinos are but a small minority.

Table 4.1 Top Five Racial/Ethnic Groups for Two States by Percentage, 2010

Racial/Ethnic Group	Maine	Hawaii
White	97.3	29.7
Latino	1.3	10.7
Asian	1.1	46.3
Native Hawaiian or Pacific Islander	—	11.9
Other[a]	0.3	1.5
Total	100.0	100.0

Source: U.S. Census Bureau, *Statistical Abstract of the United States: 2012*, Tables 18–19.

Note: a. The category "Other" counts as a racial/ethnic group.

Steps for Calculating the IQV

To calculate the IQV, we use this formula:

$$\text{IQV} = \frac{K(100^2 - \Sigma Pct^2)}{100^2(K-1)} \tag{4.1}$$

where

K = the number of categories

ΣPct^2 = the sum of all squared percentages in the distribution

In Table 4.2, we present the squared percentages for each racial/ethnic group for Maine and Hawaii.

Table 4.2 Squared Percentages for Five Racial/Ethnic Groups for Two States

	Maine		Hawaii	
Racial/Ethnic Group	%	($\%^2$)	%	($\%^2$)
White	97.3	9,467.29	29.7	882.09
Latino	1.3	1.69	10.7	114.49
Asian	1.1	1.21	46.3	2,143.69
Native Hawaiian or Pacific Islander	—	—	11.9	141.61
Other[a]	0.3	0.09	1.5	2.25
Total	100.0	9,470.28	100.0	3,284.13

Note: a. The category "Other" counts as a racial/ethnic group.

The IQV for Maine is

$$\text{IQV} = \frac{K(100^2 - \sum Pct^2)}{100^2(K-1)} = \frac{4(100^2 - 9{,}470.28)}{100^2(4-1)} = \frac{2{,}118.88}{30{,}000} = 0.07$$

The IQV for Hawaii is

$$\text{IQV} = \frac{K(100^2 - \sum Pct^2)}{100^2(K-1)} = \frac{5(100^2 - 3{,}284.13)}{100^2(5-1)} = \frac{33{,}579.35}{40{,}000} = 0.84$$

Note that the values of the IQV for the two states support our earlier observation: In Hawaii, where the IQV is 0.84, there is considerably more racial/ethnic variation than in Maine, where the IQV is 0.07.

It is important to remember that the IQV is partially a function of the number of categories. In this example, there were four and five racial/ethnic categories in Maine and Hawaii, respectively. Had we used more categories, the IQV for both states would have been considerably more.

To summarize, these are the steps we follow to calculate the IQV:

1. Construct a percentage distribution.
2. Square the percentages for each category.
3. Sum the squared percentages.
4. Calculate the IQV using the formula.

$$\text{IQV} = \frac{K(100^2 - \sum Pct^2)}{100^2(K-1)}$$

EXPRESSING THE IQV AS A PERCENTAGE The IQV can also be expressed as a percentage rather than a proportion: Simply multiply the IQV by 100. Expressed as a percentage, the IQV would reflect the percentage of racial/ethnic differences relative to the maximum possible differences in each distribution. Thus, an IQV of 0.07 indicates that the number of racial/ethnic differences in Maine is 7.0% (0.07 × 100) of the maximum possible differences. Similarly, for Hawaii, an IQV of 0.84 means that the number of racial/ethnic differences is 84.0% (0.84 × 100) of the maximum possible differences.

STATISTICS IN PRACTICE: DIVERSITY IN U.S. SOCIETY

According to demographers' projections, by the middle of this century, the United States will no longer be a predominantly white society. It is estimated that by 2044, the United States will be a minority-majority nation. While the non-Hispanic white population will still be the largest group, no racial or ethnic group will have the majority share of the population.[3] Population shifts, which began in the 1990s, indicated geographic concentration of minority groups in specific regions and metropolitan areas of the United States.[4] Demographers call it chain migration: Essentially, migrants use social capital–specific knowledge of the migration process (i.e., to move from one area and settle in another).[5] For example, in 2010, about 74% of all foreign born lived in 10 states. The states with the highest percentage of foreign born were California (27%), New York (22%), and New Jersey (21%).[6]

How do you compare the amount of diversity in different cities, states, or regions? Diversity is a characteristic of a population many of us can sense intuitively. For example, the ethnic diversity of a large city is seen in the many members of various groups encountered when walking down its streets or traveling through its neighborhoods.[7]

We can use the IQV to measure the amount of diversity in different regions. Table 4.3 displays the 2011 percentage breakdown of the population by race for all four regions of the United States. Based on these data, and using Formula 4.1 as in our earlier example, we have also calculated the IQV for each region. The advantage of using a single number to express diversity is demonstrated in Figure 4.2, which depicts the regional variations in diversity as

Table 4.3 Percentage Makeup of Population for Regions by Race, 2011

Region	White	Black	Latino	Asian	Other	IQV
Northeast	68.2	11.0	13.0	5.6	2.2	0.63
Midwest	77.5	10.2	7.1	2.6	2.6	0.48
South	59.5	19.0	16.2	2.8	2.5	0.73
West	52.3	4.4	29.0	9.2	5.0	0.79

Source: U.S. Census Bureau, *American Community Survey*, 2011.

Note: IQV = index of qualitative variation.

Figure 4.2 Racial Diversity in the United States in 2011, IQV by Region

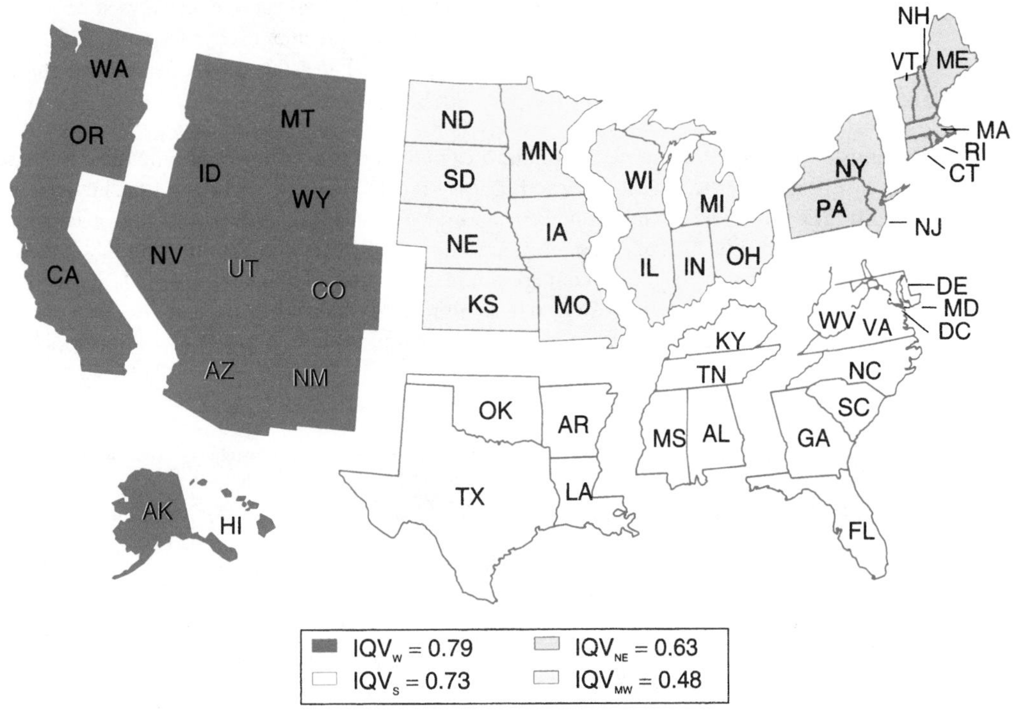

Note: IQV = index of qualitative variation.

expressed by the IQVs from Table 4.3. Figure 4.2 shows the wide variation in racial diversity that exists in the United States. Note that the West, with an IQV of 0.79, is the most diverse region. At the other extreme, the Midwest, whose population is overwhelmingly white, is the most homogeneous region with an IQV of 0.48.

THE RANGE

Range A measure of variation for interval-ratio variables. It is the difference between the highest (maximum) and the lowest (minimum) scores in the distribution.

The simplest and most straightforward measure of variation is the **range**, which measures variation in interval-ratio variables. It is the difference between the highest (maximum) and the lowest (minimum) scores in the distribution:

$$\text{Range} = \text{Highest score} - \text{Lowest score}$$

For example, in the 2014 General Social Survey (GSS), the oldest person included in the study was 89 years old and the youngest was 18. Thus, the range was 89 – 18 = 71 years.

The range can also be calculated on percentages. For example, since the 1980s, relatively large communities of the elderly have become noticeable not just in the traditional retirement meccas of the Sun Belt[8] but also in the Ozarks of Arkansas and the mountains of Colorado and Montana. The number of elderly persons increased in every state during the 1990s and the 2000s (Washington, D.C., is the exception), but by different amounts. As the baby boomers age into retirement, we would expect this trend to continue. Table 4.4 displays the percentage change in the elderly population from 2008 to 2015 by region and by state as predicted by the U.S. Census Bureau.[9]

What is the range in the percentage change in state elderly population for the United States? To find the ranges in a distribution, simply pick out the highest and the lowest scores in the distribution and subtract. Alaska has the highest percentage change, with 50%, and Washington, D.C., has the lowest change, with –14.1%. The range is 64.1 percentage points, or 50% to –14.1%.

Although the range is simple and quick to calculate, it is a rather crude measure because it is based on only the lowest and the highest scores. These two scores might be extreme and rather atypical, which might make the range a misleading indicator of the variation in the distribution. For instance, note that among the 50 states and Washington, D.C., listed in Table 4.4, no state has a percentage decrease as that of Washington, D.C., and only Nevada has a percentage increase nearly as high as Alaska's. The range of 64.1 percentage points does not give us information about the variation in states between Washington, D.C., and Alaska.

LEARNING CHECK 4.2

Why can't we use the range to describe diversity in nominal variables? The range can be used to describe diversity in ordinal variables (e.g., We can say that responses to a question ranged from "somewhat satisfied" to "very dissatisfied"), but it has no quantitative meaning. Why not?

Table 4.4 Projected Percentage Change in the Population 65 Years and Over by Region and State, 2008–2015

Region, Division, and State	Percentage Change	Region, Division, and State	Percentage Change
Northeast	**16.0**	**South (cont.)**	
Connecticut	20.9	Georgia	21.1
Delaware	22.3	Kentucky	12.5
Maine	25.6	Louisiana	23.0
Massachusetts	17.7	Maryland	23.1
New Hampshire	28.4	Mississippi	16.4
New Jersey	20.4	North Carolina	20.7
New York	12.5	Oklahoma	12.8
Pennsylvania	12.5	South Carolina	22.1
Rhode Island	18.2	Tennessee	18.2
Vermont	31.4	Texas	25.9
Midwest	**14.0**	Virginia	26.8
Indiana	11.3	Washington, D.C.	−14.1
Illinois	12.9	West Virginia	15.4
Iowa	11.2	**West**	**27.0**
Kansas	14.2	Alaska	50.0
Michigan	15.5	Arizona	36.8
Minnesota	19.2	California	27.1
Missouri	14.5	Colorado	22.7
Nebraska	12.4	Hawaii	18.8
North Dakota	12.6	Idaho	20.2
Ohio	12.4	Montana	27.0
South Dakota	9.4	Nevada	42.1
Wisconsin	17.6	New Mexico	31.9
South	**22.8**	Oregon	17.1
Alabama	15.1	Utah	13.8
Arkansas	14.7	Washington	23.2
Florida	29.7	Wyoming	36.9

Source: U.S. Census Bureau, *Statistical Abstract of the United States: 2010*, Tables 16 and 18.

THE INTERQUARTILE RANGE

Interquartile range (IQR) The width of the middle 50% of the distribution. It is defined as the difference between the lower and upper quartiles (Q_1 and Q_3). IQR can be calculated for interval-ratio and ordinal data.

To remedy the limitation of the range, we can employ an alternative—the *interquartile range*. The **interquartile range (IQR)**, a measure of variation for interval-ratio and ordinal variables, is the width of the middle 50% of the distribution. It is defined as the difference between the lower and upper quartiles (Q_1 and Q_3).

$$\text{IQR} = Q_3 - Q_1$$

Recall that the first quartile (Q_1) is the 25th percentile, the point at which 25% of the cases fall below it and 75% above it. The third quartile (Q_3) is the 75th percentile, the point at which 75% of the cases fall below it and 25% above it. The IQR, therefore, defines variation for the middle 50% of the cases.

Like the range, the IQR is based on only two scores. However, because it is based on intermediate scores, rather than on the extreme scores in the distribution, it avoids some of the instability associated with the range.

These are the steps for calculating the IQR

1. To find Q_1 and Q_3, order the scores in the distribution from the highest to the lowest score, or vice versa. Table 4.5 presents the data of Table 4.4 arranged in order from Alaska (50.0%) to Washington, D.C. (–14.1%).
2. Next, we need to identify the first quartile, Q_1 or the 25th percentile. We have to identify the percentage increase in the elderly population associated with the state that divides the distribution so that 25% of the states are below it and 75% of the states are above it. To find Q_1, we multiply N by 0.25:

   $$(N)(0.25) = (51)(0.25) = 12.75$$

   The first quartile falls between the 12th and the 13th states. Counting from the bottom, the 12th state is Illinois, and the percentage increase associated with it is 12.9. The 13th state is Utah, with a percentage increase of 13.8. To find the first quartile, we take the average of 12.9 and 13.8. Therefore, $(12.9 + 13.8)/2 = 13.35$ is the first quartile (Q_1).
3. To find Q_3, we have to identify the state that divides the distribution in such a way that 75% of the states are below it and 25% of the states are above it. We multiply N this time by 0.75:

   $$(N)(0.75) = (51)(0.75) = 38.25$$

   The third quartile falls between the 38th and the 39th states. Counting from the bottom, the 38th state is Washington, and the percentage increase associated with it is 23.2. The 39th state is Maine, with a percentage increase of 25.6. To find the third quartile, we take the average of 23.2 and 25.6. Therefore, $(23.2 + 25.6)/2 = 24.4$ is the third quartile (Q_3).
4. We are now ready to find the IQR:

   $$\text{IQR} = Q_3 - Q_1 = 24.4 - 13.35 = 11.05$$

   It may be more useful to report the full IQR (24.4 to 13.35) rather than the single value (11.05). The IQR tells us that half the states are clustered between 24.4 and 13.35, a narrower (and more meaningful) spread than the range of 64.1 points (50% to –14.1%).

LEARNING CHECK 4.3

Why is the IQR better than the range as a measure of variability, especially when there are extreme scores in the distribution? To answer this question, you may want to examine Figure 4.3.

Figure 4.3 The Range Versus the Interquartile Range: Number of Children Among Two Groups of Women

		Group 1: IQR = 1-3	Group 2: IQR = 1-6	
	Number of Children	Less Variable	More Variable	
	0			
Q_1 ⇨	1			⇦ Q_1
	2			
Q_3 ⇨	3			
	4			
	5			
	6			⇦ Q_3
	7			
	8			
	9			
	10			
		Range = 10	Range = 10	
		Interquartile range = 2	Interquartile range = 5	

THE BOX PLOT

A graphic device called the box plot can visually present the range, the IQR, the median, the lowest (minimum) score, and the highest (maximum) score. The box plot provides us with a way to visually examine the center, the variation, and the shape of distributions of interval-ratio variables.

Figure 4.4 is a box plot of the distribution of the 2008–2015 projected percentage increase in the elderly population displayed in Table 4.5. To construct the box plot in Figure 4.4, we used

Table 4.5 Projected Percentage Change in the Population 65 Years and Over, 2008–2015, by State, Ordered From the Highest to the Lowest					
State	Percentage Change	State	Percentage Change	State	Percentage Change
Alaska	50.0	Delaware	22.3	Alabama	15.1
Nevada	42.1	South Carolina	22.1	Arkansas	14.7
Wyoming	36.9	Georgia	21.1	Missouri	14.5
Arizona	36.8	Connecticut	20.9	Kansas	14.2
New Mexico	31.9	North Carolina	20.7	Utah	13.8
Vermont	31.4	New Jersey	20.4	Illinois	12.9
Florida	29.7	Idaho	20.2	New York	12.8
New Hampshire	28.4	Minnesota	19.2	Oklahoma	12.8
California	27.1	Hawaii	18.8	North Dakota	12.6
Montana	27.0	Rhode Island	18.2	Kentucky	12.5
Virginia	26.8	Tennessee	18.2	Pennsylvania	12.5
Texas	25.9	Massachusetts	17.7	Nebraska	12.4
Maine	25.6	Wisconsin	17.6	Ohio	12.4
Washington	23.2	Oregon	17.1	Indiana	11.3
Maryland	23.1	Mississippi	16.4	Iowa	11.2
Louisiana	23.0	Michigan	15.5	South Dakota	9.4
Colorado	22.7	West Virginia	15.4	Washington, D.C.	−14.1

Source: U.S. Census Bureau, *Statistical Abstract of the United States: 2010*, Tables 16 and 18.

the lowest and the highest values in the distribution, the upper and lower quartiles, and the median. We can easily draw a box plot by hand following these instructions:

1. Draw a box between the lower and upper quartiles.
2. Draw a solid line within the box to mark the median.
3. Draw vertical lines (called whiskers) outside the box, extending to the lowest and highest values.

What can we learn from creating a box plot? We can obtain a visual impression of the following properties: First, the center of the distribution is easily identified by the solid line inside the box.

Figure 4.4 Box Plot of the Distribution of the Projected Percentage Increase in the Elderly Population, 2008–2015

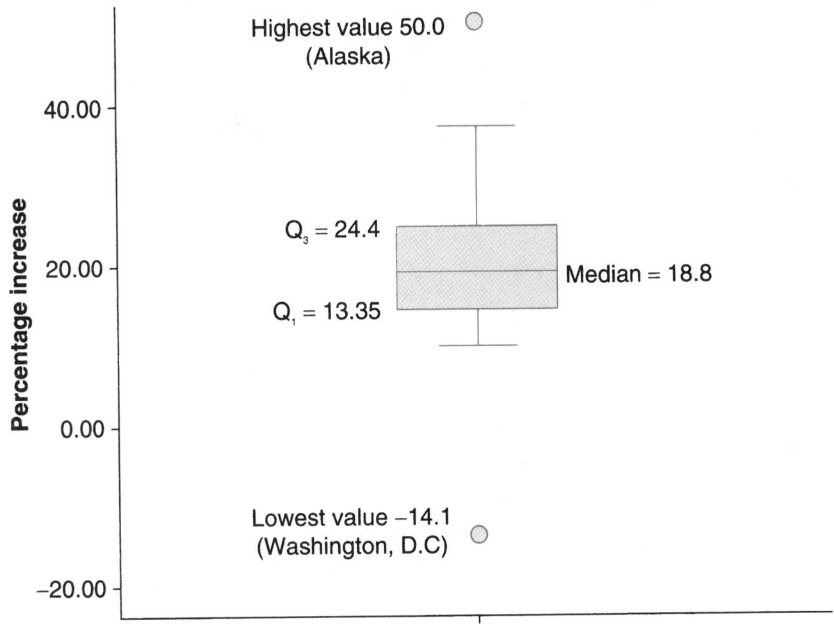

Second, since the box is drawn between the lower and upper quartiles, the IQR is reflected in the height of the box. Similarly, the length of the vertical lines drawn outside the box (on both ends) represents the range of the distribution.[10] Both the IQR and the range give us a visual impression of the spread in the distribution. Finally, the relative position of the box and the position of the median within the box tell us whether the distribution is symmetrical or skewed. A perfectly symmetrical distribution would have the box at the center of the range as well as the median in the center of the box. When the distribution departs from symmetry, the box and/or the median will not be centered; it will be closer to the lower quartile when there are more cases with lower scores or to the upper quartile when there are more cases with higher scores.

LEARNING CHECK 4.4

Is the distribution shown in the box plot in Figure 4.4 symmetrical or skewed?

Box plots are particularly useful for comparing distributions. To demonstrate box plots that are shaped quite differently, in Figure 4.5, we have used the data on the percentage increase in the elderly population (Table 4.5) to compare the pattern of change occurring between 2008 and 2015 in the northeastern and western regions of the United States.

As you can see, the box plots differ from each other considerably. First, the positions of the medians highlight the dramatic increase in the elderly population in the western United States. While the Northeast (median = 20.7%) is projected to experience a steady rise in its elderly population, the West shows a much higher projected percentage increase (median = 27%).

Figure 4.5 Box Plots of the Projected Percentage Increase in the Elderly Population, 2008–2015, for the Northeastern and Western Regions of the United States

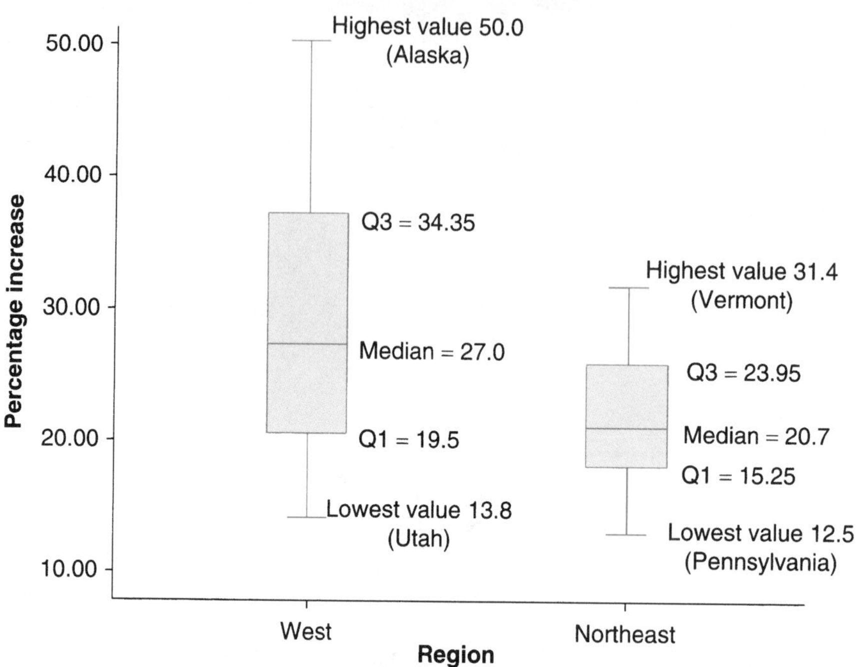

Second, both the range (illustrated by the position of the whiskers in each box plot) and the IQR (illustrated by the height of the box) are much wider in the West (range = 36.2%; IQR = 14.85%) than in the Northeast (range = 18.9%; IQR = 8.7%), indicating that there is more variability among states in the West than among those in the Northeast. Finally, the relative positions of the boxes tell us something about the different shapes of these distributions. Because its box is at about the center of its range, the Northeast distribution is almost symmetrical. In contrast, with its box off center and closer to the lower end of the distribution, the distribution of percentage change in the elderly population for the Western states is positively skewed.

THE VARIANCE AND THE STANDARD DEVIATION

As of 2010, the elderly population in the United States is 13 times as large as in 1900, and it is projected to continue to increase.[11] The pace and direction of these demographic changes will create compelling social, economic, and ethical choices for individuals, families, and governments.

Table 4.6 presents the projected percentage change in the elderly population for all regions of the United States.

Table 4.6 shows that between 2008 and 2015, the size of the elderly population in the United States is projected to increase by an average of 19.95%. But this average increase does not inform us about the regional variation in the elderly population. For example, will the Northeastern states show a smaller-than-average increase because of the out-migration of the elderly population to the warmer climate of the Sun Belt states? Is the projected increase higher in the South because of the immigration of the elderly?

Table 4.6 Projected Percentage Change in the Elderly Population by Region, 2008–2015	
Region	**Percentage**
Northeast	16.0
South	22.8
Midwest	14.0
West	27.0
Mean ($\bar{Y}$)	19.95

Source: U.S. Census Bureau, *Statistical Abstract of the United States: 2010*, Tables 16 and 18.

Although it is important to know the average projected percentage increase for the nation as a whole, you may also want to know whether regional increases might differ from the national average. If the regional projected increases are close to the national average, the figures will cluster around the mean, but if the regional increases deviate much from the national average, they will be widely dispersed around the mean.

Table 4.6 suggests that there is considerable regional variation. The percentage change ranges from 27.0% in the West to 14.0% in the Midwest, so the range is 13.0% (27.0% – 14.0% = 13.0%). Moreover, most of the regions are projected to deviate considerably from the national average of 19.95%. How large are these deviations on the average? We want a measure that will give us information about the overall variations among all regions in the United States and, unlike the range or the IQR, will not be based on only two scores.

Such a measure will reflect how much, on the average, each score in the distribution deviates from some central point, such as the mean. We use the mean as the reference point rather than other kinds of averages (the mode or the median) because the mean is based on all the scores in the distribution. Therefore, it is more useful as a basis from which to calculate average deviation. The sensitivity of the mean to extreme values carries over the calculation of the average deviation, which is based on the mean. Another reason for using the mean as a reference point is that more advanced measures of variation require the use of algebraic properties that can be assumed only by using the arithmetic mean.

The variance and the standard deviation are two closely related measures of variation that increase or decrease based on how closely the scores cluster around the mean. The **variance** is the average of the squared deviations from the center (mean) of the distribution, and the **standard deviation** is the square root of the variance. Both measure variability in interval-ratio and ordinal variables.

Variance A measure of variation for interval-ratio and ordinal variables; it is the average of the squared deviations from the mean.

Standard deviation A measure of variation for interval-ratio and ordinal variables; it is equal to the square root of the variance.

Calculating the Deviation From the Mean

Consider again the distribution of the percentage change in the elderly population for the four regions of the United States. Because we want to calculate the average difference of all the regions from the national average (the mean), it makes sense to first look at the difference between each region and the mean. This difference, called a deviation from the mean, is symbolized as $(Y-\bar{Y})$. The sum of these deviations can be symbolized as $\sum(Y-\bar{Y})$.

The calculations of these deviations for each region are displayed in Table 4.7 and Figure 4.6. We have also summed these deviations. Note that each region has either a positive or a negative deviation score. The deviation is positive when the percentage change in the elderly home population is above the mean. It is negative when the percentage change is below the mean. Thus, for example, the Northeast's deviation score of –3.95 means that its percentage change in the elderly population was 3.95 percentage points below the mean.

You may wonder if we could calculate the average of these deviations by simply adding up the deviations and dividing them. Unfortunately we cannot, because the sum of the deviations of scores from the mean is always zero, or algebraically $\sum(Y - \bar{Y})$. In other words, if we were to subtract the mean from each score and then add up all the deviations as we did in Table 4.7, the sum would be zero, which in turn would cause the average deviation (i.e., average difference) to compute to zero. This is always true because the mean is the center of gravity of the distribution.

Figure 4.6 Illustrating Deviations From the Mean

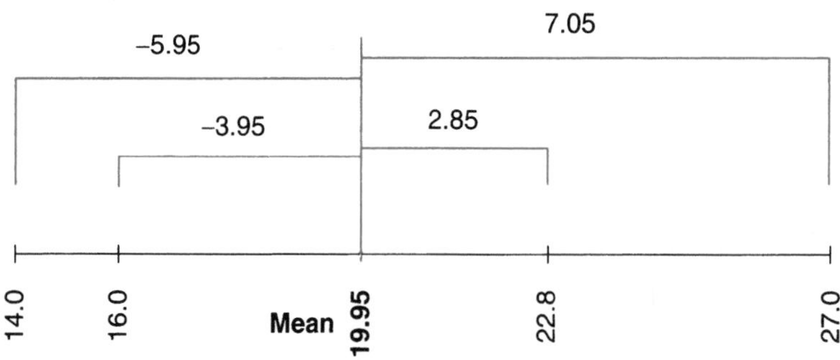

–5.95 + –3.95 + 2.85 + 7.05 = 0

Table 4.7 Projected Percentage Change in the Elderly Population, 2008–2015, by Region and Deviation From the Mean

Region	Percentage	$(Y - \bar{Y})$
Northeast	16.0	16.0 – 19.95 = –3.95
South	22.8	22.8 – 19.95 = 2.85
Midwest	14.0	14.0 – 19.95 = –5.95
West	27.0	27.0 – 19.95 = 7.05
	$\Sigma(Y) = 79.8$	$\Sigma(Y - \bar{Y}) = 0$
	$\bar{Y} = \frac{\Sigma Y}{N} = \frac{79.8}{4} = 19.95$	

Mathematically, we can overcome this problem either by ignoring the plus and minus signs, using instead the absolute values of the deviations, or by squaring the deviations—that is, multiplying each deviation by itself to get rid of the negative sign. Since absolute values are difficult to work with mathematically, the latter method is used to compensate for the problem.

Table 4.8 presents the same information as Table 4.7, but here we have squared the actual deviations from the mean and added together the squares. The sum of the squared deviations is symbolized as $\sum(Y-\bar{Y})^2$. Note that by squaring the deviations, we end up with a sum representing the deviation from the mean, which is positive. (Note that this sum will equal zero if all the cases have the same value as the mean.) In our example, this sum is $\sum(Y-\bar{Y})^2 = 108.82$.

LEARNING CHECK 4.5

Examine Table 4.8 again and note the disproportionate contribution of the western region to the sum of the squared deviations from the mean (it actually accounts for about 45% of the sum of squares). Can you explain why? (Hint: It has something to do with the sensitivity of the mean to extreme values.)

Calculating the Variance and the Standard Deviation

The average of the squared deviations from the mean is known as the variance. The variance is symbolized as s^2. Remember that we are interested in the average of the squared deviations from the mean. Therefore, we need to divide the sum of the squared deviations by the number of scores (N) in the distribution. However, unlike the calculation of the mean, we will use $N - 1$ rather than N in the denominator.[12] The formula for the variance can be stated as

$$s^2 = \frac{\sum(Y-\bar{Y})^2}{N-1} \tag{4.2}$$

Table 4.8 Projected Percentage Change in the Elderly Population, 2008–2015, by Region, Deviation From the Mean, and Deviation From the Mean Squared

Region	Percentage	$(Y-\bar{Y})$	$(Y-\bar{Y})^2$
Northeast	16.0	$16.0 - 19.95 = -3.95$	15.60
South	22.8	$22.8 - 19.95 = 2.85$	8.12
Midwest	14.0	$14.0 - 19.95 = -5.95$	35.40
West	27.0	$27.0 - 19.95 = 7.05$	49.70
	$\Sigma(Y) = 79.8$	$\Sigma(Y-\bar{Y}) = 0$	$\Sigma(Y-\bar{Y})^2 = 108.82$

$$\text{Mean} = \bar{Y} = \frac{\Sigma Y}{N} = \frac{79.8}{4} = 19.95$$

where

s^2 = the variance

$(Y - \bar{Y})$ = the deviation from the mean

$\Sigma(Y - \bar{Y})^2$ = the sum of the squared deviations from the mean

N = the number of scores

Note that the formula incorporates all the symbols we defined earlier. This formula means that the variance is equal to the average of the squared deviations from the mean.

Follow these steps to calculate the variance:

1. Calculate the mean, $\bar{Y} = \Sigma(Y) / N$.
2. Subtract the mean from each score to find the deviation, $Y - \bar{Y}$.
3. Square each deviation, $(Y - \bar{Y})^2$.
4. Sum the squared deviations, $\Sigma(Y - \bar{Y})^2$.
5. Divide the sum by $N - 1$, $\Sigma(Y - \bar{Y})^2 / (N - 1)$.
6. The answer is the variance.

To assure yourself that you understand how to calculate the variance, go back to Table 4.8 and follow this step-by-step procedure for calculating the variance. Now plug the required quantities into Formula 4.2. Your result should look like this:

$$s^2 = \frac{\Sigma(Y - \bar{Y})^2}{N - 1} = \frac{108.82}{3} = 36.27$$

One problem with the variance is that it is based on squared deviations and therefore is no longer expressed in the original units of measurement. For instance, it is difficult to interpret the variance of 36.27, which represents the distribution of the percentage change in the elderly population, because this figure is expressed in squared percentages. Thus, we often take the square root of the variance and interpret it instead. This gives us the standard deviation, symbolized as s, is the square root of the variance, or

$$s = \sqrt{s^2}$$

The standard deviation for our example is

$$s = \sqrt{36.27} = 6.02$$

The formula for the standard deviation uses the same symbols as the formula for the variance:

$$s = \sqrt{\frac{\Sigma(Y - \bar{Y})^2}{N - 1}} \qquad (4.3)$$

As we interpret the formula, we can say that the standard deviation is equal to the square root of the average of the squared deviations from the mean.

The advantage of the standard deviation is that unlike the variance, it is measured in the same units as the original data. For instance, the standard deviation for our example is 6.02. Because the original data were expressed in percentages, this number is expressed as a percentage as well. In other words, you could say, the standard deviation is 6.02%. But what does this mean? The actual number tells us very little by itself, but it allows us to evaluate the dispersion of the scores around the mean. We will explore this further in Chapter 5 ("The Normal Distribution").

In a distribution where all the scores are identical, the standard deviation is zero (0). Zero is the lowest possible value for the standard deviation; in an identical distribution, all the points would be the same, with the same mean, mode, and median. There is no variation or dispersion in the scores.

The more the standard deviation departs from zero, the more variation there is in the distribution. There is no upper limit to the value of the standard deviation. In our example, we can conclude that a standard deviation of 6.02% means that the projected percentage change in the elderly population for the four regions of the United States is widely dispersed around the mean of 19.95%.

The standard deviation can be considered a standard against which we can evaluate the positioning of scores relative to the mean and to other scores in the distribution. As we will see in more detail in Chapter 5, in most distributions, unless they are highly skewed, about 34% of all scores fall between the mean and 1 standard deviation above the mean. Another 34% of scores fall between the mean and 1 standard deviation below it. Thus, we would expect the majority of scores (68%) to fall within 1 standard deviation of the mean.

LEARNING CHECK 4.6

Take time to understand the section on standard deviation and variance. You will see these statistics in more advanced procedures. Although your instructor may require you to memorize the formulas, it is more important for you to understand how to interpret standard deviation and variance and when they can be appropriately used. Many hand calculators and all statistical software programs will calculate these measures of diversity for you, but they won't tell you what they mean. Once you understand the meaning behind these measures, the formulas will be easier to remember.

CONSIDERATIONS FOR CHOOSING A MEASURE OF VARIATION

So far, we have considered five measures of variation: (1) the IQV, (2) the range, (3) the IQR, (4) the variance, and (5) the standard deviation. Each measure can represent the degree of variability in a distribution. But which one should we use? There is no simple answer to this question. However, in general, we tend to use only one measure of variation, and the choice of the appropriate one involves a number of considerations. These considerations and how they affect our choice of the appropriate measure are presented in the form of a decision tree in Figure 4.8.

As in choosing a measure of central tendency, one of the most basic considerations in choosing a measure of variability is the variable's level of measurement. Valid use of any of the measures requires that the data are measured at the level appropriate for that measure or higher, as shown in Figure 4.8.

A CLOSER LOOK 4.1

MORE ON INTERPRETING THE STANDARD DEVIATION

The standard deviation can be used to describe the distribution of a specific variable. For example, in Table 4.9 we present descriptive statistics for the gross domestic product (GDP) per capita (measured in current U.S. dollars in millions) for a sample of 70 countries.

In the first column, we see the name of the variable *Gross Domestic Product per capita*. The next three columns tell us that there were 70 countries in our sample and that the minimum GDP per capita was $400 and the maximum was $80,700. This is quite a gap between the poorest and richest countries in our sample. The mean and standard deviation are listed in the final two columns.

The mean GDP per capita is $19,247.14, with a standard deviation of $17,628.28. We can expect about 68% of these countries to have GDP per capita values within a range of $1,618.86 ($19,247.14 – $17,628.28) to $36,875.42 ($19,247.14 + $17,628.28). Hence, based on the mean and the standard deviation, we have a pretty good indication of what would be considered a typical GDP per capita value for the majority of countries in our sample. For example, we would consider a country with a GDP per capita value of $80,700 to be extremely wealthy in comparison with other countries. More than two thirds of all countries in our sample fall closer to the mean ($19,247.14) than the country with a GDP per capita value of $80,700.

Table 4.9 Descriptive Statistics for GDP

	N	Minimum (Million $)	Maximum (Million $)	Mean	Std. Deviation
Gross Domestic Product per capita	70	400	80,700	19,247.14	17,628.277
Valid *N* (listwise)	70				

Another way to interpret the standard deviation is to compare it with another distribution. For instance, Table 4.10 displays the means and standard deviations of employee age for two samples drawn from a *Fortune 100* corporation. Samples are divided into female clerical and female technical. Note that the mean ages for both samples are about the same—approximately 39 years of age. However, the standard deviations suggest that the distribution of age is dissimilar between the two groups. Figure 4.7 loosely illustrates this dissimilarity in the two distributions.

The relatively low standard deviation for female technical indicates that this group is relatively homogenous in age. That is to say, most of the women's ages, while not identical, are fairly similar. The average deviation from the mean age of 39.87 is 3.75 years. In contrast, the standard deviation for female clerical employees is about twice the standard deviation for female technical. This suggests a wider dispersion or greater heterogeneity in the ages of clerical workers. We can say that the average deviation from the mean age of 39.46 is 7.80 years for clerical workers. The larger standard deviation indicates a wider dispersion of points below or above the mean. On average, clerical employees are farther in age from their mean of 39.46.[13]

Table 4.10 Age Characteristics of Female Clerical and Technical Employees

Characteristics	Female Clerical N = 22	Female Technical N = 39
Mean age	39.46	39.87
Standard deviation	7.80	3.75

Source: Adapted from Marjorie Armstrong-Srassen, "The Effect of Gender and Organizational Level on How Survivors Appraise and Cope with Organizational Downsizing," *Journal of Applied Behavioral Science*, 34, no. 2 (June 1998): 125–142. Reprinted with permission.

Figure 4.7 Illustrating the Means and Standard Deviations for Age Characteristics

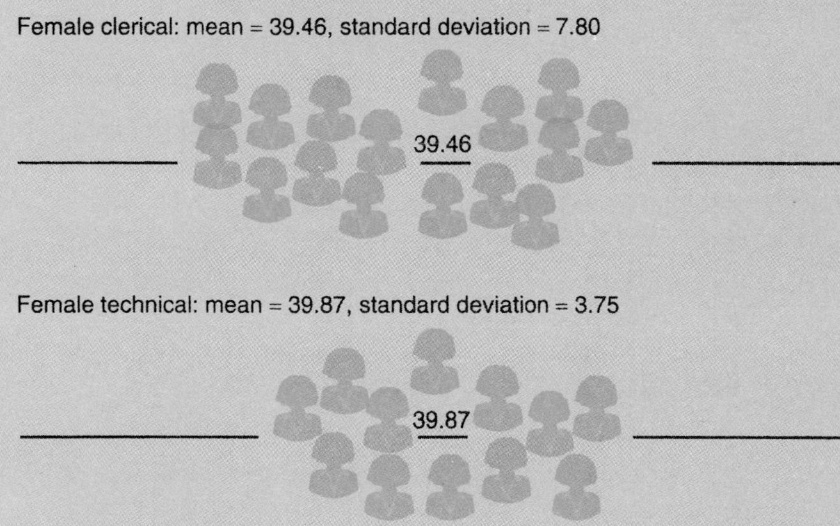

Nominal level: With nominal variables, your choice is restricted to the IQV as a measure of variability.

Ordinal level: The choice of measure of variation for ordinal variables is more problematic. The IQV can be used to reflect variability in the distributions of ordinal variables, but because IQV is sensitive to the rank-ordering of values implied in ordinal variables, it loses some information. Another possibility is to use the IQR, interpreting the IQR as the range of rank-ordered values that includes the middle 50% of the observations.[14] For example, if the IQR for income categories begins with the category \$50,000 to \$70,500 and ends with the category \$100,000 to \$120,500, the IQR can be reported as between \$50,000 and \$120,500. However, in most instances, social science researchers treat ordinal variables as interval-ratio measures, preferring to calculate variance and standard deviation.

Interval-ratio level: For interval-ratio variables, you can choose the variance, standard deviation, the range, or the IQR. Because the range, and to a lesser extent the IQR, is based on only two scores in the distribution (and therefore tends to be sensitive if either of the two points is extreme), the variance and/or standard deviation is usually preferred. However, if a distribution is extremely skewed so that the mean is no longer representative of the central tendency in the distribution, the range and the IQR can be used. The range and the IQR will also be useful when you are reading tables or quickly scanning data to get a rough idea of the extent of dispersion in the distribution.

Figure 4.8 How to Choose a Measure of Variation

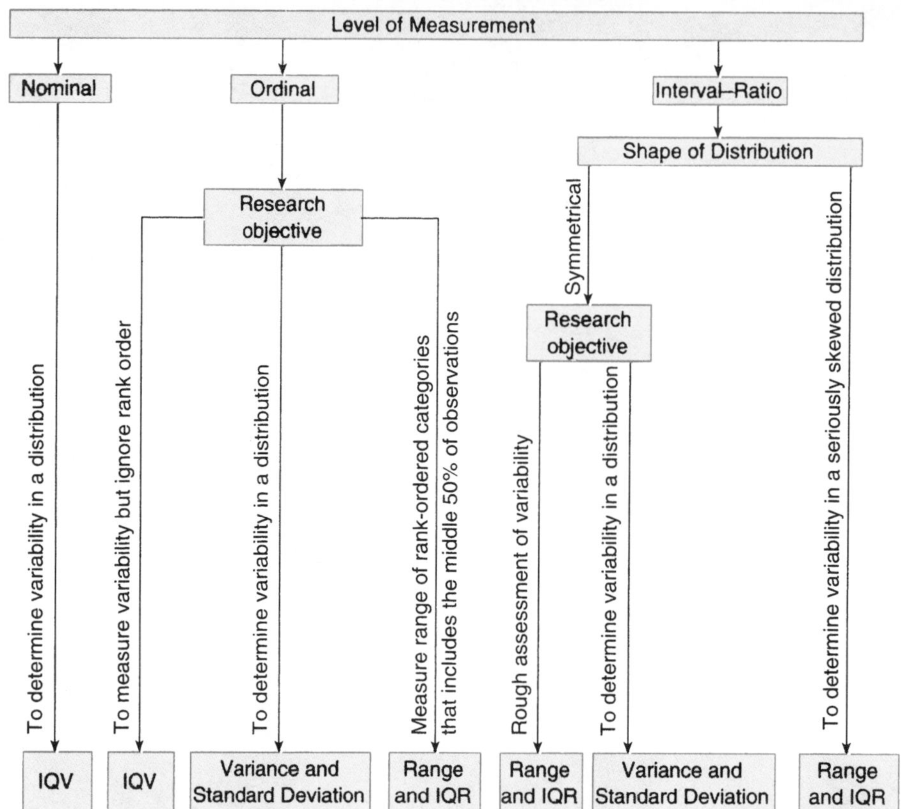

READING THE RESEARCH LITERATURE: COMMUNITY COLLEGE MENTORING

In this Reading the Research Literature, Myron Pope (2002) explores the importance of mentoring for 250 students of color enrolled in 25 different community colleges across the country. Pope argues that students of color respond best to multiple levels of mentoring—formal and informal methods of mentoring and mentoring from different sources (faculty, staff, and other students). Pope's analysis is based on a survey measuring student perceptions about campus climate, institutional diversity, mentoring, and administrative support of diversity. For this 2002 research, Pope focused specifically on statements regarding mentoring, measuring student agreement on an ordinal 5-point scale: 1 = *no agreement* to 5 = *strong agreement*.[15] Note how mean scores and standard deviations for selected statements are reported in Table 4.11.

In Table 4.11, we present statements that measure mentoring from three different sources: (1) staff, (2) peers, and (3) students themselves. The mean agreement scores and standard deviations vary by each group, that is to say, perceptions about mentoring differ by racial or ethnic identity. The standard deviations indicate the variability of responses: A smaller standard deviation reveals more consistency of responses clustered around the mean score, whereas a larger standard deviation indicates more variation, more spread from the mean. For example, for the statement, "There are persons of color in administrative roles from whom

Table 4.11 Minority Student Perception of Mentoring at Their Institution by Race (N = 254)

	African American N = 178 M (SD)	Asian N = 12 M (SD)	Hispanic N = 28 M (SD)	Native American N = 22 M (SD)	Multiethnic N = 14 M (SD)
There are persons of color in administrative roles from whom I would seek mentoring at this institution.	3.76 (1.10)	3.50 (1.31)	3.14 (1.08)	4.09 (0.68)	4.14 (0.66)
There are peer mentors who can advise me.	3.48 (1.11)	2.17 (1.40)	3.14 (1.20)	3.91 (0.68)	3.29 (1.54)
I mentor other students.	3.30 (1.25)	2.00 (1.21)	3.00 (1.09)	3.46 (1.10)	3.29 (1.07)

Source: Adapted from Myron Pope, "Community College Mentoring Minority Student Perception," *Community College Review,* 30, no. 3 (2002): 37.

Note: N = total, SD = standard deviation, M = mean.

I would seek mentoring at this institution," the larger average scores for Native American and multiethnic students also correspond to smaller standard deviations. Native American and multiethnic students were more likely to agree with the statement, and there was more consistency (less variation) in their responses. For the statement, "There are peer mentors who can advise me," Native American students had the highest mean score (3.91) with the smallest standard deviation (0.68) indicating less variation of responses. Finally, for the statement, "I mentor other students," there is a lower level of agreement among all the student groups. The highest mean is 3.46 (based on a 5-point scale) for the Native American student group; the lowest mean is 2.0 for the Asian student group. The standard deviations are all above 1.0, with the most variation in responses for the group of African American students.

Pope (2002) advocates the value of multilevel mentoring

> By way of multilevel mentoring, minority students are exposed to a variety of individuals who are committed to ensuring that they adjust to life as a college student. These individuals will be able to assist these students in overcoming some of the precollege characteristics, such as their academic preparation and first-generation college student status, along with dealing with some of the conflicts that arise as a result of their enrollment in college, such as balancing their responsibilities. . . . Mentoring programs also cannot be one dimensional, in that the mentor must provide guidance to the student in academic, personal and professional areas. The setting must incorporate an opportunity for these mentors to learn about students from various ethnic backgrounds. (pp. 42–43)[16]

Pope suggests that to improve these mentoring opportunities, community college administrators "must begin more aggressively to recruit future faculty and administrators with these ethnic backgrounds" (p. 43).[17]

We will revisit this research example in Chapter 11 ("Analysis of Variance").

DATA AT WORK

Sruthi Chandrasekaran: Senior Research Associate

Photo courtesy of Sruthi Chandrasekaran

Trained in economics and public policy, Sruthi is currently employed in a development economics–based research organization that specializes in using randomized controlled trials for impact evaluation. She emphasizes the importance of quality data as she describes her work. "As a field-based researcher, I take the lead in ensuring that the intervention follows the study design to the dot, the data collection tools elicit quality responses in an unbiased manner, the survey data is of the highest quality, the cleaning of the data is coherent and methodical and the analysis is rigorous. The results of the study are published in leading academic journals and the policy lessons are disseminated to stakeholders and hence it is crucial that the research is well designed and the quality of the data is impeccable."

Her research has broad implications on community stakeholders and policies. "On field visits as part of the study, there is so much that I learn that furthers my understanding, helping to piece together the results from the data analysis. Meeting communities and listening to their perspectives is intellectually stimulating and emotionally fulfilling. Engaging with powerful stakeholders in the decision-making process, such as donor organizations, non-profits and government officials and sharing my learnings from the field and from the data is very rewarding professionally and helps me feel like I'm doing my bit to impact policy design and implementation towards an efficient and equitable solution."

For students interested in a research career, Sruthi recommends developing the ability to focus on details and the flexibility to examine the big picture of a project. She explains, "Research can at times be painstakingly slow and frustrating, so patience and single-minded focus on the end goal can help one through the tough times. Being aware of competing methodologies and research studies in relevant fields can also prove to be quite useful in understanding the advantages and pitfalls in your own research. If you are inspired to take up research, make sure you choose a field close to your heart since this will be personally and professionally rewarding. If you are unsure, take up an internship or a short-term project to see how much you may enjoy it."

MAIN POINTS

- Measures of variability are numbers that describe how much variation or diversity there is in a distribution.
- The index of qualitative variation is used to measure variation in nominal variables. It is based on the ratio of the total number of differences in the distribution to the maximum number of possible differences within the same distribution. The index of qualitative variation can vary from 0.00 to 1.00.
- The range measures variation in interval-ratio and ordinal variables and is the difference between the highest (maximum)

and the lowest (minimum) scores in the distribution. To find the range, subtract the lowest from the highest score in a distribution. For an ordinal variable, report the lowest and the highest values without subtracting.

- The interquartile range measures the width of the middle 50% of the distribution for interval-ratio and ordinal variables. It is defined as the difference between the lower and upper quartiles (Q_1 and Q_3). In some instances, reporting the full range (the values of Q_1 and Q_3) may provide more information than the single interquartile range value.
- The box plot is a graphical device that visually presents the range, the interquartile range, the median, the lowest (minimum) score, and the highest (maximum) score. The box plot provides us with a way to visually examine the center, the variation, and the shape of a distribution.
- The variance and the standard deviation are two closely related measures of variation for interval-ratio and ordinal variables that increase or decrease based on how closely the scores cluster around the mean. The variance is the average of the squared deviations from the center (mean) of the distribution; the standard deviation is the square root of the variance.

KEY TERMS

DIGITAL RESOURCES

Get the edge on your studies. **edge.sagepub.com/frankfort8e**

Take a quiz to find out what you've learned.
Review key terms with eFlashcards.
Dive into real research with SAGE Journal Articles.

SPSS DEMONSTRATIONS [GSS14SSDS-B]

Demonstration 1: Producing Measures of Variability With Frequencies

Except for the IQV, the SPSS Frequencies procedure can produce all the measures of variability we've reviewed in this chapter. (SPSS can be programmed to calculate the IQV, but the programming procedures are beyond the scope of our book.)

We'll begin with Frequencies and calculate various statistics for AGE. If we click on *Analyze, Descriptive Statistics, Frequencies*, then on the *Statistics* button, we can select the appropriate measures of variability.

The measures of variability available are listed in the Dispersion box at the bottom of the dialog box. We've selected the standard deviation, variance, and range, plus the mean and median (in the

Central Tendency box) for reference. In the Percentile Values box, we've selected Quartiles to tell SPSS to calculate the values for the 25th, 50th, and 75th percentiles. SPSS also allows us to specify exact percentiles in this section (such as the 34th percentile) by typing a number in the box after "Percentile(s)" and then clicking on the *Add* button.

Earlier, we had seen the frequency table for the variable AGE, so after clicking on *Continue*, we click on *Format* to turn off the display table. This is done by clicking on the button for "Suppress tables with many categories" (see Figure 4.9). There are other formatting options here that you may explore later when using SPSS.

Click on *Continue*, then *OK* to run the procedure. SPSS produces the mean and the other statistics we requested (Figure 4.10). The range of age is 71 years (from 18 to 89). The standard deviation is 17.073, which indicates that there is a moderate amount of dispersion in the ages. The variance, 291.495, is the square of the standard deviation (17.073).

The value of the 25th percentile is 36, the value of the 50th percentile (which is also the median) is 50, and the value of the 75th percentile is 62. Although Frequencies does not calculate the IQR, it can easily be calculated by subtracting the value of the 25th percentile from the 75th percentile, which yields a value of 26 years. Compare this value with the standard deviation.

Figure 4.9 Format Dialog Box

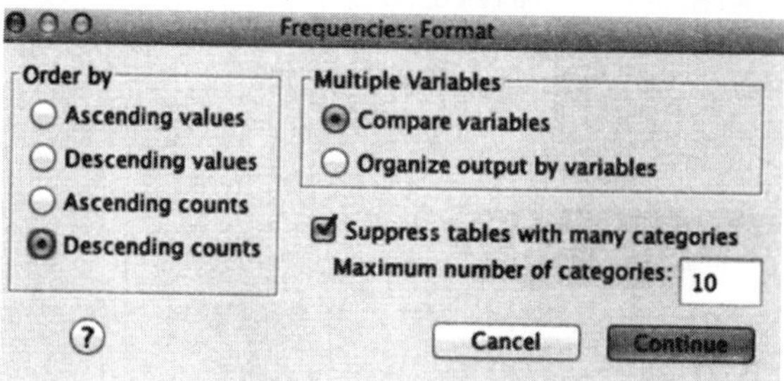

Figure 4.10 Descriptive Statistics for AGE

Statistics

age AGE OF RESPONDENT

N	Valid	1490
	Missing	10
Mean		50.12
Std. Deviation		17.073
Variance		291.495
Range		71
Percentiles	25	36.00
	50	50.00
	75	62.00

Demonstration 2: Producing Variability Measures and Box Plots With Explore

Another SPSS procedure that can produce the usual measures of variability is Explore, which also produces box plots. The Explore procedure is located in the *Descriptive Statistics* section of the *Analyze* menu. In its main dialog box (Figure 4.11), the variables for which you want statistics are placed in the Dependent List box. You have the option of putting one or more nominal variables in the Factor List box; Explore will display separate statistics for each category of the nominal variable(s) you've selected.

Place the variable HRS1 (number of hours worked last week) in the Dependent box and SEX in the Factor box to provide separate output for males and females. Click *OK*. By default, Explore will produce statistics and plots, so we don't need to make any other choices. Although our request will not produce percentiles or create a histogram, Explore has options to do both plus several other tasks.

Selected output for males is shown in Figure 4.12. Though not replicated here, you'll notice that the first table is the Case Processing Summary Table. It indicates that 456 males answered this question. The valid sample of females is also reported, 439. Based on the second table, Descriptives, we know that for males, the mean number of hours worked last week is 43.92; the median is 40.00. The standard deviation is 15.528, the range is 88, and the IQR is 10, which is quite narrow compared with the range. (A stem-and-leaf plot—another way to visually present and review data—is also displayed by default. However, we will not cover stem-and-leaf plots in this textbook. The option for the stem-and-leaf plot can be changed so that it will not be displayed.)

Although not displayed here, the mean number of hours worked last week for females is 38.92; the median is 40. The standard deviation is 14.085, the IQR is 13, and the range, 88—values somewhat smaller than those for males with the exception of the range and the IQR. The variation in the number of hours worked last week is also slightly smaller for females than those for males.

Explore displays separate box plots for males and females in the same window for easy comparison. Although the SPSS box plot has some differences from those discussed in this chapter, some things are the same. The solid dark line is the value of the median. The width of the shaded box (in color on the screen) is the IQR (10 for males, 13 for females).

Note that SPSS only extends whiskers from the box edges to 1½ times the box width (the IQR). If there are additional values beyond 1½ times the IQR, SPSS displays the individual cases. Those that are somewhat extreme (1½ to 3 box widths from the edge of the box) are marked with an open circle; those considered very extreme (more than 3 box widths from the box edge) are marked with an asterisk.

Figure 4.11 Explore Dialog Box

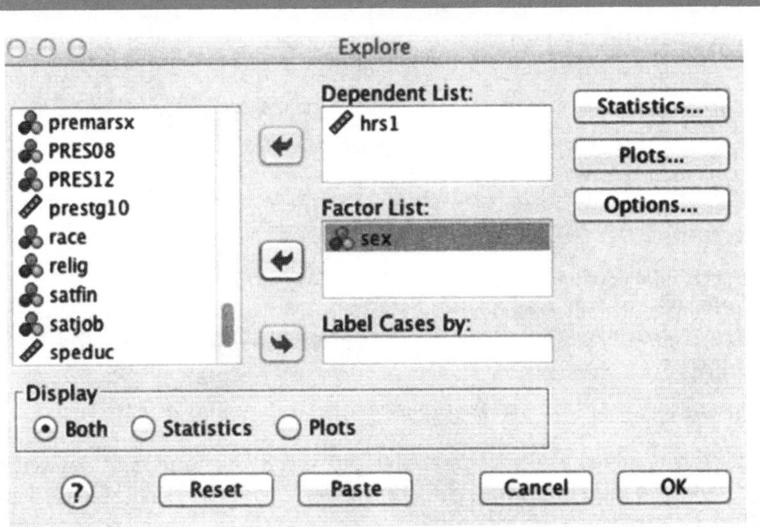

Figure 4.12 Descriptive Statistics for HRS1, Men Only

Descriptives

	sex RESPONDENTS SEX			Statistic	Std. Error
hrs1 NUMBER OF HOURS WORKED LAST WEEK	1 MALE	Mean		43.92	.727
		95% Confidence Interval for Mean	Lower Bound	42.49	
			Upper Bound	45.35	
		5% Trimmed Mean		43.75	
		Median		40.00	
		Variance		241.108	
		Std. Deviation		15.528	
		Minimum		1	
		Maximum		89	
		Range		88	
		Interquartile Range		10	
		Skewness		.234	.114
		Kurtosis		.876	.228

Visually, the box plot shows us that variability in hours worked last week is smaller for females than for males. Note that the box is slightly larger for females than for males. The IQR for males runs from 40 to 50 hours, while the IQR for females runs from 32 to 45 hours. Both genders have outlying cases beyond the edge of the whiskers.

SPSS PROBLEMS [GSS14SSDS-B]

1. Use the Frequencies procedure to investigate the variability of the respondent's current age (AGE). Click on *Analyze, Descriptive Statistics, Frequencies*, and then *Statistics*. Select the appropriate measures of variability. How would you describe the distribution of AGE?
2. Using the Explore procedure, separate the statistics for EDUC (education) and PRESTG10 (occupational prestige score) for men and women, selecting SEX as a factor variable in the Explore window. Click on *Analyze, Descriptive Statistics, Explore*, and then insert EDUC and PRESTG10 into the Dependent List and SEX in the Factor List. What differences exist in the educational attainment and occupational prestige of men and women? Assess the differences between men and women based on measures of central tendency and variability.
3. Repeat the procedure in Exercise 2, investigating the dispersion in NRINCOME06 (recoded income). Select your own factor (nominal) variable to make the comparison (such as CLASS, RACE, or some other factor). Click on *Analyze, Descriptive Statistics, Explore*, and insert NRINCOME06 into the Dependent List and your factor variable of choice in the Factor List. In a paragraph or two, use appropriate measures of variability to summarize the results.
4. Examine the number of hours that blacks and whites work each week. The variable HRS1 measures the number of hours a respondent worked the week before the interview. Use the Explore procedure to study the variability of hours worked, comparing blacks and whites (RACE) in the GSS sample.
   a. Is there a difference between the two groups in the variability of work hours?
   b. Write a short paragraph describing the box plot that SPSS created as if you were writing a report and had included the box plot as a chart to support your conclusions about the difference between blacks and whites in the variability (and central tendency) of hours worked.

CHAPTER EXERCISES

1. Americans often think of themselves as quite diverse in their political opinions, within the continuum of liberal to conservative. Let's use GSS 2014 data to investigate the diversity of political views. The percentage distribution shown displays respondents' self-rating of their political position. (The statistics box is not displayed; cases with no response were removed for this example.)

Political Views	f	Percentage (%)
Extremely liberal	41	3.6
Liberal	144	12.7
Slightly liberal	126	11.1
Moderate	447	39.5
Slightly conservative	163	14.4
Conservative	169	14.9
Extremely conservative	43	3.8
Total	1,133	100.0

   a. How many categories (K) are we working with?

   b. Calculate the sum of the squared percentages, or ΣPct^2.

   c. What is the IQV for this variable? Do you find it to be higher (closer to 1) or lower (closer to 0) than you might have expected for political views? Or to put it another way, did you expect that Americans would be diverse in their political views or more narrowly concentrated in certain categories?

2. Using the information listed below, explore the educational attainment of GSS 2014 respondents.

   a. Calculate the IQR for both groups. What do the IQRs reveal about the degree diversity for males and females?

   b. What is the limitation to applying IQR to ordinal data?

Highest Educational Degree	Male Frequency/%	Female Frequency/%
Less than high school	56 10.7%	84 12.8%
High school graduate	267 50.9%	316 48.3%
Junior college	28 5.3%	61 9.3%
Bachelor's degree	106 20.2%	120 18.3%
Graduate degree	68 13.0%	73 11.2%
Total	525 100%	654 100%

3. Public corruption continues to be a concern. Let's examine data from the U.S. Department of Justice to explore the variability in public corruption in the years 1990 and 2009. All the numbers below are of those convicted of public corruption.

Number of Public Corruption Convictions by Year

1990		2009	
Govt. Level	No. of Convictions	Govt. Level	No. of Convictions
Federal	583	Federal	426
State	79	State	102
Local	225	Local	257

Source: U.S. Census Bureau, *Statistical Abstract of the United States: 2012*, Table 338.

a. What is the range of convictions in 1990? In 2009? Which is greater?

b. What is the mean number of convictions in 1990 and 2009?

c. Calculate the standard deviation for 1990 and 2009.

d. Which year appears to have more variability in number of convictions as measured by the standard deviation? Are the results consistent with what you found using the range?

4. Your task is to construct a report regarding criminal offenses investigated by U.S. attorneys by offense and year using the following data from the U.S. Department of Justice. Identify the appropriate measures of central tendency and measures of variability that should be applied to these data.

Type of Offense	2009 No. of Suspects	2012 No. of Suspects
Violent	5,463	3,528
Property	26,161	14,491
Drug	37,721	25,929
Public order	23,067	8,712
Weapon	11,749	7,672
Immigration	88,313	85,458

Source: U.S. Department of Justice, *Federal Justice Statistics 2009*, Table 4; *Federal Justice Statistics 2012*, Table 4.

5. The output below depicts data for projected elderly population change in Midwestern and Western states between 2008 and 2015 from Table 4.4.

Descriptives

	Region		Statistic
Population_Change	Midwest	Mean	13.600
		Std. Deviation	2.7831
		Minimum	9.4
		Maximum	19.2
		Range	9.8
		Interquartile Range	3.7
	West	Mean	28.277
		Std. Deviation	10.6948
		Minimum	13.8
		Maximum	50.0
		Range	36.2
		Interquartile Range	17.3

a. Compare the range for the Western states with that of the Midwest. Which region had a greater range?

b. Examine the IQR for each region. Which is greater?

c. Use the statistics to characterize the variability in population increase of the elderly in the two regions. Does one region have more variability than another? If yes, why do you think that is?

6. Occupational prestige is a statistic developed by sociologists to measure the status of one's occupation. Occupational prestige is also a component of what sociologists call socioeconomic status, a composite measure of one's status in society. On average, people with more education tend to have higher occupational prestige than people with less education. We investigate this using the GSS 2014 variable PRESTG80 and the Explore procedure to generate the SPSS output.

Descriptive Statistics for Occupational Prestige Score by Highest Degree Earned

Descriptives

	degree RS HIGHEST DEGREE			Statistic	Std. Error
prestg10 Rs occupational prestige score (2010)	1 HIGH SCHOOL	Mean		38.82	.473
		95% Confidence Interval for Mean	Lower Bound	37.89	
			Upper Bound	39.75	
		5% Trimmed Mean		38.38	
		Median		38.00	
		Variance		126.725	
		Std. Deviation		11.257	
		Minimum		16	
		Maximum		75	
		Range		59	
		Interquartile Range		16	
		Skewness		.517	.103
		Kurtosis		.116	.205

Descriptives

	degree RS HIGHEST DEGREE			Statistic	Std. Error
prestg10 Rs occupational prestige score (2010)	3 BACHELOR	Mean		50.02	.879
		95% Confidence Interval for Mean	Lower Bound	48.29	
			Upper Bound	51.75	
		5% Trimmed Mean		50.33	
		Median		50.00	
		Variance		172.360	
		Std. Deviation		13.129	
		Minimum		16	
		Maximum		75	
		Range		59	
		Interquartile Range		21	
		Skewness		-.393	.163
		Kurtosis		-.490	.324

a. Note that SPSS supplies the IQR, the median, and the minimum and maximum values of each group. Looking at the values of the mean and median, do you think the distribution of prestige is skewed for respondents with a high school diploma? For respondents with a bachelor's degree? Why or why not?

b. Explain why you think there is more variability of prestige for either group, or why the variability of prestige is similar for the two groups.

7. The U.S. Census Bureau collects information about divorce rates. The following table summarizes the divorce rate for 10 U.S. states in 2007. Use the table to answer the questions that follow.

State	Divorce Rate per 1,000 Population
Alaska	4.3
Florida	4.7
Idaho	4.9
Maine	4.5
Maryland	3.1
Nevada	6.5
New Jersey	3.0
Texas	3.3
Vermont	3.8
Wisconsin	2.9

Source: U.S. Census Bureau, *Statistical Abstract of the United States: 2010*, Table 126.

a. Calculate and interpret the range and the IQR. Which is a better measure of variability? Why?

b. Calculate and interpret the mean and standard deviation.

c. Identify two possible explanations for the variation in divorce rates across the 10 states.

8. Individuals with higher levels of education tend to delay parenting, having children at an older age in comparison with individuals with lower levels of education. We examine this relationship based on GSS 2014 data. In the following table, the mean, standard deviation,

and variance for respondent's age when first child was born (AGEKDBRN) is reported for five categories (DEGREE).

a. Identify the level of measurement for DEGREE and AGEKDBRN.

b. Describe the relationship between respondent degree and age when first child was born.

	Less Than High School	High School	Some College	Bachelor's Degree	Graduate Degree
Mean	20.72	23.34	23.46	27.98	28.99
Standard deviation	4.745	5.542	5.575	6.185	6.205
Variance	22.512	30.709	31.082	38.259	38.496

9. You are interested in studying the variability of crimes committed (including violent and property crimes) and police expenditures in the eastern and Midwestern United States. The U.S. Census Bureau collected the following statistics on these two variables for 21 states in the East and Midwest in 2008.

State	Number of Crimes per 100,000 Population	Police Protection Expenditures (in Millions of Dollars)
Maine	2,583	233
New Hampshire	2,384	317
Vermont	2,761	141
Massachusetts	2,860	1,843
Rhode Island	3,098	317
Connecticut	2,798	996
New York	2,407	8,164
New Jersey	2,618	3,087
Pennsylvania	2,842	2,840
Ohio	3,982	3,157
Indiana	3,947	1,223
Illinois[a]	3,498	4,242
Michigan	3,492	2,425
Wisconsin	3,047	1,552
Minnesota[b]	2,893	1,527
Iowa	2,820	614
Missouri	4,188	1,632
North Dakota	2,343	120
South Dakota	2,181	141
Nebraska	3,275	528
Kansas	3,800	684

Source: U.S. Census Bureau, *Statistical Abstract of the United States: 2012*, Tables 308 and 443.

Notes: 

a. Limited data for Illinois during 2008 were available.

b. Limited data for Minnesota during 2008 were available.

The SPSS output showing the mean and the standard deviation for both variables is presented below.

Descriptive Statistics

	N	Minimum	Maximum	Mean	Std. Deviation
Number of Crimes per 100,000 Population	21	2181	4188	3038.90	583.004
Police Protection Expenditures (in millions of dollars)	21	120	8164	1703.95	1895.214
Valid N (listwise)	21				

a. What are the means? The standard deviations?

b. Compare the mean with the standard deviation for each variable. Does there appear to be more variability in the number of crimes or in police expenditures per capita in these states? Which states contribute more to this greater variability?

c. Suggest why one variable has more variability than the other. In other words, what social forces would cause one variable to have a relatively large standard deviation?

10. The following table summarizes the racial differences in education and the ideal number of children for GSS 2010 Chinese Americans and Filipino Americans. Based on the means and standard deviations (in parentheses), what conclusions can be drawn about differences in the ideal number of children?

	Chinese Americans	Filipino Americans
Education (years)	15.55 (3.643)	13.42 (3.704)
Ideal number of children	2.88 (2.167)	4.00 (2.098)

11. Based on the Monitoring the Future 2014 survey, we investigate the type of paid work for 8th and 10th graders. Percentages for each category are reported.

Type of Work	Grade 8 % (N = 326)	Grade 10 % (N = 228)
Lawn work	28	20
Food service	3	10
Babysitting	37	28
Other	32	42

a. What is the appropriate measure of variability for these variables? Why?

b. Calculate the appropriate measure of variability for each variable.

c. Was there more variability in type of job for 8th or 10th graders? Offer an explanation for your findings.

12. The 2015 average life expectancy for the total population is reported for 10 countries. Calculate the appropriate measures of central tendency and variability for both European countries and non-European countries. Is there more variability in life expectancy for European countries or non-European countries? If so, what might explain these differences?

Country	Life Expectancy at Birth
European countries	
France	81.8
Germany	80.6
Netherlands	81.2
Spain	81.6
Turkey	74.6
Non-European countries	
Japan	84.7
Australia	82.1
Mexico	75.7
Iceland	83.0
Israel	82.3

Source: CIA *Workbook*, 2015.

13. We examine education (measured in years), age (measured in years), and frequency of religious services (measured on an ordinal scale: 0 = never, 4 = once a month to 8 = more than once a week) for males and females who voted for Barack Obama and John McCain in the 2008 Presidential election. Using the GSS 2014 statistics, describe the characteristics of Obama and McCain voters.

	Obama		McCain	
	Males N = 165	Females N = 277	Males N = 148	Females N = 142
Education	14.84 (3.07)	14.35 (2.79)	14.60 (2.41)	14.21 (2.66)
Age	51.71 (15.99)	50.99 (16.62)	55.73 (15.61)	59.31 (15.70)
Frequency of religious services	2.70 (2.66)	3.55 (2.86)	3.93 (2.80)	4.64 (2.76)

5

THE NORMAL DISTRIBUTION

Chapter Learning Objectives

1. Explain the importance and use of the normal distribution in statistics
2. Describe the properties of the normal distribution
3. Transform a raw score into standard (Z) score and vice versa
4. Transform a Z score into proportion (or percentage) and vice versa
5. Calculate and interpret the percentile rank of a score

We have learned some important things about distributions: how to organize them into frequency distributions, how to display them using graphs, and how to describe their central tendencies and variation using measures such as the mean and the standard deviation. The distributions that we have described so far are all empirical distributions—that is, they are all based on real data.

On the other hand, the focus of this chapter is the distribution known as the normal curve or the **normal distribution**. The normal distribution is a theoretical distribution, similar to an empirical distribution in that it can be organized into frequency distributions, displayed using graphs, and described by its central tendency and variation using measures such as the mean and the standard deviation. However, unlike an empirical distribution, a theoretical distribution is based on theory rather than on real data. The value of the theoretical normal distribution lies in the fact that many empirical distributions that we study seem to approximate it. We can often learn a lot about the characteristics of these empirical distributions based on our knowledge of the theoretical normal distribution.

Normal distribution A bell-shaped and symmetrical theoretical distribution with the mean, the median, and the mode all coinciding at its peak and with the frequencies gradually decreasing at both ends of the curve.

PROPERTIES OF THE NORMAL DISTRIBUTION

The normal curve (Figure 5.1) is bell-shaped. One of the most striking characteristics of the normal distribution is its perfect symmetry. If you fold Figure 5.1 exactly in the middle, you have two equal halves, each the mirror image of the other. This means that precisely half the observations fall on each side of the middle of the distribution. In addition, the midpoint of the normal curve is the point having the maximum frequency. This is also the point at which three measures coincide: (1) the mode (the point of the highest frequency), (2) the median (the point that divides the distribution into two equal halves), and (3) the mean (the average of all the scores). Notice also that most of the observations are clustered around the middle, with the frequencies gradually decreasing at both ends of the distribution.

Figure 5.1 The Normal Curve

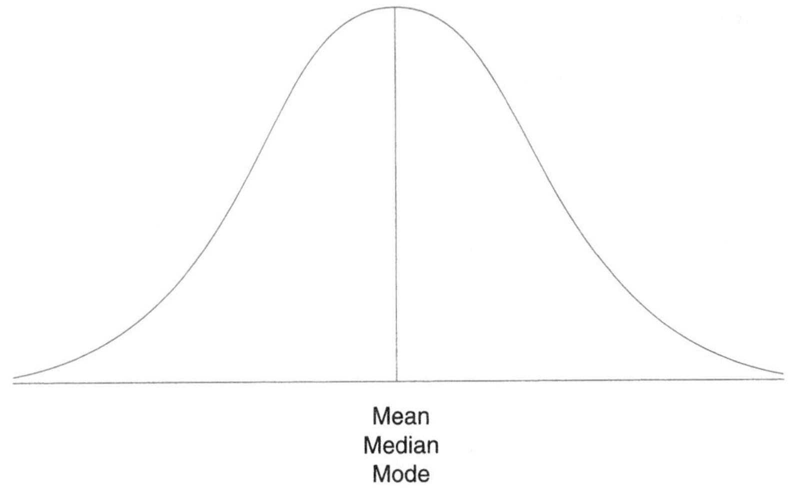

Empirical Distributions Approximating the Normal Distribution

The normal curve is a theoretical ideal, and real-life distributions never match this model perfectly. However, researchers study many variables (e.g., standardized tests such as the SAT, ACT, or GRE) that closely resemble this theoretical model. When we say that a variable is "normally distributed," we mean that the graphic display will reveal an approximately bell-shaped and symmetrical distribution closely resembling the idealized model shown in Figure 5.1. This property makes it possible for us to describe many empirical distributions based on our knowledge of the normal curve.

Areas Under the Normal Curve

In all normal or nearly normal curves, we find a constant proportion of the area under the curve lying between the mean and any given distance from the mean when measured in standard deviation units.

The area under the normal curve may be conceptualized as a proportion or percentage of the number of observations in the sample. Thus, the entire area under the curve is equal to 1.00 or 100% (1.00 × 100) of the observations. Because the normal curve is perfectly symmetrical, exactly 0.50 or 50% of the observations lie above or to the right of the center, which is the mean of the distribution, and 50% lie below or to the left of the mean.

In Figure 5.2, note the percentage of cases that will be included between the mean and 1, 2, and 3 standard deviations above and below the mean. The mean of the distribution divides it exactly into half; 34.13% is included between the mean and 1 standard deviation to the right of the mean, and the same percentage is included between the mean and 1 standard deviation to the left of the mean. The plus signs indicate standard deviations above the mean; the minus signs denote standard deviations below the mean. Thus, between the mean and ±1 standard deviation, 68.26% of all the observations in the distribution occur; between the mean and ±2 standard deviations, 95.46% of all observations in the distribution occur; and between the mean and ±3 standard deviations, 99.72% of the observations occur.

LEARNING CHECK 5.1

Review the properties of the normal curve. What is the area underneath the curve equal to? What percentage of the distribution is within 1 standard deviation? Within 2 and 3 standard deviations? Verify the percentage of cases by summing the percentages in Figure 5.2.

Figure 5.2 Percentages Under the Normal Curve

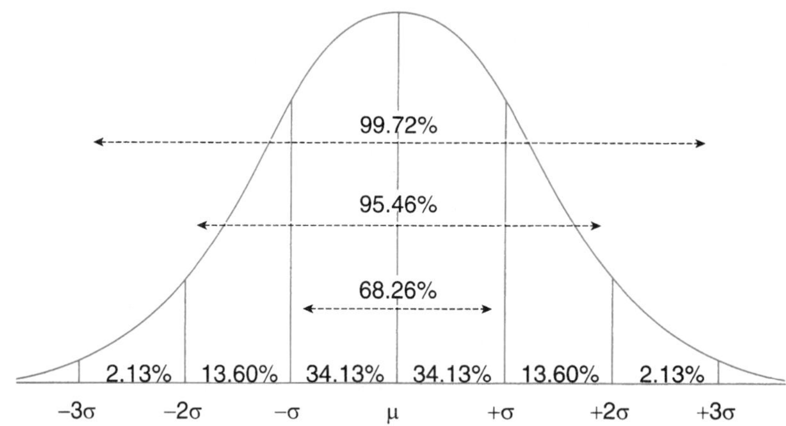

Interpreting the Standard Deviation

The fixed relationship between the distance from the mean and the areas under the curve represents a property of the normal curve that has highly practical applications. As long as a distribution is normal and we know the mean and the standard deviation, we can determine the proportion or percentage of cases that fall between any score and the mean.

This property provides an important interpretation for the standard deviation of empirical distributions that are approximately normal. For such distributions, when we know the mean and the standard deviation, we can determine the percentage or proportion of scores that are within any distance, measured in standard deviation units, from that distribution's mean.

Not every empirical distribution is normal. We've learned that the distributions of some common variables, such as income, are skewed and therefore not normal. The fixed relationship between the distance from the mean and the areas under the curve applies only to distributions that are normal or approximately normal.

AN APPLICATION OF THE NORMAL CURVE

For the rest of this chapter discussion, we rely on the results of the 2014–2015 SAT examination. You may have taken the SAT exam as part of your college admission process. Though there is much debate on the predictive value of SAT scores on college success and some schools have revised their SAT requirements, the exam is still widely regarded as the standardized assessment test to measure college readiness and student quality.

Table 5.1 2014–2015 SAT Component Means and Standard Deviations for High School Seniors						
Number of Test Takers	Critical Reading		Mathematics		Writing	
	Mean	Standard Deviation	Mean	Standard Deviation	Mean	Standard Deviation
1,108,165	485	110	501	117	475	109

Source: College Board, *2015 College-Bound Seniors Total Group Profile Report*, Table 3, 2015. The College Board. www.collegeboard.org.

The current SAT includes three components: (1) critical reading, (2) mathematics, and (3) writing. The perfect score for each component is 800, for a total possible of 2,400. Table 5.1 presents mean and standard deviation statistics for all 2014–2015 senior test takers. The results of the SAT exam, combined or for each component, are assumed to be normally distributed. Throughout this chapter, we will use the normal (theoretical) curve to describe and better understand the characteristics of the SAT writing empirical (real data) distribution.

Transforming a Raw Score Into a *Z* Score

We can express the difference between any score in a distribution and the mean in terms of standard scores, also known as *Z* scores. A **standard (*Z*) score** is the number of standard deviations that a given raw score (or the observed score) is above or below the mean. A raw score can be transformed into a *Z* score to find how many standard deviations it is above or below the mean.

Standard (*Z*) score The number of standard deviations that a given raw score is above or below the mean.

To transform a raw score into a *Z* score, we divide the difference between the score and the mean by the standard deviation. For example, if we want to transform a 584 SAT writing score into a *Z* score, we subtract the mean writing score of 475 from 584 and divide the difference by the standard deviation of 109 (mean and standard deviation reported in Table 5.1).

This calculation gives us a method of standardization known as transforming a raw score into a *Z* score (also known as a standard score). The *Z*-score formula is

$$Z = \frac{Y - \bar{Y}}{s} \tag{5.1}$$

Thus, the *Z* score of 584 is

$$\frac{584 - 475}{109} = \frac{109}{109} = 1.00$$

or 1 standard deviation above the mean. Similarly, for a 366 SAT writing score, the *Z* score is

$$\frac{366 - 475}{109} = \frac{-109}{109} = -1.00$$

or 1 standard deviation below the mean. The negative sign indicates that this score is below (on the left side of) the mean.

A *Z* score allows us to represent a raw score in terms of its relationship to the mean and to the standard deviation of the distribution. It represents how far a given raw score is from the mean in standard deviation units. A positive *Z* indicates that a score is larger than the mean, and a negative *Z* indicates that it is smaller than the mean. The larger the *Z* score, the larger the difference between the score and the mean.

Figure 5.3 The Standard Normal Distribution

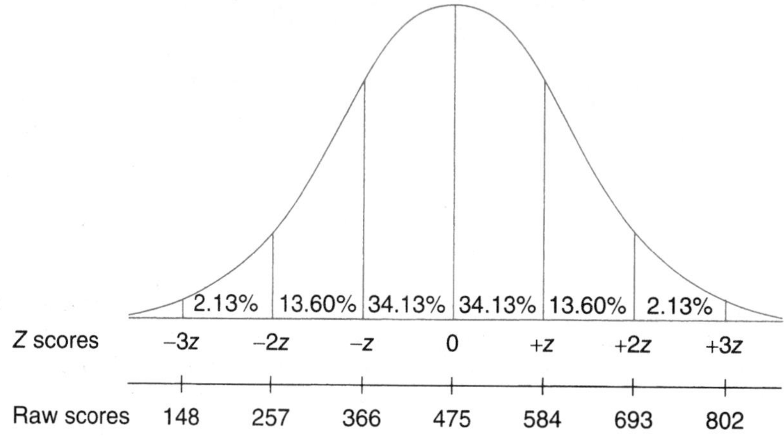

THE STANDARD NORMAL DISTRIBUTION

Standard normal distribution A normal distribution represented in standard (*Z*) scores, with mean = 0 and standard deviation = 1.

When a normal distribution is represented in standard scores (*Z* scores), we call it the **standard normal distribution**. Standard scores, or *Z* scores, are the numbers that tell us the distance between an actual score and the mean in terms of standard deviation units. The standard normal distribution has a mean of 0.0 and a standard deviation of 1.0.

Figure 5.3 shows a standard normal distribution with areas under the curve associated with 1, 2, and 3 standard scores above and below the mean. To help you understand the relationship between raw scores of a distribution and their respective standard *Z* scores, we also show the SAT writing scores that correspond to these standard scores. For example, notice that the mean for the SAT writing score distribution is 475 and the corresponding *Z* score—the mean of the standard normal distribution—is 0. As we've already calculated, the score of 584 is 1 standard deviation above the mean (475 + 109 = 584); therefore, its corresponding *Z* score is +1. Similarly, the score of 366 is 1 standard deviation below the mean (475 − 109 = 366), and its *Z*-score equivalent is −1.

THE STANDARD NORMAL TABLE

We can use *Z* scores to determine the proportion of cases that are included between the mean and any *Z* score in a normal distribution. The areas or proportions under the standard normal curve, corresponding to any *Z* score or its fraction, are organized into a special table called the **standard normal table**. The table is presented in Appendix B. In this section, we discuss how to use this table.

Standard normal table A table showing the area (as a proportion, which can be translated into a percentage) under the standard normal curve corresponding to any *Z* score or its fraction.

Table 5.2 reproduces a small part of the standard normal table. Note that the table consists of three columns (rather than having one long table, we have moved the second half of the table next to the first half, so the three columns are presented in a six-column format).

Column A lists positive *Z* scores. (Note that *Z* scores are presented with two decimal places. In our chapter calculations, we will do the same.) Because the normal curve is symmetrical, the proportions that correspond to positive *Z* scores are identical to the proportions corresponding to negative *Z* scores.

Table 5.2 The Standard Normal Table

(A)	(B)	(C)	(A)	(B)	(C)
Z	Area Between Mean and Z	Area Beyond Z	Z	Area Between Mean and Z	Area Beyond Z
0.00	0.0000	0.5000	0.21	0.0832	0.4168
0.01	0.0040	0.4960	0.22	0.0871	0.4129
0.02	0.0080	0.4920	0.23	0.0910	0.4090
0.03	0.0120	0.4880	0.24	0.0948	0.4052
0.04	0.0160	0.4840	0.25	0.0987	0.4013
0.05	0.0199	0.4801	0.26	0.1026	0.3974
0.06	0.0239	0.4761	0.27	0.1064	0.3936
0.07	0.0279	0.4721	0.28	0.1103	0.3897
0.08	0.0319	0.4681	0.29	0.1141	0.3859
0.09	0.0359	0.4641	0.30	0.1179	0.3821
0.10	0.0398	0.4602	0.31	0.1217	0.3783

Column B shows the area included between the mean and the Z score listed in Column A. Note that when Z is positive, the area is located on the right side of the mean (see Figure 5.4a), whereas for a negative Z score, the same area is located left of the mean (Figure 5.4b).

Column C shows the proportion of the area that is beyond the Z score listed in Column A. Areas corresponding to positive Z scores are on the right side of the curve (see Figure 5.4a). Areas corresponding to negative Z scores are identical except that they are on the left side of the curve (Figure 5.4b).

In Sections 1–4, we present examples of how to transform Z scores into proportions or percentages to describe different areas of the empirical distribution of SAT writing scores.

Figure 5.4 Areas Between Mean and Z (B) and Beyond Z (C)

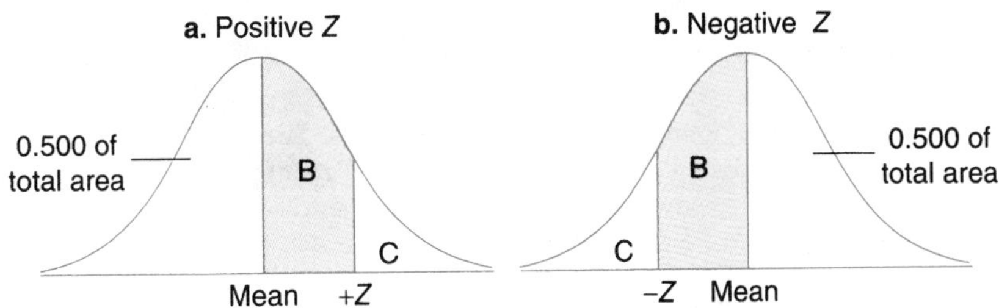

1. Finding the Area Between the Mean and a Positive or Negative *Z* Score

We can use the standard normal table to find the area between the mean and specific *Z* scores.

To find the area between 475 and 675, follow these steps.

1. Convert 675 to a *Z* score:

$$\frac{675-475}{109}=\frac{200}{109}=1.83$$

2. Look up 1.83 in Column A (in Appendix B) and find the corresponding area in Column B, 0.4664. We can translate this proportion into a percentage ($0.4664 \times 100 = 46.64\%$) of the area under the curve included between the mean and a *Z* score of 1.83 (Figure 5.5).

3. Thus, 46.64% of the total area lies between 475 and 675.

Figure 5.5 Finding the Area Between the Mean and a Specified Positive Z Score

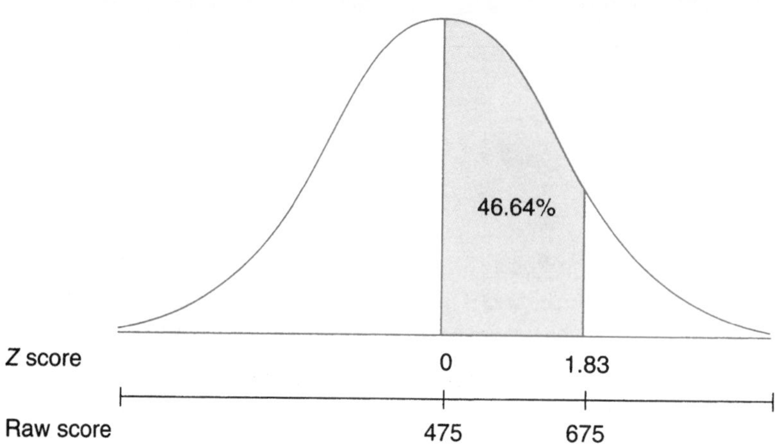

To find the actual number of students who scored between 475 and 675, multiply the proportion 0.4664 by the total number of students. Thus, 516,848 students ($0.4664 \times 1{,}108{,}165 = 516{,}848$) obtained a score between 475 and 675.

For a score lower than the mean, such as 305, we can use the standard normal table and the following steps.

1. Convert 305 to a *Z* score:

$$\frac{305-475}{109}=\frac{-170}{109}=-1.56$$

2. Because the proportions that correspond to positive *Z* scores are identical to the proportions corresponding to negative *Z* scores, we ignore the negative sign of *Z* and look up 1.56 in Column A. The area corresponding to a *Z* score of 1.56 is .4406. This indicates that 0.4406 of the area under the curve is included between the mean and a *Z* of −1.56 (Figure 5.6). We convert this proportion to a percentage, 44.06%.

3. Thus, 44.06% of the distribution lies between the scores 305 and 475.

Figure 5.6 Finding the Area Between the Mean and a Specified Negative Z Score

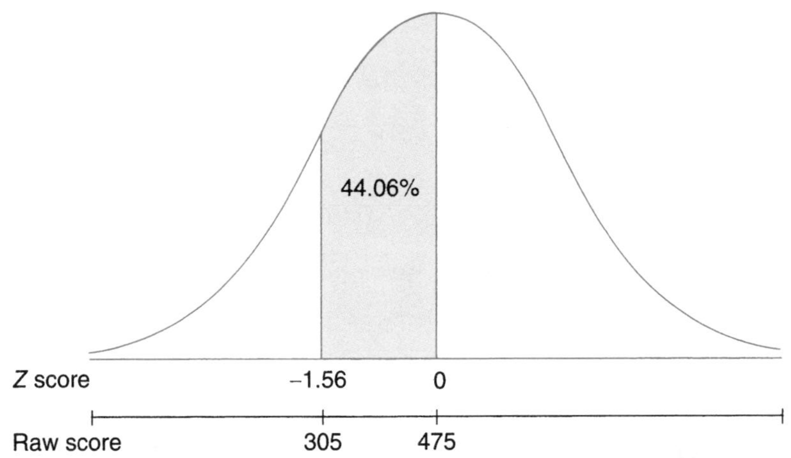

LEARNING CHECK 5.2

How many students obtained a score between 305 and 475?

2. Finding the Area Above a Positive Z Score or Below a Negative Z Score

The normal distribution table can also be used to find the area beyond a *Z* score, SAT scores that lie at the tip of the positive or negative sides of the distribution (Figure 5.7).

For example, what is the area below a score of 750? The *Z* score corresponding to a final SAT writing score of 750 is equal to 2.52.

$$\frac{750-475}{109}=\frac{275}{109}=2.52$$

The area beyond a *Z* of 2.52 includes all students who scored above 750. This area is shown in Figure 5.7. To find the proportion of students whose scores fall in this area, refer to the entry in Column C that corresponds to a *Z* of 2.52, 0.0059. This means that .59% ($0.0059 \times 100 = 0.59\%$) of the students scored above 750, a very small percentage. To find the actual number of students in this group, multiply the proportion 0.0059 by the total number of students. Thus, there were $1{,}108{,}165 \times 0.0059$, or about 6,538 students, who scored above 750.

A similar procedure can be applied to identify the number of students on the opposite end of the distribution. Let's first convert a score of 375 to a Z score:

$$\frac{375-475}{109}=\frac{-100}{109}=-0.92$$

The *Z* score corresponding to a final score of 375 is equal to −0.92. The area beyond a *Z* of −0.92 includes all students who scored below 375. This area is also shown in Figure 5.7. Locate the proportion of students in this area in Column C in the entry corresponding to a *Z* of 0.92.

Figure 5.7 Finding the Area Above a Positive Z Score or Below a Negative Z Score

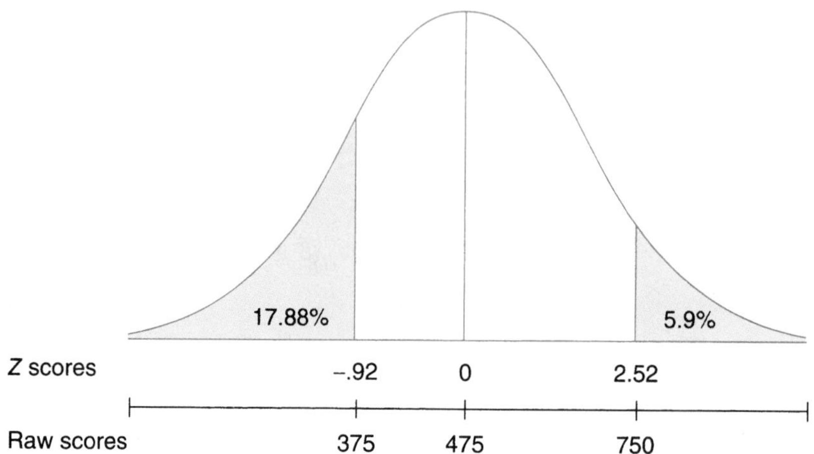

(Remember that the proportions corresponding to positive or negative *Z* scores are identical.) This proportion is equal to 0.1788. Thus, 17.88% (0.1788 × 100) of the group, or about 198,140 (0.1788 × 1,108,165) students, performed poorly on the SAT writing exam.

LEARNING CHECK 5.3

Calculate the proportion of test takers who earned a SAT writing score of 400 or less. What is the proportion of students who earned a score of 600 or higher?

3. Transforming Proportions and Percentages Into Z Scores

We can also convert proportions or percentages into *Z* scores.

FINDING A *Z* SCORE WHICH BOUNDS AN AREA ABOVE IT Let's say we are interested in identifying the score that corresponds to the top 10% of SAT test takers. We will need to identify the cutoff point for the top 10% of the class. This problem involves two steps:

1. Find the *Z* score that bounds the top 10% or 0.1000 (0.1000 × 100 = 10%) of all the students who took the writing SAT (Figure 5.8).

   Refer to the areas under the normal curve shown in Appendix B. First, look for an entry of 0.1000 (or the value closest to it) in Column C. The entry closest to 0.1000 is 0.1003. Then, locate the *Z* in Column A that corresponds to this proportion. The *Z* score associated with the proportion 0.1003 SAT is 1.28.

2. Find the score associated with a *Z* of 1.28.

This step involves transforming the Z score into a raw score. To transform a Z score into a raw score we multiply the score by the standard deviation and add that product to the mean (Formula 5.2):

$$Y = \bar{Y} + Z(s) \tag{5.2}$$

Thus,

$$Y = 475 + 1.28(109) = 475 + 139.52 = 614.52$$

The cutoff point for the top 10% of SAT writing exam test takers is 615.

Figure 5.8 Finding a Z Score Which Bounds an Area Above It

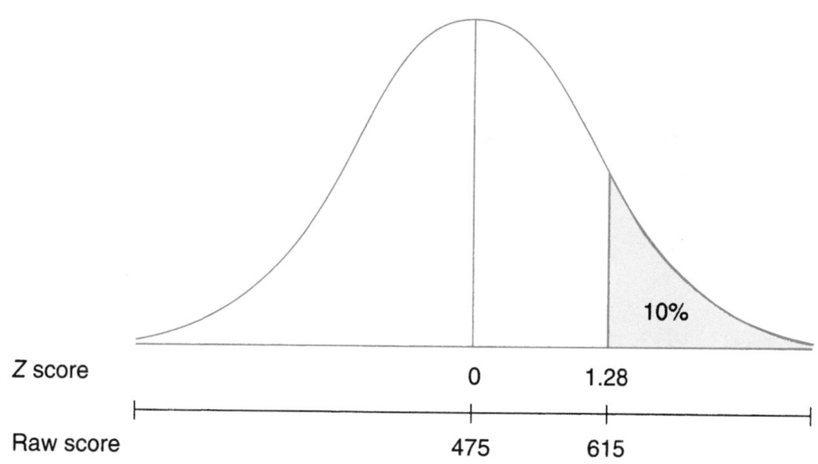

FINDING A *Z* SCORE WHICH BOUNDS AN AREA BELOW IT Now, let's identify the score which corresponds to the bottom 5% of test takers. This problem involves two steps:

1. Find the Z score that bounds the lowest 5% or 0.0500 of all the students who took the class (Figure 5.9).

   Refer to the areas under the normal curve, and look for an entry of 0.0500 (or the value closest to it) in Column C. The entry closest to 0.0500 is 0.0495. Then, locate the Z in Column A that corresponds to this proportion, 1.65. Because the area we are looking for is on the left side of the curve—that is, below the mean—the Z score is negative. Thus, the Z associated with the lowest 0.0500 (or 0.0495) is −1.65.

2. To find the final writing score associated with a Z of −1.65, convert the Z score to a raw score:

$$Y = 475 + (-1.65)(109) = 475 - 179.85 = 295.15$$

The cutoff for the lowest 5% of SAT writing scores is 295.

Figure 5.9 Finding a Z Score Which Bounds an Area Below It

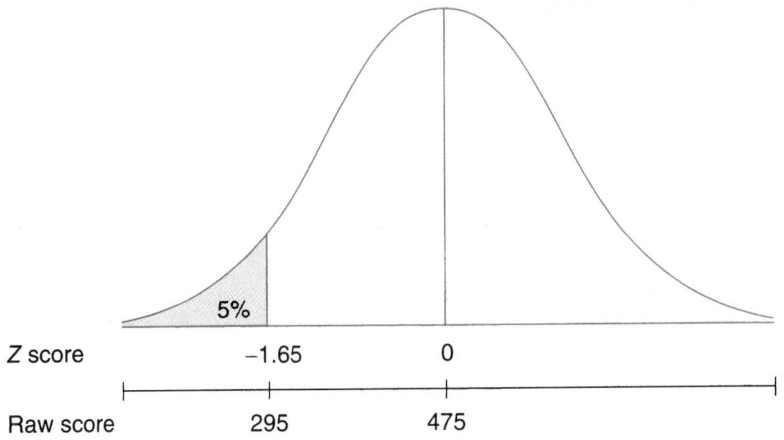

LEARNING CHECK 5.4

Which score corresponds to the top 5% of SAT writing test takers?

4. Working With Percentiles in a Normal Distribution

In Chapter 2 ("The Organization and Graphic Presentation of Data"), we defined percentiles as scores below which a specific percentage of the distribution falls. For example, the 95th percentile is a score that divides the distribution so that 95% of the cases are below it and 5% of the cases are above it. How are percentile ranks determined? How do you convert a percentile rank to a raw score? To determine the percentile rank of a raw score requires transforming Z scores into proportions or percentages. Converting percentile ranks to raw scores is based on transforming proportions or percentages into Z scores. In the following examples, we illustrate both procedures based on the SAT writing scores data.

FINDING THE PERCENTILE RANK OF A SCORE HIGHER THAN THE MEAN Suppose you took the SAT writing exam during the same year. You recall that your final score was 680, but how well did you do relative to the other students who took the exam? To evaluate your performance, you need to translate your raw score into a percentile rank. Figure 5.10 illustrates this problem.

To find the percentile rank of a score higher than the mean, follow these steps:

1. Convert the raw score to a Z score:

$$\frac{680-475}{109}=\frac{205}{109}=1.88$$

The Z score corresponding to a raw score of 680 is 1.88.

2. Find the area beyond Z in Appendix B, Column C. The area beyond a Z score of 1.88 is 0.0301.

Figure 5.10 Finding the Percentile Rank of a Score Higher Than the Mean

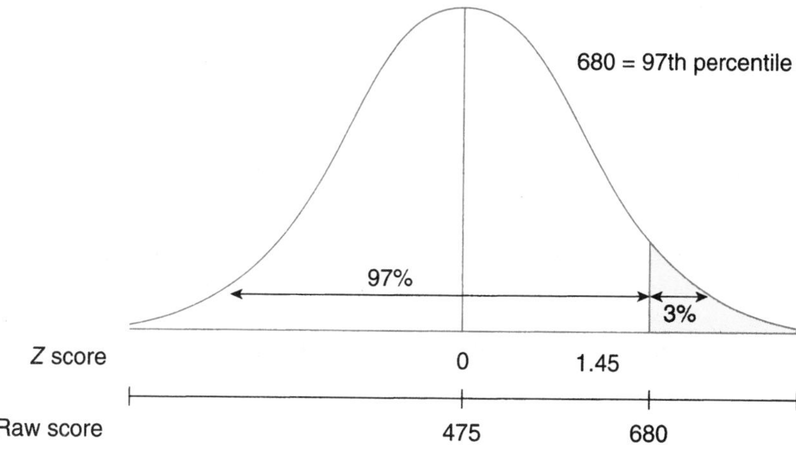

3. Subtract the area from 1.00 and multiply by 100 to obtain the percentile rank:

$$\text{Percentile rank} = (1.0000 - .0301 = 0.9699) \times 100 = 96.99\% = 97\%$$

Being in the 97th percentile means that 97% of all test takers scored lower than 680 and 3% scored higher than 680.

FINDING THE PERCENTILE RANK OF A SCORE LOWER THAN THE MEAN If your SAT score is 380, what is your percentile rank? Figure 5.11 illustrates this problem.

To find the percentile rank of a score lower than the mean, follow these steps:

1. Convert the raw score to a Z score:

$$\frac{380-475}{109} = \frac{-95}{109} = -0.87$$

Figure 5.11 Finding the Percentile Rank of a Score Lower Than the Mean

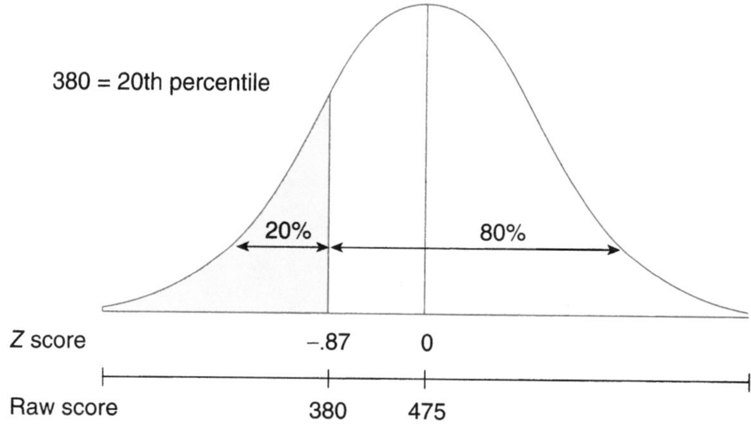

The Z score corresponding to a raw score of 380 is −0.87.

2. Find the area beyond Z in Appendix B, Column C. The area beyond a Z score of −0.87 is 0.1992.

3. Multiply the area by 100 to obtain the percentile rank:

$$\text{Percentile rank} = 0.1992(100) = 19.92\% = 20\%$$

The 20th percentile rank means that 20% of all test takers scored lower than you (i.e., 20% scored lower, but 80% scored the same or higher).

FINDING THE RAW SCORE ASSOCIATED WITH A PERCENTILE HIGHER THAN 50 Now, let's assume that for an honors English program, your university will only admit students who scored at or above the 95th percentile in the SAT writing exam. What is the cutoff point required for acceptance? Figure 5.12 illustrates this problem.

To find the score associated with a percentile higher than 50, follow these steps:

1. Divide the percentile by 100 to find the area below the percentile rank:

$$\frac{95}{100} = 0.95$$

2. Subtract the area below the percentile rank from 1.00 to find the area above the percentile rank:

$$1.00 - 0.95 = 0.05$$

3. Find the Z score associated with the area above the percentile rank.

   Refer to the area under the normal curve shown in Appendix B. First, look for an entry of 0.0500 (or the value closest to it) in Column C. The entry closest to 0.0500 is 0.0495. Now, locate the Z in Column A that corresponds to this proportion, 1.65.

Figure 5.12 Finding the Raw Score Associated With a Percentile Higher Than 50

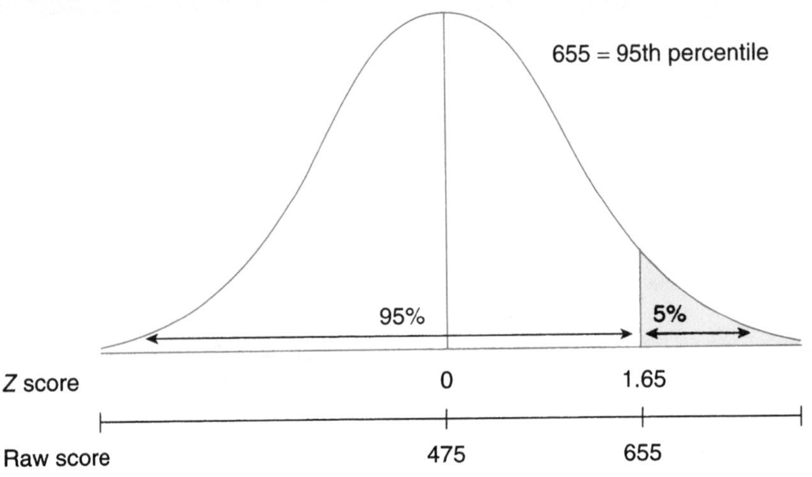

4. Convert the Z score to a raw score:

$$Y = 475 + 1.65(109) = 475 + 179.85 = 654.85$$

The final SAT writing score associated with the 95th percentile is 654.85. This means that you will need a score of 655 or higher to be admitted into the honors English program.

LEARNING CHECK 5.5

In a normal distribution, how many standard deviations from the mean is the 95th percentile?

FINDING THE RAW SCORE ASSOCIATED WITH A PERCENTILE LOWER THAN 50 Finally, what is the score associated with the 40th percentile? To find the percentile rank of a score lower than 50 follow these steps (Figure 5.13).

1. Divide the percentile by 100 to find the area below the percentile rank:

$$\frac{40}{100} = 0.40$$

2. Find the Z score associated with this area.

   Refer to the area under the normal curve shown in Appendix B. First, look for an entry of 0.4000 (or the value closest to it) in Column C. The entry closest to 0.4000 is 0.4013. Now, locate the Z in Column A that corresponds to this proportion. The Z score associated with the proportion 0.4013 is −0.25.

3. Convert the Z score to a raw score:

$$Y = 475 + (-0.25)(109) = 475 - 27.25 = 447.75$$

Figure 5.13 Finding the Raw Score Associated With a Percentile Lower Than 50

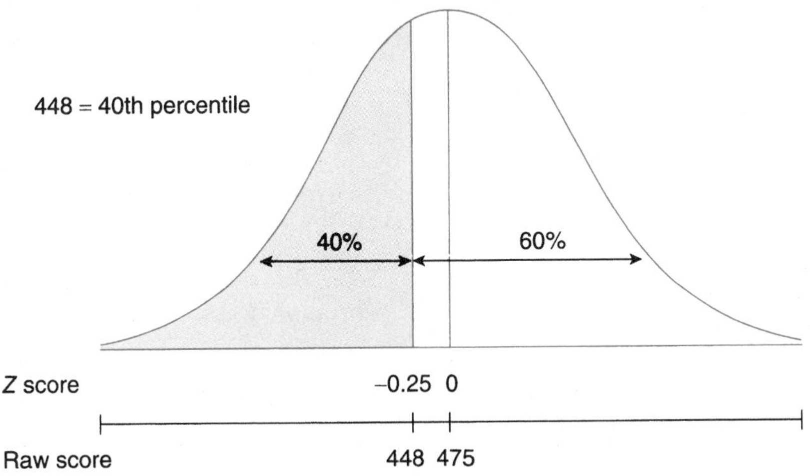

The SAT writing score associated with the 40th percentile is 448. This means that 40% of the students scored below 448 and 60% scored above it.

LEARNING CHECK 5.6

What is the raw SAT writing score associated with the 50th percentile?

READING THE RESEARCH LITERATURE: CHILD HEALTH AND ACADEMIC ACHIEVEMENT

Margot Jackson (2015) relied on data from the British National Child Development Study 1958–1974 to examine the intersection of economic disadvantage, poor health, and academic achievement for children aged 7 to 16 years. The longitudinal data set is comprehensive, tracking child health, educational progress, income, and family relationships. Jackson suggests that the role of health in producing academic inequality depends on when, and for how long, children are in poor health.[1]

A CLOSER LOOK 5.1

PERCENTAGES, PROPORTIONS, AND PROBABILITIES

We take a moment to note the relationship between the theoretical normal curve and the estimation of probabilities, a topic that we'll explore in more detail in Chapter 6 ("Sampling and Sampling Distributions").

We consider probabilities in many instances. What is the probability of winning the lottery? Of selecting the Queen of Hearts out of a deck of 52 cards? Of getting your favorite parking spot on campus? But we rarely make the connection to some statistical computation or a normal curve.

A probability is a quantitative measure that a particular event will occur. Probability can be calculated as follows:

Number of times an event will occur/Total number of events

Probabilities range in value from 0 (the event will not occur) to 1 (the event will certainly occur).

In fact, the shape of the normal curve and the percentages beneath it (refer to Figure 5.2) can be used to determine probabilities. By definition we know that the majority of cases are near the mean, within 1 to 3 standard deviation units. Thus, it is common—or a high probability occurrence—to find a case near the mean. Rare events—with smaller corresponding probabilities—are further way from the mean, toward the tail ends of the normal curve.

In our chapter example of SAT writing scores, we've determined the proportion or percentage of cases that fall within a certain area of the empirical distribution. But these same calculations tell us the probability of the occurrence of a specific score or set of scores based on their distance from the mean. We calculated the proportion of cases between the mean of 475 and a test score of 675 as .4664. We can say that the probability of earning a score between 475 and 675 is .4664 (at least 47 times out of a 100 events). What percentage of scores were 375 or less on the SAT writing exam? According to our calculations, it is 17.88%. The probability of earning a score of 375 or less is 17.88% (18 times out of a 100 events). Notice how the calculations are unchanged, but we are shifting our interpretation from a percentage or a proportion to a probability.

The relationship between probabilities and sampling methods will be the focus of Chapter 6.

Table 5.3 Academic Achievement by Health, Birth to Age 16 Sample: National Child Development Study, 1958–1974 (N 9,252)

	No Health Condition	Low Birth Weight	Medium/ Variable Smoking	Heavy Prenatal Smoking	Condition at Age 7	Condition at Ages 7, 11, and 16
Age 7						
Mean reading *Z* score	0.139	−0.304	−0.046	−0.084	−0.661	−1.561
Mean math *Z* score	0.087	−0.321	−0.053	−0.085	−0.439	−1.026
Age 11						
Mean reading *Z* score	0.102	−0.337	−0.101	−0.144	−0.454	−1.196
Mean math *Z* score	0.101	−0.367	−0.081	−0.160	−0.411	−0.952
Age 16						
Mean reading *Z* score	0.115	−.317	−0.115	−0.160	−0.432	−1.206
Mean math *Z* score	0.084	−.321	−0.149	−0.196	−0.388	−0.706
N	7,806	445	419	1,080	586	126

Source: Margot Jackson, "Cumulative Inequality in Child Health and Academic Achievement," *Journal of Health and Social Behavior* 56, no. 2 (2015), 269.

Jackson examined how standardized reading and math scores vary by the child's health condition at ages 7, 11, and 16 (the presence of a slight, moderate, severe, or no health condition impeding the child's normal functioning; asthma was the most common health condition), low child birth weight (weight below 5.5 pounds), and maternal smoking (amount of smoking by the mother after the fourth month of pregnancy).[2]

A portion of her study analyses is presented in Table 5.3. Jackson converts reading and math scores into *Z* scores, measuring the distance from the overall mean test score in standard deviation units. A positive *Z* score indicates that the group's test score is higher than the mean; a negative score indicates that the test score is lower.

Jackson confirms her hypothesis about the cumulative effects of health on a child's academic performance:

> Table 5.3, which disaggregates average achievement by health status and age, reveals clear variation in reading and math achievement across health categories. Respondents with no childhood health conditions score highest on reading and math assessments at all ages. In contrast, low-birth-weight respondents, those exposed to heavy prenatal smoking late in utero, and those with early school-age health limitations perform more poorly, ranging from .10 to .5 of a standard deviation below average. Children with health conditions at all school ages perform nearly a full standard deviation lower in math and reading (p. 269).[3]

LEARNING CHECK 5.7

Review the mean math Z scores for the variable "conditions at age 7, 11, and 16" (the last column of Table 5.3). From ages 7, 11, and 16, was there an improvement in their math scores? Explain.

DATA AT WORK

Claire Wulf Winiarek: Director of Collaborative Policy Engagement

Photo courtesy of Claire Wulf Winiarek

Claire has had an impressive career in public policy. She's worked for a member of Congress, coordinated international human rights advocacy initiatives, and led a public policy team. Her experiences have led her to her current position with a *Fortune 50* health insurance company. Research is a constant in her work. "The critical and analytic thinking a strong foundation in research methods allows informs my work—from analyzing draft legislation and proposed regulation to determining next year's department budget, from estimating potential growth to making the case for a new program. Research is part of my every day."

Claire was drawn to a career in research because she wanted to make a difference in the public sector. "Early in my career, the frequency with which I returned to and leveraged research methods surprised me—these were not necessarily research positions. However, as government and its private sector partners increasingly rely on data and evidence-based decision-making, research methods and the ability to analyze their output have become more critical in public affairs."

"Whether you pursue a research career or not, the importance of research methods—especially with regard to data—will be necessary for success. The information revolution is impacting all industries and sectors, as well as government and our communities. With this ever growing and ever richer set of information, today's professionals must have the know-how to understand and apply this data in a meaningful way. Research methods will create the critical and analytical foundation to meet the challenge, but internships or special research projects in your career field will inform that foundation with practical experience. Always look for that connection between research and reality."

MAIN POINTS

- The normal distribution is central to the theory of inferential statistics. It also provides a model for many empirical distributions that approximate normality.
- In all normal or nearly normal curves, we find a constant proportion of the area under the curve lying between the mean and any given distance from the mean when measured in standard deviation units.
- The standard normal distribution is a normal distribution represented in standard scores, or Z scores, with mean = 0 and standard deviation = 1. Z scores express the number of standard deviations that a given score is located above or below the mean. The proportions corresponding to any Z score or its fraction are organized into a special table called the standard normal table.

KEY TERMS

normal distribution 128

standard normal distribution 132

standard normal table 132

standard (*Z*) score 131

DIGITAL RESOURCES

Get the edge on your studies. **edge.sagepub.com/frankfort8e**

Take a quiz to find out what you've learned.
Review key terms with eFlashcards.
Dive into real research with SAGE Journal Articles.

SPSS DEMONSTRATION [GSS14SSDS-B]

Producing *Z* Scores With SPSS

In this chapter, we have discussed the theoretical normal curve, *Z* scores, and the relationship between raw scores and *Z* scores. The SPSS Descriptives procedure can calculate *Z* scores for any distribution. We'll use it to study the distribution of education in the GSS 2014 file. Locate the Descriptives procedure in the *Analyze* menu, under *Descriptive Statistics*, then click *Descriptives*. We can select one or more variables to place in the Variable(s) box; for now, we'll just place EDUC (years of education) in this box. Check the box in the bottom left corner (*Save standardized values as variables*), to create standardized values, or *Z* scores, as new variables. Any new variable is placed in a new Column in the Data View window and will then be available for additional analyses. Click on *OK* to run the procedure.

The output from Descriptives (Figure 5.14) is brief, listing the mean and standard deviation for EDUC, plus the minimum and maximum values and the number of valid cases.

Figure 5.14 Descriptives for Education

Descriptive Statistics

	N	Minimum	Maximum	Mean	Std. Deviation
educ HIGHEST YEAR OF SCHOOL COMPLETED	1500	0	20	13.77	3.071
Valid N (listwise)	1500				

Though not indicated in the Output window, SPSS has created a new Z-score variable for EDUC. To see this new variable, switch to the Data View screen. Then, go to the last Column, scrolling all the way to the right (Figure 5.15). By default, SPSS appends a Z to the variable name, so the new variable is called ZEDUC. The first case in the file has a Z score of –0.25199, so the education years for this person must be below the mean of 13.77. If we locate the respondent's EDUC score, we see that the score for this person was 13 (not pictured), or below the mean as we expected. There may be missing values for ZEDUC. Missing values include those that the question did not apply to, those that outright refused to provide occupational information, or those data entry errors that resulted in an invalid answer.

Figure 5.15 The Creation of the Z-Score Variable for EDUC

wwwhr	Zeduc
-1	-.25119
1	-.57685
-1	-1.87947
1	-.25119
-1	.72578
1	.07447
-1	.07447
80	1.37709

If the data file is saved, the new Z-score variable will be saved along with the original data and then can be used in analyses. In addition, if we have SPSS calculate the mean and standard deviation of ZEDUC, we find that they are equal to 0 and 1.00, respectively.

SPSS PROBLEMS [GSS14SSDS-B]

1. The majority of variables that social scientists study are not normally distributed. This doesn't typically cause problems in analysis when the goal of a study is to calculate means and standard deviations—as long as sample sizes are greater than about 50. (This will be discussed in later chapters.) However, when characterizing the distribution of scores in one sample, or in a complete population (if this information is available), a non-normal distribution can cause complications. We can illustrate this point by examining the distribution of age in the GSS data file.
   a. Create a histogram for AGE. Click on *Analyze*, *Frequencies* (select AGE), *Charts*, and *Histograms* (select *Show normal curve on histogram*). How does the distribution of AGE deviate from the theoretical normal curve?
   b. Calculate the mean and standard deviation for AGE in this sample, using either the Frequencies or Descriptives procedure.
   c. Assuming the distribution of AGE is normal, calculate the number of people who should be 25 years of age or less.
   d. Use the Frequencies procedure to construct a table of the percentage of cases at each value of AGE. Compare the theoretical calculation in (c) with the actual distribution of age in the sample. What percentage of people in the sample are 25 years old or less? Is this value close to what you calculated?

2. In the SPSS Demonstration, we examined the distribution of EDUC (years of school completed).

   a. What is the equivalent Z score for someone who has completed 18 years of education?

   b. Use the Frequencies procedure to find the percentile rank for a score of 18.

   c. Does the percentile rank that you found from Frequencies correspond to the Z score for a value of 18? In other words, is the distribution for years of education normal? If so, then the Z score that SPSS calculates should be very close, after transforming it into an appropriate area, to the percentile rank for that same score.

   d. Create histograms for EDUC and the new variable ZEDUC. Explain why they have the same shape.

3. Run separate analyses for men versus women (SEX) based on the variables EDUC and ZEDUC. (Click on *Data*, *Split File*, *Organize Output by Groups*, and select SEX.) Answer Questions 2a–d separately for men and women.

CHAPTER EXERCISES

1. We discovered that 1,001 GSS 2014 respondents watched television for an average of 2.94 hours per day, with a standard deviation of 2.60 hours. Answer the following questions assuming the distribution of the number of television hours is normal.

   a. What is the Z score for a person who watches more than 8 hours per day?

   b. What proportion of people watch television less than 5 hours per day? How many does this correspond to in the sample?

   c. What number of television hours per day corresponds to a Z score of +1?

   d. What is the percentage of people who watch between 1 and 6 hours of television per day?

2. You are asked to do a study of shelters for abused and battered women to determine the necessary capacity in your city to provide housing for most of these women. After recording data for a whole year, you find that the mean number of women in shelters each night is 250, with a standard deviation of 75. Fortunately, the distribution of the number of women in the shelters each night is normal, so you can answer the following questions posed by the city council.

   a. If the city's shelters have a capacity of 350, will that be enough places for abused women on 95% of all nights? If not, what number of shelter openings will be needed?

   b. The current capacity is only 220 openings, because some shelters have been closed. What is the percentage of nights that the number of abused women seeking shelter will exceed current capacity?

3. Based on the SPSS Demonstration, we find the mean number of years of education is 13.77 with a standard deviation of 3.07. A total of 1,500 GSS 2014 respondents were included in the survey. Assuming that years of education is normally distributed, answer the following questions.

   a. If you have 13.77 years of education, that is, the mean number of years of education, what is your Z score?

   b. If your friend is in the 60th percentile, how many years of education does she have?

   c. How many people have between your years of education (13.77) and your friend's years of education?

4. A criminologist developed a test to measure recidivism, where low scores indicated a lower probability of repeating the undesirable behavior. The test is normed so that it has a mean of 140 and a standard deviation of 40.

   a. What is the percentile rank of a score of 172?

   b. What is the Z score for a test score of 200?

   c. What percentage of scores falls between 100 and 160?

   d. What proportion of respondents should score above 190?

   e. Suppose an individual is in the 67th percentile in this test, what is his or her corresponding recidivism score?

5. We report the average years of education for a subsample of GSS 2014 respondents by their social class—lower, working, middle, and upper. Standard deviations are also reported for each class.

	Mean	Standard Deviation	N
Lower class	12.11	2.83	122
Working class	13.01	2.91	541
Middle class	14.99	2.93	475
Upper class	15.44	2.83	34

   a. Assuming that years of education is normally distributed in the population, what proportion of working-class respondents have 12 to 16 years of education? What proportion of upper-class respondents have 12 to 16 years of education?

   b. What is the probability that a working-class respondent, drawn at random from the population, will have more than 16 years of education? What is the equivalent probability for a middle-class respondent drawn at random?

   c. What is the probability that a lower-class respondent will have less than 10 years of education?

   d. If years of education is actually positively skewed in the population, how would that change your other answers?

6. As reported in Table 5.1, the mean SAT reading score was 485 with a standard deviation of 110 in 2014–2015.

   a. What percentage of students scored above 625?

   b. What percentage of students scored between 400 and 625?

   c. A college decides to liberalize its admission policy. As a first step, the admissions committee decides to exclude student applicants scoring below the 20th percentile on the reading SAT. Translate this percentile into a Z score. Then, calculate the equivalent SAT reading test score.

7. The standardized IQ test is described as a normal distribution with 100 as the mean score and a 15-point standard deviation.

   a. What is the Z score for a score of 150?

   b. What percentage of scores are above 150?

c. What percentage of scores fall between 85 and 150?

d. Explain what is meant by scoring in the 95th percentile? What is the corresponding score?

8. We'll examine the results of the 2014–2015 SAT math exam with a mean of 501 and standard deviation of 117, as reported in Table 5.1.

   a. What percentage of seniors scored lower than 300 on the math SAT?

   b. What percentage scored between 600 and 700 points?

   c. Your score is 725. What is your percentile rank?

9. The Hate Crime Statistics Act of 1990 requires the Attorney General to collect national data about crimes that manifest evidence of prejudice based on race, religion, sexual orientation, or ethnicity, including the crimes of murder and non-negligent manslaughter, forcible rape, aggravated assault, simple assault, intimidation, arson, and destruction, damage, or vandalism of property. The Hate Crime Data collected in 2007 reveals, based on a randomly selected sample of 300 incidents, that the mean number of victims in a particular type of hate crime was 1.28, with a standard deviation of 0.82. Assuming that the number of victims was normally distributed, answer the following questions.

   a. What proportion of crime incidents had more than two victims?

   b. What is the probability that there was more than one victim in an incident?

   c. What proportion of crime incidents had less than four victims?

10. The number of hours people work each week varies widely for many reasons. Using the GSS 2014, you find that the mean number of hours worked last week was 41.47, with a standard deviation of 15.04 hours, based on a sample size of 895.

   a. Assume that hours worked is approximately normally distributed in the sample. What is the probability that someone in the sample will work 60 hours or more in a week? How many people in the sample should have worked 60 hours or more?

   b. What is the probability that someone will work 30 hours or fewer in a week (i.e., work part time)? How many people does this represent in the sample?

   c. What number of hours worked per week corresponds to the 60th percentile?

11. The National Collegiate Athletic Association has a public access database on each Division I sports team in the United States, which contains data on team-level Academic Progress Rates (APRs), eligibility rates, and retention rates. The APR score combines team rates for academic eligibility and retention. The mean APR of all reporting men's and women's teams for the 2013–2014 academic year was 981 (based on a 1,000-point scale), with a standard deviation of 27.3. Assuming that the distribution of APRs for the teams is approximately normal:

   a. Would a team be at the upper quartile (the top 25%) of the APR distribution with an APR score of 990?

   b. What APR score should a team have to be more successful than 75% of all the teams?

   c. What is the Z value for this score?

12. According to the same National Collegiate Athletic Association data, the means and standard deviations of eligibility and retention rates (based on a 1,000-point scale) for the 2013–2014 academic year are presented, along with the fictional scores for two basketball teams, A and B. Assume that rates are normally distributed.

	Mean	Standard Deviation	Team A	Team B
Eligibility	983	33	971	987
Retention	976	34.9	958	970

a. On which criterion (eligibility or retention) did Team A do better than Team B? Calculate appropriate statistics to answer this question.

b. What proportion of the teams have retention rates below Team B?

c. What is the percentile rank of Team A's eligibility rate?

13. We present data from the 2014 International Social Survey Programme for five European countries. The average number of completed years of education, standard deviations, and sample size are reported in the table. Assuming that each data are normally distributed, for each country, calculate the number of years of education that corresponds to the 95th percentile.

Country	Mean	Standard Deviation	N
Hungary	11.76	2.91	501
Czech Republic	12.82	2.29	914
Denmark	13.93	5.83	651
France	14.12	5.73	975
Ireland	15.15	3.90	581

6

SAMPLING AND SAMPLING DISTRIBUTIONS

Until now, we have ignored the question of who or what should be observed when we collect data or whether the conclusions based on our observations can be generalized to a larger group of observations. In truth, we are rarely able to study or observe everyone or everything we are interested in. Although we have learned about various methods to analyze observations, remember that these observations represent a fraction of all the possible observations we might have chosen. Consider the following research examples.

Example 1: The Muslim Student Association on your campus is interested in conducting a study of experiences with campus diversity. The association has enough funds to survey 300 students from the more than 20,000 enrolled students at your school.

Example 2: Environmental activists would like to assess recycling practices in 2-year and 4-year colleges and universities. There are more than 4,700 colleges and universities nationwide.[1]

Example 3: The Academic Advising Office is trying to determine how to better address the needs of more than 15,000 commuter students, but determines that it has only enough time and money to survey 500 students.

The primary problem in each situation is that there is too much information and not enough resources to collect and analyze it.

Chapter Learning Objectives

1. Describe the aims of sampling and basic principles of probability
2. Explain the relationship between a sample and a population
3. Identify and apply different sampling designs
4. Apply the concept of the sampling distribution
5. Describe the central limit theorem

AIMS OF SAMPLING[2]

Researchers in the social sciences rarely have enough time or money to collect information about the entire group that interests them. Known as the **population**, this group includes all the cases (individuals, groups, or objects) in which the researcher is interested. For example, in our first illustration, there are more than 20,000 students; the population in the second illustration consists of 4,700 colleges and universities; and in the third illustration, the population is 15,000 commuter students.

Population A group that includes all the cases (individuals, objects, or groups) in which the researcher is interested.

Sample A subset of cases selected from a population.

Sampling The process of identifying and selecting a subset of the population for study.

Parameter A measure (e.g., mean, standard deviation) used to describe the population distribution.

Fortunately, we can learn a lot about a population if we carefully select a subset of it. This subset is called a **sample**. Through the process of **sampling**—selecting a subset of observations from the population—we attempt to generalize the characteristics of the larger group (population) based on what we learn from the smaller group (the sample). This is the basis of inferential statistics—making predictions or inferences about a population from observations based on a sample. Thus, it is important how we select our sample.

The term **parameter**, associated with the population, refers to measures used to describe the population we are interested in. For instance, the average commuting time for the 15,000 commuter students on your campus is a population parameter because it refers to a population characteristic. In previous chapters, we have learned the many ways of describing a distribution, such as a proportion, a mean, or a standard deviation. When used to describe the population distribution, these measures are referred to as parameters. Thus, a population mean, a population proportion, and a population standard deviation are all parameters.

Statistic A measure (e.g., mean, standard deviation) used to describe the sample distribution.

We use the term **statistic** when referring to a corresponding characteristic calculated for the sample. For example, the average commuting time for a sample of commuter students is a sample statistic. Similarly, a sample mean, a sample proportion, and a sample standard deviation are all statistics.

In this chapter and in the remaining chapters of this text, we discuss some of the principles involved in generalizing results from samples to the population. We will use different notations when referring to sample statistics and population parameters in our discussion. Table 6.1 presents the sample notation and the corresponding population notation.

Table 6.1 Sample and Population Notations

Measure Notation	Sample Notation	Population
Mean	$\bar{Y}$	μ
Proportion	p	π
Standard deviation	s	σ
Variance	s^2	σ^2

The distinctions between a sample and a population and between a parameter and a statistic are illustrated in Figure 6.1. We've included for illustration the population parameter of 0.60—the proportion of white respondents in the population. However, since we almost never have enough resources to collect information about the population, it is rare that we know the value of a parameter. The goal of most research is to find the population parameter. Researchers usually select a sample from the population to obtain an estimate of the population parameter. Thus, the major objective of sampling theory and statistical inference is to provide estimates of unknown parameters from sample statistics that can be easily obtained and calculated.

LEARNING CHECK 6.1

Take a moment to review the definitions of population, sample, parameter, and statistic mean. Use your own words so that the concepts make sense to you. Also review the sample and population notations. These concepts and notations will be used throughout the rest of the text in our discussion of inferential statistics.

Figure 6.1 The Proportion of White Respondents in a Population and in a Sample

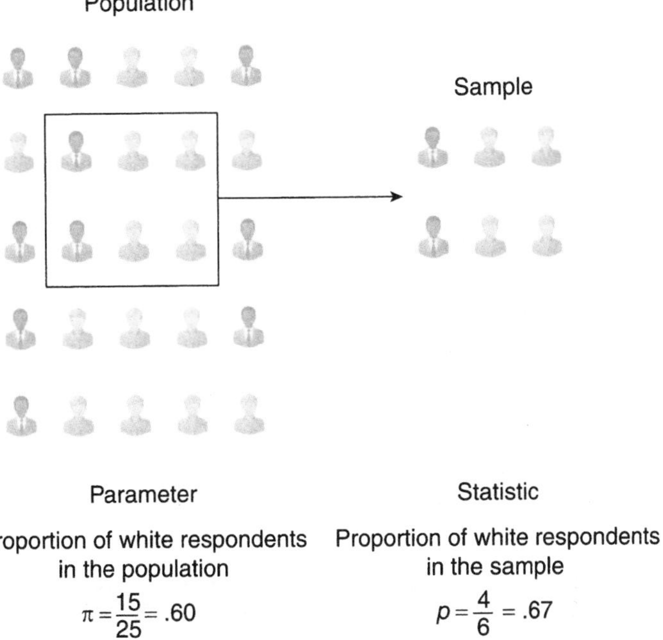

Parameter

Proportion of white respondents in the population

$\pi = \frac{15}{25} = .60$

Statistic

Proportion of white respondents in the sample

$p = \frac{4}{6} = .67$

BASIC PROBABILITY PRINCIPLES

We all use the concept of probability in everyday conversation. You might ask, "What is the probability that it will rain tomorrow?" or "What is the likelihood that I will do well on a test?" In everyday conversations, our answers to these questions are rarely systematic, but in the study of statistics, probability has a far more precise meaning.

In the following sections, we will discuss a variety of techniques adopted by social scientists to select samples from populations. The techniques follow a general approach called probability sampling. Before we discuss these techniques, we will briefly review some theories and principles of probability.

A probability is a quantitative measure that a particular event will occur. It is expressed as a ratio of the number of times an event will occur relative to the set of all possible and equally likely outcomes. Probability is represented by a lower case p.

Probability A quantitative measure that a particular event will occur.

p = Number of times an event will occur/Total number of events

Probabilities range in value from 0 (the event will not occur) to 1 (the event will certainly occur). As first discussed in A Closer Look 5.1, probabilities can be expressed as proportions or percentages. Consider, for example, the outcome of rolling a 3 with a six-sided, equally

Table 6.2 How Often Respondent Uses Media to Get Political News or Information, GSS 2014		
	Frequency	Proportion
Several times a day	96	.26
Once a day	110	.30
5–6 days a week	29	.08
3–4 days a week	20	.05
1–2 days a week	30	.08
Less than 1 day a week	42	.11
Never	40	.11
Total	367	.99

weighted die. The probability of rolling a 3 is 1/6 or 0.17, because this outcome can occur only once out of a total of six possible outcomes: 1, 2, 3, 4, 5, or 6.

$$p\,(\text{rolling a 3}) = 1/6 = .1667 = .17$$

Over many rolls of the die, the chances of rolling a 3 is .17. So for every 100 rolls, a 3 would come up 17 times. The other 83 times we would see the other values of the die. We can also convert the proportion to a percentage (.17 × 100) and conclude that the probability of rolling a 3 is 17%.

Sometimes we use information from past events to help us predict the likelihood of future events. Such a method is called the relative frequency method. Let's consider, for example, a sample of 367 respondents from the 2014 General Social Survey. Respondents were asked how often they use media (including television, newspapers, radio, and the Internet) to get their political news or information; their responses are summarized in Table 6.2.

The ratio of respondents who use the media once a day is 110:367, or when reduced, approximately 1:3. To convert a ratio to a proportion, we divide the numerator (110) by the denominator (367), as shown in Table 6.2. Thus, the probability 110/367 is equivalent to .30. Now, imagine that we wrote down each of the 367 respondents' names and placed them in a hat. Because the proportion of .3 is closer to 0 than it is to 1, there is a low likelihood that we would select a respondent who uses the media once a day to get political news.

LEARNING CHECK 6.2

What is the probability of drawing an ace out of a normal deck of 52 playing cards? It's not 1/52. There are four aces, so the probability is 4/52 or 1/13. The proportion is .08. The probability of drawing the specific ace, like the ace of spades is 1/52 or .02.

The observed relative frequencies are just an approximation of the true probability of identifying how often a respondent uses the media for political news. The true probabilities can only be determined if we were to repeat the study many times under the same conditions. Then, our long-run relative frequency (or probability) will approximate the true probability.

In Chapter 5 ("The Normal Distribution"), we converted the areas under the normal distribution into proportions or percentages of the number of observations in a sample based on standard deviation units from the mean. These proportions make it possible to estimate the probability of occurrence of these observations. For example, a study of 200 teen girls on the prevalence of texting found the average number of messages a teen girl texts per day to be 70 with a standard deviation of 10. We can estimate that the probability of randomly selecting a teen girl who texts between 70 and 80 messages per day is approximately .3413 (based on the definition of the normal distribution discussed in Chapter 5). We can also say that there is a 34.13% chance that any teen girl drawn randomly from the sample of 200 girls would text between 70 and 80 messages per day.

PROBABILITY SAMPLING

Social researchers are systematic in their efforts to obtain samples that are representative of the population. Such researchers have adopted a number of approaches for selecting samples from populations. Only one general approach, probability sampling, allows the researcher to use the principles of statistical inference to generalize from the sample to the population.

Probability sampling is a method that enables the researcher to specify for each case in the population the probability of its inclusion in the sample. The purpose of probability sampling is to select a sample that is as representative as possible of the population. The sample is selected in such a way as to allow the use of the principles of probability to evaluate the generalizations made from the sample to the population. A probability sample design enables the researcher to estimate the extent to which the findings based on one sample are likely to differ from what would be found by studying the entire population.

Probability sampling A method of sampling that enables the researcher to specify for each case in the population the probability of its inclusion in the sample.

Although accurate estimates of sampling error can be made only from probability samples, social scientists often use nonprobability samples because they are more convenient and cheaper to collect. Nonprobability samples are useful under many circumstances for a variety of research purposes. Their main limitation is that they do not allow the use of the method of inferential statistics to generalize from the sample to the population. Because through the rest of this text we deal only with inferential statistics, we will not review nonprobability sampling. In the following sections, we will learn about three sampling designs that follow the principles of probability sampling: (1) the simple random sample, (2) the systematic random sample, and (3) the stratified random sample.[3]

The Simple Random Sample

The simple random sample is the most basic probability sampling design, and it is incorporated into even more elaborate probability sampling designs. A **simple random sample** is a sample design chosen in such a way as to ensure that (a) every member of the population has an equal chance of being chosen and (b) every combination of N members has an equal chance of being chosen.

Simple random sample A sample designed in such a way as to ensure that (a) every member of the population has an equal chance of being chosen and (b) every combination of N members has an equal chance of being chosen.

Let's take a very simple example to illustrate. Suppose we are conducting a cost-containment study of the 10 hospitals in our region, and we want to draw a sample of 2 hospitals to study intensively. We can put into a hat 10 slips of paper, each representing 1 of the 10 hospitals, and mix the slips carefully. We select one slip out of the hat and identify the hospital it represents. We then make the second draw and select another slip out of the hat and identify it. The two hospitals we identified on the two draws become the two members of our sample:

(1) Assuming that we made sure the slips were really well mixed, pure chance determined which hospital was selected on each draw. The sample is a simple random sample because every hospital had the same chance of being selected as a member of our sample of two and (2) every combination of ($N = 2$) hospitals was equally likely to be chosen.

Researchers usually use computer programs or tables of random numbers in selecting random samples. An abridged table of random numbers is reproduced in Appendix A. To use a random number table, list each member of the population and assign the member a number. Begin anywhere on the table and read each digit that appears in the table in order—up, down, or sideways; the direction does not matter, as long as it follows a consistent path. Whenever we come across a digit in the table of random digits that corresponds to the number of a member in the population of interest, that member is selected for the sample. Continue this process until the desired sample size is reached.

Suppose now that, in your job as a hospital administrator, you are planning to conduct a cost-containment study by examining patients' records. Out of a total of 300 patients' records, you want to draw a simple random sample of five. You follow these steps:

1. Number the patient accounts, beginning with 001 for the first account and ending with 300, which represents the 300th account.
2. Use some random process to enter Appendix A (you might close your eyes and point a pencil). For our illustration, let's start with the first column of numbers. Note that each column lists five-digit numbers. Because your population contains only three-digit numbers (001 to 300), drop the last two digits of each number and read only the first three digits in each group of numbers. (Alternatively, you could choose any other group of three-digit numbers in this block—e.g., the last three digits in the block.)
3. Dropping the last two digits of each five-digit block and proceeding down the column, you obtain the following three-digit numbers:

104*	375	963	289*
223*	779	895	635
241*	995	854	094*
421			

Among these numbers, five correspond to numbers within the range of numbers assigned to the patient records. These are marked with asterisk symbols. The last number listed is 094 from Line 13. You do not need to list more numbers because you already have five different numbers that qualify for inclusion in the sample. The asterisked numbers represent the records you will choose for your sample because these are the only ones that fall between 001 and 300, the range you specified. We now have five records in our simple random sample. Let's list them: 104, 223, 241, 289, and 094.

The Systematic Random Sample

Now let's look at a sampling method that is easier to implement than a simple random sample. The systematic random sample, although not a true probability sample, provides results very similar to those obtained with a simple random sample. It uses a ratio, K, obtained by dividing the population size by the desired sample size:

$$K = \frac{\text{Population size}}{\text{Sample size}}$$

Systematic random sampling is a method of sampling in which every Kth member in the total population is chosen for inclusion in the sample after the first member of the sample is selected at random from among the first K members in the population.

> **Systematic random sampling** A method of sampling in which every Kth member (K is a ratio obtained by dividing the population size by the desired sample size) in the total population is chosen for inclusion in the sample after the first member of the sample is selected at random from among the first K members in the population.

Recall our opening example in which we had a population of 15,000 commuting students and our sample was limited to 500. In this example,

$$K = \frac{15{,}000}{500} = 30$$

Using a systematic random sampling method, we first choose any one student at random from among the first 30 students on the list of commuting students. Then, we select every 30th student after that until we reach 500, our desired sample size. Suppose that our first student selected at random happens to be the eighth student on the list. The second student in our sample is then 38th on the list (8 + 30 = 38). The third would be 38 + 30 = 68, the fourth, 68 + 30 = 98, and so on. An example of a systematic random sample is illustrated in Figure 6.2.

LEARNING CHECK 6.3

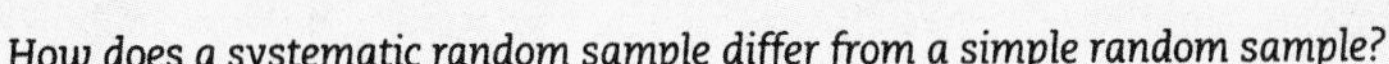

How does a systematic random sample differ from a simple random sample?

Figure 6.2 Systematic Random Sampling

From a population of 40 students, let's select a systematic random sample of 8 students. Our value of K will be 5 (40 ÷ 8 = 5). Using a random number table, we first choose a number between 1 and 5. Let's say we choose 4. We then start with student 4 and pick every 5th student:

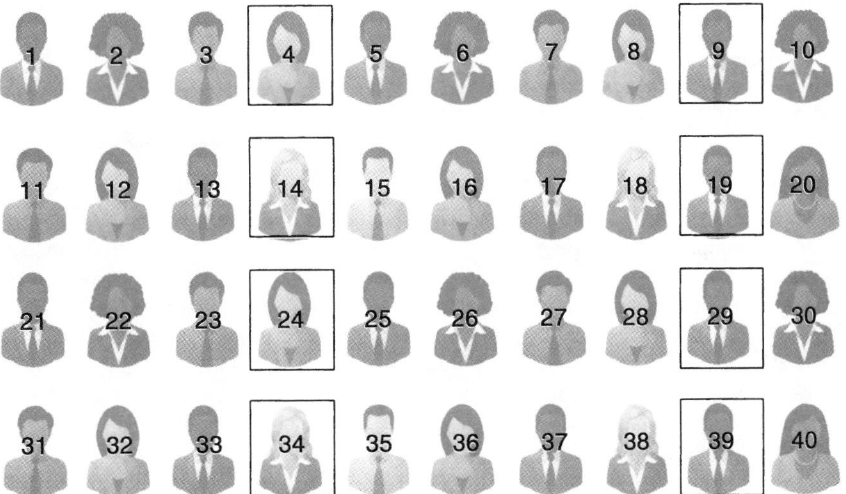

Our trip to the random number table could have just as easily given us a 1 or a 5, so all the students do have a chance to end up in our sample.

The Stratified Random Sample

Stratified random sample A method of sampling obtained by (a) dividing the population into subgroups based on one or more variables central to our analysis and (b) then drawing a simple random sample from each of the subgroups.

Proportionate stratified sample The size of the sample selected from each subgroup is proportional to the size of that subgroup in the entire population.

Disproportionate stratified sample The size of the sample selected from each subgroup is disproportional to the size of the subgroup in the population.

Suppose we want to examine the frequency of media access for political news by race and ethnicity. Our population of interest consists of 1,000 individuals, with 700 (or 70%) whites, 200 (or 20%) blacks, and 100 (10%) Latinos. A third type of probability sampling is the stratified random sample. We obtain a **stratified random sample** by (a) dividing the population into subgroups based on one or more variables central to our analysis and then (b) drawing a simple random sample from each of the subgroups. The choice of subgroups is based on what variables are known and what variables are of interest to us.

For our example, the subgroup we are interested in is race and ethnicity. We could divide the population into different racial/ethnic groups and then draw a simple random sample from each group. In a **proportionate stratified sample**, the size of the sample selected from each subgroup is proportional to the size of that subgroup in the entire population. For a sample of 180 individuals, we would select 126 whites (70%), 36 blacks (20%), and 18 Latinos (10%). Proportional sampling ensures the representation of the subgroup variable.

In a **disproportionate stratified sample**, the size of the sample selected from each subgroup is deliberately made disproportional to the size of that subgroup in the population. For instance, for our example, we could select a sample ($N = 180$) consisting of 90 whites (50%), 45 blacks (25%), and 45 Latinos (25%). In such a sampling design, although the sampling probabilities for each population member are not equal (they vary between groups), they are known, and therefore, we can make accurate estimates of error in the inference process.[4] Disproportionate stratified sampling is especially useful when we want to compare subgroups with each other, and when the size of some of the subgroups in the population is relatively small. Proportionate sampling can result in the sample having too few members from a small subgroup to yield reliable information about them.

LEARNING CHECK 6.4

Can you think of some research questions that could best be studied using a disproportionate stratified random sample? When might it be important to use a proportionate stratified random sample?

THE CONCEPT OF THE SAMPLING DISTRIBUTION

We began this chapter with a few examples illustrating why researchers in the social sciences almost never collect information on the entire population that interests them. Instead, they usually select a sample from that population and use the principles of statistical inference to estimate the characteristics, or parameters, of that population based on the characteristics, or statistics, of the sample. In this section, we describe one of the most important concepts in statistical inference—sampling distribution. The sampling distribution helps estimate the likelihood of our sample statistics and, therefore, enables us to generalize from the sample to the population.

The Population

To illustrate the concept of the sampling distribution, let's consider as our population the 20 individuals listed in Table 6.3.[6] Our variable, Y, is the income (in dollars) of these 20 individuals, and the parameter we are trying to estimate is the mean income.

DISPROPORTIONATE STRATIFIED SAMPLES AND DIVERSITY

Disproportionate stratified sampling is especially useful given the increasing diversity of American society. In a diverse society, factors such as race, ethnicity, class, and gender, as well as other categories of experience such as age, religion, and sexual orientation become central in shaping our experiences and defining the differences among us. These factors are an important dimension of the social structure, and they not only operate independently but also are experienced simultaneously by all of us.[5] For example, if you are a white woman, you may share some common experiences with a woman of color based on your gender, but your racial experiences are going to be different. Moreover, your experiences within the race/gender system are further shaped by your social class. Similarly, if you are a man, your experiences are shaped as much by your class, race, and sexual orientation as they are by your gender. If you are a black gay man, for instance, you might not benefit equally from patriarchy compared with a classmate who is a white heterosexual male.

What are the research implications of an inclusive approach that emphasizes social differences? Such an approach will include women and men in a study of race, Latinos and people of color when considering class, and women and men of color when studying gender. Such an approach makes the experience of previously excluded groups more visible and central because it puts those who have been excluded at the center of the analysis so that we can better understand the experience of all groups, including those with privilege and power.

What are the sampling implications of such an approach? Suppose you are looking at the labor force experiences of black women and Latinas who are above 50 years of age, and you want to compare these experiences with those of white women in the same age group. Both Latinas and black women comprise a small proportion of the population. A proportional sample probably would not include enough Latinas or black women to provide an adequate basis for comparison with white women. To make such comparisons, it would be desirable to draw a disproportionate stratified sample that deliberately overrepresents both Latinas and black women so that these subsamples will be of sufficient size (Figure 6.3).

Figure 6.3 A Random Sample Stratified by Race/Ethnicity

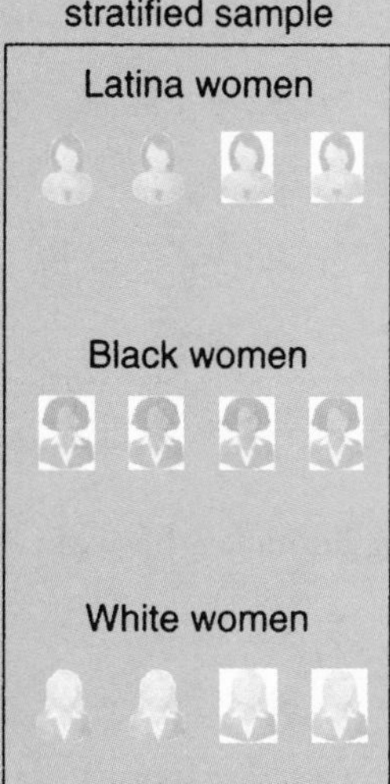

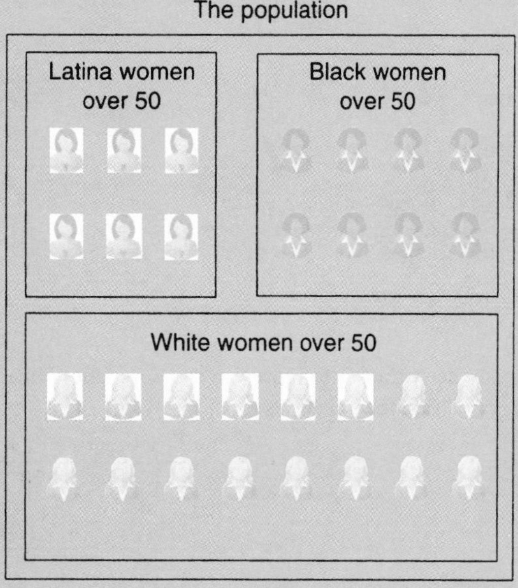

Table 6.3 The Population: Personal Income (in Dollars) for 20 Individuals (Hypothetical Data)

Individual	Income (Y)
Case 1	11,350 (Y_1)
Case 2	7,859 (Y_2)
Case 3	41,654 (Y_3)
Case 4	13,445 (Y_4)
Case 5	17,458 (Y_5)
Case 6	8,451 (Y_6)
Case 7	15,436 (Y_7)
Case 8	18,342 (Y_8)
Case 9	19,354 (Y_9)
Case 10	22,545 (Y_{10})
Case 11	25,345 (Y_{11})
Case 12	68,100 (Y_{12})
Case 13	9,368 (Y_{13})
Case 14	47,567 (Y_{14})
Case 15	18,923 (Y_{15})
Case 16	16,456 (Y_{16})
Case 17	27,654 (Y_{17})
Case 18	16,452 (Y_{18})
Case 19	23,890 (Y_{19})
Case 20	25,671 (Y_{20})
Mean (μ) = 22,766	Standard deviation (σ) = 14,687

We use the symbol μ to represent the population mean. Using Formula 3.1, we can calculate the population mean:

$$\mu = \frac{\Sigma Y}{Y} = \frac{Y_1 + Y_2 + Y_3 + Y_4 + Y_5 + \cdots + Y_{20}}{20}$$

$$= \frac{11,350 + 7,859 + 41,654 + 13,445 + 17,458 + \cdots + 25,671}{20}$$

$$= 22,766$$

Using Formula 4.3, we can also calculate the standard deviation for this population distribution. We use the Greek symbol sigma (σ) to represent the population's standard deviation:

$$\sigma = 14{,}687$$

Of course, most of the time, we do not have access to the population. So instead, we draw one sample, compute the mean—the statistic—for that sample, and use it to estimate the population mean—the parameter.

The Sample

Let's assume that μ is unknown and that we estimate its value by drawing a random sample of three individuals ($N = 3$) from the population of 20 individuals and calculate the mean income for that sample. The incomes included in that sample are as follows:

Case 8	18,342
Case 16	16,456
Case 17	27,654

Now let's calculate the mean for that sample:

$$\bar{Y} = \frac{18{,}342 + 16{,}456 + 27{,}654}{3} = 20{,}817$$

Note that our sample mean, $\bar{Y}$ = \$20,817, differs from the actual population parameter, \$22,766. This discrepancy is due to sampling error. **Sampling error** is the discrepancy between a sample estimate of a population parameter and the real population parameter. By comparing the sample statistic with the population parameter, we can determine the sampling error. The sampling error for our example is 1,949 (22,766 – 20,817 = 1,949).

Sampling error The discrepancy between a sample estimate of a population parameter and the real population parameter.

Now let's select another random sample of three individuals. This time, the incomes included are as follows:

Case 15	18,923
Case 5	17,458
Case 17	27,654

The mean for this sample is

$$\bar{Y} = \frac{18{,}923 + 17{,}458 + 27{,}654}{3} = 21{,}345$$

The sampling error for this sample is 1,421 (22,766 – 21,345 = 1,421), somewhat less than the error for the first sample we selected.

The Dilemma

Although comparing the sample estimates of the average income with the actual population average is a perfect way to evaluate the accuracy of our estimate, in practice, we rarely have information about the actual population parameter. If we did, we would not need to conduct a study! Moreover, few, if any, sample estimates correspond exactly to the actual population parameter. This, then, is our dilemma: If sample estimates vary and if most estimates result in some sort of sampling error, how much confidence can we place in the estimate? On what basis can we infer from the sample to the population?

The Sampling Distribution

Sampling distribution The sampling distribution is a theoretical probability distribution of all possible sample values for the statistics in which we are interested.

The answer to this dilemma is to use a device known as the sampling distribution. The **sampling distribution** is a theoretical probability distribution of all possible sample values for the statistic in which we are interested. If we were to draw all possible random samples of the same size from our population of interest, compute the statistic for each sample, and plot the frequency distribution for that statistic, we would obtain an approximation of the sampling distribution. Every statistic—for example, a proportion, a mean, or a variance—has a sampling distribution. Because it includes all possible sample values, the sampling distribution enables us to compare our sample result with other sample values and determine the likelihood associated with that result.[7]

THE SAMPLING DISTRIBUTION OF THE MEAN

Sampling distributions are theoretical distributions, which means that they are never really observed. Constructing an actual sampling distribution would involve taking all possible random samples of a fixed size from the population. This process would be very tedious because it would involve a very large number of samples. However, to help grasp the concept of the sampling distribution, let's illustrate how one could be generated from a limited number of samples.

An Illustration

Sampling distribution of the mean A theoretical probability distribution of sample means that would be obtained by drawing from the population all possible samples of the same size.

For our illustration, we use one of the most common sampling distributions—the sampling distribution of the mean. The **sampling distribution of the mean** is a theoretical distribution of sample means that would be obtained by drawing from the population all possible samples of the same size.

Let's go back to our example in which our population is made up of 20 individuals and their incomes. From that population (Table 6.3), we now randomly draw 50 possible samples of size 3 ($N = 3$), computing the mean income for each sample and replacing it before drawing another.

In our first sample of $N = 3$, we draw three incomes: \$8,451, \$41,654, and \$18,923. The mean income for this sample is

$$\bar{Y} = \frac{8,451 + 41,654 + 18,923}{3} = 23,009$$

Now we restore these individuals to the original list and select a second sample of three individuals. The mean income for this sample is

$$\bar{Y} = \frac{15,436 + 25,345 + 16,456}{3} = 19,079$$

We repeat this process 48 more times, each time computing the sample mean and restoring the sample to the original list. Table 6.4 lists the means of the first five and the 50th samples of $N = 3$ that were drawn from the population of 20 individuals. (Note that $\Sigma\bar{Y}$ refers to the sum of all the means computed for each of the samples and M refers to the total number of samples that were drawn.)

The grouped frequency distribution for all 50 sample means ($M = 50$) is displayed in Table 6.5; Figure 6.4 is a histogram of this distribution. This distribution is an example of a sampling distribution of the mean. Note that in its structure, the sampling distribution

Table 6.4 Mean Income of 50 Samples of Size 3

Sample	Mean ($\bar{Y}$)
First	23,009
Second	19,079
Third	18,873
Fourth	26,885
Fifth	21,847
⋮	⋮
Fiftieth	26,645
Total (M) = 50	$\Sigma\bar{Y} = 1{,}237{,}482$

resembles a frequency distribution of raw scores, except that here each score is a sample mean, and the corresponding frequencies are the number of samples with that particular mean value. For example, the third interval in Table 6.5 ranges from \$19,500 to \$23,500, with a corresponding frequency of 14, or 28%. This means that we drew 14 samples (28%) with means ranging between \$19,500 and \$23,500.

Remember that the distribution depicted in Table 6.5 and Figure 6.4 is an empirical distribution, whereas the sampling distribution is a theoretical distribution. In reality, we never really

Figure 6.4 Sampling Distribution of Sample Means for Sample Size N = 3 Drawn From the Population of 20 Individuals' Incomes

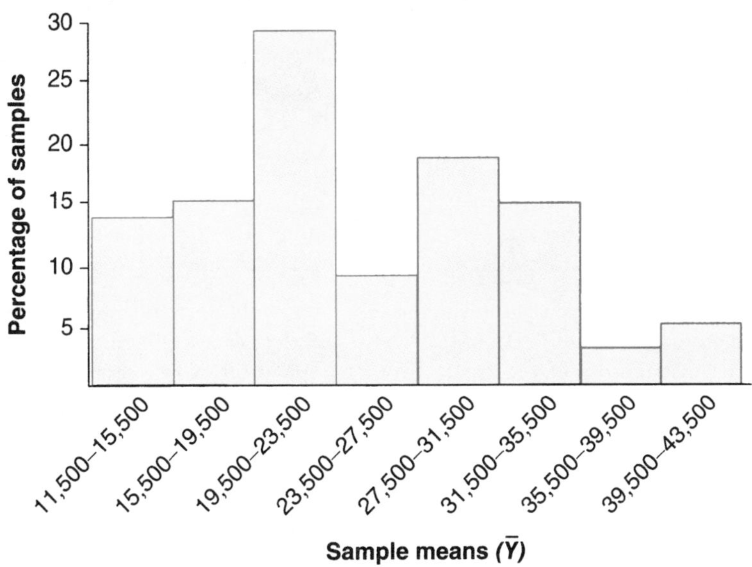

Table 6.5 Sampling Distribution of Sample Means for Sample Size N = 3 Drawn From the Population of 20 Individuals' Incomes

Sample Mean Intervals	Frequency	Percentage
11,500–15,500	6	12
15,500–19,500	7	14
19,500–23,500	14	28
23,500–27,500	4	8
27,500–31,500	9	18
31,500–35,500	7	14
35,500–39,500	1	2
39,500–43,500	2	4
Total (*M*)	50	100

construct a sampling distribution. However, even this simple empirical example serves to illustrate some of the most important characteristics of the sampling distribution.

Review

Before we continue, let's take a moment to review the three distinct types of distribution.

The Population: We began with the population distribution of 20 individuals. This distribution actually exists. It is an empirical distribution that is usually unknown to us. We are interested in estimating the mean income for this population.

The Sample: We drew a sample from that population. The sample distribution is an empirical distribution that is known to us and is used to help us estimate the mean of the population. We selected 50 samples of $N = 3$ and calculated the mean income. We generally use the sample mean ($\bar{Y}$) as an estimate of the population mean (μ).

The Sampling Distribution of the Mean: For illustration, we generated an approximation of the sampling distribution of the mean, consisting of 50 samples of $N = 3$. The sampling distribution of the mean does not really exist. It is a theoretical distribution.

To help you understand the relationship among the population, the sample, and the sampling distribution, we have illustrated in Figure 6.5 the process of generating an empirical sampling distribution of the mean. From a population of raw scores (Ys), we draw M samples of size N and calculate the mean of each sample. The resulting sampling distribution of the mean, based on M samples of size N, shows the values that the mean could take and the frequency (number of samples) associated with each value. Make sure you understand these relationships. The concept of the sampling distribution is crucial to understanding statistical inference. In this and the following chapter, we learn how to

Figure 6.5 Generating the Sampling Distribution of the Mean

From a population (with a population mean of μ) we start drawing samples and calculating the means for those samples:

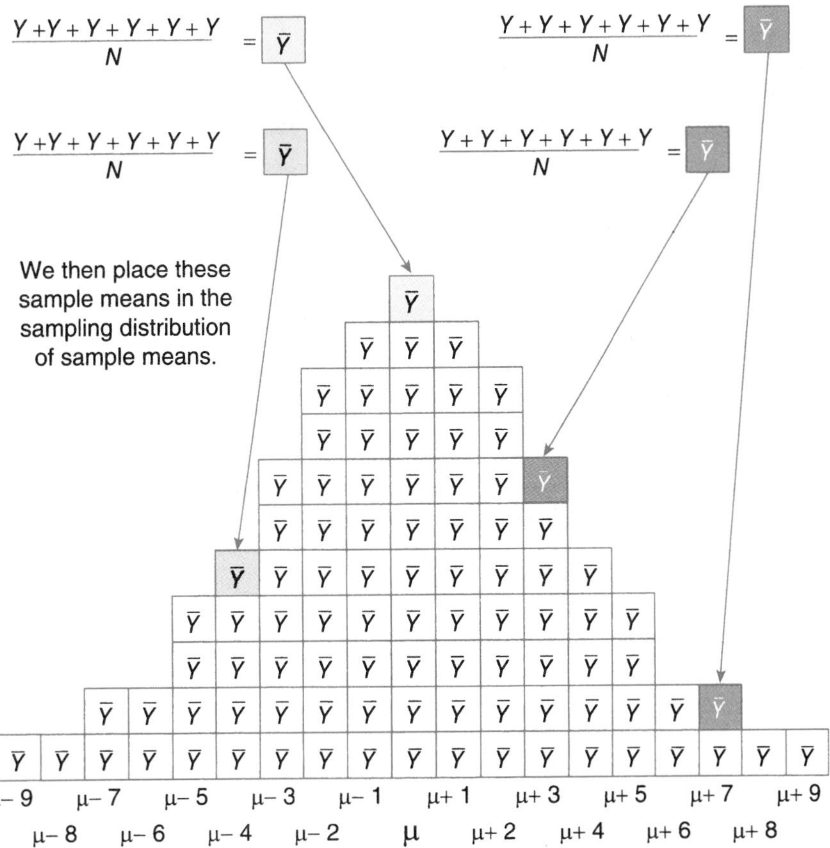

employ the sampling distribution to draw inferences about the population on the basis of sample statistics.

The Mean of the Sampling Distribution

Like the population and sample distributions, the sampling distribution can be described in terms of its mean and standard deviation. We use the symbol $\mu_{\bar{Y}}$ to represent the mean of the sampling distribution. The subscript indicates the specific variable of this sampling distribution. To obtain the mean of the sampling distribution, add all the individual sample means $\left(\Sigma\bar{Y} = 1{,}237{,}482\right)$ and divide by the number of samples (M = 50). Thus, the mean of the sampling distribution of the mean is actually the mean of means:

$$\mu_{\bar{Y}} = \frac{\Sigma\bar{Y}}{M} = \frac{1{,}237{,}482}{50} = 24{,}750$$

The Standard Error of the Mean

Standard error of the mean The standard deviation of the sampling distribution of the mean. It describes how much dispersion there is in the sampling distribution of the mean.

The standard deviation of the sampling distribution is also called the **standard error of the mean**. The standard error of the mean describes how much dispersion there is in the sampling distribution, or how much variability there is in the value of the mean from sample to sample:

$$\sigma_{\bar{Y}} = \frac{\sigma}{\sqrt{N}}$$

This formula tells us that the standard error of the mean is equal to the standard deviation of the population σ divided by the square root of the sample size (N). For our example, because the population standard deviation is 14,687 and our sample size is 3, the standard error of the mean is

$$\sigma_{\bar{Y}} = \frac{14,687}{\sqrt{3}} = 8,480$$

THE CENTRAL LIMIT THEOREM

In Figure 6.6a and b, we compare the histograms for the population and sampling distributions of Tables 6.3 and 6.4. Figure 6.6a shows the population distribution of 20 incomes, with a mean $\mu = 22,766$ and a standard deviation $\sigma = 14,687$. Figure 6.6b shows the sampling distribution of the means from 50 samples of $N = 3$ with a mean $\mu_{\bar{Y}} = 24,750$ and a standard deviation (the standard error of the mean) $\sigma_{\bar{Y}} = 8,480$. These two figures illustrate some of the basic properties of sampling distributions in general and the sampling distribution of the mean in particular.

First, as can be seen from Figure 6.6a and b, the shapes of the two distributions differ considerably. Whereas the population distribution is skewed to the right, the sampling distribution of the mean is less skewed—that is, it is closer to a symmetrical, normal distribution.

Second, whereas only a few of the sample means coincide exactly with the population mean, \$22,766, the sampling distribution centers on this value. The mean of the sampling distribution is a pretty good approximation of the population mean.

In the discussions that follow, we make frequent references to the mean and standard deviation of the three distributions. To distinguish among the different distributions, we use certain conventional symbols to refer to the means and standard deviations of the sample, the population, and the sampling distribution. Note that we use Greek letters to refer to both the sampling and the population distributions.

The Population: We began with the population distribution of 20 individuals. This distribution actually exists. It is an empirical distribution that is usually unknown to us. We are interested in estimating the mean income for this population.

The Sample: We drew a sample from that population. The sample distribution is an empirical distribution that is known to us and is used to help us estimate the mean of the population. We selected 50 samples of $N = 3$ and calculated the mean income. We mostly use the sample mean as an estimate of the population mean μ.

The Sampling Distribution of the Mean: For illustration, we generated an approximation of the sampling distribution of the mean, consisting of 50 samples of $N = 3$. The sampling distribution of the mean does not really exist. It is a theoretical distribution.

Figure 6.6 Three Income Distributions

a. Population distribution of personal income for 20 individuals (hypothetical data)

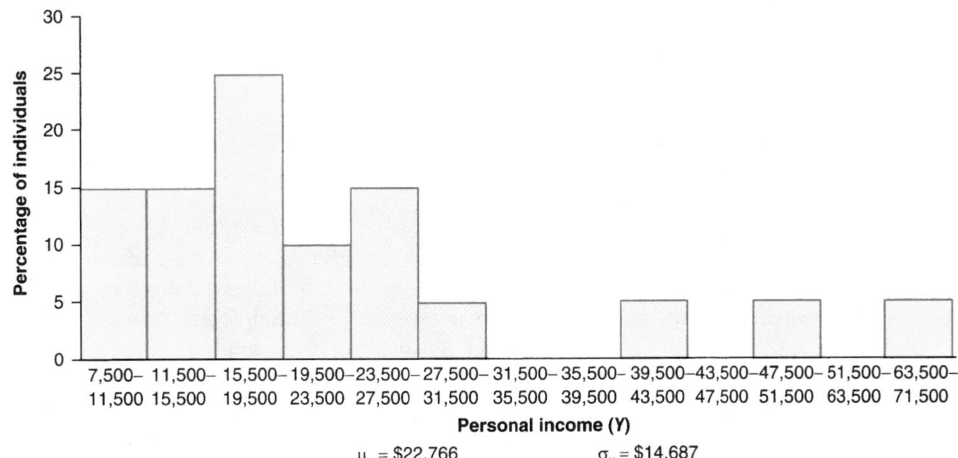

$\mu_Y = \$22{,}766$ $\sigma_Y = \$14{,}687$

b. Sampling distribution of sample means for sample size $N = 3$ drawn from the population of 20 individuals' incomes

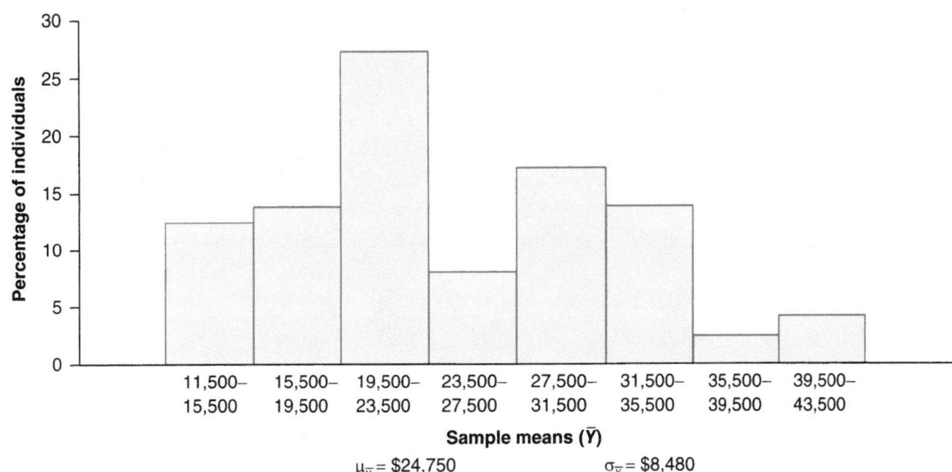

$\mu_{\bar{Y}} = \$24{,}750$ $\sigma_{\bar{Y}} = \$8{,}480$

c. Sampling distribution of sample means for sample size $N = 6$ drawn from the population of 20 individuals' incomes

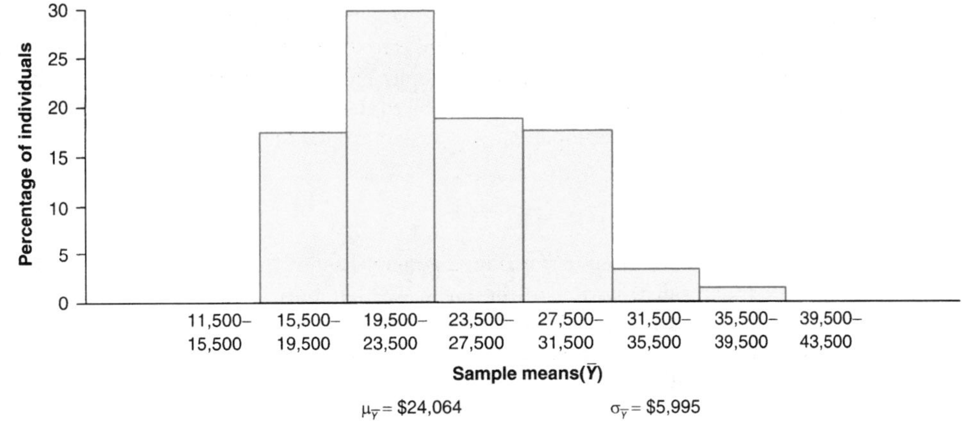

$\mu_{\bar{Y}} = \$24{,}064$ $\sigma_{\bar{Y}} = \$5{,}995$

	Mean	Standard Deviation
Sample distribution	$\bar{Y}$	s
Population distribution	μ	σ
Sampling distribution of the mean	$\mu_{\bar{Y}}$	$\sigma_{\bar{Y}}$

Third, the variability of the sampling distribution is considerably smaller than the variability of the population distribution. Note that the standard deviation for the sampling distribution ($\sigma_{\bar{Y}} = 8,480$) is almost half that for the population ($\sigma = 14,687$).

These properties of the sampling distribution are even more striking as the sample size increases. To illustrate the effect of a larger sample on the shape and properties of the sampling distribution, we went back to our population of 20 individual incomes and drew 50 additional samples of $N = 6$. We calculated the mean for each sample and constructed another sampling distribution. This sampling distribution is shown in Figure 6.6c. It has a mean $\mu_{\bar{Y}} = 24,064$ and a standard deviation $\sigma_{\bar{Y}} = 5,995$. Note that as the sample size increased, the sampling distribution became more compact. This decrease in the variability of the sampling distribution is reflected in a smaller standard deviation: With an increase in sample size from $N = 3$ to $N = 6$, the standard deviation of the sampling distribution decreased from 8,480 to 5,995. Furthermore, with a larger sample size, the sampling distribution of the mean is an even better approximation of the normal curve.

Central limit theorem If all possible random samples of size *N* are drawn from a population with a mean μ and a standard deviation σ, then as *N* becomes larger, the sampling distribution of sample means becomes approximately normal, with mean $\mu_{\bar{Y}}$ equal to the population mean and a standard deviation equal to

$$\sigma_{\bar{Y}} = \frac{\sigma}{\sqrt{N}}$$

These properties of the sampling distribution of the mean are summarized more systematically in one of the most important statistical principles underlying statistical inference. It is called the **central limit theorem**, and it states that if all possible random samples of size N are drawn from a population with a mean μ and a standard deviation σ, then as N becomes larger, the sampling distribution of sample means becomes approximately normal, with mean $\mu_{\bar{Y}}$ equal to the population mean and a standard deviation equal to

$$\sigma_{\bar{Y}} = \frac{\sigma}{\sqrt{N}}$$

The significance of the central limit theorem is that it tells us that with a sufficient sample size the sampling distribution of the mean will be normal regardless of the shape of the population distribution. Therefore, even when the population distribution is skewed, we can still assume that the sampling distribution of the mean is normal, given random samples of large enough size. Furthermore, the central limit theorem also assures us that (a) as the sample size gets larger, the mean of the sampling distribution becomes equal to the population mean and (b) as the sample size gets larger, the standard error of the mean (the standard deviation of the sampling distribution of the mean) decreases in size. The standard error of the mean tells how much variability in the sample estimates there is from sample to sample. The smaller the standard error of the mean, the closer (on average) the sample means will be to the population mean. Thus, the larger the sample, the more closely the sample statistic clusters around the population parameter.

The Size of the Sample

Although there is no hard-and-fast rule, a general rule of thumb is that when N is 50 or more, the sampling distribution of the mean will be approximately normal regardless of the shape of the distribution. However, we can assume that the sampling distribution will be normal even with samples as small as 30 if we know that the population distribution approximates normality.

LEARNING CHECK 6.5

What is a normal population distribution? If you can't answer this question, go back to Chapter 5. You must understand the concept of a normal distribution before you can understand the techniques involved in inferential statistics.

The Significance of the Sampling Distribution and the Central Limit Theorem

In the preceding sections, we have covered a lot of abstract material. You may have a number of questions at this time. Why is the concept of the sampling distribution so important? What is the significance of the central limit theorem? To answer these questions, let's go back and review our 20 incomes example.

To estimate the mean income of a population of 20 individuals, we drew a sample of three cases and calculated the mean income for that sample. Our first sample mean, $\bar{Y} = 20{,}817$, differs from the actual population parameter, $\mu = 22{,}766$. When we selected different samples, we found each time that the sample mean differed from the population mean. These discrepancies are due to sampling errors. Had we taken a number of additional samples, we probably would have found that the mean was different each time because every sample differs slightly. Few, if any, sample means would correspond exactly to the actual population mean. Usually we have only one sample statistic as our best estimate of the population parameter.

So now let's restate our dilemma: If sample estimates vary and if most result in some sort of sampling error, how much confidence can we place in the estimate? On what basis can we infer from the sample to the population?

The solution lies in the sampling distribution and its properties. Because the sampling distribution is a theoretical distribution that includes all possible sample outcomes, we can compare our sample outcome with it and estimate the likelihood of its occurrence.

Since the sampling distribution is theoretical, how can we know its shape and properties so that we can make these comparisons? Our knowledge is based on what the central limit theorem tells us about the properties of the sampling distribution of the mean. We know that if our sample size is large enough (at least 50 cases), most sample means will be quite close to the true population mean. It is highly unlikely that our sample mean would deviate much from the actual population mean.

In Chapter 5, we saw that in all normal curves, a constant proportion of the area under the curve lies between the mean and any given distance from the mean when measured in standard deviation units, or Z scores. We can find this proportion in the standard normal table (Appendix B).

Knowing that the sampling distribution of the means is approximately normal, with a mean $\mu_{\bar{Y}}$ and a standard deviation $\sigma / \sqrt{N}$ (the standard error of the mean), we can use Appendix B to determine the probability that a sample mean will fall within a certain distance—measured in standard deviation units, or Z scores—of $\mu_{\bar{Y}}$ or μ. For example, we can expect approximately 68% (or we can say the probability is approximately 0.68) of all sample means to fall within ±1 standard error $\left(\sigma / \sqrt{N}\right)$, or the standard deviation of the sampling distribution of the mean of $\mu_{\bar{Y}}$ or μ. Similarly, the probability is about 0.95 that the sample mean will fall within ±2 standard errors of $\mu_{\bar{Y}}$ or μ. In the next chapter, we will see how this information helps us evaluate the accuracy of our sample estimates.

LEARNING CHECK 6.6

Suppose a population distribution has a mean $\mu = 150$ and a standard deviation $s = 30$, and you draw a simple random sample of $N = 100$ cases. What is the probability that the mean is between 147 and 153? What is the probability that the sample mean exceeds 153? Would you be surprised to find a mean score of 159? Why? (Hint: To answer these questions, you need to apply what you learned in Chapter 5 about Z scores and areas under the normal curve [Appendix B].) To translate a raw score into a Z score we used this formula:

$$Z = \frac{Y - \bar{Y}}{s}$$

However, because here we are dealing with a sampling distribution, replace Y with the sample mean $\bar{Y}$, $\bar{Y}$ with the sampling distribution's mean $\mu_{\bar{Y}}$, and σ with the standard error of the mean.

$$Z = \frac{\bar{Y} - \mu_{\bar{Y}}}{\sigma / \sqrt{N}}$$

STATISTICS IN PRACTICE: A SAMPLING LESSON

There are numerous applications of the central limit theorem in research, business, medicine, and popular media. As varied as these applications may be, what they have in common is that the data are derived from relatively small random samples taken from considerably larger and often varied populations. And the data have consequence—informing our understanding of the social world, influencing decisions, shaping social policy, and predicting social behavior.

In November 6, 2012, Barack Obama was reelected president of the United States with 49% of the vote. Governor Mitt Romney, the Republican candidate, received 46% of the votes. Weeks before the election took place, several surveys correctly predicted an Obama victory within 2 or 3 percentage points of the actual result. These predictions were based on interviews conducted with samples no larger than about 2,000 registered voters. What is astounding about these surveys is that their predictions were based on a single, smaller sample of the voting population.

But not all election polls predicted an Obama victory. Romney and his campaign staff believed that he would win the election as the campaign's internal polling showed Romney leading in several key and swing states. Days before the election, their survey results indicated that Romney was 2.5 points ahead of Obama in Colorado. In the end, the Republican candidate lost the state by 5.4 points. After the election, the campaign's chief pollster, Neil Newhouse, admitted that the biggest flaw of their polling was "the failure to predict the demographic composition of the electorate." As described by Norm Scheiber (2012), "The people who showed up to vote on November 6 were younger and less white than Team Romney anticipated, and far more Democratic as a result."[8]

Romney campaign pollsters were not the only ones who erred. Throughout the presidential campaign, the Gallup Poll consistently reported a lead by the Republican candidate. The day before the election, Gallup's final preelection survey gave Romney a one-point lead over Obama, 49% versus 48%. After a postelection assessment, Gallup identified four factors that contributed to the difference between its estimates and the final election results. Though part of Gallup's prediction problem involved the mathematical weighting of

Emily Treichler: Postdoctoral Fellow

Photo courtesy of Emily Treichler

As an undergraduate, Dr. Treichler wanted to figure out a way to make mental health treatment more effective and more accessible. Having completed her Ph.D., currently she is postdoctoral fellow conducting research on schizophrenia and other related disorders in a VA hospital. "I divide my time between research, clinical work, and other kinds of training, including learning new methods. I conduct research in clinical settings working with people who are experiencing mental health problems, and use the results of my research and other research literature to try to improve mental health treatment."

"I use statistics and methods constantly. I read research literature in order to learn more about my area, to apply in clinical situations, and to apply it to my own research. I conduct clinical research, using both qualitative and quantitative methodology, and conducting statistics on quantitative data. I collect data in settings I work as a clinician and conduct statistics on that data in order to understand how our services are working, and how to improve clinical services."

According to Treichler, "Quantitative research can be an incredibly fun area." For students interested in the field, she advises, "Get a wide range of training in statistics and methods so you can understand the literature in your area, and have access to multiple methods for your own studies. Choosing appropriate methods and statistics given your research question and the literature in your area is key to creating a successful project."

DATA AT WORK

responses (not the focus of our discussion), Gallup admitted to serious sampling missteps. The organization reported that it (a) overestimated the number of voters most likely to vote for Romney, (b) completed more interviews in pro-Romney geographic regions, (c) sampled too many white voters while undersampling Hispanic and black voters, and (d) relied on a listed landline sample that included older and more Republican voters.[9]

The Romney campaign and Gallup's presidential polling failures help underscore the value of representative samples. Since most social science research is based on sample data, it is imperative that our samples accurately reflect the populations we're interested in. If not, we won't be able to make appropriate and meaningful inferences about the population, the primary goal of inferential statistics.

Gallup implemented new sampling and calling procedures to improve its polling. So it was a surprise when Gallup Editor-in-Chief Frank Newport announced in late 2015 that the organization would not conduct any polling for the 2016 presidential primary or general election. According to Newport, Gallup would still conduct polls about broader social and political issues.

MAIN POINTS

- Through the process of sampling, researchers attempt to generalize the characteristics of a large group (the population) from a subset (sample) selected from that group. The term parameter, associated with the population, refers to the information we are interested in finding out. Statistic refers to a corresponding calculated sample statistic.
- A probability sample design allows us to estimate the extent to which the findings based on one sample are likely to differ from what we would find by studying the entire population.
- A simple random sample is chosen in such a way as to ensure that every member of the population and every combination of N members have an equal chance of being chosen.
- In systematic sampling, every Kth member in the total population is chosen for inclusion in the sample after the first member of the sample is selected at random from the first K members in the population.
- A stratified random sample is obtained by (a) dividing the population into subgroups based on one or more variables central to our analysis and (b) then drawing a simple random sample from each of the subgroups.
- The sampling distribution is a theoretical probability distribution of all possible sample values for the statistic in which we are interested. The sampling distribution of the mean is a frequency distribution of all possible sample means of the same size that can be drawn from the population of interest.
- According to the central limit theorem, if all possible random samples of size N are drawn from a population with a mean μ and a standard deviation σ, then as N becomes larger, the sampling distribution of sample means becomes approximately normal, with mean μ and standard deviation $\sigma / \sqrt{N}$.
- The central limit theorem tells us that with sufficient sample size, the sampling distribution of the mean will be normal regardless of the shape of the population distribution. Therefore, even when the population distribution is skewed, we can still assume that the sampling distribution of the mean is normal, given a large enough randomly selected sample size.

KEY TERMS

central limit theorem 168
disproportionate stratified sample 158
parameter 152
population 151
probability 153
probability sampling 155
proportionate stratified sample 158
sample 152
sampling 152
sampling distribution 162
sampling distribution of the mean 162
sampling error 161
simple random sample 155
standard error of the mean 166
statistic 152
stratified random sample 158
systematic random sampling 157

DIGITAL RESOURCES

Get the edge on your studies. **edge.sagepub.com/frankfort8e**

Take a quiz to find out what you've learned.
Review key terms with eFlashcards.
Dive into real research with SAGE Journal Articles.

SPSS DEMONSTRATION [GSS14SSDS-B]

Selecting a Random Sample

In this chapter, we've discussed various types of samples and the definition of the standard error of the mean. Usually, data entered into SPSS have already been sampled from some larger population. However, SPSS does have a sampling procedure that can take random samples of data. Systematic samples and stratified samples can also be drawn with SPSS, but they require the use of the SPSS command language.

When might it be worthwhile to use the SPSS Sample procedure? One instance is when doing preliminary analysis of a very large data set. For example, if you worked for your local hospital and had complete data records for all patients (tens of thousands), there would be no need to use *all* the data during initial analysis. You could select a random sample of individuals and use the subset of data for preliminary analysis. Later, the complete patient data set could be used for completing your final analyses.

To use the Sample procedure, click on *Data* from the main menu, then click on *Select Cases.* The opening dialog box (Figure 6.7) has five choices that will select a subset of cases via various

Figure 6.7 Select Cases Dialog Box

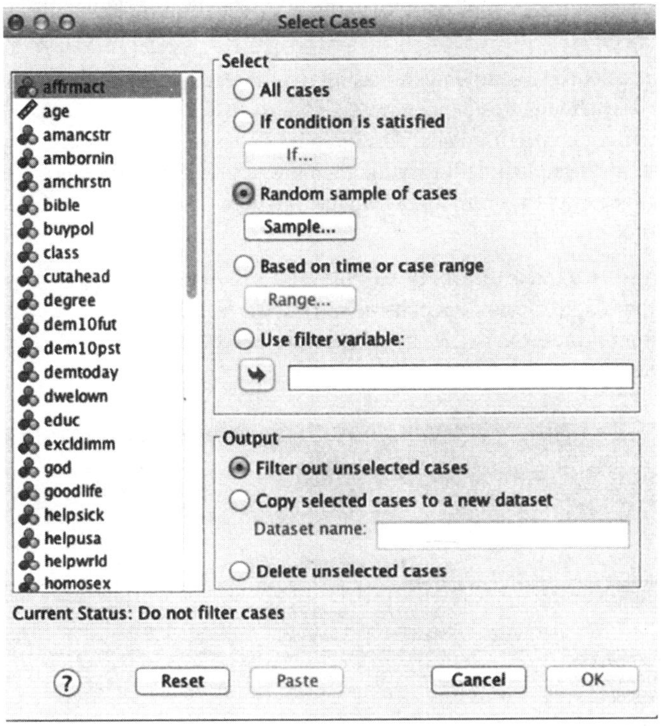

Figure 6.8 Specifying Sample Size When Selecting Cases

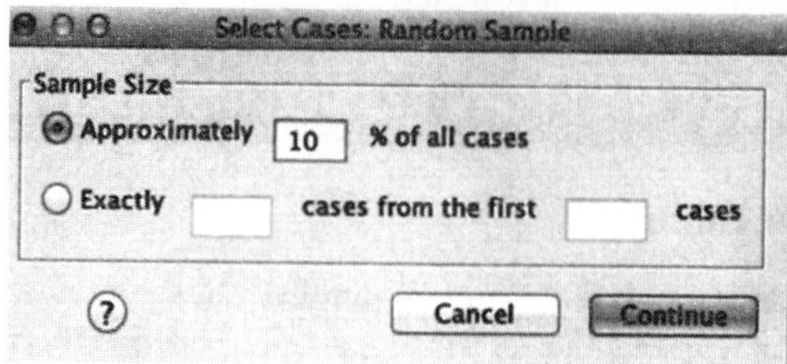

methods. By default, the *All cases* button is checked. We click on the *Random sample of cases* button, then on the *Sample* button to give SPSS our specification.

The next dialog box (Figure 6.8) provides two options to create a random sample. The most convenient one is the first, where we tell SPSS what percentage of cases to select from the larger file. Alternatively, we can tell SPSS to take an exact number of cases. The second option is available because SPSS will only take approximately the percentage specified in the first option.

We type "10" in the box to ask for 10% of the original sample of 1,500 respondents from the GSS. Then, click on *Continue* and *OK*, as usual, to process the request.

SPSS does not delete the cases from the active data file that aren't selected for the sample. Instead, they are filtered out (you can identify them in the Data View window by the slash across their row number). This means that we can always return to the full data file by going back to the Select Cases dialog box and selecting the *All cases* button.

When SPSS processes our request, it tells us that the data have been filtered by putting the words "Filter On" in the status area at the bottom of the SPSS window (the status area has many helpful messages from SPSS).

To demonstrate the effect of sampling, we ask for univariate statistics for the variable HRS1, measuring the number of hours a respondent worked last week. Click on *Analyze, Descriptive Statistics,* and then *Descriptives* to open this dialog box. Place HRS1 in the variable list. Click on the *Options* button to select the mean, standard deviation, minimum, and maximum values. In addition, we'll add the standard error of the mean by clicking the *S.E. mean* box. Then, click *Continue* and *OK* to put SPSS to work.

The results (Figure 6.9) show that the number of valid cases is exactly 87, or 10% of the valid cases (those who responded to the number of hours worked last week). The mean of HRS1 is 42.38, and the standard error of the mean is 1.78. If we repeat the process, this time asking for a 25% sample, we obtain the results shown in Figure 6.10.

Figure 6.9 Descriptive Statistics for Number of Hours Worked Last Week, 10% Sample

Descriptive Statistics

	N	Minimum	Maximum	Mean		Std. Deviation
	Statistic	Statistic	Statistic	Statistic	Std. Error	Statistic
hrs1 NUMBER OF HOURS WORKED LAST WEEK	87	1	81	42.38	1.780	16.599
Valid N (listwise)	87					

Figure 6.10 Descriptive Statistics for Number of Hours Worked Last Week, 25% Sample

Descriptive Statistics

	N	Minimum	Maximum	Mean		Std. Deviation
	Statistic	Statistic	Statistic	Statistic	Std. Error	Statistic
hrs1 NUMBER OF HOURS WORKED LAST WEEK	200	4	89	40.82	1.070	15.131
Valid N (listwise)	200					

Your results may differ from the results presented here. We are asking SPSS to generate a random selection of cases, and you may not get the same selection of cases as we did.

How closely does the mean for HRS1 from these two random samples match that of the full file? The mean for all 895 respondents (the other 605 respondents did not have valid responses) is 41.47 years. Both samples produced means and standard deviations that are within the range of the population parameters.

SPSS PROBLEMS [GSS14SSDS-B]

Using GSS14SSDS-B, repeat the SPSS demonstration, selecting 25%, 50%, 75%, and 100% samples and requesting descriptives for MAEDUC and PAEDUC. Compare your descriptive statistics with descriptives for the entire sample. What can you say about the accuracy of your random samples?

CHAPTER EXERCISES

1. Explain which of the following is a statistic and which is a parameter.
   a. The mean age of Americans from the 2010 decennial census
   b. The unemployment rate for the population of U.S. adults, estimated by the government from a large sample
   c. The percentage of Texans opposed to the health care reform bill from a poll of 1,000 residents
   d. The mean salaries of employees at your school (e.g., administrators, faculty, maintenance)
   e. The percentage of students at your school who receive financial aid
2. The mayor of your city has been talking about the need for a tax hike. The city's newspaper uses letters sent to the editor to judge public opinion about this possible hike, reporting on their results in an article.
   a. Do you think that these letters represent a random sample? Why or why not?
   b. What alternative sampling method would you recommend to the mayor?
3. The following four common situation scenarios involve selecting a sample and understanding how a sample relates to a population.
   a. A friend interviews every 10th shopper who passes by her as she stands outside one entrance of a major department store in a shopping mall. What type of sample is she selecting? How might you define the population from which she is selecting the sample?

b. A political polling firm samples 50 potential voters from a list of registered voters in each county in a state to interview for an upcoming election. What type of sample is this? Do you have enough information to tell?

c. Another political polling firm in the same state selects potential voters from the same list of registered voters with a very different method. First, they alphabetize the list of last names, then pick the first 20 names that begin with an A, the first 20 that begin with a B, and so on until Z (the sample size is thus 20 × 26, or 520). Is this a probability sample?

d. A social scientist gathers a carefully chosen group of 20 people whom she has selected to represent a broad cross-section of the population in New York City. She interviews them in depth for a study she is doing on race relations in the city. Is this a probability sample?

4. An upper-level sociology class has 120 registered students: 34 seniors, 57 juniors, 22 sophomores, and 7 freshmen.

   a. Imagine that you choose one random student from the classroom (perhaps by using a random number table). What is the probability that the student will be a junior?

   b. What is the probability that the student will be a freshman?

   c. If you are asked to select a proportionate stratified sample of size 30 from the classroom, stratified by class level (senior, junior, etc.), how many students from each group will there be in the sample?

   d. If instead you are to select a disproportionate sample of size 20 from the classroom, with equal numbers of students from each class level in the sample, how many freshmen will there be in the sample?

5. Can the standard error of a variable ever be larger than, or even equal in size to, the standard deviation for the same variable? Justify your answer by means of both a formula and a discussion of the relationship between these two concepts.

6. When taking a random sample from a very large population, how does the standard error of the mean change when

   a. the sample size is increased from 100 to 1,600?

   b. the sample size is decreased from 300 to 150?

   c. the sample size is multiplied by 4?

7. Many television news shows conduct "instant" polls by providing an 800 number and asking an interesting question of the day for viewers to call and answer.

   a. Is this poll a probability sample? Why or why not?

   b. Specify the population from which the sample of calls is drawn.

8. The following table shows the number of active military personnel in 2009, by region (including the District of Columbia).

Pacific	229,634	Mountain	89,816	West South Central	177,336
West North Central	64,564	East North Central	26,384	East South Central	68,440
South Atlantic	376,034	Middle Atlantic	41,441	New England	8,579

Source: U.S. Census Bureau, *Statistical Abstract of the United States: 2012*, Table 508 (data) and U.S. Census Bureau, Census Regions and Divisions of the United States (regions).

a. Calculate the mean and standard deviation for the population.

b. Now take 10 samples of size 3 from the population. Use either simple random sampling or systematic sampling with the help of the table of random numbers in Appendix A. Calculate the mean for each sample.

c. Once you have calculated the mean for each sample, calculate the mean of means (i.e., add up your 10 sample means and divide by 10). How does this mean compare with the mean for all states?

d. How does the value of the standard deviation that you calculated in Exercise 8a compare with the value of the standard error (i.e., the standard deviation of the sampling distribution)?

e. Construct two histograms, one for the distribution of values in the population and the other for the various sample means taken from Exercise 8b. Describe and explain any differences you observe between the two distributions.

f. It is important that you have a clear sense of the population that we are working with in this exercise. What is the population?

9. You've been asked to determine the percentage of students who would support gay marriage. You want to take a random sample of fellow students to make the estimate. Explain whether each of the following scenarios describes a random sample.

   a. You ask all students eating lunch in the cafeteria on a Tuesday at 12:30 p.m.

   b. You ask every 10th student from the list of enrolled students.

   c. You ask every 10th student passing by the student union.

   d. What sampling procedure would you recommend to complete your study?

10. Imagine that you are working with a total population of 21,473 respondents. You assign each respondent a value from 0 to 21,473 and proceed to select your sample using the random number table in Appendix A. Starting at Column 7, Line 1 in Appendix A and going down, which are the first five respondents that will be included in your sample?

11. A small population of $N = 10$ has values of 4, 7, 2, 11, 5, 3, 4, 6, 10, and 1.

    a. Calculate the mean and standard deviation for the population.

    b. Take 10 simple random samples of size 3, and calculate the mean for each.

    c. Calculate the mean and standard deviation of all these sample means. How closely does the mean of all sample means match the population mean? How is the standard deviation of the means related to the standard deviation for the population?

12. The following table presents the number of parolees (per 100,000 people) for 12 of the most populous states as of July 2015.

State	Parolees (per 100,000 People)
California	292
Texas	556
New York	288
Florida	28

(Continued)

(Continued)

State	Parolees (per 100,000 People)
Illinois	299
Pennsylvania	1,035
Ohio	193
Georgia	334
Michigan	239
North Carolina	130
New Jersey	214
Virginia	27

Source: National Institute of Corrections, Correction Statistics by State, 2016.

a. Assume that $\sigma = 226.83$ for the entire population of 50 states. Calculate and interpret the standard error. (Consider the formula for the standard error. Since we provided the population standard deviation, calculating the standard error requires only minor calculations.)

b. Write a brief statement on the following: the standard error compared with the standard deviation of the population, the shape of the sampling distribution, and suggestions for reducing the standard error.

7

ESTIMATION

Chapter Learning Objectives

1. Explain the concepts of estimation, point estimates, confidence level, and confidence interval
2. Calculate and interpret confidence intervals for means
3. Describe the concept of risk and how to reduce it
4. Calculate and interpret confidence intervals for proportions

In this chapter, we discuss the procedures involved in estimating population means and proportions based on the principles of sampling and statistical inference discussed in Chapter 6 ("Sampling and Sampling Distributions"). Knowledge about the sampling distribution allows us to estimate population means and proportions from sample outcomes and to assess the accuracy of these estimates. Consider three examples of information derived from samples.

Example 1: Based on a random sample of 1,019 U.S. adults, a March 2016 Gallup poll found that the percentage of Americans who identify as environmentalists has decreased. Compared with the 1991 high of 78%, in 2016 only 42% of Americans self-identified as environmentalists. In its report, Gallup attributed the decline to several factors, including the adoption of routine environmental friendly practices and the politicization of environmental issues.[1]

Example 2: Every other year, the National Opinion Research Center conducts the General Social Survey (GSS) on a representative sample of about 1,500 respondents. The GSS, from which many of the examples in this book are selected, is designed to provide social science researchers with a readily accessible database of socially relevant attitudes, behaviors, and attributes of a cross-section of the U.S. adult population. For example, in analyzing the responses to the 2014 GSS, researchers found that the average respondent's education was about 13.77 years. This average probably differs from the average of the population from which the GSS sample was drawn. However, we can establish that in most cases the sample mean (in this case, 13.77 years) is fairly close to the actual true average in the population.

Example 3: In 2016, North Carolina legislators passed House Bill 2, prohibiting transgender people from using bathrooms and locker rooms that do not match the gender on their birth certificate. The law quickly drew protests from civil rights and LGBT (lesbian, gay, bisexual, transgender) rights groups. A CNN/ORC poll of 1,001 Americans revealed that 39% of those surveyed strongly oppose laws that require transgender individuals to use restroom facilities that correspond on their gender at birth rather than their gender identity. Seventy-five percent favor laws guaranteeing equal protection for transgender people in jobs, housing, and public accomodations.[2]

The percentage of Americans who identify as environmentalists as approximated by the Gallup organization, the average level of education in the United States as calculated from the GSS, and the percentage of Americans who oppose laws requiring transgender people to use bathrooms that correspond to their gender at birth based on the CNN/ORC poll are all sample estimates of population parameters. Population parameters are the actual percentage of Americans who identify as environmentalists or the actual average level of education in the United States. The 39% who oppose laws that require transgender individuals to use restrooms that correspond to their birth gender can be used to estimate the actual percentage of all Americans who oppose such laws.

Estimation A process whereby we select a random sample from a population and use a sample statistic to estimate a population parameter.

These are illustrations of estimation. **Estimation** is a process whereby we select a random sample from a population and use a sample statistic to estimate a population parameter. We can use sample proportions as estimates of population proportions, sample means as estimates of population means, or sample variances as estimates of population variances.

Why estimate? The goal of most research is to find the population parameter. Yet we hardly ever have enough resources to collect information about the entire population. We rarely know the actual value of the population parameter. On the other hand, we can learn a lot about a population by randomly selecting a sample from that population and obtaining an estimate of the population parameter. The major objective of sampling theory and statistical inference is to provide estimates of unknown population parameters from sample statistics.

Point and Interval Estimation

Point estimate A sample statistic used to estimate the exact value of a population parameter.

Confidence interval (CI) A range of values defined by the confidence level within which the population parameter is estimated to fall. A confidence interval may also be referred to as a margin of error.

Confidence level The likelihood, expressed as a percentage or a probability, that a specified interval will contain the population parameter.

Estimates of population characteristics can be divided into two types: (1) point estimates and (2) interval estimates. **Point estimates** are sample statistics used to estimate the exact value of a population parameter. When the Gallup organization reports that 42% of Americans identify as environmentalists, they are using a point estimate. Similarly, if we reported the average level of education of the population of adult Americans to be exactly 13.77 years, we would be using a point estimate.

The problem with point estimates is that sample statistics vary, usually resulting in some sort of sampling error. Thus, we never really know how accurate they are. As a result we rarely rely on them as estimators of population parameters such as average income or percentage of the population who are in favor of gay and lesbian relations.

One method of increasing accuracy is to use an interval estimate rather than a point estimate. In interval estimation, we identify a range of values within which the population parameter may fall. This range of values is called a **confidence interval (CI)**. Instead of using a single value, 13.77 years, as an estimate of the mean education of adult Americans, we could say that the population mean is somewhere between 12 and 14 years.

When we use confidence intervals to estimate population parameters, such as mean educational levels, we can also evaluate the accuracy of this estimate by assessing the likelihood that any given interval will contain the mean. This likelihood, expressed as a percentage or a probability, is called a **confidence level**. Confidence intervals are defined in terms of confidence levels. Thus, by selecting a 95% confidence level, we are saying that there is a .95 probability—or 95 chances out of 100—that a specified interval will contain the population mean. Confidence intervals can be constructed for any level of confidence, but the most common ones are the 90%, 95%, and 99% levels. You should also know that confidence intervals are sometimes referred to in terms of **margin of error**. In short, margin of error is simply the radius of a confidence interval. If we select a 95% confidence level, we would have a 5% chance of our interval being incorrect.

Margin of error The radius of a confidence interval.

Confidence intervals can be constructed for many different parameters based on their corresponding sample statistics. In this chapter, we describe the rationale and the procedure for the construction of confidence intervals for means and proportions.

LEARNING CHECK 7.1

What is the difference between a point estimate and a confidence interval?

CONFIDENCE INTERVALS FOR MEANS

To illustrate the procedure for establishing confidence intervals for means, we'll reintroduce one of the research examples mentioned in Chapter 6—assessing the needs of commuter students.

Recall that we have been given enough money to survey a random sample of 500 students. One of our tasks is to estimate the average commuting time of all 15,000 commuters on our campus—the population parameter. To obtain this estimate, we calculate the average commuting time for the sample. Suppose the sample average is $\bar{Y} = 7.5 \text{ hours / week}$, and we want to use it as an estimate of the true average commuting time for the entire population of commuting students.

Because it is based on a sample, this estimate is subject to sampling error. We do not know how close it is to the true population mean. However, based on what the central limit theorem tells us about the properties of the sampling distribution of the mean, we know that with a large enough sample size, most sample means will tend to be close to the true population mean. Therefore, it is unlikely that our sample mean, $\bar{Y} = 7.5 \text{ hours / week}$, deviates much from the true population mean.

We know that the sampling distribution of the mean is approximately normal with a mean equal to the population mean μ and a standard error $\sigma_{\bar{Y}}$ (standard deviation of the sampling distribution) as follows:

$$\sigma_{\bar{Y}} = \frac{\sigma}{\sqrt{N}} \tag{7.1}$$

This information allows us to use the normal distribution to determine the probability that a sample mean will fall within a certain distance—measured in standard deviation (standard error) units or Z scores—of μ or $\mu_{\bar{Y}}$. We can make the following assumptions:

- A total of 68% of all random sample means will fall within ±1 standard error of the true population mean.
- A total of 95% of all random sample means will fall within ±1.96 standard errors of the true population mean.
- A total of 99% of all random sample means will fall within ±2.58 standard errors of the true population mean.

A CLOSER LOOK 7.1

ESTIMATION AS A TYPE OF INFERENCE

Using inferential statistics, a researcher is able to describe a population based entirely on information from a sample of that population. A confidence interval is an example of this—by knowing a sample mean, sample size, and sample standard deviation, we are able to say something about the population from which that sample was drawn.

Combining this information gives us a range within which we can confidently say that the population mean falls.

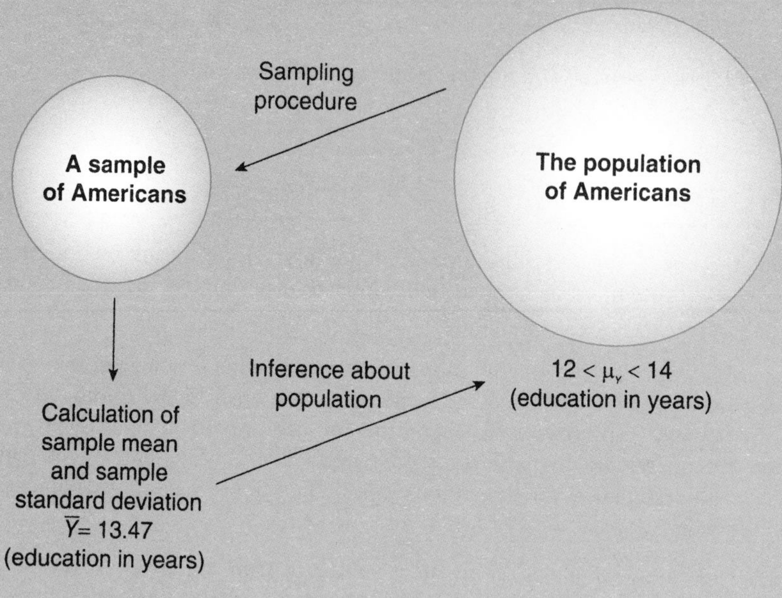

On the basis of these assumptions and the value of the standard error, we can establish a range of values—a confidence interval—that is likely to contain the actual population mean. We can also evaluate the accuracy of this estimate by assessing the likelihood that this range of values will actually contain the population mean.

The general formula for constructing a confidence interval (CI) for any level is

$$\text{CI} = \bar{Y} \pm Z(\sigma_{\bar{Y}}) \qquad (7.2)$$

Note that to calculate a confidence interval, we take the sample mean and add to or subtract from it the product of a Z value and the standard error.

The Z score we choose depends on the desired confidence level. For example, to obtain a 95% confidence interval we would choose a Z of 1.96 because we know (from Appendix B) that 95% of the area under the curve lies between ±1.96. Similarly, for a 99% confidence level, we would choose a Z of 2.58. The relationship between the confidence level and Z is illustrated in Figure 7.1 for the 95% and 99% confidence levels.

LEARNING CHECK 7.2

To understand the relationship between the confidence level and Z, review the material in Chapter 5. What would be the corresponding Z value for a 98% confidence interval?

Determining the Confidence Interval

To determine the confidence interval for means, follow these steps:

1. Calculate the standard error of the mean.
2. Decide on the level of confidence, and find the corresponding Z value.
3. Calculate the confidence interval.
4. Interpret the results.

Let's return to the problem of estimating the mean commuting time of the population of students on our campus. How would you find the 95% confidence interval?

CALCULATING THE STANDARD ERROR OF THE MEAN Let's suppose that the standard deviation for our population of commuters is $\sigma = 1.5$. We calculate the standard error for the sampling distribution of the mean:

$$\sigma_{\bar{Y}} = \frac{\sigma}{\sqrt{N}} = \frac{1.5}{\sqrt{500}} = 0.07$$

DECIDING ON THE LEVEL OF CONFIDENCE AND FINDING THE CORRESPONDING *Z* VALUE We decide on a 95% confidence level. The Z value corresponding to a 95% confidence level is 1.96.

CALCULATING THE CONFIDENCE INTERVAL The confidence interval is calculated by adding and subtracting from the observed sample mean the product of the standard error and Z:

$$\begin{aligned} 95\%\ \text{CI} &= 7.5 \pm 1.96(0.07) \\ &= 7.5 \pm 0.14 \\ &= 7.36 \text{ to } 7.64 \end{aligned}$$

The 95% CI for the mean commuting time is illustrated in Figure 7.2.

Figure 7.1 Relationship Between Confidence Level and Z for 95% and 99% Confidence Intervals

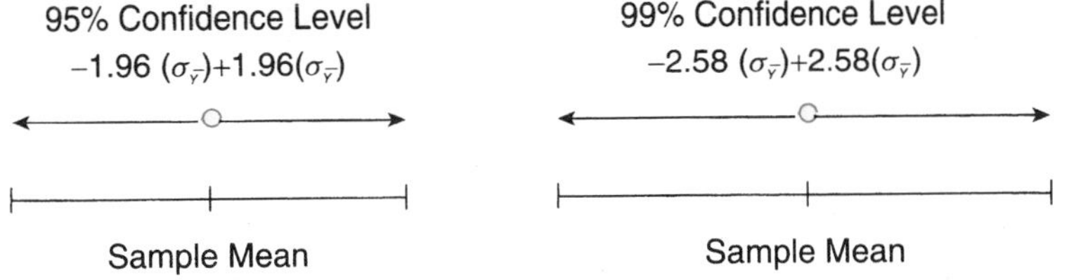

Source: David Freedman, Robert Pisani, Roger Purves, and Ani Akhikari, Statistics, 2nd ed. (New York: Norton, 1991).

Figure 7.2 Ninety-Five Percent Confidence Interval for the Mean Commuting Time ($N = 500$)

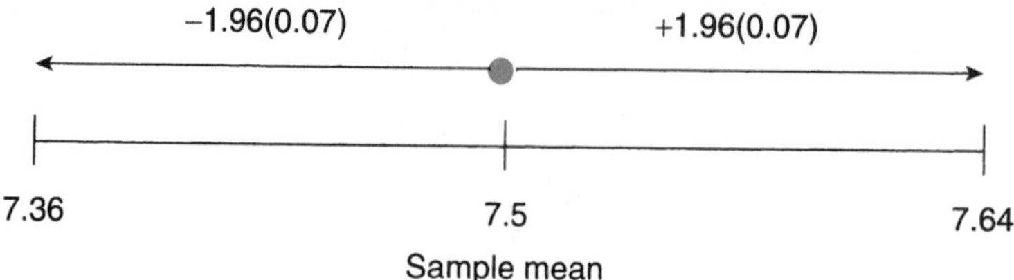

INTERPRETING THE RESULTS We can be 95% confident that the actual mean commuting time—the true population mean—is not less than 7.36 hours and not greater than 7.64 hours. In other words, if we collected a large number of samples ($N = 500$) from the population of commuting students, 95 times out of 100, the true population mean would be included within our computed interval. With a 95% confidence level, there is a 5% risk that we are wrong. Five times out of 100, the true population mean will not be included in the specified interval.

Remember that we can never be sure whether the population mean is actually contained within the confidence interval. Once the sample is selected and the confidence interval defined, the confidence interval either does or does not contain the population mean—but we will never be sure.

LEARNING CHECK 7.3

What is the 90% confidence interval for the mean commuting time? First, find the Z value associated with a 90% confidence level.

To further illustrate the concept of confidence intervals, let's suppose that we draw 10 different samples ($N = 500$) from the population of commuting students. For each sample mean, we construct a 95% confidence interval. Figure 7.3 displays these confidence intervals. Each horizontal line represents a 95% confidence interval constructed around a sample mean (marked with a circle).

The vertical line represents the population mean. Note that the horizontal lines that intersect the vertical line are the intervals that contain the true population mean. Only 1 out of the 10 confidence intervals does not intersect the vertical line, meaning it does not contain the population mean. What would happen if we continued to draw samples of the same size from this population and constructed a 95% confidence interval for each sample? For about 95% of all samples, the specified interval would contain the true population mean, but for 5% of all samples it would not.

Reducing Risk

One way to reduce the risk of being incorrect is by increasing the level of confidence. For instance, we can increase our confidence level from 95% to 99%. The 99% confidence interval for our commuting example is

Figure 7.3 Ninety-Five Percent Confidence Intervals for 10 Samples

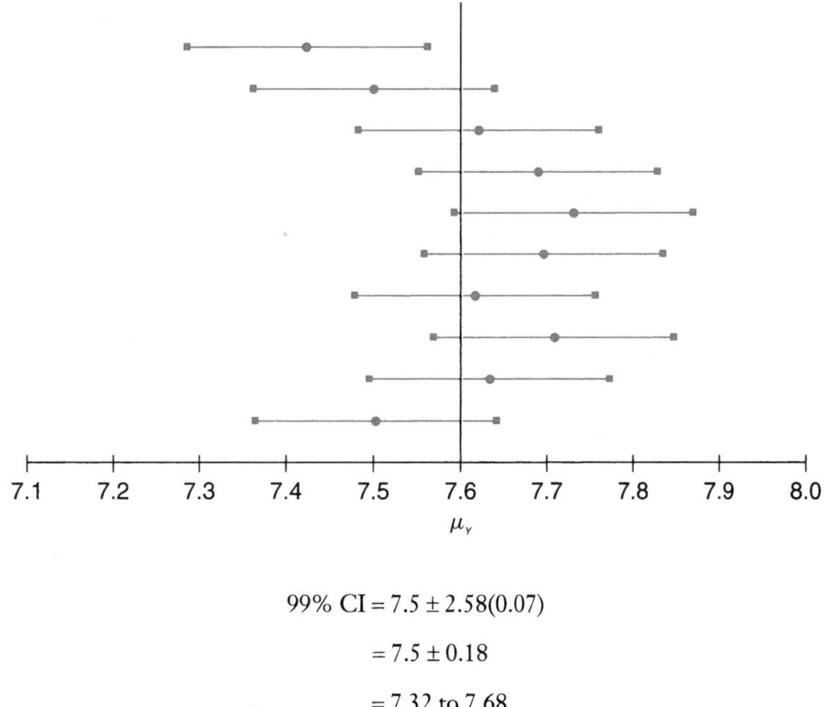

$$99\%\ \text{CI} = 7.5 \pm 2.58(0.07)$$
$$= 7.5 \pm 0.18$$
$$= 7.32 \text{ to } 7.68$$

When using the 99% confidence interval, there is only a 1% risk that we are wrong and the specified interval does not contain the true population mean. We can be almost certain that the true population mean is included in the interval ranging from 7.32 to 7.68 hours/week. Note that by increasing the confidence level, we have also increased the width of the confidence interval from 0.28 (7.36–7.64) to 0.36 hours (7.32–7.68), thereby making our estimate less precise.

This is the trade-off between achieving greater confidence in an estimate and the precision of that estimate. Although using a higher level of confidence increases our confidence that the true population mean is included in our confidence interval, the estimate becomes less precise as the width of the interval increases. Although we are only 95% confident that the interval ranging between 7.36 and 7.64 hours includes the true population mean, it is a more precise estimate than the 99% interval ranging from 7.32 to 7.68 hours. The relationship between the confidence level and the precision of the confidence interval is illustrated in Figure 7.4. Table 7.1 lists three commonly used confidence levels along with their corresponding Z values.

Table 7.1 Confidence Levels and Corresponding Z Values

Confidence Level	Z Value
90%	1.65
95%	1.96
99%	2.58

Figure 7.4 Confidence Intervals, 95% Versus 99% (Mean Commuting Time)

A 95% Confidence Interval

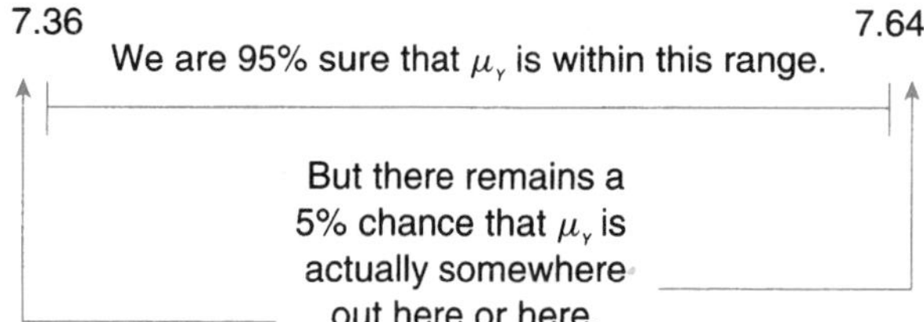

A 99% Confidence Interval

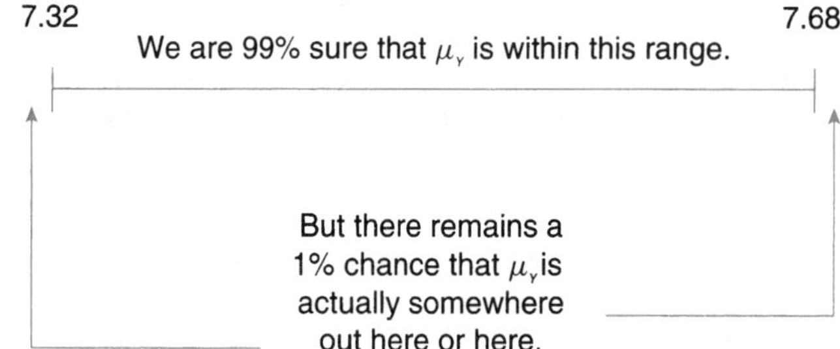

Estimating Sigma

To calculate confidence intervals, we need to know the standard error of the sampling distribution. The standard error is a function of the population standard deviation and the sample size:

$$\sigma_{\bar{Y}} = \frac{\sigma}{\sqrt{N}}$$

In our commuting example, we have been using a hypothetical value, $\sigma = 1.5$, for the population standard deviation. Typically, both the mean (μ) and the standard deviation (σ) of the population are unknown to us. When $N \geq 50$, however, the sample standard deviation, s, is a good estimate of $\sigma_{\bar{Y}}$. The standard error is then calculated as follows:

$$s_{\bar{Y}} = \frac{s}{\sqrt{N}} \tag{7.3}$$

As an example, we'll estimate the mean hours per day that Americans spend watching television based on the 2014 GSS. The mean hours per day spent watching television for a sample of $N = 1{,}001$ is $\bar{Y} = 2.94$, and the standard deviation $s = 2.60$ hours. Let's determine the 95% confidence interval for these data.

CALCULATING THE ESTIMATED STANDARD ERROR OF THE MEAN The estimated standard error for the sampling distribution of the mean is

$$s_{\bar{Y}} = \frac{2.60}{\sqrt{1{,}001}} = 0.08$$

DECIDING ON THE LEVEL OF CONFIDENCE AND FINDING THE CORRESPONDING *Z* VALUE We decide on a 95% confidence level. The *Z* value corresponding to a 95% confidence level is 1.96.

CALCULATING THE CONFIDENCE INTERVAL The confidence interval is calculated by adding to and subtracting from the observed sample mean the product of the standard error and *Z*:

$$\begin{aligned} 95\%\ \text{CI} &= 2.94 \pm 1.96(0.08) \\ &= 2.94 \pm 0.16 \\ &= 2.78 \text{ to } 3.10 \end{aligned}$$

INTERPRETING THE RESULTS We can be 95% confident that the actual mean hours spent watching television by Americans from which the GSS sample was taken is not less than 2.78 hours and not greater than 3.10 hours. In other words, if we drew a large number of samples ($N = 1{,}001$) from this population, then 95 times out of 100, the true population mean would be included within our computed interval.

Sample Size and Confidence Intervals

Researchers can increase the precision of their estimate by increasing the sample size. In Chapter 6, we learned that larger samples result in smaller standard errors and, therefore, sampling distributions are more clustered around the population mean (Figure 6.6). A more tightly clustered sampling distribution means that our confidence intervals will be narrower and more precise. To illustrate the relationship between sample size and the standard error, and thus the confidence interval, let's calculate the 95% confidence interval for our GSS data with (a) a sample of $N = 150$ and (b) a sample of $N = 1{,}987$.

With a sample size $N = 150$, the estimated standard error for the sampling distribution is

$$s_{\bar{Y}} = \frac{s}{\sqrt{N}} = \frac{2.60}{\sqrt{150}} = 0.21$$

and the 95% confidence interval is

$$\begin{aligned} 95\%\ \text{CI} &= 2.94 \pm 1.96(0.21) \\ &= 2.94 \pm 0.41 \\ &= 2.53 \text{ to } 3.35 \end{aligned}$$

With a sample size $N = 1{,}987$, the estimated standard error for the sampling distribution is

$$s_{\bar{Y}} = \frac{s}{\sqrt{N}} = \frac{2.60}{\sqrt{1{,}987}} = 0.06$$

and the 95% confidence interval is

$$\begin{aligned} 95\%\ \text{CI} &= 2.94 \pm 1.96(0.06) \\ &= 2.94 \pm 0.12 \\ &= 2.82 \text{ to } 3.06 \end{aligned}$$

In Table 7.2, we summarize the 95% confidence intervals for the mean number of hours watching television for these three sample sizes: $N = 150$, $N = 1{,}001$, and $N = 1{,}987$.

Table 7.2 Ninety-Five Percent Confidence Interval and Width for Mean Number of Hours per Day Watching Television for Three Different Sample Sizes

Sample Size (N)	Confidence Interval	Interval Width	s	$s_{\bar{Y}}$
150	2.53–3.35	0.82	2.60	0.21
1,001	2.78–3.10	0.32	2.60	0.08
1,987	2.82–3.06	0.24	2.60	0.12

Note that there is an inverse relationship between sample size and the width of the confidence interval. The increase in sample size is linked with increased precision of the confidence interval. The 95% confidence interval for the GSS sample of 150 cases is 0.82 hours. But the interval widths decrease to 0.32 and 0.24 hours, respectively, as the sample sizes increase to $N = 1{,}001$ and then to $N = 1{,}987$. We had to nearly double the size of the sample (from 1,001 to 1,987) to reduce the confidence interval by about one fourth (from 0.32 to 0.24 hours). In general, although the precision of estimates increases steadily with sample size, the gains would appear to be rather modest after N reaches 1,987. An important factor to keep in mind is the increased cost associated with a larger sample. Researchers have to consider at what point the increase in precision is too small to justify the additional cost associated with a larger sample.

LEARNING CHECK 7.4

Why do smaller sample sizes produce wider confidence intervals? (See Figure 7.5.) Compare the standard errors of the mean for the three sample sizes.

STATISTICS IN PRACTICE: HISPANIC MIGRATION AND EARNINGS

There were nearly 55 million people of Hispanic or Latino ethnicity in the United States in 2014. Mexican-origin Hispanics comprise the single largest group of Hispanics in the country. But the origins of the Hispanic population have diversified with the addition of immigrants from other Latin American nations and Puerto Rico.[3]

During the past few decades, numerous studies have noted the discrepancy in earnings between these groups.[4] The gap in earnings has been attributed mainly to differences in migration status and in level of education. In this classic study, Marta Tienda and Franklin Wilson argued that Mexicans, Puerto Ricans, and Cubans varied markedly in socioeconomic characteristics because of differences in the timing and circumstances of their immigration to the United States.[5] The period of entry and the circumstances prompting migration affected the geographical distribution and the employment opportunities of each group. For example, Puerto Ricans were disproportionately located in the Northeast, where the labor market was characterized by the highest unemployment rates, whereas the majority of Cuban immigrants resided in the Southeast, where the unemployment rate was the lowest in the United States.

Tienda and Wilson also noted persistent differences in educational levels among Mexicans and Puerto Ricans compared with Cubans.[6] Only about 9% of Mexicans and 16% of Puerto

A CLOSER LOOK 7.2

WHAT AFFECTS CONFIDENCE INTERVAL WIDTH? SUMMARY

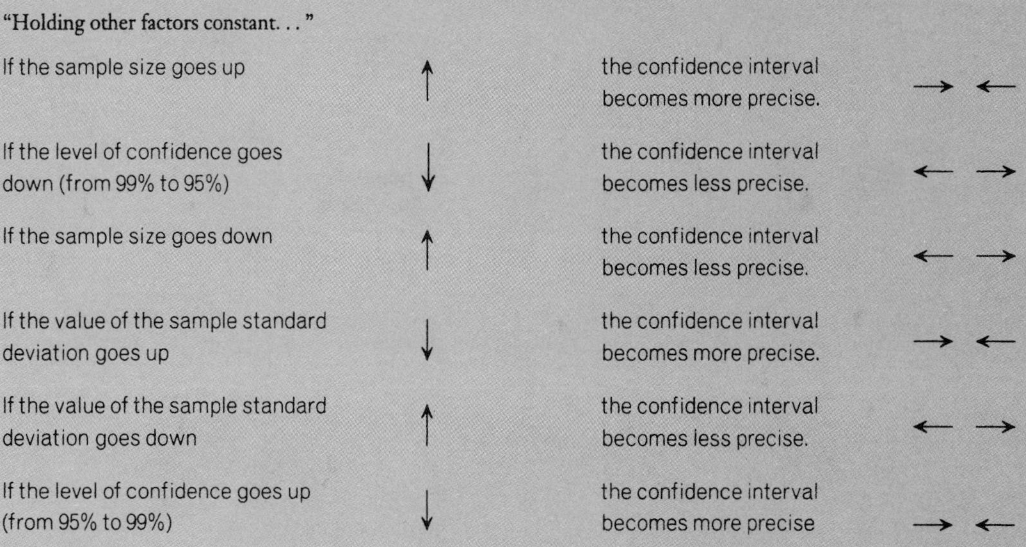

"Holding other factors constant. . ."

If the sample size goes up	↑	the confidence interval becomes more precise.	→ ←
If the level of confidence goes down (from 99% to 95%)	↓	the confidence interval becomes less precise.	← →
If the sample size goes down	↑	the confidence interval becomes less precise.	← →
If the value of the sample standard deviation goes up	↓	the confidence interval becomes more precise.	→ ←
If the value of the sample standard deviation goes down	↑	the confidence interval becomes less precise.	← →
If the level of confidence goes up (from 95% to 99%)	↓	the confidence interval becomes more precise	→ ←

Ricans have graduated college, compared with 25% of Cuban men.[7] These differences in migrant status and educational level were likely to be reflected in disparities in earnings among the three groups. We would anticipate that the earnings of Cubans would be higher than the earnings of Mexicans and Puerto Ricans.

We tested the ideas of Tienda and Wilson based on a sample of men from the 2000 Census that included 29,233 Cubans, 34,620 Mexican Americans, and 66,933 Puerto Ricans. As hypothesized, with average earnings of \$24,018 (s = \$36,298), Cubans were at the top of the income hierarchy. Puerto Ricans were intermediate among the groups with earnings averaging \$18,748 (s = \$25,694). Mexican men were at the bottom of the income hierarchy with average annual earnings of \$16,537 (s = \$23,502). Although Tienda and Wilson did not calculate confidence intervals for their estimates, we use the data from the 2000 Census to calculate a 95% confidence interval for the mean income of the three groups of Hispanic men.[8]

To find the 95% confidence interval for Cuban income, we first estimate the standard error:

$$s_{\bar{Y}} = \frac{36,298}{\sqrt{29,233}} = 212.30$$

Then, we calculate the confidence interval:

$$\begin{aligned} 95\%\ \text{CI} &= 24,018 \pm 1.96(212.30) \\ &= 24,018 \pm 416 \\ &= 23,602 \text{ to } 24,434 \end{aligned}$$

For Puerto Rican income, the estimated standard error is

$$s_{\bar{Y}} = \frac{25,694}{\sqrt{66,933}} = 99.31$$

Figure 7.5 The Relationship Between Sample Size and Confidence Interval Width

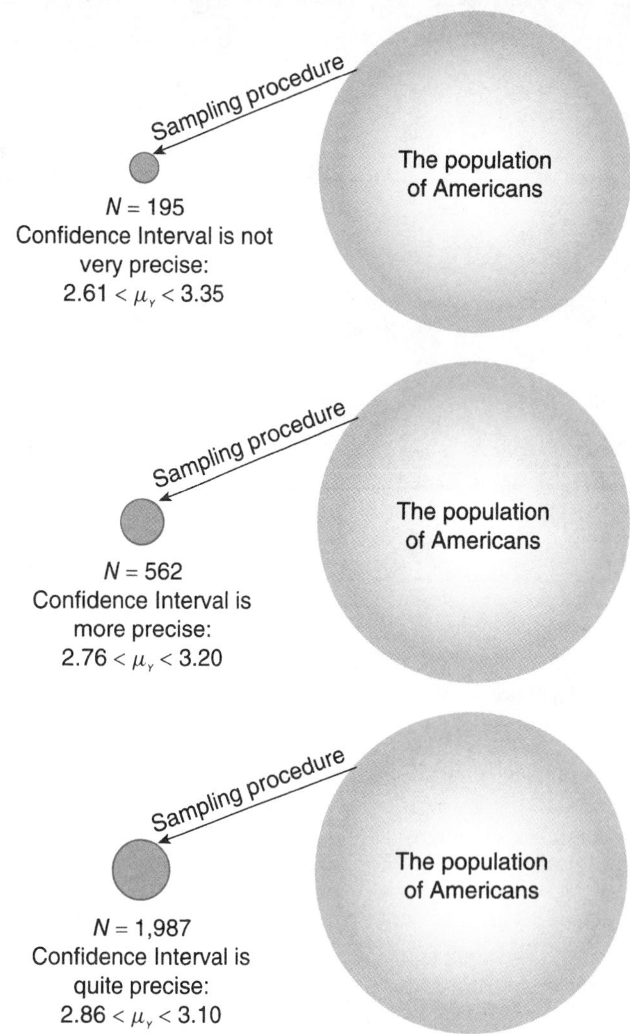

and the 95% confidence interval is

$$\begin{aligned} 95\%\ \text{CI} &= 18{,}748 \pm 1.96(99.31) \\ &= 18{,}748 \pm 195 \\ &= 18{,}553 \text{ to } 18{,}943 \end{aligned}$$

Finally, for Mexican income, the estimated standard error is

$$s_{\bar{Y}} = \frac{23{,}502}{\sqrt{34{,}620}} = 126.31$$

Figure 7.6 Ninety-Five Percent Confidence Intervals for the Mean Income of Puerto Ricans, Mexicans, and Cubans

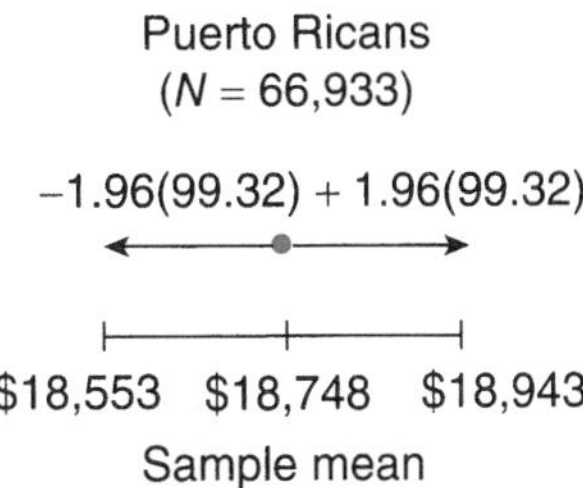

and the 95% confidence interval is

$$\begin{aligned}95\%\ \text{CI} &= 16{,}537 \pm 1.96(126.31)\\ &= 16{,}537 \pm 248\\ &= 16{,}289 \text{ to } 16{,}785\end{aligned}$$

The confidence intervals for mean annual income of Cuban, Puerto Rican, and Mexican immigrants are illustrated in Figure 7.6. We can say with 95% confidence that the true income mean for each Hispanic group lies somewhere within the corresponding confidence interval. Note that the confidence intervals do not overlap, thus revealing great disparities in earnings among the three groups. Highest interval estimates are for Cubans, followed by Mexicans and then Puerto Ricans.

CONFIDENCE INTERVALS FOR PROPORTIONS

You may already be familiar with confidence intervals, having seen them applied in opinion and election polls like those conducted by Gallup or CNN/ORC. Pollsters interview a random sample representative of a defined population to assess their opinion on a certain issue or their voting preference. Sample proportions or percentages are usually reported along with a margin error, plus or minus a particular value. The margin of error is the confidence interval and is used to estimate the population proportions or percentages. The same conceptual foundations of sampling and statistical inference that are central to the estimation of population means—the selection of random samples and the special properties of the sampling distribution—are also central to the estimation of population proportions.

Earlier, we saw that the sampling distribution of the means underlies the process of estimating population means from sample means. Similarly, the sampling distribution of proportions underlies the estimation of population proportions from sample proportions. Based on the central limit theorem, we know that with sufficient sample size the sampling distribution of proportions is approximately normal, with mean μ_p equal to the population proportion π and with a standard error of proportions (the standard deviation of the sampling distribution of proportions) equal to

$$\sigma_p = \sqrt{\frac{(\pi)(1-\pi)}{N}} \tag{7.4}$$

where

σ_p = the standard error of proportions

π = the population proportion

N = the population size

However, since the population proportion, π, is unknown to us (that is what we are trying to estimate), we can use the sample proportion, p, as an estimate of π. The estimated standard error then becomes

$$s_p = \sqrt{\frac{(p)(1-p)}{N}} \tag{7.5}$$

where

s_p = the estimated standard error of proportions

p = the sample proportion

N = the sample size

Let's calculate the estimated standard error for the 2016 Gallup survey about environmentalist identification. Based on a random sample of 1,019 adults, the percentage who identify as an environmentalist was reported at 42%. Based on Formula 7.5, with p = 0.42, 1 − p = (1 − 0.42) = 0.58, and N = 1,019, the standard error is $s_p = \sqrt{.42(1-.42)/1{,}019} = 0.015 = 0.02$. We will have to consider two factors to meet the assumption of normality with the sampling distribution of proportions: (1) the sample size N and (2) the sample proportions p and 1 − p. When p and 1 − p are about 0.50, a sample size of at least 50 is sufficient. But when $p > 0.50$ (or $1 - p < 0.50$), a larger sample is required to meet the assumption of normality. Usually, a sample of 100 or more is adequate for any single estimate of a population proportion.

Determining the Confidence Interval

Because the sampling distribution of proportions is approximately normal, we can use the normal distribution to establish confidence intervals for proportions in the same manner that we used the normal distribution to establish confidence intervals or means.

The general formula for constructing confidence intervals for proportions for any level of confidence is

$$\text{CI} = p \pm Z(s_p) \tag{7.6}$$

where

CI = the confidence interval

p = the observed sample proportion

Z = the Z corresponding to the confidence level

s_p = the estimated standard error of proportions

Let's examine this formula in more detail. Note that to obtain a confidence interval at a certain level, we take the sample proportion and add to or subtract from it the product of a Z value and the standard error. The Z value we choose depends on the desired confidence level. We want the area between the mean and the selected $\pm Z$ to be equal to the confidence level.

For example, to obtain a 95% confidence interval, we would choose a Z of 1.96 because we know (from Appendix B) that 95% of the area under the curve is included between ±1.96. Similarly, for a 99% confidence level, we would choose a Z of 2.58. (The relationship between confidence level and Z values is illustrated in Figure 7.1.)

To determine the confidence interval for a proportion, we follow the same steps that were used to find confidence intervals for means:

1. Calculate the estimated standard error of the proportion.
2. Decide on the desired level of confidence, and find the corresponding Z value.
3. Calculate the confidence interval.
4. Interpret the results.

To illustrate these steps, we use the Gallup survey results about the percentage of Americans who identify as environmentalists.

CALCULATING THE ESTIMATED STANDARD ERROR OF THE PROPORTION The standard error of the proportion 0.42 (42%) with a sample N = 1,019 is 0.02.

DECIDING ON THE DESIRED LEVEL OF CONFIDENCE AND FINDING THE CORRESPONDING Z VALUE We choose the 95% confidence level. The Z corresponding to a 95% confidence level is 1.96.

CALCULATING THE CONFIDENCE INTERVAL We calculate the confidence interval by adding to and subtracting from the observed sample proportion the product of the standard error and Z:

$$95\%\ CI = 0.42 \pm 1.96(0.02)$$
$$= 0.42 \pm 0.04$$
$$= 0.38 \text{ to } 0.46$$

INTERPRETING THE RESULTS We are 95% confident that the true population proportion is somewhere between 0.38 and 0.46. In other words, if we drew a large number of samples from the population of adults, then 95 times out of 100, the confidence interval we obtained would contain the true population proportion. We can also express this result in percentages and say that we are 95% confident that the true population percentage of Americans who identify as environmentalists is between 38% and 46%.

LEARNING CHECK 7.5

Calculate the 95% confidence interval for the CNN/ORC survey results for those who do not support anti-trans bathroom legislation.

Note that with a 95% confidence level, there is a 5% risk that we are wrong. If we continued to draw large samples from this population, in 5 out of 100 samples the true population proportion would not be included in the specified interval.

We can decrease our risk by increasing the confidence level from 95% to 99%.

$$\begin{aligned} 99\%\ \text{CI} &= 0.42 \pm 2.58(0.02) \\ &= 0.42 \pm 0.05 \\ &= .37 \text{ to } .47 \end{aligned}$$

When using the 99% confidence interval, we can be almost certain (99 times out of 100) that the true population proportion is included in the interval ranging from .37 to .47 (or 37% to 47%). However, as we saw earlier, there is a trade-off between achieving greater confidence in making an estimate and the precision of that estimate. Although using a 99% level increased our confidence level from 95% to 99% (thereby reducing our risk of being wrong from 5% to 1%), the estimate became less precise as the width of the interval increased.[9]

READING THE RESEARCH LITERATURE: WOMEN VICTIMS OF INTIMATE VIOLENCE

Janet Fanslow and Elizabeth Robinson (2010)[10] studied help-seeking behavior and motivation among women victims of intimate partner violence in New Zealand. The researchers argue that

> historically, responses to victims have been developed on the basis of identified need and active advocacy work rather than driven by data. . . .Questions remain, however, in terms of whether the responses that have been developed are the most appropriate ways to deliver help to victims of intimate partner violence according to victims' personal perceptions of who they would like to receive help from and the types and nature of help they would like to receive. (p. 930)

Fanslow and Robinson relied on data from the New Zealand Violence Against Women Study to document the reasons why victims sought help or left their partner due to domestic violence.

We present one of the tables featured in Fanslow and Robinson's study (see Table 7.3). Note that 95% confidence intervals are reported for each reason category. The confidence intervals are based on the confidence level, the standard error of the proportion (which can be estimated from *p*), and the sample size. For example, we know that based on their sample of 486 women, 48.5% reported that "could not endure more" was a reason for seeking help. Based on the 95% confidence interval, we can say that the actual proportion of women victims who identify that they "could not endure more" as a reason for seeking help lies somewhere between 43.6% and 53.3%.

Fanslow and Robinson identify the categories with the highest percentages for each sample: for seeking help (could not endure more, encouraged by friends or family, children suffering and badly injured) and for leaving (could not endure more, he threatened to kill her, children suffering and badly injured). They write as follows:

> The majority of women who sought help, and the majority of women who left violent relationships reported doing so because they "could not endure more". Where and when this line is drawn will undoubtedly differ from person to person . . . but factors that may affect it include realistic assessment of the man's behavior and his likelihood to change, and recognition of the seriousness of the violence they experienced. Other commonly reported reasons for leaving and/or seeking help included because women experienced serious injury or feared for their lives. This emphasizes that the violence experienced by many women in the context of intimate relationships is not trivial. (p. 946)[11]

Concern for children suffering was also identified as an important reason for female victims to seek help and/or to leave their abuser.

When estimates are reported for subgroups, the confidence intervals are likely to vary. Even when a confidence interval is reported only for the overall sample, we can easily compute separate confidence intervals for each of the subgroups if the confidence level and the size of each of the subgroups are included.

Table 7.3 Percentage of Women With Lifetime Experience of Physical and/or Sexual Intimate Partner Violence who Reported Reasons for Asking for Help With, and for Leaving Violent Relationships

	Reasons That Made You Go for Help (*n* = 486) Percentage (95% CI)	Reasons for Leaving the Last Time (*n* = 508) Percentage (95% CI)
Could not endure more	48.5 (43.6–53.3)	64.2 (59.8–68.6)
Encouraged by friends/family	17.7 (14.0–21.5)	6.7 (4.4–9.0)
Badly injured	15.4 (12.0–18.7)	7.1 (4.2–9.9)
He threated to kill her	11.3 (8.1–14.5)	10.2 (7.0–13.3)
Afraid he would kill her	11.4 (8.3–14.6)	5.9 (3.8–7.9)
Children suffering	17.2 (13.5–20.9)	8.6 (5.9–11.3)
He threatened or hit children	7.9 (5.2–10.5)	5.0 (3.0–7.0)
She was afraid she would kill him	2.1 (0.8–3.5)	1.2 (0.2–2.2)
She was thrown out of the home	2.0 (0.6–3.3)	2.2 (0.7–3.7)
For her mental health/save sanity	8.2 (5.5–10.9)	—
To get information/legal help	8.1 (5.5–10.6)	—
Encouraged by organization	—	1.7 (0.1–3.3)
No particular incident	—	5.3 (3.3–7.4)
He was unfaithful	—	3.8 (2.1–5.5)
She was pregnant	—	1.4 (0.4–2.3)
To have time out/break from relationships	—	1.4 (0.3–2.4)
Other	22.4 (18.5–26.2)	8.3 (5.6–10.9)

Source: Adapted from Janet Fanslow and Elizabeth Robinson, "Help Seeking Behaviors and Reasons for Help Seeking Reported by a Representative Sample of Women Victims of Intimate Partner Violence in New Zealand," *Journal of Interpersonal Violence*, 25, no. 5 (2010), 929–951.

Note: Percentages sum to greater than 100% because individuals could provide multiple responses.

DATA AT WORK

Laurel Person Mecca: Research Specialist

Photo courtesy of Laurel Person Mecca

Laurel works as a research specialist in a university center for social and urban research. The center provides support and consultation to behavioral and social science investigators. She first connected with the center while she was recruiting subjects for her master's thesis research.

"Interacting with human subjects offers a unique view into peoples' lives," says Laurel, "thereby providing insights into one's own life and a richer understanding of the human condition." She's consulted on an array of projects: testing prototypes of technologies designed to enable older adults and persons with disabilities to live independently, facilitating focus groups with low-income individuals to explore their barriers to Supplemental Nutrition Assistance Program participation, and evaluating an intervention designed to improve parent-adolescent communication about sexual behaviors to reduce STDs and unintended pregnancies among teens.

For students interested in a career in research and data analysis, she offers this advice: "Gain on-the-job experience while in college, even if it is an unpaid internship. Find researchers who are conducting studies that interest you, and inquire about working for them. Even if they are not posting an available position, they may bring you on board (as I have done with students). Persistence pays off! You are much more likely to be selected for a position if you demonstrate a genuine interest in the work and if you continue to show your enthusiasm by following up. Definitely check out the National Science Foundation's Research Experience for Undergraduates program. Though most of these internships are in the "hard" sciences, there are plenty of openings in social sciences disciplines. These internships include a stipend (YES!), and oftentimes, assistance with travel and housing. They are wonderful opportunities to work directly on a research project, and may provide the additional benefit of a conference presentation and/or publication."

MAIN POINTS

- The goal of most research is to find population parameters. The major objective of sampling theory and statistical inference is to provide estimates of unknown parameters from sample statistics.
- Researchers make point estimates and interval estimates. Point estimates are sample statistics used to estimate the exact value of a population parameter. Interval estimates are ranges of values within which the population parameter may fall.
- Confidence intervals can be used to estimate population parameters such as means or proportions. Their accuracy is defined with the confidence level. The most common confidence levels are 90%, 95%, and 99%.
- To establish a confidence interval for a mean or a proportion, add or subtract from the mean or the proportion the product of the standard error and the *Z* value corresponding to the confidence level.

KEY TERMS

confidence interval (CI) 180
confidence level 180
estimation 180
margin of error 181
point estimate 180

DIGITAL RESOURCES

Get the edge on your studies. **edge.sagepub.com/frankfort8e**

Take a quiz to find out what you've learned.
Review key terms with eFlashcards.
Dive into real research with SAGE Journal Articles.

SPSS DEMONSTRATION [GSS14SSDS-B]

Producing Confidence Intervals Around a Mean

SPSS calculates confidence intervals around a sample mean or proportion with the Explore procedure. Activate the Explore procedure by selecting the *Analyze* menu, *Descriptive Statistics*, then *Explore*. The opening dialog box has spaces for both dependent and independent variables.

Place HRSRELAX (after an average work day, about how many hours do you have to relax or pursue the activities you enjoy?) in the Dependent List box, and SEX (respondent's sex) in the Factor List box, as shown in Figure 7.7. We expect a gender difference in average relaxation hours,

Figure 7.7 Explore Dialog Box for HRSRELAX and SEX

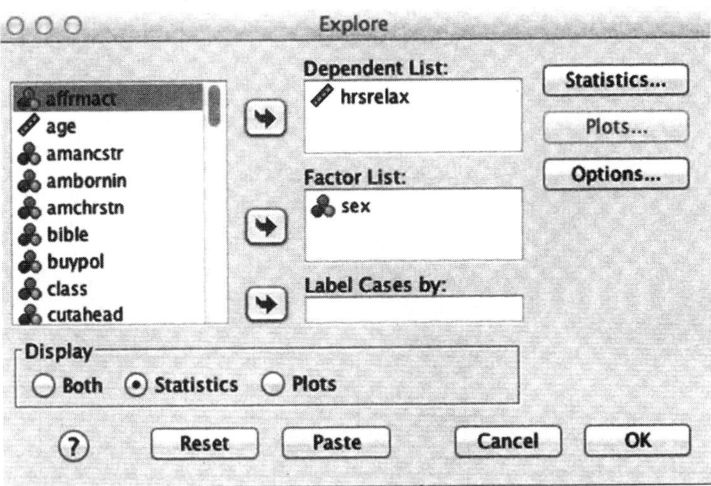

with women having less hours than men. The GSS asked respondents about their relaxation time after an average workday. In fact, social scientists have documented how women (not men) assume a second shift after work, managing family responsibilities at home, and consequently having less time for themselves.

Click on the *Statistics* button. Note that the Descriptives choice also includes the confidence interval for the mean, which by default is calculated at the 95% confidence level. Let's change that to the 99% level by erasing the "95" and substituting "99".

Click on *Continue* to return to the main dialog box. Recall that Explore produces several statistics and plots by default. For this example, we don't need to view the graphics, so click on the *Statistics* button in the *Display* section. Click on *OK* to run the procedure.

The output from the Explore procedure (Figure 7.8) is divided into two parts, one for males and the other for females. The mean number of HRSRELAX for males is 3.68; for females, it's 3.18. Our data indicate that, on average, men have slightly more time to relax in a day.

The 99% confidence interval for males runs from 3.26 to 4.11 hours. One way to interpret this result is to state that, in 100 samples each of size 244 males from the U.S. adult population, we would expect the confidence interval to include the true population value for the mean ideal number of children 99 times out of those 100. We can never be sure that in this particular sample the

Figure 7.8 SPSS Output for HRSRELAX by SEX

Descriptives

	sex RESPONDENTS SEX			Statistic	Std. Error
hrsrelax HOURS PER DAY R HAVE TO RELAX	1 MALE	Mean		3.68	.163
		99% Confidence Interval for Mean	Lower Bound	3.26	
			Upper Bound	4.11	
		5% Trimmed Mean		3.48	
		Median		3.00	
		Variance		6.513	
		Std. Deviation		2.552	
		Minimum		0	
		Maximum		16	
		Range		16	
		Interquartile Range		3	
		Skewness		1.417	.156
		Kurtosis		3.330	.310
	2 FEMALE	Mean		3.18	.151
		99% Confidence Interval for Mean	Lower Bound	2.79	
			Upper Bound	3.57	
		5% Trimmed Mean		2.97	
		Median		3.00	
		Variance		5.826	
		Std. Deviation		2.414	
		Minimum		0	
		Maximum		18	
		Range		18	
		Interquartile Range		2	
		Skewness		2.092	.152
		Kurtosis		8.607	.303

confidence interval includes the population mean. Still, our best estimate for the average relaxation hours per day falls within a narrow range of 0.85 (4.11–3.26). For females, the 99% confidence interval is 2.79 to 3.57 hours, with a range of 0.78 (3.57–2.79).

We'll continue to explore the relationship between gender and relaxation hours in Chapter 8 ("Testing Hypotheses").

SPSS PROBLEMS [GSS14SSDS-B]

1. Recall that the GSS sample includes men and women from 18 to 89 years of age. Does it matter that we have responses from men and women of diverse ages? Would our HRSRELAX results change if we selected a younger sample of men and women?
   a. To take the SPSS demonstration one step further, use the Select Cases procedure to select respondents based on the variable AGE who are less than or equal to 35 years old. Do this by selecting *Data* and then *Select Cases*. Next, select *If Condition is satisfied* and then click on *If*. Find and highlight the variable AGE in the scroll-down box on the left of your screen. Click the arrow next to the scroll-down box. AGE will now appear in the box on the right. Now, tell SPSS that you want to select respondents who are 35 years of age or less. The box on the right should now read AGE <= 35. Click *Continue* and then *OK*.
   b. Using this younger sample, repeat the Explore procedure (with the 99% confidence interval) that we just completed in the demonstration. What differences exist between men and women in this younger sample on hours per day the respondent has to relax? How do these results compare with those based on the entire sample?
2. Calculate the 90% confidence interval for the following variables, comparing lower, working, middle, and upper classes (CLASS) in the GSS sample. Use the Explore procedure using CLASS as your factor variable (*Analyze, Descriptive Statistics, Explore*). Make a summary statement of your findings. (Reset Select Cases to *All cases* before completing this exercise.)
   a. HRSRELAX (hours to relax per day)
   b. EDUC (Respondent's highest year of school completed)
   c. HRS1 (work hours per week)
   d. MAEDUC (Mother's highest year of school completed)

CHAPTER EXERCISES

1. In the 2013 National Crime Victimization Study, the Federal Bureau of Investigation found that 23% of Americans age 12 or older had been victims of crime during a 1-year period. This result was based on a sample of 160,040 persons.[12]
   a. Estimate the percentage of U.S. adults who were victims at the 90% confidence level. Provide an interpretation of the confidence interval.
   b. Estimate the percentage of victims at the 99% confidence level. Provide an interpretation of the confidence interval.
2. Use the GSS 2014 data on education from Chapter 5 ("The Normal Distribution"), Exercise 5.

	Mean	Standard Deviation	N
Lower class	12.11	2.83	122
Working class	13.01	2.91	541
Middle class	14.99	2.93	475
Upper class	15.44	2.83	34

a. Construct the 95% confidence interval for the mean number of years of education for lower-class and working-class respondents.

b. Construct the 99% confidence interval for the mean number of years of education for lower-class and middle-class respondents.

c. As our confidence in the result increases, how does the size of the confidence interval change? Explain why this is so.

3. In 2016, the Pew Research Center conducted a survey of 1,004 Canadians and 1,003 Americans to assess their opinion of climate change. The data show that 51% of Canadians and 45% of Americans believe climate change is a very serious problem.[13]

a. Estimate the proportion of all Canadians who believe climate change is a very serious problem at the 95% confidence interval.

b. Estimate the proportion of all Americans who believe climate change is a very serious problem at the 95% confidence interval.

c. Would you be confident in reporting that the majority (51% or higher) of Canadians and Americans believe climate change is a very serious problem? Explain.

4. Though 70% of women with children younger than 18 years participate in the labor force,[14] society still upholds the stay-at-home mother as the traditional model. Some believe that employment distracts mothers from their parenting role, affecting the well-being of children.

a. In the GSS 2014, respondents were asked to indicate their level of agreement to the statement, "A working mother hurts children". Of the 435 male respondents who answered the question, 18% strongly agreed that a working mother does not hurt children. Construct a 90% confidence interval for this statistic.

b. Of the 566 female respondents who answered the question, 40% strongly agreed that a working mother does not hurt children. Construct a 90% confidence interval for this statistic.

c. Why do you think there is a difference between men and women on this issue?

5. Gallup conducted a survey in April 1 to 25, 2010, to determine the congressional vote preference of the American voters.[15] They found that 51% of the male voters preferred a Republican candidate to a Democratic candidate in a sample of 5,490 registered voters. Gallup asks you, their statistical consultant, to tell them whether you could declare the Republican candidate as the likely winner of the votes coming from men if there was an election today. What is your advice? Why?

6. You have been doing research for your statistics class on the prevalence of binge drinking among teens.

a. According to 2011 Monitoring the Future data, the average binge drinking score, for this sample of 914 teens, is 1.27, with a standard deviation of 0.80. Binge drinking is defined as the number of times the teen drank five or more alcoholic drinks during the past week. Construct the 95% confidence interval for the true average severe binge drinking score.

b. Your roommate is concerned about your confidence interval calculation, arguing that severe binge drinking scores are not normally distributed, which in turn makes the confidence interval calculation meaningless. Assume your roommate is correct about the distribution of severe binge drinking scores. Does that imply that the calculation of a confidence interval is not appropriate? Why or why not?

7. From the GSS 2014 subsample, we find that 64% of respondents favor the death penalty for murder (N = 1,403).

   a. What is the 95% confidence interval for the percentage of the U.S. population who favor the death penalty for murder?

   b. Without doing any calculations, estimate the lower and upper bounds of 90% and 99% confidence intervals.

8. A social service agency plans to conduct a survey to determine the mean income of its clients. The director of the agency prefers that you measure the mean income very accurately, to within ±$500. From a sample taken 2 years ago, you estimate that the standard deviation of income for this population is about $5,000. Your job is to figure out the necessary sample size to reduce sampling error to ±$500.

   a. Do you need to have an estimate of the current mean income to answer this question? Why or why not?

   b. What sample size should be drawn to meet the director's requirement at the 95% level of confidence? (*Hint:* Use the formula for a confidence interval and solve for N, the sample size.)

   c. What sample size should be drawn to meet the director's requirement at the 99% level of confidence?

9. Education data (measured in years) from the ISSP 2014 are presented below for four countries. Calculate the 90% confidence interval for each country.

Country	Mean	Standard Deviation	N
France	14.12	5.73	975
Japan	12.48	2.53	528
Croatia	12.18	2.71	480
Turkey	9.15	11.98	783

10. Throughout the 2016 Presidential election primaries, Millennials (those aged 20 to 36 years) consistently supported Senator Bernie Sanders over Secretary Hillary Clinton. According to the 2016 Gallup poll of 1,754 Millennials, 55% had a favorable opinion of Sanders than Hillary Clinton (38%).[16] Calculate the 90% confidence interval for both reported percentages.

11. According to a 2014 survey by the Pew Research Center, 18% of registered Republicans and 15% of registered Democrats follow political candidates on social media.[17] These data are based on a national survey of 446 registered Republicans and 522 registered Democrats. What is the 95% confidence interval for the percentage of Republicans who follow political candidates on social media? The 95% confidence interval for Democrats?

12. According to a report published by the Pew Research Center in February 2010, 61% of Millennials (Americans in their teens and 20s) think that their generation has a unique and distinctive identity ($N = 527$).[18]

    a. Calculate the 95% confidence interval to estimate the percentage of Millennials who believe that their generation has a distinctive identity as compared with the other generations (Generation X, baby boomers, or the Silent Generation).

    b. Calculate the 99% confidence interval.

    c. Are both these results compatible with the conclusion that the majority of Millennials believe that they have a unique identity that separates them from the previous generations?

13. In 2014, GSS respondents ($N = 950$) were asked whether homosexual relations were wrong. The data show that 40% believed that homosexual relations were always wrong, while 49% believed that homosexual relations were not wrong at all.

    a. For each reported percentage, calculate the 95% confidence interval.

    b. Approximately 10% of GSS respondents were in the middle, some saying that homosexual relations were almost always wrong or sometimes wrong. Calculate the 95% confidence interval.

    c. Based on your calculations, what conclusions can you draw about the public's opinions of homosexual behavior?

8

TESTING HYPOTHESES

Chapter Learning Objectives

1. Describe the assumptions of statistical hypothesis testing
2. Define and apply the components in hypothesis testing
3. Explain what it means to reject or fail to reject a null hypothesis
4. Calculate and interpret a test for two sample cases with means or proportions
5. Determine the significance of t-test and Z-test statistics

According to economist Ethan Harris, "People may not remember too many numbers about the economy, but there are certain sign-posts they do pay attention to. As a short hard way to assess how the economy is doing, everybody notices the price of gas."[1]

The impact of high and volatile fuel prices is felt across the nation, affecting consumer spending and the economy, but the burden remains greater among distinct social economic groups and geographic areas. Lower-income Americans spend eight times more of their disposable income on gasoline than wealthier Americans do.[2] For example, in Wilcox, Alabama, individuals spend 12.72% of their income to fuel one vehicle, while in Hunterdon Co., New Jersey, people spend 1.52%. Nationally, Americans spend 3.8% of their income fueling one vehicle.

The first state to reach the $5 per gallon milestone was California in 2012. California's drivers were especially hit hard by the rising price of gas, due in part to their reliance on automobiles, especially for work commuters. In 2016, gasoline prices remained higher for states along the West Coast, particularly in Alaska, Hawaii, and California.

Let's say we drew a random sample of California gas stations ($N = 100$) and calculated the mean price for a gallon of regular gas, $2.78. Based on consumer information,[3] we also know that nationally the mean price of a gallon was $2.32 with a standard deviation of 0.17 for the same week. We can thus compare the mean price of gas in California with the mean price of all gas stations in May 2016. By comparing these means, we are asking whether it is reasonable to consider our random sample of California gas as representative of the population of gas stations in the United States. Actually, we expect to find that the average price of gas from a sample of California gas stations will be unrepresentative of the population of gas stations because we assume higher gas prices in California.

The sample mean of $2.78 is higher than the population mean of $2.32, but it is an estimate based on a single sample. Thus, it could mean one of two things: (1) the average price of gas in California is indeed higher than the national average or (2) the average price of gas in California is about the same as the national average, and this sample happens to show a particularly high mean.

How can we decide which explanation makes more sense? Because most estimates are based on single samples and different samples may result in different estimates, sampling results cannot be used directly to make statements about a population. We need a procedure that allows us to evaluate hypotheses about population parameters based on sample statistics. In Chapter 7 ("Estimation"), we saw that population parameters can be estimated from sample statistics. In this chapter, we will learn how to use sample statistics to make decisions about population parameters. This procedure is called **statistical hypothesis testing.**

Statistical hypothesis testing A procedure that allows us to evaluate hypotheses about population parameters based on sample statistics.

ASSUMPTIONS OF STATISTICAL HYPOTHESIS TESTING

Statistical hypothesis testing requires several assumptions. These assumptions include considerations of the level of measurement of the variable, the method of sampling, the shape of the population distribution, and the sample size. The specific assumptions may vary, depending on the test or the conditions of testing. However, without exception, all statistical tests assume random sampling. Tests of hypotheses about means also assume interval-ratio level of measurement and require that the population under consideration be normally distributed or that the sample size be larger than 50.

Based on our data, we can test the hypothesis that the average price of gas in California is higher than the average national price of gas. The test we are considering meets these conditions:

1. The sample of California gas stations was randomly selected.
2. The variable *price per gallon* is measured at the interval-ratio level.
3. We cannot assume that the population is normally distributed. However, because our sample size is sufficiently large ($N > 50$), we know, based on the central limit theorem, that the sampling distribution of the mean will be approximately normal.

STATING THE RESEARCH AND NULL HYPOTHESES

Hypotheses are usually defined in terms of interrelations between variables and are often based on a substantive theory. Earlier, we defined hypotheses as tentative answers to research questions. They are tentative because we can find evidence for them only after being empirically tested. The testing of hypotheses is an important step in this evidence-gathering process.

The Research Hypothesis (H_1)

Our first step is to formally express the hypothesis in a way that makes it amenable to a statistical test. The substantive hypothesis is called the **research hypothesis** and is symbolized as H_1. Research hypotheses are always expressed in terms of population parameters because we are interested in making statements about population parameters based on our sample statistics.

Research hypothesis (H_1) A statement reflecting the substantive hypothesis. It is always expressed in terms of population parameters, but its specific form varies from test to test.

In our research hypothesis (H_1), we state that the average price of gas in California is higher than the average price of gas nationally. Symbolically, we use μ to represent the population mean; our hypothesis can be expressed as

$$H_1: \mu > \$2.32$$

In general, the research hypothesis (H_1) specifies that the population parameter is one of the following:

1. Not equal to some specified value: $\mu \neq$ some specified value
2. Greater than some specified value: $\mu >$ some specified value
3. Less than some specified value: $\mu <$ some specified value

In a **one-tailed test**, the research hypothesis is directional; that is, it specifies that a population mean is either less than (<) or greater than (>) some specified value. We can express our research hypothesis as either

$$H_1: \mu < \text{some specified value}$$

or

$$H_1: \mu > \text{some specified value}$$

One-tailed test A type of hypothesis test that involves a directional research hypothesis. It specifies that the values of one group are either larger or smaller than some specified population value.

The research hypothesis we've stated for the average price of a gallon of regular gas in California is a one-tailed test.

When a one-tailed test specifies that the population mean is greater than some specified value, we call it a **right-tailed test** because we will evaluate the outcome at the right tail of the sampling distribution. If the research hypothesis specifies that the population mean is less than some specified value, it is called a **left-tailed test** because the outcome will be evaluated at the left tail of the sampling distribution. Our example is a right-tailed test because the research hypothesis states that the mean gas prices in California are higher than \$2.32. (Refer to Figure 8.1 on page 207.)

Right-tailed test A one-tailed test in which the sample outcome is hypothesized to be at the right tail of the sampling distribution.

Left-tailed test A one-tailed test in which the sample outcome is hypothesized to be at the left tail of the sampling distribution.

Sometimes, we have some theoretical basis to believe that there is a difference between groups, but we cannot anticipate the direction of that difference. For example, we may have reason to

Figure 8.1 Sampling Distribution of Sample Means Assuming H_0 Is True for a Sample N = 100

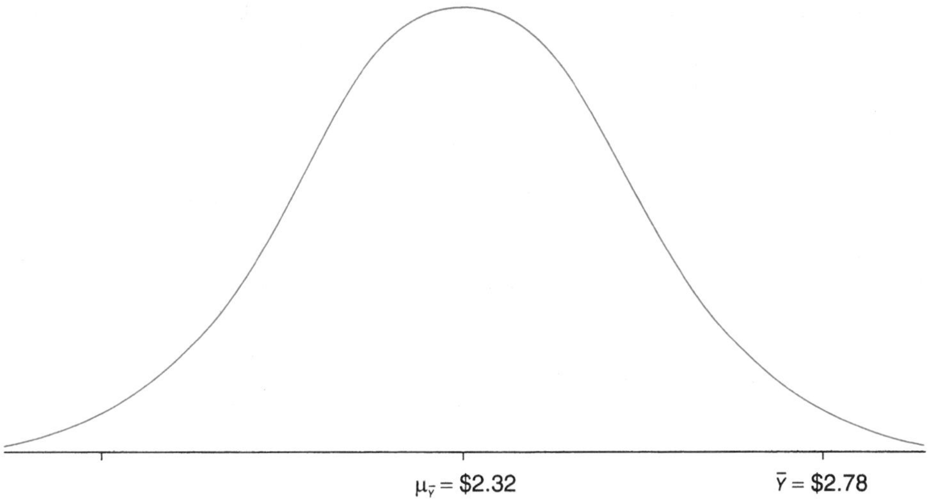

believe that the average price of California gas is different from that of the general population, but we may not have enough research or support to predict whether it is higher or lower. When we have no theoretical reason for specifying a direction in the research hypothesis, we conduct a **two-tailed test**. The research hypothesis specifies that the population mean is not equal to some specified value. For example, we can express the research hypothesis about the mean price of gas as

Two-tailed test A type of hypothesis test that involves a nondirectional research hypothesis. We are equally interested in whether the values are less than or greater than one another. The sample outcome may be located at both the lower and the higher ends of the sampling distribution.

$$H_1: \mu \neq \$2.32$$

With both one- and two-tailed tests, our null hypothesis of no difference remains the same. It can be expressed as

$$H_0: \mu = \text{some specified value}$$

The Null Hypothesis (H_0)

Is it possible that in the population there is no real difference between the mean price of gas in California and the mean price of gas in the nation and that the observed difference of 0.46 is actually due to the fact that this particular sample happened to contain California gas stations with higher prices? Since statistical inference is based on probability theory, it is not possible to prove or disprove the research hypothesis directly. We can, at best, estimate the likelihood that it is true or false.

To assess this likelihood, statisticians set up a hypothesis that is counter to the research hypothesis. The **null hypothesis**, symbolized as H_0, contradicts the research hypothesis and states that there is no difference between the population mean and some specified value. It is also referred to as the hypothesis of "no difference." Our null hypothesis can be stated symbolically as

Null hypothesis (H_0) A statement of "no difference" that contradicts the research hypothesis and is always expressed in terms of population parameters.

$$H_0: \mu = \$2.32$$

Rather than directly testing the substantive hypothesis (H_1) that there is a difference between the mean price of gas in California and the mean price nationally, we test the null hypothesis (H_0) that there is no difference in prices. In hypothesis testing, we hope to reject the null hypothesis to provide indirect support for the research hypothesis. Rejection of the null hypothesis will strengthen our belief in the research hypothesis and increase our confidence in the importance and utility of the broader theory from which the research hypothesis was derived.

PROBABILITY VALUES AND ALPHA

Now let's put all our information together. We're assuming that our null hypothesis ($\mu = \$2.32$) is true, and we want to determine whether our sample evidence casts doubt on that assumption, suggesting that there is evidence for research hypothesis, $\mu > \$2.32$. What are the chances that we would have randomly selected a sample of California gas stations such that the average price per gallon is higher than \$2.32, the average for the nation? We can determine the chances or probability because of what we know about the sampling distribution and its properties. We know, based on the central limit theorem, that if our sample size is larger than 50, the sampling distribution of the mean is approximately normal, with a mean and a standard deviation (standard error) of

$$\sigma_{\bar{Y}} = \frac{\sigma}{\sqrt{N}}$$

We are going to assume that the null hypothesis is true and then see if our sample evidence casts doubt on that assumption. We have a population mean $\mu = \$2.32$ and a standard deviation $\sigma = 0.17$. Our sample size is $N = 100$, and the sample mean is \$2.78. We can assume that the distribution of means of all possible samples of size $N = 100$ drawn from this distribution would be approximately normal, with a mean of \$2.32 and a standard deviation of

$$\sigma_{\bar{Y}} = \frac{0.17}{\sqrt{100}} = 0.02$$

This sampling distribution is shown in Figure 8.1. Also shown in Figure 8.1 is the mean gas price we observed for our sample of California gas stations.

Because this distribution of sample means is normal, we can use Appendix B to determine the probability of drawing a sample mean of \$2.78 or higher from this population. We will translate our sample mean into a Z score so that we can determine its location relative to the population mean. In Chapter 5 ("The Normal Distribution"), we learned how to translate a raw score into a Z score by using Formula 5.1:

$$Z = \frac{Y - \bar{Y}}{s}$$

Because we are dealing with a sampling distribution in which our raw score is $\bar{Y}$ (the mean), and the standard deviation (standard error) is $\sigma / \sqrt{N}$, we need to modify the formula somewhat:

$$Z = \frac{\bar{Y} - \mu_{\bar{Y}}}{\sigma / \sqrt{N}} \qquad (8.1)$$

Converting the sample mean to a Z-score equivalent is called computing the test statistic. The Z value we obtain is called the **Z statistic (obtained)**. The obtained Z gives us the number of standard deviations (standard errors) that our sample is from the hypothesized value (μ or $\mu_{\bar{Y}}$), assuming the null hypothesis is true. For our example, the obtained Z is

Z statistic (obtained) The test statistic computed by converting a sample statistic (such as the mean) to a Z score. The formula for obtaining Z varies from test to test.

$$Z = \frac{2.78 - 2.32}{0.17 / \sqrt{100}} = \frac{0.46}{0.02} = 23.00$$

Before we determine the probability of our obtained Z statistic, let's determine whether it is consistent with our research hypothesis. Recall that we defined our research hypothesis as a right-tailed test ($\mu > = \$2.32$), predicting that the difference would be assessed on the right tail of the sampling distribution. The positive value of our obtained Z statistic confirms that we will be evaluating the difference on the right tail. (If we had a negative obtained Z, it would mean the difference would have to be evaluated at the left tail of the distribution, contrary to our research hypothesis.)

To determine the probability of observing a Z value of 23.00, assuming that the null hypothesis is true, look up the value in Appendix B to find the area to the right of (above) the Z of 23.00. Our calculated Z value is not listed in Appendix B, so we'll need to rely on the last Z value reported in the table, 4.00. Recall from Chapter 5, where we calculated Z scores and their probability, that the Z values are located in Column A. The p value is the probability to the right of the obtained Z, or the "area beyond Z" in Column C. This area includes the proportion of all sample means that are \$2.78 or higher. The proportion is less than .0001 (Figure 8.2). This value is the probability of getting a result as extreme as the sample result if the null hypothesis is true; it is symbolized as p. Thus, for our example, $p \leq .0001$.

p value The probability associated with the obtained value of Z.

A **p value** can be defined as the probability associated with the obtained value of Z. It is a measure of how unusual or rare our obtained statistic is compared with what is stated in our

Figure 8.2 The Probability (p) Associated With $Z \geq 23.00$

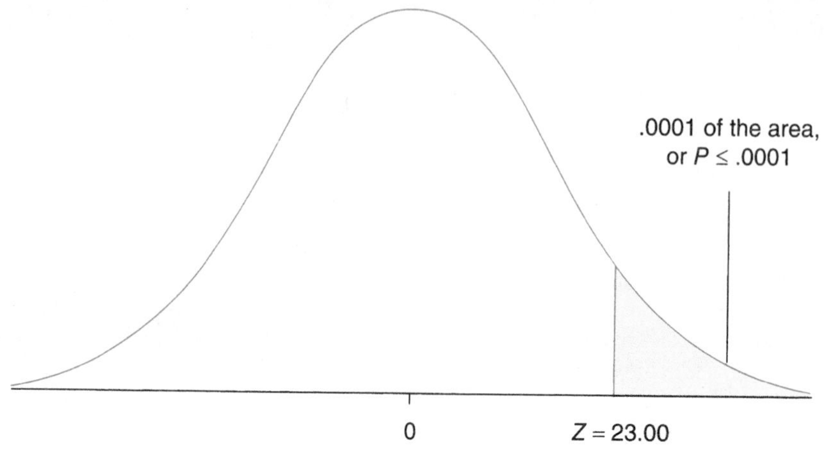

null hypothesis. The smaller the p value, the more evidence we have that the null hypothesis should be rejected in favor of the research hypothesis. The larger the p value, we can assume that the null hypothesis is true and fail to reject it. Based on the p value, we can also make a statement regarding the significance of the results. A result is deemed "statistically significant" if the probability is less than or equal to the alpha level.

Alpha (α) The level of probability at which the null hypothesis is rejected. It is customary to set alpha at the .05, .01, or .001 level.

Researchers usually define in advance what a sufficiently improbable Z value is by specifying a cutoff point below which p must fall to reject the null hypothesis. This cutoff point, called **alpha** and denoted by the Greek letter α, is customarily set at the .05, .01, or .001 level. Let's say that we decide to reject the null hypothesis if $p \leq .05$. The value .05 is referred to as alpha (α); it defines for us what result is sufficiently improbable to allow us to take the risk and reject the null hypothesis. An alpha (α) of .05 means that even if the obtained Z statistic is due to sampling error, so that the null hypothesis is true, we would allow a 5% risk of rejecting it. Alpha values of .01 and .001 are more cautionary levels of risk. The difference between p and alpha is that p is the actual probability associated with the obtained value of Z, whereas alpha is the level of probability determined in advance at which the null hypothesis is rejected. The null hypothesis is rejected when $p \leq \alpha$.

We have already determined that our obtained Z has a probability value less than .0001. Since our observed p is less than .05 ($p = .0001 < \alpha = .05$), we reject the null hypothesis. The value of .0001 means that fewer than 1 out of 10,000 samples drawn from this population are likely to have a mean that is 23.00 Z scores above the hypothesized mean of \$2.78. Another way to say it is as follows: There is only 1 chance out of 10,000 (or .0001%) that we would draw a random sample with a $Z \geq 23.00$ if the mean price of California gas were equal to the national mean price. We can state that the difference between the average price of gas in California and nationally is statistically significant at the .05 level, or specify the level of significance by saying that the level of significance is less than .0001. For more about significance, refer to A Closer Look 8.1.

Recall that our hypothesis was a one-tailed test ($\mu > \$2.32$). In a two-tailed test, sample outcomes may be located at both the higher and the lower ends of the sampling distribution. Thus, the null hypothesis will be rejected if our sample outcome falls either at the left or right tail of the sampling distribution. For instance, a .05 alpha or p level means that H_0 will

A CLOSER LOOK 8.1

MORE ABOUT SIGNIFICANCE

Just because a relationship between two variables is statistically significant does not mean that the relationship is important theoretically or practically. Recall that we are relying on information from a sample to infer characteristics about the population. If you decide to reject the null hypothesis, you must still determine what inferences you can make about the population. Ronald Wasserstein and Nicole Lazar (2016) advise, "Researchers should bring many contextual factors into play to derive scientific inferences, including the design of a study, the quality of the measurements, the external evidence for the phenomenon under study, and the validity of assumptions that underlies the data analysis."[4] Indeed, determining significance is just one part of the research process.

The application of hypothesis testing and significance presented in this text reflects how our discipline currently utilizes and reports hypothesis testing. Yet scholars and statisticians have expressed concern about reducing scientific inquiry to the pursuit of single measure; that is to say, the only result that matters is when $p < .05$ or some arbitrary level of significance. According to demographer Jan Hoem (2008), "The scientific importance of an empirical finding depends much more on its contribution to the development or falsification of a substantive theory than on the values of indicators of statistical significance."(p. 438)[5]

Many have argued how hypothesis testing is problematic because it fails to provide definitive evidence about the existence of real relationships in the data. Despite these criticisms, hypothesis testing remains the primary model by which we derive statistical inference. Several academic journals have adopted new standards for data (e.g., eliminating p values, reporting nonsignificant findings along with significant ones), in hopes of improving the quality and integrity of research.

be rejected if our sample outcome falls among either the lowest or the highest 5% of the sampling distribution.

Suppose we had expressed our research hypothesis about the mean price of gas as

$$H_1: \mu \neq \$2.32$$

The null hypothesis to be directly tested still takes the form $H_0: \mu = \$2.32$ and our obtained Z is calculated using the same formula (Formula 8.1) as was used with a one-tailed test. To find p for a two-tailed test, look up the area in Column C of Appendix B that corresponds to your obtained Z (as we did earlier) and then multiply it by 2 to obtain the two-tailed probability. Thus, the two-tailed p value for $Z = 23.00$ is $.0001 \times 2 = .0002$. This probability is less than our stated alpha (.05), and thus, we reject the null hypothesis.

THE FIVE STEPS IN HYPOTHESIS TESTING: A SUMMARY

Statistical hypothesis testing can be organized into five basic steps. Let's summarize these steps:

1. Making assumptions
2. Stating the research and null hypotheses and selecting alpha
3. Selecting the sampling distribution and specifying the test statistic
4. Computing the test statistic
5. Making a decision and interpreting the results

1. *Making Assumptions:* Statistical hypothesis testing involves making several assumptions regarding the level of measurement of the variable, the method of sampling, the shape of the population distribution, and the sample size. In our example, we made the following assumptions:

- A random sample was used.
- The variable *price per gallon* is measured on an interval-ratio level of measurement.
- Because $N > 50$, the assumption of normal population is not required.

2. *Stating the Research and Null Hypotheses and Selecting Alpha:* The substantive hypothesis is called the research hypothesis and is symbolized as H_1. Research hypotheses are always expressed in terms of population parameters because we are interested in making statements about population parameters based on sample statistics. Our research hypothesis was

$$H_1: \mu > \$2.32$$

The null hypothesis, symbolized as H_0, contradicts the research hypothesis in a statement of no difference between the population mean and our hypothesized value. For our example, the null hypothesis was stated symbolically as

$$H_0: \mu = \$2.32$$

We set alpha at .05, meaning that we would reject the null hypothesis if the probability of our obtained Z was less than or equal to .05.

3. *Selecting the Sampling Distribution and Specifying the Test Statistic:* The normal distribution and the Z statistic are used to test the null hypothesis.

4. *Computing the Test Statistic:* Based on Formula 8.1, our Z statistic is 23.00.

5. *Making a Decision and Interpreting the Results:* We confirm that our obtained Z is on the right tail of the distribution, consistent with our research hypothesis. We determine that the p value of 23.00 is less than .0001, less than our .05 alpha level. We have evidence to reject the null hypothesis of no difference between the mean price of California gas and the mean price of gas nationally. Based on these data, we conclude that the average price of California gas is significantly higher than the national average.

ERRORS IN HYPOTHESIS TESTING

We should emphasize that because our conclusion is based on sample data, we will never really know if the null hypothesis is true or false. In fact, as we have seen, there is a 0.01% chance that the null hypothesis is true and that we are making an error by rejecting it.

Type I error The probability associated with rejecting a null hypothesis when it is true.

Type II error The probability associated with failing to reject a null hypothesis when it is false.

The null hypothesis can be either true or false, and in either case, it can be rejected or not rejected. If the null hypothesis is true and we reject it nonetheless, we are making an incorrect decision. This type of error is called a **Type I error**. Conversely, if the null hypothesis is false but we fail to reject it, this incorrect decision is a **Type II error.**

In Table 8.1, we show the relationship between the two types of errors and the decisions we make regarding the null hypothesis. The probability of a Type I error—rejecting a true hypothesis—is equal to the chosen alpha level. For example, when we set alpha at the .05 level, we know that the probability that the null hypothesis is in fact true is .05 (or 5%).

Table 8.1 Type I and Type II Errors		
	True State of Affairs	
Decision Made	H_0 is True	H_0 is False
Reject H_0	Type I error (α)	Correct decision
Do not reject H_0	Correct decision	Type II error

We can control the risk of rejecting a true hypothesis by manipulating alpha. For example, by setting alpha at .01, we are reducing the risk of making a Type I error to 1%. Unfortunately, however, Type I and Type II errors are inversely related; thus, by reducing alpha and lowering the risk of making a Type I error, we are increasing the risk of making a Type II error (Table 8.1).

As long as we base our decisions on sample statistics and not population parameters, we have to accept a degree of uncertainty as part of the process of statistical inference.

LEARNING CHECK 8.1

The implications of research findings are not created equal. For example, researchers might hypothesize that eating spinach increases the strength of weight lifters. Little harm will be done if the null hypothesis that eating spinach has no effect on the strength of weight lifters is rejected in error. The researchers would most likely be willing to risk a high probability of a Type I error, and all weight lifters would eat spinach. However, when the implications of research have important consequences (funding of social programs or medical testing), the balancing act between Type I and Type II errors becomes more important. Can you think of some examples where researchers would want to minimize Type I errors? When might they want to minimize Type II errors?

The *t* Statistic and Estimating the Standard Error

The Z statistic we have calculated (Formula 8.1) to test the hypothesis involving a sample of California gas stations assumes that the population standard deviation (σ) is known. The value of σ is required to calculate the standard error

$$\sigma / \sqrt{N}$$

In most situations, σ will not be known, and we will need to estimate it using the sample standard deviation s. We then use the t statistic instead of the Z statistic to test the null hypothesis. The formula for computing the t statistic is

$$t = \frac{\bar{Y} - \mu}{s / \sqrt{N}} \quad (8.2)$$

The t value we calculate is called the **t statistic (obtained)**. The obtained t represents the number of standard deviation units (or standard error units) that our sample mean is from the hypothesized value of μ, assuming that the null hypothesis is true.

***t* statistic (obtained)** The test statistic computed to test the null hypothesis about a population mean when the population standard deviation is unknown and is estimated using the sample standard deviation.

The *t* Distribution and Degrees of Freedom

***t* distribution** A family of curves, each determined by its degrees of freedom (*df*). It is used when the population standard deviation is unknown and the standard error is estimated from the sample standard deviation.

Degrees of freedom (*df*) The number of scores that are free to vary in calculating a statistic.

To understand the *t* statistic, we should first be familiar with its distribution. The ***t* distribution** is actually a family of curves, each determined by its degrees of freedom. The concept of degrees of freedom is used in calculating several statistics, including the *t* statistic. The **degrees of freedom (*df*)** represent the number of scores that are free to vary in calculating each statistic.

To calculate the degrees of freedom, we must know the sample size and whether there are any restrictions in calculating that statistic. The number of restrictions is then subtracted from the sample size to determine the degrees of freedom. When calculating the *t* statistic for a one-sample test, we start with the sample size *N* and lose 1 degree of freedom for the population standard deviation we estimate.[6] Note that the degrees of freedom will increase as the sample size increases. In the case of a single-sample mean, the *df* is calculated as follows:

$$df = N - 1 \tag{8.3}$$

Comparing the *t* and *Z* Statistics

Notice the similarities between the formulas for the *t* and *Z* statistics. The only apparent difference is in the denominator. The denominator of *Z* is the standard error based on the population standard deviation σ. For the denominator of *t*, we replace $\sigma / \sqrt{N}$ with $s / \sqrt{N}$, the estimated standard error based on the sample standard deviation.

However, there is another important difference between the *Z* and *t* statistics: Because it is estimated from sample data, the denominator of the *t* statistic is subject to sampling error. The sampling distribution of the test statistic is not normal, and the standard normal distribution cannot be used to determine probabilities associated with it.

In Figure 8.3, we present the *t* distribution for several *df*s. Like the standard normal distribution, the *t* distribution is bell shaped. The *t* statistic, similar to the *Z* statistic, can have positive and

Figure 8.3 The Normal Distribution and t Distributions for 1, 5, 20, and ∞ Degrees of Freedom

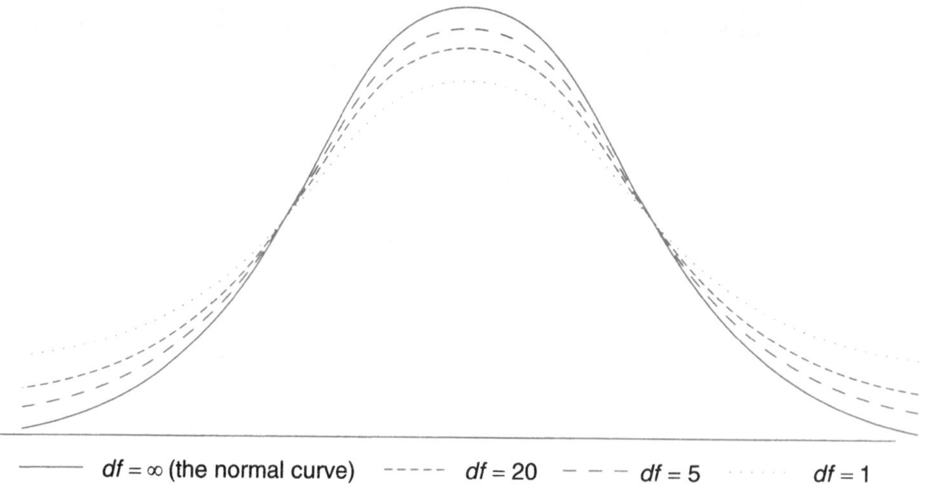

negative values. A positive t statistic corresponds to the right tail of the distribution; a negative value corresponds to the left tail. Note that when the df is small, the t distribution is much flatter than the normal curve. But as the degrees of freedom increases, the shape of the t distribution gets closer to the normal distribution, until the two are almost identical when df is greater than 120.

Appendix C summarizes the t distribution. Note that the t table differs from the normal (Z) table in several ways. First, the column on the left side of the table shows the degrees of freedom. The t statistic will vary depending on the degrees of freedom, which must first be computed ($df = N - 1$). Second, the probabilities or alpha, denoted as significance levels, are arrayed across the top of the table in two rows, the first for a one-tailed and the second for a two-tailed test. Finally, the values of t, listed as the entries of this table, are a function of (a) the degrees of freedom, (b) the level of significance (or probability), and (c) whether the test is a one- or a two-tailed test.

To illustrate the use of this table, let's determine the probability of observing a t value of 2.021 with 40 degrees of freedom and a two-tailed test. Locating the proper row ($df = 40$) and column (two-tailed test), we find the t statistic of 2.021 corresponding to the .05 level of significance. Restated, we can say that the probability of obtaining a t statistic of 2.021 is .05, or that there are less than 5 chances out of 100 that we would have drawn a random sample with an obtained t of 2.021 if the null hypothesis were correct.

HYPOTHESIS TESTING WITH ONE SAMPLE AND POPULATION VARIANCE UNKNOWN

To illustrate the application of the t statistic, let's test a two-tailed hypothesis about a population mean μ. Let's say we drew a random sample of 280 white females who worked full time in 2014. We found their mean earnings to be \$41,653, with a standard deviation, s = \$29,563. Based on data from the U.S. Census Bureau,[7] we also know that the 2014 mean earnings nationally for all women was μ = \$39,621. However, we do not know the value of the population standard deviation. We want to determine whether the sample of white women was representative of the population of all full-time women workers in 2014. Although we suspect that white American women experienced a relative advantage in earnings, we are not sure enough to predict that their earnings were indeed higher than the earnings of all women nationally. Therefore, the statistical test is two tailed.

Let's apply the five-step model to test the hypothesis that the average earnings of white women differed from the average earnings of all women working full-time in the United States in 2014.

1. *Making Assumptions:* Our assumptions are as follows:
   - A random sample is selected.
   - Because $N > 50$, the assumption of normal population is not required.
   - The level of measurement of the variable *income* is interval ratio.
2. *Stating the Research and the Null Hypotheses and Selecting Alpha:* The research hypothesis is

$$H_1: \mu > \$39{,}621$$

and the null hypothesis is

$$H_0: \mu = \$39{,}621$$

We'll set alpha at .05, meaning that we will reject the null hypothesis if the probability of our obtained statistic is less than or equal to .05.

3. *Selecting the Sampling Distribution and Specifying the Test Statistic:* We use the t distribution and the t statistic to test the null hypothesis.

4. *Computing the Test Statistic:* We first calculate the df associated with our test:

$$df = (N - 1) = (280 - 1) = 279$$

To evaluate the probability of obtaining a sample mean of $41,653, assuming the average earnings of white women were equal to the national average of $39,621, we need to calculate the obtained t statistic by using Formula 8.2:

$$t = \frac{\bar{Y} - \mu}{s / \sqrt{N}} = \frac{41{,}653 - 39{,}621}{29{,}563 / \sqrt{280}} = \frac{2{,}032}{1766.73} = 1.15$$

5. *Making a Decision and Interpreting the Results:* Given our research hypothesis, we will conduct a two-tailed test. To determine the probability of observing a t value of 1.15 with 279 degrees of freedom, let's refer to Appendix C. From the first column, we can see that 279 degrees of freedom is not listed, so we'll have to use the last row, $df = \infty$, to assess the significance of our obtained t statistic.

Our obtained t statistic of 1.15 is not listed in the last row. It is less than 1.645 (t critical for .05 one-tailed test) and 1.282 (t critical for .10 one-tailed test). The probability of 1.15 can be estimated as $p > .10$, leading to the conclusion that we fail to reject the null hypothesis. We do not have sufficient evidence to reject the null hypothesis.

HYPOTHESIS TESTING WITH TWO SAMPLE MEANS

The two examples that we reviewed at the beginning of this chapter dealt with data from one sample compared with data from the population. In practice, social scientists are often more interested in situations involving two (sample) parameters than those involving one, such as the differences between men and women, Democrats and Republicans, whites and nonwhites, or high school or college graduates. Specifically, we may be interested in finding out whether the average years of education for one racial/ethnic group is the same, lower, or higher than another group.

U.S. data on educational attainment reveal that Asian and Pacific Islanders have more years of education than any other racial/ethnic groups; this includes the percentage of those earning a high school degree or higher or a college degree or higher. Though years of education have steadily increased for blacks and Hispanics since 1990, their numbers remain behind Asian and Pacific Islanders and whites.

Using data from the 2014 General Social Survey (GSS), we examine the difference in white and black educational attainment. From the GSS sample, white respondents reported an average of 13.88 years of education and blacks, an average of 13.00 years as shown in Table 8.2. These sample averages could mean either (a) the average number of years of education for whites is higher than the average for blacks or (b) the average for whites is actually about the same as for blacks, but our sample just happens to indicate a higher average for whites. What we are applying here is a bivariate analysis (for more information, refer to Chapter 9 ["Bivariate Tables"]),

Table 8.2 Years of Education for White and Black Men and Women, GSS 2014

	Whites (Sample 1)	Blacks (Sample 2)
Mean	13.88	13.00
Standard deviation	2.99	2.28
Variance	8.94	5.20
N	445	88

a method to detect and describe the relationship between two variables—*race/ethnicity* and *educational attainment*.

The statistical procedures discussed in the following sections allow us to test whether the differences that we observe between two samples are large enough for us to conclude that the populations from which these samples are drawn are different as well. We present tests for the significance of the differences between two groups. Primarily, we consider differences between sample means and differences between sample proportions.

Hypothesis testing with two samples follows the same structure as for one-sample tests: The assumptions of the test are stated, the research and null hypotheses are formulated and the alpha level selected, the sampling distribution and the test statistic are specified, the test statistic is computed, and a decision is made whether or not to reject the null hypothesis.

The Assumption of Independent Samples

One important difference between one- and two-sample hypothesis testing involves sampling procedures. With a two-sample case, we assume that the samples are independent of each other. The choice of sample members from one population has no effect on the choice of sample members from the second population. In our comparison of whites and blacks, we are assuming that the selection of whites is independent of the selection of black individuals. (The requirement of independence is also satisfied by selecting one sample randomly, then dividing the sample into appropriate subgroups. For example, we could randomly select a sample and then divide it into groups based on gender, religion, income, or any other attribute that we are interested in.)

Stating the Research and Null Hypotheses

The second difference between one- and two-sample tests is in the form taken by the research and the null hypotheses. In one-sample tests, both the null and the research hypotheses are statements about a single population parameter, μ. In contrast, with two-sample tests, we compare two population parameters.

Our research hypothesis (H_1) is that the average years of education for whites is not equal to the average years of education for black respondents. We are stating a hypothesis about the relationship between race/ethnicity and education in the general population by comparing the mean educational attainment of whites with the mean educational attainment of blacks.

Symbolically, we use μ to represent the population mean; the subscript 1 refers to our first sample (whites) and subscript 2 to our second sample (blacks). Our research hypothesis can then be expressed as

$$H_1: \mu_1 \neq \mu_2$$

Because H_1 specifies that the mean education for whites is not equal to the mean education for blacks, it is a nondirectional hypothesis. Thus, our test will be a two-tailed test. Alternatively, if there were sufficient basis for deciding which population mean score is larger (or smaller), the research hypothesis for our test would be a one-tailed test:

$$H_1: \mu_1 < \mu_2 \text{ or } H_1: \mu_1 > \mu_2$$

In either case, the null hypothesis states that there are no differences between the two population means:

$$H_0: \mu_1 = \mu_2$$

We are interested in finding evidence to reject the null hypothesis of no difference so that we have sufficient support for our research hypothesis.

LEARNING CHECK 8.2

For the following research situations, state your research and null hypotheses:

- *There is a difference between the mean statistics grades of social science majors and the mean statistics grades of business majors.*
- *The average number of children in two-parent black families is lower than the average number of children in two-parent nonblack families.*
- *Grade point averages are higher among girls who participate in organized sports than among girls who do not.*

Sampling distribution of the difference between means A theoretical probability distribution that would be obtained by calculating all the possible mean differences that would be obtained by drawing all the possible independent random samples of size N_1 and N_2 from two populations where N_1 and N_2 are both greater than 50.

THE SAMPLING DISTRIBUTION OF THE DIFFERENCE BETWEEN MEANS

The sampling distribution allows us to compare our sample results with all possible sample outcomes and estimate the likelihood of their occurrence. Tests about differences between two sample means are based on the **sampling distribution of the difference between means**. The sampling distribution of the difference between two sample means is a theoretical probability distribution that would be obtained by calculating all the possible mean differences by drawing all possible independent random samples of size N_1 and N_2 from two populations.

The properties of the sampling distribution of the difference between two sample means are determined by a corollary to the central limit theorem. This theorem assumes that our samples are independently drawn from normal populations, but that with sufficient sample size ($N_1 > 50$, $N_2 > 50$) the sampling distribution of the difference between means will be approximately normal, even if the original populations are not normal. This sampling distribution has a mean $\mu_{Y_1} - \mu_{Y_2}$ and a standard deviation (standard error)

$$\sigma_{\bar{Y}_1-\bar{Y}_2} = \sqrt{\frac{\sigma_1^2}{N_1} + \frac{\sigma_2^2}{N_2}} \tag{8.4}$$

which is based on the variances in each of the two populations (σ_1^2 and σ_2^2).

Estimating the Standard Error

Formula 8.4 assumes that the population variances are known and that we can calculate the standard error $\sigma_{\bar{Y}_1-\bar{Y}_2}$ (the standard deviation of the sampling distribution). However, in most situations, the only data we have are based on sample data, and we do not know the true value of the population variances, σ_1^2 and σ_2^2. Thus, we need to estimate the standard error from the sample variances, s_1^2 and s_2^2. The estimated standard error of the difference between means is symbolized as $S_{\bar{Y}_1-\bar{Y}_2}$ (instead of $\sigma_{\bar{Y}_1-\bar{Y}_2}$).

Calculating the Estimated Standard Error

When we can assume that the two population variances are equal, we combine information from the two sample variances to calculate the estimated standard error.

$$S_{\bar{Y}_1-\bar{Y}_2} = \sqrt{\frac{(N_1-1)s_1^2 + (N_2-1)s_2^2}{(N_1+N_2)-2}}\sqrt{\frac{N_1+N_2}{N_1N_2}} \tag{8.5}$$

where $S_{\bar{Y}_1-\bar{Y}_2}$ is the estimated standard error of the difference between means, and s_1^2 and s_2^2 are the variances of the two samples. As a rule of thumb, when either sample variance is more than twice as large as the other, we can no longer assume that the two population variances are equal and would need to use Formula 8.8 in A Closer Look 8.2.

The *t* Statistic

As with single sample means, we use the *t* distribution and the *t* statistic whenever we estimate the standard error for a difference between means test. The *t* value we calculate is the obtained *t*. It represents the number of standard deviation units (or standard error units) that our mean difference $\bar{Y}_1 - \bar{Y}_2$ is from the hypothesized value of $\mu_1 - \mu_2$, assuming that the null hypothesis is true.

The formula for computing the *t* statistic for a difference between means test is

$$t = \frac{\bar{Y}_1 - \bar{Y}_2}{S_{\bar{Y}_1-\bar{Y}_2}} \tag{8.6}$$

where $S_{\bar{Y}_1-\bar{Y}_2}$ is the estimated standard error.

Calculating the Degrees of Freedom for a Difference Between Means Test

To use the *t* distribution for testing the difference between two sample means, we need to calculate the degrees of freedom. As we saw earlier, the degrees of freedom (*df*) represent the number of scores that are free to vary in calculating each statistic. When calculating the *t* statistic for the two-sample test, we lose 2 degrees of freedom, one for every population variance we estimate. When population variances are assumed to be equal or if the size of both samples is greater than 50, the *df* is calculated as follows:

$$df = (N_1 + N_2) - 2 \tag{8.7}$$

When we cannot assume that the population variances are equal and when the size of one or both samples is equal to or less than 50, we use Formula 8.9 in A Closer Look 8.2 to calculate the degrees of freedom.

THE FIVE STEPS IN HYPOTHESIS TESTING ABOUT DIFFERENCE BETWEEN MEANS: A SUMMARY

As with single-sample tests, statistical hypothesis testing involving two sample means can be organized into five steps.

1. *Making Assumptions:* In our example, we made the following assumptions:
    - Independent random samples are used.
    - The variable *years of education* is measured at an interval-ratio level of measurement.
    - Because $N_1 > 50$ and $N_2 > 50$, the assumption of normal population is not required.
    - The population variances are assumed to be equal.

A CLOSER LOOK 8.2

CALCULATING THE ESTIMATED STANDARD ERROR AND THE DEGREES OF FREEDOM (*df*) WHEN THE POPULATION VARIANCES ARE ASSUMED TO BE UNEQUAL

If the variances of the two samples (s_1^2 and s_2^2) are very different (one variance is twice as large as the other), the formula for the estimated standard error becomes

$$S_{\bar{Y}_1 - \bar{Y}_2} = \sqrt{\frac{s_1^2}{N_1} + \frac{s_2^2}{N_2}} \tag{8.8}$$

When the population variances are unequal and the size of one or both samples is equal to or less than 50, we use another formula to calculate the degrees of freedom associated with the *t* statistic:[8]

$$df = \frac{(s_1^2 / N_1 + s_2^2 / N_2)^2}{(s_1^2 / N_1)/(N_1 - 1) + (s_2^2 / N_1)/(N_2 - 1)} \tag{8.9}$$

2. *Stating the Research and Null Hypotheses and Selecting Alpha:* Our research hypothesis is that the mean education of whites is different from the mean education of blacks, indicating a two-tailed test. Symbolically, the research hypothesis is expressed as

$$H_1: \mu_1 \neq \mu_2$$

with μ_1 representing the mean education of whites and μ_2 the mean education of blacks.

The null hypothesis states that there are no differences between the two population means, or

$$H_0: \mu_1 = \mu_2$$

We are interested in finding evidence to reject the null hypothesis of no difference so that we have sufficient support for our research hypothesis. We will reject the null hypothesis if the probability of t (obtained) is less than or equal to .05 (our alpha value).

3. *Selecting the Sampling Distribution and Specifying the Test Statistic:* The t distribution and the t statistic are used to test the significance of the difference between the two sample means.

4. *Computing the Test Statistic:* To test the null hypothesis about the differences between the mean education of whites and blacks, we need to translate the ratio of the observed differences to its standard error into a t statistic (based on data presented in Table 8.2). The obtained t statistic is calculated using Formula 8.6:

$$t = \frac{\bar{Y}_1 - \bar{Y}_2}{S_{\bar{Y}_1 - \bar{Y}_2}}$$

where $S_{\bar{Y}_1 - \bar{Y}_2}$ is the estimated standard error of the sampling distribution. Because the population variances are assumed to be equal, df is $(N_1 + N_2) - 2 = (445 + 88) - 2 = 531$ and we can combine information from the two sample variances to estimate the standard error (Formula 8.5):

$$S_{\bar{Y}_1 - \bar{Y}_2} = \sqrt{\frac{(445-1)(2.99)^2 + (88-1)(2.28)^2}{(445+88)-2}}\sqrt{\frac{445+88}{(445)(88)}} = (2.89)(0.12) = 0.35$$

We substitute this value into the denominator for the t statistic (Formula 8.6):

$$t = \frac{13.88 - 13.00}{0.35} = 2.51$$

5. *Making a Decision and Interpreting the Results:* We confirm that our obtained t is on the right tail of the distribution. Since our obtained t statistic of 2.51 is greater than $t = 1.96$ ($df = \infty$, two tailed; see Appendix C), we can state that its probability is less than .05. We can reject the null hypothesis of no difference between the educational attainment of whites and blacks. We conclude that based on our sample data, white men and women, on average, have significantly higher years of education than black men and women do.

LEARNING CHECK 8.3

Would you change your decision in the previous example if alpha was .01? Why or why not?

STATISTICS IN PRACTICE: CIGARETTE USE AMONG TEENS

Administered annually since 1975, the Monitoring the Future (MTF) survey measures the extent of and beliefs regarding drug use among 8th, 10th, and 12th graders. In recent years, data collected from the MTF surveys revealed decreases or stability in drug use among youths, particularly for cigarettes, alcohol, marijuana, cocaine, and methamphetamine.[9]

Let's examine data from the MTF 2014 survey, comparing first-time cigarette use between black and white students.

We will rely on SPSS to calculate the *t* obtained for the data. We will not present the complete five-step model and *t*-test calculation because we want to focus here on interpreting the SPSS output. However, we will need a research hypothesis and an alpha level to guide our interpretation. SPSS always estimates a two-tailed test, namely, does the gap of 1.47 (7.2844 – 5.8095) indicate a difference in when black and white adolescents first smoke cigarettes? We'll set alpha at .05.

The output includes two tables. The Group Statistics table (Figure 8.4) presents descriptive statistics for each group. The survey results indicate that black students are more likely to smoke cigarettes later (in earlier grades) than white students. The mean grade of first use of cigarettes is 5.8095 for black students and 7.2844 for white students.

In the second table (Figure 8.5), labeled Independent Samples Test, *t* statistics are presented for equal variances assumed (–3.444) and equal variances not assumed (–3.665). Both *t*-obtained statistics are negative, indicating that the average grade for black students is lower than the average grade for white students. In order to determine which *t* statistic to use, review the results of the Levene's test for Equality of Variances. The Levene's test (a calculation that we will not cover in this text) tests the null hypothesis that the population variances are equal. If the significance of the reported *F* statistic is equal to or less than .05 (the baseline alpha for the Levene's test), we can reject the null hypothesis that the variances are equal; if the significance is greater than .05, we fail to reject the null hypothesis. (In other words, if the significance

Figure 8.4 Group Statistics, MTF 2014

Group Statistics

	RACE 2014 RACE--B/W/H F1234	N	Mean	Std. Deviation	Std. Error Mean
NGradeSmoke New Grade Smoke	1 BLACK:(1)	21	5.8095	1.66190	.36266
	2 WHITE:(2)	109	7.2844	1.82113	.17443

Figure 8.5 Independent Samples Test, MTF 2014

Independent Samples Test

		Levene's Test for Equality of Variances		t-test for Equality of Means						
									95% Confidence Interval of the Difference	
		F	Sig.	t	df	Sig. (2-tailed)	Mean Difference	Std. Error Difference	Lower	Upper
NGradeSmoke New Grade Smoke	Equal variances assumed	.077	.782	-3.444	128	.001	-1.47488	.42829	-2.32233	-.62743
	Equal variances not assumed			-3.665	30.027	.001	-1.47488	.40243	-2.29671	-.65305

for the Levene's test is greater than .05, refer to the t obtained for equal variances assumed; if the significance is less than .05, refer to the t obtained for equal variances not assumed.) Since the significance of F is $.782 > .05$, we fail to reject the null hypothesis and conclude that the variances are equal. Thus, the t obtained that we will use for this model is −3.444 (the one corresponding to equal variances assumed).

SPSS calculates the exact probability of the t obtained for a two-tailed test. There is no need to estimate it based on Appendix C (as we did in our previous example). The significance of −3.444 is .001, which is less than our alpha level of .05. We reject the null hypothesis of no difference for grade of first-time cigarette use between white and black students. On average, black students first use cigarettes at a later grade (1.47 grades earlier) than white students.

LEARNING CHECK 8.4

State the null and research hypothesis for this SPSS example.

Would you change your decision in the previous example if alpha was .01? Why or why not?

HYPOTHESIS TESTING WITH TWO SAMPLE PROPORTIONS

In the preceding sections, we have learned how to test for the significance of the difference between two population means when the variable is measured at an interval-ratio level. Yet numerous variables in the social sciences are measured at a nominal or an ordinal level. These variables are often described in terms of proportions or percentages. For example, we might be interested in comparing the proportion of those who support immigrant policy reform among Hispanics and non-Hispanics or the proportion of men and women who supported the Democratic candidate during the last presidential election. In this section, we present statistical inference techniques to test for significant differences between two sample proportions.

Hypothesis testing with two sample proportions follows the same structure as the statistical tests presented earlier: The assumptions of the test are stated, the research and null hypotheses are formulated, the sampling distribution and the test statistic are specified, the test statistic is calculated, and a decision is made whether or not to reject the null hypothesis.

In 2013, the Pew Research Center[10] presented a comparison of first-generation Americans (immigrants who were foreign born) and second-generation Americans (adults who have at least one immigrant parent) on several key demographic variables. Based on several measures of success, the Center documented social mobility between the generations, confirming that second-generation Americans were doing better than the first-generation Americans. The statistical question we examine here is whether the difference between the generations is significant.

For example, according to the Center's report, the proportion of first-generation Hispanic Americans who earned a bachelor's degree or higher was 0.11 (p_1); the proportion of second-generation Hispanic Americans with the same response was 0.21 (p_2). A total of 899 first-generation Hispanic Americans (N_1) and 351 second-generation Hispanic Americans (N_2) answered this question. We use the five-step model to determine whether the difference between the two proportions is significant.

1. *Making Assumptions:* Our assumptions are as follows:

- Independent random samples of $N_1 > 50$ and $N_2 > 50$ are used.
- The level of measurement of the variable is nominal.

2. *Stating the Research and Null Hypotheses and Selecting Alpha:* We propose a two-tailed test that the population proportions for first-generation and second-generation Hispanic Americans are not equal.

$$H_1: \pi_1 \neq \pi_2$$
$$H_0: \pi_1 = \pi_2$$

We decide to set alpha at .05.

3. *Selecting the Sampling Distribution and Specifying the Test Statistic:* The population distributions of dichotomies are not normal. However, based on the central limit theorem, we know that the sampling distribution of the difference between sample proportions is normally distributed when the sample size is large (when $N_1 > 50$ and $N_2 > 50$), with mean $\mu_{p_1-p_2}$ and the estimated standard error $S_{p_1-p_2}$. Therefore, we can use the normal distribution as the sampling distribution, and we can calculate Z as the test statistic.[11]

The formula for computing the Z statistic for a difference between proportions test is

$$Z = \frac{p_1 - p_2}{S_{p_1-p_2}} \tag{8.10}$$

where p_1 and p_2 are the sample proportions for first- and second-generation Hispanic Americans, and $S_{p_1-p_2}$ is the estimated standard error of the sampling distribution of the difference between sample proportions.

The estimated standard error is calculated using the following formula:

$$S_{p_1-p_2} = \sqrt{\frac{p_1(1-p_1)}{N_1} + \frac{p_2(1-p_2)}{N_2}} \tag{8.11}$$

4. *Calculating the Test Statistic:* We calculate the standard error using Formula 8.11:

$$S_{p_1-p_2} = \sqrt{\frac{0.11(1-0.11)}{899} + \frac{0.21(1-0.21)}{351}} = \sqrt{0.000581547} = 0.02$$

Substituting this value into the denominator of Formula 8.10, we get

$$Z = \frac{0.11 - 0.21}{0.02} = -5.00$$

5. *Making a Decision and Interpreting the Results:* Our obtained Z of −5.00 indicates that the difference between the two proportions will be evaluated at the left tail (the negative side) of the Z distribution. To determine the probability of observing a Z value of −5.00 if the null hypothesis is true, look up the value in Appendix B (Column C) to find the area to the right of (above) the obtained Z.

Note that a Z score of 5.00 is not listed in Appendix B; however, the value exceeds the largest Z reported in the table, 4.00. The p value corresponding to a Z score of –5.00 would be less than .0001. For a two-tailed test, we'll have to multiply p by 2 ($.0001 \times 2 = .0002$). If this were a one-tailed test, we would not have to multiply the p value by 2. The probability of –5.00 for a two-tailed test is less than our alpha level of .05 ($.0002 < .05$).

Thus, we reject the null hypothesis of no difference. Based on the Pew Research data, we conclude that there is a significantly higher proportion of college graduates among second-generation Hispanic Americans compared with first-generation Hispanic Americans.

LEARNING CHECK 8.5

If alpha was changed to .01, two-tailed test, would your final decision change? Explain.

We continue our analysis of the 2013 Pew Research Center data, this time examining the difference in educational attainment between first- and second-generation Asian Americans presented in Table 8.3. Our research hypothesis is whether there is a lower proportion of college graduates among first-generation Asian Americans than second-generation Asian Americans, indicating a one-tailed test. We'll set alpha at .05.

The final calculation for Z is

$$Z = \frac{0.50 - 0.55}{0.02} = -2.50$$

The one-tailed probability of –2.50 is .0062. Comparing .0062 to our alpha, we reject the null hypothesis of no difference. We conclude that a significantly higher proportion of second-generation Asian Americans (55%) have a bachelor's degree or higher compared with first-generation Asian Americans (50%). The 5% difference is significant at the .05 level.

LEARNING CHECK 8.6

If alpha was changed to .01, one-tailed test, would your final decision change? Explain.

Table 8.3 Proportion of College Graduates Among First-Generation and Second-Generation Asian Americans

First-Generation Asian Americans	Second-Generation Asian Americans
$p_1 = .50$	$p_2 = .55$
$N_1 = 2{,}684$	$N_2 = 566$

Source: Pew Research Center, *Second-Generation Americans: A Portrait of the Adult Children of Immigrants*. Pew Research Center, Washington, D.C. February 7, 2013. http://www.pewsocialtrends.org/2013/02/07/second-generation-americans/

READING THE RESEARCH LITERATURE: REPORTING THE RESULTS OF HYPOTHESIS TESTING

Let's conclude with an example of how the results of statistical hypothesis testing are presented in the social science research literature. Keep in mind that the research literature does not follow the same format or the degree of detail that we've presented in this chapter. For example, most research articles do not include a formal discussion of the null hypothesis or the sampling distribution. The presentation of statistical analyses and detail will vary according to the journal's editorial policy or the standard format for the discipline.

It is not uncommon for a single research article to include the results of 10 to 20 statistical tests. Results have to be presented succinctly and in summary form. An author's findings are usually presented in a summary table that may include the sample statistics (e.g., the sample means), the obtained test statistics (t or Z), the p level, and an indication of whether or not the results are statistically significant.

Robert Emmet Jones and Shirley A. Rainey (2006) examined the relationship between race, environmental attitudes, and perceptions about environmental health and justice.[12] Researchers have documented how people of color and the poor are more likely than whites and more affluent groups to live in areas with poor environmental quality and protection, exposing them to greater health risks. Yet little is known about how this disproportional exposure and risk are perceived by those affected. Jones and Rainey studied black and white residents from the Red River community in Tennessee, collecting data from interviews and a mail survey during 2001 to 2003.

They created a series of index scales measuring residents' attitudes pertaining to environmental problems and issues. The Environmental Concern (EC) Index measures public concern for specific environmental problems in the neighborhood. It includes questions on drinking water quality, landfills, loss of trees, lead paint and poisoning, the condition of green areas, and stream and river conditions. EC-II measures public concern (very unconcerned to very concerned) for the overall environmental quality in the neighborhood. EC-III measures the seriousness (not serious at all to very serious) of environmental problems in the neighborhood. Higher scores on all EC indicators indicate greater concern for environmental problems in their neighborhood. The Environmental Health (EH) Index measures public perceptions of certain physical side effects, such as headaches, nervous disorders, significant weight loss or gain, skin rashes, and breathing problems. The EH Index measures the likelihood (very unlikely to very likely) that the person believes that he or she or a household member experienced health problems due to exposure to environmental contaminants in his or her neighborhood. Higher EH scores reflect a greater likelihood that respondents believe that they have experienced health problems from exposure to environmental contaminants. Finally, the Environmental Justice (EJ) Index measures public perceptions about environmental justice, measuring the extent to which they agreed (or disagreed) that public officials had informed residents about environmental problems, enforced environmental laws, or held meetings to address residents' concerns. A higher mean EJ score indicates a greater likelihood that respondents think public officials failed to deal with environmental problems in their neighborhood.[13] Index score comparisons between black and white respondents are presented in Table 8.4.

Table 8.4 Environmental Concern (EC), Environmental Health (EH), and Environmental Justice (EJ)					
Indicator	**Group**	**Mean**	**Standard Deviation**	**t**	**Significance (One Tailed)**
EC Index	Blacks	56.2	13.7	6.2	<0.001
	Whites	42.6	15.5		
EC-II	Blacks	4.4	1.0	5.6	<0.001
	Whites	3.5	1.3		
EC-III	Blacks	3.4	1.1	6.7	<0.001
	Whites	2.3	1.0		
EH Index	Blacks	23.0	10.5	5.1	<0.001
	Whites	16.0	7.3		
EJ Index	Blacks	31.0	7.3	3.8	<0.001
	Whites	27.2	6.3		

Source: Robert E. Jones and Shirley A. Rainey, "Examining Linkages Between Race, Environmental Concern, Health and Justice in a Highly Polluted Community of Color," *Journal of Black Studies* 36, no. 4 (2006): 473–496.

Note: N = 78 blacks, 113 whites.

LEARNING CHECK 8.7

Based on Table 8.4, what would be the t critical at the .05 level for the first indicator, EC Index? Assume a two-tailed test.

Let's examine the table carefully. Each row represents a single index measurement, reporting means and standard deviations separately for black and white residents. Obtained *t*-test statistics are reported in the second to last column. The probability of each *t* test is reported in the last column ($p < .001$), indicating a significant difference in responses between the two groups. All index score comparisons are significant at the .001 level. (*Note:* Researchers will use "n.s." to indicate non-significant results.)

While not referring to specific differences in index scores or to *t*-test results, Jones and Rainey use data from this table to summarize the differences between black and white residents on the three environmental index measurements:

> The results presented [in Table 1] suggest that as a group, Blacks are significantly more concerned than Whites about local environmental conditions (EC Index). . . . The results . . . also indicate that as a group, Blacks believe they have suffered more health problems from exposure to poor environmental conditions in their neighborhood than Whites (EH Index). . . . [T]here is greater likelihood that Blacks feel local public agencies and officials failed to deal with environmental problems in their neighborhood in a fair, just, and effective manner (EJ Index). (p. 485)[14]

DATA AT WORK

Stephanie Wood: Campus Visit Coordinator

Photo courtesy of Stephanie Wood

At a mid-west liberal arts university, Stephanie coordinates the campus visit program for the Office of Admission, partnering with other university members (faculty, administrators, coaches, and alumni) to ensure that each prospective student visit is tailored to the student's needs. Stephanie says her work allows her to "think both creatively and strategically in developing innovative and successful events while also providing the opportunity to mentor a group of over fifty college students."

She explains how she uses statistical data and methods to improve the campus visit program. "Emphasis is placed on analyzing the success of each event by tracking the number of campus visitors and event attendees who progress further through the enrollment funnel by later applying, being admitted, and eventually enrolling to the institution. Events that have high yield (a large number of attendees who later enroll) are duplicated while events with low yield are deconstructed and examined to discover what aspects factored in to the low yield. Variables examined typically include, ambassador to student/family ratios, number of students who met with faculty in their major of interest, number of student-athletes able to meet with athletics, university events occurring at competing universities on the same day, weather, and various other factors. After the analysis is complete, conclusions regarding the low yield are made and new strategies are developed to help combat the findings."

Stephanie examines these variables on a daily basis. "I am constantly doing bivariate and multivariate analyses to ensure all events are contributing to increased enrollment across all student profiles."

"Regardless of whether a student *wants* to work with statistics, it is likely they will have to, to some extent. I would advise students to look at statistics in a much simpler and less scary mindset. Measuring office efficiencies, project successes, and understanding biases is incredibly important in a professional setting."

MAIN POINTS

- Statistical hypothesis testing is a decision-making process that enables us to determine whether a particular sample result falls within a range that can occur by an acceptable level of chance. The process of statistical hypothesis testing consists of five steps: (1) making assumptions, (2) stating the research and null hypotheses and selecting alpha, (3) selecting a sampling distribution and a test statistic, (4) computing the test statistic, and (5) making a decision and interpreting the results.
- Statistical hypothesis testing may involve a comparison between a sample mean and a population mean or a comparison between two sample means. If we know the population variance(s) when testing for differences between means, we can use the Z statistic and the normal distribution.

However, in practice, we are unlikely to have this information.

- When testing for differences between means when the population variance(s) are unknown, we use the t statistic and the t distribution.
- Tests involving differences between proportions follow the same procedure as tests for differences between means when population variances are known. The test statistic is Z, and the sampling distribution is approximated by the normal distribution.

KEY TERMS

alpha (α) 208
degrees of freedom (df) 212
left-tailed test 205
null hypothesis (H_0) 206
one-tailed test 205
p value 207
research hypothesis (H_1) 204
right-tailed test 205
sampling distribution of the difference between means 216
statistical hypothesis testing 204
t distribution 212
t statistic (obtained) 211
two-tailed test 206
Type I error 210
Type II error 210
Z statistic (obtained) 207

DIGITAL RESOURCES

SAGE edge™

Get the edge on your studies. **edge.sagepub.com/frankfort8e**

Take a quiz to find out what you've learned.
Review key terms with eFlashcards.
Dive into real research with SAGE Journal Articles.

SPSS DEMONSTRATIONS [GSS14SSDS-B]

Demonstration 1: Producing a One-Sample T Test

In this chapter, we discussed methods of testing differences in means between a sample and a population value. SPSS includes a One-Sample T Test procedure to do this test. SPSS does not compute the test with the Z statistic; instead, it uses the t statistic to test for all mean differences. The One-Sample T Test procedure can be found under the *Analyze* menu choice, then under *Compare Means*, where it is labeled *One-Sample T Test*. The opening dialog box (Figure 8.6) requires that you place at least one variable in the Test Variable(s) box. Then a test value must be specified.

We'll use the GSS2014-B data set for this demonstration. The standard workweek is thought to be 40 hours, so let's test to see whether American adults work that many hours each week. In this example, place HRS1 in the Test Variable(s) box and "40" in the Test Value box. Then click on *OK* to run the procedure.

The output from the One-Sample T Test procedure is not very extensive (see Figure 8.7). A total of 895 people answered the question about number of hours worked per week. The mean number of hours worked is 41.47, with a standard deviation of 15.039. Below this, SPSS lists the test value, 40. It includes the two-tailed significance, or probability, for the one-sample test. This value is .004, given the calculated *t* statistic of 2.918, with 894 degrees of freedom. Thus, at the .01 significance level, we would reject the null hypothesis and conclude that American adults work more than 40 hours per week.

SPSS also supplies a 95% confidence interval for the mean difference between the test value and the sample mean. Here, the confidence interval runs from 0.48 to 2.45, providing estimates of how much more than 40 hours per week Americans work.

Figure 8.6 One-Sample T Test Dialog Box

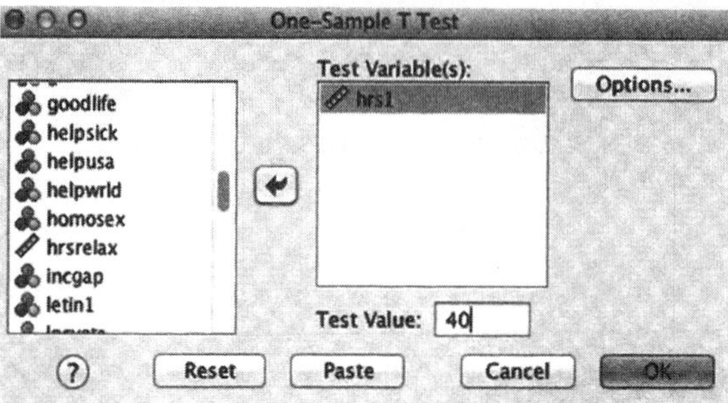

Figure 8.7 One-Sample T Test Output

One-Sample Statistics

	N	Mean	Std. Deviation	Std. Error Mean
hrs1 NUMBER OF HOURS WORKED LAST WEEK	895	41.47	15.039	.503

One-Sample Test

	Test Value = 40					
					95% Confidence Interval of the Difference	
	t	df	Sig. (2-tailed)	Mean Difference	Lower	Upper
hrs1 NUMBER OF HOURS WORKED LAST WEEK	2.918	894	.004	1.467	.48	2.45

Demonstration 2: Producing a Test of Mean Differences

In this chapter, we have also discussed methods of testing differences in means or proportions between two samples (or groups). The Two-Sample T Test procedure can be found under the *Analyze* menu choice, then under *Compare Means*, where it is labeled *Independent-Samples T Test*.

The opening dialog box requires that you specify various test variables (the dependent variable) and one independent or grouping variable (Figure 8.8). We'll test the null hypothesis that men and women work the same number of hours each week by using the variable HRS1. Place that variable in the Test Variable(s) box and SEX in the Grouping Variable box. When you do so, question marks appear next to SEX indicating that you must supply two values to define the two groups (independent samples). Click on *Define Groups*. Then put "1" in the first box and "2" in the second box (1 = male and 2 = female), as shown in Figure 8.9. Then click on *Continue* and *OK* to run the procedure.

Figure 8.8 Independent-Samples T Test Dialog Box

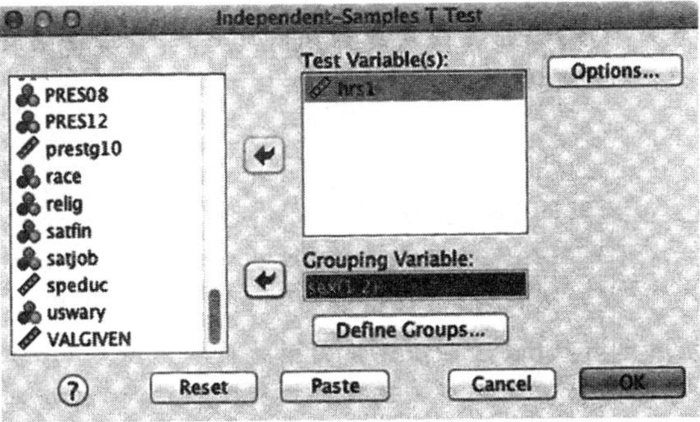

Figure 8.9 Define Groups Dialog Box

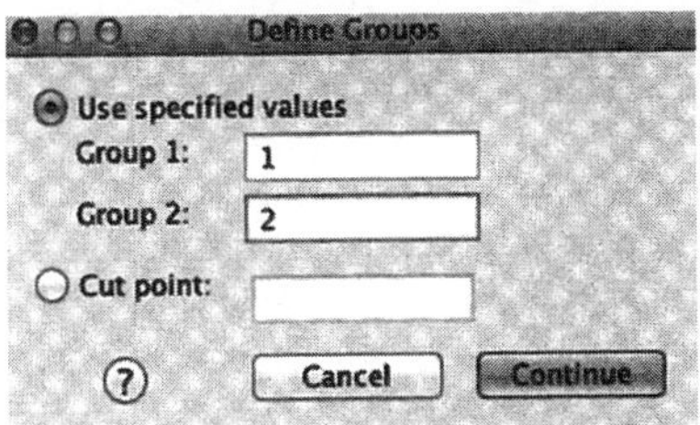

The output from Independent Samples T Test (Figure 8.10) is detailed and contains more information than we have reviewed in this chapter. The first part of the output displays the mean number of hours worked for whites and blacks, the number of respondents in each group, the standard deviation, and the standard error of the mean. We see that males worked 5.00 hours more per week than females (43.92 – 38.92 = 5.00).

Figure 8.10 Independent-Samples T Test Output

Group Statistics

	sex RESPONDENTS SEX	N	Mean	Std. Deviation	Std. Error Mean
hrs1 NUMBER OF HOURS WORKED LAST WEEK	1 MALE	456	43.92	15.528	.727
	2 FEMALE	439	38.92	14.085	.672

Independent Samples Test

		Levene's Test for Equality of Variances		t-test for Equality of Means						
									95% Confidence Interval of the Difference	
		F	Sig.	t	df	Sig. (2-tailed)	Mean Difference	Std. Error Difference	Lower	Upper
hrs1 NUMBER OF HOURS WORKED LAST WEEK	Equal variances assumed	4.931	.027	5.038	893	.000	4.999	.992	3.051	6.946
	Equal variances not assumed			5.048	889.868	.000	4.999	.990	3.055	6.942

Earlier in the chapter, we reviewed the Levene's test and how to determine whether the variances of the two groups are equal. In this case, we reject the null hypothesis of equal variances (the significance of F is .027 < .05 alpha). The t obtained is 5.048 (equal variances not assumed) with a probability of .000 (smaller than .05 or .01). We can reject the null hypothesis of no difference and conclude that men work significantly more hours per week than women. The difference of 5.00 hours is significant at the .000 level.

What if we wanted to do a one-tailed test instead? SPSS does not directly list the probability for a one-tailed test, but it is easy to calculate. If we had specified a directional research hypothesis—such as that men work more hours than women—we would simply take the probability reported by SPSS and divide it into half for a one-tailed test. Because the probability is so large in this case, our conclusion will be the same whether we do a one- or a two-tailed test.

The last portion of output on each line is the 95% confidence interval for the mean difference in hours worked between the two groups. (Confidence intervals were reviewed in Chapter 7.) It is helpful information when testing mean differences because the actual mean difference will vary from sample to sample. The 95% confidence interval gives us a range over which the sample mean differences are likely to vary.

SPSS PROBLEMS [GSS14SSDS-B]

1. Use the GSS file to investigate whether or not Americans use the Internet at least 7 hours per week (estimating an hour per day). Perform the One Sample T Test procedure (as presented in SPSS Demonstration 1) to do this test with the variable WWWHR. Do the test at the .01 significance level. What did you find? Do Americans use the Internet 7 hours per week, more or less?
2. The GSS includes a measure of highest educational degree completed (DEGREE). Test whether there is a significant difference between those with less than high school (coded 0) and those with a bachelor's degree (coded 3) in the number of hours on the Internet per week (WWWHR). Assume α is .05 for a two-tailed test. Summarize your findings.
3. Investigate the difference between individuals who support legalization of marijuana from those who do not based on data from the GSS. Use the variable PRES12 as your independent or grouping variable (1 = Obama and 2 = Romney). Investigate whether there is a significant difference between these two groups in terms of their age (AGE), education (EDUC), and respondent income (NRINCOME06). Assume that α is .05 for a two-tailed test. Based on your analysis, write three Step 5–type statements summarizing your findings.
4. For this analysis, use the variable GOD as your independent variable, comparing individuals who believe in some higher power (3) or know God exists (6). Use the same dependent variables, AGE, EDUC, and NRINCOME06, to estimate t tests. Assume a is .05 for a two-tailed test. Prepare a statement to summarize your findings.

CHAPTER EXERCISES

1. It is known that, nationally, doctors working for health maintenance organizations (HMOs) average 13.5 years of experience in their specialties, with a standard deviation of 7.6 years. The executive director of an HMO in a Western state is interested in determining whether or not its doctors have less experience than the national average. A random sample of 150 doctors from HMOs shows a mean of only 10.9 years of experience.

a. State the research and the null hypotheses to test whether or not doctors in this HMO have less experience than the national average.

b. Using an alpha level of .01, calculate this test.

2. In this chapter, we examined the difference in educational attainment between first- and second-generation Hispanic and Asian Americans based on the proportion of each group with a bachelor's degree. We present additional data from the Pew Research Center's 2013 report, measuring the percentage of each group that owns a home.

	Percentage Owning a Home
First-Generation Hispanic Americans $N = 899$	43
Second-Generation Hispanic Americans $N = 351$	50
First-Generation Asian Americans $N = 2{,}684$	58
Second-Generation Asian Americans $N = 566$	51

Source: Pew Research Center, Second-Generation Americans: A Portrait of the Adult Children of Immigrants. Pew Research Center, Washington, D.C. February 7, 2013. http://www.pewsocialtrends.org/2013/02/07/second-generation-americans/

a. Test whether there is a significant difference in the proportion of homeowners between first- and second-generation Hispanic Americans. Set alpha at .05.

b. Test whether there is a significant difference in the proportion of homeowners between first- and second-generation Asian Americans. Set alpha at .01.

3. For each of the following situations determine whether a one- or a two-tailed test is appropriate. Also, state the research and the null hypotheses.

a. You are interested in finding out if the average household income of residents in your state is different from the national average household. According to the U.S. Census, for 2014, the national average household income is $53,657.[15]

b. You believe that students in small liberal arts colleges attend more parties per month than students nationwide. It is known that nationally undergraduate students attend an average of 3.2 parties per month. The average number of parties per month will be calculated from a random sample of students from small liberal arts colleges.

c. A sociologist believes that the average income of elderly women is lower than the average income of elderly men.

d. Is there a difference in the amount of study time on-campus and off-campus students devote to their schoolwork during an average week? You prepare a survey to determine the average number of study hours for each group of students.

e. Reading scores for a group of third graders enrolled in an accelerated reading program are predicted to be higher than the scores for nonenrolled third graders.

f. Stress (measured on an ordinal scale) is predicted to be lower for adults who own dogs (or other pets) than for non–pet owners.

4. In 2016, the Pew Research Center[16] surveyed 1,799 white and 1,001 black Americans about their views on race and inequality. Pew researchers found "profound differences between black and white adults in their views on racial discrimination, barriers to black progress and the prospects for change." White and black respondents also disagreed about the best methods to achieve

racial equality. For example, 34% of whites and 41% of blacks said that "bringing people of different racial backgrounds together to talk about race" would be a very effective tactic for groups striving to help blacks achieve equality. Test whether the proportion of white respondents who support this tactic is significantly less than the proportion of black respondents.

a. State the null and research hypotheses.

b. Calculate the Z statistic and test the hypothesis at the .05 level. What is your Step 5 decision?

5. One way to check on how representative a survey is of the population from which it was drawn is to compare various characteristics of the sample with the population characteristics. A typical variable used for this purpose is age. The GSS 2014 found a mean age of 50.12 and a standard deviation of 17.07 for its sample of 1,490 American adults. Assume that we know from census data that the mean age of all American adults is 37.20. Use this information to answer the following questions.

   a. State the research and the null hypotheses for a two-tailed test of means.

   b. Calculate the t statistic and test the null hypothesis at the .001 significance level. What did you find?

   c. What is your decision about the null hypothesis? What does this tell us about how representative the sample is of the American adult population?

6. Is there a significant difference in the level of community service participation between college and high school graduates? According to the GSS 2014, 44% of 88 college graduates reported volunteering in the previous month compared with 30% of 245 high school graduates.

   a. What is the research hypothesis? Should you conduct a one- or a two-tailed test? Why?

   b. Present the five-step model, testing your hypothesis at the .05 level. What do you conclude?

7. GSS 2014 respondents were asked, "Some people say the following things are important for being truly American. Others say they are not important. How important do you think each of the following is—to be a Christian?" Responses were measured on a 4-point scale: 1 = very important, 2 = fairly important, 3 = not very important, and 4 = not important at all. Those with a high school degree had an average score of 2.35 ($s = 1.21, N = 189$) while respondents with a bachelor's degree had an average score of 3.05 ($s = 1.05, N = 61$).

   a. What is the appropriate test statistic? Why?

   b. Test the null hypothesis with a one-tailed test (conservatives are less likely to believe being Christian is not important at all); $\alpha = .05$. What do you conclude about the difference in attitudes between high school and bachelor's degree graduates?

   c. If you conducted a two-tailed test with $\alpha = .05$, would your decision have been different?

8. We compare the proportion who indicated that it was "very important" to be born in this country to be American for two GSS 2014 groups: respondents (1) born in the United States (native born) and (2) not born in the United States (foreign born). Test the research hypothesis that a higher proportion of native-born respondents than foreign-born respondents indicated being born in the United States was "very important" to be American. Set alpha at .05.

	Native Born Sample 1	Foreign Born Sample 2
Proportion	.48	.36
N	338	59

9. In surveys conducted during August 2016 (months before the election), the Pew Research Center reported that among 752 men, 55% indicated that regardless of how they felt about Hillary Clinton, the election of a women as president would be very important historically. Among 815 women, 65% reported the same. Do these differences reflect a significant gender gap?

 a. If you wanted to test the research hypothesis that the proportion of male voters who believe in the historical importance of the election of a woman as president is less than the proportion of female voters who believe the same, would you conduct a one- or a two-tailed test?

 b. Test the research hypothesis at the .05 alpha level. What do you conclude?

 c. If alpha were changed to .01, would your decision remain the same?

10. In the chapter, we examined the difference between white and black students in the timing of when they first tried cigarettes. In this SPSS output, we examine the grade when MTF 2014 white and black students first tried alcohol. Present Step 5 (final decision) for these data. Assume alpha = .05, two-tailed test.

T Test Output for RACE and NGradeAlcohol

Group Statistics

	RACE 2014 RACE--B/W/H F1234	N	Mean	Std. Deviation	Std. Error Mean
NGradeAlcohol New Grade Alcohol	1 BLACK:(1)	49	7.0408	1.70733	.24390
	2 WHITE:(2)	224	7.8125	1.67027	.11160

Independent Samples Test

		Levene's Test for Equality of Variances		t-test for Equality of Means					95% Confidence Interval of the Difference	
		F	Sig.	t	df	Sig. (2-tailed)	Mean Difference	Std. Error Difference	Lower	Upper
NGradeAlcohol New Grade Alcohol	Equal variances assumed	.009	.925	-2.918	271	.004	-.77168	.26446	-1.29235	-.25102
	Equal variances not assumed			-2.877	69.546	.005	-.77168	.26822	-1.30670	-.23667

11. Research indicates that charitable giving is more common among older adults, though increased giving by Millennials is part of a growing trend. We examine charitable giving (measured in dollars) for two age groups: (1) 30–39 years and (2) 50–59 years of age, based on data from the GSS2014. Assume alpha = .05 for a two-tailed test. What can you conclude about the difference in giving between the two age groups?

Group Statistics

	recoded Age	N	Mean	Std. Deviation	Std. Error Mean
TOTAL DONATIONS PAST YEAR R AND IMMEDIATE FAMILY	30-39	62	1145.32	2611.793	331.698
	50-59	82	1583.24	3661.567	404.352

Independent Samples Test

		Levene's Test for Equality of Variances		t-		
		F	Sig.	t	df	Sig. (2-tailed)
TOTAL DONATIONS PAST YEAR R AND IMMEDIATE FAMILY	Equal variances assumed	1.318	.253	-.800	142	.425
	Equal variances not assumed			-.837	141.568	.404

12. Based on the 2014 MTF survey, we compare social network media usage (measured by an ordinal scale: 1 = none, 2 = less than an hour, 3 = 1–2 hours, 4 = 3–5 hours, 5 = 6–9 hours, 6 = 10–19 hours, 7 = 20–29 hours, 8 = 30–39 hours, and 9 = 40+ hours) between males and females. (Recall that the MTF 2014 is a survey of teens in the 8th, 10th, and 12th grades.)

a. Interpret the group means for males and females. Which group spends more time on social media?

b. Assume alpha = .05 for a two-tailed test. What can you conclude about the difference in social network usage between the two groups?

c. If alpha were changed to .01, would your Step 5 decision change? Explain.

Group Statistics

	sex 2014 R01 R'S SEX F1234	N	Mean	Std. Deviation	Std. Error Mean
SocialNetHr 2014 C09 #HR/W SOCIAL NET WEB F1!	1 MALE:(1)	184	3.60	2.382	.176
	2 FEMALE:(2)	220	5.05	2.568	.173

Independent Samples Test

		Levene's Test for Equality of Variances		t-test for Equality of Means						
									95% Confidence Interval of the Difference	
		F	Sig.	t	df	Sig. (2-tailed)	Mean Difference	Std. Error Difference	Lower	Upper
SocialNetHr 2014 C09 #HR/W SOCIAL NET WEB F1!	Equal variances assumed	2.866	.091	-5.828	402	.000	-1.447	.248	-1.935	-.959
	Equal variances not assumed			-5.867	397.706	.000	-1.447	.247	-1.932	-.962

13. In Chapter 7's SPSS Demonstration, we used the Explore command to calculate the confidence intervals for HRSRELAX for men and women. The GSS 2014 asked respondents "after an average work day, about how many hours do you have to relax or pursue the activities you enjoy"? In this exercise, we selected married GSS respondents and calculated the *t* test for HRSRELAX.

a. Is there a significant difference between married men and married women in the number of hours they have to relax during the day? Set alpha at .05.

b. If alpha was changed to .01, would your Step 5 decision change? Explain.

Group Statistics

	RESPONDENTS SEX	N	Mean	Std. Deviation	Std. Error Mean
HOURS PER DAY R HAVE TO RELAX	MALE	126	3.56	2.566	.229
	FEMALE	113	2.88	2.164	.204

Independent Samples Test

		Levene's Test for Equality of Variances		t-test for Equality of Means						
									95% Confidence Interval of the Difference	
		F	Sig.	t	df	Sig. (2-tailed)	Mean Difference	Std. Error Difference	Lower	Upper
HOURS PER DAY R HAVE TO RELAX	Equal variances assumed	2.596	.108	2.225	237	.027	.687	.309	.079	1.296
	Equal variances not assumed			2.246	236.126	.026	.687	.306	.084	1.290

9

BIVARIATE TABLES

One of the main objectives of social science is to make sense out of human and social experience by uncovering regular patterns among events. Therefore, the language of relationships is at the heart of social science inquiry. Consider the following examples from articles and research reports:

Example 1: Americans 50 years and older are more likely to oppose creating a path to citizenship for illegal immigrants than are younger Americans.[1] (This example indicates a relationship between age and immigration reform.)

Example 2: Contrary to the stereotype, whites use government safety net programs more than blacks or Latinos, and they are more likely than minorities to be lifted out of poverty by the taxpayer money that they get.[2] (This example indicates a relationship between race and receipt of government aid.)

Example 3: On average, blacks, Asians, and Hispanics are more likely than whites not to have health insurance.[3] (This example indicates a relationship between race and access to health care.)

In each of these examples, certain values of one variable are related with certain values of the other variable. In Chapter 1 ("The What and the Why of Statistics"), we described a relationship in terms of an independent and a dependent variable. For Example 1, the purpose of the research is to explain support for *immigration reform*, the dependent variable. Age is associated with immigration reform, specifically being younger is associated with support of a path to citizenship. *Age* is the independent variable.

Chapter Learning Objectives

1. Create and analyze a bivariate table
2. Identify the properties of a bivariate relationship: existence, strength, and direction
3. Explain how to elaborate the relationship between variables: nonspuriousness, intervening, and conditional relationships

LEARNING CHECK 9.1

Identify the independent and dependent variables in Examples 2 and 3.

Cross-tabulation A technique for analyzing the relationship between two nominal or ordinal variables that have been organized in a table.

Bivariate analysis A statistical method designed to detect and describe the relationship between two nominal or ordinal variables.

Bivariate table A table that displays the distribution of one variable across the categories of another variable.

In this chapter, we introduce one of the most common techniques used in the analysis of relationships between two variables: cross-tabulation. **Cross-tabulation** is a technique for analyzing the relationship between two variables (an independent and a dependent variable) that have been organized in a table. A cross-tabulation is a type of **bivariate analysis**, a method designed to detect and describe the relationship between two nominal or ordinal variables. We demonstrate not only how to detect whether two variables are associated but also how to determine the strength of the association and, when appropriate, its direction.[4]

HOW TO CONSTRUCT A BIVARIATE TABLE

A **bivariate table** displays the distribution of one variable across the categories of another variable. It is obtained by classifying cases based on their joint scores on two nominal or ordinal variables. It can be thought of as a series of frequency distributions joined to make one

Table 9.1 Race and Home Ownership for 20 GSS Respondents

Respondent	Race	Home Ownership
1	Black	Own
2	Black	Own
3	White	Rent
4	White	Rent
5	White	Own
6	White	Own
7	White	Own
8	Black	Rent
9	Black	Rent
10	Black	Rent
11	White	Own
12	White	Own
13	White	Rent
14	White	Own
15	Black	Rent
16	White	Own
17	Black	Rent
18	White	Rent
19	Black	Own
20	Black	Rent

Table 9.2 Home Ownership by Race (Absolute Frequencies), GSS

	Race: Black	Race: White	
Own	3	7	10 (Row Total)
Rent	6	4	10 (Row Total)
(Column Total)	9	11	20 Total cases (*N*)

table. The data in Table 9.1 represent a sample of General Social Survey (GSS) respondents by race and whether they own or rent their home (in this case, both variables are nominal-level measurements).

To make sense out of these data, we must first construct the table in which these individual scores will be classified. In Table 9.2, the 20 respondents have been classified according to joint scores on race and home ownership.

The table has the following features typical of most bivariate tables:

1. The table's title is descriptive, identifying its content in terms of the two variables.
2. It has two dimensions, one for race and one for home ownership. The variable *home ownership* is represented in the rows of the table, with one row for owners and another for renters. The variable *race* makes up the columns of the table, with one column for each racial group. A table may have more columns and more rows, depending on how many categories the variables represent. For example, had we included a group of Latinos, there would have been three columns (not including the Row Total column). Usually, the independent variable is the **column variable** and the dependent variable is the **row variable.**
3. The intersection of a row and a column is called a **cell**. For example, the two individuals represented in the upper left cell are blacks who are also homeowners.
4. The column and row totals are the frequency distribution for each variable, respectively. The column total is the frequency distribution for *race*, the row total for *home ownership*. Row and column totals are sometimes called **marginals**. The total number of cases (N) is the number reported at the intersection of the row and column totals. (These elements are all labeled in the table.)
5. The table is a 2 × 2 table because it has two rows and two columns (not counting the marginals). We usually refer to this as an $r \times c$ table, in which r represents the number of rows and c the number of columns. Thus, a table in which the row variable has three categories and the column variable has two categories would be designated as a 3 × 2 table.

Column variable A variable whose categories are the columns of a bivariate table.

Row variable A variable whose categories are the rows of a bivariate table.

Cell The intersection of a row and a column in a bivariate table.

Marginals The row and column totals in a bivariate table.

6. The source of the data should also be clearly noted in a source note to the table. This is consistent with what we reviewed in Chapter 2 ("The Organization and Graphic Presentation of Data").

LEARNING CHECK 9.2

Examine Table 9.2. Make sure you can identify all the parts just described and that you understand how the numbers were obtained. Can you identify the independent and dependent variables in the table? You will need to know this to convert the frequencies to percentages.

HOW TO COMPUTE PERCENTAGES IN A BIVARIATE TABLE

To compare home ownership status for blacks and whites, we need to convert the raw frequencies to percentages because the column totals are not equal. Recall from Chapter 2 that percentages are especially useful for comparing two or more groups that differ in size. There are two basic rules for computing and analyzing percentages in a bivariate table:

1. Calculate percentages within each category of the independent variable.
2. Interpret the table by comparing the percentage point difference for different categories of the independent variable.

Calculating Percentages Within Each Category of the Independent Variable

The first rule means that we have to calculate percentages within each category of the variable that the investigator defines as the independent variable. When the independent variable is arrayed in the columns, we compute percentages within each column separately. The frequencies within each cell and the row marginals are divided by the total of the column in which they are located, and the column totals should sum to 100%. When the independent variable is arrayed in the rows, we compute percentages within each row separately. The frequencies within each cell and the column marginals are divided by the total of the row in which they are located, and the row totals should sum to 100%.

Table 9.3 Home Ownership by Race (in Percentages)

	Race		
Home Ownership	Black	White	Total
Own	33%	64%	50%
Rent	67%	36%	50%
Total	100%	100%	100%
(*N*)	(9)	(11)	(20)

In our example, we are interested in *race* as the independent variable and in its relationship with *home ownership*. Therefore, we are going to calculate percentages by using the column total of each racial group as the base of the percentage. For example, the percentage of black respondents who own their homes is obtained by dividing the number of black homeowners by the total number of blacks in the sample.

Table 9.3 presents percentages based on the data in Table 9.2. Notice that the percentages in each column add up to 100%, including the total column percentages. Always show the *N*s that are used to compute the percentages—in this case, the column totals.

Comparing the Percentages Across Different Categories of the Independent Variable

The second rule tells us to compare how home ownership varies between blacks and whites. Comparisons are made by examining differences between percentage points across different categories of the independent variable. Some researchers limit their comparisons to categories with at least a 10 percentage point difference. In our comparison, we can see that there is a 31 percentage point difference between the percentage of white homeowners (64%) and black homeowners (33%). In other words, in this group, whites are more likely to be homeowners than blacks.[5] Therefore, we can conclude that one's race appears to be associated with the likelihood of being a homeowner.

Note that the same conclusion would be drawn had we compared the percentage of black and white renters. However, since the percentages of homeowners and renters within each racial group sum to 100%, we need to make only one comparison. In fact, for any 2 × 2 table, only one comparison needs to be made to interpret the table. For a larger table, more than one comparison can be made and used in interpretation.

LEARNING CHECK 9.3

Practice constructing a bivariate table. Use Table 9.1 to create a percentage bivariate table. Compare your table with Table 9.3. Did you remember all the parts? Are your calculations correct? If not, go back and review this section. It might be helpful to examine A Closer Look 9.1 below. It illustrates the process of constructing and percentaging bivariate tables. Remember, you must correctly identify the independent variable so that you know whether to percentage across the rows or down the columns.

READING THE RESEARCH LITERATURE: HISPANIC AND NON-HISPANIC HOMELESS POPULATIONS

The guidelines for constructing and interpreting bivariate tables discussed in this chapter are not always strictly followed. Most bivariate tables presented in the professional literature are more complex than those we have just been describing. Let's conclude this section with an example of how bivariate tables are presented in social science literature.

This example is from Ernest Castañeda, Jonathan Klassen, and Curtis Smith's (2014) research on the homeless population in El Paso, Texas. According to Castañeda and his colleagues, Hispanics are underrepresented in many local homeless populations, due to methodological

A CLOSER LOOK 9.1

HOW TO DEAL WITH AMBIGUOUS RELATIONSHIPS BETWEEN VARIABLES

Sometimes it isn't apparent which variable is independent or dependent; sometimes the data can be viewed either way. In this case, you might compute both row and column percentages. For example, Table 9.4 presents three sets of figures for the variables SPANKING and FEFAM for a sample of 106 GSS respondents: (a) the absolute frequencies, (b) the column percentages, and (c) the row percentages. SPANKING is measured with the survey question "Do you favor spanking to discipline a child?" The variable FEFAM measures whether the respondent agrees or disagrees with the statement "a man should work and a woman should stay at home." Table 9.4b shows that respondents who strongly disagree with spanking a child are less likely to agree to the FEFAM statement than those who strongly agree with spanking (11% compared with 49%). Table 9.4c shows that individuals who strongly agree that a man should work and a woman should stay at home are more likely to agree to spanking than those who disagree with the statement on men and women's roles (93% compared with 63%).

Table 9.4 The Different Ways Percentages Can Be Computed: SPANKING by FEFAM

	SPANKING		
FEFAM	Strongly Agree	Strongly Disagree	Row Total
a. Absolute frequencies			
Strongly agree	39	3	42
Strongly disagree	40	24	64
Column total	79	27	106
b. Column percentages (column totals as base)			
Strongly agree	49%	11%	40%
Strongly disagree	51%	89%	60%
Column total	100%	100%	100%
	(79)	(27)	(106)
c. Row percentages (row totals as base)			
Strongly agree	93%	7%	100%
			(42)
Strongly disagree	63%	38%	101%
			(64)
Column total	75%	25%	100%
			(106)

Thus, percentaging within each column (Table 9.4b) allows us to examine the hypothesis that spanking (the independent variable) is associated with agreement to the FEFAM statement (dependent variable). When we percentage within each row (Table 9.4c), the hypothesis is that agreement or disagreement with the FEFAM statement (the independent variable) may be related to SPANKING (the dependent variable).[6]

Finally, it is important to understand that ultimately what guides the construction and interpretation of bivariate tables is the theoretical question posed by the researcher. Although the particular example in Table 9.4 makes sense if interpreted using row or column percentages, not all data can be interpreted this way. For example, a table comparing women's and men's attitudes toward sexual harassment in the workplace could provide a sensible explanation in only one direction. Gender might influence a person's attitude toward sexual harassment; however, a person's attitude toward sexual harassment certainly couldn't influence her or his gender. Therefore, either row or column percentages are appropriate, depending on the way the variables are arrayed, but not both.

data collection biases. Hispanic homeless, they observe, are likely to sleep and live in places with family members rather than live in the streets or utilize homeless shelters. Thus, when homeless census counts are conducted in shelters and on streets, Hispanic homeless men and women are often omitted. For their study, the researchers used a snowball sampling technique canvasing Hispanic neighborhoods, day-labor, and agricultural worksites.[7] Demographic characteristics of the two samples—(1) Hispanic and (2) non-Hispanic homeless—are reported in Table 9.5.

Notice how the table is percentaged by ethnic group (by column). With the exception of percentage enrolled in school, the percentages sum to 100% by ethnic category, not by the demographic characteristic (by rows). The researchers compare demographic characteristics for each ethnic group.

> Our study found no substantial difference in gender ratios between the Hispanic and non-Hispanic populations, with much larger percentages of males than females in both the Hispanic (79.9%) and non-Hispanic (84.6%) populations. Approximately 42.3% of Hispanic and 38.0% of non-Hispanic populations were more than 50 years old. However, there are significant differences in several other demographics. (p. 490)[8]
>
> Hispanic homeless were more likely to have been raised in the El Paso region (40.3%) or abroad (49.1%) than non-Hispanic homeless, the majority of whom (68.0%) were raised outside of the El Paso region, a point that the researchers return to in their conclusions. Homeless Hispanics were much more likely to have lived in El Paso for more than 5 years than non-Hispanics (70% vs. 43.3%). There are also differences in education levels, with a larger percentage of Hispanics having a sixth-grade education or less than non-Hispanics (27.6% vs. 10.2%). More non-Hispanics (45.7%) completed high school than Hispanics (29.9%). Twice as many Hispanics (13.4%) were likely to be currently enrolled in a trade school or working on a degree than non-Hispanics (6.4%).[9]

Regarding the impact of place of origin and the homeless experience, the researchers conclude:

> International and internal migration plays an important yet understudied role in the composition of local homeless populations at any given point in time. Most Hispanics, including those who had been raised abroad, reported having been in El Paso for more than five years. In contrast, most non-Hispanics were raised in the United States, but not in the El Paso region.

Table 9.5 Demographic Comparison Between Hispanic and Non-Hispanic Homeless in El Paso, Texas	Hispanic (%) (N = 445)	Non-Hispanic (%) (N = 225)
Gender		
Male	79.9	84.6
Female	20.1	15.4
Age		
25 and less	17.5	8.6
25–50	40.2	53.4
Above 50	42.3	38.0
Raised		
El Paso Region	40.3	28.4
In the United States	10.7	68.0
Abroad	49.1	3.6
Time in El Paso		
Less than 4 months	3.4	13.8
4–6 months	3.2	4.6
7–12 months	3.2	4.1
1–2 years	6.6	11.5
2–5 years	11.9	17.5
Above 5 years	70.0	43.3
Enrolled in school	13.4	6.4
Education level		
Up to sixth grade	27.6	10.2
More than sixth and less than high school	22.9	22.3
Completed high school/GED	29.9	45.7
Trade/tech	11.2	13.2
Bachelor's degree	7.5	6.1
Graduate/Professional degree	0.9	2.5
Primary language		
English	20.2	95.7
Spanish	79.8	4.3

Source: Adapted from Ernest Castañeda, Jonathan Klassen, and Curtis Smith, "Hispanic and Non-Hispanic Homeless Populations in El Paso, Texas," *Hispanic Journal of Behavioral Sciences* 36 (2014): 491.

More than 40% of non-Hispanics reported having been in El Paso for more than 5 years, which demonstrates that a larger percentage of non-Hispanic homeless individuals are transient, while demonstrating that El Paso is attractive even to non-Hispanic individuals who are not originally from this area. Our research did not address what causes homeless individuals to stay for extended periods in the El Paso region, but reasons for this could include: the fact that being in the southwest, El Paso has relatively pleasant weather for those living on the street, especially in the winter; that given the location of Fort Bliss in the area and services relatively accessible to homeless veterans; or that the local homeless services operate relatively effectively. Some also suggest that Hispanic neighborhoods in El Paso provide accepting and helping environments for the homeless population. (p. 498)[10]

LEARNING CHECK 9.4

Using the percentages reported under "Time in El Paso" in Table 9.5, calculate the cumulative percentages for each homeless group. What percentage of each group was in El Paso for a year or less? Which group has been in El Paso for a longer period of time?

THE PROPERTIES OF A BIVARIATE RELATIONSHIP

So far, we have looked at the general principles of a bivariate relationship as well as the more specific "mechanics" involved in examining bivariate tables. In this section, we present some detailed observations that we may want to make about the "properties" of a bivariate association. These properties can be expressed as three questions to ask when examining a bivariate relationship:[11]

1. Does there appear to be a relationship?
2. How strong is it?
3. What is the direction of the relationship?

The Existence of the Relationship

We have seen earlier in this chapter that calculating percentages and comparing them are the two operations necessary to analyze a bivariate table. Based on Table 9.6, we want to examine whether the frequency of church attendance by respondents had an effect on their support for abortion. Support for abortion was measured with the following question: "Please tell me whether or not you think it should be possible for a pregnant woman to obtain a legal abortion if the woman wants it for any reason." Frequency of church attendance was determined by asking respondents to indicate how often they attend religious services.

Table 9.6 Support for Abortion by Church Attendance

	Church Attendance			
Abortion	Never	Infrequently	Frequently	Total
Yes	55%	50%	26%	43%
No	45%	50%	74%	57%
Total	100%	100%	100%	100%
(*N*)	(111)	(212)	(157)	(480)

Let's hypothesize that those who attend church frequently are more likely to be pro-life. We are not suggesting that church attendance necessarily causes pro-life attitudes, but that perhaps, there is an indirect connection between the two. For example, perhaps those who attend church less frequently are more likely to want decisions about the body to be made on an individual basis through the right to choose an abortion.

In this formulation, *church attendance* is said to influence attitudes toward abortion, so it is the independent variable; therefore, percentages are calculated within each category of church attendance (*church attendance* is the column variable).

A relationship is said to exist between two variables in a bivariate table if the percentage distributions vary across the different categories of the independent variable, in this case church attendance. We can easily see that the percentage that supports abortion changes across the different levels of church attendance. Of those who never attend church, 55% are pro-choice; of those who infrequently attend church, 50% are pro-choice; and of those who frequently attend church, 26% are pro-choice.

Table 9.6 indicates that church attendance and support for abortion are associated as hypothesized.

If church attendance were unrelated to attitudes toward abortion among GSS respondents, then we would expect to find equal percentages of respondents who are pro-choice (or anti-choice) regardless of the level of church attendance. Table 9.7 is a fictional representation of a strictly hypothetical pattern of no association between abortion attitudes and church attendance. The percentage of respondents who are pro-choice in each category of church attendance is equal to the overall percentage of respondents in the sample who are pro-choice (43%).

Table 9.7 Support for Abortion by Church Attendance (a Hypothetical Illustration of No Relationship)

	Church Attendance			
Abortion	Never	Infrequently	Frequently	Total
Yes	43%	43%	43%	43%
No	57%	57%	57%	57%
Total	100%	100%	100%	100%
(*N*)	(111)	(212)	(157)	(480)

The Strength of the Relationship

In the preceding section, we saw how to establish whether an association exists in a bivariate table. If it does, how do we determine the strength of the association between the two variables? A quick method is to examine the percentage difference across the different categories of the independent variable. The larger the percentage difference across the categories, the stronger the association. Percentage differences are a rough indicator of the strength of a relationship between two variables.

In the hypothetical example of no relationship between church attendance and attitude toward abortion (Table 9.7), there is a 0% difference between the columns. At the other extreme, if all respondents who never attended church were pro-choice and none of the respondents who frequently attended church were pro-choice, a perfect relationship would be manifested in a 100%

difference. Most relationships, however, will be somewhere in between these two extremes. In fact, we rarely see a situation with either a 0% or a 100% difference. Going back to the observed percentages in Table 9.6, we find the largest percentage difference between respondents who never attend church and respondents who frequently attend church (55% – 26% = 29%). The difference between respondents who infrequently attend church and respondents who frequently attend church (50% – 26% = 24%), though not as large, is nonetheless substantial, indicating a moderate relationship between church attendance and attitudes toward abortion.

The Direction of the Relationship

When both the independent and dependent variables in a bivariate table are measured at the ordinal level or the interval-ratio level, we can talk about the relationship between the variables as being either positive or negative. A positive bivariate relationship exists when the variables vary in the same direction. Higher values of one variable go together with higher values of the other variable. In a negative bivariate relationship, the variables vary in opposite directions: Higher values of one variable go together with lower values of the other variable (and the lower values of one go together with the higher values of the other).

Positive relationship A bivariate relationship between two variables measured at the ordinal level or higher in which the variables vary in the same direction.

Negative relationship A bivariate relationship between two variables measured at the ordinal level or higher in which the variables vary in opposite directions.

Table 9.8 displays a positive relationship between willingness to pay higher taxes and willingness to pay higher prices based on data from the International Social Survey Programme (ISSP). Examine each category separately. For respondents who are unwilling to pay higher prices, an unwillingness to pay higher taxes is most typical (91.5%). For respondents who are indifferent to paying higher prices, the most common response is to be indifferent to paying higher taxes (55.1%); and finally, for respondents who are willing to pay higher prices, a willingness to pay higher taxes is most typical (57.8%). This is a positive relationship, with a willingness to pay higher prices associated with a willingness to pay higher taxes and an unwillingness to pay higher prices associated with an unwillingness to pay higher taxes.

Table 9.9, also from the ISSP, shows a negative association between educational level and attendance of religious services for a sample of about 400 international respondents. Individuals with no education typically attended religious services two to three times per month or more (66.2%). Individuals with a secondary degree (i.e., roughly, the U.S. equivalent to high school) typically attended religious services infrequently, ranging from monthly to several times a year (35.0%); and for individuals who had completed work at a university, the most common category was "never," meaning they never attend religious services (37.3%). The relationship is a negative one because as educational level increases, the frequency of attendance of religious services decreases.

Table 9.8 Willingness to Pay Higher Taxes by Willingness to Pay Higher Prices: A Positive Relationship, ISSP

Willingness to Pay Higher Taxes	Willingness to Pay Higher Prices		
	Unwilling	Indifferent	Willing
Unwilling	91.5%	36.4%	23.6%
Indifferent	5.1%	55.1%	18.6%
Willing	3.4%	8.5%	57.8%
Total	100%	100%	100%
(*N*)	(529)	(352)	(532)

Table 9.9 Support for Attendance of Religious Services by Educational Level: A Negative Relationship, ISSP

	Educational Level		
Attendance of Religious Services	None	Secondary Degree	University Degree
Never	5.2%	32.5%	37.3%
Infrequently	28.6%	35.0%	34.9%
2–3 times per month or more	66.2%	32.5%	27.8%
Total	100%	100%	100%
(*N*)	(77)	(237)	(126)

ELABORATION

Elaboration A process designed to further explore a bivariate relationship; it involves the introduction of control variables.

Control variable An additional variable considered in a bivariate relationship. The variable is controlled for when we take into account its effect on the variables in the bivariate relationship.

Having established through bivariate analysis that the independent and dependent variables are associated, we seek to further interpret and understand the nature of this relationship. In this section, we discuss a procedure called elaboration. **Elaboration** is a process designed to further explore a bivariate relationship, involving the introduction of additional variables, called **control variables**. By adding a control variable to our analysis, we are considering or "controlling" for the variable's effect on the bivariate relationship. Each potential control variable represents an alternative explanation for the bivariate relationship under consideration.

The introduction of additional control variables into a bivariate relationship serves three primary goals in data analysis.

1. Elaboration allows us to test for nonspuriousness. Establishing cause-and-effect relations requires not only showing that an independent and a dependent variable are associated but also establishing the time order between them and providing theoretical and empirical evidence that the association is nonspurious—that is, it cannot be "explained away" by other variables.
2. Elaboration clarifies the causal sequence of bivariate relationships by introducing variables hypothesized to intervene between the independent and dependent variables.
3. Elaboration specifies the different conditions under which the original bivariate relationship might hold.

Testing for Nonspuriousness: Firefighters and Property Damage

Let's begin with a favorite example of a spurious relationship. Researchers have confirmed a strong bivariate relationship between *number of firefighters* (the independent variable) at a fire site and *amount of property damage* (the dependent variable). The more firefighters at the site, the greater the amount of damage. This association might lead you to the embarrassing conclusion (depicted in Figure 9.1) that firefighters cause property damage at fire sites.

Figure 9.1 The Bivariate Relation Between Number of Firefighters and Property Damage

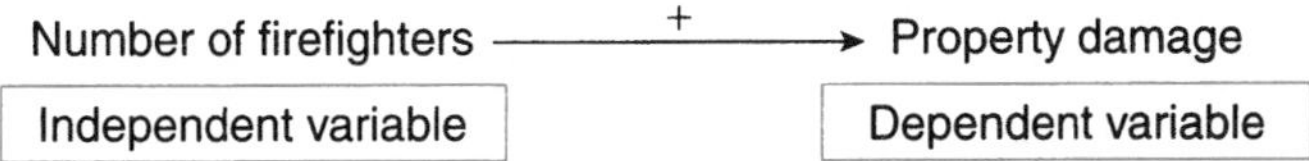

Figure 9.1 depicts what might be a *direct causal relationship* between firefighters and the amount of damage. The relationship between two variables is said to be a direct causal relationship when it cannot be accounted for by other theoretically relevant variables. Clearly, in this case, the relationship between the number of firefighters and amount of damage can be accounted for by a third, causally prior variable—the size of the fire. When the fire is large, more firefighters are sent to the site, and there is a great deal of property damage. Similarly, when the fire is small, fewer firefighters are at the site, and there is probably very little damage.

Direct causal relationship A bivariate relationship that cannot be accounted for by other theoretically relevant variables.

This alternative explanation is shown in Figure 9.2. Note that according to the hypothesized causal order suggested in Figure 9.2, the number of firefighters and the extent of property damage are both related to the variable *size of fire* but are not related to each other. The size of the fire is called a *control variable*, and the relation between the number of firefighters and property damage as depicted in Figure 9.1 is spurious. A spurious relationship is a relationship between two variables in which both the independent and dependent variables are influenced by a causally prior control variable, and there is no causal link between them. The bivariate relationship between the independent and dependent variables can thus be explained away through the introduction of the control variable.

Spurious relationship A relationship in which both the independent and dependent variables are influenced by a causally prior control variable, and there is no causal link between them. The relationship between the independent and dependent variables is said to be "explained away" by the control variable.

Figure 9.2 Spurious Relationship

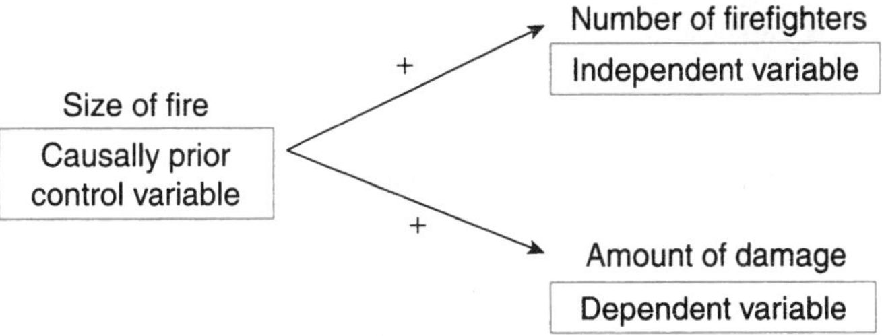

Researchers have adopted the following rule of thumb for determining whether a relationship between two variables is either direct (causal) or spurious: If the bivariate relationship between the two variables remains about the same after controlling for the effect of one or more causally prior and theoretically relevant variables, then the original bivariate relationship is said to be a direct (causal relationship) association. Conversely, if the original bivariate relationship decreases considerably (or vanishes), then the bivariate relationship is said to be spurious.

Let's see how we can apply this rule of thumb to the firefighter example. One way to control for the effect of the size of the fire on the relationship between the number of firefighters and the extent of damage is to divide the fire sites into large and small fires and then reexamine the bivariate association between the other two variables within each group of fire sites. If the original bivariate relationship vanishes (or diminishes considerably), then the explanation suggested by Figure 9.2 would seem more likely. If, however, the original relationship is maintained, then we may need to hold on to the original explanation suggested by Figure 9.1 or go back to the drawing board and think of other alternative explanations for the puzzling relationship between the number of firefighters and the extent of property damage.

Figure 9.3 Elaborating a Bivariate Relationship

1. A bivariate relationship between the number of firefighters and the extent of the property damage at 20 fire sites.

(a)

	Few firefighters	Many firefighters
Low property damage	70%	30%
High property damage	30%	70%
Total	10	10

= small fire

= large fire

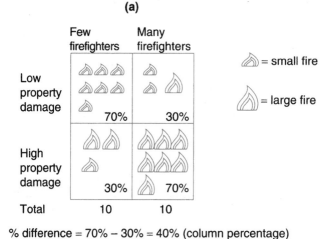

% difference = 70% – 30% = 40% (column percentage)

2. Control for size of fire: divide fire sites into small and large fires. In each group, recalculate the bivariate relationship between the number of firefighters and the extent of the property damage.

(b)

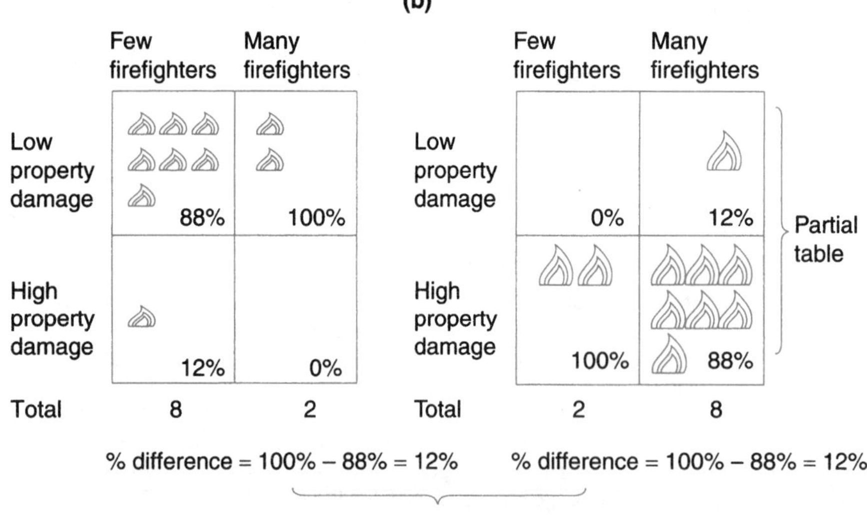

3. Compare the partial relationships with the original relationship: 40% compared with 12%.

Figure 9.3 illustrates the bivariate association between the number of firefighters and the extent of property damage (Figure 9.3a) and the process of controlling for the variable size of fire (Figure 9.3b). Note that the control for size of fire resulted in a substantial decrease (from 40% to 12% difference) in the size of the relationship between the number of firefighters and property damage. This result supports the notion, as depicted in Figure 9.2, that the size of the fire explains both the number of firefighters and the extent of property damage and that the relationship between the number of firefighters and property damage is therefore spurious.

The introduction of the control variable *size of fire* into the original bivariate relationship between *number of firefighters* and *amount of damage* illustrates the process of elaboration. These are the three steps:

1. Divide the observations into subgroups on the basis of the control variable. We have as many subgroups as there are categories in the control variable. (In our case, there were two subgroups: small and large fires.)
2. Reexamine the relationship between the original two variables separately for the control variable subgroups. The separate tables are called partial tables; they display the partial relationship between the independent (number of firefighters) and dependent (amount of damage) variables within each specific category of the control variable (small vs. large fire size).
3. Compare the partial relationships with the original bivariate relationship for the total group. In a direct causal pattern, the partial relationships will be very close to the original bivariate relationship. In a spurious pattern, the partial relationship will be much weaker than the original bivariate relationship.

Partial tables Bivariate tables that display the relationship between the independent and dependent variables while controlling for a third variable.

Partial relationship The relationship between the independent and dependent variables shown in a partial table.

An Intervening Relationship: Religion and Attitude Toward Abortion

The research on the relationship between religious affiliation and attitudes toward abortion has shown a consistent pattern: Religious affiliation is related to the level of support for abortion.[12] In particular, it has been shown that Catholics oppose abortion more than Protestants or Jews do.[13]

To test the hypothesis that religion and abortion attitudes are related, we used data from the 1988 to 1991 GSS sample. We limited our analysis to Catholics and Protestants because of the small numbers of respondents with other religious affiliation. Attitudes toward abortion are measured in terms of respondents' approval or disapproval of the following three situations: (1) the woman does not want the baby because the family has a very low income and cannot afford more children; (2) the woman is not married and does not want to marry the father; and (3) the woman does not want to have more children.[14]

The findings are presented in Table 9.10 and illustrated in Figure 9.4. Since, according to the hypothesis, religious affiliation is the independent variable, we use column percentages for our analysis. The results provide some support for the hypothesis that religion is related to attitudes toward abortion. We see that 45% of Protestants compared with 34% of Catholics support a woman's right to an abortion for these cited reasons.

These results may suggest the existence of a causal relationship between religion and attitudes toward abortion. According to this interpretation of the relationship, being either Protestant or Catholic leads to a different abortion orientation regardless of other factors. Graphically, this hypothesized relationship is shown in Figure 9.5.

Figure 9.4 Percentage Who Support Abortion by Religious Affiliation

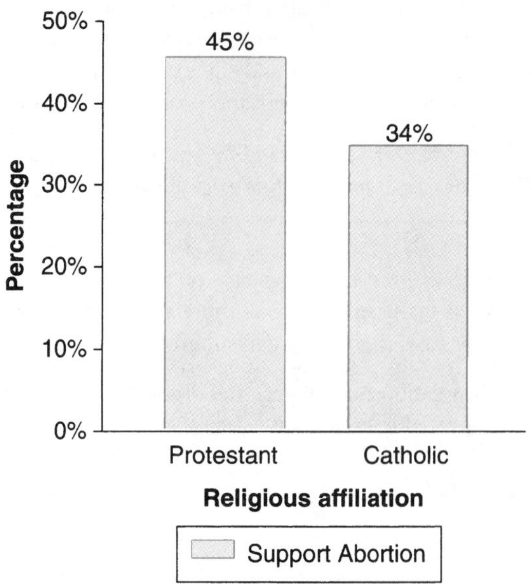

Source: GSS, 1988–1991.

Another body of research findings dealing with religion challenges the conclusion that there is a direct causal link (as suggested by Figure 9.5) between religious affiliation and support for abortion. According to this research literature, some of the differences between Catholics and Protestants can be explained by the variable *preferred family size.*[15] It is argued that religion is systematically related to desired family size: Catholics prefer larger numbers of children than non-Catholics. Similarly, if one conceptualizes abortion as an alternative device to control family size, then support for abortion may also be associated with preferred family size. Therefore, preferred family size operates as an intervening mechanism through which the relationship between religion and abortion attitudes occurs.

Table 9.10 Religious Affiliation and Support for Abortion

	Religious Affiliation		
Support	Catholic	Protestant	Total
Yes	34%	45%	41%
	(56)	(109)	
No	66%	55%	59%
	(107)	(131)	
Total	100%	100%	100%
(*N*)	(163)	(240)	(403)

Source: GSS, 1988–1991.

Figure 9.5 The Bivariate Relationship Between Religion and Support for Abortion

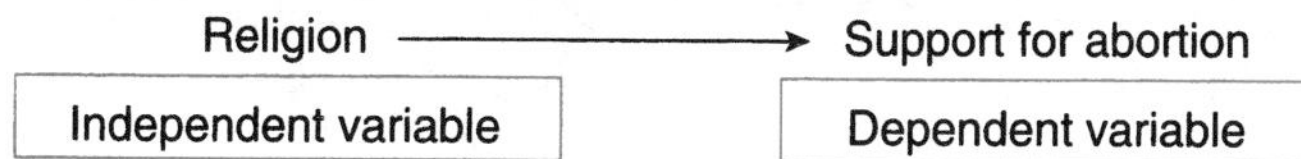

To check these ideas, we analyzed the bivariate associations between preferred family size and religion (Table 9.11) and between preferred family size and support for abortion (Table 9.12).[16] Note that because the theory suggests that preferred family size operates as an intervening mechanism between religious affiliation and support for abortion, it is analyzed as the dependent variable in Table 9.11 and as the independent variable in Table 9.12.

The data in Tables 9.11 and 9.12 confirm the linkages between preferred family size and religion and preferred family size and support for abortion. First, more Catholics (52%) than Protestants (27%) prefer larger families (Table 9.11). Second, more respondents who prefer

Table 9.11 Religious Affiliation and Preferred Family Size

	Religious Affiliation		
Preferred Family Size	Catholic	Protestant	Total
More than 2 children	52%	27%	37%
	(85)	(65)	
2 or fewer children	48%	73%	63%
	(78)	(175)	
Total	100%	100%	100%
(*N*)	(163)	(240)	(403)

Source: GSS, 1988–1991.

Table 9.12 Preferred Family Size and Support for Abortion

	Preferred Family Size		
Support	More Than 2 Children	2 or Fewer Children	Total
Yes	25%	50%	41%
	(38)	(127)	
No	75%	50%	59%
	(112)	(126)	
Total	100%	100%	100%
(*N*)	(150)	(253)	(403)

Source: GSS, 1988–1991.

smaller families support a woman's right to abortion (50%) compared with those who prefer larger families (25%) (Table 9.12). According to this interpretation of the relationship between religion and abortion attitudes, preferred family size is not only associated with both religious affiliation and support for abortion but also intervenes between religious affiliation and support for abortion. Thus, it is hypothesized that the relation between religion and attitudes toward abortion is indirect and linked via the control variable—preferred family size.

The hypothetical causal sequence suggested by this interpretation is shown in Figure 9.6. In this formulation, the control variable (preferred family size) is called an intervening variable. An **intervening variable** is a control variable that follows an independent variable but precedes the dependent variable in a causal sequence. Because preferred family size follows the independent variable, *religion*, but precedes the dependent variable, *abortion attitudes*, it is considered an intervening variable. The relationship between religion and support for abortion is called an intervening relationship. An **intervening relationship** is one between two variables in which a control variable intervenes between the independent and dependent variables.

Intervening variable A control variable that follows an independent variable but precedes the dependent variable in a causal sequence.

Intervening relationship A relationship in which the control variable intervenes between the independent and dependent variables.

We can test the model shown in Figure 9.6 by controlling for preferred family size and repeating the original bivariate analysis between religious affiliation and support for

Figure 9.6 Intervening Relationship

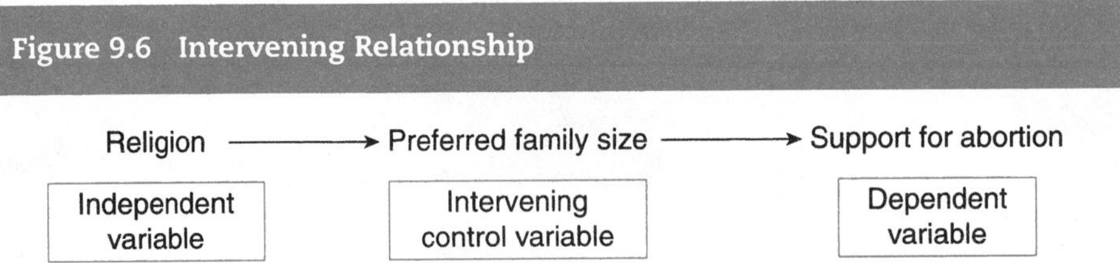

Table 9.13 Religious Affiliation and Support for Abortion After Controlling for Preferred Family Size

	Religious Affiliation		
Support	Catholic	Protestant	Total
Preferred family size: 2 or fewer children			
Yes	46% (36)	52% (91)	50%
No	54% (42)	48% (84)	50%
Total	100%	100%	100%
(*N*)	(78)	(175)	(253)
Preferred family size: more than 2 children			
Yes	24% (20)	28% (18)	25%
No	76% (65)	72% (47)	75%
Total	100%	100%	100%
(*N*)	(85)	(65)	(150)

abortion. We control for preferred family size by separating the respondents who indicated that they preferred larger families from those who preferred smaller families. If the causal sequence hypothesized by Figure 9.6 is correct, then the association between religion and abortion attitudes should disappear or diminish considerably once preferred family size has been controlled.

The results presented in Table 9.13 and Figure 9.7 support the notion, as depicted in Figure 9.6, that preferred family size intervenes between religion and abortion attitudes. The associations between religion and abortion attitudes in the two partial tables are smaller than the original bivariate table (Table 9.10). Among respondents who prefer larger families, there are smaller differences between Catholics and Protestants regarding a woman's right to an abortion. A total of 28% of Protestants and 24% of Catholics support legal abortion. Among those who prefer smaller families, there are also small differences between the two religious groups. A total of 52% of Protestants and 46% of Catholics are in support of abortion. Thus, we would conclude that Catholics are less favorable to abortion (than Protestants) because they prefer larger families. These findings increase our understanding of the original bivariate relationship between religious affiliation and attitudes toward abortion.

LEARNING CHECK 9.5

You may have noticed that the tests for spuriousness and for an intervening relationship are identical: They both require that the partial associations disappear or diminish considerably! So how can you differentiate between the two? The differentiation is made on theoretical rather than empirical grounds. When a relationship is spurious, there is no causal link between the independent and dependent variables; both are influenced by a causally prior control variable. In an intervening relationship, there is an indirect causal link between the independent and dependent variables; the control variable follows the independent variable but precedes the dependent variable in the causal sequence.

Figure 9.7 Percentage Supporting Abortion by Religious Affiliation After Controlling for Preferred Family Size

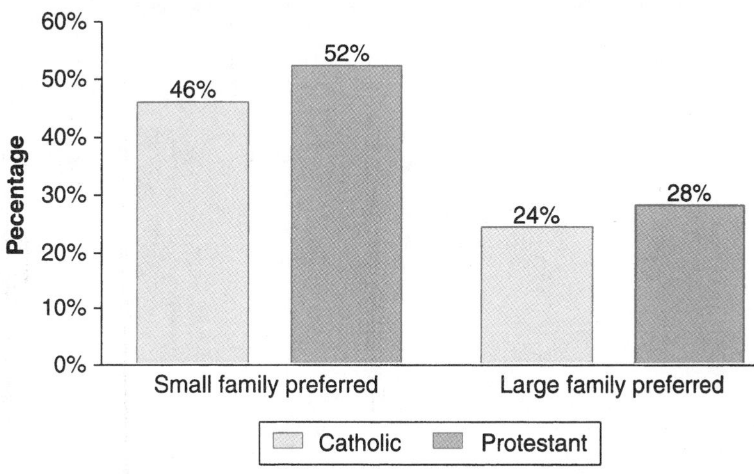

Conditional Relationships: More on Abortion

In their research on abortion attitudes, William Arney and William Trescher (1976) found that when religious participation is controlled for, there is little difference in abortion attitudes between Catholics and Protestants who attend church less than once a month.[17] In contrast, among Catholics and Protestants who attend church more than once a month, Catholics were more likely than Protestants to oppose abortion.[18] Other researchers note that age and gender may also influence the relationship between religion and abortion attitudes.

What do these examples have in common? They all specify different conditions under which the relationship between religion and abortion attitudes is expected to hold. For example, Arney and Trescher (1976) indicate that the differences in abortion attitudes between Protestants and Catholics might hold under one condition (attend church more than once a month) of the control variable religious participation but not under another (attend church less than once a month). Similarly, the relationship may differ for men and women or for older and younger individuals. When a bivariate relationship differs for different conditions of the control variable, we say that it is a **conditional relationship**. Another way to describe a conditional relationship is to say that there is a statistical interaction between the control variable and the independent variable.

Conditional relationship A relationship in which the control variable's effect on the dependent variable is conditional on its interaction with the independent variable. The relationship between the independent and dependent variables will change according to the different conditions of the control variable.

Because conditional relationships are very common, sociology offers many research examples illustrating this pattern of elaboration. One such example comes from a 1989 study by Jacqueline Scott on the relationship between stance on legal abortion and opinions about the morality of abortion. The study shows that although nearly all opponents of legal abortion view abortion as morally wrong, not all pro-choice supporters view abortion as morally right. Instead, many pro-choice supporters favor legal abortion despite personal moral reservations.[19] This bivariate relationship between abortion morality and stance on legal abortion is displayed in Table 9.14.

Because stance on legal abortion is the independent variable, percentages are calculated in the columns. The results of this analysis support Scott's hypothesis. Among those who oppose abortion, there is almost unanimous agreement (98%) that abortion is morally wrong. Among those who favor legal abortion, however, the level of incongruence is relatively high: A total of 37% support legal abortion despite viewing it as morally wrong or ambiguous.[20]

Although there is little difference between men's and women's attitudes toward the legality of abortion, some argue that women are far more likely to feel that abortion is morally wrong.

Table 9.14 Abortion Morality and Stance on Legal Abortion

	Stance on Legal Abortion		
Abortion Morality	Pro-Choice	Pro-Life	Total
Always wrong or depends	37%	98%	57%
Not wrong	63%	2%	43%
Total	100%	100%	100%
(*N*)	(337)	(162)	(499)

Source: Adapted from Jacqueline Scott, "Conflicting Belief About Abortion: Legal Approval and Moral Doubts," *Social Psychology Quarterly* 52, no. 4 (1989): 319–326. Copyright © 1989 by the American Sociological Association. Published by SAGE.

Table 9.15 Abortion Morality and Stance on Legal Abortion After Controlling for Gender

Abortion Morality	Men's Stance on Legal Abortion		Total	Abortion Morality	Women's Stance on Legal Abortion		Total
	Pro-Choice	Pro-Life			Pro-Choice	Pro-Life	
Always wrong or depends	29%	96%	50%	Always wrong or depends	46%	100%	64%
Not wrong	71%	4%	50%	Not wrong	54%	0%	36%
Total	100%	100%	100%	Total	100%	100%	100%
(*N*)	(172)	(78)	(250)	(*N*)	(165)	(84)	(249)

Source: Adapted from Jacqueline Scott, "Conflicting Belief About Abortion: Legal Approval and Moral Doubts," *Social Psychology Quarterly* 52, no. 4 (1989): 319–326. Copyright © 1989 by the American Sociological Association. Published by SAGE.

For example, Carol Gilligan (1982) argues that whereas men tend to be more concerned with rights and rules, women are more concerned with caring and relationships.[21] Abortion, therefore, may pose a greater moral dilemma for women than for men. To examine the hypothesis that women are more likely than men to favor legal abortion despite moral reservations, Scott controlled for gender and compared the original relationship between stance on legal abortion and abortion morality among men and women. The cross-tabulation of abortion morality by stance on legal abortion, controlling for gender, is given in Table 9.15. The table shows a marked gender difference in the relationship between abortion morality and stance on legal abortion. Although we can still conclude from Table 9.15 that the stance on legal abortion and the stance on abortion morality are associated, we need to qualify this conclusion by saying that this association is stronger for men (the percentage difference is 96% – 29% = 67%) than for women (the percentage difference is 100% – 46% = 54%).

Because the relationship between the independent and dependent variables is different in each of the partial tables, the relationship is said to be a conditional relationship—that is, the original bivariate relationship depends on the control variable. In our example, the strength of the relationship between abortion morality and stance on legal abortion is conditioned on gender. The conditional relationship between stance on abortion and abortion morality is depicted in Figure 9.8.

The Limitations of Elaboration

In the illustrations presented in this section, we looked at bivariate relationships that were clarified and reinterpreted when a control variable was introduced. One of the goals of social science is to untangle the complex relationships between variables. Elaboration helps us untangle these bivariate relations.

How do we know which variables to control for? In reality, theory provides significant guidance as to the relationships that we look for and the sorts of variables that should be introduced as controls. Without theory as a guide, elaboration can become a series of exercises that more closely resembles random shots in the dark than scientific analysis. Even with theory as

Figure 9.8 A Conditional Relationship

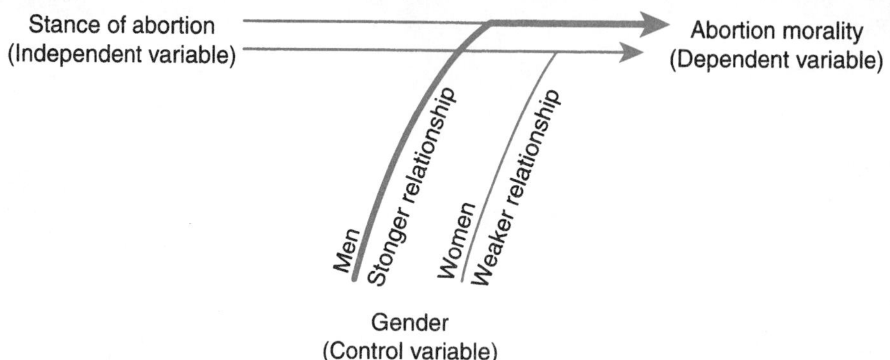

our guide, the statistical analysis is often more complex than the presentation in this section may suggest. In our examples, when the control variable was introduced, the real nature of the relationship is revealed. It's not always that easy. Most often there is a perilous gap between theory and analysis. This does not mean that you have to abandon your effort to untangle bivariate relationships, only that you should be aware of both the importance of theory as a guide to your analysis and the limitations of the statistical analysis.

READING THE RESEARCH LITERATURE: THE DIGITAL DIVIDE

We each possess a particular combination of race or ethnic identity, social class, age, and gender. These social characteristics shape our experiences, behaviors, and beliefs. Keep in mind that we aren't just one characteristic at a time, but an intersection of many characteristics at once. The methods of bivariate analysis and the statistical techniques of elaboration are especially suitable for understanding how our social characteristics affect how we experience our world.

To illustrate, let's consider the digital divide. Though the overall proportion of U.S. households with Internet access has increased, such access has not increased or been evenly distributed among all Americans at the same rate. This digital divide, the differential access to information technology, has been attributed to differences in income and educational attainment closely related to race and ethnic identity. Studies have also shown that men are more likely to access the Internet than women, due in part to gendered stereotypes regarding normatively appropriate use of technology. It is worth noting that women and racial and ethnic minorities across other countries also have the lowest levels of Internet access.[22]

In her 2015 research, Celeste Campos-Castillo compares Internet access among U.S. adults from 2007 to 2012. She writes about the importance of monitoring the racial and gender divide. Specifically, she argues that the intersection of gender and race has received little attention, especially since "the intersection of gender and race uncovers unique experiences of advantage and disadvantage that are often masked in research that collapses across these two axes" (p. 426).[23]

A comparison of Internet access by race and ethnicity, gender, and the intersections of race/ethnicity and gender are reported in Table 9.16. The table also includes a column labeled "significance of difference" based on a comparison of 2007 and 2012 percentages for each group.

Table 9.16 Percentage of Respondents Reporting Internet Access From 2007 to 2012

	% (Frequency) Reporting Internet Access		
	2007	2012	Significance of Difference
Race/ethnicity			
White	78.6 (1,661)	85.2 (3,195)	***
Black	58.7 (226)	76.4 (640)	***
Latino	62.8 (188)	77.0 (584)	*
Gender			
Male	72.0 (781)	81.9 (1,869)	***
Female	76.0 (1,294)	83.9 (2,679)	***
Intersections			
White female	80.5 (1,010)	86.7 (1,869)	***
White male	76.6 (651)	83.7 (1,326)	***
Black female	62.6 (162)	76.0 (453)	**
Black male	53.7 (64)	76.8 (187)	**
Latino female	64.2 (122)	77.0 (357)	*
Latino male	61.5 (66)	77.0 (227)	†

Source: Adapted from Celeste Campos-Castillo, "Revisiting the First-Level Digital Divide in the United States: Gender and Race/Ethnicity Patterns, 2007-2012," *Social Science Computer Review*, 33, no. 4 (2015): 429.

$^{\dagger}p < .10$; $^{*}p < .05$; $^{**}p < .01$; $^{***}p < .0001$.

Campos-Castillo offers this summary of the data:

> Table 2 shows that all of the racial and ethnic groups pertinent to the analysis exhibited significant increases in Internet [access] during this time period. Latinos' increase in access was less statistically significant than the changes for other groups. Both men and women showed significant increases in Internet access. Focusing on the intersections of gender and race and ethnicity reveals a more nuanced picture of changes in Internet access. The greatest increase in Internet access occurred among Black men. Changes in Internet access among Latino men and women were the least statistically significant. While the change in reports of Internet access among men was the second highest in magnitude, the change is only marginally significant. Meanwhile, changes in Internet access among the other intersections were statistically significant. (p. 429)[24]

She suggests that there is much more to be learned about Internet access. Future research should examine how gender and race intersect with class and gender patterns among other racial and ethnic groups. The interaction of our social characteristics—race, ethnicity, gender, social class, and age—shapes who we are and our life experiences.

DATA AT WORK

Spencer Westby: Senior Editorial Analyst

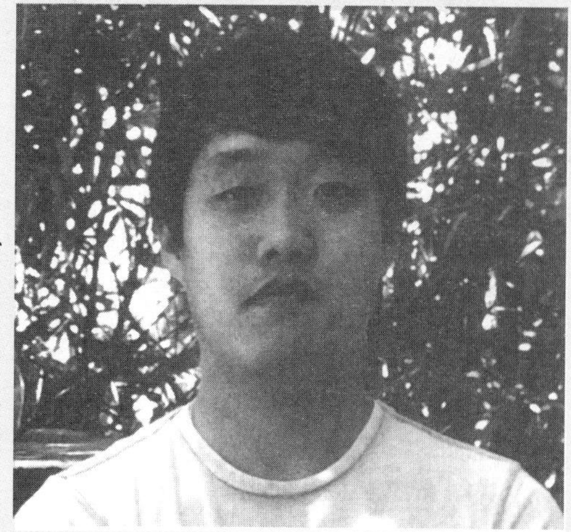

Photo courtesy of Spencer Westby

As a senior editorial analyst for an academic publishing company, Spencer uses data to examine the driving factors behind a successful journal publication. He tracks journal usage, article submissions, and citations to determine ways to improve reader outreach and revenue.

"I use bivariate tables and pie charts more than anything else as they are the quickest way to display relationships between variables. It is a simple way to display complex data for the publishing editors I am working with. Having worked at this position for a while now, I find it is just as important to make sure the data and analysis are understandable by someone who does not know statistics well. The work needs to be beneficial to the whole business."

Spencer was introduced to this work through an internship. He hoped to gain career experience for college, but during his internship, he discovered an interest in publishing. "It was especially interesting to see how this industry worked from the inside compared to how simple it seemed on the outside as a student."

"If you are interested in a career using quantitative research, my biggest advice would be to make sure that it is something that you at least find interesting," says Spencer. "Working with numbers all day can be fairly demanding mental work if you are not ready for it. However, an inquisitive mind can turn any analytical project into a puzzle waiting to be solved. A career utilizing statistics is very satisfying for those who pursue it with creative minds."

MAIN POINTS

- A bivariate table displays the distribution of one variable across the categories of another variable. It is obtained by classifying cases based on their joint scores for two variables. Percentaging bivariate tables are used to examine the relationship between two variables that have been organized in a bivariate table. The percentages are always calculated within each category of the independent variable.
- A relationship is said to exist when certain values of one variable are associated with certain values of the other variable. Bivariate tables are interpreted by comparing percentages across different categories of the independent variable. A relationship is said to exist if the percentage distributions vary across the categories of the independent variable. Variables measured at the ordinal or interval-ratio levels may be positively or negatively associated. With a positive association, higher values of one variable correspond to higher values of the other variable. When there is a negative association between variables, higher values of one variable correspond to lower values of the other variable.
- Elaboration is a technique designed to clarify bivariate associations. It involves the introduction of control variables to interpret the links between the independent and dependent variables. In a spurious relationship,

both the independent and dependent variables are influenced by a causally prior control variable, and there is no causal link between them. In an intervening relationship, the control variable follows the independent variable but precedes the dependent variable in the causal sequence. In a conditional relationship, the bivariate relationship between the independent and dependent variables is different in each of the partial tables.

KEY TERMS

bivariate analysis 236
bivariate table 236
cell 237
column variable 237
conditional relationship 254
control variable 246
cross-tabulation 236
direct causal relationship 247
elaboration 246
intervening relationship 252
intervening variable 252
marginals 237
negative relationship 245
partial relationship 249
partial tables 249
positive relationship 245
row variable 237
spurious relationship 247

DIGITAL RESOURCES

Get the edge on your studies. **edge.sagepub.com/frankfort8e**

Take a quiz to find out what you've learned.
Review key terms with eFlashcards.
Dive into real research with SAGE Journal Articles.

SPSS DEMONSTRATIONS [GSS14SSDS-B]

Demonstration 1: Producing Bivariate Tables

SPSS has a separate procedure designed specifically to produce cross-tabulation tables. It is called the Crosstabs procedure and can be found under *Descriptive Statistics* in the *Analyze* menu (*Analyze*, *Descriptive Statistics*, *Crosstabs*). The dialog box for *Crosstabs* requires us to specify both a variable that will define the rows and one that defines the columns of a table. We will investigate the relationship between the importance of being a Christian in order to be truly American (AMCHRSTN) and attitudes toward homosexuality (HOMOSEX). Select AMCHRSTN for the column variable and HOMOSEX for the row variable.

By default, SPSS displays the count in each cell of the table. Click on the *Cells* button to request percentages (Figure 9.9). As usual, we percentage the table based on the independent or predictor variable, which is religious affiliation. The independent variable is placed in the columns, while the dependent variable is placed in rows. We click on the checkbox for "Column" to percentage the table by AMCHRSTN. (Note that "Observed" is already checked by .default in the Counts section. In the Noninteger Weights section, "Round cell counts" is checked by default.)

Click on *Continue*, then *OK*, to obtain the table shown in Figure 9.10. SPSS displays both the count and the column percentage in each cell. In the upper left corner of the table, the labels "Count" and "% within AMCHRSTN" are displayed as a reminder of what SPSS has placed in each cell. Row totals and column totals are supplied automatically, as is the overall total (339 respondents gave valid responses to both questions).

As you review the table, note how the higher percentages are in opposite corners of the table. In the row for "always wrong" for HOMOSEX—respondents who believe being a Christian is "very important" or "fairly important" are more likely to think homosexual relations is "always wrong" (69.4% and 51.4%) when compared with those who believe being a Christian is "not very important" (38.6%) or "not important at all" (10.7%). How would you describe the results for the row "not wrong at all" for HOMOSEX? What is the relationship between AMCHRSTN and HOMOSEX?

Figure 9.9 Crosstabs: Cell Display Dialog Box

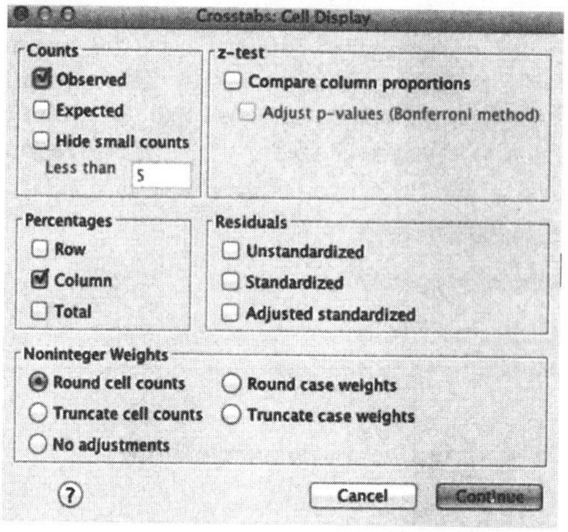

Crosstabs: Cell Display

Counts: Observed (checked); Expected; Hide small counts — Less than 5

z-test: Compare column proportions; Adjust p-values (Bonferroni method)

Percentages: Row; Column (checked); Total

Residuals: Unstandardized; Standardized; Adjusted standardized

Noninteger Weights: Round cell counts (selected); Round case weights; Truncate cell counts; Truncate case weights; No adjustments

Cancel | Continue

Figure 9.10 Cross-Tabulation Output: AMCHRSTN and HOMOSEX

homosex HOMOSEXUAL SEX RELATIONS * amchrstn HOW IMPORTANT TO BE A CHRISTIAN Crosstabulation

			amchrstn HOW IMPORTANT TO BE A CHRISTIAN				
			1 VERY IMPORTANT	2 FAIRLY IMPORTANT	3 NOT VERY IMPORTANT	4 NOT IMPORTANT AT ALL	Total
homosex HOMOSEXUAL SEX RELATIONS	1 ALWAYS WRONG	Count	77	19	34	11	141
		% within amchrstn HOW IMPORTANT TO BE A CHRISTIAN	69.4%	51.4%	38.6%	10.7%	41.6%
	2 ALMST ALWAYS WRG	Count	4	3	4	2	13
		% within amchrstn HOW IMPORTANT TO BE A CHRISTIAN	3.6%	8.1%	4.5%	1.9%	3.8%
	3 SOMETIMES WRONG	Count	8	7	4	4	23
		% within amchrstn HOW IMPORTANT TO BE A CHRISTIAN	7.2%	18.9%	4.5%	3.9%	6.8%
	4 NOT WRONG AT ALL	Count	22	8	46	86	162
		% within amchrstn HOW IMPORTANT TO BE A CHRISTIAN	19.8%	21.6%	52.3%	83.5%	47.8%
Total		Count	111	37	88	103	339
		% within amchrstn HOW IMPORTANT TO BE A CHRISTIAN	100.0%	100.0%	100.0%	100.0%	100.0%

Demonstration 2: Producing Tables With a Control Variable

As we've seen in this chapter, the analysis of data is enhanced when a third variable—a control variable—is added to a bivariate table. In the Crosstabs procedure, the third variable is added

Figure 9.11 Crosstabs Dialog Box

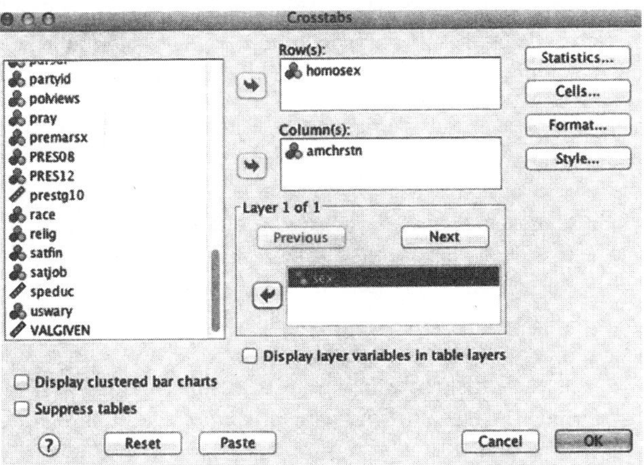

Figure 9.12 Cross-Tabulation Output: AMCHRSTN by HOMOSEX Controlling for SEX

homosex HOMOSEXUAL SEX RELATIONS * amchrstn HOW IMPORTANT TO BE A CHRISTIAN * sex RESPONDENTS SEX Crosstabulation

sex RESPONDENTS SEX				amchrstn HOW IMPORTANT TO BE A CHRISTIAN 1 VERY IMPORTANT	2 FAIRLY IMPORTANT	3 NOT VERY IMPORTANT	4 NOT IMPORTANT AT ALL	Total
1 MALE	homosex HOMOSEXUAL SEX RELATIONS	1 ALWAYS WRONG	Count	30	12	25	7	74
			% within amchrstn HOW IMPORTANT TO BE A CHRISTIAN	75.0%	60.0%	48.1%	13.5%	45.1%
		2 ALMST ALWAYS WRG	Count	1	1	4	0	6
			% within amchrstn HOW IMPORTANT TO BE A CHRISTIAN	2.5%	5.0%	7.7%	0.0%	3.7%
		3 SOMETIMES WRONG	Count	6	5	3	3	17
			% within amchrstn HOW IMPORTANT TO BE A CHRISTIAN	15.0%	25.0%	5.8%	5.8%	10.4%
		4 NOT WRONG AT ALL	Count	3	2	20	42	67
			% within amchrstn HOW IMPORTANT TO BE A CHRISTIAN	7.5%	10.0%	38.5%	80.8%	40.9%
	Total		Count	40	20	52	52	164
			% within amchrstn HOW IMPORTANT TO BE A CHRISTIAN	100.0%	100.0%	100.0%	100.0%	100.0%
2 FEMALE	homosex HOMOSEXUAL SEX RELATIONS	1 ALWAYS WRONG	Count	47	7	9	4	67
			% within amchrstn HOW IMPORTANT TO BE A CHRISTIAN	66.2%	41.2%	25.0%	7.8%	38.3%
		2 ALMST ALWAYS WRG	Count	3	2	0	2	7
			% within amchrstn HOW IMPORTANT TO BE A CHRISTIAN	4.2%	11.8%	0.0%	3.9%	4.0%
		3 SOMETIMES WRONG	Count	2	2	1	1	6
			% within amchrstn HOW IMPORTANT TO BE A CHRISTIAN	2.8%	11.8%	2.8%	2.0%	3.4%
		4 NOT WRONG AT ALL	Count	19	6	26	44	95
			% within amchrstn HOW IMPORTANT TO BE A CHRISTIAN	26.8%	35.3%	72.2%	86.3%	54.3%
	Total		Count	71	17	36	51	175
			% within amchrstn HOW IMPORTANT TO BE A CHRISTIAN	100.0%	100.0%	100.0%	100.0%	100.0%

in the Layer section of the main dialog box (Figure 9.11). (This box is labeled "Layer 1 of 1" because it is possible to have additional levels of control, which are accessed by clicking on the *Next* button.) We will not change HOMOSEX and AMCHRSTN, but will add SEX as the control variable. There is no need to change the numbers displayed in the cells: The observed count and column percentages are still correct choices. Figure 9.12 shows the bivariate tables for men and women separately.

The relationship we observed in the original table (Figure 9.10) is present in this analysis—if respondents believe being a Christian is important to being an American, they are more likely to indicate that homosexuality is always wrong. But when controlling for sex, note how most men believe that homosexuality is "always wrong" (three out of four of the AMCHRSTN modes—75%, 60%, and 48.1%—are in the HOMOSEX category "always wrong"). In contrast, for women, the AMCHRSTN modes are split in two HOMOSEX categories—"always wrong" (66.2% and 41.2%) and "not wrong at all" (72.2% and 86.3%). The relationship between AMCHRSTN and HOMOSEX appears to be slightly stronger for women. In the next chapter, we will use the Statistics button in the Crosstabs dialog box to request additional output to further interpret and evaluate bivariate tables.

SPSS PROBLEMS [GSS14SSDS-B]

1. The GSS data set includes responses to questions about the respondent's homeownership status (DWELOWN) and his or her subjective class identification (CLASS). Analyze the relationship between responses to these two questions with the SPSS Crosstabs procedure, requesting counts and appropriate cell percentages. (Click on *Analyze*, *Descriptive Statistics*, and *Crosstabs* to get started.)
   a. What percentage of the working-class group responded that they "pay rent"?
   b. What percentage of the lower-class group were homeowners?
   c. What percentage of those who were homeowners were also from the middle and upper classes?
   d. Is there a relationship between perceived class and homeownership? If there is a relationship, describe it.
   e. Rerun your analysis, this time adding RACE as a control variable. Is there a difference in the relationship between perceived class and homeownership for whites and blacks?
2. We continue to explore attitudes toward homosexuality, this time using BIBLE (feelings about the Bible) as an independent variable. Use SPSS to construct a table showing the relationship between HOMOSEX and BIBLE. Explain the relationship between HOMOSEX and BIBLE.
3. GSS respondents were asked to report which candidate they voted for in the 2012 presidential election (PRES12). Examine the relationship between PRES12, CLASS, and SEX. Use SEX as the control variable. Does presidential voting vary by one's social class and sex? Explain.
4. In this exercise, we test the relationship between 2008 and 2012 presidential election voting (PRES08 and PRES12) and respondent's feelings about the Bible (BIBLE).
   a. Which variable should be defined as the dependent variable? Explain your answer.
   b. Using SPSS Crosstabs, create two tables with BIBLE and each of the PRES variables. Explain the relationship between the two variables for 2008 and 2012. (When you discuss your findings, exclude those respondents who did not vote.) If the respondent believes the Bible is the word of God, how did the respondent vote in 2008 or 2012?

c. Examine the relationship between BIBLE and one of the PRES variables with a control variable of your choice.

5. Describe the relationship between PRES12 and agreement to the statement, "America should exclude illegal immigrants" (EXCLDIMM). Define PRES12 as the dependent variable.

CHAPTER EXERCISES

1. We present data for 20 men and women. In addition to measuring respondent's sex (M = male, F = female), we also measured their home ownership status (O = own, R = rent), and fear of walking alone at night (Y = yes, N = no).

Sex	Fear	Rent/Own
M	N	O
M	N	O
F	Y	O
F	Y	O
M	N	R
F	Y	O
M	N	R
F	Y	R
M	N	R
F	N	R
F	N	R
F	N	O
M	Y	R
M	Y	O
F	Y	R
F	Y	R
F	Y	R
M	N	O
F	Y	R
M	N	O

a. Construct a bivariate table of frequencies for sex and fear of walking alone at night. Which is the independent variable?

b. Calculate percentages for the table based on the independent variable. Describe the relationship between sex and fear of walking alone using the table. What sampling issues are involved here?

c. Use the data to construct a bivariate table to compare fear of walking alone at night between people who own their homes and those who rent. Treat home ownership as your independent variable.

2. The elderly are characterized as being more politically engaged than younger individuals. We will test this relationship by examining the relationship between RAGE (age categories) and CNTCTGOV (how often have you contacted a politician or civil servant) based on GSS 2014 data.

cntctgov CONTACTED POLITICIAN OR CIVIL SERVANT TO EXPRESS VIEW * RAge recoded Age Crosstabulation

			RAge recoded Age				Total
			1.00 18-29	2.00 30-39	3.00 40-49	4.00 50-59	
cntctgov CONTACTED POLITICIAN OR CIVIL SERVANT TO EXPRESS VIEW	1 Have done it in the past yr	Count	5	8	7	14	34
		% within RAge recoded Age	10.2%	10.4%	12.1%	19.7%	13.3%
	2 Have done it in the more distant past	Count	3	9	15	17	44
		% within RAge recoded Age	6.1%	11.7%	25.9%	23.9%	17.3%
	3 Have not done it but might do it	Count	21	34	21	19	95
		% within RAge recoded Age	42.9%	44.2%	36.2%	26.8%	37.3%
	4 Have not done it and would never do it	Count	20	26	15	21	82
		% within RAge recoded Age	40.8%	33.8%	25.9%	29.6%	32.2%
Total		Count	49	77	58	71	255
		% within RAge recoded Age	100.0%	100.0%	100.0%	100.0%	100.0%

a. Which is the independent variable?

b. How would you describe the relationship between the two variables?

c. What might be some other social factors related to contacting politicians to express one's view? Identify two reasons.

3. One of your classmates argues that attitudes about homosexuality influence political views. The classmate hypothesizes that those who believe homosexual relations are wrong tend to be more conservative compared with those who do not think that homosexual relations are wrong. Use these GSS 2014 data to test your classmate's hypothesis.

	Homosexual Relations		
Political Views	Always Wrong	Not Wrong at All	Total
Liberal	43	149	192
	15%	41%	30%
Moderate	98	145	243
	34%	40%	38%
Conservative	144	66	210
	51%	18%	32%
Total	285	360	645
	100%	99%	100%

a. Based on your classmate's argument, what is the dependent variable? The independent variable?

b. What percentage of those surveyed think that homosexual relations are always wrong?

c. Using the percentages in the table, describe the relationship between views about homosexual relations and political orientation?

4. We continue our examination of attitudes regarding homosexuality. Suppose that a classmate of yours suggests that views about homosexual relations can be explained by the frequency of church attendance. Your classmate shows you the following table taken from the GSS 2014 sample. (Frequencies are shown below.)

Homosexual Relations	Church Attendance			Total
	Never	Several Times a Year	Every Week	
Always wrong	42	26	87	155
Not wrong at all	134	36	30	200
Total	176	62	117	355

a. Which is the dependent variable in this table? Which is the independent variable?

b. Calculate the percentages using church attendance as the independent variable for each cell in the table. Is there a relationship between church attendance and views about homosexual relations? If so, how strong is it?

c. Suppose that you respond to your classmate by stating that it is not church attendance that explains views about homosexual relations; rather, it is one's opinion about the nature of right and wrong (i.e., morality) that explains attitudes about homosexual relations. Why might there be a potential problem with your argument? Think in terms of assigning variables to the independent and dependent categories.

5. Youth were asked in the Monitoring the Future (MTF) 2014 survey to report how often they were drunk in the past 12 months. Responses for 544 males are reported by race.

Drunk in the Last 12 Months	Race			Total
	Black	White	Hispanic	
None	75	282	119	476
1–2 times	6	23	5	34
3–5 times	0	13	3	16
6 or more times	2	11	5	18
Total	83	329	132	544

Calculate the percentages using *race* as the independent variable. Is there a relationship between student race and frequency of drunkenness?

6. Amy Stauffer and her colleagues (2006) examined the interactive effects of victim race and gender on capital murder death sentence outcomes in North Carolina. Their analysis is based on sentences rendered from 1979 to 2002. Demographic statistics are presented in the following table. Row percentages equal 100%.

Describe the relationship between victim race and gender, separately and combined (an interaction), on capital murder sentences. Are offenders more likely to be sentenced to death if their victims were female or white?

Demographic Characteristics	No Death Sentence		Death Sentence	
	%	N	%	N
Victim gender				
Female	42.5	174	57.5	235
Male	54.6	297	45.4	247

(Conitnued)

(Conitnued)

Demographic Characteristics	No Death Sentence		Death Sentence	
	%	N	%	N
Victim race				
White	47.3	296	52.7	330
Black	53.5	175	46.5	152
Victim race and gender				
White female	41.2	105	58.8	150
White male	51.5	191	48.5	180
Black female	44.8	69	55.2	85
Black male	61.3	106	38.7	67

Source: Adapted from Amy Stauffer, M. Dwayne Smith, John K. Cochran, Sondra Fogel, and Beth Bjerregaard, "The Interaction Between Race and Gender in Sentencing Outcomes in Capital Murder Trials," *Homicide Studies* 10, no. 2 (2009): 108.

7. In 2004, high school seniors were surveyed about their postsecondary expectations and plans. U.S. Department of Education data are presented for male and female students. Which group of students has higher educational expectations? Refer to the data to support your answer. (The row total for males will not equal to 100% due to rounding.)

Sex	Students' Educational Expectations (Percentages Reported)				
	Do Not Know Yet	High School or Less	Some College	Bachelor's Degree	Graduate/ Advanced Degree
Males	9.4	6.9	20.5	34.4	28.9
Females	7.4	3.1	15.6	32.6	41.3

Source: Xianglei Chen, Joanna Wu, Shayna Tasoff, and Thomas Weko, *Postsecondary Expectations and Plans of the High School Senior Class of 2003–2004*, U.S. Department of Education NCES 2010–070 rev, 2010.

8. In Exercise 1, you found that more women than men are likely to fear walking alone in their neighborhoods. You now wonder if this difference exists because women are more likely to own their own homes and so live in safer neighborhoods. In other words, you want to try some elaboration.

    a. Use the data from Exercise 1 to construct tables showing the relationship between fear of walking alone and sex, controlling for whether the individual rents or owns his or her dwelling.

    b. Does renting versus owning one's dwelling explain the difference in fear between women and men? (Use percentage differences to support your answer.)

    c. Has introducing home ownership shown that the relationship between sex and fear is spurious or is home ownership an intervening variable? Explain.

9. Daniel Rocke and his colleagues (2014) assessed support of the Patient Protection and Affordable Care Act among a sample of 647 otolaryngology (ear, nose, and throat) physicians. They divided physicians by political party affiliation—Democrat, Other, and Republican (refer to the following table). Is there a relationship between political party affiliation and attitudes toward the Affordable Care Act? Explain.

Attitude Toward the Affordable Care Act	N (%)			
	Total	Democratic	Other	Republican
Strongly against	162 (26.87)	14 (11.20)	70 (30.84)	78 (31.08)
Against	293 (48.59)	45 (36.00)	115 (50.66)	133 (52.99)
Favors	128 (21.23)	56 (44.80)	35 (15.42)	37 (14.74)
Strongly favors	20 (3.32)	10 (8.00)	7 (3.08)	3 (1.20)

Source: Adapted from Daniel Rocke, Steven Thomas, Liana Puscas, and Walter Lee, "Physician Knowledge of and Attitudes Toward the Patient Protection and Affordable Care Act," *Otolaryngology—Head and Neck Surgery*, 150, no. 2 (2014): 230.

10. In 2013 ISSP, respondents in several European countries were asked their level of agreement to the statement, "Immigrants take jobs away from people born in their country." Their responses (frequencies only) are presented below.

Immigrants Take Jobs Away	Czech Republic	France	Denmark	Finland	Germany
Strongly agree	648	251	108	93	125
Agree	658	310	211	245	254
Neither	355	490	309	309	459
Disagree	190	472	325	440	616
Disagree strongly	40	407	342	100	199
Total	1,891	1,930	1,295	1,187	1,653

a. Is there a relationship between a respondent's country of residence and their level of agreement to the statement on immigrants?

b. Could we characterize the relationship as positive or negative? Why or why not?

c. Combining the strongly agree and agree categories, 69.1% (648 + 658/1,891) of Czechs agree that immigrants take away jobs from those born in the Czech Republic, much higher than responses from other countries. What hypothesis can you offer to explain the difference in responses?

11. We continue our examination of high school senior educational expectations (Exercise 7), this time examining the relationship between highest level of parents' education and seniors' educational expectations. How would you characterize the relationship between the two variables? Is it a positive or negative relationship?

Highest Level of Parents' Education	Students' Educational Expectations (Percentages Reported)				
	Do Not Know Yet	High School or Less	Some College	Bachelor's Degree	Graduate/ Advanced Degree
High school or less	11.4	9.4	27.2	30.0	22.0
Some college	9.0	5.1	21.0	35.4	29.5
College graduation	6.2	2.6	12.6	38.5	40.1
Graduate/ Professional degree	5.7	1.5	6.7	28.2	57.9

Source: Xianglei Chen, Joanna Wu, Shayna Tasoff, and Thomas Weko, *Postsecondary Expectations and Plans of the High School Senior Class of 2003–2004*, U.S. Department of Education NCES 2010–070 rev, 2010.

12. We consider one more variable—2001 family income—and its relationship with students' educational expectations. What direction is the relationship between the two variables? Explain your answer. (*Note:* Some row percentages will not equal 100% due to rounding.)

Family Income in 2001	Students' Educational Expectations (Percentages Reported)				
	Do Not Know Yet	High School or Less	Some College	Bachelor's Degree	Graduate/ Advanced Degree
$35,000 or lower	11.3	7.8	24.3	30.2	26.3
$35,001–75,000	8.4	5.1	18.7	35.0	32.9
More than $75,000	5.1	1.8	10.3	34.8	48.0

Source: Xianglei Chen, Joanna Wu, Shayna Tasoff, and Thomas Weko, *Postsecondary Expectations and Plans of the High School Senior Class of 2003–2004*, U.S. Department of Education NCES 2010–070 rev, 2010.

13. In Exercise 5, we presented MTF 2014 data for male students. In this exercise, we present the data for 554 female students and their self-report of drunkenness.

Drunk in the Last 12 Months	Race			Total
	Black	White	Hispanic	
None	76	286	100	462
1–2 times	6	33	11	50
3–5 times	4	12	7	23
6 or more times	1	14	4	19
Total	87	345	122	554

Compare this table to the one presented in Exercise 5. Do females report the same frequency of drunkenness as male students? Explain your answer.

10

THE CHI-SQUARE TEST AND MEASURES OF ASSOCIATION

Figures collected by the U.S. Census Bureau indicate that educational attainment is increasing in the United States. The percentage of Americans who completed 4 years of high school or more increased from 52.3% in 1970 to 88.2% in 2013. In 1970, only about 11% of Americans completed 4 years or more of college compared with 31% in 2013.[1] Despite this overall increase, educational attainment and one's educational experience still vary by demographic factors such as race/ethnicity, class, or gender.

In the first part of this chapter, we focus on first-generation college students—that is, students whose parents never completed a post-secondary education. The proportion of first-generation students has declined within the total population of first-year, full-time-entering college freshmen, reflecting the overall increase in educational attainment in the U.S. population.[2]

Most first-generation students begin college at 2-year programs or at community colleges. According to W. Elliot Inman and Larry Mayes (1999), since first-generation college students represent a large segment of the community college population, they bring with them a set of distinct goals and constraints. Understanding their experiences and their demographic backgrounds may allow for more intentional recruiting, retention, and graduation efforts. Inman and Mayes set out to examine first-generation college students' experiences, but they began first by determining who was most likely to be a first-generation college student.

Data from Inman and Mayes's study are presented in Table 10.1, a bivariate table, which includes gender and first-generation college status. From the table, we know that a higher percentage of women than men reported being first-generation college students, 46.6% versus 35.4%.

The percentage differences between males and females in first-generation college status, shown in Table 10.1, suggest that there is a relationship. In inferential statistics, we base our statements about the larger population on what we observe in our sample. How do we know whether the gender differences in Table 10.1 reflect a real

Chapter Learning Objectives

1. Summarize the application of a chi-square test
2. Calculate and interpret a test for the bivariate relationship between nominal or ordinal variables
3. Determine the significance of a chi-square test statistic
4. Explain the concept of proportional reduction of error
5. Apply and interpret measures of association: lambda, Cramer's V, gamma, and Kendall's tau-*b*
6. Interpret SPSS output for chi-square and measures of association

Table 10.1 Percentage of Men and Women Who Are First-Generation College Students			
First Generation	Men	Women	Total
Firsts	35.4%	46.6%	41.9%
	(691)	(1,245)	(1,936)
Nonfirsts	64.6%	53.4%	58.1%
	(1,259)	(1,425)	(2,684)
Total (*N*)	100.0%	100.0%	100.0%
	(1,950)	(2,670)	(4,620)

Source: Adapted from W. Elliot Inman and Larry Mayes, "The Importance of Being First: Unique Characteristics of First Generation Community College Students," *Community College Review* 26, no. 3 (1999): 8. Copyright © North Carolina State University. Published by SAGE.

difference in first-generation college status among the larger population? How can we be sure that these differences are not just a quirk of sampling? If we took another sample, would these differences be wiped out or be even reversed?

Let's assume that men and women are equally likely to be first-generation college students—that in the population from which this sample was drawn, there are no real differences between them. What would be the expected percentages of men and women who are first-generation college students versus those who are not?

If gender and first-generation college status were not associated, we would expect the same percentage of men and women to be first-generation college students. Similarly, we would expect to see the same percentage of men and women who are nonfirsts. These percentages should be equal to the percentage of "firsts" and "nonfirsts" respondents in the sample as a whole (categories used by Inman and Mayes). The last column of Table 10.1—the row marginals—displays these percentages: 41.9% of all respondents were first-generation students, whereas 58.1% were nonfirsts. Therefore, if there were no association between gender and first-generation college status, we would expect to see 41.9% of the men and 41.9% of the women in the sample as first-generation students. Similarly, 58.1% of the men and 58.1% of the women would not be.

Table 10.2 shows these hypothetical expected percentages. Because the percentage distributions of the variable *first-generation college status* are identical for men and women, we can say that Table 10.2 demonstrates a perfect model of "no association" between the variable *first-generation college status* and the variable *gender*.

If there is an association between gender and first-generation college status, then at least some of the observed percentages in Table 10.1 should differ from the hypothetical expected percentages shown in Table 10.2. Conversely, if gender and first-generation college status are not associated, the observed percentages should approximate the expected percentages shown in Table 10.2. In a cell-by-cell comparison of Tables 10.1 and 10.2, you can see that there is quite a disparity between the observed percentages and the hypothetical percentages. For example, in Table 10.1, 35.4% of the men reported that they were first-generation college students, whereas the corresponding cell for Table 10.2 shows that 41.9% of the men reported the same. The remaining three cells reveal similar discrepancies.

Table 10.2 Percentage of Men and Women Who Are First-Generation College Students: Hypothetical Data Showing No Association

First Generation	Men	Women	Total
Firsts	41.9%	41.9%	41.9%
			(1,936)
Nonfirsts	58.1%	58.1%	58.1%
			(2,684)
Total (*N*)	100.0%	100.0%	100.0%
	(1,950)	(2,670)	(4,620)

Are the disparities between the observed and expected percentages large enough to convince us that there is a genuine pattern in the population? The chi-square statistic helps us answer this question. It is obtained by comparing the actual observed frequencies in a bivariate table with the frequencies that are generated under an assumption that the two variables in the cross-tabulation are not associated with each other. If the observed and expected values are very close, the chi-square statistic will be small. If the disparities between the observed and expected values are large, the chi-square statistic will be large. In the following sections, we will learn how to compute the chi-square statistic to determine whether the differences between men's and women's first-generation college status could have occurred simply by chance.

THE CONCEPT OF CHI-SQUARE AS A STATISTICAL TEST

The **chi-square test** (pronounced kai-square and written as χ^2) is an inferential statistical technique designed to test for significant relationships between two variables organized in a bivariate table. The test has a variety of research applications and is one of the most widely used tests in the social sciences. Chi-square requires no assumptions about the shape of the population distribution from which a sample is drawn. It can be applied to nominal or ordinal data (including grouped interval-level data).

Chi-square test An inferential statistical technique designed to test for significant relationships between two nominal or ordinal variables organized in a bivariate table.

The chi-square test can also be applied to the distribution of scores for a single variable. Also referred to as the goodness-of-fit test, the chi-square can compare the actual distribution of a variable with a set of expected frequencies. This application is not presented in this chapter.

THE CONCEPT OF STATISTICAL INDEPENDENCE

Statistical independence The absence of association between two cross-tabulated variables. The percentage distributions of the dependent variable within each category of the independent variable are identical.

When two variables are not associated (as in Table 10.2), one can say that they are **statistically independent**. That is, an individual's score on one variable is independent of his or her score on the second variable. We identify statistical independence in a bivariate table by comparing the distribution of the dependent variable in each category of the independent variable. When two variables are statistically independent, the percentage distributions of the dependent variable within each category of the independent variable are identical. The hypothetical data presented in Table 10.2 illustrate the notion of statistical independence. Based on Table 10.2, we would say that first-generation college status is independent of one's gender.[3]

LEARNING CHECK 10.1

The data we will use to practice calculating chi-square are also from Inman and Mayes's research. We will examine the relationship between age (independent variable) and first-generation college status (the dependent variable), as shown in the following bivariate table:

Age and First-Generation College Status

First-Generation Status	Years of Age		Total
	19 Years or Younger	20 Years or Older	
Firsts	916 (33.7%)	1,018 (53.6%)	1,934 (41.9%)
Nonfirsts	1,802 (66.3%)	881 (46.4%)	2,683 (58.1%)
Total (*N*)	2,718 (100.0%)	1,899 (100.0%)	4,617 (100.0%)

Source: Adapted from W. Elliot Inman and Larry Mayes, "The Importance of Being First: Unique Characteristics of First Generation Community College Students," *Community College Review* 26, no. 3 (1999): 8.

Construct a bivariate table (in percentages) showing no association between age and first-generation college status.

THE STRUCTURE OF HYPOTHESIS TESTING WITH CHI-SQUARE

The chi-square test follows the same five basic steps as the statistical tests presented in Chapter 9 ("Bivariate Tables"): (1) making assumptions, (2) stating the research and null hypotheses and selecting alpha, (3) selecting the sampling distribution and specifying the test statistic, (4) computing the test statistic, and (5) making a decision and interpreting the results. Before we apply the five-step model to a specific example, let's discuss some of the elements that are specific to the chi-square test.

The Assumptions

The chi-square test requires no assumptions about the shape of the population distribution from which the sample was drawn. However, like all inferential techniques, it assumes random sampling. It can be applied to variables measured at a nominal and/or an ordinal level of measurement.

Stating the Research and the Null Hypotheses

The research hypothesis (H_1) proposes that the two variables are related in the population.

H_1: The two variables are related in the population. (*Gender* and *first-generation college status* are statistically dependent.)

Like all other tests of statistical significance, the chi-square is a test of the null hypothesis. The null hypothesis (H_0) states that no association exists between two cross-tabulated variables in the population, and therefore, the variables are statistically independent.

H_0: There is no association between the two variables in the population. (*Gender* and *first-generation college status* are statistically independent.)

LEARNING CHECK 10.2

Refer to the data in the previous Learning Check. Are the variables age and first-generation college status statistically independent? Write out the research and the null hypotheses for your practice data.

The Concept of Expected Frequencies

Assuming that the null hypothesis is true, we compute the cell frequencies that we would expect to find if the variables are statistically independent. These frequencies are called expected frequencies (and are symbolized as f_e). The chi-square test is based on cell-by-cell comparisons between the expected frequencies (f_e) and the frequencies actually observed (observed frequencies are symbolized as f_o).

Expected frequencies (f_e) The cell frequencies that would be expected in a bivariate table if the two variables were statistically independent.

Observed frequencies (f_o) The cell frequencies actually observed in a bivariate table.

Calculating the Expected Frequencies

The difference between f_o and f_e will determine the likelihood that the null hypothesis is true and that the variables are, in fact, statistically independent. When there is a large difference between f_o and f_e, it is unlikely that the two variables are independent, and we will probably reject the null hypothesis. On the other hand, if there is little difference between f_o and f_e, the variables are probably independent of each other, as stated by the null hypothesis (and therefore, we will not reject the null hypothesis).

The most important element in using chi-square to test for the statistical significance of cross-tabulated data is the determination of the expected frequencies. Because chi-square is computed on actual frequencies instead of on percentages, we need to calculate the expected frequencies based on the null hypothesis.

In practice, the expected frequencies are more easily computed directly from the row and column frequencies than from the percentages. We can calculate the expected frequencies using this formula:

$$f_e = \frac{(\text{Column marginal})(\text{Row marginal})}{N} \qquad (10.1)$$

To obtain the expected frequencies for any cell in any cross-tabulation in which the two variables are assumed independent, multiply the row and column totals for that cell and divide the product by the total number of cases in the table.

Let's use this formula to recalculate the expected frequencies for our data on gender and first-generation college status as displayed in Table 10.1. Consider the men who were first-generation

Table 10.3 Expected Frequencies of Men and Women and First-Generation College Status

First Generation	Men	Women	Total
Firsts	817.14	1,118.86	1,936
Nonfirsts	1,132.86	1,551.14	2,684
Total (*N*)	1,950	2,670	4,620

college students (the upper left cell). The expected frequency for this cell is the product of the column total (1,950) and the row total (1,936) divided by all the cases in the table (4,620):

$$f_e = \frac{(1{,}936)(1{,}950)}{4{,}620} = 817.14$$

For men who are nonfirsts (the lower left cell), the expected frequency is

$$f_e = \frac{(2{,}684)(1{,}950)}{4{,}620} = 1{,}132.86$$

Next, let's compute the expected frequencies for women who are first-generation college students (the upper right cell):

$$f_e = \frac{(1{,}936)(2{,}670)}{4{,}620} = 1{,}118.86$$

Finally, the expected frequency for women who are nonfirsts (the lower right cell) is

$$f_e = \frac{(2{,}684)(2{,}670)}{4{,}620} = 1{,}551.14$$

These expected frequencies are displayed in Table 10.3.

Note that the table of expected frequencies contains identical row and column marginals as the original table (Table 10.1). Although the expected frequencies usually differ from the observed frequencies (depending on the degree of relationship between the variables), the row and column marginals must always be identical with the marginals in the original table.

LEARNING CHECK 10.3

Refer to the data in the Learning Check on page 272. Calculate the expected frequencies for age and first-generation college status and construct a bivariate table. Are your column and row marginals the same as in the original table?

Calculating the Obtained Chi-Square

The next step in calculating chi-square is to compare the differences between the expected and observed frequencies across all cells in the table. In Table 10.4, the expected frequencies are shown next to the corresponding observed frequencies. Note that the difference between

Table 10.4 Observed and Expected Frequencies of Men and Women Who Are First-Generation College Students

First Generation	Men		Women		Total
	f_o	f_e	f_o	f_e	
Firsts	691	817.14	1,245	1,118.86	1,936
Nonfirsts	1,259	1,132.86	1,425	1,551.14	2,684
Total (N)	1,950		2,670		4,620

Table 10.5 Calculating Chi-Square

Gender and First-Generation College Status	f_o	f_e	$f_o - f_e$	$(f_o - f_e)^2$	$\frac{(f_o - f_e)^2}{f_e}$
Men/firsts	691	817.14	−126.14	15,911.2996	19.47
Men/nonfirsts	1,259	1,132.86	126.14	15,911.2996	14.05
Women/firsts	1,245	1,118.86	126.14	15,911.2996	14.22
Women/nonfirsts	1,425	1,551.14	−126.14	15,911.2996	10.26
$\chi^2 = \Sigma \frac{(f_o - f_e)^2}{f_e} = 58.00$					

the observed and expected frequencies in each cell is quite large. Is it large enough to be significant? The way we decide is by calculating the **obtained chi-square** statistic:

Chi-square (obtained) The test statistic that summarizes the differences between the observed (f_o) and the expected (f_e) frequencies in a bivariate table.

$$\chi^2 = \Sigma \frac{(f_o - f_e)^2}{f_e} \quad (10.2)$$

where

f_o = observed frequencies

f_e = expected frequencies

According to this formula, for each cell, subtract the expected frequency from the observed frequency, square the difference, and divide by the expected frequency. After performing this operation for every cell, sum the results to obtain the chi-square statistic.

Let's follow these procedures using the observed and expected frequencies from Table 10.4. Our calculations are displayed in Table 10.5. The obtained chi-square statistic, 58.00, summarizes the differences between the observed frequencies and the frequencies that we would expect to see if the null hypothesis were true and the variables—*gender* and *first-generation college status*—were not associated. Next, we need to interpret our obtained chi-square statistic and decide whether it is large enough to allow us to reject the null hypothesis.

LEARNING CHECK 10.4

Using the format of Table 10.5, construct a table to calculate chi-square for age and educational attainment.

The Sampling Distribution of Chi-Square

In Chapter 8 ("Testing Hypotheses"), we learned that test statistics such as Z and t have characteristic sampling distributions that tell us the probability of obtaining a statistic, assuming that the null hypothesis is true. In the same way, the sampling distribution of chi-square tells the probability of getting values of chi-square, assuming no relationship exists in the population.

Like other sampling distributions, the chi-square sampling distributions depend on the degrees of freedom. In fact, the chi-square sampling distribution is not one distribution, but—like the t distribution—is a family of distributions. The shape of a particular chi-square distribution depends on the number of degrees of freedom. This is illustrated in Figure 10.1, which shows chi-square distributions for 1, 5, and 9 degrees of freedom. Here are some of the main properties of the chi-square distributions that can be observed in this figure:

- The distributions are positively skewed.
- Chi-square values are always positive. The minimum possible value is zero, with no upper limit to its maximum value. A chi-square of zero means that the variables are completely independent and the observed frequencies in every cell are equal to the corresponding expected frequencies.
- As the number of degrees of freedom increases, the chi-square distribution becomes more symmetrical and, with degrees of freedom greater than 30, begins to resemble the normal curve.

Determining the Degrees of Freedom

In Chapter 8, we defined degrees of freedom (df) as the number of values that are free to vary. With cross-tabulation data, we find the degrees of freedom by using Formula 10.3:

$$df = (r - 1)(c - 1) \tag{10.3}$$

where

r = the number of rows

c = the number of columns

Thus, Table 10.1 with 2 rows and 2 columns has (2 − 1)(2 − 1) or 1 degree of freedom. If the table had 3 rows and 2 columns, it would have (3 − 1)(2 − 1) or 2 degrees of freedom.

Appendix D shows values of the chi-square distribution for various degrees of freedom. Notice how the table is arranged with the degrees of freedom listed down the first column and the level of significance (or p values) arrayed across the top. For example, with 5 degrees of freedom, the probability associated with a chi-square as large as 15.086 is .01. An obtained chi-square as large as 15.086 would occur only once in 100 samples.

Figure 10.1 Chi-Square Distributions for 1, 5, and 9 Degrees of Freedom

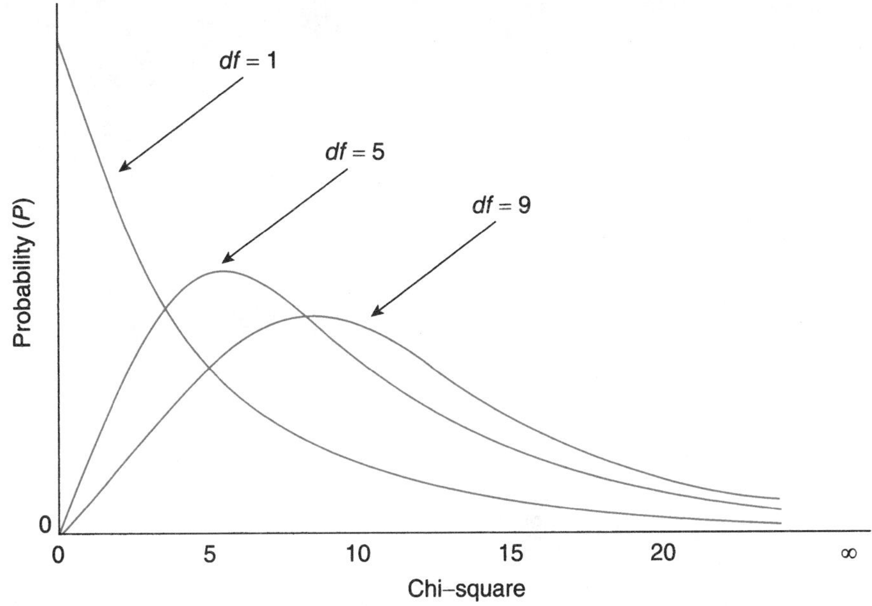

The degrees of freedom in a bivariate table can be interpreted as the number of cells in the table for which the expected frequencies are free to vary, given that the marginal totals are already set. Based on our data in Table 10.3, suppose we first calculate the expected frequencies for men who are first-generation college students (f_e = 817.14). Because the sum of the expected frequencies in the first column is set at 1,950, the expected frequency of men who are nonfirsts has to be 1,132.86 (1,950 – 817.14). Similarly, all other cells are predetermined by the marginal totals and are not free to vary. Therefore, this table has only 1 degree of freedom.

Data in a bivariate table can be distorted if by chance one cell is over- or undersampled and may therefore influence the chi-square calculation. Calculation of the degrees of freedom compensates for this, but in the case of a 2 × 2 table with just 1 degree of freedom, the value of chi-square should be adjusted by applying the Yates's correction for continuity. Formula 10.4 reduces the absolute value of each ($f_o - f_e$) by .5, then the difference is squared and then divided by the expected frequency for each cell. The formula for the Yates's correction for continuity is as follows:

$$\chi_c^2 = \Sigma \frac{(|f_o - f_e| - 0.5)^2}{f_e} \quad (10.4)$$

LEARNING CHECK 10.5

Based on Appendix D, identify the probability for each chi-square value (df in parentheses):

- 12.307 (15)
- 20.337 (21)
- 54.052 (24)

Table 10.6 Calculating Yates's Correction

Gender and First-Generation College Status	$\|f_o - f_e\|$	$(\|f_o - f_e\| - 0.50)^2$	f_e	$\chi_c^2 = \sum \frac{(\|f_o - f_e\| - 0.5)^2}{f_e}$
Men firsts	126.14	$(125.64)^2 = 15{,}785.41$	817.14	19.32
Men nonfirsts	126.14	$(125.64)^2 = 15{,}785.41$	1,132.86	13.93
Women firsts	126.14	$(125.64)^2 = 15{,}785.41$	1,118.86	14.11
Women nonfirsts	126.14	$(125.64)^2 = 15{,}785.41$	1,551.14	10.18
Total				57.54

Making a Final Decision

With the Yates's correction, the corrected chi-square is 57.54. Refer to Table 10.6 for calculations.

We can see that 57.54 does not appear on the first row ($df = 1$); in fact, it exceeds the largest chi-square value of 10.827 ($p = .001$). We can establish that the probability of obtaining a chi-square of 57.54 is less than .001 if the null hypothesis were true. If our alpha was preset at .05, the probability of 10.827 would be well below this. Therefore, we can reject the null hypothesis that gender and first-generation college status are not associated in the population from which our sample was drawn. Remember, the larger the chi-square statistic, the smaller the p value providing us with more evidence to reject the null hypothesis. We can be very confident of our conclusion that there is a relationship between gender and first-generation college status in the population because the probability of this result occurring owing to sampling error is less than .001, a very rare occurrence.

Review

To summarize our discussion, let's apply the five-step process of hypothesis testing.

1. *Making Assumptions:*
   - A random sample of $N = 4{,}620$ was selected.
   - The level of measurement of the variable gender is nominal.
   - The level of measurement of the variable *first-generation college status* is nominal.

2. *Stating the Research and Null Hypotheses and Selecting Alpha*: The research hypothesis, H_1, is that there is a relationship between gender and first-generation college status (i.e., gender and first-generation college status are statistically dependent). The null hypothesis, H_0, is that there is no relationship between gender and first-generation college status in the population (i.e., gender and first-generation college status are statistically independent). Alpha is set at .05.

3. *Selecting the Sampling Distribution and Specifying the Test Statistic:* Both the sampling distribution and the test statistic are chi-square.

4. *Computing the Test Statistic:* We should first determine the degrees of freedom associated with our test statistic:

$$df = (r-1)(c-1) = (2-1)(2-1) = (1)(1) = 1$$

Next, to calculate chi-square, we calculate the expected frequencies under the assumption of statistical independence. To obtain the expected frequencies for each cell, we multiply its row and column marginal totals and divide the product by *N*. The expected frequencies are displayed in Table 10.3.

Are these expected frequencies different enough from the observed frequencies presented in Table 10.1 to justify rejection of the null hypothesis? To find out, we calculate the chi-square statistic of 57.54 (with the Yates's correction). The calculations are shown in Table 10.6.

5. *Making a Decision and Interpreting the Results*: To determine the probability of obtaining our chi-square of 57.54, we refer to Appendix D. With 1 degree of freedom, the probability of obtaining 57.54 is less than .001 (less than our alpha of .05). We reject the null hypothesis that there is no difference in first-generation college status among men and women. Thus, we can conclude that in the population from which our sample was drawn, first-generation college status does vary by gender. Based on our sample data, we know that women are more likely to report being first-generation college students than men.

LEARNING CHECK 10.6

What decision can you make about the association between age and first-generation college status? Should you reject the null hypothesis at the .05 alpha level or at the .01 level?

STATISTICS IN PRACTICE: RESPONDENT AND FATHER EDUCATION

Each year the General Social Survey collects data on individual degree attainment along with the highest degrees attained by both parents. We know that parental education is an important predictor of a child's educational attainment. For this Statistics in Practice, we will take a look at father and individual degree attainment as shown in Table 10.7. Based on a sample of 897 men and women, the bivariate table shows a pattern of positive association between father's education (the independent variable) and respondent's education (the dependent variable)—as father's education increases, so does the respondent's education. Among those with a father who earned less than a high school degree, only 24.2% reported some college education. In contrast, among those with a father with some college education or more, 75.1% reported having some college education.

It is not clear whether these differences are owing to chance or to sampling fluctuations, or whether they reflect a real pattern of association in the population. In the following discussion, we will not review our calculations (though they are presented in Table 10.8). Rather, our focus will be on the five-step model and drawing conclusions about the relationship between father's and respondent's educational degrees.

A CLOSER LOOK 10.1

A CAUTIONARY NOTE: SAMPLE SIZE AND STATISTICAL SIGNIFICANCE FOR CHI-SQUARE

Although we found the relationship between gender and first-generation college status to be statistically significant, this in itself does not give us much information about the strength of the relationship or its substantive significance in the population. Statistical significance only helps us evaluate whether the argument (the null hypothesis) that the observed relationship occurred by chance is reasonable. It does not tell us anything about the relationship's theoretical importance or even if it is worth further investigation.

The distinction between statistical and substantive significance is important in applying any of the statistical tests discussed in Chapter 8. However, this distinction is of particular relevance for the chi-square test because of its sensitivity to sample size. The size of the calculated chi-square is directly proportional to the size of the sample, independent of the strength of the relationship between the variables.

For instance, suppose that we cut the observed frequencies for every cell in Table 10.1 exactly into half—which is equivalent to reducing the sample size by one half. This change will not affect the percentage distribution of firsts among men and women; therefore, the size of the percentage difference and the strength of the association between gender and first-generation college status will remain the same. However, reducing the observed frequencies by half will cut down our calculated chi-square by exactly half, from 57.54 to 28.77. (Can you verify this calculation?) Conversely, had we doubled the frequencies in each cell, the size of the calculated chi-square would have doubled, thereby making it easier to reject the null hypothesis.

This sensitivity of the chi-square test to the size of the sample means that a relatively strong association between the variables may not be significant when the sample size is small. Similarly, even when the association between variables is very weak, a large sample may result in a statistically significant relationship. However, just because the calculated chi-square is large and we are able to reject the null hypothesis by a large margin does not imply that the relationship between the variables is strong and substantively important.

Another limitation of the chi-square test is that it is sensitive to small expected frequencies in one or more of the cells in the table. Generally, when the expected frequency in one or more of the cells is below 5, the chi-square statistic may be unstable and lead to erroneous conclusions. There is no hard-and-fast rule regarding the size of the expected frequencies. Most researchers limit the use of chi-square to tables that either have no f_e values below 5 or have no more than 20% of the f_e values below 5.

Testing the statistical significance of a bivariate relationship is only a small step, although an important one, in examining a relationship between two variables. A significant chi-square suggests that a relationship, weak or strong, probably exists in the population and is not due to sampling fluctuation. However, to establish the strength of the association, we need to employ measures of association such as gamma, lambda (both discussed later in this chapter), or Pearson's r (refer to Chapter 12 ["Regression and Correlation"]). Used in conjunction, statistical tests of significance and measures of association can help determine the importance of the relationship and whether it is worth additional investigation.

1. *Making Assumptions:*
    1. A random sample of $N = 897$ is selected.
    2. The level of measurement of the variable respondent's degree is ordinal.
    3. The level of measurement of the variable father's degree is ordinal.
2. *Stating the Research and Null Hypotheses and Selecting Alpha:*

    H_1: There is a relationship between father's educational attainment and respondent's educational attainment in the population. (Father's degree and respondent's degree are statistically dependent.)

Table 10.7 Father's Degree by Respondent's Degree, GSS Subsample				
	Father's Degree			
Respondent's Degree	Less Than High School	High School Degree	Some College or More	Total
Less than high school	66	20	3	89
	(22.1%)	(5.2%)	(1.4%)	(9.9%)
High school degree	160	215	50	425
	(53.7%)	(55.7%)	(23.5%)	(47.4%)
Some college or more	72	151	160	383
	(24.2%)	(39.1%)	(75.1%)	(42.7%)
Total	298	386	213	897
	(100%)	(100%)	(99.9%)	(100%)

Table 10.8 Calculating Chi-Square for Respondent's and Father's Educational Degree

Respondent's Degree and Father's Degree	f_o	f_e	$f_o - f_e$	$(f_o - f_e)^2$	$\frac{f_o - f_e}{f_e}$
Less than high school/less than high school	66	29.57	36.43	1327.14	44.88
Less than high school/high school	20	38.30	−18.30	334.89	8.74
Less than high school/some college or more	3	21.13	−18.13	328.70	15.56
High school/less than high school	160	141.19	18.81	353.82	2.51
High school/high school	215	182.89	32.11	1031.05	5.64
High school/some college or more	50	100.92	−50.92	2592.85	25.69
Some college or more/less than high school	72	127.24	−55.24	3051.46	23.98
Some college or more/high school	151	164.81	−13.81	190.72	1.16
Some college or more/some college or more	160	90.95	69.05	4767.90	52.42

$$\chi^2 = \Sigma \frac{(f_o - f_e)^2}{f_e} = 180.58$$

> H_0: There is no relationship between father's educational attainment and respondent's educational attainment in the population. (Father's degree and respondent's degree are statistically independent.)

For this test, we'll select an alpha of .01.

3. *Selecting the Sampling Distribution and Specifying the Test Statistic:* The sampling distribution is chi-square; the test statistic is also chi-square.

4. *Computing the Test Statistic*: The degrees of freedom for Table 10.7 is

$$df = (r - 1)(c - 1) = (3 - 1)(3 - 1) = (2)(2) = 4$$

The chi-square obtained is 180.58. The detailed calculations are shown in Table 10.8.

5. *Making a Decision and Interpreting the Results*: To determine if the observed frequencies are significantly different from the expected frequencies, we compare our calculated chi-square with Appendix D. With 4 degrees of freedom, our chi-square of 180.58 exceeds the largest listed chi-square value of 22.457 (p = .001). We determine that the probability of observing our obtained chi-square of 180.58 is less than .001, and less than our alpha of .01. We can reject the null hypothesis that there are no differences in health among the different educational groups. Thus, we conclude that in the population from which our sample was drawn, respondent's degree is related to father's degree. The positive relationship between the two variables is significant.

LEARNING CHECK 10.7

For the bivariate table with age and first-generation college status (first presented in the Learning Check on page 272), the value of the obtained chi-square is 181.15 with 1 degree of freedom. Based on Appendix D, we determine that its probability is less than .001. This probability is less than our alpha level of .05. We reject the null hypothesis of no relationship between age and first-generation college status. If we reduce our sample size by half, the obtained chi-square is 90.58. Determine the p value for 90.58. What decision can you make about the null hypothesis?

PROPORTIONAL REDUCTION OF ERROR

Measure of association A single summarizing number that reflects the strength of a relationship, indicates the usefulness of predicting the dependent variable from the independent variable, and often shows the direction of the relationship.

In this section, we review special measures of association for nominal and ordinal variables. These measures enable us to use a single summarizing measure or number for analyzing the pattern of relationship between two variables. Unlike chi-square, measures of association reflect the strength of the relationship and, at times, its direction (whether it is positive or negative). They also indicate the usefulness of predicting the dependent variable from the independent variable.

We discuss four measures of association: (1) lambda (measures of association for nominal variables), (2) gamma and (3) Kendall's tau-*b* (measures of association between ordinal variables), and (4) Cramer's *V* (a chi-square–related measure of association). In Chapter 12, we introduce Pearson's correlation coefficient, which is used for measuring bivariate association between interval-ratio variables.

Proportional reduction of error (PRE) A measure that tells us how much we can improve predicting the value of a dependent variable based on information about an independent variable.

All the measures of association discussed here and in Chapter 12 are based on the concept of the proportional reduction of error, often abbreviated as PRE. According to the concept of PRE, two variables are associated when information about one variable (an independent variable) can help us improve our prediction of the other variable (a dependent variable).

Table 10.9 may help us grasp intuitively the general concept of PRE. Using General Social Survey (GSS) 2010 data, Table 10.9 shows a moderate relationship between the independent variable, educational attainment, and the dependent variable, support for abortion if the woman is poor and can't afford any more children. The table shows that 69.0% of the respondents who did not receive a bachelor's degree were antiabortion, compared with only 45.9% of the respondents who had a bachelor's degree or more.

A CLOSER LOOK 10.2

WHAT IS STRONG? WHAT IS WEAK? A GUIDE TO INTERPRETATION

The more you work with various measures of association, the better feel you will have for what particular values mean. Until you develop this skill, here are some guidelines regarding what is generally considered a strong relationship and what is considered a weak relationship.

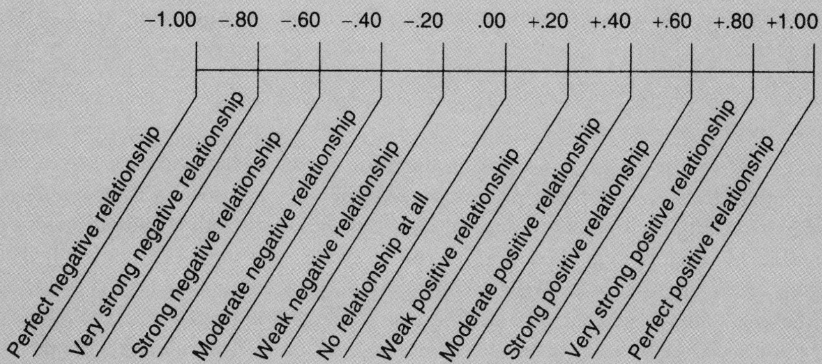

Keep in mind that these are only rough guidelines. Often, the interpretation for a measure of association will depend on the research context. A +0.30 in one research field will mean something a little different from a +0.30 in another research field. Zero, however, always means the same thing: no relationship.

Table 10.9 Support for Abortion by Degree, GSS 2010

Support for Abortion	Degree: Less Than Bachelor's	Degree: Bachelor's or More	Total
No	462	124	586
	69.0%	45.9%	62.3%
Yes	208	146	354
	31.0%	54.1%	37.7%
Total	670	270	940
	100.0%	100.0%	100.0%

The conceptual formula for all[4] PRE measures of association is

$$\text{PRE} = \frac{E_1 - E_2}{E_1} \tag{10.5}$$

where

E_1 = errors of prediction made when the independent variable is ignored (Prediction 1)

E_2 = errors of prediction made when the prediction is based on the independent variable (Prediction 2)

All PRE measures are based on comparing predictive error levels that result from each of the two methods of prediction. Let's say that we want to predict a respondent's position on abortion, but we do not know anything about the degree he or she has. Based on the row totals in Table 10.9, we could predict that every respondent in the sample is antiabortion because this is the modal category of the variable *abortion position*. With this prediction, we would make 354 errors because in fact 586 respondents in this group are antiabortion but 354 respondents are pro-choice. Thus,

$$E_1 = 940 - 586 = 354$$

How can we improve this prediction by using the information we have on each respondent's educational attainment? For our new prediction, we will use the following rule: If a respondent has less than a bachelor's degree, we predict that he or she will be antiabortion; if a respondent has a bachelor's degree or more, we predict that he or she is pro-choice. It makes sense to use this rule because we know, based on Table 10.9, that respondents with a lower educational attainment are more likely to be antiabortion, while respondents who have a bachelor's degree or more are more likely to be pro-choice. Using this prediction rule, we will make 332 errors (instead of 354) because 124 of the respondents who have a bachelor's degree or more are actually antiabortion, whereas 208 of the respondents who have less than a bachelor's degree are pro-choice (124 + 208 = 332). Thus,

$$E_2 = 124 + 208 = 332$$

Our first prediction method, ignoring the independent variable (*educational attainment*), resulted in 354 errors. Our second prediction method, using information we have about the independent variable (*educational attainment*), resulted in 332 errors. If the variables are associated, the second method will result in fewer errors of prediction than the first method. The stronger the relationship is between the variables, the larger will be the reduction in the number of errors of prediction.

Let's calculate the PRE for Table 10.9 using Formula 10.5. The PRE resulting from using educational attainment to predict position on abortion is

$$\text{PRE} = \frac{354 - 332}{354} = 0.06$$

PRE measures of association can range from 0.0 to ±1.0. A PRE of zero indicates that the two variables are not associated; information about the independent variable will not improve predictions about the dependent variable. A PRE of ±1.0 indicates a perfect positive or negative association between the variables; we can predict the dependent variable without error using information about the independent variable. Intermediate values of PRE will reflect the strength of the association between the two variables and therefore the utility of using one to predict the other. The more the measure of association departs from 0.00 in either direction, the stronger the association. PRE measures of association can be multiplied by 100 to indicate the percentage improvement in prediction.

A PRE of 0.06 indicates that there is a weak relationship between respondents' educational attainment and their position on abortion. (Refer to A Closer Look 10.2 for a discussion of the strength of a relationship.) A PRE of 0.06 means that we have improved our prediction of respondents' position on abortion by just 6% (0.06 × 100 = 6.0%) by using information on their educational attainment.

LAMBDA: A MEASURE OF ASSOCIATION FOR NOMINAL VARIABLES

Lambda is an asymmetrical measure used to determine the strength of the relationship between two nominal variables. An **asymmetrical measure** will vary depending on which variable is considered the independent variable and which the dependent variable.

Lambda An asymmetrical measure of association, lambda is suitable for use with nominal variables and may range from 0.0 to 1.0. It provides us with an indication of the strength of an association between the independent and dependent variables.

Asymmetrical measure of association A measure whose value may vary depending on which variable is considered the independent variable and which the dependent variable.

In U.S. colleges, there is a difference in the rate of first-generation college students by race and ethnicity. Specifically Latinos have a higher percentage of first-generation college students (38.2%) at 4-year colleges than any other racial/ethnic group.[5]

In Table 10.10, we present fictional data on the relationship between Latino ethnic identity and first-generation college student status.

Examine the row totals, which show the subtotals by first-generation student status, firsts versus nonfirsts. If we had to predict one first-generation category, our best bet would be nonfirsts (132), the largest category or mode. This prediction will result in the smallest possible error. The number of wrong predictions or errors we would make is 109 (241 – 132).

Now take another look at Table 10.10, but this time let's consider student Latino ethnic identity when we predict first-generation college student status. We can use the mode, but this time we will identify it separately for Latinos and non-Latinos. The mode for Latino is "first generation"; therefore, we can predict that all Latino students would be non-first-generation college students. With this method of prediction, we make 32 errors, since 55 out of 87 Latinos were first-generation college students. Next let's examine the group of non-Latinos. The mode for non-Latinos is "non-first generation"; this will be our prediction, our best guess. This method of prediction results in 54 errors (154 – 100 = 54). The total number of errors is 86 (32 + 54).

Let's put it all together and calculate lambda.

1. Find E_1, the errors of prediction made when the independent variable is ignored. To find E_1, find the mode of the dependent variable and subtract its frequency from N. For Table 10.1,

$$E_1 = N - \text{Modal frequency}$$

$$E_1 = 241 - 132 = 109$$

2. Find E_2, the errors made when the prediction is based on the independent variable. To find E_2, find the modal frequency for each category of the independent variable, subtract it from the category total to find the number of errors, and then add up all the errors. For Table 10.10,

Table 10.10 Latino Ethnic Identity and First-Generation College Status

	Latino	Non-Latino	Row Total
First Generation	55	54	109
Non–First Generation	32	100	132
Column Total	87	154	241

$$E_2 = N_k - \text{Mode}_k$$

$$\text{Latinos} = 87 - 55 = 32$$

$$\text{Non-Latinos} = 154 - 100 = 54$$

$$E_2 = 32 + 54 = 86$$

3. Calculate lambda (denoted by the Greek symbol λ) using Formula 10.5

$$\lambda = \frac{E_1 - E_2}{E_1} = \frac{109 - 86}{109} = 0.21$$

Lambda may range in value from 0.0 to 1.0. Zero indicates that there is nothing to be gained by using the independent variable to predict the dependent variable. A lambda of 1.0 indicates that by using the independent variable as a predictor, we are able to predict the dependent variable without any error. In our case, a lambda of 0.21 indicates that for this sample of respondents, there is a weak association between Latino identity and first-generation college status.

The *PRE* when multiplied by 100 can be interpreted as follows: By using information on respondent's Latino ethnic identity to predict first-generation college status, we reduced our error of prediction by 21%. In other words, if we rely on students' Latino identity to predict their first-generation status, we would reduce the error by 21%.

A reminder that lambda is an asymmetrical measure. If we considered *Latino identity* as the dependent variable and *first-generation status* as the independent variable, we would have obtained a slightly different lambda value.

Lambda is always zero in situations in which the mode for each category of the independent variable falls into the same category of the dependent variable. A problem with interpreting lambda arises in situations in which lambda is zero, but other measures of association indicate that the variables are associated. To avoid this potential problem, examine the percentage differences in the table whenever lambda is exactly equal to zero. If the percentage differences are very small (usually 5% or less), lambda is an appropriate measure of association for the table. However, if the percentage differences are larger, indicating that the two variables may be associated, lambda will be a poor choice as a measure of association. In such cases, we may want to discuss the association in terms of the percentage differences or select an alternative measure of association.

We've presented the lambda calculation based on the dependent variable as the row variable. The method of calculation is the same when the variables are switched (the independent variable presented in columns and the dependent variable presented in rows). Although lambda can be calculated either way, ultimately what guides the decision of which variables to consider as independent or dependent is the researcher's theory.

CRAMER'S *V*: A CHI-SQUARE–RELATED MEASURE OF ASSOCIATION FOR NOMINAL VARIABLES

Cramer's *V* A chi square related measure of association for nominal variables. Cramer's *V* is based on the value of chi-square and ranges between 0 and 1.

Cramer's *V* is an alternative measure of association that can be used for nominal variables. It is based on the value of chi-square and ranges between 0 to 1, with 0 indicating no association and 1 indicating perfect association. Because it cannot take negative values, it is considered a nondirectional measure. Unfortunately, Cramer's *V* is somewhat limited because the results cannot be interpreted using the *PRE* framework. It is calculated using Formula 10.6:

$$V = \sqrt{\frac{\chi^2}{N(m)}} \qquad (10.6)$$

where m = smaller of $(r - 1)$ or $(c - 1)$.

Earlier, we tested the hypothesis that first-generation college enrollment was related to student gender. The analysis yielded a chi-square value of 57.54, leading us to reject the null hypothesis that there are no differences between men and women. We concluded that in the population from which our sample was drawn, first-generation college student status does vary by student sex.

We can use Cramer's V to measure the relative strength of the association between student gender and first-generation college student status using Formula 10.6.

$$V = \sqrt{\frac{\chi^2}{N(m)}} = \sqrt{\frac{57.54}{4620(1)}} = .11$$

A Cramer's V of 0.11 tells us that there is a weak association between these two variables.

GAMMA AND KENDALL'S TAU-*B*: SYMMETRICAL MEASURES OF ASSOCIATION FOR ORDINAL VARIABLES

Gamma and **Kendall's tau-*b*** are **symmetrical measures of association** suitable for use with ordinal variables or with dichotomous nominal variables. This means that their value will be the same regardless of which variable is the independent variable or the dependent variable. Both gamma and Kendall's tau-*b* can vary from 0.0 to ±1.0 and provide us with an indication of the strength and direction of the association between the variables. Gamma and Kendall's tau-*b* can be positive or negative. A gamma or Kendall's tau-*b* of 1.0 indicates that the relationship between the variables is positive and that the dependent variable can be predicted without any errors based on the independent variable. A gamma of −1.0 indicates a perfect, negative association between the variables. A gamma or a Kendall's tau-*b* of zero reflects no association between the two variables; hence, there is nothing to be gained by using the independent variable to predict the dependent variable.

Gamma A symmetrical measure of association suitable for use with ordinal variables or with dichotomous nominal variables. It can vary from 0.0 to ±1.0 and provides us with an indication of the strength and direction of the association between the variables. Gamma is also referred to as Goodman and Kruskal's gamma.

Kendall's tau-*b* A symmetrical measure of association suitable for use with ordinal variables. It can vary from 0.0 to ±1.0. It provides an indication of the strength and direction of the association between the variables. Kendall's tau-*b* will always be lower than gamma.

Symmetrical measure of association A measure whose value will be the same when either variable is considered the independent variable or the dependent variable.

Ordinal variables are very common in social science research. The GSS contains many questions that ask people to indicate their responses on an ordinal scale—for example, strongly agree, agree, neutral, disagree, and strongly disagree.

Let's consider the association between two ordinal variables. We hypothesize that as one's educational attainment increases, the frequency of political discussion will increase. Our analysis is based on two variables: (1) education (EDUC) with five degree categories and (2) frequency of discussing politics (DISCPOL) measured in four categories—(1) never, (2) rarely, (3) sometimes, and (4) often.

Table 10.11 displays the cross-tabulation of these two variables, with *education* as the independent variable and *frequency of political discussions* as the dependent variable. We find that 44% of those with less than a high school degree never talk about politics, as compared with 2% of those with a graduate degree. The percentage difference (44% − 2% = 42%) suggests that the variables are related. We can examine the percentages for those who often talk about politics by their educational attainment (2% − 21% = −19%), and reach the same conclusion.

Since both variables are ordinal measures, we select gamma to assess the strength and the direction of the relationship between education and political discussions. We will not demonstrate how to calculate gamma, rather we will rely on SPSS output to interpret gamma.

The SPSS output reports that the gamma for the table is 0.351, indicating a weak-moderate positive relationship between education and political discussion. The positive sign of gamma indicates that as education increases, so does the level of political discussion. By using education to predict frequency of political discussion, we've reduced our prediction error by 35.1% (Figure 10.2).

Table 10.11 How Often Discuss Politics by Education, GSS 2014

	Less than High School	High School	Junior College	Bachelor	Graduate	Total
Never	23	51	6	15	1	96
	44%	29%	30%	20%	2%	26%
Rarely	20	64	10	21	16	131
	39%	36%	50%	28%	37%	36%
Sometimes	8	52	4	25	17	106
	15%	29%	20%	34%	40%	29%
Often	1	12	0	13	9	35
	2%	7%	0%	18%	21%	10%
Total	52	179	20	74	43	368
	100%	101%	100%	100%	100%	101%

Figure 10.2 Symmetric Measures for EDUC and DISCPOL, GSS 2014

Symmetric Measures

		Value	Asymptotic Standardized Error[a]	Approximate T[b]	Approximate Significance
Ordinal by Ordinal	Kendall's tau-b	.248	.040	6.048	.000
	Gamma	.351	.055	6.048	.000
N of Valid Cases		368			

a. Not assuming the null hypothesis.

b. Using the asymptotic standard error assuming the null hypothesis.

Measures of association for ordinal data are not influenced by the modal category as is lambda. Consequently, an ordinal measure of association might be preferable for tables when an association cannot be detected by lambda. We can use an ordinal measure for some tables where one or both variables would appear to be measured on a nominal scale. Dichotomous variables (those with only two categories) can be treated as ordinal variables for most purposes. In this chapter, we calculated lambda to examine the association between abortion attitudes and educational attainment (Table 10.9). Although both variables might be considered as nominal variables—because both are dichotomized (yes/no; high school or less/more than high school)—they could also be treated as ordinal variables. Thus, the association might also be examined using gamma, an ordinal measure of association.

READING THE RESEARCH LITERATURE: INDIA'S INTERNET-USING POPULATION

Most social science research considers multivariate causal relationships, much more complex than the bivariate relationships we considered in this chapter. Thus, gamma or Kendall's tau-*b* are not often presented in scholarly research. These statistics are most appropriate for descriptive, rather than inferential, analyses.

For example, Bharti Varshney, Prashant Kumar, Vivek Sapre, and Sanjeev Vanrshey (2014) present a demographic summary of Internet usage habits among the online population of India.

India has more than 74 million Internet users out of a total population of 1.2 billion. The researchers test the hypothesis that usage varies by age, gender, occupation, and city/town tier.[6] Table 10.12 presents their results for age and city/town tier with Internet use and duration.

Table 10.12 Crosstab Results for Age and Tier With Internet Usage Frequency and Duration

Independent Variable	Dependent Variable	Kendall's Tau-b	Sig.	Gamma	Sig.
Age	Internet access in a week	0.257	.000	0.356	.000
	Average session length	0.174	.002	0.225	.002
	Weekly time spent on net	0.166	.004	0.230	.004
Tier	Internet access in a week	0.187	.002	0.288	.002
	Average session length	0.115	.008	0.226	.008
	Weekly time spent on net	0.153	.009	0.234	.009

Source: Adapted from Bharti Varshney, Prashant Kumar, Vivek Sapre, and Sanjeev Varshney, "Demographic Profile of the Internet-Using Population of India," *Management and Labour Studies* 39, no. 4 (2014): 431.

Age was measured as an ordinal variable. *Tier* is also an ordinal measure, identifying city or town of residence by population and technology infrastructure (Internet connection at home). Categories for both independent variables and for all dependent variables were not reported in the article.[7]

The researchers summarize Table 10.12, by first describing why they utilized cross-tabulations, then explaining the relationship between *age*, *tier*, and the dependent variables.

> In [the] present study, cross tabulations were performed to find up to what extent usage and activity variables are related to the demographic variables. The cross tabulation table is the basic technique for examining the relationship between two categorical (nominal or ordinal) variables. The purpose of a cross tabulation is to show the relationship (or lack thereof) between two variables. . . . with age group and tier being the ordinal measure, cross tab was carried out with [Gamma and Kendall's tau-b]. For statistically significant and strong relationship, significance value of each measure should be less than or equal to .05 and the value of each measure should be greater than 0.150.
>
> Based on the above outputs, for cross tab on age group to Internet access days in a week and for age group to weekly actual time spent on the Net, statistically significant and strong relationship is obtained.
>
> For cross tab with independent variable city/town tier, for all of the variables, that is, city/town tier to Internet access days in a week, city/town tier to average session length and city/town tier to weekly actual time spent on the Net, statistically significant and strong relationship is obtained. The possible reason being the usage rate goes down with the decreasing size of the city. Most likely because the infrastructure and surfing speed get poorer while the surfing charges increase with the decreasing size of the city. (pp. 431–432)[8]

DATA AT WORK

Patricio Cumsille: Professor

Photo courtesy of Patricio Cumsille

Dr. Cumsille became a clinical psychologist because he wanted to understand and help people. Along with his Ph.D. in Human Development and Family Studies, he has a minor in statistics. When asked about using statistics in his work, he explains, "As a developmental researcher it is essential to collect longitudinal data and use appropriate techniques to uncover how developmental processes unfold over time. So, statistics is an essential part of what I do, both in my teaching and research activities." Based in Chile, he applies advanced statistical techniques and longitudinal methods in his research.

Cumsille offers four recommendations to undergraduates interested in pursuing a career in quantitative research or statistics. "This is a fascinating field, with new research methods developing and expanding. The first thing you need to do is to get a solid training in the basics of statistics. Second, you need to get involved in research projects from very early in your career, so you get exposed to the multiple details that are part of a research project. Starting as a research assistant doing the most basic tasks required in a research project is essential to become a seasoned researcher later on. Third, make sure to get exposed to as many perspectives on how to develop a research project. Finally, it is important to have a solid theoretical training in order for your research to be informed by theory."

MAIN POINTS

- The chi-square test is an inferential statistical technique designed to test for a significant relationship between nominal and ordinal variables organized in a bivariate table. This is conducted by testing the null hypothesis that no association exists between two cross-tabulated variables in the population, and therefore, the variables are statistically independent.
- The obtained chi-square (χ^2) statistic summarizes the differences between the observed frequencies (f_o) and the expected frequencies (f_e)—the frequencies we would have expected to see if the null hypothesis were true and the variables were not associated. The Yates's correction for continuity is applied to all 2 × 2 tables.
- The sampling distribution of chi-square tells the probability of getting values of chi-square, assuming no relationship exists in the population. The shape of a particular chi-square sampling distribution depends on the number of degrees of freedom.
- Measures of association are single summarizing numbers that reflect the strength of the relationship between variables, indicate the usefulness of predicting the dependent from the independent variable, and often show the direction of the relationship.

- Proportional reduction of error (*PRE*) underlies the definition and interpretation of several measures of association. *PRE* measures are derived by comparing the errors made in predicting the dependent variable while ignoring the independent variable with errors made when making predictions that use information about the independent variable.
- Measures of association may be symmetrical or asymmetrical. When the measure is symmetrical, its value will be the same regardless of which of the two variables is considered the independent or dependent variable. In contrast, the value of asymmetrical measures of association may vary depending on which variable is considered the independent variable and which the dependent variable.
- Lambda is an asymmetrical measure of association suitable for use with nominal variables. It can range from 0.0 to 1.0 and gives an indication of the strength of an association between the independent and the dependent variables.
- Gamma is a symmetrical measure of association suitable for ordinal variables or for dichotomous nominal variables. It can vary from 0.0 to ±1.0 and reflects both the strength and direction of the association between two variables.
- Kendall's tau-*b* is a symmetrical measure of association suitable for use with ordinal variables. Unlike gamma, it accounts for pairs tied on the independent and dependent variable. It can vary from 0.0 to ±1.0. It provides an indication of the strength and direction of the association between two variables.
- Cramer's *V* is a measure of association for nominal variables. It is based on the value of chi-square and ranges between 0.0 to 1.0. Because it cannot take negative values, it is considered a nondirectional measure.

KEY TERMS

asymmetrical measure of association 285
chi-square (obtained) 275
chi-square test 271
Cramer's *V* 286
expected frequencies (f_e) 273
gamma 287
Kendall's tau-*b* 287
lambda 285
measure of association 282
observed frequencies (f_o) 273
proportional reduction of error 282
statistical independence 271
symmetrical measure of association 287

DIGITAL RESOURCES

Get the edge on your studies. **edge.sagepub.com/frankfort8e**

Take a quiz to find out what you've learned.
Review key terms with eFlashcards.
Dive into real research with SAGE Journal Articles.

SPSS DEMONSTRATION [GSS14SSDS-A]

Demonstration 1: Producing the Chi-Square Statistic for Cross-Tabulations

The SPSS Crosstabs procedure was previously demonstrated in Chapter 9. This procedure can also be used to calculate a chi-square value for a bivariate table.

Click on *Analyze*, *Descriptive Statistics*, and *Crosstabs*, then on the *Statistics* button. You will see the Dialog box shown in Figure 10.3. To request the chi-square statistic, click on the Chi-square box in the upper left corner. You can also request expected frequencies via the Cells button.

Click on *Continue*. In this demonstration, we will look at the relationship between educational degree (DEGREE) and political views (POLVIEWS). Place POLVIEWS in the Row(s) box and DEGREE in the Column(s) box. Then, click on *OK* to run the procedure.

The resulting output includes the chi-square statistics as shown in Figure 10.4. SPSS produces quite a bit of output, perhaps more than what is expected. We will concentrate on the first row of information, the Pearson chi-square.

The Pearson chi-square has a value of 53.733 with 24 degrees of freedom. SPSS calculates the significance of this chi-square to be .000. Educational degree and political views are related. Specifically, as educational degree increases (graduate degree attainment), it appears that men and women are more likely to report being "extremely liberal."

The last portion of the output from SPSS allows us to check for the assumption that all expected values in each cell of the table are 5 or greater. The output indicates that two of the cells or 5.7% have a value less than 5. This is lower than our threshold of 20%.

Figure 10.3 Crosstabs Statistics Dialog Box

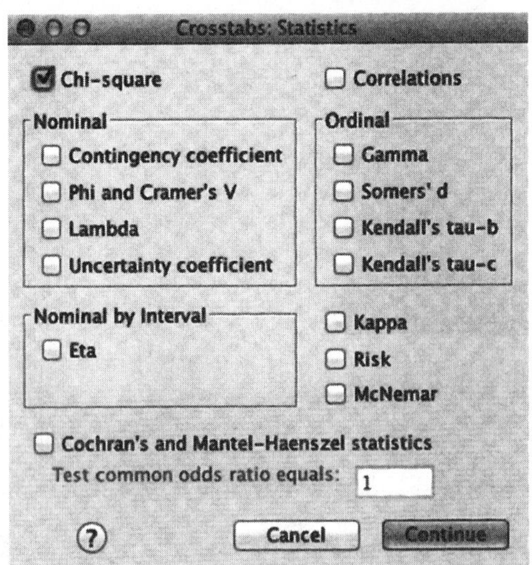

Figure 10.4 Chi-Square Test Output for DEGREE by POLVIEWS

Chi-Square Tests

	Value	df	Asymptotic Significance (2-sided)
Pearson Chi-Square	53.733[a]	24	.000
Likelihood Ratio	53.533	24	.000
Linear-by-Linear Association	6.892	1	.009
N of Valid Cases	1442		

a. 2 cells (5.7%) have expected count less than 5. The minimum expected count is 3.95.

Demonstration 2: Producing Nominal and Ordinal Measures of Association for Bivariate Tables

The SPSS Crosstabs procedure can also be used to calculate measures of association. We'll begin by investigating the relationship between belief in the Bible (BIBLE) and support for legal abortions for women for any reason (ABANY).

Click on *Analyze*, *Descriptive Statistics*, then *Crosstabs* to get to the Crosstabs dialog box. Put ABANY in the Row(s) box and BIBLE in the Column(s) box. Then click on the Statistics button. The Statistics dialog box (Figure 10.3) has about a dozen statistics from which to choose. Note that four statistics are listed in separate categories for "Nominal" and "Ordinal" data. Lambda is listed in the former, and gamma and Kendall's tau-*b* in the latter. Cramer's *V* can be easily obtained by checking the Phi and Cramer's *V* box. The other measures of association, such as Somer's *d* and Phi, will not be discussed in this textbook.

Since both variables are nominal, check the box for lambda. It is critical that we, as users of statistical programs, understand which statistics to select in any procedure. SPSS, like most programs, can't help us select the appropriate statistic for an analysis. Now click on Continue and then OK to create the table.

The first table is Case Processing Summary showing the number of valid and missing cases (not shown here). The second table should be a bivariate table of our two variables (not shown). Below is a table labeled "Directional Measures" (Figure 10.5). For now, we will only concern ourselves with the first two columns. Lambda is listed with three values. We've learned that the value of lambda depends on which variable is considered the dependent variable. In our example, attitude toward abortion for any reason is dependent, so lambda is .216. This indicates a weak relationship between the two variables. We can conclude that knowing the respondent's belief about the Bible increases the ability to predict his or her abortion attitude by just 21.6%.

SPSS also calculates a symmetrical lambda for those tables, where there is no independent or dependent variable. This calculation goes beyond the scope of this book. In addition, SPSS provides the Goodman and Kruskal tau statistic, another nominal measure of association, even though it was not requested. These measures will always be produced when lambda is requested.

If we checked the box for the Phi and Cramer's *V* in the Statistics dialog box, the Symmetric Measures table should be included in the output (Figure 10.5).

Cramer's *V* is .338, which indicates a moderate association between belief in the Bible and support for legal abortions for women for any reason.

Figure 10.5 Measures of Association for BIBLE and ABANY

Directional Measures

			Value	Asymptotic Standardized Error[a]	Approximate T[b]	Approximate Significance
Nominal by Nominal	Lambda	Symmetric	.100	.015	6.364	.000
		abany ABORTION IF WOMAN WANTS FOR ANY REASON Dependent	.216	.031	6.364	.000
		bible FEELINGS ABOUT THE BIBLE Dependent	.000	.000	.[c]	.[c]
	Goodman and Kruskal tau	abany ABORTION IF WOMAN WANTS FOR ANY REASON Dependent	.114	.020		.000[d]
		bible FEELINGS ABOUT THE BIBLE Dependent	.045	.008		.000[d]

a. Not assuming the null hypothesis.

b. Using the asymptotic standard error assuming the null hypothesis.

c. Cannot be computed because the asymptotic standard error equals zero.

d. Based on chi-square approximation

Symmetric Measures

		Value	Approximate Significance
Nominal by Nominal	Phi	.338	.000
	Cramer's V	.338	.000
N of Valid Cases		936	

We can also use the same procedures to calculate gamma for ordinal measures. For this demonstration, we'll examine the relationship between educational attainment (DEGREE) and attitudes toward same-sex marriage (MARHOMO). Respondents were asked whether homosexuals should have the right to marry (strongly agree, agree, neither, disagree, strongly agree). Both variables are ordinal measurements.

Click on *Analyze*, *Descriptive Statistics*, then *Crosstabs* to get to the Crosstabs dialog box. Put MARHOMO in the Row(s) box and DEGREE in the Column(s) box. Then click on the Statistics button. The Statistics dialog box has about a dozen statistics from which to choose. Click on gamma and Kendall's tau-*b* listed in the ordinal box. SPSS produces two separate tables (other than Case Processing Summary), the first is the bivariate table between MARHOMO and DEGREE, and the second is the table of symmetric measures, gamma and Kendall's tau-b, which we requested (Figure 10.6).

Figure 10.6 SPSS Output Displaying the Relationship Between DEGREE and MARHOMO

Symmetric Measures

		Value	Asymptotic Standardized Error[a]	Approximate T[b]	Approximate Significance
Ordinal by Ordinal	Kendall's tau-b	-.219	.026	-8.481	.000
	Gamma	-.299	.035	-8.481	.000
N of Valid Cases		976			

a. Not assuming the null hypothesis.

b. Using the asymptotic standard error assuming the null hypothesis.

The Kendall's tau-*b* statistic is in the first row under the column labeled "Value" followed by the gamma statistic. For this bivariate table, both the Kendall's tau-*b* statistic (−.219) and the gamma statistic (−.299) indicate a weak negative relationship between educational level and attitudes toward same-sex marriage. Using Kendall's tau-*b*, we can reduce about 22% of our error in predicting attitudes toward same-sex marriage by using information about respondent's education. Using gamma, about 30% of the error in predicting attitudes toward same-sex marriage would be reduced if we had information about respondent's educational attainment. Note that given how MARHOMO is coded, the negative gamma indicates that as DEGREE increases, respondents are more likely to strongly agree/agree that homosexuals should have the right to marry.

SPSS PROBLEMS [GSS2014SSDS-A]

1. Does marital happiness vary by respondent's sex?
   a. Use SPSS to investigate the relationship between SEX and HAPMAR (happiness of marriage). Create a bivariate table, and ask for appropriate percentages and expected values. Does the table have a large number of cells with expected values less than 5? Are there any surprises in the data?
   b. Have SPSS calculate chi-square for the table.
   c. Test the null hypothesis at the .05 significance level. What do you conclude?
   d. Select another demographic variable (DEGREE or CLASS) and investigate its relationship with HAPMAR.
2. Investigate the relationship between social class (CLASS) and general happiness rating (HAPPY)? Does money buy happiness? Have SPSS calculate the cross-tabulation, along with chi-square (set alpha at .05). What can you conclude?
3. Examine the relationships between respondent's health (HEALTH) and educational degree (DEGREE). Define DEGREE as your independent variable.
   a. Request the appropriate measures of association to describe the relationship between these two variables. Interpret your measures of association.
   b. Calculate the chi-square for the table. Test the null hypothesis at the .05 level. What do you conclude?
4. Reexamine the relationship between the importance of being a Christian in order to be truly American (AMCHRSTN) and attitudes toward homosexuality (HOMOSEX), which we first explored in the SPSS Demonstration of Chapter 9. Use the GSS14SSDS-B data set.
   a. Which variable is the dependent variable? Explain.
   b. Identify and calculate the appropriate measure of association to describe the relationship between the two variables.
   c. Add SEX as a control variable and calculate the gamma for each partial table. Is the relationship stronger for women or men? Can you think of reasons why this might be so?
5. Investigate the relationship between the abortion attitudes in GSS14SSDS-A (e.g., ABANY, ABMORE, ABSINGLE, and ABPOOR) and various demographic variables (you might begin with gender, age, or race). Examine the relationship of these variables based on the appropriate measures of association. For example, you might examine whether attitude toward each of the abortion items has a similar relationship to gender. That is, if females are supportive of abortion for rape victims, are they also supportive of abortion in other circumstances? Try

exploring these relationships further by adding control variables. You might create tables of abortion attitude by race and by gender. When you have finished the analysis, write a short report summarizing the findings. Suggest possible causes for the relationships you found.

CHAPTER EXERCISES

1. We examine the relationship between gender and fear of walking at night in their neighborhood (FEAR) based on GSS 2014 data.

Afraid to Walk at Night in Your Neighborhood	Men	Women	Total
Yes	77	175	252
No	270	259	529
Total	347	434	781

   a. What is the number of degrees of freedom for this table?

   b. Test the null hypothesis that gender and fear of walking alone are independent (alpha = .05). What do you conclude?

   c. If alpha were set at .01, would your decision change? Explain.

   d. Calculate lambda for the table. Interpret this measure of association.

2. Income inequality in the United States is a complex matter, and people have diverse and conflicting ideas on how to best address it. For this exercise, we present GSS 2014 SPSS analysis of political party identification and the variable HELPPOOR, which measures support of the statement whether the government in Washington should do everything possible to improve the standard of living of all poor Americans. HELPPOOR is measured on a scale 1 = *government action* to 5 = *each person should take care of himself.* A score of 3 indicates *agreement to both strategies.*

   a. What percentage of Democrats indicate that government action is necessary to help poor Americans? What percentage of Republicans indicated the same?

   b. The chi-square obtained is 119.53. Based on an alpha of .01, what can you conclude about the relationship between political party identification and HELPPOOR?

	Government Action	2	Agree to Both	4	People Help Themselves	Total
Democrat	69	50	142	30	33	324
Independent	40	18	77	15	13	163
Republican	15	10	84	70	66	245
Total	124	78	303	115	112	732

3. We extend our analysis of fear and gender, from Exercise 1, with the addition of a control variable, race. Bivariate tables for whites and blacks are presented.

For Whites			
Afraid to Walk at Night in Your Neighborhood	**Men**	**Women**	**Total**
Yes	61	129	190
No	221	190	411
Total	282	319	601

For Blacks			
Afraid to Walk at Night in Your Neighborhood	Men	Women	Total
Yes	8	30	38
No	26	47	73
Total	34	77	111

a. Which racial group has a higher percentage of respondents indicating that they are afraid to walk at night in their neighborhood?

b. Regardless of race, are women more likely to report than men that they are afraid to walk at night in their neighborhood?

c. For each table, test the hypothesis that gender and fear to walk at night are independent (alpha = .01). What do you conclude?

4. We continue our analysis from Exercise 2, this time examining the relationship between educational attainment (RDEGREE: 0 = *less than high school*, 1 = *high school degree*, 2 = *some college or more*) and help for the poor (HELPPOOR). The obtained chi-square is 40.43. Based on an alpha of .05, do you reject the null hypothesis? Explain.

helppoor SHOULD GOVT IMPROVE STANDARD OF LIVING? * RDegree Recoded Degree Crosstabulation

Count

		RDegree Recoded Degree			
		.00	1.00	2.00	Total
helppoor SHOULD GOVT IMPROVE STANDARD OF LIVING?	1 GOVT ACTION	30	65	32	127
	2	6	32	41	79
	3 AGREE WITH BOTH	32	153	126	311
	4	6	56	58	120
	5 PEOPLE HELP SELVES	14	69	35	118
Total		88	375	292	755

5. Is there a relationship between the race of violent offenders and the race of their victims? Data from the U.S. Department of Justice for 2011 are presented below.

Characteristics of Victim	Characteristics of Offender		
	White	Black	Other
White	2,630	448	33
Black	193	2,447	9
Other	180	45	99

Source: U.S. Department of Justice, *Expanded Homicide Data*, Table 6, 2011.

a. Let's treat race of offenders as the independent variable and race of victims as the dependent variable. If we first ignore the independent variable and try to predict race of victim, how many errors will we make?

b. If we now take into account the independent variable, how many errors of prediction will we make for those offenders who are white? Black offenders? Other offenders?

c. Combine the answers in (a) and (b) to calculate the proportional reduction in error for this table based on the independent variable. How does this statistic improve our understanding of the relationship between the two variables?

6. Let's continue our analysis of offenders and victims of violent crime. In the following table, U.S. Department of Justice 2011 data for the sex of offenders and the sex of victims are reported.

	Sex of Offender	
Sex of Victim	Male	Female
Male	3,760	450
Female	1,590	140

Source: U.S. Department of Justice, *Expanded Homicide Data*, Table 6, 2011.

a. Treating sex of offender as the independent variable, how many errors of prediction will be made if the independent variable is ignored?

b. How many fewer errors will be made if the independent variable is taken into account?

c. Combine your answers in (a) and (b) to calculate lambda. Discuss the relationship between these two variables.

d. Which lambda is stronger, the one for sex of offenders/victims or race of offenders/victims (Exercise 5)?

7. Earlier in this chapter, we reviewed Inman and Mayes' (1999) research on first-generation college students. They also examined the relationship between student race and first-generation college status. Based on their data, test whether race is independent of first-generation college status (alpha = .01).

First-Generation College Status	Student Race					Total
	White	Black	Native American	Hispanic	Asian American	
Firsts	1,742	102	41	19	6	1,910
Nonfirsts	2,392	119	45	25	22	2,603
Total	4,134	221	86	44	28	4,513

Source: Adapted from W. Elliot Inman and Larry Mayes, "The Importance of Being First: Unique Characteristics of First Generation Community College Students," *Community College Review* 26, no. 3 (1999): 8.

8. GSS 2014 respondents were asked to rate their level of agreement to the statement, "Scientific research is necessary and should be supported by the federal government" (ADVFRONT). Responses are cross-tabulated by educational attainment (DEGREE).

a. What percentage of those with a graduate degree strongly agree or agree with the statement?

b. Interpret the gamma statistic.

c. Test the null hypothesis that DEGREE and ADVFRONT are statistically independent. Set alpha at .05.

advfront SCI RSCH IS NECESSARY AND SHOULD BE SUPPORTED BY FEDERAL GOVT * degree RS HIGHEST DEGREE Crosstabulation

Count

		degree RS HIGHEST DEGREE					
		0 LT HIGH SCHOOL	1 HIGH SCHOOL	2 JUNIOR COLLEGE	3 BACHELOR	4 GRADUATE	Total
advfront SCI RSCH IS NECESSARY AND SHOULD BE SUPPORTED BY FEDERAL GOVT	1 Strongly agree	10	61	7	39	31	148
	2 Agree	43	205	27	69	41	385
	3 Disagree	17	49	5	11	8	90
	4 Strongly disagree	1	7	1	2	0	11
Total		71	322	40	121	80	634

Chi-Square Tests

	Value	df	Asymptotic Significance (2-sided)
Pearson Chi-Square	30.520[a]	12	.002
Likelihood Ratio	30.419	12	.002
Linear-by-Linear Association	22.921	1	.000
N of Valid Cases	634		

a. 4 cells (20.0%) have expected count less than 5. The minimum expected count is .69.

Symmetric Measures

		Value	Asymptotic Standardized Error[a]	Approximate T[b]	Approximate Significance
Ordinal by Ordinal	Gamma	-.276	.055	-4.858	.000
N of Valid Cases		634			

a. Not assuming the null hypothesis.

b. Using the asymptotic standard error assuming the null hypothesis.

9. Data from the ISSP 2014 are presented below for 975 French respondents, cross-tabulating highest completed educational level (DEGREE) with religious service attendance (ATTEND). Notice the international categories for degree. Test the null hypothesis that the variables are not related. Set alpha at .05.

ATTEND Attendance of religious services * DEGREE Highest completed education level: Categories for international comparison Crosstabulation

Count

		DEGREE Highest completed education level: Categories for international comparison						
		0 No formal education	1 Primary school	2 Lower secondary (secondary completed does not allow entry to	3 Upper secondary (programs that allows entry to university	5 Lower level tertiary, first stage (also technical schools at	6 Upper level tertiary (Master, Doctor)	Total
ATTEND Attendance of religious services	1 Several times a week or more often (incl. every day, several	1	0	10	4	4	4	23
	2 Once a week	1	2	24	4	5	12	48
	3 2 or 3 times a month	1	3	12	4	3	4	27
	4 Once a month	0	3	14	1	1	6	25
	5 Several times a year	3	3	80	21	23	34	164
	6 Once a year	0	6	44	16	22	22	110
	7 Less frequently than once a year	1	6	54	18	26	14	119
	8 Never	3	9	175	70	91	111	459
Total		10	32	413	138	175	207	975

Chi-Square Tests

	Value	df	Asymptotic Significance (2-sided)
Pearson Chi-Square	52.047[a]	35	.032
Likelihood Ratio	51.313	35	.037
Linear-by-Linear Association	8.439	1	.004
N of Valid Cases	975		

a. 21 cells (43.8%) have expected count less than 5. The minimum expected count is .24.

10. We test the same relationship between DEGREE and ATTEND, this time with the GSS 2014 sample of 914 men and women. Test the null hypothesis that there is no relationship between the two variables. Set alpha at .05.

attend HOW OFTEN R ATTENDS RELIGIOUS SERVICES * degree RS HIGHEST DEGREE Crosstabulation

Count

		degree RS HIGHEST DEGREE					
		0 LT HIGH SCHOOL	1 HIGH SCHOOL	2 JUNIOR COLLEGE	3 BACHELOR	4 GRADUATE	Total
attend HOW OFTEN R ATTENDS RELIGIOUS SERVICES	0 NEVER	39	160	23	55	31	308
	1 LT ONCE A YEAR	10	41	12	11	9	83
	2 ONCE A YEAR	12	92	7	37	25	173
	3 SEVRL TIMES A YR	11	61	8	20	17	117
	4 ONCE A MONTH	10	22	8	12	7	59
	5 2-3X A MONTH	9	43	5	27	13	97
	6 NRLY EVERY WEEK	10	20	6	13	4	53
	7 EVERY WEEK	24	101	15	42	25	207
	8 MORE THN ONCE WK	15	42	5	9	9	80
Total		140	582	89	226	140	1177

Chi-Square Tests

	Value	df	Asymptotic Significance (2-sided)
Pearson Chi-Square	42.866[a]	32	.095
Likelihood Ratio	42.023	32	.111
Linear-by-Linear Association	.054	1	.816
N of Valid Cases	1177		

a. 2 cells (4.4%) have expected count less than 5. The minimum expected count is 4.01.

11. The GSS 2014 included a question on the importance of providing health care for everyone (HLTHALL). HLTHALL is an ordinal measure: 1 = not important at all to 7 = very important. We present HLTHALL with two independent variables—social class (CLASS) and 2012 presidential candidate support (PRES12). Interpret each measure of association.

HLTHALL HEALTHCARE PROVIDED FOR EVERYONE * PRES12 VOTE OBAMA OR ROMNEY Crosstabulation

Count

		PRES12 VOTE OBAMA OR ROMNEY		
		1 Obama	2 Romney	Total
HLTHALL HEALTHCARE PROVIDED FOR EVERYONE	1 Not at all important	2	15	17
	2	0	6	6
	3	2	5	7
	4	9	22	31
	5	10	5	15
	6	17	5	22
	7 Very imporant	96	17	113
Total		136	75	211

Directional Measures

			Value	Asymptotic Standardized Error[a]	Approximate T[b]	Approximate Significance
Nominal by Nominal	Lambda	Symmetric	.231	.060	3.425	.001
		HLTHALL HEALTHCARE PROVIDED FOR EVERYONE Dependent	.051	.062	.802	.423
		PRES12 VOTE OBAMA OR ROMNEY Dependent	.467	.076	4.711	.000
	Goodman and Kruskal tau	HLTHALL HEALTHCARE PROVIDED FOR EVERYONE Dependent	.113	.026		.000[c]
		PRES12 VOTE OBAMA OR ROMNEY Dependent	.354	.062		.000[c]

a. Not assuming the null hypothesis.

b. Using the asymptotic standard error assuming the null hypothesis.

c. Based on chi-square approximation

HLTHALL HEALTHCARE PROVIDED FOR EVERYONE * class SUBJECTIVE CLASS IDENTIFICATION Crosstabulation

Count

		class SUBJECTIVE CLASS IDENTIFICATION				
		1 LOWER CLASS	2 WORKING CLASS	3 MIDDLE CLASS	4 UPPER CLASS	Total
HLTHALL HEALTHCARE PROVIDED FOR EVERYONE	1 Not at all important	4	10	8	0	22
	2	0	6	5	0	11
	3	1	7	4	0	12
	4	3	13	23	1	40
	5	2	8	13	0	23
	6	0	16	16	3	35
	7 Very imporant	27	110	66	4	207
Total		37	170	135	8	350

Symmetric Measures

		Value	Asymptotic Standardized Error[a]	Approximate T[b]	Approximate Significance
Ordinal by Ordinal	Gamma	-.198	.076	-2.606	.009
N of Valid Cases		350			

a. Not assuming the null hypothesis.

b. Using the asymptotic standard error assuming the null hypothesis.

12. We take another look at the frequency of political discussions (DISCPOL), first presented in Table 10.11 (based on GSS 2014). DISCPOL is presented with two independent variables—(1) respondent sex and (2) age (measured in categories as reported in corresponding tables). Interpret each measure of association. Which variable—age or sex—has a higher proportional reduction of error?

discpol HOW OFTEN R DISCUSS POLITICS * RAge recoded Age Crosstabulation

Count

		RAge recoded Age				
		1.00 18-29	2.00 30-39	3.00 40-49	4.00 50-59	Total
discpol HOW OFTEN R DISCUSS POLITICS	1 OFTEN	3	5	4	8	20
	2 SOMETIMES	12	17	16	26	71
	3 RARELY	19	25	23	24	91
	4 NEVER	18	31	15	14	78
Total		52	78	58	72	260

Symmetric Measures

		Value	Asymptotic Standardized Error[a]	Approximate T[b]	Approximate Significance
Ordinal by Ordinal	Gamma	-.206	.070	-2.932	.003
N of Valid Cases		260			

a. Not assuming the null hypothesis.

b. Using the asymptotic standard error assuming the null hypothesis.

discpol HOW OFTEN R DISCUSS POLITICS * sex RESPONDENTS SEX Crosstabulation

Count

		sex RESPONDENTS SEX		
		1 MALE	2 FEMALE	Total
discpol HOW OFTEN R DISCUSS POLITICS	1 OFTEN	21	14	35
	2 SOMETIMES	57	49	106
	3 RARELY	49	82	131
	4 NEVER	32	64	96
Total		159	209	368

Directional Measures

			Value	Asymptotic Standardized Error[a]	Approximate T[b]	Approximate Significance
Nominal by Nominal	Lambda	Symmetric	.058	.047	1.213	.225
		discpol HOW OFTEN R DISCUSS POLITICS Dependent	.034	.043	.778	.437
		sex RESPONDENTS SEX Dependent	.094	.071	1.266	.206
	Goodman and Kruskal tau	discpol HOW OFTEN R DISCUSS POLITICS Dependent	.013	.007		.003[c]
		sex RESPONDENTS SEX Dependent	.039	.020		.002[c]

a. Not assuming the null hypothesis.

b. Using the asymptotic standard error assuming the null hypothesis.

c. Based on chi-square approximation

13. Paul Mazerolle, Alex Piquero, and Robert Brame (2010)[9] examined whether violent onset offenders have distinct career dimensions from offenders whose initial offending involves nonviolence. In this table, the researchers investigate the relationship between gender, race, and age, and nonviolent versus violent onset using chi-square analysis. Their data are based on 1,503 juvenile offenders in Queensland, Australia. The independent variables are reported in rows.

    The chi-square models for gender and age at first offense are significant at the .01 level. Interpret the relationship between gender and age at first offense with a nonviolent or violent initial offense.

Violent Offense Onset by Gender, Race, and Age

	Nonviolent Onset N (%)	Violent Onset N (%)	Total N (%)
Gender			
Male	1,146 (88.29)	152 (11.71)	1,298 (100)
Female	156 (81.68)	35 (18.32)	191 (100)
Total	1,302	187	1,489
			$\chi^2 = 6.331^{**}$
Indigenous status			
Nonindigenous	815 (87.17)	120 (12.83)	935 (100)
Indigenous	477 (88.17)	64 (11.83)	541 (100)
			$\chi^2 = 0.317$
Age at first offense			
Less than 14 years	579 (90.33)	62 (9.67)	641 (100)
14 years and older	723 (85.26)	125 (14.74)	848 (100)
			$\chi^2 = 8.539^{**}$

Source: Paul Mazerolle, Alex Piquero, and Robert Brame, "Violent Onset Offenders: Do Initial Experiences Shape Criminal Career Dimensions?" *International Criminal Justice Review*, 20, no. 2 (2010): 132–146.

$^{**}p < .01$.

11

ANALYSIS OF VARIANCE

Chapter Learning Objectives

1. Explain the application of a one-way analysis of variance (ANOVA) model
2. Define the concepts of between and within total variance
3. Calculate and interpret a test for two or more sample cases with means
4. Determine the significance of an F-ratio test statistic
5. Interpret SPSS output for ANOVA

Many research questions require us to look at multiple samples or groups, at least more than two at a time. We may be interested in studying the relationship between ethnic identity (white, African American, Asian American, Latino/Latina) and church attendance, the influence of one's social class (lower, working, middle, and upper) on President Barack Obama's job approval ratings, or the effect of educational attainment (less than high school, high school graduate, some college, and college graduate) on household income. Note that each of these examples requires a comparison between multiple demographic or ethnic groups, more than the two-group comparisons we reviewed in Chapter 8 ("Testing Hypotheses"). While it would be easy to confine our analyses between two groups, our social world is much more complex and diverse.

Let's say that we're interested in examining educational attainment—on average, how many years of education do Americans achieve? For 2013, the U.S. Census reported that 88.2% of adults (25 years and older) completed at least a high school degree, and 31% of all adults attained at least a bachelor's degree.[1] During his first term of office, President Obama pledged that the United States would have the world's highest proportion of college graduates by 2020. Special attention has been paid to the educational achievement of Latino students. Data from the U.S. Census, as well as from the U.S. Department of Education, confirm that Latino students continue to have lower levels of educational achievement than other racial or ethnic groups.

In Chapter 8, we introduced statistical techniques to assess the difference between two sample means or proportions. In Table 8.2, we compared the difference in educational attainment for blacks and whites. But what if we wanted to examine more than two racial or ethnic groups?

Suppose we collect a random sample of 23 men and women, grouped them into four demographic categories, and included their educational attainment in Table 11.1. With the t-test statistic we discussed in Chapter 8, we could analyze only two samples at a time. We would have to analyze the mean educational attainment of whites

Table 11.1 Educational Attainment (Measured in Years) for Four Racial/Ethnic Groups

White	Black	Asian	Latino
$n_1 = 6$	$n_2 = 5$	$n_3 = 6$	$n_4 = 6$
12	16	16	11
12	12	18	12
14	13	16	12
12	13	14	13
12	14	16	16
16		20	11

and blacks, whites and Asians, whites and Latinos, blacks and Asians, and so on. (Confirm that we would have to analyze six different pairs.) In the end, we would have a series of *t*-test statistic calculations, and we still wouldn't be able to answer our original question: Is there a difference in educational attainment among all *four* demographic groups?

LEARNING CHECK 11.1

Identify the independent and dependent variables in Table 11.1.

Analysis of variance (ANOVA) An inferential statistics technique designed to test for a significant relationship between two variables in two or more groups or samples.

There is a statistical technique that will allow us to examine all the four groups or samples simultaneously. This technique is called analysis of variance (ANOVA). ANOVA follows the same five-step model of hypothesis testing that we used with *t* test for means and *Z* test for proportions (in Chapter 8) and chi-square (in Chapter 10 ["The Chi-Square Test and Measures of Association"]). In this chapter, we review the calculations for ANOVA and discuss two applications of ANOVA from the research literature.

UNDERSTANDING ANALYSIS OF VARIANCE

Recall that the *t* test examines the difference between two means, $\bar{Y}_1 - \bar{Y}_2$, while the null hypothesis assumed that there was no difference between them: $\mu_1 = \mu_2$. Rejecting the null hypothesis meant that there was a significant difference between the two mean scores (or the populations from which the samples were drawn).

The logic of ANOVA is the same but extending to two or more groups. For the data presented in Table 11.1, ANOVA will allow us to examine the variation among four means $(\bar{Y}_1, \bar{Y}_2, \bar{Y}_3, \bar{Y}_4)$, and the null hypothesis can be stated as follows: $\mu_1 = \mu_2 = \mu_3 = \mu_4$. Rejecting the null hypothesis for ANOVA indicates that there is a significant variation among the four samples (or the four populations from which the samples were drawn) and that at least one of the sample means is significantly different from the others. In our example, it suggests that years of education (dependent variable) do vary by group membership (independent variable).

When ANOVA procedures are applied to data with one dependent and one independent variable, it is called a one-way ANOVA.

One-way ANOVA Analysis of variance application with one dependent and one independent variable.

The means, standard deviations, and variances for the samples have been calculated and are shown in Table 11.2. Note that the four mean educational years are not identical, with Asians having the highest educational attainment. Also, based on the standard deviations, we can tell that the samples are relatively homogeneous with deviations within 1.00 to 2.07 years of the mean. We already know that there is a difference between the samples, but the question remains: Is this difference significant? Do the samples reflect a relationship between demographic group membership and educational attainment in the general population?

LEARNING CHECK 11.2

We've calculated the mean and standard deviation scores for each group in Table 11.2. Compute each mean (Chapter 3) and standard deviation (Chapter 4) and confirm that our statistics are correct.

To determine whether the differences are significant, ANOVA examines the differences *between* our four samples, as well as the differences *within* a single sample. The differences can also be referred to as variance or variation, which is why ANOVA is the analysis of *variance*. What is the difference between one sample's mean score and the overall mean? What

Table 11.2 Years of Education, Means, Standard Deviations, and Variances for Four Racial/Ethnic Groups

White	Black	Asian	Latino
$n_1 = 6$	$n_2 = 5$	$n_3 = 6$	$n_4 = 6$
12	16	16	11
12	12	18	12
14	13	16	12
12	13	14	13
12	14	16	16
16		20	11
$\bar{Y}_1 = 13.00$	$\bar{Y}_2 = 13.60$	$\bar{Y}_3 = 16.67$	$\bar{Y}_4 = 12.50$
$s_1 = 1.67$	$s_2 = 1.51$	$s_3 = 2.07$	$s_4 = 1.87$
$s_1^2 = 2.79$	$s_2^2 = 2.28$	$s_3^2 = 4.28$	$s_4^2 = 3.50$
$\bar{Y} = 13.96$			

is the variation of individual scores within one sample? Are all the scores alike (no variation), or is there a broad variation in scores? ANOVA allows us to determine whether the variance between samples is larger than the variance within the samples. If the variance is larger between samples than the variance within samples, we know that educational attainment varies significantly across the samples. It would support the notion that group membership explains the variation in educational attainment.

THE STRUCTURE OF HYPOTHESIS TESTING WITH ANOVA

The Assumptions

ANOVA requires several assumptions regarding the method of sampling, the level of measurement, the shape of the population distribution, and the homogeneity of variance.

> Independent random samples are used. Our choice of sample members from one population has no effect on the choice of sample members from the second, third, or fourth population. For example, the selection of Asians has no effect on the selection of any other sample.
>
> The dependent variable, years of education, is an interval-ratio level of measurement. Some researchers also apply ANOVA to ordinal-level measurements.
>
> The population is normally distributed. Although we cannot confirm whether the populations are normal, given that our N is so small, we must assume that the population is normally distributed to proceed with our analysis.
>
> The population variances are equal. Based on our calculations in Table 11.2, we see that the sample variances, although not identical, are relatively homogeneous.[2]

Stating the Research and the Null Hypotheses and Setting Alpha

The research hypothesis (H_1) proposes that at least one of the means is different. We do not identify which one(s) will be different, or larger or smaller, we only predict that a difference does exist.

H_1: At least one mean is different from the others.

ANOVA is a test of the null hypothesis of no difference between any of the means. Since we're working with four samples, we include four μs in our null hypothesis.

H_0: $\mu_1 = \mu_2 = \mu_3 = \mu_4$

As we did in other models of hypothesis testing, we'll have to set our alpha. Alpha is the level of probability at which we'll reject our null hypothesis. For this example, we'll set alpha at .05.

The Concepts of Between and Within Total Variance

A word of caution before we proceed: Since we're working with four different samples and a total of 21 respondents, we'll have a lot of calculations. It's important to be consistent with your notations (don't mix up numbers for the different samples) and be careful with your calculations.

Our primary set of calculations has to do with the two types of variance: (1) between-group variance and (2) within-group variance. The estimate of each variance has two parts, the sum of squares and degrees of freedom (*df*).

The **between-group sum of squares** or *SSB* measures the difference in average years of education between our four groups. Sum of squares is the abbreviation for "sum of squared deviations." For *SSB*, what we're measuring is the sum of squared deviations between each sample mean to the overall mean score. The formula for the *SSB* can be presented as follows:

Between-group sum of squares (SSB) The sum of squared deviations between each sample mean to the overall mean score.

$$SSB = \sum n_k \left(\bar{Y}_k - \bar{Y}\right)^2 \tag{11.1}$$

where

n_k = the number of cases in a sample (k represents the number of different samples)

$\bar{Y}_k$ = the mean of a sample

$\bar{Y}$ = the overall mean

SSB can also be understood as the amount of variation in the dependent variable (years of education) that can be attributed to or explained by the independent variable (the four demographic groups).

Within-group sum of squares or *SSW* measures the variation of scores within a single sample or, as in our example, the variation in years of education within one group. *SSW* is also referred to as the amount of unexplained variance, since this is what remains after we consider the effect of the specified independent variable. The formula for *SSW* measures the sum of squared deviations within each group, between each individual score with its sample mean.

Within-group sum of squares (SSW) Sum of squared deviations within each group, calculated between each individual score and the sample mean.

$$SSW = \sum \left(Y_i - \bar{Y}_k\right)^2 \tag{11.2}$$

where

Y_i = each individual score in a sample

$\bar{Y}_k$ = the mean of a sample

Even with our small sample size, if we were to use Formula 11.2, we'd have a tedious and cumbersome set of calculations. Instead, we suggest using the following computational formula for within-group variation or *SSW*:

$$SSW = \sum Y_i^2 - \sum \frac{\left(\sum Y_k\right)^2}{n_k} \tag{11.3}$$

where

Y_i^2 = the squared scores from each sample

$\sum Y_k$ = the sum of the scores of each sample

n_k = the number of cases in a sample

Total sum of squares (SST) The total variation in scores, calculated by adding *SSB* and *SSW*.

Together, the explained (*SSB*) and unexplained (*SSW*) variances compose the amount of total variation in scores. The **total sum of squares** or *SST* can be represented by

$$SST = \sum\left(Y_i - \bar{Y}\right)^2 = SSB + SSW \quad (11.4)$$

where

Y_i = each individual score

$\bar{Y}$ = the overall mean

The second part of estimating the between-group and within-group variances is calculating the degrees of freedom. Degrees of freedom are also discussed in Chapters 8 and 10. For ANOVA, we have to calculate two degrees of freedom. For *SSB*, the degrees of freedom are determined by

$$df_{\text{b}} = k - 1 \quad (11.5)$$

where k is the number of samples.

For *SSW*, the degrees of freedom are determined by

$$df_{\text{w}} = N - k \quad (11.6)$$

where

N = total number of cases

k = number of samples

Mean square between Sum of squares between divided by its corresponding degrees of freedom.

Mean square within Sum of squares within divided by its corresponding degrees of freedom.

Finally, we can estimate the between-group variance by calculating **mean square between**. Simply stated, mean squares are averages computed by dividing each sum of squares by its corresponding degrees of freedom. Mean square between can be represented by

$$\text{Mean square between} = SSB/df_{\text{b}} \quad (11.7)$$

and the within-group variance or **mean square within** can be represented by

$$\text{Mean square within} = SSW/df_{\text{w}} \quad (11.8)$$

The *F* Statistic

***F* ratio or *F* statistic** The test statistic for ANOVA, calculated by the ratio of mean square between to mean square within.

Together the mean square between (Formula 11.7) and mean square within (Formula 11.8) compose the ***F* ratio obtained** or ***F* statistic**. Developed by R. A. Fisher, the *F* statistic is the ratio of between-group variance to within-group variance and is determined by Formula 11.9:

$$F = \frac{\text{Mean square between}}{\text{Mean square within}} = \frac{SSB/\,df_{\text{b}}}{SSW/df_{\text{w}}} \quad (11.9)$$

We know that a larger *F*-obtained statistic means that there is more between-group variance than within-group variance, increasing the chances of rejecting our null hypothesis. In Table 11.3, we present additional calculations to compute *F*.

Let's calculate between-group sum of squares and degrees of freedom based on Formulas 11.1 and 11.5. The calculation for *SSB* is

DECOMPOSITION OF *SST*

A CLOSER LOOK 11.1

According to Formula 11.4, sum of squares total (*SST*) is equal to

$$SST = \sum(Y_i - \bar{Y})^2 = SSB + SSW$$

You can see that the between sum of squares (explained variance) and within sum of squares (unexplained variance) account for the total variance (*SST*) in a particular dependent variable. How does that apply to a single case in our educational attainment example? Let's take the first black respondent in Table 11.1 with 16 years of education.

This respondent's total deviation (corresponding to *SST*) is based on the difference between the years of education from the overall mean (Formula 11.4). The individual mean is quite a bit higher than the overall mean education of 8 years. The difference of the individual from the overall mean is 2.04 years (16 – 13.96). Between-group deviation (corresponding to *SSB*) can be determined by measuring the difference between the group average from the overall mean (Formula 11.1). The deviation between the group average and overall average for blacks is –.36 years (13.60 – 13.96). Finally, the within-group deviation (corresponding to *SSW*, Formula 11.2) is based on the difference between the first black person's years of education and the group average for blacks: 2.40 years (16 – 13.60). So for the first black person in our sample, *SSB* + *SSW* = *SST* or 2.40 + –.36 = 2.04. In a complete ANOVA problem, we're computing these two sources of deviation (*SSB* and *SSW*) to obtain *SST* (Formula 11.4) for everyone in the sample.

Table 11.3 Computational Worksheet for ANOVA

White	Black	Asian	Hispanic
$n_1 = 6$	$n_2 = 5$	$n_3 = 6$	$n_4 = 6$
12	16	16	11
12	12	18	12
14	13	16	12
12	13	14	13
12	14	16	16
16	———	20	11
$\bar{Y}_1 = 13.00$	$\bar{Y}_2 = 13.60$	$\bar{Y}_3 = 16.67$	$\bar{Y}_4 = 12.50$
$s_1 = 1.67$	$s_2 = 1.51$	$s_3 = 2.07$	$s_4 = 1.87$
$s_1^2 = 2.79$	$s_2^2 = 2.28$	$s_3^2 = 4.28$	$s_4^2 = 3.50$
$Y_1 = 78$	$Y_2 = 68$	$Y_3 = 100$	$Y_4 = 75$
$Y_1^2 = 1028$	$Y_2^2 = 934$	$Y_3^2 = 1{,}688$	$Y_4^2 = 955$
$\bar{Y} = 13.96$			

$$\Sigma n_k(\bar{Y}_k - \bar{Y})^2 = 6(13-13.96)^2 + 5(13.6-13.96)^2 + 6(16.67-13.96)^2 + 6(12.5-13.96)^2$$
$$= 5.53 + .65 + 44.06 + 12.79$$
$$= 63.03$$

The degrees of freedom for *SSB* is $k - 1$ or $4 - 1 = 3$. Based on Formula 11.7, the mean square between is

$$\text{Mean square between} = 63.03/3 = 21.01$$

The within-group sum of squares and degrees of freedom are based on Formulas 11.3 and 11.6. The calculation for *SSW* is

$$\Sigma Y_i^2 - \Sigma \frac{(\Sigma Y_k)^2}{n_k} = (1{,}028 + 934 + 1{,}688 + 955) - \left(\frac{78^2}{6} + \frac{68^2}{5} + \frac{100^2}{6} + \frac{75^2}{6}\right)$$
$$= 4{,}605 - (1014 + 924.8 + 1666.67 + 937.50)$$
$$= 4{,}605 - 4542.97$$
$$= 62.03$$

The degrees of freedom for *SSW* is $N - k = 23 - 4 = 19$. Based on Formula 11.8, the mean square within is

$$\text{Mean square within} = 62.03/19 = 3.26$$

Finally, our calculation of *F* is based on Formula 11.9:

$$F \text{ ratio} = 21.01/3.26 = 6.44$$

Making a Decision

To determine the probability of calculating an *F* statistic of 6.44, we rely on Appendix E, the distribution of the *F* statistic. Appendix E lists the corresponding values of the *F* distribution for various degrees of freedom and two levels of significance, .05 and .01.

Since we set alpha at .05, we'll refer to the table marked "$p = .05$." Note that Appendix E includes two *df*s. These refer to our degrees of freedom, $df_1 = df_b$ and $df_2 = df_w$.

Because of the two degrees of freedom, we'll have to determine the probability of our *F* obtained differently than we did with *t* test or chi-square. For this ANOVA example, we'll have to determine the corresponding *F*, also called the *F* critical, when $df_b = 3$ and $df_w = 19$, and $\alpha = .05$.

F critical The *F*-test statistic that corresponds to the alpha level, df_w, and df_b (as in Appendix E).

F obtained The *F*-test statistic that is calculated.

Based on Appendix E, the **F critical** is 3.13, while our **F obtained** (the one that we calculated) is 6.44. Since our *F* obtained is greater than the *F* critical (6.44 > 3.13), we know that its probability is < .05, extending into the shaded area. (If our *F* obtained was <3.13, we could determine that its probability was greater than our alpha of .05, in the unshaded area of the *F*-distribution curve. Refer to Figure 11.1.) We can reject the null hypothesis of no difference and conclude that there is a significant difference in educational attainment between the four groups.

THE FIVE STEPS IN HYPOTHESIS TESTING: A SUMMARY

To summarize, we've calculated an ANOVA test examining the difference between four demographic groups and their average years of education.

Figure 11.1 Comparing F Obtained Versus F Critical

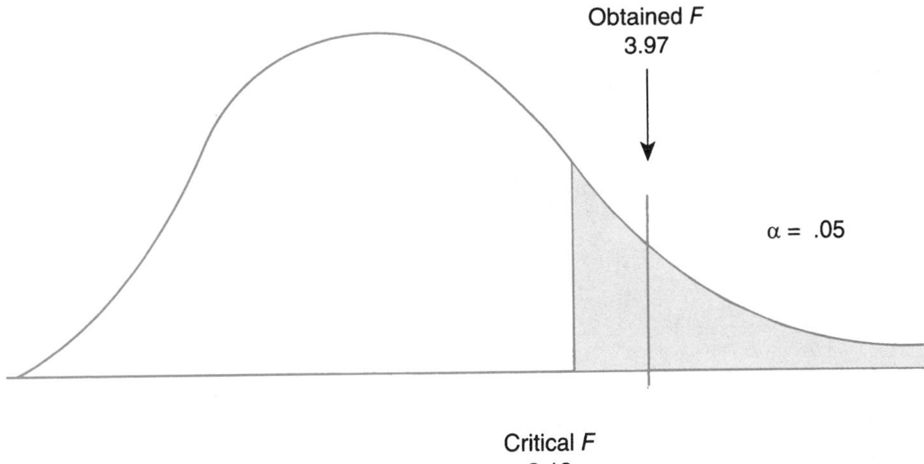

1. *Making Assumptions:*

- Independent random samples are used.
- The dependent variable, years of education, is an interval-ratio level of measurement.
- The population is normally distributed.
- The population variances are equal.

2. *Stating the Research and Null Hypothesis and Selecting Alpha:*

H_1: At least one mean is different from the others.

H_0: $\mu_1 = \mu_2 = \mu_3 = \mu_4$

$$\alpha = .05$$

3. *Selecting the Sampling Distribution and Specifying the Test Statistic:* The *F* distribution and *F* statistic are used to test the significance of the difference between the four sample means.

4. *Computing the Test Statistic:* We need to calculate the between-group and within-group variation (sum of squares and degrees of freedom). We estimate $SSB = 21.01$ ($df_b = 3$) and $SSW = 3.26$ ($df_w = 19$).

Based on Formula 11.9,

$$F = 21.01/3.26 = 6.44$$

5. *Making a Decision and Interpreting the Results:* We reject the null hypothesis of no difference. Our *F* obtained of 6.44 is greater than the *F* critical of 3.13. The probability of 6.44 is <.05. *F* doesn't advise us about which groups are different, only that educational attainment

does differ significantly by demographic group members. Based on the sample data, we know that the only group to achieve a college education average was Asians (16.67 years). If we were to rank the other group means, second highest educational attainment was among blacks (13.60), followed by whites (13.00) and Latinos (12.50).

LEARNING CHECK 11.3

If alpha were changed to .01, would our final decision change?

STATISTICS IN PRACTICE: THE ETHICAL CONSUMER

Consumers increasingly avoid products that are perceived as having a negative social or environmental impact. By purchasing fair labor, organic or environmentally safe products, consumers express their politics through their purchases, a practice that has been referred to as ethical consumerism. The GSS2014 includes a series of questions on what it takes to be a good citizen. Respondents were asked how important it was to "choose products for political, ethical or environmental reasons, even if they cost a bit more." Answers were ranked on a 7-point scale: 1 = not at all important to 7 = very important. We use SPSS and the GSS2014 data to examine the relationship between responses to this question and political party identification (Democrat, Independent, or Republican). We will set alpha at .05 to assess our results. SPSS output are presented as Figure 11.2.

A CLOSER LOOK 11.2

ASSESSING THE RELATIONSHIP BETWEEN VARIABLES

Based on our five-step model of *F*, we've determined that there is a significant difference between the four demographic groups in their educational attainment. We rejected the null hypothesis and concluded that the years of education (our dependent variable) do vary by group membership (our independent variable). But can we say anything about how strong the relationship is between the variables?

The correlation ratio or eta square (η^2) allows us to make a statement about the strength of the relationship or the effect size. Eta square is determined by the following:

$$\eta^2 = \frac{SSB}{SST} \quad (11.10)$$

The ratio of *SSB* to *SST* (*SSB* + *SSW*) represents the proportion of variance that is explained by the group (or independent) variable. Eta square indicates the strength of the relationship between the independent and dependent variables, ranging in value from 0 to 1.0. As eta square approaches 0, the relationship between the variables is weaker, and as eta square approaches 1, the relationship between the variables is stronger.

Based on our ANOVA example,

$$\eta^2 = \frac{63.03}{63.03 + 62.03} = .50$$

We can state that 50% of the variation in educational attainment can be attributed to demographic group membership. Or we can say that 50% of the variation in the dependent variable (educational attainment) can be explained by the independent variable (group membership). So how strong is this relationship? We can base our determination of the strength on A Closer Look 10.2 from Chapter 10, the same scale that we used to assess gamma. We conclude that there is a very strong relationship between group membership and educational attainment.

Figure 11.2 SPSS ANOVA Output: Political Party Identification and Choosing Products for Political Reasons

Descriptives

buypol HOW IMPORTANT TO CHOOSE PRODUCTS FOR POL REASONS

	N	Mean	Std. Deviation	Std. Error	95% Confidence Interval for Mean		Minimum	Maximum
					Lower Bound	Upper Bound		
1.00 Democrat	208	5.11	1.648	.114	4.89	5.34	1	7
2.00 Independent	98	4.85	1.852	.187	4.48	5.22	1	7
3.00 Republican	135	4.78	1.718	.148	4.49	5.07	1	7
Total	441	4.95	1.719	.082	4.79	5.11	1	7

ANOVA

buypol HOW IMPORTANT TO CHOOSE PRODUCTS FOR POL REASONS

	Sum of Squares	df	Mean Square	F	Sig.
Between Groups	10.408	2	5.204	1.766	.172
Within Groups	1290.494	438	2.946		
Total	1300.902	440			

The ANOVA output includes two tables: (1) Descriptives and (2) ANOVA. In the Descriptives table, the *N*, mean, and standard deviation are reported for each group and the entire sample, along with the 95% confidence interval for each mean.

The *F* obtained is reported in the ANOVA table, along with its level of significance (or probability). For this data, *F* obtained is 1.766 with a significance of. 172. Since the level of significance is greater than our alpha (.172 > .05), we fail to reject the null hypothesis. Though the means are different (Democrats had the highest mean of 5.11), these differences are not significant.

LEARNING CHECK 11.4

Calculate eta-squared for the model presented in Figure 11.2.

READING THE RESEARCH LITERATURE: EMERGING ADULTHOOD

Like bivariate, *t* test, or chi-square analyses, ANOVA can help us understand how the categories of experience—race, age, class, and/or gender—shape our social lives. ANOVA allows us to investigate a variety of social categories by comparing the differences between them. We conclude this chapter with an example of how ANOVA is presented and interpreted in the social science literature.

Anna Oleszkowicz and Anna Misztela (2015)[3] investigated the process by which young Polish men and women emerge into adulthood. Increasingly, the pathway to adulthood is taking longer, as there is a trend among young adults to postpone the roles characteristic of adult life—marriage, parenthood, or living independently. This prolonged period has been described as emerging adulthood, a development stage between adolescence and adulthood. The researchers hypothesize that there is a difference in the sense of adulthood between these three age-groups.

Table 11.4 Frequencies of Emerging Adulthood Features Across the Age-Groups

	Late Adolescents N = 349	Emerging Adults N = 207	Young Adults N = 128	F
Identity Exploration	$M = 3.07$ $SD = 0.44$	$M = 3.16$ $SD = 0.5$	$M = 2.91$ $SD = 0.66$	9.24***
Experimentation/Possibilities	$M = 3.16$ $SD = 0.43$	$M = 3.05$ $SD = 0.44$	$M = 2.86$ $SD = 0.51$	28.09***
Negativity/Instability	$M = 2.53$ $SD = 0.51$	$M = 2.39$ $SD = 0.51$	$M = 2.27$ $SD = 0.47$	13.46***
Self-Focus Concerns	$M = 2.82$ $SD = 0.44$	$M = 3.07$ $SD = 0.39$	$M = 3.07$ $SD = 0.42$	31.13***
Feeling "In-Between"	$M = 3.06$ $SD = 0.5$	$M = 2.80$ $SD = 0.63$	$M = 2.40$ $SD = 0.69$	61.22***

Source: Adapted from Anna Oleszkowicz and Anna Misztela, "How do Young Poles Perceive Their Adulthood?", *Journal of Adolescent Research* 30, no. 6 (2015), 695.

Note: M = mean, SD = standard deviation.

***$p < .001$.

Their sample is composed of 684 young Poles, identified by three distinct age-groups: (1) 349 late adolescents (aged 17–19 years), (2) 207 emerging adults (aged 21–26 years), and (3) 128 young adults (aged 28–34 years). Oleszkowicz and Misztela measured emerging adulthood with the Polish version of the Inventory of the Dimensions of Emerging Adulthood. There are five dimensions of emerging adulthood: (1) Identity Exploration (learning more about themselves), (2) Experimentation/Possibilities (contemplating future possibilities), (3) Negativity/Instability (revising future goals and plans), (4) Self-Focused Concerns (development of personal identity and making decisions for themselves), and (5) Feeling "In Between" (in between adolescent and adult statuses). All dimensions were measured on a 4-point scale: 1 = strongly disagree, 2 = somewhat disagree, 3 = somewhat agree, and 4 = strongly agree. Their results are presented in Table 11.4.[4]

The table presents ANOVA results for five models, one for each emerging adulthood dimension. The mean and standard deviation for each group are reported in the table along with the obtained F ratio and its significance. The researchers explain as follows:

> With respect to Identity Exploration, emerging adults functioned similiarly to late adolescents, with significantly higher scores obtained for this feature as compared with young adults. In contrast, emerging adults shared similarities with young adults with regard to Negativity/Instability and Self-Focused Concerns, although, while both groups scored significantly lower on the former feature when compared with late adolescents, they also obtained significantly higher scores on the latter than did the youngest of the three groups. In respect to the remaining two features—Experimentation/Possibilities and Feeling "In Between"—the scores obtained by the emerging adults ranked them between late adolescents and young adults. (p. 695)[5]

Kevin Hemminger: Sales Support Manager/Graduate Program in Research Methods and Statistics

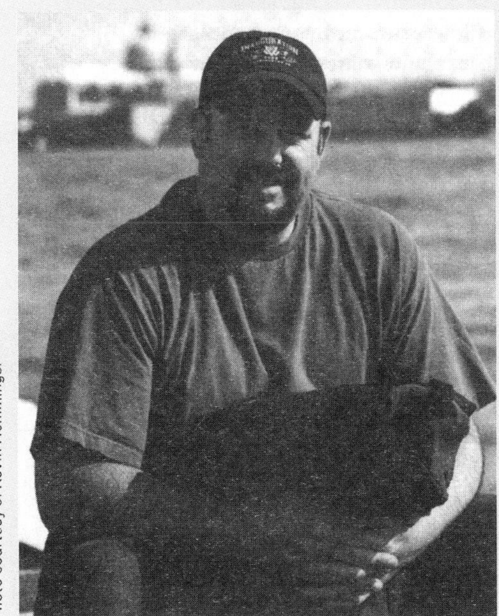

Photo courtesy of Kevin Hemminger

While working as a sales support manager for a travel management company, Kevin decided to return to school to pursue a degree in criminal justice. Though originally he intended to become a probation officer for the juvenile court system, his career trajectory went into a different direction after taking a statistics course. "[D]ue in great part to an incredible professor who made the subject enjoyable and interesting, I decided to pursue a Ph.D. in Research Methods and Statistics in order to teach research methods and statistics. . . . My hope is to teach on either the graduate level, or to gifted high school students preparing for college."

Kevin has incorporated what he's learned about methods and statistics into his sales support work. "Being a very customer-focused company in a very customer-centric field, the idea of surveying customers is critical and being able to incorporate a knowledgeable administration of surveys has been integral to my team's success. Knowing research best practices and understanding what constitutes good, valid research has made a tremendous impact on the value of the data I provide to my leaders. My knowledge in the field has also given me a confidence level in speaking about quantitative data that I never had before. I work with enormous data sets and spreadsheets on a daily basis and understanding even the most basic concepts such as mean, median, mode, standard deviation, and variance has allowed me to lead projects and present findings in a much more intelligent way."

He recently completed his master's degree and is currently working on his doctorate. Kevin offers these fine words of encouragement for anyone considering data and statistical work: "If you're thinking about pursuing a career involving statistics, my recommendation is to dive full throttle into a study or project you're incredibly passionate about. Watching your study move from an idea, to a literature review, to a hypothesis, data collection, and then data analysis is one of the best ways to confirm your interest—and, by far, the best way to experience the power behind statistics as a discipline. If you get excited watching your data come in, and even more excited wondering [what] you're going to do with that data, I think you've confirmed there is no question you'd enjoy the field! If you're learning stats concepts and all you can think about is how you'd teach that concept to others—it's over! You're perfect for the field."

DATA AT WORK

They conclude that "the differences observed between the three age groups' frequencies of emerging adulthood features do not support the thesis that these would be highest for people between 20 and 26 years of age. In constrast, it has been found that Polish emerging adults share a number of similiarities with both late adolescents and young adults—in other words, the way they function places them somewhere in-between these two groups." (p. 702)[6]

LEARNING CHECK 11.5

For the ANOVA model for Identity Formation, what is the F critical? What information do you need to determine the F critical? Assume alpha = .05.

MAIN POINTS

- Analysis of variance (ANOVA) procedures allow us to examine the variation in means in more than two samples. To determine whether the difference in mean scores is significant, ANOVA examines the differences between multiple samples, as well as the differences within a single sample.
- One-way ANOVA is a procedure using one dependent variable and one independent variable. The five-step hypothesis testing model is applied to one-way ANOVA.
- The test statistic for ANOVA is *F*. The *F* statistic is the ratio of between-group variance to within-group variance.

KEY TERMS

analysis of variance (ANOVA) 304
between-group sum of squares (*SSB*) 307
F critical 310
F obtained 310
F ratio or *F* statistic 308
mean square between 308
mean square within 308
one-way ANOVA 305
total sum of squares (*SST*) 307
within-group sum of squares (*SSW*) 307

DIGITAL RESOURCES

Get the edge on your studies. **edge.sagepub.com/frankfort8e**

Take a quiz to find out what you've learned.
Review key terms with eFlashcards.
Dive into real research with SAGE Journal Articles.

SPSS DEMONSTRATION [GSS14SSDS-A]

Computing Analysis of Variance Models

Social scientists have examined the association between a woman's fertility decisions (deciding whether and/or when to have a child) and her wages, employment status, and education, along with other socioeconomic and demographic factors. Research has indicated that different social groups may have different norms and values about fertility.[7]

In this example, we'll investigate the relationship between a woman's educational attainment and the age at which her first child was born using GSS2014SSDS-A. We first analyzed this relationship in Exercise 8 of Chapter 4 ("Measures of Variability"). Using education as the independent variable and age at which her first child was born as the dependent variable, we can assess whether there is a relationship between educational attainment and age at first childbirth.

We'll use two variables for our analysis, the variable DEGREE (five categories of educational attainment) and AGEKDBRN (respondent's age when her first child was born). But first, we'll restrict our analysis to women in the GSS sample (using *Data—Select Cases* command. You will have to select the option "If the condition is satisfied," then type SEX = 2 to restrict your analysis to women).

We can compute the ANOVA model by clicking on *Analyze*, *Compare Means*, then *One-Way ANOVA*. The opening dialog box requires that we insert AGEKDBRN in the box labeled "Dependent List" and in the box labeled "Factor" insert DEGREE.

Click on the *Options* button at the upper right. Click on *Descriptive* in the Statistics box. This will produce a table of means and standard deviations along with the ANOVA statistics. Click on *Continue* in the Options box, then *OK* in the One-Way ANOVA box.

We are interested in the F statistic and significance in the ANOVA table (Figure 11.3). Based on the output, F is 49.311 significant at the .000 level. The data reveals a positive relationship—the higher one's educational attainment, the higher the age of first childbirth. The oldest average age at first childbirth is for women with graduate degrees (28.36 years of age), followed by women with bachelor's degrees (26.46 years of age). The youngest group of first-time mothers is women with less than a high school diploma. On average, women with less than a high school diploma had their first child at 19.62 years of age. When compared with the age of graduate-degree first-time mothers, there is a difference of 8.74 years.

Figure 11.3 ANOVA Output for Age at First Childbirth and Education, Women Only

Descriptives

agekdbrn R'S AGE WHEN 1ST CHILD BORN

	N	Mean	Std. Deviation	Std. Error	95% Confidence Interval for Mean		Minimum	Maximum
					Lower Bound	Upper Bound		
0 LT HIGH SCHOOL	98	19.62	4.359	.440	18.75	20.50	14	45
1 HIGH SCHOOL	324	22.02	4.569	.254	21.53	22.52	15	37
2 JUNIOR COLLEGE	64	22.52	5.182	.648	21.22	23.81	15	36
3 BACHELOR	115	26.46	5.760	.537	25.40	27.52	16	45
4 GRADUATE	69	28.36	5.547	.668	27.03	29.69	18	42
Total	670	23.13	5.595	.216	22.71	23.56	14	45

ANOVA

agekdbrn R'S AGE WHEN 1ST CHILD BORN

	Sum of Squares	df	Mean Square	F	Sig.
Between Groups	4790.577	4	1197.644	49.311	.000
Within Groups	16151.333	665	24.288		
Total	20941.910	669			

SPSS PROBLEMS [GSS14SSDS-A AND B]

1. Let's continue to examine the relationship between fertility decisions and education using GSS14SSDS-A. But this time, we'll analyze the relationship for men.

   a. Run a Select Cases, selecting only men for the analysis.

   b. Compute an ANOVA model for men, using age at first-born child (AGEKDBRN) as the dependent variable and educational degree (DEGREE) as the independent variable. Based on the SPSS output, what can you conclude about the relationship between degree attainment and AGEKDBRN for men? How do these results compare with the results for women in the SPSS demonstration? Use alpha = .05.

2. Repeat Exercise 1b, substituting respondent's social class (CLASS) as the independent variable in separate models for men and women. What can you conclude about the relationship between CLASS and AGEKDBRN based on an alpha of .01?

3. What is the ideal number of children a family should have (variable CHLDIDEL)? Use CHLDIDEL as your dependent variable and DEGREE as your independent variable. Is there a significant difference in the number of ideal children among different educational groups? (*Option*: You can run three sets of analyses—first, for all GSS respondents; second, an ANOVA model for women only; and finally, a model for men. Make sure to select the Descriptives option.) Evaluate your model results based on an alpha of .05.

4. Using GSS14SSDS-B, investigate other social factors that may be associated with ethical consumerism. Using BUYPOL (important to buy products for political, ethical, and environmental reasons) as your dependent variable, assess the relationship with factor variables DEGREE (respondent's educational degree) and RACE (respondent's reported race). Using alpha = .05, assess the significance of both models.

5. Repeat Exercise 4, separating results by SEX. Does the relationship change when including SEX as a control variable? Explain.

CHAPTER EXERCISES

1. For a random sample of 32 GSS cases, health is measured according to a 4-point scale: 1 = excellent, 2 = good, 3 = fair, and 4 = poor. Four social classes are reported here: 1 = lower, 2 = working, 3 = middle, and 4 = upper. Present the five-step model for these data, using alpha = .05.

Lower Class	Working Class	Middle Class	Upper Class
3	2	2	2
2	1	3	1
2	3	1	1
2	2	1	2
3	2	2	1
3	2	3	1
4	3	3	1
4	3	1	2

2. We take another look at health, this time examining the relationship between educational attainment and perceived quality of health care. Data for three groups are presented based on the Health Information National Trends Survey (HINTS) 2012 data set. HINTS is an annual survey measuring the use of cancer-related information for adults 18 years and older. Present the five-step model for these data, using alpha = .01. QUALITYCARE is measured on a 5-point scale: 1 = excellent, 2 = very good, 3 = good, 4 = fair, and 5 = poor. Note how a lower score indicates a higher quality of care.

   Present the five-step model for these data, using alpha = .05.

Less Than High School	Some College	College Graduate
1	2	1
4	3	1
2	2	1
2	2	2
3	4	1
3	2	2

3. We selected a sample of 30 International Social Science Programme respondents, noting their educational status (no degree, secondary degree, and university degree) and their level of church attendance (0 = never, 1 = infrequently, and 2 = two to three times per month or more). Is there a relationship between educational attainment and church attendance?

   Complete the five-step model for these data, using alpha = .01.

No Degree	Secondary Degree	University Degree
2	2	0
1	2	0
1	2	0
2	1	0
2	1	1
2	0	1
0	2	0
2	1	1
2	1	2
2	2	1

4. Based on a sample of 21 Monitoring the Future respondents, we present their racial/ethnic background and the numbers of school days missed in the past 4 weeks.

   a. Complete the five-step model for these data, set alpha at .05.

   b. If alpha were set at .01, would your decision change? Explain.

White	Black	Hispanic
4	1	4
5	2	3
3	2	5
4	1	1
4	3	5
4	4	2
6	3	2

5. We selected a sample of 14 Monitoring the Future respondents. We present their number of moving (traffic) violations in the past 12 months along with their residential area (residential area is the independent variable). Complete the five-step model for these data, using alpha = .05.

Small Town	Medium-Sized City	Large City
0	2	3
0	3	4
1	1	4
2	1	3
1		2

6. The GSS 2014 asked respondents to identify what was important for "truly being American." When asked "How important to have American ancestry?", answers were measured on a 4-point scale: 1 = very important, 2 = fairly important, 3 = not very important, and 4 = not important at all. We selected a sample of 20 GSS respondents and present their individual responses. Complete the five-step model for these data, using alpha = .01 to assess the significance of the model.

White	Black	Other
3	1	4
2	2	2
2	2	2
2	2	2
3	1	3
4	1	2
4	2	—

7. Nan Sook Park and her colleagues (2012) investigated racial/ethnic differences in predictors of self-rating health and the use of sociocultural resources. Their data are based on the Survey of Older Floridians, a statewide sample of white, African American, Cuban, and non-Cuban Hispanic seniors.

We present ANOVA results for two sociocultural resources. Social support was measured with the question: In times of trouble, can you count on at least some of your family and friends? (1 = hardly ever, 2 = some of the time, and 3 = most of the time). Religious attendance was measured according to the scale: 1 = never or almost never to 5 = more than once a week. Mean scores are presented for each racial/ethnic group, along with the standard deviation in parentheses. Review each measure of sociocultural resource and determine whether the null hypothesis would be rejected. Set alpha at .05 for each.

	Racial/Ethnic Group Mean (Standard Deviation)				
Variable	Whites (n = 503)	African Americans (n = 360)	Cubans (n = 328)	Non-Cuban Hispanics (n = 241)	F
Social Support	2.85 (0.47)	2.75 (0.57)	2.73 (0.60)	2.58 (0.70)	12.17***
Religious Attendance	2.79 (1.57)	3.94 (1.21)	2.74 (1.49)	3.37 (1.43)	56.43***

Source: Nan Sook Park, Yuri Jan, Beom Lee, and David Chiriboga. "Racial/Ethnic Differences in Predictors of Self-Rated Health: Findings from the Survey of Older Floridians." *Research on Aging* 35, no. 1 (2012): 207.

*** $p < .001$.

8. The GSS 2014 included a series of questions about what it takes to be a good citizen. Respondents were asked to be a good citizen how important was it "to help people in America who are worse off than yourself" (HELPUSA) and "to help people in the rest of the world who are worse off than yourself" (HELPWRLD). Answers were measured on a 7-point scale:1 = not important at all to 7 = very important. We ran ANOVA models for each with respondent's political party (RPartyId) as the independent variable. Set alpha at .05 to assess the significance of each model.

Descriptives

		N	Mean	Std. Deviation	Std. Error	95% Confidence Interval for Mean Lower Bound	95% Confidence Interval for Mean Upper Bound	Minimum	Maximum
helpusa HOW IMPORTANT TO HELP WORSE OFF PPL IN AMERICA	1.00 Democrat	167	6.15	1.117	.086	5.98	6.32	1	7
	2.00 Independent	87	5.94	1.214	.130	5.68	6.20	2	7
	3.00 Republican	101	5.76	1.184	.118	5.53	6.00	3	7
	Total	355	5.99	1.169	.062	5.87	6.11	1	7
helpwrld HOW IMPORTANT TO HELP WORSE OFF PPL IN REST OF WORLD	1.00 Democrat	166	4.91	1.712	.133	4.65	5.17	1	7
	2.00 Independent	83	4.82	1.829	.201	4.42	5.22	1	7
	3.00 Republican	102	4.45	1.614	.160	4.13	4.77	1	7
	Total	351	4.75	1.720	.092	4.57	4.94	1	7

ANOVA

		Sum of Squares	df	Mean Square	F	Sig.
helpusa HOW IMPORTANT TO HELP WORSE OFF PPL IN AMERICA	Between Groups	9.688	2	4.844	3.595	.028
	Within Groups	474.267	352	1.347		
	Total	483.955	354			
helpwrld HOW IMPORTANT TO HELP WORSE OFF PPL IN REST OF WORLD	Between Groups	13.740	2	6.870	2.341	.098
	Within Groups	1021.189	348	2.934		
	Total	1034.929	350			

9. The following ANOVA model examines the relationship between DEGREE (respondent's educational degree) and VALGIVEN (total dollar value of all donations made in the past year). Data are from the GSS 2014. Is there a significant difference in donation amount by educational degree? Set alpha at .01.

Descriptives

VALGIVEN TOTAL DONATIONS PAST YEAR R AND IMMEDIATE FAMILY

	N	Mean	Std. Deviation	Std. Error	95% Confidence Interval for Mean		Minimum	Maximum
					Lower Bound	Upper Bound		
0 LT HIGH SCHOOL	54	593.85	1229.945	167.374	258.14	929.56	0	7000
1 HIGH SCHOOL	177	1164.01	2904.570	218.321	733.15	1594.88	0	23000
2 JUNIOR COLLEGE	40	857.50	1826.298	288.763	273.42	1441.58	0	10000
3 BACHELOR	52	3397.40	9054.431	1255.624	876.63	5918.17	0	59300
4 GRADUATE	41	5590.61	13340.635	2083.457	1379.79	9801.43	0	70000
Total	364	1863.40	6188.306	324.355	1225.55	2501.25	0	70000

ANOVA

VALGIVEN TOTAL DONATIONS PAST YEAR R AND IMMEDIATE FAMILY

	Sum of Squares	df	Mean Square	F	Sig.
Between Groups	906027134	4	226506784	6.257	.000
Within Groups	1.300E+10	359	36198062.6		
Total	1.390E+10	363			

10. Is there a significant difference in e-mail hours per week among the same educational groups? Using data from the GSS 2014, we ran an ANOVA model using DEGREE (educational attainment) as the independent variable and EMAILHR (e-mail hours per week) as the dependent variable. Based on an alpha of .05, what do you conclude?

Descriptives

emailhr EMAIL HOURS PER WEEK

	N	Mean	Std. Deviation	Std. Error	95% Confidence Interval for Mean		Minimum	Maximum
					Lower Bound	Upper Bound		
0 LT HIGH SCHOOL	43	1.72	4.002	.610	.49	2.95	0	20
1 HIGH SCHOOL	220	5.60	14.731	.993	3.64	7.56	0	150
2 JUNIOR COLLEGE	43	5.67	8.687	1.325	3.00	8.35	0	40
3 BACHELOR	84	8.39	8.819	.962	6.48	10.31	0	35
4 GRADUATE	55	11.13	16.573	2.235	6.65	15.61	0	99
Total	445	6.44	13.025	.617	5.23	7.66	0	150

ANOVA

emailhr EMAIL HOURS PER WEEK

	Sum of Squares	df	Mean Square	F	Sig.
Between Groups	2666.751	4	666.688	4.037	.003
Within Groups	72655.038	440	165.125		
Total	75321.789	444			

11. We examine the relationship between satisfaction with one's finances and agreement to the statement, "Immigrants take jobs away from people born in America" as measured in the GSS 2014. Responses to the immigrant statement (IMMJOBS) are measured on an ordinal scale: 1 = strongly agree, 2 = agree, 3 = neither, 4 = disagree, and 5 = strongly disagree. Does agreement to the statement vary by how satisfied the individual is with his or her financial situation?

Descriptives

immjobs IMMIGRANTS TAKE JOBS AWAY

	N	Mean	Std. Deviation	Std. Error	95% Confidence Interval for Mean		Minimum	Maximum
					Lower Bound	Upper Bound		
1 SATISFIED	100	3.20	1.119	.112	2.98	3.42	1	5
2 MORE OR LESS	191	3.12	1.055	.076	2.96	3.27	1	5
3 NOT AT ALL SAT	106	2.72	1.201	.117	2.49	2.95	1	5
Total	397	3.03	1.126	.056	2.92	3.14	1	5

ANOVA

immjobs IMMIGRANTS TAKE JOBS AWAY

	Sum of Squares	df	Mean Square	F	Sig.
Between Groups	14.662	2	7.331	5.931	.003
Within Groups	486.975	394	1.236		
Total	501.637	396			

a. Set alpha at .01, and test the null hypothesis of equal means.

b. What is the eta-squared for this model?

12. Using GSS 2014 data, we take another look at BUYPOL, buying products for political, ethical, and environmental reasons. Earlier in this chapter, we examined the relationship with political party identification and BUYPOL, finding no significant relationship between the variables. Here we identify social class (CLASS) as the independent variable and BUYPOL as the dependent. SPSS Anova results are presented.

Descriptives

buypol HOW IMPORTANT TO CHOOSE PRODUCTS FOR POL REASONS

	N	Mean	Std. Deviation	Std. Error	95% Confidence Interval for Mean		Minimum	Maximum
					Lower Bound	Upper Bound		
1 LOWER CLASS	36	4.53	2.274	.379	3.76	5.30	1	7
2 WORKING CLASS	167	4.78	1.880	.145	4.49	5.07	1	7
3 MIDDLE CLASS	139	5.22	1.335	.113	5.00	5.45	1	7
4 UPPER CLASS	8	5.63	1.506	.532	4.37	6.88	3	7
Total	350	4.95	1.739	.093	4.77	5.13	1	7

ANOVA

buypol HOW IMPORTANT TO CHOOSE PRODUCTS FOR POL REASONS

	Sum of Squares	df	Mean Square	F	Sig.
Between Groups	25.338	3	8.446	2.838	.038
Within Groups	1029.736	346	2.976		
Total	1055.074	349			

a. Set alpha at .05. What do you conclude about the relationship between social class and BUYPOL?

b. What is the eta-squared for this model?

c. If alpha were set at .01, would your decision change? Explain.

13. In Chapter 4's Statistics in Practice, we reviewed Myron Pope's 2002 research on community college mentoring. Pope compared responses from four groups of minority students, measuring their perception of multilevel mentoring at their school. Student responses were based on a 5-point scale: 1 = no agreement to 5 = strong agreement. Pope's results are presented again with an additional column of F test and significance.[8]

a. What are the degrees of freedom for the models?

b. Based on an alpha of .05, assess each model. What do you conclude?

Minority Student Perception of Mentoring at Their Institution by Race (N 254)

	African American N= 178 M (SD)	Asian N = 12 M (SD)	Hispanic N = 28 M (SD)	Native American N = 22 M (SD)	Multiethnic N = 14 M (SD)	F Test Sig.
There are persons of color in administrative roles from whom I would seek mentoring at this institution.	3.76 (1.10)	3.50 (1.31)	3.14 (1.08)	4.09 (0.68)	4.14 (0.66)	3.508 0.008
There are peer mentors who can advise me.	3.48 (1.11)	2.17 (1.40)	3.14 (1.20)	3.91 (0.68)	3.29 (1.54)	5.245 0.000
I mentor other students.	3.30 (1.25)	2.00 (1.21)	3.00 (1.09)	3.46 (1.10)	3.29 (1.07)	3.702 0.006

Source: Adapted from Myron Pope, "Community College Mentoring Minority Student Perception," *Community College Review*, 30, no. 3 (2002): 37.

12

REGRESSION AND CORRELATION

As we learned in Chapter 9 ("Bivariate Tables"), the differential access to the Internet is real and persistent. Celeste Campos-Castillo's (2015) research confirmed the impact of gender and race on the digital divide. Pew researchers Andrew Perrin and Maeve Duggan (2015) documented other sources of the divide. For example, Americans with college degrees continue to have higher rates of Internet use than Americans with less than a college degree. Though less-educated adults have increased their Internet use since 2000, the percentage who use the Internet is still lower than the percentage of college graduates.[1]

In this chapter, we apply regression and correlation techniques to examine the relationship between interval-ratio variables. **Correlation** is a measure of association used to determine the existence and strength of the relationship between variables and is similar to the proportional reduction of error (*PRE*) measures reviewed in Chapter 10 ("The Chi-Square Test and Measures of Association"). **Regression** is a linear prediction model, using one or more independent variables to predict the values of a dependent variable. We will present two basic models: (1) **Bivariate regression** examines how changes in one independent variable affects the value of a dependent variable, while (2) **multiple regression** estimates how several independent variables affect one dependent variable.

We begin with calculating the bivariate regression model for educational attainment and Internet hours per week. We will use *years of educational attainment* as our independent variable (X) to predict *Internet hours per week* (our dependent variable or Y). Fictional data are presented for a sample of 10 individuals in Table 12.1.

Chapter Learning Objectives

1. Describe linear relationships and prediction rules for bivariate and multiple regression models
2. Construct and interpret straight-line graphs and best-fitting lines
3. Calculate and interpret *a* and *b*
4. Calculate and interpret the coefficient of determination (r^2) and Pearson's correlation coefficient (r)
5. Interpret SPSS multiple regression output
6. Test the significance of r^2 and R^2 using ANOVA

Correlation A measure of association used to determine the existence and strength of the relationship between interval-ratio variables.

THE SCATTER DIAGRAM

One quick visual method used to display the relationship between two interval-ratio variables is the **scatter diagram** (or **scatterplot**). Often used as a first exploratory step in regression analysis, a scatter diagram can suggest whether two variables are associated.

Regression A linear prediction model using one or more independent variables to predict the values of a dependent variable.

Bivariate regression A regression model that examines the effect of one independent variable on the values of a dependent variable.

Multiple regression A regression model that examines the effect of several independent variables on the values of one dependent variable.

Scatter diagram (scatterplot) A visual method used to display a relationship between two interval-ratio variables.

Table 12.1 Educational Attainment and Internet Hours per Week, N 10

Educational Attainment (X)	Internet Hours per Week (Y)
10	1
9	0
12	3
13	4
19	7
11	2
16	6
23	9
14	5
21	8
$\bar{X} = 14.80$	$\bar{Y} = 4.50$
$s_X^2 = 23.07$	$s_Y^2 = 9.17$
Range = 23 − 9 = 14	Range = 9 − 0 = 9

The scatter diagram showing the relationship between *educational attainment* and *Internet hours per week* is shown in Figure 12.1. In a scatter diagram, the scales for the two variables form the vertical and horizontal axes of a graph. Usually, the independent variable, *X*, is arrayed along the horizontal axis and the dependent variable, *Y*, along the vertical axis. In Figure 12.1, each dot represents a person; its location lies at the exact intersection of that person's years of education and Internet hours per week. Note that individuals with lower educational attainment have fewer hours of Internet use, while individuals with higher educational attainment spend more time on the Internet per week. Educational attainment and Internet hours are positively associated.

Linear relationship A relationship between two interval-ratio variables in which the observations displayed in a scatter diagram can be approximated with a straight line.

Deterministic (perfect) linear relationship A relationship between two interval-ratio variables in which all the observations (the dots) fall along a straight line. The line provides a predicted value of *Y* (the vertical axis) for any value of *X* (the horizontal axis).

Scatter diagrams may also reveal a negative association between two variables or no relationship at all. We will review a negative relationship between two variables later in this chapter. Nonlinear relationships are explained in A Closer Look 12.1.

LINEAR RELATIONSHIPS AND PREDICTION RULES

Though we can use a scatterplot as a first step to explore a relationship between two interval-ratio variables, we need a more systematic way to express the relationship between two interval-ratio variables. One way to express them is as a linear relationship. A linear relationship allows us to approximate the observations displayed in a scatter diagram with a straight line. In a perfectly linear relationship, all the observations (the dots) fall along a straight line (a perfect relationship is sometimes called a deterministic relationship), and the line itself

Figure 12.1 Scatter Diagram of Educational Attainment and Internet Hours per Week

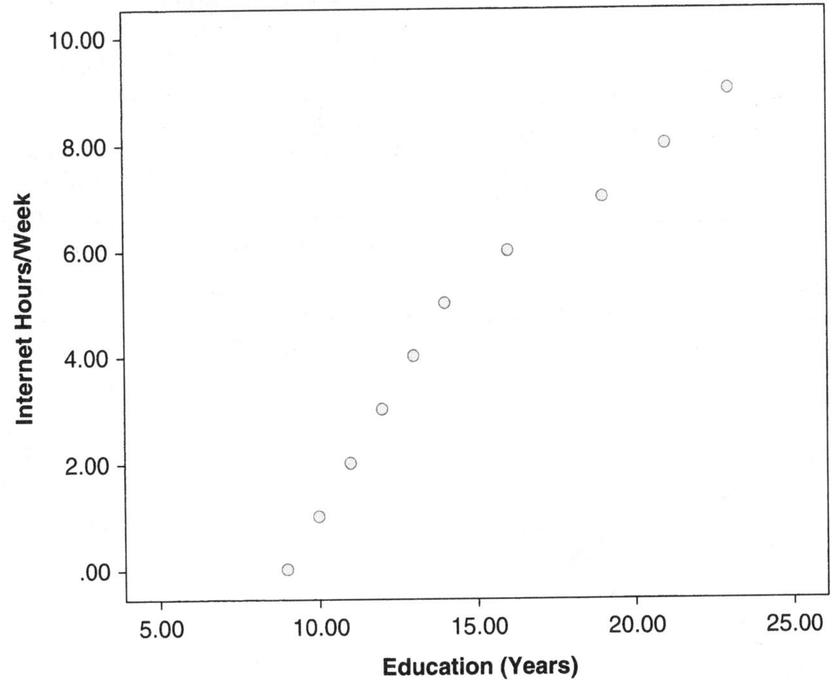

provides a predicted value of Y (the vertical axis) for any value of X (the horizontal axis). For example, in Figure 12.3, we have superimposed a straight line on the scatterplot originally displayed in Figure 12.1. Using this line, we can obtain a predicted value of Internet hours per week for any individual by starting with a value from the education axis and then moving up to the Internet hours per week axis (indicated by the dotted lines). For example, the predicted value of Internet hours per week for someone with 12 years of education is approximately 3 hours.

Finding the Best-Fitting Line

As indicated in Figure 12.3, the actual relationship between years of education and Internet hours is not perfectly linear; that is, although some individual points lie very close to the line, none fall exactly on the line. Most relationships we study in the social sciences are not deterministic, and we are not able to come up with a linear equation that allows us to predict Y from X with perfect accuracy. We are much more likely to find relationships approximating linearity, but in which numerous cases don't follow this trend perfectly.

The relationship between educational attainment and Internet hours, as depicted in Figure 12.3, can also be described with the following algebraic equation, an equation for a straight line:

$$Y = a + b(X) \tag{12.1}$$

A CLOSER LOOK 12.1

OTHER REGRESSION TECHNIQUES

The regression examples we present in this chapter reflect two assumptions.

The first assumption is that the dependent and independent variables are interval-ratio measurements. In fact, regression models often include ordinal measures such as social class, income, and attitudinal scales. (Later in the chapter we feature a regression model based on ordinal attitudinal scales.) Dummy variable techniques (creating a dichotomous variable, coded one or zero) permit the use of nominal variables, such as sex, race, religion, or political party affiliation. For example, in measuring gender, males could be coded as 0 and females coded as 1. Dummy variable techniques will not be elaborated here.

Our second assumption is that the variables have a linear or straight-line relationship. For the most part, social science relationships can be approximated using a linear equation. It is important to note, however, that sometimes a relationship cannot be approximated by a straight line and is better described by some other, nonlinear function. For example, Figure 12.2 shows a nonlinear relationship between age and hours of reading (hypothetical data). Hours of reading increase with age until the twenties, remain stable until the forties, and then tend to decrease with age.

There are regression models for many nonlinear relationships, for nominal or dichotomous dependent variables, or even when there are multiple dependent variables. These advanced regression techniques will not be covered in this text.

Figure 12.2 A Nonlinear Relationship Between Age and Hours of Reading per Week

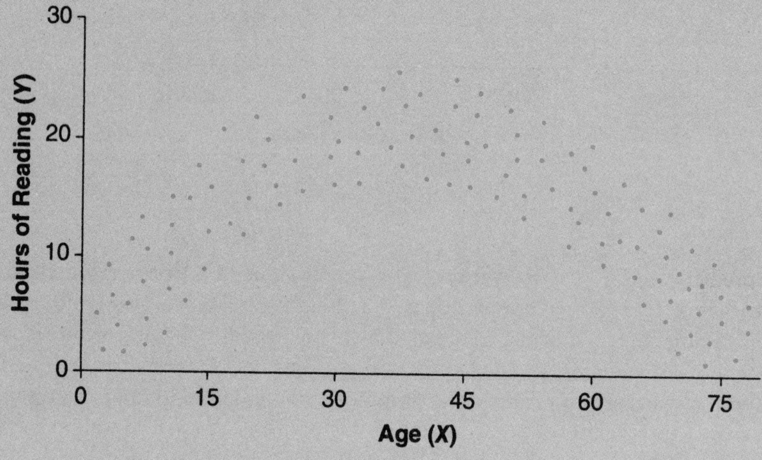

Y-intercept (a) The point where the regression line crosses the Y-axis, or the value of Y when X is 0.

Slope (b) The change in variable Y (the dependent variable) with a unit change in variable X (the independent variable).

where

Y = the predicted score on the dependent variable

X = the score on the independent variable

a = the Y-intercept, or the point where the line crosses the Y-axis; therefore, a is the value of Y when X is 0

b = the slope of the regression line, or the change in Y with a unit change in X.

Figure 12.3 A Straight-Line Graph for Educational Attainment and Internet Hours per Week

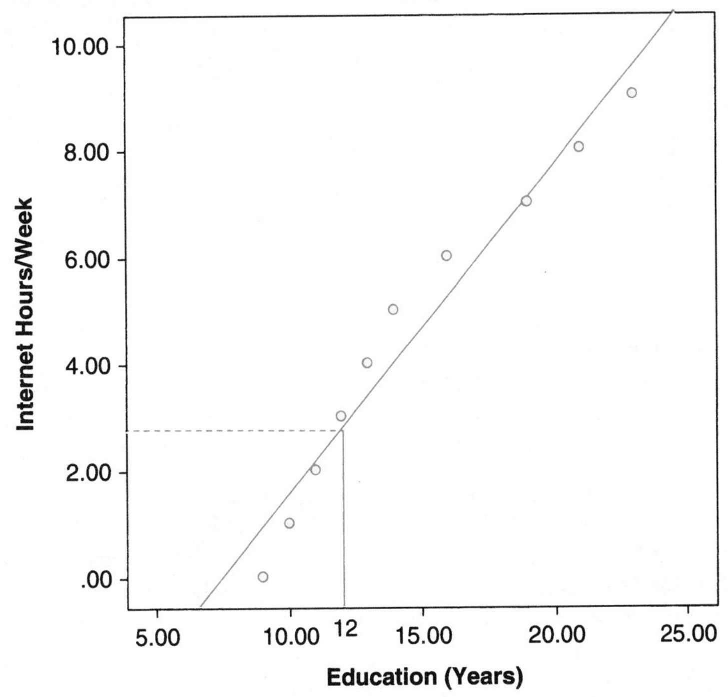

LEARNING CHECK 12.1

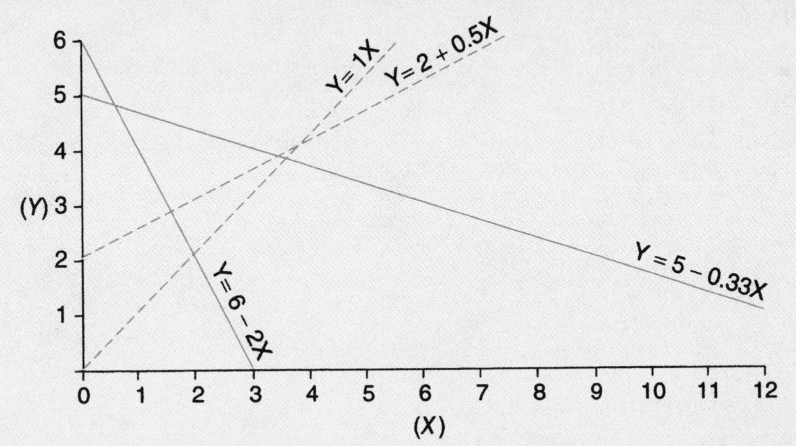

For each of these four lines, as X goes up by 1 unit, what does Y do? Be sure you can answer this question using both the equation and the line.

DEFINING ERROR The best-fitting line is the one that generates the least amount of error, also referred to as the residual. Look again at Figure 12.3. For each education level, the line (or the equation that this line represents) predicts a value of Internet hours. For example, with 21 years of education, the predicted value for Y is 8.34 hours. But we know from Table 12.1 that the actual value for 21 years of education is 8.0 hours. Thus, we have two values for Y: (1) a predicted Y, which we symbolize as $\hat{Y}$ and which is generated by the prediction equation, also called the linear regression equation $Y = a + b(X)$, and (2) the observed Y, symbolized simply as Y. Thus, for someone with 21 years of education, $\hat{Y} = 8.34$, whereas $Y = 8.0$.

We can think of the residual as the difference between the observed Y and the predicted $\hat{Y}$. If we symbolize the residual as e, then

$$e = Y - \hat{Y}$$

The residual is 8.34 - 8.0 = 0.34 hours.

THE RESIDUAL SUM OF SQUARES (Σe^2) Our goal is to identify a line or a prediction equation that minimizes the error for each individual observation. However, any line we choose will minimize the residual for some observations but may maximize it for others. We want to find a prediction equation that minimizes the residuals over all observations.

There are many mathematical ways of defining the residuals. For example, we may take the algebraic sum of residuals $\sum(Y - \hat{Y})$, the sum of the absolute residuals $\sum(|Y - \hat{Y}|)$, or the sum of the squared residuals $\sum(Y - \hat{Y})^2$. For mathematical reasons, statisticians prefer to work with the third method—squaring and summing the residuals over all observations. The result is the residual sum of squares, or Σe^2. Symbolically, Σe^2 is expressed as

$$\sum e^2 = \sum(Y - \hat{Y})^2$$

Least squares line (best-fitting line) A line where the residual sum of squares, or Σe^2, is at a minimum.

Least squares method The technique that produces the least squares line.

THE LEAST SQUARES LINE The best-fitting regression line is that line where the sum of the squared residuals, or Σe^2, is at a minimum. Such a line is called the **least squares line** (or **best-fitting line**), and the technique that produces this line is called the **least squares method**. The technique involves choosing a and b for the equation such that Σe^2 will have the smallest possible value. In the next section, we use the data from the 10 individuals to find the least squares equation.

Computing a and b

Through the use of calculus, it can be shown that to figure out the values of a and b in a way that minimizes Σe^2, we need to apply the following formulas:

$$b = \frac{s_{XY}}{s_X^2} \qquad (12.2)$$

$$a = \bar{Y} - b(\bar{X}) \qquad (12.3)$$

where

s_{XY} = the covariance of X and Y

s_X^2 = the variance of X

$\bar{Y}$ = the mean of Y

$\bar{X}$ = the mean of X

Table 12.2 Worksheet for Calculating *a* and *b* for the Regression Equation

(1)	(2)	(3)	(4)	(5)	(6)	(7)
Educational Attainment	Internet Hours per Week					
X	Y	$(X-\bar{X})$	$(X-\bar{X})^2$	$(Y-\bar{Y})$	$(Y-\bar{Y})^2$	$(X-\bar{X})(Y-\bar{Y})$
10	1	−4.8	23.04	−3.5	12.25	16.80
9	0	−5.8	33.64	−4.5	20.25	26.10
12	3	−2.8	7.84	−1.5	2.25	4.20
13	4	−1.8	3.24	−0.5	.25	0.90
19	7	4.2	17.64	2.5	6.25	10.50
11	2	−3.8	14.44	−2.5	6.25	9.50
16	6	1.2	1.44	1.5	2.25	1.80
23	9	8.2	67.24	4.5	20.25	36.90
14	5	−0.8	.64	0.5	0.25	−0.40
21	8	6.2	38.44	3.5	12.25	21.70
$\Sigma X = 148$	$\Sigma Y = 45$	0[a]	207.60	0[a]	82.50	128

$$\bar{X} = \frac{\Sigma X}{N} = \frac{148}{10} = 14.8$$

$$\bar{Y} = \frac{\Sigma Y}{N} = \frac{45}{10} = 4.5$$

$$s_X^2 = \frac{\Sigma(X-\bar{X})^2}{N-1} = \frac{207.60}{9} = 23.07$$

$$s_X = \sqrt{23.07} = 4.80$$

$$s_Y^2 = \frac{\Sigma(Y-\bar{Y})^2}{N-1} = \frac{82.50}{9} = 9.17$$

$$s_Y = \sqrt{9.17} = 3.03$$

$$s_{XY} = \frac{\Sigma(X-\bar{X})(Y-\bar{Y})}{N-1} = \frac{128}{9} = 14.22$$

Note:

a. Answers may differ due to rounding; however, the exact value of these column totals, properly calculated, will always be equal to zero.

a = the Y-intercept

b = the slope of the line

These formulas assume that X is the independent variable and Y is the dependent variable.

Before we compute a and b, let's examine these formulas. The denominator for b is the variance of the variable X. It is defined as follows:

$$\text{Variance } (X) = s_X^2 = \frac{\Sigma\left(X - \bar{X}\right)^2}{N - 1}$$

This formula should be familiar to you from Chapter 4 ("Measures of Variability"). The numerator (s_{XY}), however, is a new term. It is the covariance of X and Y and is defined as

$$\text{Covariance } (X,Y) = s_{XY} = \frac{\Sigma(X - \bar{X})(Y - \bar{Y})}{N - 1} \qquad (12.4)$$

The covariance is a measure of how X and Y vary together. Essentially, the covariance tells us to what extent higher values of one variable are associated with higher values of the second variable (in which case we have a positive covariation) or with lower values of the second variable (which is a negative covariation). Based on the formula, we subtract the mean of X from each X score and the mean of Y from each Y score, and then take the product of the two deviations. The results are then summed for all the cases and divided by $N - 1$.

In Table 12.2, we show the computations necessary to calculate the values of a and b for our 10 individuals. The means for educational attainment and Internet hours per week are obtained by summing Column 1 and Column 2, respectively, and dividing each sum by N. To calculate the covariance, we first subtract from each X score (Column 3) and from each Y score (Column 5) to obtain the mean deviations. We then multiply these deviations for every observation. The products of the mean deviations are shown in Column 7.

The covariance is a measure of the linear relationship between two variables, and its value reflects both the strength and the direction of the relationship. The covariance will be close to zero when X and Y are unrelated; it will be larger than zero when the relationship is positive and smaller than zero when the relationship is negative.

Now, let's substitute the values for the covariance and the variance from Table 12.2 to calculate b:

$$b = \frac{s_{XY}}{s_X^2} = \frac{14.22}{23.07} = 0.62$$

Once b has been calculated, we can solve for a, the intercept:

$$a = \bar{Y} - b(\bar{X}) = 4.5 - .62(14.8) = -4.68$$

The prediction equation is therefore

$$\hat{Y} = -4.68 + .62(X)$$

This equation can be used to obtain a predicted value for Internet hours per week given an individual's years of education. For example, for a person with 15 years of education, the predicted Internet hours is

$$\hat{Y} = -4.68 + 0.62(15) = 4.62$$

A CLOSER LOOK 12.2

UNDERSTANDING THE COVARIANCE

Let's say we have a set of eight data points for which the mean of *X* is 6 and the mean of *Y* is 3.

So the covariance in this case will be positive, giving us a positive *b* and a positive *r*.

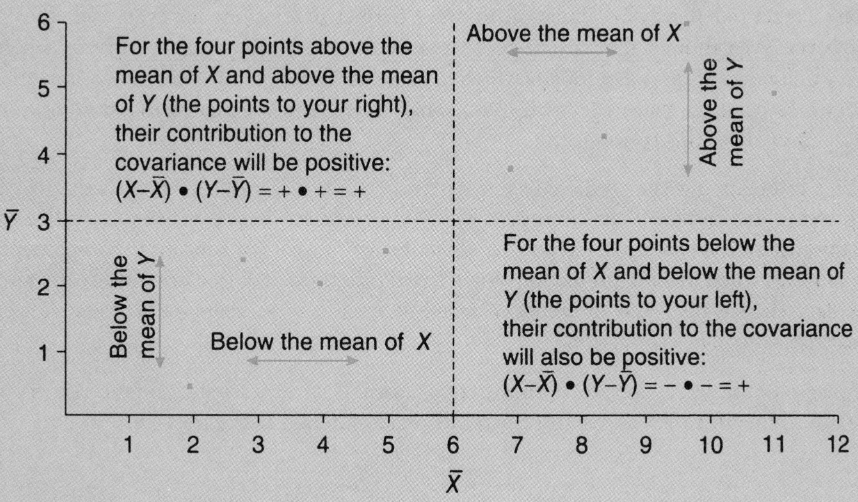

Now let's say we have a set of eight points that look like this:

So the covariance in this case will be negative, giving us a negative *b*.

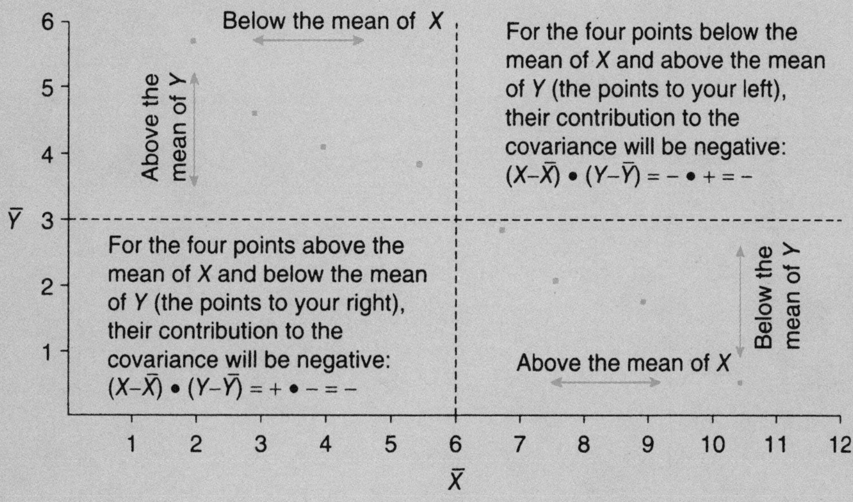

We can plot the straight-line graph corresponding to the regression equation. To plot a straight line, we need only two points, where each point corresponds to an *X*, *Y* value predicted.

Interpreting *a* and *b*

The *b* coefficient is equal to 0.62. This tells us that with each additional year of educational attainment, Internet hours per week is predicted to increase by 0.62 hours.

Note that because the relationships between variables in the social sciences are inexact, we don't expect our regression equation to make perfect predictions for every individual case. However, even though the pattern suggested by the regression equation may not hold for every individual, it gives us a tool by which to make the best possible guess about how Internet usage is associated, on average, with educational attainment. We can say that the slope of 0.62 is the estimate of this relationship.

The *Y* intercept *a* is the predicted value of *Y*, when $X = 0$. Thus, it is the point at which the regression line and the *Y*-axis intersect. The *Y* intercept can have positive or negative values. In this instance, it is unusual to consider someone with 0 years of education. As a general rule, be cautious when making predictions for *Y* based on values of *X* that are outside the range of the data, such as the –4.68 intercept calculated for our model. The intercept may not have a clear substantive interpretation.

We can plot the regression equation with two points: (1) the mean of *X* and the mean of *Y* and (2) 0 and the value of *a*. We've displayed this regression line in Figure 12.4.

Figure 12.4 The Best-Fitting Line for Educational Attainment and Internet Hours per Week

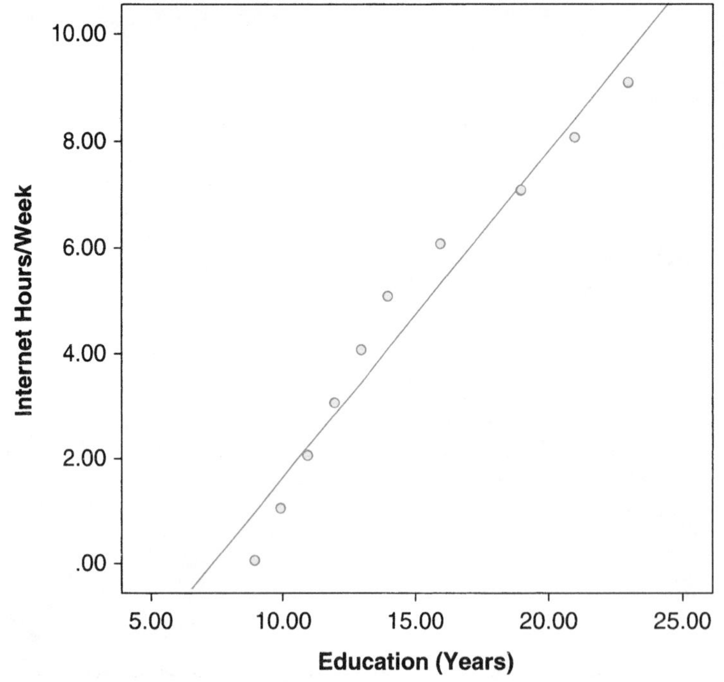

LEARNING CHECK 12.2

Use the prediction equation to calculate the predicted values of Y if X equals 9, 11, or 14. Verify that the regression line in Figure 12.3 passes through these points.

A NEGATIVE RELATIONSHIP: AGE AND INTERNET HOURS PER WEEK

Pew researchers Perrin and Duggan (2015) also documented how older adults have lagged behind younger adults in their Internet adoption. The majority of seniors, about 58%, currently use the Internet.[2] In this section, we'll examine the relationship between respondent age and Internet hours per week, defining *Internet hours* as the dependent variable (Y) and *age* as the independent variable (X). The fictional data are presented in Table 12.3 and the corresponding scatter diagram in Figure 12.5.

The scatter diagram reveals that age and Internet hours per week are linearly related. It also illustrates that these variables are negatively associated; that is, as age increases the number of hours of Internet access decreases. (Compare Figure 12.5 with Figure 12.4. Notice how the regression lines are in opposite direction—one positive, the other negative.)

For a more systematic analysis of the association, we will estimate the least squares regression equation for these data. Table 12.3 shows the calculations necessary to find a and b for our data on age and hours spent weekly on the Internet.

Now, let's substitute the values for the covariance and the variance from Table 12.3 to calculate b:

$$b = \frac{s_{XY}}{s_X^2} = \frac{-34.44}{167.73} = -.205 = -.21$$

Interpreting the slope, we can say with each one year increase in age, Internet hours per week will decline by .21. This indicates a negative relationship between age and Internet hours. Once b has been calculated, we can solve for a, the intercept:

$$a = \bar{Y} - b(\bar{X}) = 4.5 - (-.21)(37.8) = 12.44$$

The prediction equation is therefore

$$\hat{Y} = 12.44 - .21(X)$$

This equation can be used to obtain a predicted value for Internet hours per week given respondent's age. In Figure 12.5, the regression line is plotted over our original scatter diagram.

METHODS FOR ASSESSING THE ACCURACY OF PREDICTIONS

So far, we calculated two regression equations that help us predict Internet usage per week based on educational attainment or age. In both cases, our predictions are far from perfect. If we examine Figures 12.4 and 12.5, we can see that we fail to make accurate predictions in every case. Though some of the individual points lie fairly close to the regression line, not all

Table 12.3 Age and Internet Hours per Week, N = 10; Worksheet for Calculating *a* and *b* for the Regression Equation

(1)	(2)	(3)	(4)	(5)	(6)	(7)
Age	Internet Hours per Week					
X	Y	$(X-\bar{X})$	$(X-\bar{X})^2$	$(Y-\bar{Y})$	$(Y-\bar{Y})^2$	$(X-\bar{X})(Y-\bar{Y})$
55	1	17.2	295.84	−3.5	12.25	−60.2
60	0	22.2	492.84	−4.5	20.25	−99.9
45	3	7.2	51.84	−1.5	2.25	−10.8
35	4	−2.8	7.84	−0.5	.25	1.4
23	7	−14.8	219.04	2.5	6.25	−37
40	2	2.20	4.84	−2.5	6.25	−5.5
22	6	−15.8	249.64	1.5	2.25	−23.7
27	9	−10.8	116.64	4.5	20.25	−48.6
41	5	3.2	10.24	0.5	.25	1.6
30	8	−7.8	60.84	3.5	12.25	−27.3
$\sum X = 378$	$\sum Y = 45$	0[a]	1509.60	0[a]	82.50	−310

$$\bar{X} = \frac{\sum X}{N} = \frac{378}{10} = 37.8$$

$$\bar{Y} = \frac{\sum Y}{N} = \frac{45}{10} = 4.5$$

$$s_X^2 = \frac{\sum(X-\bar{X})^2}{N-1} = \frac{1509.60}{9} = 167.73$$

$$s_X = \sqrt{167.73} = 12.95$$

$$s_Y^2 = \frac{\sum(Y-\bar{Y})^2}{N-1} = \frac{82.50}{9} = 9.17$$

$$s_Y = \sqrt{9.17} = 3.03$$

$$s_{XY} = \frac{\sum(X-\bar{X})(Y-\bar{Y})}{N-1} = \frac{-310}{9} = -34.44$$

Note:

a. Answers may differ due to rounding; however, the exact value of these column totals, properly calculated, will always be equal to zero.

Figure 12.5 The Best-Fitting Line for Age and Internet Hours per Week, N = 10

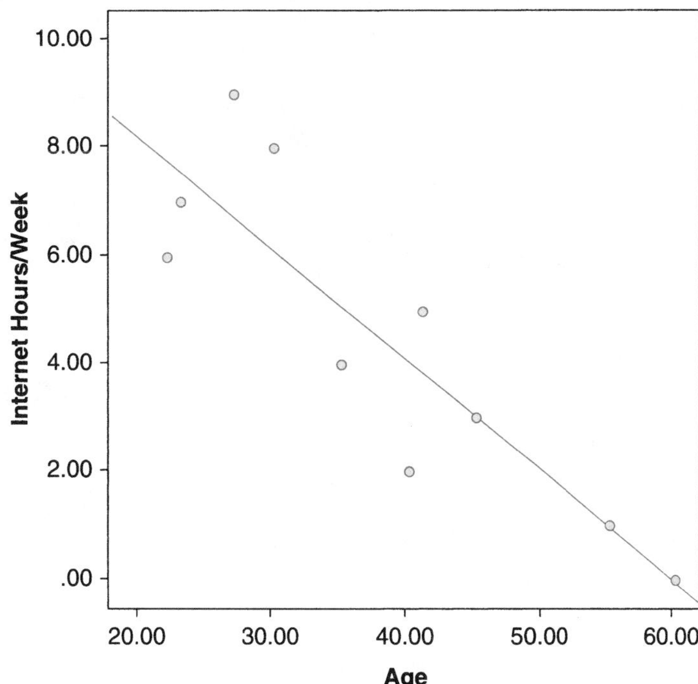

lie directly on the line—an indication that some prediction error was made. We have a model that helps us make predictions, but how can we assess the accuracy of these predictions?

We saw earlier that one way to judge our accuracy is to review the scatterplot. The closer the observations are to the regression line, the better the fit between the predictions and the actual observations. Still we need a more systematic method for making such a judgment. We need a measure that tells us how accurate a prediction the regression model provides. The coefficient of determination, or r^2, is such a measure. The coefficient of determination measures the improvement in the prediction error based on our use of the linear prediction equation. The coefficient of determination is a *PRE* measure of association. Recall from Chapter 10 that *PRE* measures adhere to the following formula:

$$PRE = \frac{E_1 - E_2}{E_1}$$

where

E_1 = prediction errors made when the independent variable is ignored

E_2 = prediction errors made when the prediction is based on the independent variable

Applying this to the regression model, we have two prediction rules and two measures of error. The first prediction rule is in the absence of information on X, predict $\bar{Y}$. The error of prediction is defined as $Y - \bar{Y}$. The second rule of prediction uses X and the regression equation to predict $\hat{Y}$. The error of prediction is defined as $Y - \hat{Y}$.

To calculate these two measures of error for all the cases in our sample, we square the deviations and sum them. Thus, for the deviations from the mean of Y we have

$$\Sigma\left(Y - \bar{Y}\right)^2$$

The sum of the squared deviations from the mean is called the *total sum of squares*, or *SST*:

$$SST = \Sigma\left(Y - \bar{Y}\right)^2$$

To measure deviation from the regression line, or $\hat{Y}$, we have

$$\Sigma\left(Y - \hat{Y}\right)^2$$

The sum of squared deviations from the regression line is denoted as the *residual sum of squares*, or *SSE:*

$$SSE = \Sigma\left(Y - \hat{Y}\right)^2$$

(We discussed this error term, the residual sum of squares, earlier in the chapter.)

Residual sum of squares (SSE) Sum of squared differences between observed and predicted *Y*.

Regression sum of squares (SSR) Reflects the improvement in the prediction error resulting from using the linear prediction equation, *SST - SSE*.

The predictive value of the linear regression equations can be assessed by the extent to which the **residual sum of squares**, or *SSE*, is smaller than the total sum of squares, *SST*. By subtracting *SSE* from *SST* we obtain the **regression sum of squares**, or *SSR*, which reflects improvement in the prediction error resulting from our use of the linear prediction equation. *SSR* is defined as

$$SSR = SST - SSE$$

Let's calculate r^2 for our regression model.

Calculating Prediction Errors

Figure 12.6 displays the regression line we calculated for educational attainment (X) and the Internet hours per week (Y) for 10 individuals, highlighting the prediction of Y for the person with 16 years of education, Subject A. Suppose we didn't know the actual Y, the number of Internet hours per week. Suppose further that we did not have knowledge of X, Subject A's years of education. Because the mean minimizes the sum of the squared errors for a set of scores, our best guess for Y would be $\bar{Y}$, or 4.5 hours. The horizontal line in Figure 12.6 represents this mean. Now, let's compare actual Y, 6 hours with this prediction:

$$Y - \bar{Y} = 6 - 4.5 = 1.5$$

With an error of 1.5, our prediction of the average score for Subject A is not accurate.

Let's see if our predictive power can be improved by using our knowledge of X—the years of education—and its linear relationship with Y—Internet hours per week. If we insert Subject A's 16 years of education into our prediction equation, as follows:

Figure 12.6 Error Terms for Subject A

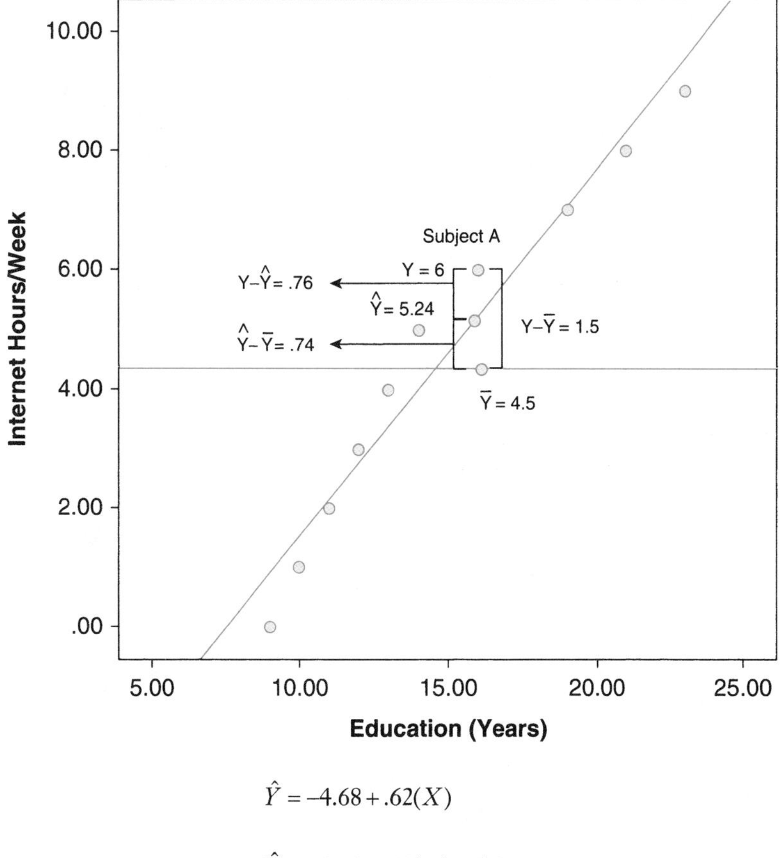

$$\hat{Y} = -4.68 + .62(X)$$

$$\hat{Y} = -4.68 + .62(16) = 5.24$$

We can now recalculate our new error of prediction by comparing the predicted $\hat{Y}$ with the actual Y:

$$Y - \hat{Y} = 6 - 5.24 = .76$$

Although this prediction is by no means perfect, it is a slight improvement of .73 (1.5 – 0.76 = 0.74) over our earlier prediction. This improvement is illustrated in Figure 12.6.

Note that this improvement is the same as $\hat{Y} - \bar{Y} = 5.24 - 4.5 = .74$. This quantity represents the improvement in the prediction error resulting from our use of the linear prediction equation.

Let's calculate these terms for our data on educational attainment (X) and Internet use (Y). We already have from Table 12.3 the total sum of squares:

$$SST = \sum(Y - \bar{Y})^2 = 82.50$$

To calculate the errors sum of squares, we will calculate the predicted $\hat{Y}$ for each individual, subtract it from the observed Y, square the differences, and sum these for all 10 individuals. These calculations are presented in Table 12.4.

The residual sum of squares is thus

$$SSE = \sum(Y - \hat{Y})^2 = 3.59$$

SSR is then given as

$$SSR = SST - SSE = 82.50 - 3.59 = 78.91$$

We have all the elements we need to construct a *PRE* measure. Because *SST* measures the prediction errors when the independent variable is ignored, we can define

$$E_1 = SST$$

Similarly, because *SSE* measures the prediction errors resulting from using the independent variable, we can define

$$E_2 = SSE$$

We are now ready to define the coefficient of determination r^2. It measures the *PRE* associated with using the linear regression equation as a rule for predicting *Y*:

$$PRE = \frac{E_1 - E_2}{E_1} = \frac{\sum(Y - \bar{Y})^2 - \sum(Y - \hat{Y})^2}{\sum(Y - \bar{Y})^2} \qquad (12.5)$$

Table 12.4 Worksheet for Calculating Errors Sum of Squares (SSE)

(1)	(2)	(3)	(4)	(5)
Educational Attainment	Internet Hours per Week	Predicted Y		
X	Y	$\hat{Y}$	$Y - \hat{Y}$	$(Y - \hat{Y})^2$
10	1	1.52	−0.52	0.27
9	0	0.90	−0.90	0.81
12	3	2.76	0.24	0.06
13	4	3.38	0.62	0.38
19	7	7.10	−0.10	0.01
11	2	2.14	−0.14	0.02
16	6	5.24	−0.76	0.58
23	9	9.58	−0.58	0.34
14	5	4.00	1	1.0
21	8	8.34	−0.34	0.12
$\sum X = 148$	$\sum Y = 45$		$\sum(Y - \hat{Y})^2 = 3.59$	

For our example,

$$r^2 = \frac{82.50 - 3.59}{82.50} = \frac{78.91}{82.50} = 0.96$$

The coefficient of determination (r^2) reflects the proportion of the total variation in the dependent variable, Y, explained by the independent variable, X. An r^2 of 0.96 means that by using educational attainment and the linear prediction rule to predict Internet hours per week, we have reduced the error of prediction by 96%. We can also say that the independent variable (*educational attainment*) explains about 96% of the variation in the dependent variable (*Internet hours per week*) as illustrated in Figure 12.7.

Coefficient of determination (r^2) A *PRE* measure reflecting the proportional reduction of error that results from using the linear regression model. It reflects the proportion of the total variation in the dependent variable, Y, explained by the independent variable, X.

The coefficient of determination ranges from 0.0 to 1.0. An r^2 of 1.0 means that by using the linear regression model, we have reduced uncertainty by 100%. It also means that the independent variable accounts for 100% of the variation in the dependent variable. With an r^2 of 1.0, all the observations fall along the regression line, and the prediction error is equal to 0.0. An r^2 of 0.0 means that using the regression equation to predict Y does not improve the prediction of Y. Figure 12.8 shows r^2 values near 0.0 and near 1.0. In Figure 12.8a, where r^2 is approximately 1.0, the regression model provides a good fit. In contrast, a very poor fit is evident in Figure 12.8b, where r^2 is near zero. An r^2 near zero indicates either poor fit or a well-fitting line with a b of zero.

CALCULATING r^2 Another method for calculating r^2 uses the following equation:

$$r^2 = \frac{[\text{Covariance}(X,Y)]^2}{[\text{Variance}(X)][\text{Variance}(Y)]} = \frac{s_{XY}^2}{s_X^2 s_Y^2} \tag{12.6}$$

This formula tells us to divide the square of the covariance of X and Y by the product of the variance of X and the variance of Y.

Figure 12.7 A Pie Graph Approach to r^2

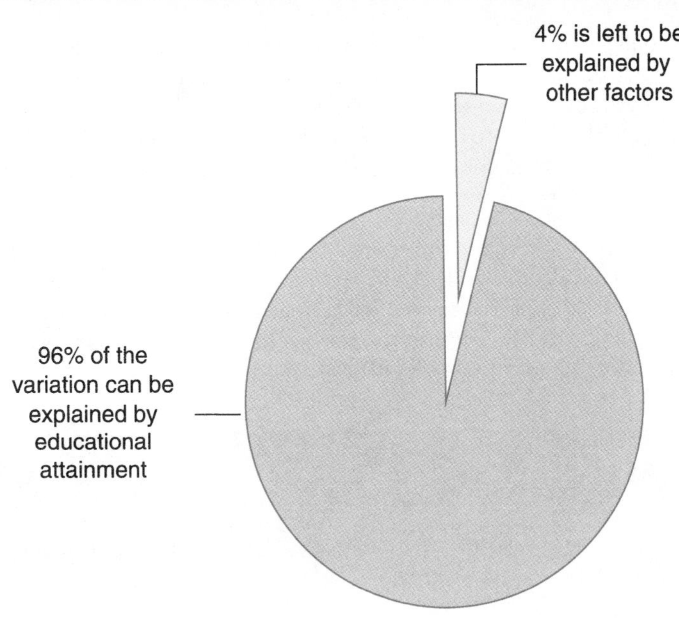
4% is left to be explained by other factors
96% of the variation can be explained by educational attainment

Figure 12.8 Examples Showing r^2 (a) Near 1.0 and (b) Near 0

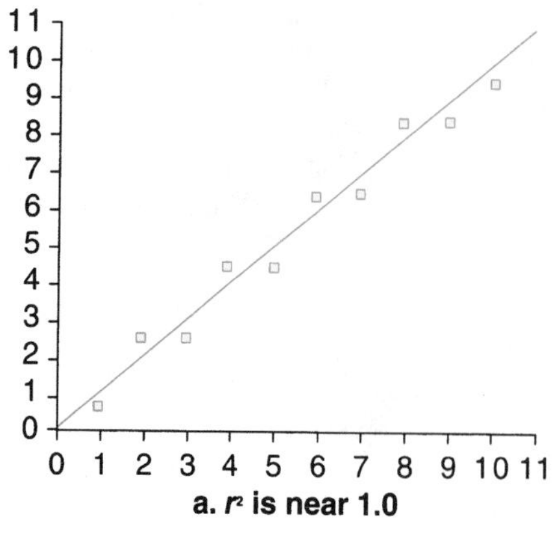

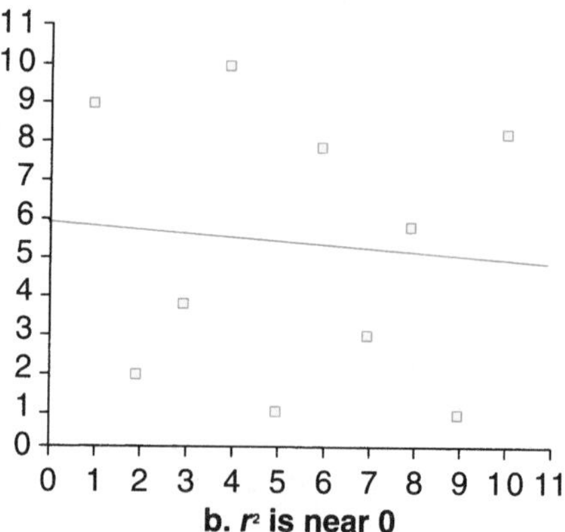

To calculate r^2 for our example, we can go back to Table 12.2, where the covariance and the variances for the two variables have already been calculated:

$$s_{XY} = 14.22$$

$$s_X^2 = 23.07$$

$$s_Y^2 = 9.17$$

Therefore,

$$r^2 = \frac{14.22^2}{23.07(9.17)} = \frac{202.21}{211.55} = .96$$

Since we are working with actual values for educational attainment, its metric, or measurement, values are different from the metric values for the dependent variable, Internet hours per week. While this hasn't been an issue until now, we must account for this measurement difference if we elect to use the variances and covariance to calculate r^2 (Formula 12.6). The remedy is actually quite simple. All we have to do is multiply our obtained r^2, 0.96, by 100 to obtain 96. Why multiply the obtained r^2 by 100?

We can multiply r^2 by 100 to obtain the percentage of variation in the dependent variable explained by the independent variable. An r^2 of 0.96 means that by using educational attainment and the linear prediction rule to predict Y, Internet hours per week, we have reduced uncertainty of prediction by 96%. We can also say that the independent variable explains 96% of the variation in the dependent variable, as illustrated in Figure 12.7.

LEARNING CHECK 12.3

Calculate r and r^2 for the age and Internet hours regression model. Interpret your results.

TESTING THE SIGNIFICANCE OF r^2 USING ANOVA

Like other descriptive statistics, r^2 is an estimate based on sample data. Once r^2 is obtained, we should assess the probability that the linear relationship between median household income and the percentage of state residents with a bachelor's degree, as expressed in r^2, is really zero in the population (given the observed sample coefficient). In other words, we must test r^2 for statistical significance. ANOVA (analysis of variance), presented earlier in Chapter 11 ("Analysis of Variance"), can easily be applied to determine the statistical significance of the regression model as expressed in r^2. In fact, when you look closely, ANOVA and regression analysis can look very much the same. In both methods, we attempt to account for variation in the dependent variable in terms of the independent variable, except that in ANOVA the independent variable is a categorical variable (nominal or ordinal, e.g., *gender* or *social class*) and with regression, it is an interval-ratio variable (e.g., *income measured in dollars*).

With ANOVA, we decomposed the total variation in the dependent variable into portions explained (*SSB*) and unexplained (*SSW*) by the independent variable. Next, we calculated the mean squares between (SSB/df_b) and mean squares within (SSW/df_w). The statistical test, *F*, is the ratio of the mean squares between to the mean squares within as shown in Formula 12.7.

$$F = \frac{\text{Mean squares between}}{\text{Mean squares within}} = \frac{SSB \,/\, df_b}{SSW \,/\, df_w} \qquad (12.7)$$

With regression analysis, we decompose the total variation in the dependent variable into portions explained, *SSR*, and unexplained, *SSE*. Similar to ANOVA, the mean squares regression and the mean squares residual are calculated by dividing each sum of squares by its corresponding degrees of freedom (*df*). The degrees of freedom associated with *SSR* (df_r) are equal to *K*, which refers to the number of independent variables in the regression equation.

$$\text{Mean squares regression} = \frac{SSR}{df_r} = \frac{SSR}{K} \qquad (12.8)$$

For *SSE*, degrees of freedom (df_e) is equal to $[N - (K + 1)]$, with *N* equal to the sample size.

$$\text{Mean squares residual} = \frac{SSE}{df_e} = \frac{SSE}{[N-(K+1)]} \qquad (12.9)$$

Mean squares regression An average computed by dividing the regression sum of squares (*SSR*) by its corresponding degrees of freedom.

Mean squares residual An average computed by dividing the residual sum of squares (*SSE*) by its corresponding degrees of freedom.

In Table 12.5 for example, we present the ANOVA summary table for educational attainment and Internet hours.

In the table, under the heading Source of Variation are displayed the regression, residual, and total sums of squares. The column marked *df* shows the degrees of freedom associated with both the regression and residual sum of squares. In the bivariate case, *SSR* has 1 degree of freedom associated with it. The degrees of freedom associated with *SSE* is $[N - (K + 1)]$, where *K* refers to the number of independent variables in the regression equation. In the bivariate case, with one independent variable—median household income—*SSE* has $N - 2$ degrees of freedom associated with it $[N - (1 + 1)]$. Finally, the **mean squares regression** (*MSR*) and the **mean squares residual** (*MSE*) are calculated by dividing each sum of squares by its corresponding degrees of freedom. For our example,

$$MSR = \frac{SSR}{1} = \frac{78.91}{1} = 78.91$$

$$MSE = \frac{SSE}{N-2} = \frac{3.57}{8} = 0.45$$

The F statistic together with the mean squares regression and the mean squares residual compose the obtained F ratio or F statistic. The F statistic is the ratio of the mean squares regression to the mean squares residual:

$$F = \frac{\text{Mean squares regression}}{\text{Mean squares residual}} = \frac{SSR / df_r}{SSE / df_e} \tag{12.10}$$

The F ratio, thus, represents the size of the mean squares regression relative to the size of the mean squares residual. The larger the mean squares regression relative to the mean squares residual, the larger the F ratio and the more likely that r^2 is significantly larger than zero in the population. We are testing the null hypothesis that r^2 is zero in the population.

The F ratio of our example is

$$F = \frac{\text{Mean squares regression}}{\text{Mean squares residual}} = \frac{78.91}{0.45} = 175.36$$

Making a Decision

To determine the probability of obtaining an F statistic of 175.36, we rely on Appendix E, Distribution of F. Appendix E lists the corresponding values of the F distribution for various degrees of freedom and two levels of significance, .05 and .01. We will set alpha at .05, and thus, we will refer to the table marked "$p < .05$." Note that Appendix E includes two *dfs*. For the numerator, df_1 refers to the df_r associated with the mean squares regression; for the denominator, df_2 refers to the df_e associated with the means squares residual. For our example, we compare our obtained F (175.36) to the F critical. When the *dfs* are 1 (numerator) and 8 (denominator), and $\alpha < .05$, the F critical is 5.32. Since our obtained F is larger than the F critical ($175.36 > 5.32$), we can reject the null hypothesis that r^2 is zero in the population. We conclude that the linear relationship between educational attainment and Internet hours per week as expressed in r^2 is probably greater than zero in the population (given our observed sample coefficient).

Table 12.5 ANOVA Summary Table for Educational Attainment and Internet Hours per Week

Source of Variation	Sum of Squares	*df*	Mean Squares	F
Regression	78.91	1	78.91	175.36
Residual	3.59	8	0.45	
Total	82.5	9		

LEARNING CHECK 12.4

Test the null hypothesis that there is a linear relationship between Internet hours and age. The mean squares regression is 63.66 with 1 degree of freedom. The mean squares residual is 2.355 with 8 degrees of freedom. Calculate the F statistic and assess its significance.

Pearson's Correlation Coefficient (r)

The square root of r^2, or r—known as **Pearson's correlation coefficient**—is most often used as a measure of association between two interval-ratio variables:

Pearson's correlation coefficient (r) The square root of r^2; it is a measure of association for interval-ratio variables, reflecting the strength and direction of the linear association between two variables. It can be positive or negative in sign.

$$r = \sqrt{r^2}$$

Pearson's r is usually computed directly by using the following definitional formula:

$$r^2 = \frac{\left[\text{Covariance}\,(X,Y)^2\right]}{\left[\text{Standard deviation }(X)\right]\left[\text{Standard deviation }(Y)\right]} = \frac{s_{XY}^2}{s_X s_Y}$$

Thus, r is defined as the ratio of the covariance of X and Y to the product of the standard deviations of X and Y.

CHARACTERISTICS OF PEARSON'S *r* Pearson's r is a measure of relationship or association for interval-ratio variables. Like gamma (introduced in Chapter 10), it ranges from 0.0 to ±1.0, with 0.0 indicating no association between the two variables. An r of +1.0 means that the two variables have a perfect positive association; –1.0 indicates that it is a perfect negative association. The absolute value of r indicates the strength of the linear association between two variables. (Refer to A Closer Look 10.2 for an interpretational guide.) Thus, a correlation of –0.75 demonstrates a stronger association than a correlation of 0.50. Figure 12.9 illustrates a strong positive relationship, a strong negative relationship, a moderate positive relationship, and a weak negative relationship.

Unlike the b coefficient, r is a symmetrical measure. That is, the correlation between X and Y is identical to the correlation between Y and X.

To calculate r for our example of the relationship between *educational attainment* and *Internet hours per week*, let's return to Table 12.2, where the covariance and the standard deviations for X and Y have already been calculated:

$$r = \frac{s_{XY}}{s_X s_Y} = \frac{14.22}{(4.80)(3.03)} = 0.98$$

A correlation coefficient of 0.98 indicates that there is a strong positive linear relationship between educational attainment and Internet hours per week.

Note that we could have taken the square root of r^2 to calculate r, because $r = \sqrt{r^2}$ or $\sqrt{0.96} = 0.98$. Similarly, if we first calculate r, we can obtain r^2 simply by squaring r (be careful not to lose the sign of r^2).

Figure 12.9 Scatter Diagrams Illustrating Weak, Moderate, and Strong Relationships as Indicated by the Absolute Value of *r*

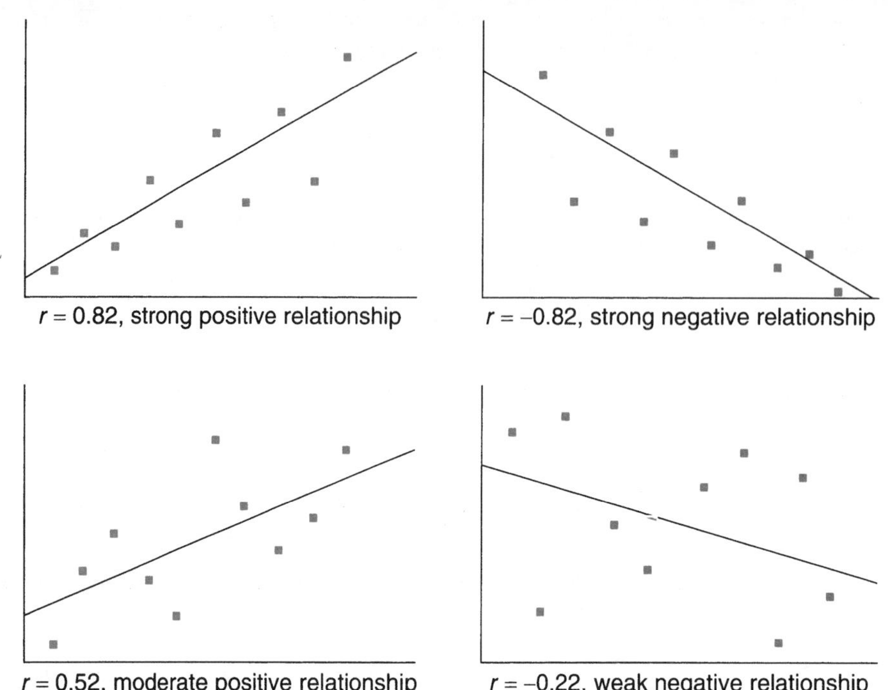

STATISTICS IN PRACTICE: MULTIPLE REGRESSION

Thus far, we have used examples that involve only two interval-ratio variables: (1) a dependent variable and (2) an independent variable. Multiple regression is an extension of bivariate regression, allowing us to examine the effect of two or more independent variables on the dependent variable.[6]

The general form of the multiple regression equation involving two independent variables is

$$\hat{Y} = a + b_1^* X_1 + b_2^* X_2 \tag{12.11}$$

where

$\hat{Y}$ = the predicted score on the dependent variable

X_1 = the score on independent variable X_1

X_2 = the score on independent variable X_2

a = the Y-intercept, or the value of Y when both X_1 and X_2 are equal to zero

b_1^* = the partial slope of Y and X_1, the change in Y with a unit change in X_1, when the other independent variable X_2 is controlled

SPURIOUS CORRELATIONS AND CONFOUNDING EFFECTS

A CLOSER LOOK 12.3

It is important to note that the existence of a correlation only denotes that the two variables are associated (they occur together or covary) and not that they are causally related. The well-known phrase "correlation is not causation" points to the fallacy of inferring that one variable causes the other based on the correlation between the variables. Such relationship is sometimes said to be spurious because both variables are influenced by a causally prior control variable, and there is no causal link between them. We can also say that a relationship between the independent and dependent variables is confounded by a third variable.

There are numerous examples in the research literature of spurious or confounded relationships. For instance, in a 2004 article, Michael Benson and his colleagues[3,4] discuss the issue of domestic violence as a correlate of race. Studies and reports have consistently found that rates of domestic abuse are higher in communities with a higher percentage of African American residents. Would this correlation indicate that race and domestic violence are causally related? To suggest that African Americans are more prone to engage in domestic violence would be erroneous if not outright racist. Benson and colleagues argue that the correlation between race and domestic violence is confounded by the level of economic distress in the community. Economically distressed communities are typically occupied by a higher percentage of African Americans. Also, rates of domestic violence tend to be higher in such communities. We can say that the relationship between race and domestic violence is confounded by a third variable—level of economic distress in the community.

Similarly, to test for the confounding effect of community economic distress on the relationship between race and domestic violence, Benson and Fox[5] calculated rates of domestic violence for African Americans and whites in communities with high and low levels of economic distress. They found that the relationship between race and domestic violence is not significant when the level of economic distress is constant. That is, the difference in the base rate of domestic violence for African Americans and whites is reduced by almost 50% in communities with high distress levels. In communities with low distress levels (and high income), the rate of domestic violence of African Americans is virtually identical to that of whites. The results showed that the correlation between race and domestic violence is accounted for in part by the level of economic distress of the community.

Uncovering spurious or confounded relations between an independent and a dependent variable can also be accomplished by using multiple regression. Multiple regression, an extension of bivariate regression, helps us examine the effect of an independent variable on a dependent variable while holding constant one or more additional variables.

b_2^* = the partial slope of Y and X_2, the change in Y with a unit change in X_2, when the other independent variable X_1 is controlled

Notice how the slopes are referred to as partial slopes. Partial slopes reflect the amount of change in Y for a unit change in a specific independent variable while controlling or holding constant the value of the other independent variables.

Partial slopes The amount of change in Y for a unit change in a specific independent variable while controlling for the other independent variable(s).

To illustrate, let's combine our investigation of Internet hours per week, educational attainment, and age. We hypothesize that individuals with higher levels of education will have higher levels of Internet use per week and that older individuals have lower hours of Internet use. We will estimate the multiple regression model data using SPSS. SPSS output are presented in Figure 12.10.

The partial slopes are reported in the Coefficients table, under the column labeled B. The intercept is also in Column B, on the (Constant) row. Putting it all together, the multiple regression equation that incorporates both educational attainment and respondent age as predictors of Internet hours per week is

Figure 12.10 SPSS Regression Output for Internet Hours per Week, Educational Attainment, and Age

Model Summary

Model	R	R Square	Adjusted R Square	Std. Error of the Estimate
1	.988[a]	.977	.970	.52203

a. Predictors: (Constant), educ, age

ANOVA[a]

Model		Sum of Squares	df	Mean Square	F	Sig.
1	Regression	80.592	2	40.296	147.870	.000[b]
	Residual	1.908	7	.273		
	Total	82.500	9			

a. Dependent Variable: internet

b. Predictors: (Constant), educ, age

Coefficients[a]

Model		Unstandardized Coefficients		Standardized Coefficients	t	Sig.
		B	Std. Error	Beta		
1	(Constant)	-.605	1.717		-.352	.735
	age	-.057	.023	-.245	-2.477	.042
	educ	.491	.062	.779	7.883	.000

a. Dependent Variable: internet

$$\hat{Y} = -.605 + .491(X_1) + -.057(X_2)$$

where

$\hat{Y}$ = number of Internet hours per week

X_1 = educational attainment

X_2 = age

This equation tells us that Internet hours increases by 0.49 per each year of education (X_1), holding age (X_2) constant. On the other hand, Internet hours decreases by 0.06 with each year increase in age (X_2) when we hold educational attainment (X_1) constant. Controlling for the effect of one variable, while examining the effect of the other, allows us to separate out the effects of each predictor independently of the other. For example, given two individuals with the same years of education, the person who might be a year older than the other is expected to use Internet 0.06 hours less. Or given two individuals of the same age, the person who has one more year of education will have 0.49 hours more of Internet use than the other.

Finally, the value of *a* (–0.60) reflects Internet hours per week when both education and age are equal to zero. Though this *Y*-intercept doesn't lend itself to a meaningful interpretation, the value of *a* is a baseline that must be added to the equation for Internet hours to be properly estimated.

When a regression model includes more than one independent variable, it is likely that the units of measurement will vary. A multiple regression model could include income (dollars), highest degree (years), and number of children (individuals), making it difficult to compare their effects on the dependent variable. The **standardized slope coefficient** or **beta** (represented by the Greek letter, β) converts the values of each score into a Z score, standardizing the units of measurement so we can interpret their relative effects. Beta, also referred to as beta weights, range from 0 to ±1.0. The largest β value (whether negative or positive) identifies the independent variable with the strongest effect. Beta is reported in the SPSS Coefficient table, under the column labeled "Standardized Coefficient/Beta."

Standardized slope coefficient or beta The slope between the dependent variable and a specific independent variable when all scores are standardized or expressed as Z scores. Beta scores range from 0 to ±1.0.

A standardized multiple regression equation can be written as

$$\hat{Y} = a + \beta_1 X_1 + \beta_2 X_2 \tag{12.12}$$

Based on this data example, the equation is

$$\hat{Y} = -.605 + .779X_1 + -.245X_2$$

We can conclude that education has the strongest effect on Internet hours as indicated by the β value of 0.779 (compared with the beta of −.245 for age).

Like bivariate regression, multiple regression analysis yields a **multiple coefficient of determination**, symbolized as R^2 (corresponding to r^2 in the bivariate case). R^2 measures the *PRE* that results from using the linear regression model. It reflects the proportion of the total variation in the dependent variable that is explained jointly by two or more independent variables. We obtained an R^2 of 0.977 (in the Model Summary table, in the column labeled R Square). This means that by using educational attainment and age, we reduced the error of predicting Internet hours by 97.7 or 98%. We can also say that the independent variables, educational attainment and age, explain 98% of the variation in Internet hours per week.

Multiple coefficient of determination (R^2) Measure that reflects the proportion of the total variation in the dependent variable that is explained jointly by two or more independent variables.

Including respondent age in our regression model did not improve the prediction of Internet hours per week. As we saw earlier, educational attainment accounted for 96% of the variation in Internet hours per week. The addition of age to the prediction equation resulted in a 2% increase in the percentage of explained variation.

As in the bivariate case, the square root of R^2, or R, is **Pearson's multiple correlation coefficient**. It measures the linear relationship between the dependent variable and the combined effect of two or more independent variables. For our model $R = 0.988$ or 0.99. This indicates that there is a strong relationship between the dependent variable and both independent variables.

Pearson's multiple correlation coefficient (R) Measure of the linear relationship between the independent variable and the combined effect of two or more independent variables.

LEARNING CHECK 12.5

Use the prediction equation describing the relationship between Internet hours per week and both educational attainment and age to calculate Internet hours per week for someone with 20 years of education who is 35 years old.

SPSS can also produce a correlation matrix, a table that presents the Pearson's correlation coefficient for all pairs of variables in the multiple regression model. A correlation matrix provides a baseline summary of the relationships between variables, identifying relationships or hypotheses that are usually the main research objective. Extensive correlation matrices are often presented in social science literature, but in this example, we have three pairs: (1) Internet hours with educational attainment, (2) Internet hours with age, and (3) educational attainment with age. Refer to Figure 12.11.

Figure 12.11 Correlation Matrix for Internet Hours per Week, Educational Attainment, and Age

Correlations

		internet	educ	age
internet	Pearson Correlation	1	.978**	-.878**
	Sig. (2-tailed)		.000	.001
	N	10	10	10
educ	Pearson Correlation	.978**	1	-.813**
	Sig. (2-tailed)	.000		.004
	N	10	10	10
age	Pearson Correlation	-.878**	-.813**	1
	Sig. (2-tailed)	.001	.004	
	N	10	10	10

**. Correlation is significant at the 0.01 level (2-tailed).

The matrix reports variable names in columns and rows. Note the diagonal from the upper left corner to the lower right corner reporting a correlation value of 1 (there are three 1s). This is the correlation of each variable with itself. This diagonal splits the matrix in half, creating mirrored correlations. We're interested in the intersection of the row and column variables, the cells that report their correlation coefficient for each pair. For example, the correlation coefficient for Internet and age, −0.878, is reported twice at the upper right-hand corner and at the lower left-hand corner. The other two correlations are also reported twice.

We calculated the correlation coefficients for Internet hours with educational attainment and Internet hours with age earlier in this chapter. The negative correlation between Internet hours and age is confirmed in Figure 12.10. We conclude that there is a strong negative relationship (−0.813) between these two variables. We also know that there is a strong positive correlation of 0.978 between Internet hours and educational attainment. The matrix also reports the significance of each correlation.

ANOVA FOR MULTIPLE LINEAR REGRESSION

The ANOVA summary table for multiple regression is nearly identical to the one for bivariate linear regression, except that the degrees of freedom are adjusted to reflect the number of independent variables in the model.

We conducted an ANOVA test to assess the probability that the linear relationship between Internet hours per week, educational attainment, and age as expressed by R^2, is really zero. The results of this test are reported in Figure 12.10. The obtained F statistic of 147.87 is shown in this table. With 2 and 7 degrees of freedom, we would need an F of 9.55 to reject the null hypothesis that $R^2 = 0$ at the .01 level. Since our obtained F exceeds that value (147.87 > 9.55), we can reject the null hypothesis with $p < .01$.

READING THE RESEARCH LITERATURE: ACADEMIC INTENTIONS AND SUPPORT

Katherine Purswell, Ani Yazedjian, and Michelle Toews (2008)[7] utilized regression analysis to examine academic intentions (intention to perform specific behaviors related to learning engagement and positive academic behaviors), parental support, and peer support as predictors of self-reported academic behaviors (e.g., speaking in class, completed assignments on time during their freshman year) of first- and continuing-generation college students. The researchers apply social capital theory, arguing that relationships with others (parents and peers) would predict positive academic behaviors.

They estimated three separate multiple regression models for first-generation students (Group 1), students with at least one parent with college experience but with no degree (Group 2), and students with at least one parent with a bachelor's degree or higher (Group 3). The regression models are presented in Table 12.6. All of the variables included in the analysis are ordinal measures, with responses coded on a *strongly disagree* to *strongly agree* scale.

Each model is presented with partial and standardized slopes. No intercepts are reported. The multiple correlation coefficient and F statistic are also reported for each model. The asterisk indicates significance at the .05 level.

The researchers summarize the results of each model.

> The regression model was significant for all three groups ($p < .05$). For FGCS (first generation college students), the model predicted 24% of the variance in behavior. However, intention was the only significant predictor for this group. For the second group, the model predicted 18% of the variance, with peer support significantly predicting academic behavior. Finally, the model predicted 23% of the variance in behavior for those in the third group with all three independent variables—intention, parental support, and peer support—predicting academic behavior.[8]

Table 12.6 Regression Analyses Predicting Behavior by Intention, Parental Support, and Peer Support

	First Generation Students N = 44		Group 2 N = 82		Group 3 N = 203	
	b	β	b	β	b	β
Intention	.75*	.49	.14	.15	.53*	.48
Parental Support	.00	.00	.07	.04	.06*	.13
Peer Support	−.02	−.02	.26*	.26	−.20*	−.16
R^2	.24		.18		.23	
F	3.82*		5.77*		18.74*	

Source: Adapted from Katherine Purswell, Ani Yazedjian, and Michelle Toews, "Students' Intentions and Social Support as Predictors of Self-Reported Academic Behaviors: A Comparison of First- and Continuing-Generation College Students," *Journal of College Student Retention* 10 no. 2 (2008): 200.

*$p < .05$.

DATA AT WORK

Shinichi Mizokami: Professor

Photo courtesy of Shinichi Mizokami

Dr. Mizokami is a professor of psychology and pedagogy at Kyoto University, Japan. Pedagogy is a discipline that examines educational theories and teaching methods. His current research involves two areas of study: (1) student learning and development and (2) identity formation in adolescence and young adulthood.

In 2013, his research team launched a 10-year transition survey with 45,000 second-year high school students. He uses multiple regression techniques to examine students' transition from school to work. "My team administers the surveys with the questions regarding what attitudes and distinctions competent students have or what activities they are engaged in. We analyze the data controlling the variables of gender, social class, major, kinds of university (doctoral, master's, or baccalaureate university), and find the results. In the multiple regression analysis, we carefully look at the bivariate tables and correlations between the used variables, and go back and forth between those descriptive statistics and the results [of the] multiple regression analysis."

He would be pleased to learn that you are enrolled in an undergraduate statistics course. According to Mizokami, "Many people will not have enough time to learn statistics after they start to work, so it may be worthwhile to study it in undergraduate education. Learning statistics can expand the possibilities of your job and provide many future advantages. . . . This can happen not only in academic fields but also in business. Good luck!"

MAIN POINTS

- A scatter diagram (also called scatterplot) is a quick visual method used to display relationships between two interval-ratio variables.
- Equations for all straight lines have the same general form:

$$\hat{Y} = a + b(X)$$

- The best-fitting regression line is that line where the residual sum of squares, or Σe^2, is at a minimum. Such a line is called the least squares line, and the technique that produces this line is called the least squares method.
- The coefficient of determination (r^2) and Pearson's correlation coefficient (r) measure how well the regression model fits the data. Pearson's r indicates the strength of the association between the two variables. The coefficient of determination is a *PRE* measure, identifying the reduction of error based on the regression model.

- The general form of the multiple regression equation involving two independent variables is $\hat{Y} = a + b_1^* X_1 + b_2^* X_2$. The multiple coefficient of determination (R^2) measures the proportional reduction of error based on the multiple regression model.
- The standardized multiple regression equation is $\hat{Y} = a + \beta_1 X_1 + \beta_2 X_2$. The beta coefficients allow us to assess the relative strength of all the independent variables.

KEY TERMS

bivariate regression 325
coefficient of determination (r^2) 341
correlation 325
deterministic (perfect) linear relationship 326
least squares line (best-fitting line) 330
least squares method 330
linear relationship 326
mean squares regression 343
mean squares residual 343
multiple coefficient of determination (R^2) 349
multiple regression 325
partial slopes (b^*) 347
Pearson's correlation coefficient (r) 345
Pearson's multiple correlation coefficient (R) 349
regression 325
regression sum of squares (SSR) 338
residual sum of squares (SSE) 338
scatter diagram (scatterplot) 325
slope (b) 328
standardized slope coefficient or beta 349
Y-intercept (a) 328

DIGITAL RESOURCES

SAGE edge™

Get the edge on your studies. **edge.sagepub.com/frankfort8e**

Take a quiz to find out what you've learned.
Review key terms with eFlashcards.
Dive into real research with SAGE Journal Articles.

SPSS DEMONSTRATIONS [GSS14SSDS-A]

Demonstration 1: Producing Scatterplots (Scatter Diagrams)

Do people with more education work more hours per week? Some may argue that those with lower levels of education are forced to work low-paying jobs, thereby requiring them to work more hours per week to make ends meet. Others may rebut this argument by saying those with higher levels of education are in greater positions of authority, which requires more time to ensure operations run smoothly. This question can be explored with SPSS using the techniques discussed in this chapter for interval-ratio data because *hours worked last week* (HRS1) and *number of years of education* (EDUC) are both coded at an interval-ratio level in the GSS14SSDS-A file.

Figure 12.12 Scatterplot of Hours Worked by Education, Regression Line Plotted

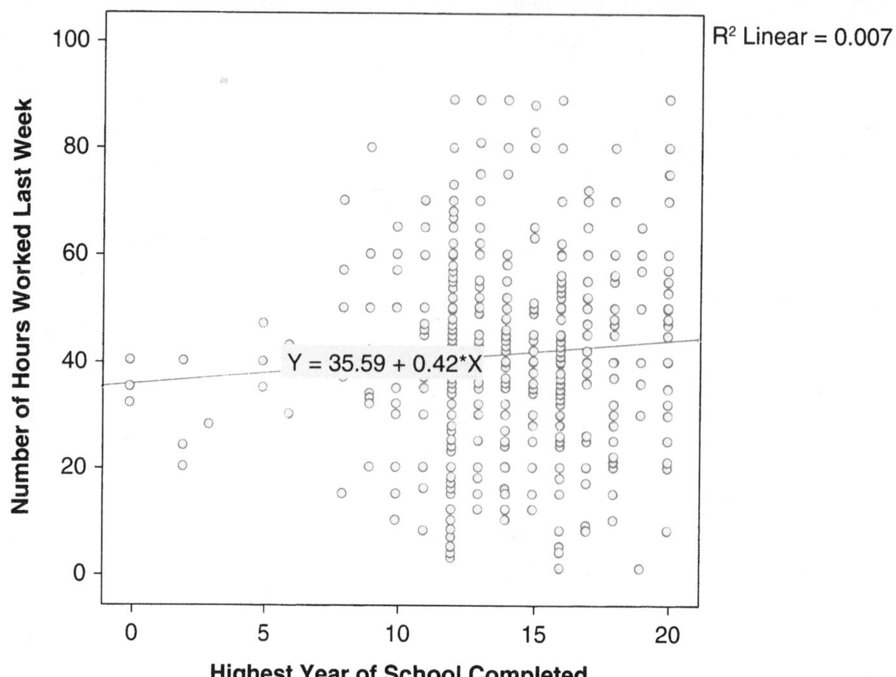

We begin by looking at a scatterplot of these two variables. The Scatter procedure can be found under the *Graphs* menu choice. In the opening dialog box, click *Legacy Dialogs* then *Scatter/Dot* (which means we want to produce a standard scatterplot with two variables), select the icon for *Simple Scatter*, and then click *Define*.

The Scatterplot dialog box requires that we specify a variable for both the *X*- and *Y*-axes. We place EDUC (number of years of education) on the *X*-axis because we consider it the independent variable and HRS1 (number of hours worked last week) on the *Y*-axis because it is the dependent variable. Then, click *OK*.

You can edit it to change its appearance by double-clicking on the chart in the viewer. The action of double-clicking displays the chart in a chart window. You can edit the chart from the menus, from the toolbar, or by double-clicking on the object you want to edit.

It is difficult to tell whether a relationship exists just by looking at points in the scatterplot, so we will ask SPSS to include the regression line. To add a regression line to the plot, we start by double-clicking on the scatterplot to open the Chart Editor. Click *Elements* from the main menu, then *Fit Line at Total*. In the section of the dialog box headed "Fit Method," select *Linear*. Click *Apply* and then *Close*. Finally, in the Chart Editor, click *File* and then *Close*. The result of these actions is shown in Figure 12.12.

Since the regression line clearly rises as number of years of education increases, we observe the positive relationship between education and number of hours worked last week. The predicted value for those with 20 years of education is about 44 hours, compared with 39.76 hours for those with 10 years of education. However, because there is a lot of scatter around the line (the points are not close to the regression line), the predictive power of the model is weak.

Demonstration 2: Producing Correlation Coefficients

To further quantify the effect of education on hours worked, we request a correlation coefficient. This statistic is available in the Bivariate procedure, which is located by clicking on *Analyze*, *Correlate*, then *Bivariate* (Figure 12.13). Place the variables you are interested in correlating, EDUC and HRS1, in the Variable(s) box, then click *OK*.

Figure 12.13 Bivariate Correlations Dialog Box

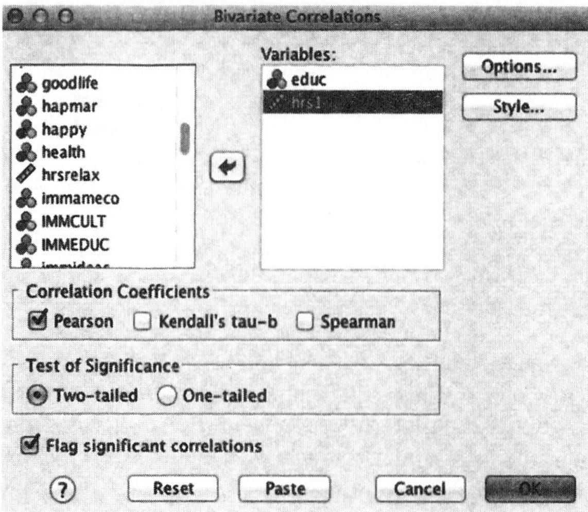

SPSS produces a matrix of correlations, shown in Figure 12.14. We are interested in the correlation in the bottom left-hand cell, .084. The correlation is significant at the .05 level (two-tailed). We see that this correlation is closer to 0 than to 1, which tells us that education is not a very good predictor of hours worked, even if it is true that those with more education work more hours per week. The number under the correlation coefficient, 895, is the number of valid cases (*N*)—those respondents who gave a valid response to both questions. The number is reduced because not everyone in the sample is working.

Figure 12.14 Correlation Matrix for Hours Worked and Education

Correlations

		educ HIGHEST YEAR OF SCHOOL COMPLETED	hrs1 NUMBER OF HOURS WORKED LAST WEEK
educ HIGHEST YEAR OF SCHOOL COMPLETED	Pearson Correlation	1	.084*
	Sig. (2-tailed)		.012
	N	1500	895
hrs1 NUMBER OF HOURS WORKED LAST WEEK	Pearson Correlation	.084*	1
	Sig. (2-tailed)	.012	
	N	895	895

*. Correlation is significant at the 0.05 level (2-tailed).

Demonstration 3: Producing a Regression Equation

Next, we will use SPSS to calculate the best-fitting regression line and the coefficient of determination. This procedure is located by clicking on *Analyze*, *Regression*, then *Linear*. The Linear Regression dialog box (Figure 12.15) provides boxes in which to enter the dependent variable, HRS1, and the independent variable, EDUC (regression allows more than one). After you place the variables in their appropriate places, click *OK* to generate the output. The Linear Regression dialog box offers many other choices, but the default output from the procedure contains all that we need.

SPSS produces a great deal of output, which is typical for many of the more advanced statistical procedures in the program. The output is presented in Figure 12.16. Under the Model Summary, the coefficient of determination is labeled "R square." Its value is .007, which is very weak. Educational attainment explains little of the variation in hours worked, less than 1%.

The regression equation coefficients are presented in the Coefficients table. The regression equation coefficients are listed in the column headed "B." The coefficient for EDUC, or b, is about .417; the intercept term, or a, identified in the "(Constant)" row, is 35.589. Thus, we would predict that every additional year of education increases the number of hours worked each week by about 25 minutes. Or we could predict that those with a high school level of education work, on average, 35.589 + (.417)(12) hours, or 40.59 hours.

The ANOVA table provides the results of the analysis of variance test. The table includes regression and residual sum of squares, as well as mean squares. To test the null hypothesis that r^2 is zero, you will only need the statistic shown in the last column labeled "Sig." This is the p value associated with the F ratio listed in the column head "F." The F statistic is 6.368, and its associated p value is .012. This means that there is a little probability (.012) that r^2 is really zero in the population, given the observed r^2 of .007. The model, though not reducing much of the variance in predicting work hours, is significant. We are therefore able to reject the null hypothesis at the .05 level.

Figure 12.15 Linear Regression Dialog Box

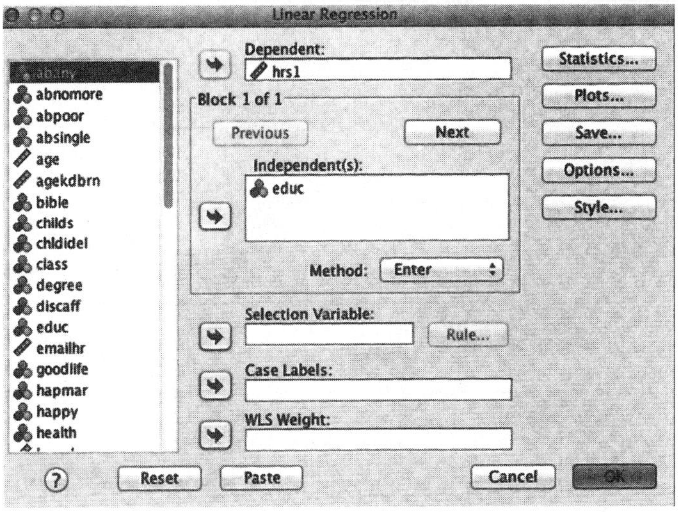

Figure 12.16 Linear Regression Output Specifying the Relationship Between Education and Number of Hours Worked Last Week

Model Summary

Model	R	R Square	Adjusted R Square	Std. Error of the Estimate
1	.084[a]	.007	.006	14.994

a. Predictors: (Constant), educ HIGHEST YEAR OF SCHOOL COMPLETED

ANOVA[a]

Model		Sum of Squares	df	Mean Square	F	Sig.
1	Regression	1431.613	1	1431.613	6.368	.012[b]
	Residual	200755.164	893	224.810		
	Total	202186.778	894			

a. Dependent Variable: hrs1 NUMBER OF HOURS WORKED LAST WEEK

b. Predictors: (Constant), educ HIGHEST YEAR OF SCHOOL COMPLETED

Coefficients[a]

Model		Unstandardized Coefficients		Standardized Coefficients	t	Sig.
		B	Std. Error	Beta		
1	(Constant)	35.589	2.383		14.936	.000
	educ HIGHEST YEAR OF SCHOOL COMPLETED	.417	.165	.084	2.524	.012

a. Dependent Variable: hrs1 NUMBER OF HOURS WORKED LAST WEEK

Demonstration 4: Producing a Multiple Regression Equation

What other variables, in addition to education, affect the number of hours worked per week? One possible answer to this question is that age (AGE) has something to do with the number of hours worked per week. To answer this question, we will use SPSS to calculate a multiple regression equation and a multiple coefficient of determination. This procedure is similar to the one used to generate the bivariate regression equation. Click *Analyze*, *Regression*, then *Linear*. We place EDUC (number of years of education) and AGE (age in years) in the box for the independent variables and HRS1 (the number of hours worked last week) in the box for the dependent variable, and click *OK*. The output is presented in Figure 12.17.

Under the Model Summary, the multiple correlation coefficient labeled "*R*" is .109. This tells us that education and age are weakly associated with hours worked last week. The coefficient of determination is labeled "R square." Its value is .012. An R^2 of .012 means that educational attainment and age jointly explain just 1% of the variation in hours worked last week. In addition, SPSS provides an "adjusted R square," which is .01. The "adjusted R square" adjusts the R^2 coefficient for the number of predictors in the equation. Generally, the adjusted R^2 will be lower, relative to R^2, the larger the number of predictors.

The regression equation coefficients are listed in the Coefficients table. The regression equation coefficients are listed in the column headed "B." The coefficient for EDUC is about .433, and for AGE it is –.077. The intercept term, or *a*, identified in the "(Constant)" row, is 38.815. Thus, we would predict that, holding age constant, every additional year of education increases the number of hours worked the previous week by about 26 minutes (.43 × 60).

Figure 12.17 Multiple Regression Output Specifying the Relationship Between Education, Age, and Number of Hours Worked Last Week

Model Summary

Model	R	R Square	Adjusted R Square	Std. Error of the Estimate
1	.109[a]	.012	.010	14.967

a. Predictors: (Constant), age AGE OF RESPONDENT, educ HIGHEST YEAR OF SCHOOL COMPLETED

ANOVA[a]

Model		Sum of Squares	df	Mean Square	F	Sig.
1	Regression	2381.351	2	1190.675	5.315	.005[b]
	Residual	198915.736	888	224.004		
	Total	201297.086	890			

a. Dependent Variable: hrs1 NUMBER OF HOURS WORKED LAST WEEK

b. Predictors: (Constant), age AGE OF RESPONDENT, educ HIGHEST YEAR OF SCHOOL COMPLETED

Coefficients[a]

Model		Unstandardized Coefficients		Standardized Coefficients	t	Sig.
		B	Std. Error	Beta		
1	(Constant)	38.815	2.854		13.600	.000
	educ HIGHEST YEAR OF SCHOOL COMPLETED	.433	.165	.087	2.615	.009
	age AGE OF RESPONDENT	-.077	.037	-.069	-2.061	.040

a. Dependent Variable: hrs1 NUMBER OF HOURS WORKED LAST WEEK

SPSS PROBLEMS [GSS14SSDS-A]

1. Explore the relationship between the number of siblings a respondent has (SIBS) and his or her number of children (CHILDS).

   a. Construct a scatterplot of these two variables in SPSS, and place the best-fit linear regression line on the scatterplot. Describe the relationship between the number of siblings a respondent has (IV) and the number of his or her children (DV).

   b. Calculate the regression equation predicting CHILDS with SIBS. What are the intercept and the slope? What are the coefficient of determination and the correlation coefficient?

   c. What is the predicted number of children for someone with three siblings?

   d. What is the predicted number of children for someone without any siblings?

2. Use the same variables as in Exercise 1, but do the analysis separately for men and women. Begin by locating the variable SEX. Click *Data*, *Split File*, and then select *Organize Output by Groups*. Insert SEX into the box and click *OK*. Now, SPSS will split your results by sex.

   a. Calculate the regression equation for men and women. (*Note:* You will need to scroll down through your output to find the results for men and women.) How similar are they?

b. What is the predicted number of children for a man with six siblings? For a woman with the same number of siblings? Which group has the higher predicted number of children?

3. Use the same variables as in Exercise 1, but do the analysis separately for white and black respondents. Click *Data*, *Split File*, and then select *Organize Output by Groups*. Insert RACECEN1 into the box and click *OK*. SPSS will split your results by RACECEN1 (focusing your analysis only on the categories for whites and blacks).

   a. Is there any difference between the regression equations for whites and blacks?

   b. What is the predicted number for whites and blacks with the same number of siblings: one sibling, four siblings, and seven siblings?

4. Use the same variables as in Exercise 1, but do the analysis separately for married and divorced respondents. Begin by locating the variable MARITAL. Click *Data*, *Split File*, and then select *Organize Output by Groups*. Insert MARITAL into the box and click *OK*. SPSS will split your results by marital status.

   a. Is there any difference between the regression equations for married and divorced respondents?

   b. What is the predicted number of children for married and divorced respondents with the following number of siblings: one sibling, four siblings, and seven siblings?

   c. What differences, if any, do you find? Is the number of siblings a better predictor of number of children for married respondents or for women?

5. Investigate the relationship between the respondent's education (EDUC) and the education received by his or her father and mother (PAEDUC and MAEDUC, respectively).

   a. Calculate the correlation coefficient, the coefficient of determination, and the regression equation predicting the respondent's education with father's education only. Interpret your results.

   b. Determine the multiple correlation coefficient, the multiple coefficient of determination, and the regression equation predicting the respondent's education with father's and mother's education. Interpret your results.

   c. Did taking into account the respondent's mother's education improve our prediction? Discuss this on the basis of the results from 5b.

   d. Using the regression equation from 5a, calculate the predicted number of years of education for a person with a father with 12 years of education. Then, repeat this procedure, adding in a mother's 12 years of education and using the regression equation from 5b.

   e. Review the ANOVA results. Can you reject the null hypothesis that $R^2 = 0$?

CHAPTER EXERCISES

1. Concerns over climate change, pollution, and a growing population has led to the formation of social action groups focused on environmental policies nationally and around the globe. A large number of these groups are funded through donor support. Based on the following eight countries, examine the data to determine the extent of the relationship between simply being concerned about the environment and actually giving money to environmental groups.

Country	Percentage Concerned	Percentage Donating Money
United States	33.8	22.8
Austria	35.5	27.8
The Netherlands	30.1	44.8
Slovenia	50.3	10.7
Russia	29.0	1.6
Philippines	50.1	6.8
Spain	35.9	7.4
Denmark	27.2	22.3

Source: International Social Survey Programme, 2000.

a. Construct a scatterplot of the two variables, placing percentage concerned about the environment on the horizontal or X-axis and the percentage donating money to environmental groups on the vertical or Y-axis.

b. Does the relationship between the two variables seem linear? Describe the relationship.

c. Find the value of the Pearson correlation coefficient that measures the association between the two variables and offer an interpretation.

2. In this exercise, we will investigate the relationships between adolescent fertility rate and female labor force participation in South America. Data are presented for 2014.

Country	Adolescent Fertility Rate	Female Labor Force Participation Rate
Argentina	40.4	63.9
Bolivia	44.6	71.1
Brazil	43.8	67.3
Chile	40.8	48.1
Colombia	42.6	51.7
Ecuador	40.4	76.2
Paraguay	39.2	58.0
Peru	45.3	49.7
Uruguay	44.5	56.5
Venezuela	39.9	79.7

Source: World Bank, 2014, Health Nutrition and Population Statistics.

a. Construct a scatterplot for adolescent fertility rate and labor force participation rate. Do you think the scatterplot can be characterized by a linear relationship?

b. Calculate the coefficient of determination and correlation coefficient.

c. Describe the relationship between the variables based on your calculations.

3. Let's examine the relationship between a country's gross national product (GNP) and the percentage of respondents willing to pay higher prices for goods to protect the environment. The following table displays information for five countries selected at random.

a. Calculate the correlation coefficient between a country's GNP and the percentage of its residents willing to pay higher prices to protect the environment. What is its value?

b. Provide an interpretation for the coefficient.

Country	GNP per Capita	Percentage Willing to Pay
United States	29.24	44.9
Ireland	18.71	53.3
The Netherlands	24.78	61.2
Norway	34.31	40.7
Sweden	25.58	32.6

Source: International Social Survey Programme, 2000.

4. In 2010, a U.S. Census Bureau report revealed that approximately 14.3% of all Americans were living below the poverty line in 2009. This figure is higher than in 2000, when the poverty rate was 12.2%. Individuals and families living below the poverty line face many obstacles, the least of which is access to health care. In many cases, those living below the poverty line are without any form of health insurance. Using data from the U.S. Census Bureau, analyze the relationship between living below the poverty line and access to health care for a random sample of 12 states. (The health insurance data are pre-Affordable Care Act implementation.)

State	Percentage Below Poverty Line (2009)	Percentage Without Health Insurance (2009)
Alabama	17.9	16.9
California	14.2	20
Idaho	14.3	15.2
Louisiana	17.3	16
New Jersey	9.4	15.8
New York	14.2	14.8
Pennsylvania	12.5	11.4
Rhode Island	11.5	12.3

(Continued)

(Continued)

State	Percentage Below Poverty Line (2009)	Percentage Without Health Insurance (2009)
South Carolina	17.1	17.0
Texas	17.2	26.1
Washington	12.3	12.9
Wisconsin	12.4	9.5

Source: U.S. Census Bureau, *The 2012 Statistical Abstract*, 2011, Tables 709 and 156.

a. Construct a scatterplot, predicting the percentage without health insurance with the percentage living below the poverty level. Does it appear that a straight-line relationship will fit the data?

b. Calculate the regression equation with percentage of the population without health insurance as the dependent variable, and draw the regression line on the scatterplot. What is its slope? What is the intercept? Has your opinion changed about whether a straight line seems to fit the data? Are there any states that fall far from the regression line? Which one(s)?

5. We test the hypothesis that as an individual's years of education increases, the individual will have fewer children. Based on a subsample from the GSS 2014, we present a scatterplot and regression output for the variables EDUC and CHILDS. Interpret the results.

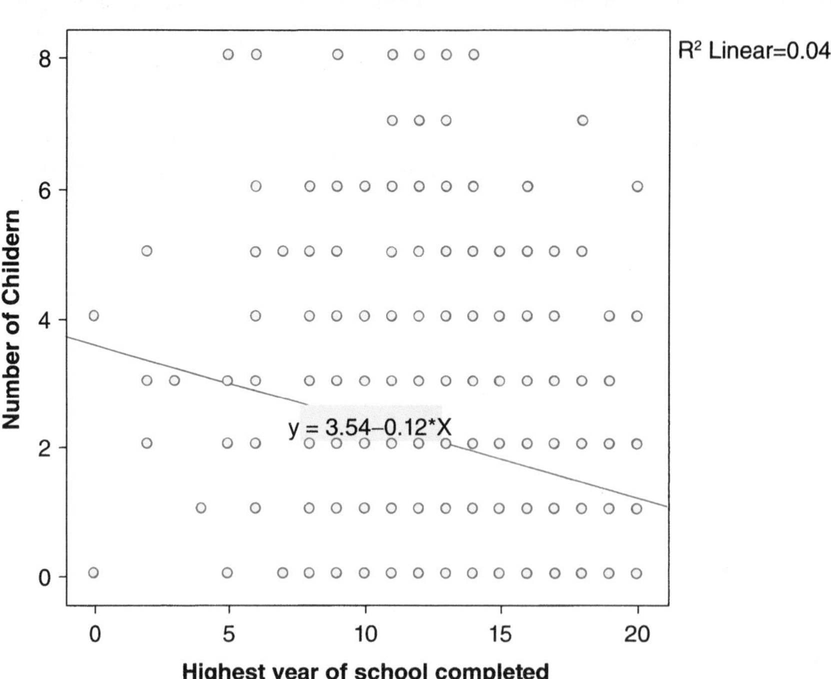

Linear Regression Output Specifying the Relationship Between Education and Number of Children

Model Summary

Model	R	R Square	Adjusted R Square	Std. Error of the Estimate
1	.220ª	.048	.047	1.625

a. Predictors: (Constant), educ HIGHEST YEAR OF SCHOOL COMPLETED

ANOVAª

Model		Sum of Squares	df	Mean Square	F	Sig.
1	Regression	156.892	1	156.892	59.418	.000ᵇ
	Residual	3091.980	1171	2.640		
	Total	3248.871	1172			

a. Dependent Variable: childs NUMBER OF CHILDREN

b. Predictors: (Constant), educ HIGHEST YEAR OF SCHOOL COMPLETED

Coefficientsª

Model		Unstandardized Coefficients		Standardized Coefficients	t	Sig.
		B	Std. Error	Beta		
1	(Constant)	3.537	.217		16.322	.000
	educ HIGHEST YEAR OF SCHOOL COMPLETED	-.118	.015	-.220	-7.708	.000

a. Dependent Variable: childs NUMBER OF CHILDREN

6. We present SPSS output examining the relationship between education (measured in years) and television viewing per day (measured in hours) based on a GSS 2014 subsample. We hypothesize that as educational attainment increases, hours of television viewing will decrease, indicating a negative relationship between the two variables. Discuss the significance of the overall model based on F and its p values. Is the relationship between education and television viewing significant?

Linear Regression Output for Hours Spent per Day Watching Television and Education

Model Summary

Model	R	R Square	Adjusted R Square	Std. Error of the Estimate
1	.196ª	.039	.037	2.555

a. Predictors: (Constant), educ HIGHEST YEAR OF SCHOOL COMPLETED

ANOVAª

Model		Sum of Squares	df	Mean Square	F	Sig.
1	Regression	206.107	1	206.107	31.576	.000ᵇ
	Residual	5136.953	787	6.527		
	Total	5343.060	788			

a. Dependent Variable: tvhours HOURS PER DAY WATCHING TV

b. Predictors: (Constant), educ HIGHEST YEAR OF SCHOOL COMPLETED

Coefficientsª

Model		Unstandardized Coefficients		Standardized Coefficients	t	Sig.
		B	Std. Error	Beta		
1	(Constant)	5.166	.412		12.530	.000
	educ HIGHEST YEAR OF SCHOOL COMPLETED	-.164	.029	-.196	-5.619	.000

a. Dependent Variable: tvhours HOURS PER DAY WATCHING TV

7. Based on the following SPSS output describe the regression model for educational attainment and amount of money given to charity based on GSS 2014.

   a. Assess the significance of the overall model based on its *F* and *p* values. What is the relationship between the two variables?

   b. Calculate the predicted charitable amount for a respondent with 14 years of education and for a respondent with 20 years of education.

Linear Regression Output for Amount of Money Given to Charity and Education

Model Summary

Model	R	R Square	Adjusted R Square	Std. Error of the Estimate
1	.169[a]	.028	.026	6108.241

a. Predictors: (Constant), educ HIGHEST YEAR OF SCHOOL COMPLETED

ANOVA[a]

Model		Sum of Squares	df	Mean Square	F	Sig.
1	Regression	394689548	1	394689548	10.578	.001[b]
	Residual	1.351E+10	362	37310613.5		
	Total	1.390E+10	363			

a. Dependent Variable: VALGIVEN TOTAL DONATIONS PAST YEAR R AND IMMEDIATE FAMILY

b. Predictors: (Constant), educ HIGHEST YEAR OF SCHOOL COMPLETED

Coefficients[a]

Model		Unstandardized Coefficients		Standardized Coefficients	t	Sig.
		B	Std. Error	Beta		
1	(Constant)	-2213.620	1293.760		-1.711	.088
	educ HIGHEST YEAR OF SCHOOL COMPLETED	304.106	93.500	.169	3.252	.001

a. Dependent Variable: VALGIVEN TOTAL DONATIONS PAST YEAR R AND IMMEDIATE FAMILY

8. Research on social mobility, status, and educational attainment has provided convincing evidence on the relationship between parents' and children's socioeconomic achievement. The GSS 2014 measures the educational level of respondents and their mothers. Use the scatterplot and regression output to describe the relationship between mothers' education and respondent's education.

Scatterplot of Respondent Level of Education by Mother's Level of Education

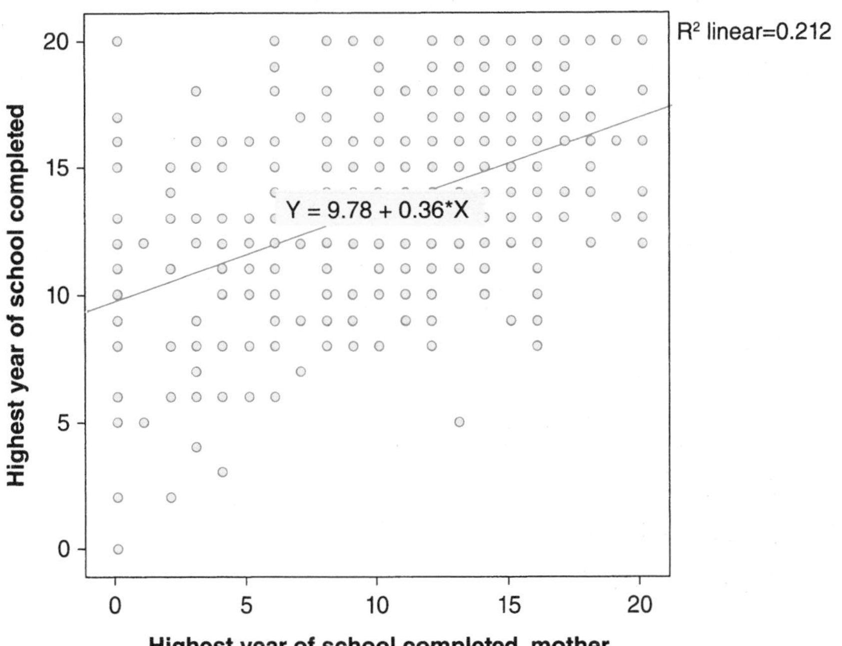

Linear Regression Output Specifying the Relationship Between Respondent's Education by Mother's Education

Model Summary

Model	R	R Square	Adjusted R Square	Std. Error of the Estimate
1	.461[a]	.212	.212	2.758

a. Predictors: (Constant), maeduc HIGHEST YEAR SCHOOL COMPLETED, MOTHER

ANOVA[a]

Model		Sum of Squares	df	Mean Square	F	Sig.
1	Regression	2188.528	1	2188.528	287.745	.000[b]
	Residual	8122.994	1068	7.606		
	Total	10311.522	1069			

a. Dependent Variable: educ HIGHEST YEAR OF SCHOOL COMPLETED

b. Predictors: (Constant), maeduc HIGHEST YEAR SCHOOL COMPLETED, MOTHER

Coefficients[a]

Model		Unstandardized Coefficients		Standardized Coefficients	t	Sig.
		B	Std. Error	Beta		
1	(Constant)	9.784	.259		37.731	.000
	maeduc HIGHEST YEAR SCHOOL COMPLETED, MOTHER	.360	.021	.461	16.963	.000

a. Dependent Variable: educ HIGHEST YEAR OF SCHOOL COMPLETED

9. We further explore the relationship between respondent's education and mother's education, computing regression models separately for males and females.

   a. Calculate the regression equation for each.

   b. What is the predicted value of respondent's education when mother's education is 20 years?

   c. For which gender group is the relationship between respondent's education and mother's education strongest? Explain.

Linear Regression Output Specifying the Relationship Between Respondent Level of Education by Mother's Level of Education: Males Only

Model Summary[a]

Model	R	R Square	Adjusted R Square	Std. Error of the Estimate
1	.450[b]	.202	.201	2.834

a. sex RESPONDENTS SEX = 1 MALE

b. Predictors: (Constant), maeduc HIGHEST YEAR SCHOOL COMPLETED, MOTHER

ANOVA[a,b]

Model		Sum of Squares	df	Mean Square	F	Sig.
1	Regression	976.149	1	976.149	121.559	.000[c]
	Residual	3846.500	479	8.030		
	Total	4822.649	480			

a. sex RESPONDENTS SEX = 1 MALE

b. Dependent Variable: educ HIGHEST YEAR OF SCHOOL COMPLETED

c. Predictors: (Constant), maeduc HIGHEST YEAR SCHOOL COMPLETED, MOTHER

Coefficients[a,b]

Model		Unstandardized Coefficients		Standardized Coefficients	t	Sig.
		B	Std. Error	Beta		
1	(Constant)	9.768	.403		24.258	.000
	maeduc HIGHEST YEAR SCHOOL COMPLETED, MOTHER	.355	.032	.450	11.025	.000

a. sex RESPONDENTS SEX = 1 MALE

b. Dependent Variable: educ HIGHEST YEAR OF SCHOOL COMPLETED

Linear Regression Output Specifying the Relationship Between Respondent Level of Education by Mother's Level of Education: Females Only

Model Summary[a]

Model	R	R Square	Adjusted R Square	Std. Error of the Estimate
1	.471[b]	.222	.221	2.697

a. sex RESPONDENTS SEX = 2 FEMALE

b. Predictors: (Constant), maeduc HIGHEST YEAR SCHOOL COMPLETED, MOTHER

ANOVA[a,b]

Model		Sum of Squares	df	Mean Square	F	Sig.
1	Regression	1217.765	1	1217.765	167.394	.000[c]
	Residual	4270.324	587	7.275		
	Total	5488.088	588			

a. sex RESPONDENTS SEX = 2 FEMALE

b. Dependent Variable: educ HIGHEST YEAR OF SCHOOL COMPLETED

c. Predictors: (Constant), maeduc HIGHEST YEAR SCHOOL COMPLETED, MOTHER

Coefficients[a,b]

Model		Unstandardized Coefficients		Standardized Coefficients	t	Sig.
		B	Std. Error	Beta		
1	(Constant)	9.770	.339		28.786	.000
	maeduc HIGHEST YEAR SCHOOL COMPLETED, MOTHER	.367	.028	.471	12.938	.000

a. sex RESPONDENTS SEX = 2 FEMALE

b. Dependent Variable: educ HIGHEST YEAR OF SCHOOL COMPLETED

10. In Exercise 6, we examined the relationship between years of education and hours of television watched per day. We saw that as education increases, hours of television viewing decreases. The number of children a family has could also affect how much television is viewed per day. Having children may lead to more shared and supervised viewing and thus increases the number of viewing hours. The following SPSS output displays the relationship between television viewing (measured in hours per day) and both education (measured in years) and number of children. We hypothesize that whereas more education may lead to less viewing, the number of children has the opposite effect: Having more children will result in more hours of viewing per day.

a. What is the b coefficient for education? For number of children? Interpret each coefficient. Is the relationship between each independent variable and hours of viewing as hypothesized?

b. Using the multiple regression equation with both education and number of children as independent variables, calculate the number of hours of television viewing for a person with 16 years of education and two children. Using the equation from Exercise 6, how do the results compare between a person with 16 years of education (number of children not included in the equation) and a person with 16 years of education with two children?

c. Compare the r^2 value from Exercise 6 with the R^2 value from this regression. Does using education and number of children jointly reduce the amount of error involved in predicting hours of television viewed per day?

Multiple Regression Output Specifying the Relationship Between Education, Number of Children, and Hours Spent per Day Watching Television

Model Summary

Model	R	R Square	Adjusted R Square	Std. Error of the Estimate
1	.200[a]	.040	.038	2.555

a. Predictors: (Constant), childs NUMBER OF CHILDREN, educ HIGHEST YEAR OF SCHOOL COMPLETED

ANOVA[a]

Model		Sum of Squares	df	Mean Square	F	Sig.
1	Regression	213.426	2	106.713	16.344	.000[b]
	Residual	5099.206	781	6.529		
	Total	5312.633	783			

a. Dependent Variable: tvhours HOURS PER DAY WATCHING TV

b. Predictors: (Constant), childs NUMBER OF CHILDREN, educ HIGHEST YEAR OF SCHOOL COMPLETED

Coefficients[a]

Model		Unstandardized Coefficients B	Unstandardized Coefficients Std. Error	Standardized Coefficients Beta	t	Sig.
1	(Constant)	5.095	.461		11.061	.000
	educ HIGHEST YEAR OF SCHOOL COMPLETED	-.164	.030	-.194	-5.422	.000
	childs NUMBER OF CHILDREN	.040	.056	.026	.714	.475

a. Dependent Variable: tvhours HOURS PER DAY WATCHING TV

11. We return to our chapter analysis of Internet hours per week (WWHR), educational attainment (EDUC), and respondent age (AGE), presenting the multiple regression model and correlation matrix based on GSS 2014 data.

a. What is the b coefficient for education? For age? Interpret each coefficient. Is the relationship between education and Internet hours as hypothesized in our chapter example? For age and Internet hours?

b. Using the multiple regression equation with both education and age as independent variables, calculate the number of Internet hours per week for a person with 16 years of education and 55 years of age.

c. Using the standardized multiple regression equation, identify which independent variable has the strongest effect on Internet hours per week.

d. Interpret the multiple coefficient of determination.

e. Interpret each correlation coefficient (based on the correlation matrix).

Multiple Regression Output for Internet Hours per Week, Educational Attainment, and Internet Hours per Week

Model Summary

Model	R	R Square	Adjusted R Square	Std. Error of the Estimate
1	.255[a]	.065	.061	15.406

a. Predictors: (Constant), age AGE OF RESPONDENT, educ HIGHEST YEAR OF SCHOOL COMPLETED

ANOVA[a]

Model		Sum of Squares	df	Mean Square	F	Sig.
1	Regression	6920.364	2	3460.182	14.579	.000[b]
	Residual	99448.621	419	237.348		
	Total	106368.986	421			

a. Dependent Variable: wwwhr WWW HOURS PER WEEK

b. Predictors: (Constant), age AGE OF RESPONDENT, educ HIGHEST YEAR OF SCHOOL COMPLETED

Coefficients[a]

Model		Unstandardized Coefficients		Standardized Coefficients	t	Sig.
		B	Std. Error	Beta		
1	(Constant)	14.395	4.202		3.426	.001
	educ HIGHEST YEAR OF SCHOOL COMPLETED	.598	.263	.108	2.271	.024
	age AGE OF RESPONDENT	-.236	.047	-.241	-5.080	.000

a. Dependent Variable: wwwhr WWW HOURS PER WEEK

Correlation Matrix for Internet Hours per Week, Educational Attainment, and Internet Hours per Week

Correlations

		wwwhr WWW HOURS PER WEEK	educ HIGHEST YEAR OF SCHOOL COMPLETED	age AGE OF RESPONDENT
wwwhr WWW HOURS PER WEEK	Pearson Correlation	1	.088	-.231**
	Sig. (2-tailed)		.071	.000
	N	423	423	422
educ HIGHEST YEAR OF SCHOOL COMPLETED	Pearson Correlation	.088	1	-.009
	Sig. (2-tailed)	.071		.749
	N	423	1179	1172
age AGE OF RESPONDENT	Pearson Correlation	-.231**	-.009	1
	Sig. (2-tailed)	.000	.749	
	N	422	1172	1172

**. Correlation is significant at the 0.01 level (2-tailed).

12. We revisit Katherine Purswell, Ani Yazedjian, and Michelle Toews' (2008)[9] research regarding the relationship between academic intentions (intention to perform specific behaviors related to learning engagement and positive academic behaviors), parental support, and peer support and self-reported academic behaviors (e.g., speaking in class, completed assignments on time during their freshman year) of first- and continuing-generation college students.

They estimated three separate models for first-generation students (Group 1), students with at least one parent with college experience but with no degree (Group 2), and students with at least one parent with a bachelor's degree or higher (Group 3). The correlation matrix is presented below.

All of the variables included in the analysis are ordinal measures, with responses coded on a *strongly disagree* to *strongly agree* scale.

Intercorrelations Between Variables Based on Parental Education Groups

	1	2	3	4
First Generation Students (n = 44)				
1. Intention	—	.34*	.11	.48**
2. Parental Support		—	.24	.15
3. Peer Support			—	.06
4. Behavior				—
Group 2 (*n* = 82)				
1. Intention	—	.30**	.49**	.32**
2. Parental Support		—	.31	.27*
3. Peer Support			—	.38**
4. Behavior				—
Group 3 (*n* = 203)				
1. Intention	—	.18*	.37**	.44*
2. Parental Support		—	.24**	.17*
3. Peer Support			—	.04
4. Behavior				—

Source: Adapted from Katherine Purswell, Ani Yazedjian, and Michelle Toews, "Students' Intentions and Social Support as Predictors of Self-Reported Academic Behaviors: A Comparison of First- and Continuing-Generation College Students," *Journal of College Student Retention* 10 no. 2 (2008): 199.

*$p < .05$, **$p < .01$.

a. Which group has the most significant correlations? Which group has the least?

b. Interpret the correlation for intention and behavior for the three groups. For which group is the relationship the strongest?

c. The correlation for peer support and intention is highest for which group? Explain.

13. We expand on the model presented in Exercise 10, adding work hours (HRS1) and respondent age (AGE) as independent variables. Data are based on the GSS 2014.

Model Summary

Model	R	R Square	Adjusted R Square	Std. Error of the Estimate
1	.289[a]	.083	.077	1.621

a. Predictors: (Constant), hrs1 NUMBER OF HOURS WORKED LAST WEEK, childs NUMBER OF CHILDREN, educ HIGHEST YEAR OF SCHOOL COMPLETED, age AGE OF RESPONDENT

ANOVA[a]

Model		Sum of Squares	df	Mean Square	F	Sig.
1	Regression	141.993	4	35.498	13.508	.000[b]
	Residual	1563.632	595	2.628		
	Total	1705.625	599			

a. Dependent Variable: tvhours HOURS PER DAY WATCHING TV

b. Predictors: (Constant), hrs1 NUMBER OF HOURS WORKED LAST WEEK, childs NUMBER OF CHILDREN, educ HIGHEST YEAR OF SCHOOL COMPLETED, age AGE OF RESPONDENT

Coefficients[a]

Model		Unstandardized Coefficients		Standardized Coefficients	t	Sig.
		B	Std. Error	Beta		
1	(Constant)	3.911	.432		9.062	.000
	educ HIGHEST YEAR OF SCHOOL COMPLETED	-.115	.023	-.202	-4.990	.000
	childs NUMBER OF CHILDREN	-.038	.048	-.034	-.788	.431
	age AGE OF RESPONDENT	.018	.005	.139	3.298	.001
	hrs1 NUMBER OF HOURS WORKED LAST WEEK	-.017	.004	-.148	-3.730	.000

a. Dependent Variable: tvhours HOURS PER DAY WATCHING TV

a. Write the multiple regression equation for the model. Interpret the slope for each independent variable.

b. Based on their beta scores, rank the independent variables according to the strength of their effect on TVHOURS (from the highest to the lowest).

c. Interpret the multiple coefficient of determination.

APPENDIX A

Table of Random Numbers

A Table of 14,000 Random Units

Line/ Col.	(1)	(2)	(3)	(4)	(5)	(6)	(7)	(8)	(9)	(10)	(11)	(12)	(13)	(14)
1	10480	15011	01536	02011	81647	91646	69179	14194	62590	36207	20969	99570	91291	90700
2	22368	46573	25595	85393	30995	89198	27982	53402	93965	34095	52666	19174	39615	99505
3	24130	48360	22527	97265	76393	64809	15179	24830	49340	32081	30680	19655	63348	58629
4	42167	93093	06243	61680	07856	16376	39440	53537	71341	57004	00849	74917	97758	16379
5	37570	39975	81837	16656	06121	91782	60468	81305	49684	60672	14110	06927	01263	54613
6	77921	06907	11008	42751	27756	53498	18602	70659	90655	15053	21916	81825	44394	42880
7	99562	72905	56420	69994	98872	31016	71194	18738	44013	48840	63213	21069	10634	12952
8	96301	91977	05463	07972	18876	20922	94595	56869	69014	60045	18425	84903	42508	32307
9	89579	14342	63661	10281	17453	18103	57740	84378	25331	12566	58678	44947	05585	56941
10	85475	36857	43342	53988	53060	59533	38867	62300	08158	17983	16439	11458	18593	64952
11	28918	69578	88231	33276	70997	79936	56865	05859	90106	31595	01547	85590	91610	78188
12	63553	40961	48235	03427	49626	69445	18663	72695	52180	20847	12234	90511	33703	90322
13	09429	93969	52636	92737	88974	33488	36320	17617	30015	08272	84115	27156	30613	74952
14	10365	61129	87529	85689	48237	52267	67689	93394	01511	26358	85104	20285	29975	89868
15	07119	97336	71048	08178	77233	13916	47564	81056	97735	85977	29372	74461	28551	90707
16	51085	12765	51821	51259	77452	16308	60756	92144	49442	53900	70960	63990	75601	40719
17	02368	21382	52404	60268	89368	19885	55322	44819	01188	65255	64835	44919	05944	55157
18	01011	54092	33362	94904	31273	04146	18594	29852	71585	85030	51132	01915	92747	64951
19	52162	53916	46369	58586	23216	14513	83149	98736	23495	64350	94738	17752	35156	35749
20	07056	97628	33787	09998	42698	06691	76988	13602	51851	46104	88916	19509	25625	58104
21	48663	91245	85828	14346	09172	30168	90229	04734	59193	22178	30421	61666	99904	32812
22	54164	58492	22421	74103	47070	25306	76468	26384	58151	06646	21524	15227	96909	44592
23	32639	32363	05597	24200	13363	38005	94342	28728	35806	06912	17012	64161	18296	22851
24	29334	27001	87637	87308	58731	00256	45834	15398	46557	41135	10367	07684	36188	18510
25	02488	33062	28834	07351	19731	92420	60952	61280	50001	67658	32586	86679	50720	94953
26	81525	72295	04839	96423	24878	82651	66566	14778	76797	14780	13300	87074	79666	95725
27	29676	20591	68086	26432	46901	20849	89768	81536	86645	12659	92259	57102	80428	25280
28	00742	57392	39064	66432	84673	40027	32832	61362	98947	96067	64760	64584	96096	98253

Line/ Col.	(1)	(2)	(3)	(4)	(5)	(6)	(7)	(8)	(9)	(10)	(11)	(12)	(13)	(14)
29	05366	04213	25669	26422	44407	44048	37937	63904	45766	66134	75470	66520	34693	90449
30	91921	26418	64117	94305	26766	25940	39972	22209	71500	64568	91402	42416	07844	69618
31	00582	04711	87917	77341	42206	35126	74087	99547	81817	42607	43808	76655	62028	76630
32	00725	69884	62797	56170	86324	88072	76222	36086	84637	93161	76038	65855	77919	88006
33	69011	65797	95876	55293	18988	27354	26575	08625	40801	59920	29841	80150	12777	48501
34	25976	57948	29888	88604	67917	48708	18912	82271	65424	69774	33611	54262	85963	03547
35	09763	83473	73577	12908	30883	18317	28290	35797	05998	41688	34952	37888	38917	88050
36	91567	42595	27958	30134	04024	86385	29880	99730	55536	84855	29080	09250	79656	73211
37	17955	56349	90999	49127	20044	59931	06115	20542	18059	02008	73708	83317	36103	42791
38	46503	18584	18845	49618	02304	51038	20655	58727	28168	15475	56942	53389	20562	87338
39	92157	89634	94824	78171	84610	82834	09922	25417	44137	48413	25555	21246	35509	20468
40	14577	62765	35605	81263	39667	47358	56873	56307	61607	49518	89656	20103	77490	18062
41	98427	07523	33362	64270	01638	92477	66969	98420	04880	45585	46565	04102	46880	45709
42	34914	63976	88720	82765	34476	17032	87589	40836	32427	70002	70663	88863	77775	69348
43	70060	28277	39475	46473	23219	53416	94970	25832	69975	94884	19661	72828	00102	66794
44	53976	54914	06990	67245	68350	82948	11398	42878	80287	88267	47363	46634	06541	97809
45	76072	29515	40980	07391	58745	25774	22987	80059	39911	96189	41151	14222	60697	59583
46	90725	52210	83974	29992	65831	38857	50490	83765	55657	14361	31720	57375	56228	41546
47	64364	67412	33339	31926	14883	24413	59744	92351	97473	89286	35931	04110	23726	51900
48	08962	00358	31662	25388	61642	34072	81249	35648	56891	69352	48373	45578	78547	81788
49	95012	68379	93526	70765	10593	04542	76463	54328	02349	17247	28865	14777	62730	92277
50	15664	10493	20492	38391	91132	21999	59516	81652	27195	48223	46751	22923	32261	85653
51	16408	81899	04153	53381	79401	21438	83035	92350	36693	31238	59649	91754	72772	02338
52	18629	81953	05520	91962	04739	13092	97662	24822	94730	06496	35090	04822	86772	98289
53	73115	35101	47498	87637	99016	71060	88824	71013	18735	20286	23153	72924	35165	43040
54	57491	16703	23167	49323	45021	33132	12544	41035	80780	45393	44812	12515	98931	91202
55	30405	83946	23792	14422	15059	45799	22716	19792	09983	74353	68668	30429	70735	25499
56	16631	35006	85900	98275	32388	52390	16815	69298	82732	38480	73817	32523	41961	44437
57	96773	20206	42559	78985	05300	22164	24369	54224	35083	19687	11052	91491	60383	19746
58	38935	64202	14349	82674	66523	44133	00697	35552	35970	19124	63318	29686	03387	59846
59	31624	76384	17403	53363	44167	64486	64758	75366	76554	31601	12614	33072	60332	92325
60	78919	19474	23632	27889	47914	02584	37680	20801	72152	39339	34806	08930	85001	87820
61	03931	33309	57047	74211	63445	17361	62825	39908	05607	91284	68833	25570	38818	46920
62	74426	33278	43972	10119	89917	15665	52872	73823	73144	88662	88970	74492	51805	99378
63	09066	00903	20795	95452	92648	45454	09552	88815	16553	51125	79375	97596	16296	66092
64	42238	12426	87025	14267	20979	04508	64535	31355	86064	29472	47689	05974	52468	16834
65	16153	08002	26504	41744	81959	65642	74240	56302	00033	67107	77510	70625	28725	34191
66	21457	40742	29820	96783	29400	21840	15035	34537	33310	06116	95240	15957	16572	06004

(Continued)

(Continued)

Line/ Col.	(1)	(2)	(3)	(4)	(5)	(6)	(7)	(8)	(9)	(10)	(11)	(12)	(13)	(14)
67	21581	57802	02050	89728	17937	37621	47075	42080	97403	48626	68995	43805	33386	21597
68	55612	78095	83197	33732	05810	24813	86902	60397	16489	03264	88525	42786	05269	92532
69	44657	66999	99324	51281	84463	60563	79312	93454	68876	25471	93911	25650	12682	73572
70	91340	84979	46949	81973	37949	61023	43997	15263	80644	43942	89203	71795	99533	50501
71	91227	21199	31935	27022	84067	05462	35216	14486	29891	68607	41867	14951	91696	85065
72	50001	38140	66321	19924	72163	09538	12151	06878	91903	18749	34405	56087	82790	70925
73	65390	05224	72958	28609	81406	39147	25549	48542	42627	45233	57202	94617	23772	07896
74	27504	96131	83944	41575	10573	08619	64482	73923	36152	05184	94142	25299	84387	34925
75	37169	94851	39117	89632	00959	16487	65536	49071	39782	17095	02330	74301	00275	48280
76	11508	70225	51111	38351	19444	66499	71945	05422	13442	78675	84081	66938	93654	59894
77	37449	30362	06694	54690	04052	53115	62757	95348	78662	11163	81651	50245	34971	52924
78	46515	70331	85922	38329	57015	15765	97161	17869	45349	61796	66345	81073	49106	79860
79	30986	81223	42416	58353	21532	30502	32305	86482	05174	07901	54339	58861	74818	46942
80	63798	64995	46583	09765	44160	78128	83991	42865	92520	83531	80377	35909	81250	54238
81	82486	84846	99254	67632	43218	50076	21361	64816	51202	88124	41870	52689	51275	83556
82	21885	32906	92431	09060	64297	51674	64126	62570	26123	05155	59194	52799	28225	85762
83	60336	98782	07408	53458	13564	59089	26445	29789	85205	41001	12535	12133	14645	23541
84	43937	46891	24010	25560	86355	33941	25786	54990	71899	15475	95434	98227	21824	19585
85	97656	63175	89303	16275	07100	92063	21942	18611	47348	20203	18534	03862	78095	50136
86	03299	01221	05418	38982	55758	92237	26759	86367	21216	98442	08303	56613	91511	75928
87	79626	06486	03574	17668	07785	76020	79924	25651	83325	88428	85076	72811	22717	50585
88	85636	68335	47539	03129	65651	11977	02510	26113	99447	68645	34327	15152	55230	93448
89	18039	14367	61337	06177	12143	46609	32989	74014	64708	00533	35398	58408	13261	47908
90	08362	15656	60627	36478	65648	16764	53412	09013	07832	41574	17639	82163	60859	75567
91	79556	29068	04142	16268	15387	12856	66227	38358	22478	73373	88732	09443	82558	05250
92	92608	82674	27072	32534	17075	27698	98204	63863	11951	34648	88022	56148	34925	57031
93	23982	25835	40055	67006	12293	02753	14827	22235	35071	99704	37543	11601	35503	85171
94	09915	96306	05908	97901	28395	14186	00821	80703	70426	75647	76310	88717	37890	40129
95	50937	33300	26695	62247	69927	76123	50842	43834	86654	70959	79725	93872	28117	19233
96	42488	78077	69882	61657	34136	79180	97526	43092	04098	73571	80799	76536	71255	64239
97	46764	86273	63003	93017	31204	36692	40202	35275	57306	55543	53203	18098	47625	88684
98	03237	45430	55417	63282	90816	17349	88298	90183	36600	78406	06216	95787	42579	90730
99	86591	81482	52667	61583	14972	90053	89534	76036	49199	43716	97548	04379	46370	28672
100	38534	01715	94964	87288	65680	43772	39560	12918	86537	62738	19636	51132	25739	56947

Source: William H. Beyer, ed., *Handbook for Probability and Statistics*, 2nd ed. Copyright © 1966 CRC Press, Boca Raton, Florida. Used by permission.

APPENDIX B

The Standard Normal Table

The values in column A are Z scores. Column B lists the proportion of area between the mean and a given Z. Column C lists the proportion of area beyond a given Z. Only positive Z scores are listed. Because the normal curve is symmetrical, the areas for negative Z scores will be exactly the same as the areas for positive Z scores.

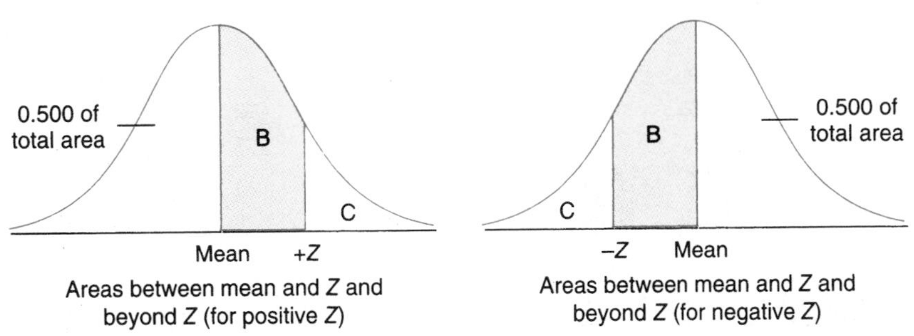

A Z	B Area Between Mean and Z	C Area Beyond Z	A Z	B Area Between Mean and Z	C Area Beyond Z	A Z	B Area Between Mean and Z	C Area Beyond Z
0.00	0.0000	0.5000	0.11	0.0438	0.4562	0.21	0.0832	0.4168
0.01	0.0040	0.4960	0.12	0.0478	0.4522	0.22	0.0871	0.4129
0.02	0.0080	0.4920	0.13	0.0517	0.4483	0.23	0.0910	0.4090
0.03	0.0120	0.4880	0.14	0.0557	0.4443	0.24	0.0948	0.4052
0.04	0.0160	0.4840	0.15	0.0596	0.4404	0.25	0.0987	0.4013
0.05	0.0199	0.4801	0.16	0.0636	0.4364	0.26	0.1026	0.3974
0.06	0.0239	0.4761	0.17	0.0675	0.4325	0.27	0.1064	0.3936
0.07	0.0279	0.4721	0.18	0.0714	0.4286	0.28	0.1103	0.3897
0.08	0.0319	0.4681	0.19	0.0753	0.4247	0.29	0.1141	0.3859
0.09	0.0359	0.4641	0.20	0.0793	0.4207	0.30	0.1179	0.3821
0.10	0.0398	0.4602						

(Continued)

(Continued)

A Z	B Area Between Mean and Z	C Area Beyond Z	A Z	B Area Between Mean and Z	C Area Beyond Z	A Z	B Area Between Mean and Z	C Area Beyond Z
0.31	0.1217	0.3783	0.71	0.2611	0.2389	1.11	0.3665	0.1335
0.32	0.1255	0.3745	0.72	0.2642	0.2358	1.12	0.3686	0.1314
0.33	0.1293	0.3707	0.73	0.2673	0.2327	1.13	0.3708	0.1292
0.34	0.1331	0.3669	0.74	0.2703	0.2297	1.14	0.3729	0.1271
0.35	0.1368	0.3632	0.75	0.2734	0.2266	1.15	0.3749	0.1251
0.36	0.1406	0.3594	0.76	0.2764	0.2236	1.16	0.3770	0.1230
0.37	0.1443	0.3557	0.77	0.2794	0.2206	1.17	0.3790	0.1210
0.38	0.1480	0.3520	0.78	0.2823	0.2177	1.18	0.3810	0.1190
0.39	0.1517	0.3483	0.79	0.2852	0.2148	1.19	0.3830	0.1170
0.40	0.1554	0.3446	0.80	0.2881	0.2119	1.20	0.3849	0.1151
0.41	0.1591	0.3409	0.81	0.2910	0.2090	1.21	0.3869	0.1131
0.42	0.1628	0.3372	0.82	0.2939	0.2061	1.22	0.3888	0.1112
0.43	0.1664	0.3336	0.83	0.2967	0.2033	1.23	0.3907	0.1093
0.44	0.1700	0.3300	0.84	0.2995	0.2005	1.24	0.3925	0.1075
0.45	0.1736	0.3264	0.85	0.3023	0.1977	1.25	0.3944	0.1056
0.46	0.1772	0.3228	0.86	0.3051	0.1949	1.26	0.3962	0.1038
0.47	0.1808	0.3192	0.87	0.3078	0.1992	1.27	0.3980	0.1020
0.48	0.1844	0.3156	0.88	0.3106	0.1894	1.28	0.3997	0.1003
0.49	0.1879	0.3121	0.89	0.3133	0.1867	1.29	0.4015	0.0985
0.50	0.1915	0.3085	0.90	0.3159	0.1841	1.30	0.4032	0.0968
0.51	0.1950	0.3050	0.91	0.3186	0.1814	1.31	0.4049	0.0951
0.52	0.1985	0.3015	0.92	0.3212	0.1788	1.32	0.4066	0.0934
0.53	0.2019	0.2981	0.93	0.3238	0.1762	1.33	0.4082	0.0918
0.54	0.2054	0.2946	0.94	0.3264	0.1736	1.34	0.4099	0.0901
0.55	0.2088	0.2912	0.95	0.3289	0.1711	1.35	0.4115	0.0885
0.56	0.2123	0.2877	0.96	0.3315	0.1685	1.36	0.4131	0.0869
0.57	0.2157	0.2843	0.97	0.3340	0.1660	1.37	0.4147	0.0853
0.58	0.2190	0.2810	0.98	0.3365	0.1635	1.38	0.4612	0.0838
0.59	0.2224	0.2776	0.99	0.3389	0.1611	1.39	0.4177	0.0823
0.60	0.2257	0.2743	1.00	0.3413	0.1587	1.40	0.4192	0.0808
0.61	0.2291	0.2709	1.01	0.3438	0.1562	1.41	0.4207	0.0793
0.62	0.2324	0.2676	1.02	0.3461	0.1539	1.42	0.4222	0.0778
0.63	0.2357	0.2643	1.03	0.3485	0.1515	1.43	0.4236	0.0764
0.64	0.2389	0.2611	1.04	0.3508	0.1492	1.44	0.4251	0.0749
0.65	0.2422	0.2578	1.05	0.3531	0.1469	1.45	0.4265	0.0735
0.66	0.2454	0.2546	1.06	0.3554	0.1446	1.46	0.4279	0.0721
0.67	0.2486	0.2514	1.07	0.3577	0.1423	1.47	0.4292	0.0708
0.68	0.2517	0.2483	1.08	0.3599	0.1401	1.48	0.4306	0.0694
0.69	0.2549	0.2451	1.09	0.3621	0.1379	1.49	0.4319	0.0681
0.70	0.2580	0.2420	1.10	0.3643	0.1357	1.50	0.4332	0.0668

A	B	C	A	B	C	A	B	C
Z	Area Between Mean and Z	Area Beyond Z	Z	Area Between Mean and Z	Area Beyond Z	Z	Area Between Mean and Z	Area Beyond Z
1.51	0.4345	0.0655	1.91	0.4719	0.0281	2.31	0.4896	0.0104
1.52	0.4357	0.0643	1.92	0.4726	0.0274	2.32	0.4898	0.0102
1.53	0.4370	0.0630	1.93	0.4732	0.0268	2.33	0.4901	0.0099
1.54	0.4382	0.0618	1.94	0.4738	0.0262	2.34	0.4904	0.0096
1.55	0.4394	0.0606	1.95	0.4744	0.0256	2.35	0.4906	0.0094
1.56	0.4406	0.0594	1.96	0.4750	0.0250	2.36	0.4909	0.0091
1.57	0.4418	0.0582	1.97	0.4756	0.0244	2.37	0.4911	0.0089
1.58	0.4429	0.0571	1.98	0.4761	0.0239	2.38	0.4913	0.0087
1.59	0.4441	0.0559	1.99	0.4767	0.0233	2.39	0.4916	0.0084
1.60	0.4452	0.0548	2.00	0.4772	0.0228	2.40	0.4918	0.0082
1.61	0.4463	0.0537	2.01	0.4778	0.0222	2.41	0.4920	0.0080
1.62	0.4474	0.0526	2.02	0.4783	0.0217	2.42	0.4922	0.0078
1.63	0.4484	0.0516	2.03	0.4788	0.0212	2.43	0.4925	0.0075
1.64	0.4495	0.0505	2.04	0.4793	0.0207	2.44	0.4927	0.0073
1.65	0.4505	0.0495	2.05	0.4798	0.0202	2.45	0.4929	0.0071
1.66	0.4515	0.0485	2.06	0.4803	0.0197	2.46	0.4931	0.0069
1.67	0.4525	0.0475	2.07	0.4808	0.0192	2.47	0.4932	0.0068
1.68	0.4535	0.0465	2.08	0.4812	0.0188	2.48	0.4934	0.0066
1.69	0.4545	0.0455	2.09	0.4817	0.0183	2.49	0.4936	0.0064
1.70	0.4554	0.0466	2.10	0.4821	0.0179	2.50	0.4938	0.0062
1.71	0.4564	0.0436	2.11	0.4826	0.0174	2.51	0.4940	0.0060
1.72	0.4573	0.0427	2.12	0.4830	0.0170	2.52	0.4941	0.0059
1.73	0.4582	0.0418	2.13	0.4834	0.0166	2.53	0.4943	0.0057
1.74	0.4591	0.0409	2.14	0.4838	0.0162	2.54	0.4945	0.0055
1.75	0.4599	0.0401	2.15	0.4842	0.0158	2.55	0.4946	0.0054
1.76	0.4608	0.0392	2.16	0.4846	0.0154	2.56	0.4948	0.0052
1.77	0.4616	0.0384	2.17	0.4850	0.0150	2.57	0.4949	0.0051
1.78	0.4625	0.0375	2.18	0.4854	0.0146	2.58	0.4951	0.0049
1.79	0.4633	0.0367	2.19	0.4857	0.0143	2.59	0.4952	0.0048
1.80	0.4641	0.0359	2.20	0.4861	0.0139	2.60	0.4953	0.0047
1.81	0.4649	0.0351	2.21	0.4864	0.0136	2.61	0.4955	0.0045
1.82	0.4656	0.0344	2.22	0.4868	0.0132	2.62	0.4956	0.0044
1.83	0.4664	0.0336	2.23	0.4871	0.0129	2.63	0.4957	0.0043
1.84	0.4671	0.0329	2.24	0.4875	0.0125	2.64	0.4959	0.0041
1.85	0.4678	0.0322	2.25	0.4878	0.0122	2.65	0.4960	0.0040
1.86	0.4686	0.0314	2.26	0.4881	0.0119	2.66	0.4961	0.0039
1.87	0.4693	0.0307	2.27	0.4884	0.0116	2.67	0.4962	0.0038
1.88	0.4699	0.0301	2.28	0.4887	0.0113	2.68	0.4963	0.0037
1.89	0.4706	0.0294	2.29	0.4890	0.0110	2.69	0.4964	0.0036
1.90	0.4713	0.0287	2.30	0.4893	0.0107	2.70	0.4965	0.0035

(Continued)

(Continued)

A Z	B Area Between Mean and Z	C Area Beyond Z	A Z	B Area Between Mean and Z	C Area Beyond Z	A Z	B Area Between Mean and Z	C Area Beyond Z
2.71	0.4966	0.0034	3.01	0.4987	0.0013	3.31	0.4995	0.0005
2.72	0.4967	0.0033	3.02	0.4987	0.0013	3.32	0.4995	0.0005
2.73	0.4968	0.0032	3.03	0.4988	0.0012	3.33	0.4996	0.0004
2.74	0.4969	0.0031	3.04	0.4988	0.0012	3.34	0.4996	0.0004
2.75	0.4970	0.0030	3.05	0.4989	0.0011	3.35	0.4996	0.0004
2.76	0.4971	0.0029	3.06	0.4989	0.0011	3.36	0.4996	0.0004
2.77	0.4972	0.0028	3.07	0.4989	0.0011	3.37	0.4996	0.0004
2.78	0.4973	0.0027	3.08	0.4990	0.0010	3.38	0.4996	0.0004
2.79	0.4974	0.0026	3.09	0.4990	0.0010	3.39	0.4997	0.0003
2.80	0.4974	0.0026	3.10	0.4990	0.0010	3.40	0.4997	0.0003
2.81	0.4975	0.0025	3.11	0.4991	0.0009	3.41	0.4997	0.0003
2.82	0.4976	0.0024	3.12	0.4991	0.0009	3.42	0.4997	0.0003
2.83	0.4977	0.0023	3.13	0.4991	0.0009	3.43	0.4997	0.0003
2.84	0.4977	0.0023	3.14	0.4992	0.0008	3.44	0.4997	0.0003
2.85	0.4978	0.0022	3.15	0.4992	0.0008	3.45	0.4997	0.0003
2.86	0.4979	0.0021	3.16	0.4992	0.0008	3.46	0.4997	0.0003
2.87	0.4979	0.0021	3.17	0.4992	0.0008	3.47	0.4997	0.0003
2.88	0.4980	0.0020	3.18	0.4993	0.0007	3.48	0.4997	0.0003
2.89	0.4981	0.0019	3.19	0.4993	0.0007	3.49	0.4998	0.0002
2.90	0.4981	0.0019	3.20	0.4993	0.0007	3.50	0.4998	0.0002
2.91	0.4982	0.0018	3.21	0.4993	0.0007	3.60	0.4998	0.0002
2.92	0.4982	0.0018	3.22	0.4994	0.0006	3.70	0.4999	0.0001
2.93	0.4983	0.0017	3.23	0.4994	0.0006	3.80	0.4999	0.0001
2.94	0.4984	0.0016	3.24	0.4994	0.0006	3.90	0.4999	<0.0001
2.95	0.4984	0.0016	3.25	0.4994	0.0006	4.00	0.4999	<0.0001
2.96	0.4985	0.0015	3.26	0.4994	0.0006			
2.97	0.4985	0.0015	3.27	0.4995	0.0005			
2.98	0.4986	0.0014	3.28	0.4995	0.0005			
2.99	0.4986	0.0014	3.29	0.4995	0.0005			
3.00	0.4986	0.0014	3.30	0.4995	0.0005			

APPENDIX C

Distribution of *t*

df	Level of Significance for One-Tailed Test					
	.10	.05	.025	.01	.005	.0005
	Level of Significance for Two-Tailed Test					
	.20	.10	.05	.02	.01	.001
1	3.078	6.314	12.706	31.821	63.657	636.619
2	1.886	2.920	4.303	6.965	9.925	31.598
3	1.638	2.353	3.182	4.541	5.841	12.941
4	1.533	2.132	2.776	3.747	4.604	8.610
5	1.476	2.015	2.571	3.365	4.032	6.859
6	1.440	1.943	2.447	3.143	3.707	5.959
7	1.415	1.895	2.365	2.998	3.499	5.405
8	1.397	1.860	2.306	2.896	3.355	5.041
9	1.383	1.833	2.262	2.821	3.250	4.781
10	1.372	1.812	2.228	2.764	3.169	4.587
11	1.363	1.796	2.201	2.718	3.106	4.437
12	1.356	1.782	2.179	2.681	3.055	4.318
13	1.350	1.771	2.160	2.650	3.012	4.221
14	1.345	1.761	2.145	2.624	2.977	4.140
15	1.341	1.753	2.131	2.602	2.947	4.073
16	1.337	1.746	2.120	2.583	2.921	4.015
17	1.333	1.740	2.110	2.567	2.898	3.965
18	1.330	1.734	2.101	2.552	2.878	3.922
19	1.328	1.729	2.093	2.539	2.861	3.883
20	1.325	1.725	2.086	2.528	2.845	3.850
21	1.323	1.721	2.080	2.518	2.831	3.819
22	1.321	1.717	2.074	2.508	2.819	3.792
23	1.319	1.714	2.069	2.500	2.807	3.767
24	1.318	1.711	2.064	2.492	2.797	3.745
25	1.316	1.708	2.060	2.485	2.787	3.725
26	1.315	1.706	2.056	2.479	2.779	3.707
27	1.314	1.703	2.052	2.473	2.771	3.690
28	1.313	1.701	2.048	2.467	2.763	3.674
29	1.311	1.699	2.045	2.462	2.756	3.659
30	1.310	1.697	2.042	2.457	2.750	3.646
40	1.303	1.684	2.021	2.423	2.704	3.551
60	1.296	1.671	2.000	2.390	2.660	3.460
120	1.289	1.658	1.980	2.358	2.617	3.373
∞	1.282	1.645	1.960	2.326	2.576	3.291

Source: Abridged from R. A. Fisher and F. Yates, *Statistical Tables for Biological, Agricultural and Medical Research*, 6th ed. Copyright © R. A. Fisher and F. Yates 1963. Reprinted by permission of Pearson Education Limited.

APPENDIX D

Distribution of Chi-Square

df	.99	.98	.95	.90	.80	.70	.50	.30	.20	.10	.05	.02	.01	.001
1	.03157	.03628	.00393	.0158	.0642	.148	.455	1.074	1.642	2.706	3.841	5.412	6.635	10.827
2	.0201	.0404	.103	.211	.446	.713	1.386	2.408	3.219	4.605	5.991	7.824	9.210	13.815
3	.115	.185	.352	.584	1.005	1.424	2.366	3.665	4.642	6.251	7.815	9.837	11.341	16.268
4	.297	.429	.711	1.064	1.649	2.195	3.357	4.878	5.989	7.779	9.488	11.668	13.277	18.465
5	.554	.752	1.145	1.610	2.343	3.000	4.351	6.064	7.289	9.236	11.070	13.388	15.086	20.517
6	.872	1.134	1.635	2.204	3.070	3.828	5.348	7.231	8.558	10.645	12.592	15.033	16.812	22.457
7	1.239	1.564	2.167	2.833	3.822	4.671	6.346	8.383	9.803	12.017	14.067	16.622	18.475	24.322
8	1.646	2.032	2.733	3.490	4.594	5.527	7.344	9.524	11.030	13.362	15.507	18.168	20.090	26.125
9	2.088	2.532	3.325	4.168	5.380	6.393	8.343	10.656	12.242	14.684	16.919	19.679	21.666	27.877
10	2.558	3.059	3.940	4.865	6.179	7.267	9.342	11.781	13.442	15.987	18.307	21.161	23.209	29.588
11	3.053	3.609	4.575	5.578	6.989	8.148	10.341	12.899	14.631	17.275	19.675	22.618	24.725	31.264
12	3.571	4.178	5.226	6.304	7.807	9.034	11.340	14.011	15.812	18.549	21.026	24.054	26.217	32.909
13	4.107	4.765	5.892	7.042	8.634	9.926	12.340	15.119	16.985	19.812	22.362	25.472	27.688	34.528
14	4.660	5.368	6.571	7.790	9.467	10.821	13.339	16.222	18.151	21.064	23.685	26.873	29.141	36.123
15	5.229	5.985	7.261	8.547	10.307	11.721	14.339	17.322	19.311	22.307	24.996	28.259	30.578	37.697
16	5.812	6.614	7.962	9.312	11.152	12.624	15.338	18.418	20.465	23.542	26.296	29.633	32.000	39.252
17	6.408	7.255	8.672	10.085	12.002	13.531	16.338	19.511	21.615	24.769	27.587	30.995	33.409	40.790
18	7.015	7.906	9.390	10.865	12.857	14.440	17.338	20.601	22.760	25.989	28.869	32.346	34.805	42.312
19	7.633	8.567	10.117	11.651	13.716	15.352	18.338	21.689	23.900	27.204	30.144	33.687	36.191	43.820
20	8.260	9.237	10.851	12.443	14.578	16.266	19.337	22.775	25.038	28.412	31.410	35.020	37.566	45.315
21	8.897	9.915	11.591	13.240	15.445	17.182	20.337	23.858	26.171	29.615	32.671	36.343	38.932	46.797
22	9.542	10.600	12.338	14.041	16.314	18.101	21.337	24.939	27.301	30.813	33.924	37.659	40.289	48.268
23	10.196	11.293	13.091	14.848	17.187	19.021	22.337	26.018	28.429	32.007	35.172	38.968	41.638	49.728
24	10.856	11.992	13.848	15.659	18.062	19.943	23.337	27.096	29.553	33.196	36.415	40.270	42.980	51.179
25	11.524	12.697	14.611	16.473	18.940	20.867	24.337	28.172	30.675	34.382	37.652	41.566	44.314	52.620
26	12.198	13.409	15.379	17.292	19.820	21.792	25.336	29.246	31.795	35.563	38.885	42.856	45.642	54.052
27	12.879	14.125	16.151	18.114	20.703	22.719	26.336	30.319	32.912	36.741	40.113	44.140	46.963	55.476
28	13.565	14.847	16.928	18.939	21.588	23.647	27.336	31.391	34.027	37.916	41.337	45.419	48.278	56.893
29	14.256	15.574	17.708	19.768	22.475	24.577	28.336	32.461	35.139	39.087	42.557	46.693	49.588	58.302
30	14.953	16.306	18.493	20.599	23.364	25.508	29.336	33.530	36.250	40.256	43.773	47.962	50.892	59.703

Source: R. A. Fisher & F. Yates, *Statistical Tables for Biological, Agricultural and Medical* Research, 6th ed.

APPENDIX E

Distribution of *F*

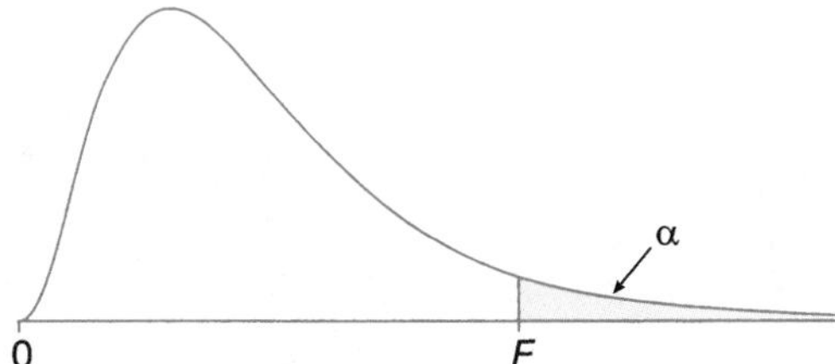

$\alpha = .05$										
	df_1									
df_2	1	2	3	4	5	6	8	12	24	∞
1	161.4	199.5	215.7	224.6	230.2	234.0	238.9	243.9	249.0	254.3
2	18.51	19.00	19.16	19.25	19.30	19.33	19.37	19.41	19.45	19.50
3	10.13	9.55	9.28	9.12	9.01	8.94	8.84	8.74	8.64	8.53
4	7.71	6.94	6.59	6.39	6.26	6.16	6.04	5.91	5.77	5.63
5	6.61	5.79	5.41	5.19	5.05	4.95	4.82	4.68	4.53	4.36
6	5.99	5.14	4.76	4.53	4.39	4.28	4.15	4.00	3.84	3.67
7	5.59	4.74	4.35	4.12	3.97	3.87	3.73	3.57	3.41	3.23
8	5.32	4.46	4.07	3.84	3.69	3.58	3.44	3.28	3.12	2.93
9	5.12	4.26	3.86	3.63	3.48	3.37	3.23	3.07	2.90	2.71
10	4.96	4.10	3.71	3.48	3.33	3.22	3.07	2.91	2.74	2.54
11	4.84	3.98	3.59	3.36	3.20	3.09	2.95	2.79	2.61	2.40
12	4.75	3.88	3.49	3.26	3.11	3.00	2.85	2.69	2.50	2.30
13	4.67	3.80	3.41	3.18	3.02	2.92	2.77	2.60	2.42	2.21
14	4.60	3.74	3.34	3.11	2.96	2.85	2.70	2.53	2.35	2.13
15	4.54	3.68	3.29	3.06	2.90	2.79	2.64	2.48	2.29	2.07
16	4.49	3.63	3.24	3.01	2.85	2.74	2.59	2.42	2.24	2.01
17	4.45	3.59	3.20	2.96	2.81	2.70	2.55	2.38	2.19	1.96
18	4.41	3.55	3.16	2.93	2.77	2.66	2.51	2.34	2.15	1.92
19	4.38	3.52	3.13	2.90	2.74	2.63	2.48	2.31	2.11	1.88
20	4.35	3.49	3.10	2.87	2.71	2.60	2.45	2.28	2.08	1.84
21	4.32	3.47	3.07	2.84	2.68	2.57	2.42	2.25	2.05	1.81
22	4.30	3.44	3.05	2.82	2.66	2.55	2.40	2.23	2.03	1.78
23	4.28	3.42	3.03	2.80	2.64	2.53	2.38	2.20	2.00	1.76
24	4.26	3.40	3.01	2.78	2.62	2.51	2.36	2.18	1.98	1.73
25	4.24	3.38	2.99	2.76	2.60	2.49	2.34	2.16	1.96	1.71
26	4.22	3.37	2.98	2.74	2.59	2.47	2.32	2.15	1.95	1.69

(Continued)

(Continued)

α = .05										
	df$_1$									
df$_2$	1	2	3	4	5	6	8	12	24	∞
27	4.21	3.35	2.96	2.73	2.57	2.46	2.30	2.13	1.93	1.67
28	4.20	3.34	2.95	2.71	2.56	2.44	2.29	2.12	1.91	1.65
29	4.18	3.33	2.93	2.70	2.54	2.43	2.28	2.10	1.90	1.64
30	4.17	3.32	2.92	2.69	2.53	2.42	2.27	2.09	1.89	1.62
40	4.08	3.23	2.84	2.61	2.45	2.34	2.18	2.00	1.79	1.51
60	4.00	3.15	2.76	2.52	2.37	2.25	2.10	1.92	1.70	1.39
120	3.92	3.07	2.68	2.45	2.29	2.17	2.02	1.83	1.61	1.25
∞	3.84	2.99	2.60	2.37	2.21	2.09	1.94	1.75	1.52	1.00

α = .01										
	df$_1$									
df$_2$	1	2	3	4	5	6	8	12	24	∞
1	4052	4999	5403	5625	5764	5859	5981	6106	6234	6366
2	98.49	99.01	99.17	99.25	99.30	99.33	99.36	99.42	99.46	99.50
3	34.12	30.81	29.46	28.71	28.24	27.91	27.49	27.05	26.60	26.12
4	21.20	18.00	16.69	15.98	15.52	15.21	14.80	14.37	13.93	13.46
5	16.26	13.27	12.06	11.39	10.97	10.67	10.27	9.89	9.47	9.02
6	13.74	10.92	9.78	9.15	8.75	8.47	8.10	7.72	7.31	6.88
7	12.25	9.55	8.45	7.85	7.46	7.19	6.84	6.47	6.07	5.65
8	11.26	8.65	7.59	7.01	6.63	6.37	6.03	5.67	5.28	4.86
9	10.56	8.02	6.99	6.42	6.06	5.80	5.47	5.11	4.73	4.31
10	10.04	7.56	6.55	5.99	5.64	5.39	5.06	4.71	4.33	3.91
11	9.65	7.20	6.22	5.67	5.32	5.07	4.74	4.40	4.02	3.60
12	9.33	6.93	5.95	5.41	5.06	4.82	4.50	4.16	3.78	3.36
13	9.07	6.70	5.74	5.20	4.86	4.62	4.30	3.96	3.59	3.16
14	8.86	6.51	5.56	5.03	4.69	4.46	4.14	3.80	3.43	3.00
15	8.68	6.36	5.42	4.89	4.56	4.32	4.00	3.67	3.29	2.87
16	8.53	6.23	5.29	4.77	4.44	4.20	3.89	3.55	3.18	2.75
17	8.40	6.11	5.18	4.67	4.34	4.10	3.79	3.45	3.08	2.65
18	8.28	6.01	5.09	4.58	4.25	4.01	3.71	3.37	3.00	2.57
19	8.18	5.93	5.01	4.50	4.17	3.94	3.63	3.30	2.92	2.49
20	8.10	5.85	4.94	4.43	4.10	3.87	3.56	3.23	2.86	2.42
21	8.02	5.78	4.87	4.37	4.04	3.81	3.51	3.17	2.80	2.36
22	7.94	5.72	4.82	4.31	3.99	3.76	3.45	3.12	2.75	2.31
23	7.88	5.66	4.76	4.23	3.94	3.71	3.41	3.07	2.70	2.26
24	7.82	5.61	4.72	4.22	3.90	3.67	3.36	3.03	2.66	2.21
25	7.77	5.57	4.68	4.18	3.86	3.63	3.32	2.99	2.62	2.17
26	7.72	5.53	4.64	4.14	3.82	3.59	3.29	2.96	2.58	2.13
27	7.68	5.49	4.60	4.11	3.78	3.56	3.26	2.93	2.55	2.10
28	7.64	5.45	4.57	4.07	3.75	3.53	3.23	2.90	2.52	2.06
29	7.60	5.42	4.54	4.04	3.73	3.50	3.20	2.87	2.49	2.03
30	7.56	5.39	4.51	4.02	3.70	3.47	3.17	2.84	2.47	2.01
40	7.31	5.18	4.31	3.83	3.51	3.29	2.99	2.66	2.29	1.80
60	7.08	4.98	4.13	3.65	3.34	3.12	2.82	2.50	2.12	1.60
120	6.85	4.79	3.95	3.48	3.17	2.96	2.66	2.34	1.95	1.38
∞	6.64	4.60	3.78	3.32	3.02	2.80	2.51	2.18	1.79	1.00

APPENDIX F

A Basic Math Review

by James Harris

You have probably already heard that there is a lot of math in statistics, and for this reason you are somewhat anxious about taking a statistics course. Although it is true that courses in statistics can involve a great deal of mathematics, you should be relieved to hear that this course will stress interpretation rather than the ability to solve complex mathematical problems. With that said, however, you will still need to know how to perform some basic mathematical operations as well as understand the meanings of certain symbols used in statistics. Following is a review of the symbols and math you will need to know to successfully complete this course.

SYMBOLS AND EXPRESSIONS USED IN STATISTICS

Statistics provides us with a set of tools for describing and analyzing *variables*. A variable is an attribute that can vary in some way. For example, a person's age is a variable because it can range from just born to more than one hundred years old. "Race" and "gender" are also variables, though with fewer categories than the variable "age." In statistics, variables you are interested in measuring are often given a symbol. For example, if we wanted to know something about the age of students in our statistics class, we would use the symbol Y to represent the variable "age." Now let's say for simplicity we asked only the students sitting in the first row their ages—19, 21, 23, and 32. These four ages would be scores of the Y variable.

Another symbol that you will frequently encounter in statistics is Σ, or uppercase sigma. Sigma is a Greek letter that stands for summation in statistics. In other words, when you see the symbol Σ, it means you should sum all of the scores. An example will make this clear. Using our sample of students' ages represented by Y, the use of sigma as in the expression ΣY (read as: the sum of Y) tells us to sum all the scores of the variable Y. Using our example, we would find the sum of the set of scores from the variable "age" by adding the scores together:

$$19 + 21 + 23 + 32 = 95$$

So, for the variable "age," $\Sigma Y = 95$.

Sigma is also often used in expressions with an exponent, as in the expression ΣY^2 (read as: the sum of squared scores). This means that we should first square all the scores of the Y

variable and then sum the squared products. So using the same set of scores, we would solve the expression by squaring each score first and then adding them together:

$$19^2 + 21^2 + 23^2 + 32^2 = 361 + 441 + 529 + 1{,}024 = 2{,}355$$

So, for the variable "age," $\Sigma Y^2 = 2{,}355$.

A similar, but slightly different, expression, which illustrates the function of parentheses, is $(\Sigma Y)^2$ (read as: the sum of scores, squared). In this expression, the parentheses tell us to first sum all the scores and then square this summed total. Parentheses are often used in expressions in statistics, and they always tell us to perform the expression within the parentheses first and then the part of the problem that is outside of the parentheses. To solve this expression, we need to sum all the scores first. However, we already found that $\Sigma Y = 95$, so to solve the expression $(\Sigma Y)^2$, we simply square this summed total,

$$95^2 = 9{,}025$$

So, for the variable "age," $(\Sigma Y)^2 = 9{,}025$.

You should also be familiar with the different symbols that denote multiplication and division. Most students are familiar with the times sign (×); however, there are several other ways to express multiplication. For example,

$$3(4) \quad (5)6 \quad (4)(2) \quad 7 \cdot 8 \quad 9 * 6$$

all symbolize the operation of multiplication. In this text, the first three are most often used to denote multiplication. There are also several ways division can be expressed. You are probably familiar with the conventional division sign (÷), but division can also be expressed in these other ways:

$$4/6 \quad \frac{6}{3}$$

This text uses the latter two forms to express division.

In statistics you are likely to encounter greater than and less than signs (>, <), greater than or equal to and less than or equal to signs (≥, ≤), and not equal to signs (≠). It is important you understand what each sign means, though admittedly it is easy to confuse them. Use the following expressions for review. Notice that numerals and symbols are often used together:

$4 > 2$ means 4 is greater than 2

$H_1 > 10$ means H_1 is greater than 10

$7 < 9$ means 7 is less than 9

$a < b$ means a is less than b

$Y \geq 10$ means that the value for Y is a value greater than or equal to 10

$a \leq b$ means that the value for a is less than or equal to the value for b

$8 \neq 10$ means 8 does not equal 10

$H_1 \neq H_2$ means H_1 does not equal H_2

PROPORTIONS AND PERCENTAGES

Proportions and percentages are commonly used in statistics and provide a quick way to express information about the relative frequency of some value. You should know how to find proportions and percentages.

Proportions are identified by *P*; to find a proportion apply this formula:

$$P = \frac{f}{N}$$

where *f* stands for the frequency of cases in a category and *N* the total number of cases in all categories. So, in our sample of four students, if we wanted to know the proportion of males in the front row, there would be a total of two categories, female and male. Because there are 3 females and 1 male in our sample, our *N* is 4; and the number of cases in our category "male" is 1. To get the proportion, divide 1 by 4:

$$P = \frac{f}{N} \qquad P = \frac{1}{4} = .25$$

So, the proportion of males in the front row is .25. To convert this to a percentage, simply multiply the proportion by 100 or use the formula for percentaging:

$$\% = \frac{f}{N} \times 100 \qquad \% = \frac{1}{4} \times 100 = 25\%$$

WORKING WITH NEGATIVES

Addition, subtraction, multiplication, division, and squared numbers are not difficult for most people; however, there are some important rules to know when working with negatives that you may need to review.

1. When adding a number that is negative, it is the same as subtracting:

$$5 + (-2) = 5 - 2 = 3$$

2. When subtracting a negative number, the sign changes:

$$8 - (-4) = 8 + 4 = 12$$

3. When multiplying or dividing a negative number, the product or quotient is always negative:

$$6 \times -4 = -24 \qquad -10 \div 5 = -2$$

4. When multiplying or dividing two negative numbers, the product or quotient is always positive:

$$-3 \times -7 = 21 \qquad -12 \div -4 = 3$$

5. Squaring a number that is negative always gives a positive product because it is the same as multiplying two negative numbers:

$$-5^2 = 25 \text{ is the same as } -5 \times -5 = 25$$

ORDER OF OPERATIONS AND COMPLEX EXPRESSIONS

In statistics you are likely to encounter some fairly lengthy equations that require several steps to solve. To know what part of the equation to work out first, follow two basic rules. The first is called the rules of precedence. They state that you should solve all squares and square roots first, then multiplication and division, and finally, all addition and subtraction from left to right. The second rule is to solve expressions in parentheses first. If there are brackets in the equation, solve the expression within parentheses first and then the expression within the brackets. This means that parentheses and brackets can override the rules of precedence. In statistics, it is common for parentheses to control the order of calculations. These rules may seem somewhat abstract here, but a brief review of their application should make them more clear.

To solve this problem,

$$4 + 6 \cdot 8 = 4 + 48 = 52$$

do the multiplication first and then the addition. Not following the rules of precedence will lead to a substantially different answer:

$$4 + 6 \cdot 8 = 10 \cdot 8 = 80$$

which is incorrect.

To solve this problem,

$$6 - 4(6)/3^2$$

first, find the square of 3,

$$6 - 4(6)/9$$

then do the multiplication and division from left to right,

$$6 - \frac{24}{9} = 6 - 2.67$$

and finally, work out the subtraction,

$$6 - 2.67 = 3.33$$

To work out the following equation, do the expressions within parentheses first:

$$(4 + 3) - 6(2)/(3 - 1)^2$$

First, solve the addition and subtraction in the parentheses,

$$(7) - 6(2)/(2)^2$$

Now that you have solved the expressions within parentheses, work out the rest of the equation based on the rules of precedence, first squaring the 2,

$$(7) - 6(2)/4$$

Then do the multiplication and division next:

$$(7)-\frac{12}{4}=(7)-3$$

Finally, work out the subtraction to solve the equation:

$$7-3=4$$

The following equation may seem intimidating at first, but by solving it in steps and following the rules, even these complex equations should become manageable:

$$\sqrt{(8(4-2)^2)/(12/4)^2}$$

For this equation, work out the expressions within parentheses first; note that there are parentheses within parentheses. In this case, work out the inner parentheses first,

$$\sqrt{(8(2)^2)/3^2}$$

Now do the outer parentheses, making sure to follow the rules of precedence within the parentheses—square first and then multiply:

$$\sqrt{\frac{32}{3^2}}$$

Now, work out the square of 3 first and then divide:

$$\sqrt{\frac{32}{9}}=\sqrt{3.55}$$

Last, take the square root:

$$1.88$$

LEARNING CHECK SOLUTIONS

CHAPTER 1

(p. 8)

Learning Check 1.3. Identify the independent and dependent variables in the following hypotheses:

- *Older Americans are more likely to support stricter immigration laws than younger Americans.*
- *People who attend church regularly are more likely to oppose abortion than people who do not attend church regularly.*
- *Elderly women are more likely to live alone than elderly men.*
- *Individuals with postgraduate education are likely to have fewer children than those with less education.*

What are the independent and dependent variables in your hypothesis?

Answer:

Independent	Dependent
Age	Support for stricter immigration laws
Church attendance	Opposition to abortion
Gender	Living arrangement
Educational attainment	Number of children

(p. 10)

Learning Check 1.4. Review the definitions of exhaustive and mutually exclusive. Now look at Table 1.2. What other categories could be added to each variable to be exhaustive and mutually exclusive?

Answer:

To the variable gender, we can include a transgender or gender neutral category. For the variable religion, we can include a category for those without any religion. For the marital status category, we could include a divorced category, though this would be covered under the Other category.

CHAPTER 2

(p. 38)

Learning Check 2.6. Inspect Table 2.12 and answer the following questions:

- *What is the source of this table?*
- *How many variables are presented? What are their names?*
- *What is represented by the numbers presented in the second column? In the last row of the table?*

Answer:

The source for the data is noted at the bottom of the table.

There are 10 variables listed in the first column of the table. The first variable name is "Prenatal care in first 3 months of pregnancy."

The second column corresponds to mothers who are Mexican immigrants. The numbers correspond to the percentage of these mothers who utilized each health and public assistance program.

The last row corresponds to WIC (Women, Infants, and Children Program) utilization.

CHAPTER 3

(p. 65)

Learning Check 3.1. Listed below are the political party affiliations of 15 individuals. Find the mode.

Democrat	Republican	Democrat	Republican	Republican
Independent	Democrat	Democrat	Democrat	Republican
Independent	Democrat	Independent	Republican	Democrat

Answer:

The mode is "Democrat," because this category has the highest frequency, which is 7.

(p. 69)

Learning Check 3.2. Find the median of the following distribution of an interval-ratio variable: 22, 15, 18, 33, 17, 5, 11, 28, 40, 19, 8, 20.

Answer:

First, we need to arrange the numbers: 5, 8, 11, 15, 17, 18, 19, 20, 22, 28, 33, 40.

$(N + 1)/2 = (12 + 1)/2 = 6.5$. So the median is the average of the sixth and the seventh numbers, which are 18 and 19. The median is 18.5.

$$\text{Median} = \frac{18+19}{2} = 18.5$$

(p. 74)

Learning Check 3.5. The following distribution is the same as the one you used to calculate the median in an earlier Learning Check: 22, 15, 18, 33, 17, 5, 11, 28, 40, 19, 8, 20. Can you calculate the mean? Is it the same as the median, or is it different?

Answer:

$$\text{Mean} = \frac{22+15+18+33+17+5+11+28+40+19+8+20}{12} = 19.67$$

So the mean, 19.67, is larger than the median, 18.5.

CHAPTER 4

(p. 100)

Learning Check 4.2. Why can't we use the range to describe diversity in nominal variables? The range can be used to describe diversity in ordinal variables (e.g., we can say that responses to a question ranged from "somewhat satisfied" to "very dissatisfied"), but it has no quantitative meaning. Why not?

Answer:

In nominal variables, the numbers are used only to represent the different categories of a variable without implying anything about the magnitude or quantitative difference between these categories. Therefore, the range, being a measure of variability that gives the quantitative difference between two values that a variable takes, is not an appropriate measure for nominal variables. Similarly, in ordinal variables, numbers corresponding with the categories of a variable are only used to rank-order these categories without having any meaning in terms of the quantitative difference between these categories. Therefore, the range does not convey any quantitative meaning when used to describe the diversity in ordinal variables.

(p. 103)

Learning Check 4.3. Why is the IQR better than the range as a measure of variability, especially when there are extreme scores in the distribution? To answer this question, you may want to examine Figure 4.3.

Answer:

Extreme scores directly affect the range—the difference between the highest and the lowest scores. Therefore, if a distribution has extreme (very high and/or very low) scores, the range does not provide an accurate description of the distribution. IQR, on the other hand, is not affected by extreme scores. Thus, it is a better measure of variability than the range when there are extreme scores in the distribution.

(p. 109)

Learning Check 4.4. Examine Table 4.8 again and note the disproportionate contribution of the Western region to the sum of the squared deviations from the mean (it actually accounts for about 45% of the sum of squares). Can you explain why? (Hint: It has something to do with the sensitivity of the mean to extreme values.)

Answer:

The Western region has the highest projected percentage change in the elderly population between 2008 and 2015, which is 27%. Therefore, it deviates more from the mean than the other regions. The more a category of a variable deviates from the mean, the larger the square of the deviation gets, and hence the more this category contributes to the sum of the squared deviations from the mean.

CHAPTER 5

(p. 135)

Learning Check 5.2. How many students obtained a score between 305 and 475?

Answer:

$0.4406 \times 1{,}108{,}165 = 488{,}257$

(p. 136)

Learning Check 5.3. Calculate the proportion of test takers who earned a SAT writing score of at least 400. What is the proportion of students who earned a score of 600 or higher?

Answer:

The proportion who earned a score of 400 or less is 0.2451 ($Z_{400} = -0.69$)

The proportion who earned a score of 600 or higher is 0.1251 ($Z_{600} = 1.15$)

(p. 138)

Learning Check 5.4. Which score corresponds to the top 5% of SAT writing test takers?

Answer:

We select a Z score of 1.65, corresponding to 0.45 (B) and 0.05 (C) areas. The formula is $Y = 475 + (1.65)(109) = 475 + 179.85 = 654.85$

(p. 141)

Learning Check 5.5. In a normal distribution, how many standard deviations from the mean is the 95th percentile?

Answer:

The number of standard deviations from the mean is what we call a Z score. The Z score associated with the 95th percentile is 1.65. So a score at the 95th percentile is 1.65 standard deviations above the mean.

(p. 142)

Learning Check 5.6. What is the raw SAT writing score associated with the 50th percentile?

Answer:

The raw score associated with the 50th percentile is the median.

(p. 143)

Learning Check 5.7. Review the mean math Z scores for the variable "conditions at age 7, 11, and 16" (the last column of Table 5.3). From ages 7, 11, and 16, was there an improvement in their math scores? Explain.

Answer:

Each group's mean math score is consistently lower than the overall mean, but over time, the distance from the mean is reduced (from −1.026 to −0.706). Recall that larger Z scores indicate a greater distance from the overall mean.

CHAPTER 6

(p. 157)

Learning Check 6.3. How does a systematic random sample differ from a simple random sample?

Answer:

In a systematic random sample, we select each case according to a predetermined number (the *K*th case). We would select each *K*th case for the study sample. For a simple random sample, there is no systematic selection. Selection could be based on a table of random numbers.

(p. 170)

Learning Check 6.6. Suppose a population distribution has a mean $\mu = 150$ *and a standard deviation* $\sigma = 30$*, and you draw a simple random sample of* $N = 100$ *cases. What is the probability that the mean is between 147 and 153? What is the probability that the sample mean exceeds 153? Would you be surprised to find a mean score of 159? Why? (Hint: To answer these questions, you need to apply what you learned in Chapter 5 about Z scores and areas under the normal curve [Appendix B].) Remember, to translate a raw score into a Z score we used this formula:*

$$Z = \frac{Y - \bar{Y}}{s}$$

However, because here we are dealing with a sampling distribution, replace Y *with the sample mean* $\bar{Y}$, $\bar{Y}$ *with the sampling distribution's mean* $\bar{Y}$, $\bar{Y}$ *and* σ *with the standard error of the mean*

$$Z = \frac{\bar{Y} - \mu_{\bar{Y}}}{s / \sqrt{N}}$$

Answer:

Z score equivalent of 147 is

$$\frac{147 - 150}{30 / \sqrt{100}} = \frac{-3}{3} = -1$$

Z score equivalent of 153 is

$$\frac{153 - 150}{30 / \sqrt{100}} = \frac{3}{3} = 1$$

Using the standard normal table (Appendix B), we can see that the probability of the area between the mean and a score 1 standard deviation above or below the mean is 0.3413. So the probability that the mean is between 147 and 153, both of which deviate from the mean by 1 standard deviation, is 0.6826 (0.3413 + 0.3413), or 68.26%.

The probability of the area beyond 1 standard deviation from the mean is 0.1587. So the probability that the mean exceeds 153 is 0.1587, or 15.87%.

Z score equivalent of 159 is

$$\frac{159 - 150}{30 / \sqrt{100}} = \frac{9}{3} = 3$$

The probability of the area beyond 3 standard deviations from the mean, according to the standard normal table, is 0.0014. Therefore, it would be surprising to find a mean score of 159, as the probability is very low (0.14%).

CHAPTER 7

(p. 181)

Learning Check 7.1. What is the difference between a point estimate and a confidence interval?

Answer:

When the estimate of a population parameter is a single number, it is called a point estimate. When the estimate is a range of scores, it is called an interval estimate. Confidence intervals are used for interval estimates.

(p. 183)

Learning Check 7.2. To understand the relationship between the confidence level and Z, review the material in Chapter 6. What would be the corresponding Z value for a 98% confidence interval?

Answer:

The appropriate Z value for a 98% confidence interval is 2.33.

(p. 184)

Learning Check 7.3. What is the 90% confidence interval for the mean commuting time? First, find the Z value associated with a 90% confidence level.

Answer:

$$\begin{aligned} 90\%\ \text{CI} &= 7.5 \pm 1.65(0.07) \\ &= 7.5 \pm 0.12 \\ &= 7.38 \text{ to } 7.62 \end{aligned}$$

(p. 188)

Learning Check 7.4. Why do smaller sample sizes produce wider confidence intervals? (See Figure 7.5.) Compare the standard errors of the mean for the three sample sizes.

Answer:

As the sample size gets smaller, the standard error of the mean gets larger, which, in turn, results in a wider confidence interval.

(p. 194)

Learning Check 7.5. Calculate the 95% confidence interval for the CNN/ORC survey results for those who do not support anti-trans bathroom legislation (refer to page 179).

Answer:

$$.39 +\!- 1.96\ (.02) = .35 - .43$$

CHAPTER 8

(p. 216)

Learning Check 8.2. For the following research situations, state your research and null hypotheses:

- *There is a difference between the mean statistics grades of social science majors and the mean statistics grades of business majors.*
- *The average number of children in two-parent black families is lower than the average number of children in two-parent nonblack families.*
- *Grade point averages are higher among girls who participate in organized sports than among girls who do not.*

Answer:

Null Hypothesis	Research Hypothesis
Means are presumed equal for all statements.	Two-tailed test. No direction is stated.
	One-tailed test, left.
	One-tailed test, right.

(p. 219)

Learning Check 8.3. Would you change your decision in the previous example if alpha were.01? Why or why not?

Answer:

For alpha = .01, the t critical is 2.576. Also, t obtained (2.51) is less than t critical. We would fail to reject the null hypothesis.

(p. 221)

Learning Check 8.4. State the null and research hypothesis for this SPSS example. Would you change your decision in the previous example if alpha was .01? Why or why not?

Answer:

The null hypothesis is: $\mu_1 = \mu_2$

The research hypothesis is: $\mu_1 \neq \mu_2$

If alpha was set at .01, we would reject the null hypothesis. The t obtained of –3.444 (equal variances assumed) is significant at the .001 < .01.

(p. 223)

Learning Check 8.5. If alpha was changed to .01, two-tailed test, would your final decision change? Explain.

Answer:

The probability of the obtained Z is .0002 < .01. We would still reject the null hypothesis of no difference.

(p. 223)

Learning Check 8.6. If alpha was changed to .01, one-tailed test, would your final decision change? Explain.

Answer:

The probability of the obtained Z is .0062 < .01. We would still reject the null hypothesis of no difference.

(p. 225)

Learning Check 8.7. Based on Table 8.4, what would be the t critical at the .05 level for the first indicator, EC Index? Assume a two-tailed test.

Answer:

The *N*s are reported as a Note in the bottom of the table. The *df* calculation would be (78 + 113) – 2 = 189. Based on Appendix C, $df = \infty$, *t* critical is 1.960.

CHAPTER 9

(p. 235)

Learning Check 9.1. Identify the independent and dependent variables in Examples 2 and 3.

Answer:

Example 2: The independent variable is *race* and dependent variable is *receipt of public aid.*

Example 3: The independent variable is *race* and *health insurance status* is the dependent variable.

(p. 238)

Learning Check 9.2. Examine Table 9.2. Make sure you can identify all the parts just described and that you understand how the numbers were obtained. Can you identify the independent and dependent variables in the table? You will need to know this to convert the frequencies to percentages.

Answer:

The dependent variable is *homeownership* and the independent variable is *race.*

(p. 243)

Learning Check 9.4. Using the percentages reported under "Time in El Paso" in Table 9.5, calculate the cumulative percentages for each homeless group. What percentage of each group was in El Paso for a year or less? Which group has been in El Paso for a longer period of time?

Answer:

Almost 10% of Hispanic homeless were in El Paso for a year or less compared with 22.5% of Non-Hispanic homeless. The Hispanic homeless have been in El Paso longer than the non-Hispanic homeless. Seventy percent were in El Paso for more than 5 years. Only 43% of non-Hispanic homeless were in El Paso for the same period of time. Note that the total percentages do not equal 100.

	Hispanic	Cumulative % (Hispanic)	Non-Hispanic	Cumulative % (Non-Hispanic)
Less than 4 months	3.4	3.4	13.8	13.8
4–6 months	3.2	6.6	4.6	18.4

(Continued)

(Continued)

	Hispanic	Cumulative % (Hispanic)	Non-Hispanic	Cumulative % (Non-Hispanic)
7–12 months	3.2	9.8	4.1	22.5
1–2 years	6.9	16.7	11.5	34
2–5 years	11.9	28.6	17.5	51.5
Above 5 years	70.0	98.6	43.3	94.8

CHAPTER 10

(p. 272)

Learning Check 10.1. Construct a bivariate table (in percentages) showing no association between age and first-generation college status.

Answer:

Age and First-Generation College Status

	19 Years or Younger	20 Years or Older	
Firsts	41.9%	41.9%	41.9% (1,934)
Nonfirsts	58.1%	58.1%	58.1% (2,683)
	100.0%	100.0%	4,617

(p. 273)

Learning Check 10.2. Refer to the data in the previous Learning Check. Are the variables age and first-generation college status statistically independent? Write out the research and the null hypotheses for your practice data.

Answer:

Null hypothesis: There is no association between age and first-generation college status.

Research hypothesis: Age and first-generation college status are statistically dependent.

(p. 274)

Learning Check 10.3. Refer to the data in the Learning Check on page 272. Calculate the expected frequencies for age and first-generation college status and construct a bivariate table. Are your column and row marginals the same as in the original table?

Answer:

Construct a table to calculate chi-square for age and educational attainment.

	f_o	f_e	$f_o - f_e$	$(f_o - f_e)^2$	$(f_o - f_e)^2/f_e$
19/Firsts	916	1138.53	−222.53	49519.60	43.49
19/Nonfirsts	1802	1579.47	222.53	49519.60	31.35
20/Firsts	1018	795.47	222.53	49519.60	62.25
20/Nonfirsts	–881	1103.53	−222.53	49519.60	44.87

Chi-square = 181.96, with Yates correction = 181.15.

(p. 277)

Learning Check 10.5. Based on Appendix D, identify the probability for each chi-square value (df in parentheses)

Answer:

- *12.307 (15)* Between .70 and .50
- *20.337 (21)* Exactly .50
- *54.052 (24)* Less than .001

(p. 279)

Learning Check 10.6. What decision can you make about the association between age and first-generation college status? Should you reject the null hypothesis at the .05 alpha level or at the .01 level?

Answer:

We would reject the null hypothesis of no difference. Our calculated chi-square is significant at the .05 and the .01 levels. We have evidence that age is related to first-generation college status—older students are more likely to be first-generation students than younger students. Fifty-four percent of students 20 years or older are first-generation students versus 34% of students 19 years or younger.

(p. 282)

Learning Check 10.7. For the bivariate table with age and first-generation college status, the value of the obtained chi-square is 181.15 with 1 degree of freedom. Based on Appendix D, we determine that its probability is less than .001. This probability is less than our alpha level of .05. We reject the null hypothesis of no relationship between age and first-generation college status. If we reduce our sample size by half, the obtained chi-square is 90.58. Determine the p *value for 90.58. What decision can you make about the null hypothesis?*

Answer:

Even if we reduce the chi-square by half, we would still reject the null hypothesis.

CHAPTER 11

(p. 304)

Learning Check 11.1. Identify the independent and dependent variables in Table 11.1.

Answer:

Race/ethnicity is the independent variable, educational attainment is the dependent variable.

(p. 312)

Learning Check 11.3. If alpha were changed to .01, would our final decision change?

Answer:

If alpha were changed to .01, the F critical would be 5.01. Our F obtained is greater than the F critical. We would still reject the null hypothesis of no difference.

(p. 313)

Learning Check 11.4. Calculate eta-squared for the model presented in Figure 11.2.

Answer:

Based on the output $\eta^2 = 10.408/1300.902 = .008$ or .01. If we know political party identification, we can predict attitudes about ethical consumerism with 1% accuracy. This is a very weak prediction model.

(p. 316)

Learning Check 11.5. For the ANOVA model for Identity Formation, what is the F critical? What information do you need to determine the F *critical? Assume alpha = .05.*

Answer:

You would need k and N. In this case, $k = 3$ (number of categories) and $N = 486$ (total sample size). There are two degrees of freedom to calculate: df(between) $= k - 1 = 3 - 1 = 2$ and df(within) $= N - k = 486 - 3 = 483$. For an alpha of .05, the F critical is 2.99 (based on Appendix E).

CHAPTER 12

(p. 329)

Learning Check 12.1. For each of these four lines, as X *goes up by 1 unit, what does* Y *do? Be sure you can answer this question using both the equation and the line.*

Answer:

For the line $Y = 1X$, as X goes up by 1 unit, Y also goes up by 1 unit. In the second line, $Y = 2 + 0.5X$, Y increases by 0.5 units as a result of 1-unit increase in X. The line $Y = 6 - 2X$ tells that every 1-unit increase in X results in 2-unit decrease in Y. Finally, in the fourth line, Y decreases by 0.33 units as a result of 1-unit increase in X.

(p. 335)

Learning Check 12.2. Use the prediction equation to calculate the predicted values of Y *if* X *equals 9, 11, and 14. Verify that the regression line in Figure 12.4 passes through these points.*

Answer:

$$Y = -4.68 + .62(9) = .90$$

$$Y = -4.68 + .62(11) = 2.14$$

$$Y = -4.68 + .62(14) = 4.00$$

(p. 342)

Learning Check 12.3. Calculate r and r^2 for the age and Internet hours regression model. Interpret your results.

Answer: $r = -.77$ and $r^2 = .88$. The correlation coefficient indicates a strong negative relationship between age and Internet hours per week. Using information about respondent's age helps reduce the error in predicting Internet hours by 88%.

(p. 345)

Learning Check 12.4. Test the null hypothesis that there is a linear relationship between age and Internet hours. The mean squares regression is 63.66 with 1 degree of freedom. The mean squares residual is 2.355 with 8 degrees of freedom. Calculate the F *statistic and assess its significance.*

Answer: $F = 63.66/2.35 = 27.09$. This exceeds the F critical (1, 8) of 5.32 (alpha = .05). We can reject the null hypothesis and conclude that the linear relationship between age and Internet hours per week as expressed in r^2 is greater than zero in the population.

(p. 349)

Learning Check 12.5. Use the prediction equation describing the relationship between Internet hours per week and both educational attainment and age to calculate Internet hours per week for someone with 20 years of education who is 35 years old.

Answer:

$$Y = -.605 + .491(20) + -.057(35) = -.605 + 9.82 + -1.20 = 8.02 \text{ Internet hours per week}$$

ANSWERS TO ODD-NUMBERED EXERCISES

CHAPTER 1

1. Once our research question, the hypothesis, and the study variables have been selected, we move on to the next stage of the research process—measuring and collecting the data. The choice of a particular data collection method or instrument depends on our study objective. After our data have been collected, we have to find a systematic way to organize and analyze our data and set up some set of procedures to decide what we mean.

3.
   a. Interval-ratio
   b. Interval-ratio
   c. Nominal
   d. Ordinal
   e. Nominal
   f. Interval-ratio
   g. Ordinal

5. There are many possible variables from which to choose. Some of the most common selections by students will probably be as follows: type of occupation or industry, work experience, and educational training or expertise. Students should first address the relationship between these variables and gender. Students may also consider measuring structural bias or discrimination.

7.
   a. Annual income
   b. Gender—nominal; Number of hours worked per week—interval-ratio; Years of education—interval-ratio; Job title—nominal.
   c. This is an application of inferential statistics. She is using information based on her sample to predict the annual income of a larger population of young graduates.

9.
   a. Individual age: This variable could be measured as an interval-ratio variable, with actual age in years reported. As discussed in the chapter, interval-ratio variables are the highest level of measurement and can also be measured at ordinal or nominal levels.
   b. Annual income: This variable could be measured as an interval-ratio variable, with actual dollar earnings reported.

c. Religiosity: This variable could be measured in several ways. For example, as church attendance, the variable could be ordinal (number of times attended church in a month: every week, at least twice a month, less than two times a month, none at all).

d. Student performance: This could be measured as an interval-ratio variable as GPA or test score.

e. Social class: This variable is an ordinal variable, with categories low, working, middle, and upper.

f. Number of children: This variable could be measured in several ways. As an interval-ratio measure, the actual number of children could be reported. As an ordinal measure, the number of children could be measured in categories: 0, 1–2, 3–4, 5 or more. This could also be a nominal measurement—do you have children? Yes or No.

CHAPTER 2

1.

a. Race is a nominal variable. Class is an ordinal variable, since the categories can be ordered. Trauma is an interval variable.

b. Frequency Table for Race

Race	Frequency (f)
White	17
Nonwhite	13
Total (*N*)	30

c. White: 17/30 = .57%; Nonwhite: 13/30 = .43

3.

Number of Traumas	Frequency (f)
0	15
1	11
2	4
Total (*N*)	30

a. Trauma is an interval or ratio-level variable, since it has a real zero point and a meaningful numeric scale.

b. People in this survey are more likely to have experienced no traumas last year (50% of the group).

c. The proportion who experienced one or more traumas is calculated by first adding 36.7% and 13.3% = 50%. Then, divide that number by 100 to obtain the proportion, 0.50, or half the group.

5. Support does vary by political party. The majority of strong Democrats (58.1%) and Independents (66%) agree/strongly agree with the statement. The group with the lowest percentage of agreement is Strong Republicans at 49%. The percentage disagreeing with the statement is highest among Strong Republicans (36.7%) compared with 12.3% of Strong Democrats and 11.3% of Independents.

7. The group with the largest increase in voting rates is blacks, from 53% in 1996 to 66.2% in 2012. Blacks are the only group that did not experience a decline in voting rates for the years presented. Hispanic voting rates exceeded the voting rates for Asians in 2000 and remained higher than Asians through 2012. Hispanics and Asians have the lowest voting rates for all groups. As noted in the exercise, in the 2012 presidential election, blacks had the highest voting rates for all groups, followed by non-Hispanic whites, Hispanics, and Asians. White voting rates declined by 2% from 2008 to 2012. The highest voting rate for whites was in 2004 (67.2%), in 2008 for Hispanics (49.9%) and for Asians (47.6%).

9. If we identify younger Americans as those in the 18 to 24 and 25 to 44 age-groups and older Americans in the 45–64, 65–74, and 75 and over categories—the data indicate that as age increases, so does the percentage of voting in a Presidential election. The group with the highest percentage of voting is the 65- to 74-year olds, with 73.5% voting. The percentage drops for the 75 and over age-group, but is still higher than the reported percentages for the age-groups: 18–24, 25–44, and 45–64.

11. Overall, the highest percentage of smokers are in the 12th-grade category; the lowest are students in the 8th grade. The highest percentage of daily smokers for all grades is between 1996 and 1997 with percentages declining through 2014. (There are no data for 8th and 10th graders pre-1990.) Since 2012, the percentage of students smoking daily was at 10% or below.

13.

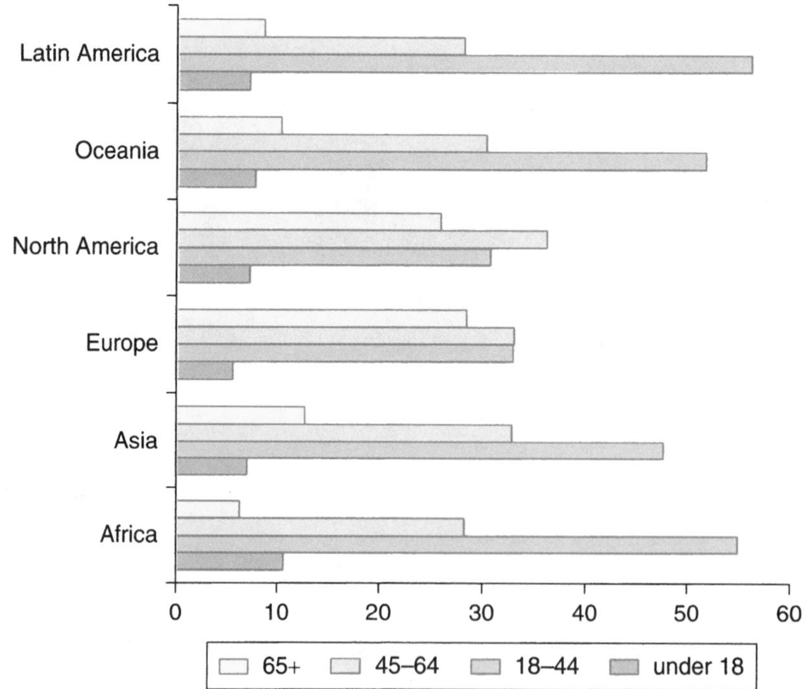

a. For Africa, Asia, Oceania, and Latin America, the largest age-group is 18 to 44 years. For Europe and North America, the age composition is slightly older; individuals aged 45 to 64 years are the largest age-group for both.

b. We display the data in a vertical bar graph. We selected a bar graph because country of origin (the basis of the percentage calculation) is nominal.

CHAPTER 3

1.

a. Mode = Routine ($f = 379$)

b. Median = Routine

c. Based on the mode and median for this variable, most respondents indicate that their lives are "routine."

d. A mean score could not be interpreted for this variable. A mean would have no meaning for a nominal measurement.

3.

a. Interval ratio. The mode can be found in two ways: by looking either for the highest frequency (14) or the highest percentage (43.8%). The mode is the category that corresponds to the value "40 hours worked last week." The median can be found in two ways: by using either the frequencies column or the cumulative percentages.

Using Frequencies	Using Cumulative Percentages
$\frac{N+1}{2} = \frac{32+1}{2} = 16.5\text{th case}$	Notice that 34.4% of the observations fall in or below the "32 hours worked last week" category; 78.1% fall in or below the "40 hours worked last week" category.
Starting with the frequency in the first category (1), add up the frequencies until you find where the 16th and 17th cases fall. Both these cases correspond to the category "40 hours worked last week," which is the median.	The 50% mark, or the median, is located somewhere within the "40 hours worked last week" category. So the median is "40 hours worked last week."

b. Since the median is merely a synonym for the 50th percentile, we already know that its value is "40 hours worked last week."

25th percentile = (32×0.25) = 8th case = 30 hours worked last week.

75th percentile = (32×0.75) = 24th case = 40 hours worked last week

5.

breakfastV8526 2014 T02 OFTN EAT BRKFST F2 * raceV1070 2014 RACE--B/W/H F1234 Crosstabulation

			raceV1070 2014 RACE--B/W/H F1234			
			1 BLACK:(1)	2 WHITE:(2)	3 HISPANIC:(3)	Total
breakfastV8526 2014 T02 OFTN EAT BRKFST F2	1 NEVER:(1)	Count	4	14	5	23
		% within raceV1070 2014 RACE--B/W/H F1234	9.3%	6.4%	7.0%	6.9%
	2 SELDOM:(2)	Count	11	22	9	42
		% within raceV1070 2014 RACE--B/W/H F1234	25.6%	10.1%	12.7%	12.7%
	3 SOMETIMES:(3)	Count	10	43	21	74
		% within raceV1070 2014 RACE--B/W/H F1234	23.3%	19.7%	29.6%	22.3%
	4 MOST DAYS:(4)	Count	2	25	9	36
		% within raceV1070 2014 RACE--B/W/H F1234	4.7%	11.5%	12.7%	10.8%
	5 NEARLY EVERY DAY:(5)	Count	7	30	2	39
		% within raceV1070 2014 RACE--B/W/H F1234	16.3%	13.8%	2.8%	11.7%
	6 EVERYDAY:(6)	Count	9	84	25	118
		% within raceV1070 2014 RACE--B/W/H F1234	20.9%	38.5%	35.2%	35.5%
Total		Count	43	218	71	332
		% within raceV1070 2014 RACE--B/W/H F1234	100.0%	100.0%	100.0%	100.0%

a.

	Mode	Median
Black	Seldom ($f = 11$)	Sometimes
White	Everyday ($f = 84$)	Nearly everyday
Hispanic	Everyday ($f = 25$)	Most days

b. Teens' breakfast habits vary by race/ethnicity. Out of the three racial/ethnic groups, black students were more likely to report seldom or sometimes eating breakfast. On the other hand, white and Hispanic students eat breakfast more frequently. The mode for white and Hispanic students is everyday.

7. We begin by multiplying each household size by its frequency.

Household Size	Frequency	Frequency × Y(fY)
1	381	381
2	526	1,052
3	227	681
4	200	800

Household Size	Frequency	Frequency × Y(fY)
5	96	480
6	42	252
7	19	133
8	5	40
9	2	18
10	2	20
Total	$N = 1{,}500$	$\Sigma fY = 3{,}857$

$$\bar{Y} = \frac{\Sigma f Y}{N} = \frac{3{,}857}{1{,}500} = 2.57$$

The mean number of people per household is 2.57.

9.

a. There appear to be a few outliers (i.e., extremely high values); this leads us to believe that the distribution is skewed in the positive direction.

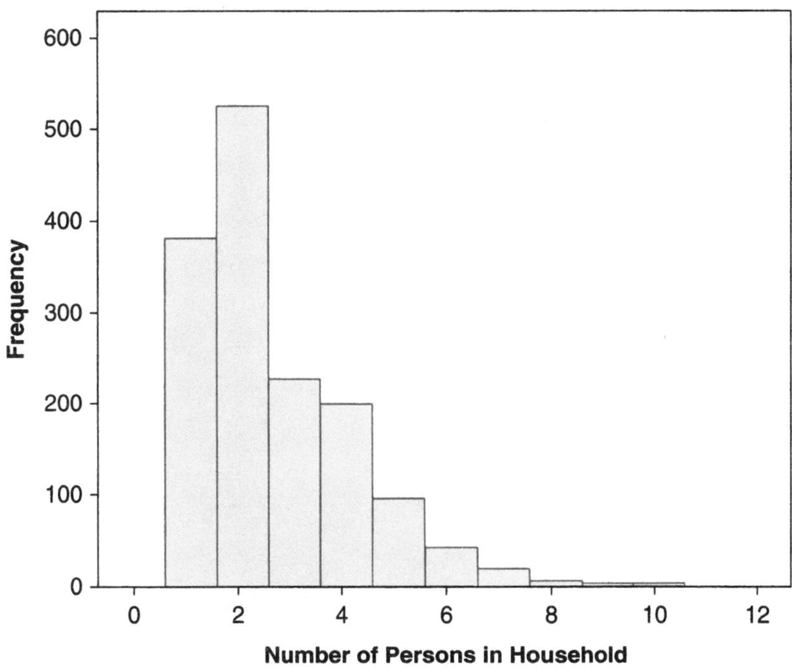

b. The median can be found in two ways: by using either the frequencies column or the cumulative percentages. The data are in frequencies; we'll use those to solve the median. Because the median (2) is less than the mean (2.57), we can conclude that the distribution is skewed in a positive direction. Our answer to Question 9a is further supported.

Using Frequencies
$\frac{N+1}{2}=\frac{1,500+1}{2}=750.5\text{th case}$
Starting with the frequency in the first category (381), add up the frequencies until you find where the 750th and 751st cases fall. Both these cases correspond to the category "2," which is the median.

11. The mean and the median represent a precise statistical middle. The mean is often referred to as the "arithmetic middle," by definition, summing everyone's income and dividing the total by the total number of people. The mean is sensitive to extremes, very low or high values and so when we consider income, the preferred measure is the median. The median is the midpoint of all collected incomes, representing the exact point where 50% of all cases are either above or below. Because Clinton and Sanders' middle-class income amount is higher than the U.S. Census estimated mean or median, their definition of middle class is not based on the statistical middle. Are they operationalizing a middle-class life style, one that includes home and car ownership, occupational status, and wealth?

13.

a. The data are reordered to calculate the median.

Infant Mortality Rates
2.52
3.43
4.65
5.87
10.41
14.58
15.61
18.87
26.11
58.19
115.08
Median = 14.58, 6th case
Mean = 275.32/11 = 25.03

b. The mean is greater than median, indicating a positively skewed distribution.

CHAPTER 4

1.

a. The table reveals seven response categories for political views.

b. The sum of the squared percentages, ΣPct^2, is equal to 2,301.52.

Political Views	Percentage (%)	Percentage Squared (%^{2})
Extremely liberal	3.6	12.96
Liberal	12.7	161.29
Slightly liberal	11.1	123.21
Moderate	39.5	1560.25
Slightly conservative	14.4	207.36
Conservative	14.9	222.01
Extremely conservative	3.8	14.44
Total	100.0	$\Sigma = 2,301.52$

c. Using the formula, we calculate the IQV as follows:

$$\text{IQV} = \frac{K(100^2 - \Sigma Pct^2)}{100^2(K-1)} = \frac{7(100^2 - 2,301.52)}{100^2(7-1)} = \frac{53,889.36}{60,000} = 0.90$$

The calculated IQV is close to 1 and suggests that Americans are fairly diverse in their political views.

3.

a. The range of convictions in 1990 is (583 – 79) = 504. The range of convictions in 2009 is (426 – 102) = 324. The range of convictions is larger in 1990 than in 2009.

b. The mean number of convictions is 295.67 in 1990 and 261.67 in 2009.

c.

1990			
Govt. Level	No. of Convictions	$(Y - \bar{Y})$	$(Y - \bar{Y})^2$
Federal	583	287.33	82,558.53
State	79	–216.67	46,645.89
Local	225	–70.67	4,994.25

(Continued)

(Continued)

Govt. Level	No. of Convictions	$(Y - \bar{Y})$	$(Y - \bar{Y})^2$
Total	887		134,498.67
	$\bar{Y} = 295.67$		
	$s = \sqrt{s^2} = \sqrt{\frac{\Sigma(Y-\bar{Y})^2}{N-1}} = \sqrt{\frac{134,498,67}{2}} = 259.32$		

2009			
Govt. Level	No. of Convictions	$(Y - \bar{Y})$	$(Y - \bar{Y})^2$
Federal	426	164.33	27,004.35
State	102	−159.67	25,494.50
Local	257	−4.67	21.80
Total	785		52,520.65
	$\bar{Y} = 261.67$		
	$s = \sqrt{s^2} = \sqrt{\frac{\Sigma(Y-\bar{Y})^2}{N-1}} = \sqrt{\frac{52,520.65}{2}} = 162.05$		

d. The standard deviation is larger in 1990 than in 2009, thus indicating more variability in number of convictions in 1990 than in 2009. This supports our results from 3a.

5.

a. The range of projected increase in the elderly population for the Western states is 36.2%. The range of percent increase for the Midwestern states is 9.8%. The Western states have a much larger range.

b. The IQR for the Western states is 17.3%. The IQR for the Midwestern states is 3.7%. Again, the value for the Western states is greater.

c. There is great variability in the projected increase in the elderly population in Western states, chiefly caused by the large increases in Nevada, Arizona, Wyoming, and Alaska, as measured by either the range or the IQR.

7.

a. The range is 3.6 (6.5 – 2.9). The 25th percentile, 3.05, means that 25% of cases fall below 3.05 divorce rate per 1,000 population. Likewise, the 75th percentile means that 75% of all cases fall below 4.6 divorce rate per 1,000 population.

25th percentile	10(0.25) = 2.5th case	So (3.0 + 3.1)/2 = 3.05
75th percentile	10(0.75) = 7.5th case	So (4.5 + 4.7)/2 = 4.6

The IQR is thus 4.6 – 3.05 = 1.55. Both measures of variability are appropriate, but the range is somewhat better, as the value for the IQR is fairly small. In other words, the range gives us a better picture of the variability of divorce rates for all states in our sample.

b.

State	Divorce Rate per 1,000 Population	$Y - \bar{Y}$	$(Y - \bar{Y})^2$
Alaska	4.3	0.2	0.04
Florida	4.7	0.6	0.36
Idaho	4.9	0.8	0.64
Maine	4.5	0.4	0.16
Maryland	3.1	−1.0	1.00
Nevada	6.5	2.4	5.76
New Jersey	3.0	−1.1	1.21
Texas	3.3	−0.8	0.64
Vermont	3.8	−0.3	0.09
Wisconsin	2.9	−1.2	1.44
Total	41	0.00	11.34
	$\bar{Y} = \frac{\Sigma Y}{N} = \frac{41}{10} = 4.1$		
	$s = \sqrt{s^2} = \sqrt{\frac{\Sigma(Y - \bar{Y})^2}{N - 1}} = \sqrt{\frac{11.34}{9}} = 1.12$		

c. Divorce rates may vary by state due to factors such as variation in religiosity, state policy (i.e., no fault divorce laws), or employment opportunities.

9.

a. The mean number of crimes is 3,038.9 and the standard deviation is 583.004. The mean amount of dollars (in millions) spent on police protection is $1,703.95 and the standard deviation is $1,895.214.

b. Because the number of crimes and police protection expenditures are measured according to different scales, it isn't appropriate to directly compare the mean and standard deviation for one variable with the other. But we can talk about each distribution separately. We know from examining the mean (3,038.90) and standard deviation (583.00) for the number of crimes that the standard deviation is large, indicating a wide dispersion of scores from the mean. For the number of crimes, states such as Missouri and South Dakota contribute more to its variability because they have values far from the mean (both above and below). With respect to police protection expenditures, we can see that there is a large dispersion from the mean of $1,703.95, as the standard deviation is $1,895.21. States such as New York and North Dakota contribute more to its variability because they have values far from the mean (both above and below).

c. Among other considerations, we need to consider the economic conditions in each state. A downturn in the local and state economy may play a part in the number of crimes and police expenditures per capita.

11.

a. Type of paid work is a nominal variable. The appropriate measure of variability would be the index of qualitative variation (IQV).

b.

Grade 8		
Type of Work	Percentage (%)	Percentage Squared (%²)
Lawn work	28	784
Food service	3	9
Babysitting	37	1369
Other	32	1,024
Total	100.0%	$\Sigma = 3186$

$$IQV = \frac{K(100^2 - \Sigma Pct^2)}{100^2(K-1)} = \frac{4(100^2 - 3{,}186)}{100^2(4-1)} = \frac{27{,}256}{30{,}000} = 0.91$$

The IQV for 8th graders is 0.91.

Grade 10		
Type of Work	Percentage (%)	Percentage Squared (%²)
Lawn work	20	400
Food service	10	100
Babysitting	28	784
Other	42	1,764
Total	100.0%	$\Sigma = 3{,}048$

Type of Work	Percentage (%)	Percentage Squared (%²)

$$IQV = \frac{K(100^2 - \sum Pct^2)}{100^2(K-1)} = \frac{4(100^2 - 3{,}048)}{100^2(4-1)} = \frac{27{,}808}{30{,}000} = 0.93$$

The IQV for 10th graders is 0.93.

c. Though both IQVs are more than 0.90, there is slightly more variation among 10th graders than 8th graders in the type of jobs they hold. The difference could be attributed to more employment options for older students. Younger students may be limited to the kind of work they can do (due to age, experience, and time), leading to more informal jobs, such as lawn work and babysitting.

13. Overall, Obama voters were younger, more educated, and attended religious services less than McCain voters. The youngest voters were female Obama voters at 50.99 years (s = 16.62), followed by male Obama voters, 51.71 years (s = 15.59). For education, males who voted for Obama had the highest mean of 14.84 (s = 3.07). Males who voted for McCain had 14.60 years of education (s = 2.41). McCain voters, both males and females, attended religious services more often than Obama voters. Mean scores were 3.93 for males (s = 2.80) and 4.64 for females (s = 2.76), indicating church attendance about once a month to 2 × 3 times per month. The standard deviations indicate a consistency in the distributions of education, age, and religious service attendance across all four groups. The largest standard deviations are for age, ranging from 15.61 to 16.62 years. These wide standard deviations indicate more dispersion around the mean age scores.

CHAPTER 5

1.

a. The Z score for a person who watches more than 8 hours per day:

$$Z = \frac{8 - 2.94}{2.60} = 1.95$$

b. We first need to calculate the Z score for a person who watches 5 hours per day:

$$Z = \frac{5 - 2.94}{2.60} = 0.79$$

The area between Z and the mean is 0.2852. We then need to add 0.50 to 0.2852 to find the proportion of people who watch television less than 5 hours per day. Thus, we conclude that the proportion of people who watch television less than 5 hours per day is 0.7852. This corresponds to 786 people (785.99 = 0.7852 × 1,001).

c. 5.54 television hours per day corresponds to a Z score of +1.

$$Y = \bar{Y} + Z(S_Y) = 2.94 + 1(2.60) = 5.54$$

d. The Z score for a person who watches 1 hour of television per day is –.75. The area between the mean and Z is 0.2734.

$$\frac{1-2.94}{2.60}=-.75$$

The Z score for a person who watches 6 hours of television per day is 1.18. The area between the mean and Z is .3810.

$$\frac{6-2.94}{2.60}=1.18$$

Therefore, the percentage of people who watch between 1 and 6 hours of television per day is 65.44% (0.2734 + 0.3810 = 0.6544 × 100).

3.

a. For an individual with 13.77 years of education, his or her Z score would be

$$Z=\frac{13.77-13.77}{3.07}=0.0$$

b. Since our friend's number of years of education completed is associated with the 60th percentile, we need to solve for Y. However, we must first use the logic of the normal distribution to find Z. For any normal distribution, 50% of all cases will fall above the mean. Since our friend is in the 60th percentile, we know that the area between the mean and our friend's score is 0.10. Similarly, the area beyond our friend's score is 0.40. We can now look in Appendix B column "B" for 0.10 or in column "C" for 0.40. We find that the Z associated with these values is 0.25. Now, we can solve for Y:

$$Y=\overline{Y}+Z(s)=13.77+0.25(307)=14.5375=14.54$$

c. Since we already know that the proportion between our number of years of education (13.77) and our friend's number of years of education (14.55) is 0.10, we can multiply N (1,500) by this proportion. Thus, 150 people have between 13.77 and 14.55 years of education.

5.

a. Among working-class respondents:

The Z score for a value of 12 is

$$Z=\frac{12-13.01}{2.91}=-0.35$$

The Z score for a value of 16 is

$$Z=\frac{16-13.01}{2.91}=1.03$$

You'll find the area between the Z scores and the mean under Column B. The total area between the scores is .1368 + .3485 = .4853. The proportion of working-class respondents with 12 to 16 years of education is .4853.

Among upper-class respondents:

The Z score for a value of 12 is

$$Z=\frac{12-15.44}{2.83}=-1.22$$

The Z score for a value of 16 is

$$Z = \frac{16 - 15.44}{2.83} = 0.20$$

The area between a Z of -1.22 and the mean is 0.3888. The area between a Z of 0.20 is 0.0793, so the total area between the scores is $0.3888 + 0.0793 = 0.4681$. The proportion of upper-class respondents with 12 to 16 years of education is 0.4681.

A higher proportion of working-class respondents have 12 to 16 years of education than upper-class respondents.

b. For working-class respondents:

As previously calculated, the Z score for a value of 16 is 1.03. The area between a Z of 1.03 and the tail of the distribution (Column C) is 0.1515. So the probability of a working-class respondent having more than 16 years of education is 15.15%.

For middle-class respondents:

The Z score for a value of 16 is

$$Z = \frac{16 - 14.99}{2.93} = .35$$

The area between a Z of .35 and the tail of the distribution (Column C) is .3632. So the probability of a middle-class respondent having more than 16 years of education is 36.32%.

c. For lower-class respondents:

The Z score for a value of 10 is

$$Z = \frac{10 - 12.11}{2.83} = -0.75$$

The area beyond Z of 0.75 is .2266. So the probability of a lower-class respondent having less than 10 years of education is .2266 (or 22.66%).

d. If years of education is positively skewed, then the proportion of cases with high levels of education will be less than that for a normal distribution. This means, for example, that the probabilities associated with high levels of education will be smaller.

7.

a. The Z score of 150 is 3.33.

b. The area beyond 3.33 is 0.0004. The percentage of scores above 150 is 0.04%, a very small percentage.

c. The Z score for 85 is -1.0. The percentage of scores between 85 and 150 is 84.09% $(0.3413 + 0.4996 = 0.8409)$.

d. Scoring in the 95th percentile means that 95% of the sample scored below this level. Identifying the 95th percentile can be calculated by this formula: $100 + 1.65(15) = 124.75$. The IQ score that is associated with the 95th percentile is 124.75.

9.

a. About 0.1894 of the distribution falls above the Z score, so that is the proportion of crime incidents with more than two victims.

$$Z = \frac{2 - 1.28}{0.82} = 0.88$$

b. The area between the mean and the Z score is about 0.1331, so the total area above one victim is 0.50 + 0.1331 = 0.6331, or 63.31%.

$$Z = \frac{1 - 1.28}{0.82} = -0.34$$

c. The area between the mean and the Z score is about 0.4995, so the total area below four victims is 0.50 + 0.4995 = 0.9995.

$$Z = \frac{4 - 1.28}{0.82} = 3.32$$

11.

a. For a team with an APR score of 990

$$Z = \frac{990 - 981}{27.3} = 0.33$$

From Appendix B, the area beyond 0.33 is 0.3707 or about the 67th percentile. The team is not in the upper quartile.

b. The Z value which corresponds to a cutoff score with an area of about 0.25 toward the tail of the distribution is 0.67. This is translated into a cutoff score:

$$981 + 0.67(27.3) = 999.29.$$

c. The Z value is 0.67.

13. The 95th percentile corresponds to a Z score of 1.65.

Hungary

11.76 + 1.65 (2.91) = 16.56 years

Czech Republic

12.82 + 1.65 (2.29) = 16.60 years

Denmark

13.93 + 1.65 (5.83) = 23.55 years

France

14.12 + 1.65 (5.73) = 23.57 years

Ireland

15.15 + 1.65 (3.90) = 21.59 years

CHAPTER 6

1.

a. Although there are problems with the collection of data from all Americans, the census is assumed to be complete, so the mean age would be a parameter.

b. A statistic because it is estimated from a sample.

c. A statistic because it is estimated from a sample.

d. A parameter because the school has information on all employees.

e. A parameter because the school would have information on all its students.

3.

a. Assuming that the population is defined as all persons shopping at that shopping mall that day of the week, she is selecting a systematic random sample. A more precise definition might limit it to all persons passing by the department store at the mall that day.

b. This is a stratified sample because voters were first grouped by county, and unless the counties have the same number of voters, it is a disproportionate stratified sample because the same number is chosen from each county. We can assume that it was a probability sample, but we are not told exactly how the 50 voters were chosen from the lists. However, assuming that the population is defined as all Americans, this sort of sampling technique would qualify as nonprobability sampling.

c. This is neither a simple random sample nor a systematic random sample. It might be thought of as a sample stratified on last name, but even then, choosing the first 20 names is not a random selection process.

d. This is not a probability sample. Instead, it is a purposive sample chosen to represent a cross-section of the population in New York City.

5. The relationship between the standard error and the standard deviation is $\sigma_{\bar{Y}} = \sigma / \sqrt{N}$. Since σ is divided by $\sqrt{N}$, $\sigma_{\bar{Y}} = \sigma / \sqrt{N}$ must always be smaller than σ, except in the trivial case where $N = 1$. Theoretically, the dispersion of the mean must be less than the dispersion of the raw scores. This implies that the standard error of the mean is less than the standard deviation.

7.

a. These polls are definitely not probability samples. No sampling is done by the television station to choose who calls the 800 number.

b. The population is all those people who watch the television channel and see the 800 number advertised.

9.

a. This is not a random sample. The students eating lunch on Tuesday are not necessarily representative of all students at the school, and you have no way of calculating the probability of inclusion of any student. Many students might, for example, rarely eat lunch at the cafeteria and, therefore, have no chance of being represented in your sample. The fact that you selected *all* the students eating lunch on Tuesday makes your selection appear to be a census of a population, but that isn't true either unless all the students ate at the cafeteria on Tuesday.

b. This is a systematic random sample because names are drawn systematically from the list of all enrolled students.

c. This would seem to be a systematic random sample as in (b), but it suffers from the same type of defect as the cafeteria sample. Unless all students pass by the students union, using that location as a selection criterion means that some students have no chance of being selected (but you don't know which ones). Samples are often drawn this way in shopping malls by choosing a central location from which to draw the sample. It is reasonable to assume that a sufficiently representative mix of shoppers will pass by a central location during any one period.

d. The second procedure (selecting every 10th student from the list of all enrolled students) is the best option because it uses a random sampling method.

11.

a. Mean = 5.3 (53/10); standard deviation = 3.27.

b. Here are 10 means from random samples of size 3: 6.33, 5.67, 3.33, 5.00, 7.33, 2.33, 6.00, 6.33, 7.00, 3.00.

c. The mean of these 10 sample means is 5.23. The standard deviation is 1.76. The mean of the sample means is very close to the mean for the population. The standard deviation of the sample means is much less than the standard deviation for the population. The standard deviation of the means from the samples is an estimate of the standard error of the mean we would find from one random sample of size 3.

CHAPTER 7

1.

a. The estimate at the 90% confidence level is 22.82% to 23.18%. This means that there are 90 chances out of 100 that the confidence interval will contain the true population percentage of victims in the American population.

Due to the large sample size, we converted the proportions to percentages, subtracting from 100, rather than 1.

$$\text{Standard error} = \sqrt{\frac{(23)\ (100-23)}{160{,}040}} = 0.105 = 0.11$$

$$\text{Confidence interval} = 23 \pm 1.65(0.11)$$

$$= 23 \pm 0.18$$

$$= 22.82 \text{ to } 23.18$$

b. The true percentage of crime victims in the American population is somewhere between 22.72% and 23.28% based on the 99% confidence interval. There are 90 chances out of 100 that the confidence interval will contain the true population percentage of crime victims.

$$\text{Confidence interval} = 23 \pm 2.58(0.11)$$

$$= 23 \pm 0.28$$

$$= 22.72 \text{ to } 23.28$$

3.

a. For Canadians

$$s_p = \sqrt{\frac{(0.51)(1-0.51)}{1{,}004}} = 0.02$$

$$\text{Confidence interval} = 0.51 \pm 1.96(0.02)$$
$$= 0.51 \pm 0.04$$
$$= 0.47 \text{ to } .55$$

b. For Americans

$$\text{Confidence interval} = 0.45 \pm 1.96(0.02)$$
$$= 0.45 \pm 0.04$$
$$= 0.39 \text{ to } 0.49$$

c. Based on the calculated 95% confidence interval, the majority of Americans do not believe climate change is a serious problem. The true percentage of Americans who believe climate change is a serious problem is under 50%, somewhere between 39% and 49%, based on this Pew Research Center sample. On the other hand, it is possible that the majority of Canadians believe climate change is a serious problem. We can be 95% confident that the true percentage of Canadians is somewhere between 47% and 55%.

5.

Due to the large sample size, we converted the proportion to full percentages, subtracting from 100 (rather than 1).

$$\text{Confidence interval} = 51 \pm 1.96(0.67)$$
$$= 49.69\% \text{ to } 52.31\%$$

We set the interval at the 95% confidence level. However, no matter whether the 90%, 95%, or 99% confidence level is chosen, the calculated interval includes values below 50% for the vote for a Republican candidate. Therefore, you should tell your supervisors that it would not be possible to declare a Republican candidate the likely winner of the votes coming from men if there was an election today because it seems quite possible that less than a majority of male voters would support her or him.

7.

a.

$$s_p = \sqrt{\frac{(0.64)(1-0.64)}{1{,}403}} = 0.01$$

$$\text{Confidence interval} = 0.64 \pm 1.96(0.01)$$
$$= 0.64 \pm 0.02$$
$$= 0.62 \text{ to } 0.66$$

b. Based on our answer in 7a, we know that a 90% confidence interval will be more precise than a 95% confidence interval that has a lower bound of 62% and an upper bound of 66%. Accordingly, a 90% confidence interval will have a lower bound that is greater than

62% and an upper bound that is less than 66%. Additionally, we know that a 99% confidence interval will be less precise than what we calculated in 7a. Thus, the lower bound for a 99% confidence interval will be less than 62% and the upper bound will be greater than 66%.

9.

Country	Mean	Standard Error	Confidence Interval
France	14.12	$5.73/\sqrt{975} = 0.18$	$14.12 + 0.18(1.65) = 14.42$ $14.12 - 0.18(1.65) = 13.82$
Japan	12.48	$2.53/\sqrt{528} = 0.11$	$12.48 + 0.11(1.65) = 12.66$ $12.48 - 0.11(1.65) = 12.30$
Croatia	12.18	$2.71/\sqrt{480} = 0.12$	$12.18 + 0.12(1.65) = 12.38$ $12.18 - 0.12(1.65) = 11.98$
Turkey	9.15	$11.98/\sqrt{783} = 0.43$	$9.15 + 0.43(1.65) = 9.86$ $9.15 - 0.43(1.65) = 8.44$

11.

For Republicans

$$s_p = \sqrt{\frac{(0.18)(1-0.18)}{446}} = 0.02$$

$$\text{Confidence interval} = 0.18 \pm 1.96(0.02)$$

$$= 0.18 \pm 0.04$$

$$= 0.14 \text{ to } 0.22$$

For Democrats

$$s_p = \sqrt{\frac{(0.15)(1-0.15)}{522}} = 0.02$$

$$\text{Confidence interval} = .15 \pm 1.96(0.02)$$

$$= 0.15 \pm 0.04$$

$$= 0.11 \text{ to } 0.19$$

13.

a. For those who thought that homosexual relations were always wrong:

$$s_p = \sqrt{\frac{(0.40)(1-.40)}{950}} = 0.02$$

$$\text{Confidence interval} = 0.40 \pm 1.96(.02)$$

$$= 0.40 \pm 0.04$$

$$= 0.36 \text{ to } 0.44$$

For those who thought that homosexual relations were not wrong at all:

$$s_p = \sqrt{\frac{(0.49)(1-0.49)}{950}} = 0.02$$

$$\text{Confidence interval} = 0.49 \pm 1.96(.02)$$

$$= 0.49 \pm 0.04$$

$$= 0.45 \text{ to } 0.53$$

b.

$$s_p = \sqrt{\frac{(0.10)(1-0.10)}{950}} = 0.01$$

$$\text{Confidence interval} = 0.10 \pm 1.96(.01)$$

$$= 0.10 \pm 0.02$$

$$= 0.08 \text{ to } 0.12$$

CHAPTER 8

1.

a. H_0: $\mu = 13.5$ years; H_1: $\mu < 13.5$ years.

b. The Z value obtained is –4.19. The p value for a Z of –4.19 is less than .001 for a one-tailed test. This is less than the alpha of .01, so we reject the null hypothesis and conclude that the doctors at the HMO do have less experience than the population of doctors at all HMOs.

3.

a. Two-tailed test, $\mu \neq \$53,657$; null hypothesis, $\mu = \$53,657$

b. One-tailed test, $\mu > 3.2$; null hypothesis, $\mu = 3.2$

c. One-tailed test, $\mu_1 < \mu_2$; null hypothesis, $\mu_1 = \mu_2$

d. Two-tailed test, $\mu_1 \neq \mu_2$; null hypothesis, $\mu_1 = \mu_2$

e. One-tailed test, $\mu_1 > \mu_2$; null hypothesis, $\mu_1 = \mu_2$

f. One-tailed test, $\mu_1 < \mu_2$; null hypothesis, $\mu_1 = \mu_2$

5.

a. Research hypothesis, $\mu \neq 37.2$; null hypothesis, $\mu = 37.2$

b. The t obtained is –29.36 and its p level is <.001 (it is greater than the last reported t critical of 3.291).

$$t = \frac{37.2 - 50.12}{17.07 / \sqrt{1490}} = \frac{-12.92}{.44} = -29.36$$

c. We conclude that we can reject the null hypothesis in favor of the research hypothesis. There is a difference between the mean age of the GSS sample and the mean age of all

American adults. Relative to age, the GSS sample is not representative of all American adults (the GSS sample is significantly older).

7.

a. The appropriate test statistic is t test for sample means.

b.

$$t = \frac{2.35 - 3.05}{.18} = -3.89$$

$$\text{Standard error} = \sqrt{\frac{188(1.21)^2 + 60(1.05)^2}{(189+61)-2}}\sqrt{\frac{189+61}{(189)(61)}} = (1.17)(.15) = 0.18$$

The t obtained of –3.89 is greater than the t critical of –1.645. We reject the null hypothesis of no difference. College graduates are more likely to indicate that being Christian is "not very important," whereas high school graduates indicate that being Christian is "fairly important."

c. For a two-tailed test, the t critical would be 1.96. The t obtained is still greater. We would reject the null hypothesis of no difference.

9.

a. "Less than" indicates a one-tailed test.

b. $Z = 3.00$. with a significance of .001. We can reject the null hypothesis and conclude that the proportion of males who believe in the historical importance of the election of a woman for president is significantly less than the proportion of female voters who believe the same.

$$\frac{.55 - .65}{.02} = -5.0$$

c. The significance of –5.00 is less than .01 (.0014 < .001). The decision to reject the null hypothesis does not change.

11. Older individuals, aged 50 to 59 years, gave more money in the past year than younger adults aged 30 to 39 years. However, the difference in giving is not significant. The t obtained is –.800 (equal variances assumed) with a probability of .425 (>.05 alpha).

13.

a. Yes, there is a significant difference between the average number of relaxation hours for married men and women. Married women have significantly less relaxation hours per day than men in the GSS 2014 sample, a difference of .68 hours (3.56 – 2.88). The t obtained of 2.225 is significant at the .025 level (less than our alpha of .05).

b. If alpha was changed to .01, we would fail to reject the null hypothesis of no difference. The probability of the t obtained is .025 > .01.

CHAPTER 9

1.

a. The independent variable is sex; the dependent variable is fear of walking alone at night.

Fear of Walking Alone at Night	Sex	
	Male F (%)	Female F (%)
Yes	2 (22%)	8 (73%)
No	7 (78%)	3 (27%)

b. Approximately 73% of women are afraid to walk alone in their neighborhoods at night, whereas approximately 22% of men said the same. This amounts to about a 51% difference between women and men who are not afraid to walk alone at night, indicating a strong relationship. It is important to keep in mind that our small sample size limits the generalizability of these results.

c. There is a relationship between homeownership and fear of walking alone at night. The majority of homeowners (56%) were not afraid of walking alone at night in their neighborhood. Among those who were not homeowners, the majority (55%) were afraid of walking alone at night.

Fear of Walking Alone at Night	Home Ownership	
	Yes F (%)	No F (%)
Yes	4 (44%)	6 (55%)
No	5 (56%)	5 (45%)

3.

a. Based on the student's argument the independent variable is *attitude toward homosexual relations* and the dependent variable is *political views*.

b. 285/645 = 44%

c. Those who believe that homosexuality is always wrong are more likely to be conservative (51%) than moderate (34%) or liberal (15%). On the other hand, those who believe homosexuality is not wrong at all are more likely to report liberal (41%) or moderate (40%) views than conservative (18%) ones.

5. The relationship is weak between race and the frequency of being drunk in the past 12 months. The majority of students are likely to report not being drunk in the past 12 months, at least 86% of each racial group. The percentage of students being drunk at least 3 or more times is highest for whites (7%), followed by Hispanic (6%), and black (2%) students.

Drunk in the Last 12 Months	Race			Total
	Black	White	Hispanic	
None	75	282	119	476
	90%	86%	90%	

(Continued)

(Continued)

Drunk in the Last 12 Months	Race			Total
	Black	White	Hispanic	
1–2 times	6	23	5	34
	7%	7%	4%	
3–5 times	0	13	3	16
		4%	2%	
6 or more times	2	11	5	18
	2%	3%	4%	
Total	83	329	132	544

7. Female seniors have higher educational expectations than male seniors. For example, 73.9% (32.6 + 41.3) of female students expected to complete a bachelor's degree or higher. This is higher than the combined percentage for male students: 63.3% (34.4 + 28.9).

9. Yes, there is a relationship between political party affiliation and attitudes toward the Affordable Care Act. The majority of physicians who reported being Republican or Other party were strongly against or against the Affordable Care Act. The largest reporting percentage was among Republicans (84.07% = 31.08 + 52.99). Only 47.2% (11.20 + 36) of Democrats were strongly against or against the act.

11. The data indicate a positive relationship between students' educational expectations and parental education. The percentage of students indicating a bachelor's degree or higher increases as the parents' educational level increases: from 52% of students with parents with a high school degree or less to 86.1% of students with parents who completed a graduate/professional degree.

13. In contrast with male students, female students are more likely to report not being drunk at all (at least 82% of each racial group). According to the data, Hispanic females (9%) are more likely to report being drunk three or more times in the last 12 months than white (7%) or black (6%) females.

Drunk in the Last 12 Months	Race			Total
	Black	White	Hispanic	
None	76	286	100	462
	87%	83%	82%	
1–2 times	6	33	11	50
	7%	10%	9%	
3–5 times	4	12	7	23
	5%	3%	6%	

Drunk in the Last 12 Months	Race			Total
	Black	White	Hispanic	
6 or more times	1	14	4	19
	1%	4%	3%	
Total	87	345	122	554

CHAPTER 10

1.

a. Degrees of freedom = (2 – 1)(2 – 1) = 1

b. Chi-square = 29.01 (with Yates's correction is 28.18). The probability of our obtained chi-square is less than our alpha (and less than 0.001). We can reject the null hypothesis and conclude that gender and fear of walking alone at night are dependent. A higher percentage of women (40%) than men (22%) report being afraid.

Sex and FEAR	f_o	f_e	$f_o - f_e$	$(f_o - f_e)^2$	$\frac{(f_o - f_e)^2}{f_e}$
Men/yes	77	111.96	–34.96	1222.20	10.92
Men/no	270	235.04	34.96	1222.20	5.20
Women/yes	175	140.04	34.96	1222.20	8.73
Women/no	259	293.96	–34.96	1222.20	4.16
$\chi^2 = 29.01$					

With the Yates correction:				
Sex and FEAR	$\lvert f_o - f_e \rvert$	$(\lvert f_o - f_e \rvert - .50)^2$	f_e	$\frac{(\lvert f_o - f_e \rvert - .5)^2}{f_e}$
Men/yes	34.96	(34.46)2 = 1187.49	111.96	10.61
Men/no	34.96	(34.46)2 = 1187.49	235.04	5.05
Women/yes	34.96	(34.46)2 = 1187.49	140.04	8.48
Women/no	34.96	(34.46)2 = 1187.49	293.96	4.04
Total				28.18

c. If α were changed to .01, we would still reject the null hypothesis. The probability of our obtained chi-square is still less than alpha.

d. The lambda is 0. There is no proportional reduction of error using sex to predict fear of walking alone at night.

3.

a. A slightly higher percentage of blacks, 34.2% (38/111), report being afraid to walk alone at night. Among whites, the percentage is 31.6% (190/601).

b. Regardless of race, women are more likely than men to report being afraid to walk alone at night. The percentage of white women indicating that they are afraid is slightly higher than black women, 40.4% (129/319) versus 39% (30/77).

c.

Whites, $\chi^2 = 23.62$; we reject the null hypothesis.

Blacks, $\chi^2 = 1.85$; we fail to reject the null hypothesis.

For Whites

Sex and FEAR	f_o	f_e	$f_o - f_e$	$(f_o - f_e)^2$	$\frac{(f_o - f_e)^2}{f_e}$
Men/yes	61	89.15	–28.15	792.42	8.89
Men/no	221	192.85	28.15	792.42	4.12
Women/yes	129	100.85	28.15	792.42	7.86
Women/no	190	218.15	–28.15	792.42	3.63
χ^2= 24.50					

With the Yates's correction, the chi-square is 23.62, as it is shown below:

Sex and FEAR	$\lvert f_o - f_e \rvert$	$(\lvert f_o - f_e \rvert - .50)^2$	f_e	$\frac{(\lvert f_o - f_e \rvert - .5)^2}{f_e}$
Men/yes	28.15	764.52	89.15	8.58
Men/no	28.15	764.52	192.85	3.96
Women/yes	28.15	764.52	100.85	7.58
Women/no	28.15	764.52	218.15	3.50

For Blacks

Sex and FEAR	f_o	f_e	$f_o - f_e$	$(f_o - f_e)^2$	$\frac{(f_o - f_e)^2}{f_e}$
Men/yes	8	11.64	–3.64	13.25	1.14
Men/no	26	22.36	3.64	13.25	.59

Sex and FEAR	f_o	f_e	$f_o - f_e$	$(f_o - f_e)^2$	$\frac{(f_o - f_e)^2}{f_e}$
Women/yes	30	26.36	3.64	13.25	.50
Women/no	47	50.64	−3.64	13.25	.26
$\chi^2 = 2.49$					

With the Yates's correction, the chi-square is 1.85:				
Sex and FEAR	$\lvert f_o - f_e \rvert$	$(\lvert f_o - f_e \rvert - .50)^2$	f_e	$\frac{(\lvert f_o - f_e \rvert - .5)^2}{f_e}$
Men/yes	3.64	9.86	11.64	0.85
Men/no	3.64	9.86	22.36	0.44
Women/yes	3.64	9.86	26.36	0.37
Women/no	3.64	9.86	50.64	0.19

5.

a. We will make 2,973 errors, because we predict that all victims fall in the modal category (white). $E_1 = 6{,}084 - 3{,}111 = 2{,}973$.

b. For white offenders, we could make 373 errors; for black offenders, 493 errors; and for other offenders, we would make 42 errors. $E_2 = 908$.

c. The proportional reduction in error is then (2,973 − 908)/2,973 = .6946. This indicates a very strong relationship between the two variables. We can reduce the error in predicting victim's race based on race of offender by 69.46%.

7.

Race/First-Generation College Status	f_o	f_e	$f_o - f_e$	$(f_o - f_e)^2$	$\frac{(f_o - f_e)^2}{f_e}$
White/first	1,742	1,749.6	−7.6	57.76	0.03
White/nonfirst	2,392	2,384.4	7.6	57.76	0.02
Black/first	102	93.5	8.5	72.25	0.77
Black/nonfirst	119	127.5	−8.5	72.25	0.57
Native American/first	41	36.4	4.6	21.16	0.58
Native American/nonfirst	45	49.6	−4.6	21.16	0.43
Hispanic/first	19	18.6	0.4	0.16	0.01
Hispanic/nonfirst	25	25.4	−0.4	0.16	0.01

(Continued)

(Continued)

Race/First-Generation College Status	f_o	f_e	$f_o - f_e$	$(f_o - f_e)^2$	$\frac{(f_o - f_e)^2}{f_e}$
Asian American/first	6	11.9	–5.9	34.81	2.93
Asian American/nonfirst	22	16.1	5.9	34.81	2.16
$\chi^2 = 7.51$					

Chi-square = 7.51, with 4 degrees of freedom [(2 – 1)(5 – 1) = 4].

We would fail to reject the null hypothesis. The probability of our obtained chi-square lies somewhere between 0.20 and 0.10, above our alpha level.

9. We would reject the null hypothesis. The chi-square obtained of 52.047 is significant at the .032 level (< .05 alpha). There is a relationship between degree and church attendance for these French respondents. Overall, as educational attainment increases, church attendance decreases.

11. The lambda of .051 for PRES12 and HLTHALL indicates a weak relationship. Only 5.1% of the error in predicting HLTHALL responses based on PRES12. Notice from the SPSS output that when PRES12 is defined as the dependent variable (HLTHALL is the independent variable), the lambda increases to .467.

    The gamma of –.198 indicates a weak negative relationship between CLASS and HLTHALL. If we rely on CLASS as an independent variable to predict HLTHALL, we would reduce our errors by 19.8%.

13. Gender: The model is significant at the .01 level, indicating a significant relationship between the variables. Though males contribute to more violent onset, in proportional terms, females exhibit a higher prevalence rate—18.32% of females exhibit violent onset compared with 11.71% of males.

    Age at first offense: The model is significant at the .01 level, indicating a significant relationship between age at first offense and violent onset. Violent onset is more likely among the group 14 years and older (14.74%) than those less than 14 years of age at first onset (9.67%).

CHAPTER 11

1.

$\bar{Y}_1 = 2.875$	$\bar{Y}_2 = 2.250$	$\bar{Y}_3 = 2.00$	$\bar{Y}_4 = 1.375$
$\Sigma Y_1 = 23$	$\Sigma Y_2 = 18$	$\Sigma Y_3 = 16$	$\Sigma Y_4 = 11$
$\Sigma Y_1^2 = 71$	$\Sigma Y_2^2 = 44$	$\Sigma Y_3^2 = 38$	$\Sigma Y_4^2 = 17$
$n_1 = 8$	$n_2 = 8$	$n_3 = 8$	$n_4 = 8$
$\bar{Y} = 2.125$			
$N = 32$			

$$SSB = 8(2.875 - 2.125)^2 + 8(2.250 - 2.125)^2 + 8(2.00 - 2.125)^2 + 8(1.375 - 2.125)^2$$
$$= 8(0.5625) + 8(.015625) + 8(.015625) + 8(.5625)$$
$$= 4.5 + .125 + .125 + 4.5$$
$$SSB = 9.25$$

$$df_b = 4 - 1$$
$$df_b = 3$$

$$\text{Mean square between} = 9.25/3 = 3.08$$

$$SSW = (71 + 44 + 38 + 17) - \left[(23^2/8) + (18^2/8) + (16^2/8) + (11^2/8)\right]$$
$$= 170 - (66.125 + 40.5 + 32 + 15.125)$$
$$= 170 - 153.75$$
$$SSW = 16.25$$

$$df_w = 32 - 4$$
$$= 28$$

$$\text{Mean square within} = 16.25/28 = 0.58$$

$$F = 3.08/0.58$$
$$= 5.31$$

Decision: If we set alpha at .05, F critical would be 2.95 ($df_1 = 3$ and $df_2 = 28$). Based on our F obtained of 5.31, we would reject the null hypothesis and conclude that at least one of the means is significantly different than the others. Upper-class respondents rate their health the highest (1.375), followed by middle- and working-class respondents (2.00 and 2.25, respectively) and lower-class respondents (2.875) on a scale where 1 = *excellent*, 4 = *poor*.

3.

$\bar{Y}_1 = 1.6$	$\bar{Y}_2 = 1.4$	$\bar{Y}_3 = 0.6$
$\Sigma Y_1 = 16$	$\Sigma Y_2 = 14$	$\Sigma Y_3 = 6$
$\Sigma Y_1^2 = 30$	$\Sigma Y_2^2 = 24$	$\Sigma Y_3^2 = 8$
$n_1 = 10$	$n_2 = 10$	$n_3 = 10$
	$\bar{Y} = 1.2$	
	$N = 30$	

$$SSB = 10(1.6 - 1.2)^2 + 10(1.4 - 1.2)^2 + 10(0.6 - 1.2)^2$$
$$= 10(0.16) + 10(0.04) + 10(0.36)$$
$$= 1.6 + 0.4 + 3.6$$
$$= 5.6$$

$$df_b = 3 - 1$$
$$= 2$$

Mean square between = 5.6/2 = 2.8

$$\begin{aligned} SSW &= (30 + 24 + 8) - (16^2/10) + (14^2/10) + (6^2/10) \\ &= 62 - (25.6 + 19.6 + 3.6) \\ &= 62 - 48.8 \\ &= 13.2 \end{aligned}$$

$$df_w = 30 - 3$$
$$df_w = 27$$

Mean square within =13.2/27 = 0.488889

$$F = 2.8/0.49$$

$$= 5.71$$

Decision: If we set alpha at .01, F critical would be 5.49 ($df_1 = 2$ and $df_2 = 27$). Based on our F obtained of 5.71, we would reject the null hypothesis and conclude that at least one of the means is significantly different than the others. Respondents with no degree rate their church attendance highest (1.6), followed by respondents with a secondary degree (1.4) and then respondents with a university degree (0.6).

5.

$\bar{Y}_1 = 0.8$	$\bar{Y}_2 = 1.75$	$\bar{Y}_3 = 3.20$
$Y_1 = 4$	$Y_2 = 7$	$Y_3 = 16$
$\Sigma Y_1^2 = 6$	$\Sigma Y_2^2 = 15$	$\Sigma Y_3^2 = 54$
$n_1 = 5$	$n_2 = 4$	$n_3 = 5$
	$\bar{Y} = 1.93$	
	$N = 14$	

$$\begin{aligned} SSB &= 5(.8 - 1.93)^2 + 4(1.75 - 1.93)^2 + 5(3.20 - 1.93)^2 \\ &= 5(1.2769) + 4(.0324) + 5(1.6129) \\ &= 6.3845 + 0.1296 + 8.0645 \\ SSB &= 14.58 \end{aligned}$$

$$df_b = 3 - 1$$
$$df_b = 2$$

$$\text{Mean square between} = 14.58/2 = 7.29$$

$$\begin{aligned} SSW &= (6+15+54) - \left[(4^2/5) + (7^2/4) + (16^2/5)\right] \\ &= 75 - (3.2 + 12.25 + 51.2) \\ &= 75 - 66.65 \\ SSW &= 8.35 \end{aligned}$$

$$\begin{aligned} df_w &= 14 - 3 \\ df_w &= 11 \end{aligned}$$

$$\text{Mean square within} = 8.35/11 = 0.76$$

$$\begin{aligned} F &= 7.29/0.76 \\ F &= 9.59 \end{aligned}$$

Decision. If we set alpha at .05, F critical would be 3.98 ($df_1 = 2$ and $df_2 = 11$). Based on our F obtained of 9.59, we would reject the null hypothesis and conclude that at least one of the means is significantly different from the others. The average number of moving violations is the highest for large-city respondents (3.2); medium-sized city residents are next (1.75), followed last by small-town respondents (0.8).

7. For each sociocultural resource, we would reject the null hypothesis. For social support, the obtained F ratio is 12.17, $p < .001$. Whites report the highest level of social support (2.85) while Non-Cuban Hispanics have the lowest (2.58). For religious attendance, the obtained F ratio is 56.43, $p < .001$. Church attendance is highest for African Americans and Non-Cuban Hispanics in the sample (3.94 and 3.37 on the 5-point scale).

9. Based on alpha = .01, we reject the null hypothesis of no difference. The average donation amount does vary by educational degree. The group with the highest average donation amount is graduate degree ($5590.61) followed by bachelor degree ($3397.40). The group with the lowest donation amount was less than high school graduates ($593.85).

11.

   a. Yes, agreement to the statement does vary by how satisfied the individual is with his or her financial situation. The ANOVA model is significant at the .003 level (< .01 alpha). All group means are between agree (2) or neither (3), but the group most likely to agree with the statement is the group which is not at all satisfied with their financial situation. This group's mean score is 2.72, between agree and neither. For the satisfied and more or less satisfied with their financial situation, average scores are slightly above 3—neither agree or disagree.

   b. Eta-squared is 14.662/501.637 = .029 = .03. Only 3% of the variation in IMMJOBS can be explained by satisfaction with finances.

13.

   a. $df_b = k - 1 = 5 - 1 = 4$; $df_w = N - k = 254 - 5 = 249$

   b. We would reject the null hypothesis for the three models. Students' perception of mentoring does vary by racial/ethnic identity. The most significant model is for the statement, "There are peer mentors who can advise me." Native American students have the highest level of agreement, followed by African American students. The lowest average score is for Asian students. The model for "I mentor other students" is significant at the .006 level. Native American students have the highest level of agreement, followed by African American students. The lowest average score is for Asian students. Finally, the model for "There are persons of color in administrative roles from whom I would seek mentoring at this institution" is significant at the .008 level. Native American students have the highest average level of agreement, followed by multiethnic students. The lowest score was reported by Hispanic students.

CHAPTER 12

1.

a. On the scatterplot below, the regression line has been plotted to make it easier to see the relationship between the two variables.

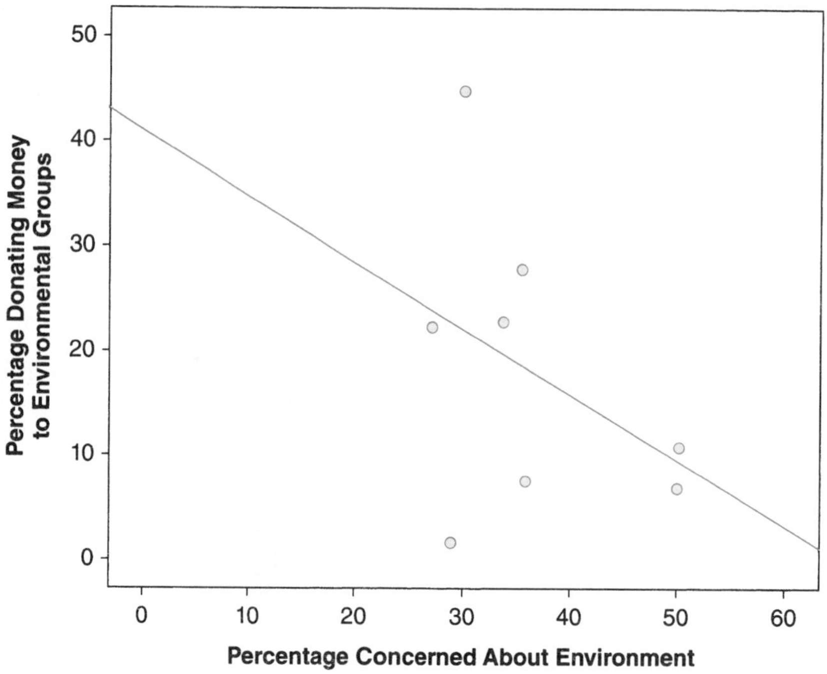

b. The scatterplot shows that there is a general linear relationship between the two variables. There is not a lot of scatter about the straight line describing the relationship. As the percentage of respondents concerned about the environment increases, the percentage of respondents donating money to environmental groups decreases.

c. The Pearson correlation coefficient between the two variables is –0.40. This is consistent with the scatterplot that indicated a negative relationship between being concerned about the environment and actually donating money to environmental groups.

	(1)	(2)	(3)	(4)	(5)	(6)	(7)
	Percentage Concerned	Percentage Donating					
Country	X	Y	$(X-\bar{X})$	$(X-\bar{X})^2$	$(Y-\bar{Y})$	$(Y-\bar{Y})^2$	$(X-\bar{X})(Y-\bar{Y})$
United States	33.8	22.8	−2.69	7.24	4.77	22.75	−12.83
Austria	35.5	27.8	−0.99	0.98	9.77	95.45	−9.67
The Netherlands	30.1	44.8	−6.39	40.83	26.77	716.63	−171.06
Slovenia	50.3	10.7	13.81	190.72	−7.33	53.73	−101.23
Russia	29.0	1.6	−7.49	56.10	−16.43	269.94	123.06
Philippines	50.1	6.8	13.61	185.23	−11.23	126.11	−152.84
Spain	35.9	7.4	−0.59	0.35	−10.63	113.00	6.27
Denmark	27.2	22.3	−9.29	86.30	4.27	18.23	−39.67
	$\Sigma X = 291.9$	$\Sigma Y = 144.2$	−0.02[a]	567.75	0.04[a]	1,415.84	−357.97

$$\text{Mean } X = \bar{X} = \frac{\Sigma X}{N} = \frac{291.9}{8} = 36.49$$

$$\text{Mean } Y = \bar{Y} = \frac{\Sigma Y}{N} = \frac{144.2}{8} = 18.03$$

$$\text{Variance }(Y) = s_Y^2 = \frac{\Sigma(Y-\bar{Y})^2}{N-1} = \frac{1{,}415.84}{7} = 202.26$$

$$\text{Standard deviation }(Y) = s_Y = \sqrt{202.26} = 14.22$$

$$\text{Variance }(X) = s_X^2 = \frac{\Sigma(X-\bar{X})^2}{N-1} = \frac{567.75}{7} = 81.11$$

$$\text{Standard deviation }(X) = s_X = \sqrt{81.11} = 9.01$$

$$\text{Covariance }(X, Y) = s_{XY} = \frac{\Sigma(X-\bar{X})(Y-\bar{Y})}{N-1} = \frac{-357.97}{7} = -51.14$$

$$r = \frac{s_{XY}}{s_X s_Y} = \frac{-51.14}{(9.01)(14.22)} = -0.40^{a}$$

Note: Answers may differ slightly due to rounding.

3.

a. The correlation coefficient is -0.45.

	(1)	(2)	(3)	(4)	(5)	(6)	(7)
Country	GNP per Capita	Percentage Willing to Pay					
State	X	Y	$(X-\bar{X})$	$(X-\bar{X})^2$	$(Y-\bar{Y})$	$(Y-\bar{Y})^2$	$(X-\bar{X})(Y-\bar{Y})$
United States	29.24	44.9	2.72	7.40	−1.64	2.69	−4.46
Ireland	18.71	53.3	−7.81	61.00	6.76	45.70	−52.80
The Netherlands	24.78	61.2	1.74	3.03	14.66	214.92	−25.51
Norway	34.31	40.7	7.79	60.68	−5.84	34.11	−45.49
Sweden	25.58	32.6	−0.94	0.88	−13.94	194.32	13.10
	$\Sigma X = 132.62$	$\Sigma Y = 232.7$	−0.02[a]	132.99	0.04[a]	491.74	−115.16
$\text{Mean } Y = \bar{Y} = \frac{\Sigma Y}{N} = \frac{232.7}{5} = 46.54$							
$\text{Variance } (X) = s_X^2 = \frac{\Sigma(X-\bar{X})^2}{N-1} = \frac{132.99}{4} = 33.25$							
$\text{Standard deviation } (X) = s_X = \sqrt{33.25} = 5.77$							
$\text{Variance } (Y) = s_Y^2 = \frac{\Sigma(Y-\bar{Y})^2}{N-1} = \frac{491.74}{4} = 122.94$							
$r = \frac{s_{XY}}{s_X s_Y} = \frac{-28.79}{(5.77)(11.09)} = -0.45$[a]							

Notes:

a. **Answers may differ slightly due to rounding.**

b. **A correlation coefficient of −0.45 means that relatively high values of GNP are moderately negatively assoicated with low values of percentage of residents willing to pay higher prices to protect the environment.**

5. The analysis reveals a negative relationship between years of education and number of children. The bivariate regression equation is $Y = 3.537 + -0.118X$. For each year increase in education, the number of children is predicted to decrease by 0.118. The model explains just 5% of the variance; however, based on the ANOVA F obtained, we can reject the null hypothesis that $r^2 = 0$.

7.

   a. The regression analysis confirms a positive relationship between years of education and total donations given in the past year. The F obtained is 10.578 (significant at .001). We can conclude that the relationship between the two variables is significant.

b. For respondent with 14 years of education: \$2043.86

For respondent with 20 years of education: \$3868.50

9.

a. For males: $Y = 9.768 + 0.355X$

For females: $Y = 9.770 + 0.367X$

b. For males, mother with 20 years of education: 9.768 + 0.355(20) = 16.87

For females, mother with 20 years of education: 9.770 + 0.367(20) = 17.11

c. The model for females has a slightly higher r^2. Mother's education explains 22% of the variance in female respondent education compared with the 20% explained for male respondent education. Based on the F-obtained statistic, both models are significant.

11.

a. Both hypotheses are confirmed.

The slope for education is 0.598. Holding age constant, for each year increase in education, Internet hours per week increases by 0.598.

The slope for age is -0.236. Holding years of education constant, for each year increase in age, Internet hours per week decreases by 0.236.

b. $Y = 14.395 + 0.598(X_1) + -0.236(X_2)$

$Y = 14.395 + 0.598(16) + -0.236(55) = 10.98$ Internet hours per week

c. $Y = 14.395 + 0.263(X_1) + -0.047(X_2)$

Education has the strongest effect on Internet hours per week (beta = .263).

d. The R^2 is 0.065. Education and age explain 6.5% of the variance in predicting Internet hours per week. This is a weak prediction model.

e. The correlation between Internet hours per week and age of respondent is –0.231, indicating a weak negative relationship. The correlation between Internet hours per week and education is 0.088, indicating a weak positive relationship. Finally, the correlation between age and education is –0.009, a weak negative relationship. The only significant correlation is the one between Internet hours and age.

13.

a. $Y = 3.91 + -0.115(X_1) + -0.038(X_2) + 0.018(X_3) + -0.017(X_4)$

(X_1 = education, X_2 = children, X_3 = age, X_4 = hours worked per week)

Holding all the other independent variables constant,

For each year of increase in education, television viewing should decrease by 0.115 hours.

For each additional child, television viewing decreases by 0.038 hours.

For each additional year of age, television viewing increases by 0.018 hours.

For each additional hour of work, television viewing decreases by 0.017 hours.

b.

Education, 0.202

Hours worked last week, –0.148

Age, 0.139

Number of children, –0.034

c. Together these four independent variables reduce the error in predicting TVHOURS by 8.3%. This is a weak prediction model.

GLOSSARY

Alpha (α) The level of probability at which the null hypothesis is rejected. It is customary to set alpha at the 0.05, 0.01, or 0.001 level

Analysis of variance (ANOVA) An inferential statistics technique designed to test for the significant relationship between two variables in two or more samples

Asymmetrical measure of association A measure of association whose value may vary depending on which variable is considered the independent variable and which the dependent variable

Bar graph A graph showing the differences in frequencies or percentages among categories of a nominal or an ordinal variable. The categories are displayed as rectangles of equal width with their height proportional to the frequency or percentage of the category

Beta (β) See standardized coefficient

Between-group sum of squares (*SSB*) The sum of squared deviations between each sample mean to the overall mean score

Bivariate analysis A statistical method designed to detect and describe the relationship between two variables

Bivariate regression A regression model that examines the effect of one independent variable on the values of a dependent variable

Bivariate table A table that displays the distribution of one variable across the categories of another variable

Cell The intersection of a row and a column in a bivariate table

Central limit theorem If all possible random samples of size N are drawn from a population with a mean μ_Y and a standard deviation σ_Y, then as N becomes larger, the sampling distribution of sample means becomes approximately normal, with mean $\mu_{\bar{Y}}$ and standard deviation, $\sigma_{\bar{Y}} = \sigma_Y / \sqrt{N}$

Chi-square (obtained) The test statistic that summarizes the differences between the observed (f_o) and the expected (f_e) frequencies in a bivariate table

Chi-square test An inferential statistics technique designed to test for a significant relationship between two variables organized in a bivariate table

Coefficient of determination (r^2) A PRE measure reflecting the proportional reduction of error that results from using the linear regression model. It reflects the proportion of the total variation in the dependent variable, Y, explained by the independent variable, X

Column variable A variable whose categories are the columns of a bivariate table

Conditional relationship A relationship in which the control variable's effect on the dependent variable is conditional on its interaction with the independent variable. The relationship between the independent and dependent variables will change according to the different conditions of the control variable

Confidence interval (CI) A range of values defined by the confidence level within which the population parameter is estimated to fall

Confidence level The likelihood, expressed as a percentage or a probability, that a specified interval will contain the population parameter

Control variable An additional variable considered in a bivariate relationship. The variable is controlled for when we take into account its effect on the variables in the bivariate relationship

Correlation A measure of association used to determine the existence and strength of the relationship between interval-ratio variables

Cramer's *V* A chi square related measure of association for nominal variables. Cramer's V is based on the value of chi-square and ranges between 0 and 1.

Cross-tabulation A technique for analyzing the relationship between two variables that have been organized in a table

Cumulative frequency distribution A distribution showing the frequency at or below each category (class interval or score) of the variable

Cumulative percentage distribution A distribution showing the percentage at or below each category (class interval or score) of the variable

Data Information represented by numbers, which can be the subject of statistical analysis

Degrees of freedom (*df*) The number of scores that are free to vary in calculating a statistic

Dependent variable The variable to be explained (the "effect")

Descriptive statistics Procedures that help us organize and describe data collected from either a sample or a population

Deterministic (perfect) linear relationship A relationship between two interval-ratio variables in which all the observations (the dots) fall along a straight line. The line provides a predicted value of Y (the vertical axis) for any value of X (the horizontal axis)

Dichotomous variable A variable that has only two values

Direct causal relationship A bivariate relationship that cannot be accounted for by other theoretically relevant variables

Disproportionate stratified sample The size of the sample selected from each subgroup is disproportional to the size of that subgroup in the population

Elaboration A process designed to further explore a bivariate relationship; it involves the introduction of control variables

Empirical research A research based on evidence that can be verified by using our direct experience

Estimation A process whereby we select a random sample from a population and use a sample statistic to estimate a population parameter

Expected frequencies (f_e) The cell frequencies that would be expected in a bivariate table if the two variables were statistically independent

F critical F-test statistic that corresponds to the alpha level, df_w, and df_b

F obtained The F-test statistic that is calculated

F ratio or F statistic The test statistic for ANOVA, calculated by the ratio of mean square to mean square within

Frequency distribution A table reporting the number of observations falling into each category of the variable

Gamma A symmetrical measure of association suitable for use with ordinal variables or with dichotomous nominal variables. It can vary from 0.0 to ±1.0 and provides us with an indication of the strength and direction of the association between the variables. Gamma is also referred to as Goodman and Kruskal's gamma

Histogram A graph showing the differences in frequencies or percentages among categories of an interval-ratio variable. The categories are displayed as contiguous bars, with width proportional to the width of the category and height proportional to the frequency or percentage of that category

Hypothesis A tentative answer to a research problem

Independent variable The variable expected to account for (the "cause" of) the dependent variable

Index of qualitative variation (IQV) A measure of variability for nominal variables. It is based on the ratio of the total number of differences in the distribution to the maximum number of possible differences within the same distribution

Inferential statistics The logic and procedures concerned with making predictions or inferences about a population from observations and analyses of a sample

Interquartile range (IQR) The width of the middle 50% of the distribution. It is defined as the difference between the lower and upper quartiles (Q_1 and Q_3). IQR can be calculated for interval-ratio and ordinal data

Interval-ratio measurement Measurements for all cases are expressed in the same units and equally spaced. Interval-ratio values can be rank-ordered

Intervening relationship A relationship in which the control variable intervenes between the independent and dependent variables

Intervening variable A control variable that follows an independent variable but precedes the dependent variable in a causal sequence

Kendall's tau-*b* A symmetrical measure of association suitable for use with ordinal variables. Unlike gamma, it accounts for pairs tied on the independent and dependent variable. It can vary from 0.0 to ±1.0. It provides an indication of the strength and direction of the association between the variables

Lambda An asymmetrical measure of association, lambda is suitable for use with nominal variables and may range from 0.0 to 1.0. It provides us with an indication of the strength of an association between the independent and dependent variables

Least squares line (best-fitting line) A line where the residual sum of squares, or $\sum e^2$, is at a minimum

Least squares method The technique that produces the least squares line

Left-tailed test A one-tailed test in which the sample outcome is hypothesized to be at the left tail of the sampling distribution

Linear relationship A relationship between two interval-ratio variables in which the observations displayed in a scatter diagram can be approximated with a straight line

Line graph A graph showing the differences in frequencies or percentages among categories of an interval-ratio variable. Points representing the frequencies of each category are placed above the midpoint of the category and are joined by a straight line

Marginals The row and column totals in a bivariate table

Margin of error The radius of a confidence interval

Mean A measure typically used to describe central tendency in interval-ratio variables. The arithmetic average obtained by adding up all the scores and dividing by the total number of scores

Mean square between Sum of squares between divided by its corresponding degrees of freedom

Mean squares regression An average computed by dividing the regression sum of squares (*SSR*) by its corresponding degrees of freedom

Mean squares residual An average computed by dividing the residual sum of squares (*SSE*) by its corresponding degrees of freedom

Mean square within Sum of squares within divided by its corresponding degrees of freedom

Measure of association A single summarizing number that reflects the strength of a relationship, indicates the usefulness of predicting the dependent variable from the independent variable, and often shows the direction of the relationship

Measures of central tendency Numbers that describe what is average or typical of the distribution

Measures of variability Numbers that describe diversity or variability in the distribution

Median A measure of central tendency. The score that divides the distribution into two equal parts so that half the cases are above and half below

Mode A measure of central tendency. The category or score with the highest frequency (or percentage) in the distribution of main points

Multiple coefficient of determination (R^2) Measure that reflects the proportion of the total variation in the dependent variable that is explained jointly by two or more independent variables

Multiple regression A regression model that examines the effects of several independent variables on the values of one dependent variable

Negatively skewed distribution A distribution with a few extremely low values

Negative relationship A bivariate relationship between two variables measured at the ordinal level or higher in which the variables vary in opposite directions

Nominal measurement Numbers or other symbols are assigned to a set of categories for the purpose of naming, labeling, or classifying the observations. Nominal categories cannot be rank-ordered

Normal distribution A bell-shaped and symmetrical theoretical distribution with the mean, the median, and the mode all coinciding at its peak and with the frequencies gradually decreasing at both ends of the curve

Null hypothesis (H_0) A statement of "no difference," which contradicts the research hypothesis and is always expressed in terms of population parameters

Observed frequencies (f_o) The cell frequencies actually observed in a bivariate table

One-tailed test A type of hypothesis test that involves a directional hypothesis. It specifies that the values of one group are either larger or smaller than some specified population value

One-way ANOVA Analysis of variance application with one dependent variable and one independent variable

Ordinal measurement Numbers are assigned to rank-ordered categories ranging from low to high

Parameter A measure (e.g., mean or standard deviation) used to describe the population distribution

Partial relationship The relationship between the independent and dependent variables shown in a partial table

Partial slopes The amount of change in *Y* for a unit change in a specific independent variable while controlling for the other independent variable(s)

Partial tables Bivariate tables that display the relationship between the independent and dependent variables while controlling for a third variable

Pearson's correlation coefficient (*r*) The square root of r^2; it is a measure of association for interval-ratio variables, reflecting the strength and direction of the linear association between two interval-ratio variables. It can be positive or negative in sign

Pearson's multiple correlation coefficient (*R*) Measure of the linear relationship between the independent variable and the combined effect of two or more independent variables

Percentage A relative frequency obtained by dividing the frequency in each category by the total number of cases and multiplying by 100

Percentage distribution A table showing the percentage of observations falling into each category of the variable

Percentile A score below which a specific percentage of the distribution falls

Pie chart A graph showing the differences in frequencies or percentages among categories of a nominal or an ordinal variable. The categories are displayed as segments of a circle whose pieces add up to 100% of the total frequencies

Point estimate A sample statistic used to estimate the exact value of a population parameter

Population The total set of individuals, objects, groups, or events in which the researcher is interested

Positively skewed distribution A distribution with a few extremely high values

Positive relationship A bivariate relationship between two variables measured at the ordinal level or higher in which the variables vary in the same direction

Probability A quantitative measure that a particular event will occur

Probability sampling A method of sampling that enables the researcher to specify for each case in the population the probability of its inclusion in the sample

Proportion A relative frequency obtained by dividing the frequency in each category by the total number of cases

Proportional reduction of error (PRE) A measure that tells us how much we can improve predicting the value of a dependent variable based on information about an independent variable

Proportionate stratified sample The size of the sample selected from each subgroup is proportional to the size of that subgroup in the entire population

***p* value** The probability associated with the obtained value of Z

Range A measure of variation in interval-ratio variables. It is the difference between the highest (maximum) and the lowest (minimum) scores in the distribution

Rate A number obtained by dividing the number of actual occurrences in a given time period by the number of possible occurrences

Regression A linear prediction model using one or more independent variables to predict the values of a dependent variable

Regression sum of squares (*SSR*) Reflects the improvement in the prediction error resulting from using the linear prediction equation, SST (sum of squared total) – SSE (residual sum of squares)

Research hypothesis (H_1) A statement reflecting the substantive hypothesis. It is always expressed in terms of population parameters, but its specific form varies from test to test

Research process A set of activities in which social scientists engage to answer questions, examine ideas, or test theories

Residual sum of squares (*SSE*) Sum of squared differences between observed and predicted Y

Right-tailed test A one-tailed test in which the sample outcome is hypothesized to be at the right tail of the sampling distribution

Row variable A variable whose categories are the rows of a bivariate table

Sample A subset of cases selected from a population

Sampling The process of identifying and selecting the subset of the population for study

Sampling distribution The sampling distribution is a theoretical probability distribution of all possible sample values for the statistics in which we are interested

Sampling distribution of the difference between means A theoretical probability distribution that would be obtained by calculating all the possible mean differences $(\bar{Y}_1 - \bar{Y}_2)$ that would be obtained by drawing all the possible independent random samples of size N_1 and N_2 from two populations where N_1 and N_2 are each greater than 50

Sampling distribution of the mean A theoretical probability distribution of sample means that would be obtained by drawing from the population all possible samples of the same size

Sampling error The discrepancy between a sample estimate of a population parameter and the real population parameter

Scatter diagram (scatterplot) A visual method used to display a relationship between two interval-ratio variables

Simple random sample A sample designed in such a way as to ensure that (a) every member of the population has an equal chance of being chosen and (b) every combination of N members has an equal chance of being chosen

Skewed distribution A distribution with a few extreme values on one side of the distribution

Slope (*b*) The amount of change in a dependent variable per unit change in an independent variable

Spurious relationship A relationship in which both the independent and dependent variables are influenced by a causally prior-control variable, and there is no causal link between them. The relationship between the independent and dependent variables is said to be "explained away" by the control variable

Standard deviation A measure of variation for interval-ratio and ordinal variables; it is equal to the square root of the variance

Standard error of the mean The standard deviation of the sampling distribution of the mean. It describes how much dispersion there is in the sampling distribution of the mean

Standard normal distribution A normal distribution represented in standard (Z) scores

Standard normal table A table showing the area (as a proportion, which can be translated into a percentage) under the standard normal curve corresponding to any Z score or its fraction

Standard (Z) score The number of standard deviations that a given raw score is above or below the mean

Standardized slope coefficient (or beta) The slope between the dependent variable and a specific independent variable when all scores are standardized or expressed as Z scores. Beta scores range from 0 to ±1.0

Statistic A specific measure used to describe the sample distribution

Statistics A set of procedures used by social scientists to organize, summarize, and communicate numerical information

Statistical hypothesis testing A procedure that allows us to evaluate hypotheses about population parameters based on sample statistics

Statistical independence The absence of association between two cross-tabulated variables. The percentage distributions of the dependent variable within each category of the independent variable are identical

Statistical map A visual presentation of geographic data patterns or variations, such as the population distribution

Stratified random sample A method of sampling obtained by (a) dividing the population into subgroups based on one or more variables central to our analysis and (b) then drawing a simple random sample from each of the subgroups

Symmetrical distribution The frequencies at the right and left tails of the distribution are identical; each half of the distribution is the mirror image of the other

Symmetrical measure of association A measure of association whose value will be the same when either variable is considered the independent variable or the dependent variable

Systematic random sampling A method of sampling in which every Kth member (K is a ratio obtained by dividing the population size by the desired sample size) in the total population is chosen for inclusion in the sample after the first member of the sample is selected at random from among the first members in the population

t distribution A family of curves, each determined by its degrees of freedom (df). It is used when the population standard deviation is unknown and the standard error is estimated from the sample standard deviation

Theory A set of assumptions and propositions used to explain, predict, and understand social phenomena

Time-series chart A graph displaying changes in a variable at different points in time. It shows time (measured in units such as years or months) on the horizontal axis and the frequencies (percentages or rates) of another variable on the vertical axis

Total sum of squares (SST) The total variation in scores, calculated by adding SSB (between-group sum of squares) and SSW (within-group sum of squares)

t statistic (obtained) The test statistic computed to test the null hypothesis about a population mean when the population standard deviation is unknown and is estimated using the sample standard deviation

Two-tailed test A type of hypothesis test that involves a nondirectional research hypothesis. We are equally interested in whether the values are less than or greater than one another. The sample outcome may be located at both the low and high ends of the sampling distribution

Type I error The probability associated with rejecting a null hypothesis when it is true

Type II error The probability associated with failing to reject a null hypothesis when it is false

Unit of analysis The object of research, such as individuals, groups, organizations, or social artifacts

Variable A property of people or objects that takes on two or more values

Variance A measure of variation for interval-ratio and ordinal variables; it is the average of the squared deviations from the mean

Within-group sum of squares (*SSW*) Sum of squared deviations within each group, calculated between each individual score and the sample mean

***Y*-intercept (*a*)** The point where the regression line crosses the Y-axis and where $X = 0$

***Z* statistic (obtained)** The test statistic computed by converting a sample statistic (such as the mean) to a Z score. The formula for obtaining Z varies from test to test

NOTES

Chapter 1—The What and the Why of Statistics

1. U.S. Bureau of Labor Statistics, *Economic News Release: Usual Weekly Earnings Summary*, January 22, 2016.
2. U.S. Department of Labor, "Traditional and Nontraditional Occupations," 2015. Retrieved from http://www.dol.gov/wb/stats/nontra_traditional_occupations.htm
3. Catherine Rampell, "Women Now a Majority in American Workplaces," *The New York Times*, February 5, 2010. Retrieved from http://www.nytimes.com/2010/02/06/business/economy/06women.html
4. Anna Leon-Guerrero, *Social Problems: Community, Policy and Social Action* (Thousand Oaks, CA: Sage, 2015).
5. Chava Frankfort-Nachmias and David Nachmias, *Research Methods in the Social Sciences* (New York: Worth Publishers, 2000), p. 56.
6. Barbara Reskin and Irene Padavic, *Women and Men at Work* (Thousand Oaks, CA: Pine Forge Press, 2002), pp. 65, 144.
7. Frankfort-Nachmias and Nachmias, 2000, p. 50.
8. Ibid., p. 52.
9. *Working Woman*, January 1991, p. 45.
10. Patricia Hill Collins, "Toward a New Vision: Race, Class and Gender as Categories of Analysis and Connection" (Keynote address at Integrating Race and Gender Into the College Curriculum, a workshop sponsored by the Center for Research on Women, Memphis State University, Memphis, TN, 1989).
11. This discussion is based on Sheila Tobias' pioneering work on mathematics anxiety. See especially Chapters 2 and 8 of Tobias' (1995) *Overcoming Math Anxiety*.
12. For instructors and students using the SPSS Student Edition, a reminder that the maximum number of variables in a dataset is 50. We've created 49 variable datasets to allow students to create/save one additional variable.
13. Adela García-Aracil, "Gender Earnings Gap Among Young European Higher Education Graduates," *Higher Education* 53, no. 4 (2007), pp. 431–455.

Chapter 2—The Organization and Graphic Presentation of Data

1. Anna Leon-Guerrero, *Social Problems: Community, Policy and Social Action* (Thousand Oaks, CA: Sage, 2015).
2. Jennifer Medina, "New Suburban Dream Born of Asia and Southern California" (*The New York Times*, April 29, 2012), p. A9.
3. Gary Hytrek and Kristine Zentgraf, *America Transformed: Globalization, Inequality and Power* (New York: Oxford University Press, 2007).
4. Anna Brown and Eileen Patton, *Statistical Portrait of the Foreign-Born Population of the United States, 2012*, 2014. Retrieved from http://www.pewhispanic.org/2014/04/29/statistical-portrait-of-the-foreign-born-population-in-the-united-states-2012/.
5. David Knoke and George W. Bohrnstedt, *Basic Social Statistics* (New York: Peacock, 1991), p. 25.
6. Yolanda Padilla, Melissa Dalton Radey, Robert Hummer, and Eunjeong Kim, "The Living Conditions of U.S.-Born Children of Mexican Immigrants in

Unmarried Families," *Hispanic Journal of Behavioral Sciences* 28, no. 3 (2006), pp. 343–344.

7. Harry Moody, *Aging: Concepts and Controversies* (Thousand Oaks, CA: Sage, 2010), p. xxiii.

8. U.S. Census Bureau, *Marital Status and Living Arrangements: March 1996*, Current Population Reports, P20-496, 1998, p. 5.

9. U.S. Census Bureau, *65+ in America*, Current Population Reports, Special Studies, P23-190, 1996, pp. 2–3.

10. Edward R. Tufte, *The Visual Display of Quantitative Information* (Cheshire, CT: Graphics Press, 1983), p. 53.

Chapter 3—Measures of Central Tendency

1. U.S. Census Bureau, *Census Bureau Reports at Least 350 Languages Spoken in U.S. Homes*, 2015. Retrieved from http://www.census.gov/newsroom/press-releases/2015/cb15-185.html

2. U.S. Bureau of Labor Statistics, *Usual Weekly Earnings of Wage and Salary Workers Fourth Quarter 2015*, 2015. Retrieved from http://www.bls.gov/news.release/pdf/wkyeng.pdf http://www.bls.gov/news.release/archives/wkyeng_01222016.pdf

3. Federal Bureau of Investigation. *Uniform Crime Report—Hate Crime Statistics 2014*. Table 12, Agency Hate Crime Reporting by State, 2014. The states associated with the number of reported hate crimes are: Texas, California, Florida, New York, Pennsylvania, Illinois, Michigan, New Jersey, and North Carolina (as listed).

4. This rule was adapted from David Knoke and George W. Bohrnstedt, *Basic Statistics* (New York: Peacock Publishers, 1991), pp. 56–57.

5. The rates presented in Table 3.4 are computed for aggregate units (states) of different sizes. The mean of 423.6 is referred to as an unweighted mean. It is not the same as the incarceration rate for the population in the combined states.

6. Carmen DeNavas-Walt and Bernadette Proctor, *Income and Poverty in the United States: 2014*, Current Population Reports, P60-252, 2015.

Chapter 4—Measures of Variability

1. Johnneta B. Cole, "Commonalities and Differences," in *Race, Class, and Gender*, eds. Margaret L. Andersen and Patricia Hill Collins (Belmont, CA: Wadsworth, 1998), pp. 128–129.

2. Ibid., pp. 129–130.

3. Sandra Colby and Jennifer Ortman, *Projections of the Size and Composition of the U.S. Population: 2014 to 2060*, Current Population Reports, P25-1143, 2014.

4. Peter Dreier, John Mollenkopf, and Todd Swanstrom, *Place Matters: Metropolitics for the Twenty-First Century*, 2nd ed. (Lawrence, KS: University Press of Kansas, 2004).

5. Silvia Domínguez, *Getting Ahead: Social Mobility, Public Housing, and Immigrant Networks* (New York: New York University Press, 2011).

6. Elizabeth Grieco, Yesenia Acosta, G. Patricia de la Cruz, Christine Gambino, Thomas Gryn, Luke Larsen, Edward Trevelyan, and Nathan Walters, *The Foreign Born Population in the United States: 2010*, American Community Survey Reports, ACS-19, 2012.

7. Douglas S. Massey, *Categorically Unequal: The American Stratification System* (New York: Russell Sage Foundation, 2007).

8. U.S. Census data indicate that the recession of 2008–2009 halted this dominant migration trend.

9. The percentage increase in the population 65 years and above for each state and region was obtained by the following formula:

Percentage increase = [(2015 population – 2008 population)/2008 population] × 100

10. The extreme values at either end are referred to as outliers. SPSS will include

outliers in box plots and in the calculation of the IQR; however, SPSS extends whiskers from the box edges to 1.5 times the box width (the IQR). If there are additional values beyond 1.5 times the IQR, SPSS displays the individual cases. It is important to keep this in mind when examining the shape of a distribution from a box plot.

11. U.S. Census Bureau, *The Older Population: 2010*, p. 3.

12. $N - 1$ is used in the formula for computing variance because usually we are computing from a sample with the intention of generalizing to a larger population. $N - 1$ in the formula gives a better estimate and is also the formula used in SPSS.

13. A good discussion of the relationship between the standard deviation and the mean can be found in Stephen Gould's "The Median Isn't the Message," *Discover Magazine*, June 1985.

14. Herman J. Loether and Donald G. McTavish, *Descriptive and Inferential Statistics: An Introduction* (Boston: Allyn and Bacon, 1980), pp. 160–161.

15. Myron Pope, "Community College Mentoring Minority Student Perception," *Community College Review*, 30, no. 3 (2002): 31–45.

16. Ibid.

17. Ibid.

Chapter 5—The Normal Distribution

1. Margot Jackson, "Cumulative Inequality in Child Health and Academic Achievement," *Journal of Health and Social Behavior*, 56, no. 2 (2015), pp. 262–280.

2. Ibid.

3. Ibid.

Chapter 6—Sampling and Sampling Distributions

1. U.S. Department of Education, National Center for Education Statistics, *Digest of Education Statistics, 2014*, 2016.

2. This discussion has benefited from a more extensive presentation on the aims of sampling in Richard Maisel and Caroline Hodges Persell, *How Sampling Works* (Thousand Oaks, CA: Pine Forge Press, 1996).

3. The discussion in these sections is based on Chava Frankfort-Nachmias and David Nachmias, *Research Methods in the Social Sciences* (New York: Worth Publishers, 2007), pp. 167–177.

4. We discuss sampling error in the next section.

5. Margaret L. Andersen and Patricia Hill Collins, *Race, Class, and Gender* (Belmont, CA: Wadsworth, 2009).

6. The population of the 20 individuals presented in Table 6.3 is considered a finite population. A finite population consists of a finite (countable) number of elements (observations). Other examples of finite populations include all women in the labor force in 2008 and all public hospitals in New York City. A population is considered infinite when there is no limit to the number of elements it can include. Examples of infinite populations include all women in the labor force, in the past or the future. Most samples studied by social scientists come from finite populations. However, it is also possible to form a sample from an infinite population.

7. Here we are using an idealized example in which the sampling distribution is actually computed. However, please bear in mind that in practice one never computes a sampling distribution because it is also infinite.

8. Noam Scheiber, "The Internal Polls That Made Mitt Romney Think He'd Win," *The New Republic*, November 28, 2012.

9. Gallup Poll, *Gallup 2012 Presidential Election Polling Review*, June 4, 2013.

Chapter 7—Estimation

1. Jeffrey Jones, *Americans' Identification as 'Environmentalists' Down to 42%*, Gallup Poll, April 22, 2016.

2. CNN/ORC International Poll, April 28-May 1, 2016.

3. Renee Stepler and Anna Brown, *Statistical Portrait of Hispanics in the United States*, April 19, 2016.

4. Marta Tienda, "The Ghetto Underclass: Social Science Perspectives," *Annals of the American Academy of Political and Social Science* 501 (January 1989): 105–119.

5. Adapted from Marta Tienda and Franklin D. Wilson, "Migration and the Earnings of Hispanic Men," *American Sociological Review* 57 (1992): 661–678.

6. Ibid.

7. Pew Hispanic Center, *Cubans in the United States*, August 2006.

8. The U.S. Census 2000, IPUMS (Integrated Public Use Micro data Series).

9. The relationship between sample size and interval width when estimating means also holds true for sample proportions. When the sample size increases, the standard error of the proportion decreases, and therefore, the width of the confidence interval decreases as well.

10. Janet Fanslow and Elizabeth Robinson, "Help Seeking Behaviors and Reasons for Help Seeking Reported by a Representative Sample of Women Victims of Intimate Partner Violence in New Zealand," *Journal of Interpersonal Violence*, 25, no. 5 (2010), 929–951.

11. Ibid.

12. Jennifer Truman and Lynn Langton. *Criminal Victimization, 2013*. NCH 247648, Bureau of Justice Statistics, September 19, 2014.

13. Jacob Poushter, *Americans, Canadians Differ in Concern about Climate Change*, Pew Research Center, March 9, 2016.

14. Women's Bureau, U.S. Department of Labor, Mothers and Families: Labor Force Participation Chart 1, 2016.

15. Data from Enthusiastic' Voters Prefer GOP by 20 Points in 2010 Vote, Gallup Organization, April 27, 2010.

16. Jim Norman, *Millennials Like Sanders, Dislike Election Process*, Gallup Organization, May 11, 2016.

17. Aaron Smith, *Cell Phones, Social Media and Campaign 2014*, Pew Research Center, November 3, 2014.

18. Data from *The Millennials: Confident. Connected. Open to Change*, Pew Research Center, February 24, 2010. *Note:* Pew operationalizes Millennials differently from the Gallup Organization as presented in Exercise 10.

Chapter 8—Testing Hypotheses

1. Jeff Somer, "Numbers That Sway Markets and Voters," 2012. Retrieved from http://www.nytimes.com/2012/03/04/your-money/rising-gasoline-prices-could-soon-have-economic-effects.html?pagewanted=all&_r=0.

2. Steve Hargreaves, "Gas Prices Hit Working Class," 2007. Retrieved from http://money.cnn.com/2007/11/13/news/economy/gas_burden/index.htm.

3. American Automobile Association, *Daily Fuel Gauge Report*, May 28, 2016. Retrieved from www.fuelgaugereport.com.

4. Ronald Wasserstein and Nicole Lazar, "The ASA's Statement on *p*-values: context, process, and purpose," *The American Statistician*, DOI: 10.1080/00031305.2016.1154108, 2016

5. Jan Hoem, "The Reporting of Statistical Significance in Scientific Journals," *Demographic Research*, 18 (2008), 438.

6. To compute the sample variance for any particular sample, we must first compute the sample mean. Since the sum of the deviations about the mean must equal 0, only $N - 1$ of the deviation scores are free to vary with each variance estimate.

7. Carmen DeNavas-Walt and Bernadette Proctor, *Income and Poverty in the United States: 2014*, Current Population Reports, P60-252, 2015.

8. Degrees of freedom formula based on Dennis Hinkle, William Wiersma, and Stephen Jurs, *Applied Statistics for the Behavioral Sciences* (Boston: Houghton Mifflin, 1998), p. 268.

9. Lloyd D. Johnson, Patrick M. O'Malley, Jerald G. Bachman, and John E. Schulenberg, *Monitoring the Future National Results on Adolescent Drug Use: Overview of Key Findings, 2008* (Bethesda, MD: National Institute on Drug Abuse, 2009).

10. Pew Research Center, *Second-Generation Americans: A Portrait of the Adult Children of Immigrants*, February 7, 2013.

11. The sample proportions are unbiased estimates of the corresponding population proportions. Therefore, we can use the Z statistic, although our standard error is estimated from the sample proportions.

12. Robert E. Jones and Shirley A. Rainey, "Examining Linkages Between Race, Environmental Concern, Health and Justice in a Highly Polluted Community of Color," *Journal of Black Studies* 36, no. 4 (2006): 473–496.

13. Ibid.

14. Ibid.

15. Carmen DeNavas-Walt and Bernadette Proctor, *Income and Poverty in the United States: 2014*, Current Population Reports, P60-252, 2015.

16. Pew Research Center, *On Views of Race and Inequality, Blacks and Whites are Worlds Apart*, June 27, 2016.

17. Pew Research Center, *Clinton, Trump Supporters Have Starkly Different Views of a Changing Nation*, August 18, 2016.

Chapter 9— Bivariate Tables

1. Pew Research Center, *Immigration: Key Data Points from Pew Research*. Washington, DC: Pew Research Center, 2013.

2. *USA Today*, October 9, 1992.

3. Carmen DeNavas-Walt, Bernadette Proctor, and Jessica Smith, *Income, Poverty and Health Insurance Coverage in the United States: 2011*, Current Population Reports P60-243, 2012.

4. Full consideration of the question of detecting the presence of a bivariate relationship requires the use of inferential statistics.

5. The relationship between home ownership and race noted here may not necessarily hold true in other (larger) samples.

6. Another way in which percentages are sometimes expressed is with the total number of cases (N) used as the base. These overall percentages express the proportion of the sample who share two properties. Overall percentages do not have as much research utility as row and column percentages and are used less frequently.

7. Ernest Castañeda, Jonathan Klassen, and Curtis Smith, "Hispanic and Non-Hispanic Homeless Populations in El Paso, Texas," *Hispanic Journal of Behavioral Sciences* 36 (2014): 488–505.

8. Ibid, p. 490.

9. Ibid, p. 490.

10. Ibid, p. 498.

11. The same three properties are also discussed by Joseph F. Healey in *Statistics: A Tool for Social Research*. (Belmont, CA: Cengage, 2012), pp. 308–337.

12. For purposes of illustration, only selected categories of educational level and attendance of religious services are shown.

13. For example, see Harris Mills, "Religion, Values, and Attitudes Toward Abortion," *Journal for the Scientific Study of Religion* 24, no. 2 (1985): 119–236.

14. Mario Renzi, "Ideal Family Size as an Intervening Variable Between Religion and Attitudes Toward Abortion," *Journal for the Scientific Study of Religion* 14 (1975): 23–27.

15. Ibid.

16. Preferred family size was measured by responses to a question about the ideal number of children for a family. Those respondents who said two or fewer children were ideal were classified as preferring small families; those who answered

three or more were classified as preferring large families.

17. William R. Arney and William H. Trescher, "Trends in Attitudes Toward Abortion, 1972–1975," *Family Planning Perspective* 8 (1976): 117–124.

18. William V. D'Antonio and Steven Stack, "Religion, Ideal Family Size, and Abortion: Extending Renzi's Hypothesis," *Journal for the Scientific Study of Religion* 19 (1980): 397–408.

19. Jacqueline Scott, "Conflicting Belief About Abortion: Legal Approval and Moral Doubts," *Social Psychology Quarterly* 52, no. 4 (1989): 319–326.

20. Ibid., p. 322.

21. Carol Gilligan, *In a Different Voice* (Cambridge, MA: Harvard University Press, 1982).

22. Celeste Campos-Castillo, "Revisiting the First-Level Digital Divide in the United States: Gender and Race/Ethnicity Patterns, 2007-2012," *Social Science Computer Review*, *33*, no. 4 (2015): 423–439.

23. Ibid, p. 426.

24. Ibid, p. 429.

Chapter 10—The Chi-Square Test and Measures of Association

1. U.S. Census Bureau, *CPS Historical Time Series Tables*, Table A-2, 2014.

2. Victor B. Saenz, Sylvia Hurtado, Doug Barrera, De'Sha Wolf, and Fanny Young., *First in My Family: A Profile of First-Generation College Students at Four-Year Institutions Since 1971* (Los Angeles, CA: Higher Education Research Institute, 2007).

3. Because statistical independence is a symmetrical property, the distribution of the independent variable within each category of the dependent variable will also be identical. That is, if first-generation status and gender were statistically independent, we would also expect to see the distribution of first-generation status identical in each gender category.

4. Although this general formula provides a framework for all PRE measures of association, only lambda is illustrated with this formula. Gamma, which is discussed in the next section, is calculated with a different formula. Both are interpreted as PRE measures.

5. Victor Saenz et al., *First in My Family: A Profile of First-Generation College Students at Four-Year Institutions Since 1971* (Los Angeles, CA: Higher Education Research Institute, 2007).

6. Bharti Varshney, Prashant Kumar, Vivek Sapre, and Sanjeev Varshney, "Demographic Profile of the Internet-Using Population of India," *Management and Labour Studies 39*, no. 4 (2014): 423–427.

7. Ibid.

8. Ibid.

9. Paul Mazerolle, Alex Piquero, and Robert Brame, "Violent Onset Offenders: Do Initial Experiences Shape Criminal Career Dimensions?" *International Criminal Justice Review*, *20*, no. 2 (2010): 132–146.

Chapter 11—Analysis of Variance

1. U.S. Census Bureau, *CPS Historical Time Series Tables*, Table A-2, 2014.

2. Since the N in our computational example is small ($N = 21$), the assumptions of normality and homogeneity of variance are required. We've selected a small N to demonstrate the calculations for F and have proceeded with Assumptions 3 and 4. If a researcher is not comfortable with making these assumptions for a small sample, she or he can increase the size of N. In general, the F test is known to be robust with respect to moderate violations of these assumptions. A larger N increases the F test's robustness to severe departures from the normality and homogeneity of variance assumptions.

3. Anna Oleszkowicz and Anna Misztela, "How do Young Poles Perceive Their Adulthood?", *Journal of Adolescent Research* 30, no. 6 (2015), 683–709.

4. Ibid, p. 695.

5. Ibid, p. 695.

6. Ibid, p. 702.

7. Sandra Hofferth, "Childbearing Decision Making and Family Well-Being: A Dynamic, Sequential Model," *American Sociological Review* 48, no. 4 (1983): 533–545.

8. Myron Pope, "Community College Mentoring Minority Student Perception," *Community College Review*, 30, no. 3 (2002): 31–45.

Chapter 12—Regression and Correlation

1. Andrew Perrin and Maeve Duggan, *Americans' Internet Access: 2000–2015*, June 6, 2015.

2. Ibid.

3. Michael L. Benson, John Wooldredge, Amy B. Thistlethwaite, and Greer Litton Fox, "The Correlation Between Race and Domestic Violence Is Confounded With Community Context," *Social Problems* 51 no. 3 (2004): 326–342.

4. Michael L. Benson and Greer L. Fox, *Economic Distress, Community Context and Intimate Violence: An Application and Extension of Social Disorganization Theory*, U.S. Department of Justice, Document No.: 193433, 2002.

5. Ibid.

6. Refer to Paul Allison's *Multiple Regression: A Primer* (Thousand Oaks, CA: Pine Forge Press, 1999) for a complete discussion of multiple regression—statistical methods and techniques that consider the relationship between one dependent variable and one or more independent variables.

7. Katherine Purswell, Ani Yazedjian, and Michelle Toews, "Students' Intentions and Social Support as Predictors of Self-Reported Academic Behaviors: A Comparison of First- and Continuing-Generation College Students," *Journal of College Student Retention* 10 no. 2 (2008): 191-206.

8. Ibid, pp. 199-200.

9. Ibid, p. 199.

INDEX